Level 2

TEACHER EDITION

Units 7–12

LANGUAGE!® Live

VOYAGER SOPRIS LEARNING™

Louisa Moats, Ed.D., Author

Based on the original work of Jane Fell Greene, Ed.D.

7 8 9 10 11 B&B 19 18 17 16

978-1-4916-9014-7
1-4916-9014-3
333403

Printed in the United States of America
Published and Distributed by

17855 Dallas Parkway, Suite 400 • Dallas, TX 75287 • 800 547-6747
www.voyagersopris.com

Table of Contents

Authors and Program Contributors vi
Program Overview viii
Program Implementation ix
Program Components x
Instructional Design xii
Sample Lessons xiv
Texts at a Glance xx
Assessments xxi
Instructional Routines xxv
Training and Support Services xxix

Unit 7

Excerpt from *White Fang*
by Jack London
Text type: literature

"Return of the Wolves"
Text type: informational

Unit Plan 2
Lesson 1 4
Lesson 2 17
Lesson 3 25
Lesson 4 31
Lesson 5 38
Lesson 6 42
Lesson 7 52
Lesson 8 60
Lesson 9 65
Lesson 10 71

Unit 8

"The White Wolf of the Hartz Mountains"
by Captain Frederick Marryat
Text type: literature—short story

Who Speaks for Wolf
by Paula Underwood
Text type: literature—learning story

Unit Plan 78
Lesson 1 80
Lesson 2 97
Lesson 3 105
Lesson 4 110
Lesson 5 122
Lesson 6 129
Lesson 7 149
Lesson 8 156
Lesson 9 161
Lesson 10 177

Table of Contents

Unit 9

"The Mysterious Human Brain"
Text type: informational

Graphic Novel of *The Strange Case of Dr. Jekyll and Mr. Hyde*
by Robert L. Stevenson; Carl Bowen
Text type: graphic novel

Unit Plan 186
Lesson 1 188
Lesson 2 202
Lesson 3 211
Lesson 4 216
Lesson 5 226
Lesson 6 231
Lesson 7 239
Lesson 8 247
Lesson 9 252
Lesson 10 264

Unit 10

North High School letter
Text type: letter and policy—persuasive/informational

"Say Yes to Free Dress!"
Text type: persuasive

Unit Plan 274
Lesson 1 276
Lesson 2 290
Lesson 3 298
Lesson 4 302
Lesson 5 312
Lesson 6 317
Lesson 7 331
Lesson 8 337
Lesson 9 342
Lesson 10 351

Unit 11

Excerpt from *The Good Earth*
by Pearl S. Buck
Text type: literature—novel

Excerpt from *Nectar in a Sieve*
by Kamala Markandaya
Text type: literature—novel

Unit Plan 364
Lesson 1 366
Lesson 2 380
Lesson 3 390
Lesson 4 394
Lesson 5 404
Lesson 6 409
Lesson 7 421
Lesson 8 428
Lesson 9 433
Lesson 10 440

Unit 12

Part 1 of the Excerpt from
My Sister's Keeper
by Jodi Picoult
Text type: literature—novel

Part 2 of the Excerpt from
My Sister's Keeper
by Jodi Picoult
Text type: literature—novel

Unit Plan 450
Lesson 1 452
Lesson 2 467
Lesson 3 477
Lesson 4 481
Lesson 5 491
Lesson 6 496
Lesson 7 507
Lesson 8 513
Lesson 9 518
Lesson 10 525

Additional Resources 537
Posters 538
Writing Rubrics 544
Sight Words 549
Vocabulary 550
Research and Evidence of Effectiveness 552
Index 556

About the Author

Louisa Moats, Ed.D., has been a teacher, psychologist, researcher, graduate school faculty member, and author of many influential scientific journal articles, books, and policy papers on the topics of reading, spelling, language, and teacher preparation. After a first job as a neuropsychology technician, she became a teacher of students with learning and reading difficulties, earning her Master's degree at Peabody College of Vanderbilt. Later, after realizing how much more she needed to know about teaching, she earned a doctorate in Reading and Human Development from the Harvard Graduate School of Education. Dr. Moats spent the next fifteen years in private practice as a licensed psychologist in Vermont, specializing in evaluation and consultation with individuals of all ages and walks of life who experienced reading, writing, and language difficulties. At that time, she trained psychology interns in the Dartmouth Medical School Department of Psychiatry. Dr. Moats spent one year as resident expert for the California Reading Initiative, and four years as site director of the NICHD Early Interventions Project in Washington, DC, where she was invited to testify to Congress three times on issues of teacher preparation and reading instruction in high poverty schools. Recently, she concluded ten years as research adviser and consultant with Sopris Learning, serving as Principle Investigator on two Small Business Innovation Research (SBIR) grants from the National Institutes of Health.

Dr. Moats was a contributing writer of the Common Core State Standards, Foundational Reading Skills, for grades K–5. In addition to the *LETRS* professional development series, Dr. Moats's books include *Speech to Print: Language Essentials for Teachers* (Brookes Publishing); *Spelling: Development, Disability, and Instruction* (Pro-Ed); *Straight Talk About Reading* (with Susan Hall, Contemporary Books), and *Basic Facts about Dyslexia*. Dr. Moats's awards include the prestigious Samuel T. and June L. Orton award from the International Dyslexia Association, for outstanding contributions to the field.

Based on the original work of Jane Fell Greene, Ed.D.

Jane Fell Greene has been at the forefront of the nation's literacy movement for many years. Prior to creating *LANGUAGE!®, The Comprehensive Literacy Curriculum*—used to teach reading, writing, vocabulary, grammar, spelling and language to at-risk and ESL students since 1995 and now in its 4th edition—Dr. Greene earned credentials in and taught English, speech, and ESL at both middle and high school levels for twenty years. Subsequently, she taught undergraduate and graduate courses in reading, reading disabilities, ESL, and clinical diagnosis for another ten years.

A tireless advocate for students who experience delays in literacy acquisition, Dr. Greene has been a frequent presenter at national and international conferences. She oversaw the *National Council of LANGUAGE! Trainers* until 2010. She has served on the Board of Directors of the International Dyslexia Association and is a Fellow of the Orton Gillingham Academy of Practitioners and Educators.

Program Contributors

Contributing Author

Anne Whitney, Ed.D., CCC-SLP
Clinical Professor
University of Colorado
Speech, Language, Hearing Department

Program Validation

Charleston County School District
Charleston, South Carolina
ARMS Academy at Morningside Middle
Baptist Hill High School
Burke High School
Burke Middle School
C E Williams Middle School
Cairo Middle School
Daniel Jenkins Creative Learning Center
Ellington Elementary School
EXCEL Academy at Morningside Middle School
Ft. Johnson Middle School
Garrett Academy of Technology
Haut Gap Middle School
James Island Middle School
Jerry Zucker Middle School
Laing Middle School
Liberty Hill Academy
Lincoln Middle-High School
Military Magnet Academy
Moultrie Middle School
North Charleston High School
Northwoods Middle School
R. B. Stall High School
Sanders-Clyde School
St. John's High School
St. Andrew's Middle School
West Ashley High School
West Ashley Middle School

Cohoes City School District
Cohoes, New York
Cohoes High School
Cohoes Middle School

Kansas City Public Schools
Kansas City, Missouri
African Centered College Preparatory Academy
East High School

Contributing Developer

Sheryl Ferlito, Ed.S.
Co-author of *Sortegories*
Secondary Special Education Literacy Teacher

New York City Department of Education
Cluster D75
New York, New York
P.S. K753 - School For Career Development
P.S. M138
P.S. M751 - Manhattan School for Career Development
P.S. R037
P.S. X721 - Stephen McSweeney School

Orange Unified School District
Orange, California
El Ranch Charter School
Portola Middle School

Paulding County School District
Dallas, Georgia
Dobbins Middle School
East Paulding Middle School
McClure Middle School

Schenectady City School District
Schenectady, New York
Steinmetz Career & Leadership Academy
Success Academy for Middle School Students

Walla Walla Public Schools
Walla Walla, Washington
Garrison Middle School

Washington Unified School District
Fresno, California
Washington Union High School
West Fresno Middle School

Program Overview

Welcome to *LANGUAGE! Live* Level 2! This exciting new program blends personalized, online learning with teacher-directed instruction to empower struggling learners to close the learning gap. The carefully crafted learning progression in *LANGUAGE! Live* Level 2 improves students' word analysis, spelling, grammar, comprehension, vocabulary, and writing. The flexible and easy-to-implement program allows students in grades 6–12 to move at their own pace online to improve their reading, writing, and language skills while being exposed to high-interest, complex text with rigorous vocabulary through teacher-directed instruction. This combination ensures accelerated learning and exposure to grade-equivalent text that moves students to grade-level independence.

Why *LANGUAGE! Live* Level 2?

- an emphasis on multisyllabic words and morphology that expands reading skills and builds vocabulary
- technology that allows students to move at their own pace to accelerate learning
- all-inclusive system to support a broad range of academic levels that simplifies intervention and teacher training
- user-friendly, flexible implementation model
- embedded assessment system to track and measure progress and differentiate instruction

Program Implementation

Students with gaps in their reading and writing need targeted instruction to accelerate learning to meet grade-level expectations. Time on instruction is critical!

The blended approach of *LANGUAGE! Live* lessons is designed for a 90-minute instructional block each day. However, the *LANGUAGE! Live* blended program provides flexible implementation opportunities to fit a 45-minute instructional block and different schedules.

The recommended computer classroom configuration is a 1:1 or 2:1 student-to-computer ratio. These two options provide the best personalization, ease of classroom management, and teacher flexibility for delivering instruction.

▶ **In School:** Recommended 90 min. class period

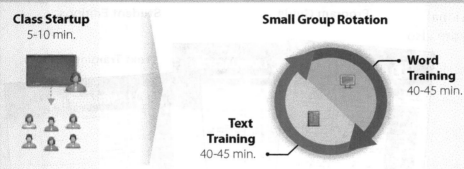

Class Startup
5-10 min.

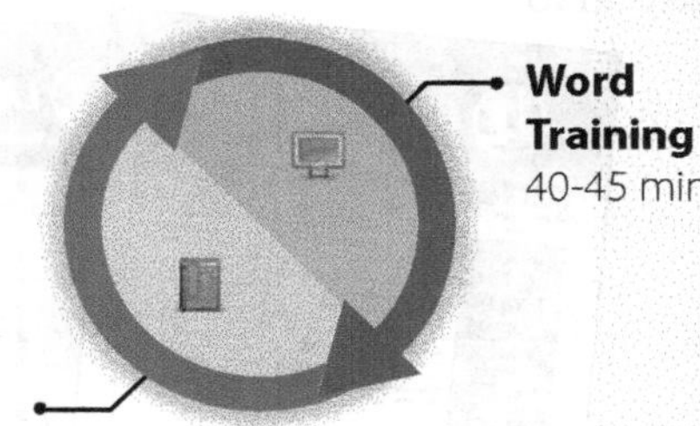

There are two core components to the program, Word Training and Text Training. It is recommended that classroom time be split between both components. Other implementation models and pacing guides are available through our online resources.

Text Training

The easy-to-use printed Teacher Editions provide everything a teacher needs to implement the Text Training component of the instruction during the allotted time period. The Text Training component includes:

- Unit Planners to provide a content snapshot and instructional roadmap for the 10 lessons.
- scripted lessons for ease of planning and implementation.
- clear guidance and support for teachers for effective instruction.
- daily opportunities to encourage collaborative discussions and link to Word Training.
- online Text Training.

Text Training

The online Text Training Practice activities and assessments are teacher-released upon completion of the corresponding lessons or at the end of the Unit. The Text Training component includes:

- Practice activities that include a short tutorial or reminder and are auto-scored.
- Content Mastery quizzes that assess mastery of skills taught in each unit.
- Power Pass quizzes that challenge students to read text analytically and respond to comprehension and vocabulary questions while familiarizing students with a standardized test-like format.

Word Training

Word Training is the highly engaging online platform. This student-centered, adaptive learning environment includes:

- motivating social media and online peer collaboration.
- game-like activities that encourage students to work at a steady pace.
- the ability for students to monitor their own progress and work at their own pace to accelerate or slow down instruction based on individual needs.

Program Components

Text Training

The easy-to-use Teacher Editions provide a carefully crafted learning progression integrating the literacy strands that provide a full menu of English Language Arts areas.

The easily accessible Student Editions and Text Training Posters correlate to the teacher instruction. Additional support materials are also available in the student material.

Level 2 Text Training Teacher Editions and Program Guide

Level 2 Text Training Student Editions

Text Training Posters

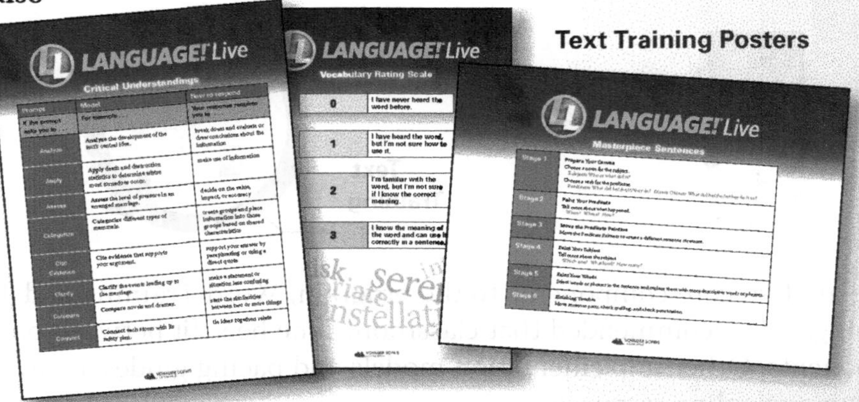

The online Resources are organized into three areas: Program Planning, Text Training, and Word Training. Resources include videos, guides, posters, and digital editions of print materials to help a teacher optimize instruction. These components can be displayed for whole class instruction or printed for extra practice, review, or homework.

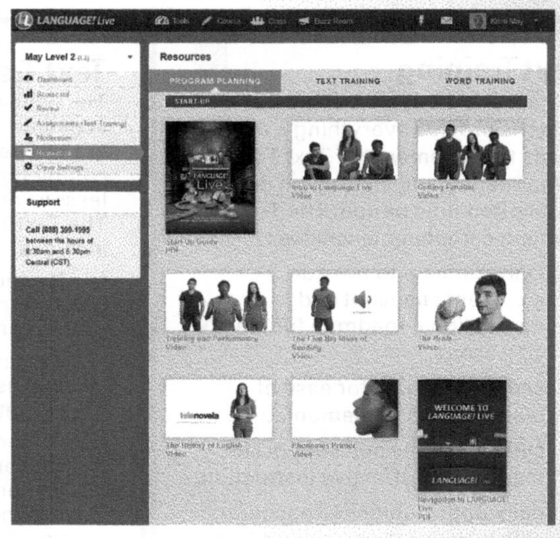

The online Practice activities, Content Mastery assessments, and Power Pass assessments are teacher-released and correspond directly to the skills taught in each Unit of Text Training.

Word Training

Each Word Training Lesson includes video tutorials; quick checks for understanding; engaging, interactive, cumulative word study activities; and fluency passages that allow students to practice and record their reading.

Instructional video on closed syllables

Engaging peer video on suffixes

Blend and Read activity in which student is asked to find vowels, then divide syllables

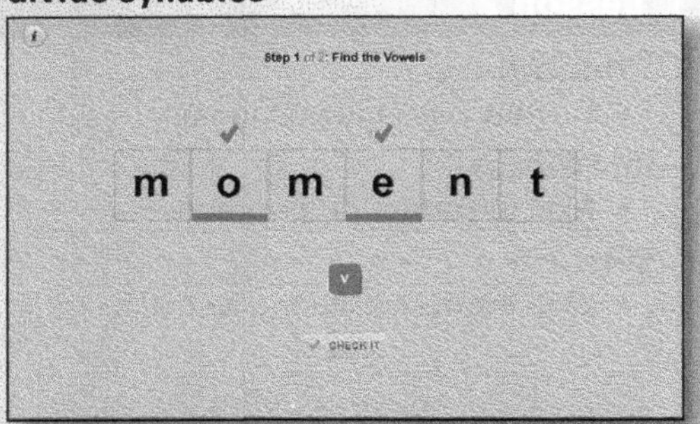

Shuffle activity in which student reconstructs a shuffled sentence

The online Course Guide provides a breakdown of all the Word Training Lessons and Unit Goals. Links are provided for all the lesson activities in each Unit. Use these resources to present to the class, review with a student, or preview what students will be learning.

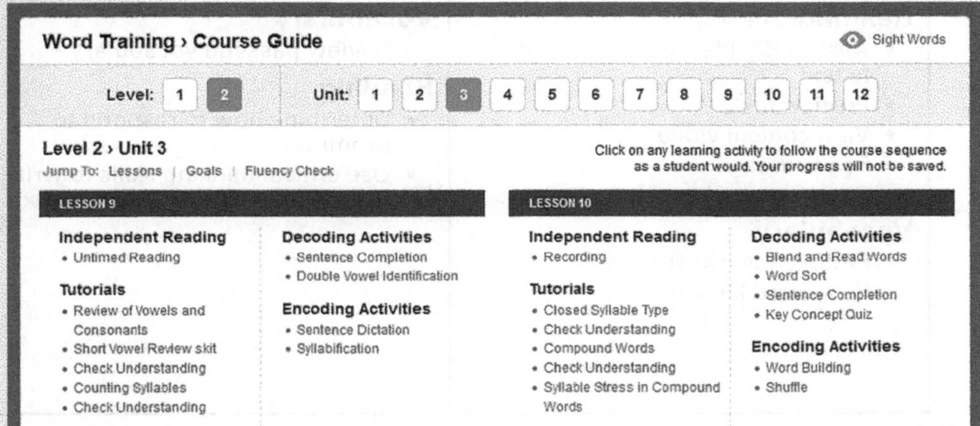

Instructional Design

Word Training—Online 

Lessons 1–4, self-paced

Independent Read
Decodable passages on Unit topics

Tutorials and Check for Understanding
Introduction of new skills through instructional videos and immediate practice

Cumulative Practice
Interactive decoding, encoding, and fluency practice activities including sentence completion, dictation, and syllabification

Unit Goals
End-of-unit area for practice, adaptation, and assessment.
Unit Goals include Read Words, Spell Words, Sentence Completion, and Stressed Syllables.

Sight Words
Fun gaming environment for students to practice reading and spelling sight words.

Text Training—Print

Lesson 1	Lesson 2
Reading • Answer Big Idea questions related to text • Preview text • View content video • Read passage • Check comprehension **Vocabulary** • Preteach words from text • Rate word knowledge	**Vocabulary** • Review passage vocabulary **Grammar** • Skill introduction or practice **Writing** • Skill introduction or practice

Lesson 6	Lesson 7
Reading • Answer Big Idea questions related to text • Preview text • View content video • Read passage • Check comprehension **Vocabulary** • Preteach words from text • Rate word knowledge	**Vocabulary** • Review passage vocabulary **Reading** • Determine how to respond to prompts • Use critical thinking skills to write responses to prompts about text

Text Training—Online 

Assigned at teacher's discretion

Practice Activities

Review of previously taught grammar, vocabulary, and reading skills through interactive activities

Content Mastery

Assessments targeting specific skills taught in Text Training

Power Pass

Provides practice reading text and answering questions in high-stakes assessment format

Lesson 3	Lesson 4	Lesson 5
Reading • Establish a purpose for rereading text • Reread text • Use critical thinking skills to write responses to prompts about text • Support written answers with evidence from text	**Vocabulary** • Review passage vocabulary **Reading** • Complete close reading of text • Dissect syntax, word meaning, and author's craft to foster comprehension of text	**Vocabulary** • Review key passage vocabulary **Writing** • Use text to write in response to reading **Reading** • Answer questions to demonstrate comprehension of text • Engage in class discussion • Identify the enduring understandings from a piece of text
Lesson 8	**Lesson 9**	**Lesson 10**
Reading • Establish a purpose for rereading text • Reread text • Use critical thinking skills to write responses to prompts about text • Support written answers with evidence from text	**Vocabulary** • Review passage vocabulary **Reading** • Complete close reading of text • Dissect syntax, word meaning, and author's craft to foster comprehension of text	**Writing** • Plan • Craft • Review • Use a rubric to guide and assess writing **Reading** • Answer questions to demonstrate comprehension of text • Engage in class discussion • Identify the enduring understandings from a piece of text

Sample Lessons

The Unit Plan shows how the instructional design strategically weaves all the English Language Arts strands into a cohesive ten-lesson cycle.

The text references provide a quick glance at the passage selections and text types read in the Unit.

The colored headings under the lesson headers correlate to the ELA strands taught within each lesson.

The objectives and skills taught within a literacy strand are part of the overall learning progression across each lesson. (Pages are referenced when the number of objectives exceed the limit.)

Word Study and fluency elements taught online are listed within each Unit Plan, although students may work at their own pace on these activities. The grammar and vocabulary practices, as well as the Content Mastery assessments, are included to inform the teacher what he or she will assign online for student completion.

Unit 5 **Unit Plan**

Primary Texts:
Excerpt from *Breaking Night*
by Liz Murray
Text type: informational—memoir

"From Homeless to Harvard"
Text type: informational

***Language! Live* Online**

Grammar Practice
- Identify the function of linking verbs, helping verbs, and action verbs in sentences.
- Use verb tenses correctly.
- Use coordinating conjunctions to combine sentence elements.
- Use *to be* verbs correctly.

Vocabulary Practice
- Distinguish between commonly confused words and use them correctly.
- Determine the meaning of derivations of words.
- Determine the meaning of similes.

Content Mastery
- Demonstrate an understanding of . . .
  - word meaning by answering questions and using words in sentences.
  - the multiple functions of nouns.
  - coordinating conjunctions in compound sentence elements.
  - how to analyze and answer questions about text.

Word Study
- Discuss Anglo-Saxon, Greek, and Latin layers of English and the meaning of morphemes.
- Blend, read, and spell multisyllabic words with open syllables; words with prefixes pre-, re-, and super- and suffixes -er and -est; words with spellings wr-, kn-, gn-, -ch as /k/ and -ph as /f/; contractions containing the words *had* and *have*.
- Read connected text to build fluency.

Lesson 1

Reading
- Determine and discuss the topic of a text.
- Determine and discuss the author' purpose.
- Use text features to preview text.

Vocabulary
- Evaluate word knowledge.
- Determine the meaning of key passage vocabulary.

Reading
- Read an excerpt from a memoir.
- Monitor comprehension during tex reading.

Lesson 6

Reading
- Determine and discuss the topic of a text.
- Determine and discuss the author's purpose.
- Use text features to preview text.

Vocabulary
- Evaluate word knowledge.
- Determine the meaning of key passage vocabulary.

Reading
- Read informational text.
- Monitor comprehension during tex reading.

Writing Project, Units 4–6: A

358 Unit 5 • Unit Plan

		Lesson 3	Lesson 4	Lesson 5
ocabulary. as direct preposition, orrectly. mpound redicates, and f co[illegible]inating ces. of a sentence. verbs correctly ces for clarity compound		**Reading** • Objectively summarize informational text. • Determine the central idea of informational text. • Reread a memoir for comprehension. • Establish a purpose for rereading text. • Determine the central idea of text. • Use critical thinking skills to write responses to prompts about text. • Support written answers with evidence from text. • Draw inferences from text and support with evidence.	**Vocabulary** • Review key passage vocabulary. **Reading** • Read with purpose and understanding. • Answer questions to demonstrate comprehension of text. • Monitor comprehension of text during reading. • Determine the meaning of figurative language in text. • Identify coordinate adjectives in text and the punctuation used to separate them. • Identify the conditional tense in writing and understand its meaning. • Identify stereotyping in text. • Determine the impact of imperative verbs in text. ** See p. 390 for additional lesson objectives.*	**Vocabulary** • Review key passage vocabulary. **Writing** • Use text to write coherent paragraphs in response to reading. • Analyze a character and how the character's traits affect the events in the text. **Reading** • Self-correct as comprehension of text deepens. • Answer questions to demonstrate comprehension of text. • Engage in class discussion. • Identify the enduring understandings from a piece of text. • Identify the influence individuals have on ideas and events. • Identify the impact of perspective and mood.

		Lesson 8	Lesson 9	Lesson 10
ocabulary. oond to kills to write about text. ers with in informational ext.		**Reading** • Establish a purpose for rereading informational text. • Monitor comprehension during text reading. • Use critical thinking skills to write responses to prompts about text. • Support written answers with evidence from text. • Use text evidence to support claims. • Analyze the effect a person has on events. • Sequence events.	**Vocabulary** • Review key passage vocabulary. **Reading** • Read informational text. • Read with purpose and understanding. • Answer questions to demonstrate comprehension of text. • Monitor comprehension during text reading. • Distinguish between the subjective point of view and the objective point of view. • Identify how text is organized and how each section contributes to the whole text. • Identify the conditional tense in writing and understand its meaning.	**Vocabulary** • Review key passage vocabulary. **Writing** • Use two texts to write coherently. • Use a process to write. • Compare and contrast one author's presentation of events with that of another. • Use a rubric to guide and evaluate writing. **Reading** • Self-correct as comprehension of text deepens. • Answer questions to demonstrate comprehension of text. • Engage in class discussion. • Identify the enduring understandings from a piece of text. • Compare and contrast two portrayals of a place or historical account. • Identify the influence individuals have on ideas and events. • Identify the impact of perspective and mood.

Sample Lessons

The carefully crafted lessons provide clear guidance and support for effective instruction.

The Lesson Opener provides several prompts to begin the class with collaborative conversation about previous learning. The prompts can be presented either online or as class discussion.

The colored headings and objectives show the ELA strand and learning objective for that specific portion of the lesson.

Passage Vocabulary is introduced and reviewed multiple times for students to internalize the word meaning.

Annotated student materials are pictured at point of use to support planning and provide a real-time resource.

Scripted lessons make it easier to plan and implement instruction.

Unit 11 Lesson 5

Lesson Opener

Before the lesson, choose one of the following activiti
on the *LANGUAGE! Live* Class Wall online.

- *Write four sentences with at least two vocabulary meanings. (fruition, fashion, delicately, cease, pre mutinous, acknowledgment)*
- *Write three simple sentences that describe Wang following questions in your sentences: When doe How does he bathe? Combine the three sentence*
- *What would you have done if you were Wang Lun your father?*

Vocabulary

Objective

- Review key passage vocabulary.

Recontextualize Passage Vocabulary

Direct students to page 290 in their Student Books. following questions to review the vocabulary words excerpt from *The Good Earth.*

- You release the lever too late and the pinball d hole. Did you *divert* the pinball? (no) Your fri across the classroom. He's concentrating on ar You signal to him but can't get his attention. D his attention? (no) Your family has the TV tu need to study. You stuff cotton balls in your ea concentration won't be what? (diverted)
- If the wind picks up speed, will the tree branch waving? (no) The alarm goes off, and you pus Does the buzzing *cease*? (yes) The people beh the movie are laughing and carrying on. You w
- You pin tiny flowers carefully into your friend' them *delicately*? (yes) You toss a stack of old Have you put them in the bin *delicately*? (no) thread through the eye of a needle. You have t
- You plan a cookout in the park for your dad's b come to *fruition*? (no) You buy one of those c from seeds inside the body. You water your "p green covering. Did your pet's fur come to *fru* your favorite celebrity for three years, and he f have come to what? (fruition)

404 Unit 11 • Lesson 5

Margin notes alert the teacher when assignments or assessments can be released online for students to complete during computer time.

Reading

Objectives

- Self-correct as comprehension of text deepens.
- Answer questions to demonstrate comprehension of text.
- Engage in class discussion.
- Identify the enduring understandings from a piece of text.

Revisit Passage Comprehension

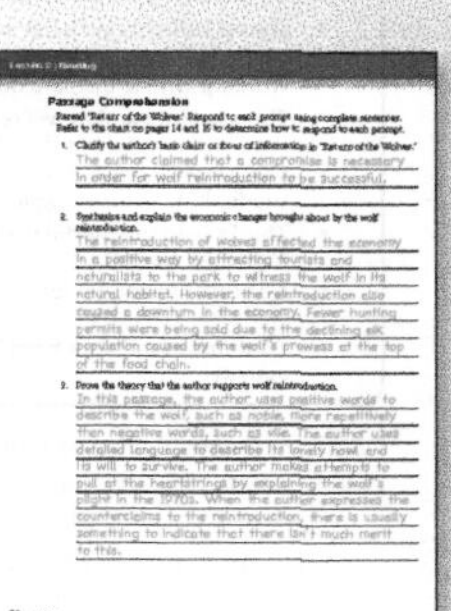

Direct students back to pages 30 and 31 in their Student Books. Have students review their answers and make any necessary changes. Then, have partners share their answers and collaborate to perfect them.

Enduring Understandings

Direct students back to page 23 in their Student Books. Reread the Big Idea questions.

How do stereotypes of wolves affect their image and perhaps even their existence?

Should humans interfere with nature? Explain.

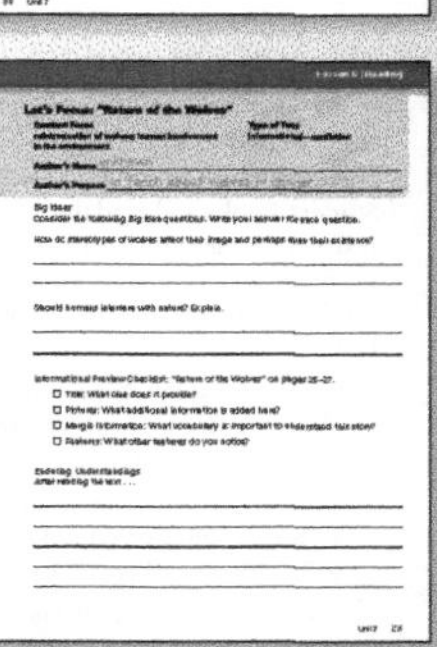

Generate a class discussion about the questions and answers students came up with in Lesson 6. Have them consider whether their answers have changed any after reading the text.

Use the following talking points to foster conversation. Then, have students write their enduring understandings from the unit.

- Wolves are shown as villains in storybooks and horror movies. In reality, wolves are insecure and at risk. It is important to educate ourselves beyond fiction, horror, and fairy tales in order to be knowledgeable about the issues that impact our ecology. It is also important to see past prejudices and understand that misconceptions exist among all species.
- Human interference impacts the ecosystem in ways that man did not fully realize. Is all human interference bad interference? Are humans at the top of the food chain? Are we simply following the natural order of life by interfering in animal habitats for our benefit? Or, is it possible that human interference can be positive, such as by bringing wolves out of jeopardy of extinction?

What we read should make us think. Use our discussion and your thoughts about the text to determine what you will "walk away with." Has it made you think about a personal experience or someone you know? Has your perspective or opinion on a specific topic changed? Do you have any lingering thoughts or questions? Write these ideas as your enduring understandings. What will you take with you from this text?

Assign online Unit 7 ***Content Mastery*** *quizzes and* ***Power Pass*** *from the Text Training link on the left menu of your teacher dashboard.*

Discuss the enduring understandings with the class. If time permits, have students post a personal response about their enduring understandings to the online class wall.

Remind students to consider why the author wrote the passage and whether he or she was successful.

Sample Lessons

The reading strand builds comprehension through explicit systematic instruction of academic vocabulary to ask and answer questions.

Chart Reading Procedure

- Group students with partners or in triads.
- Have students count off as 1s or 2s. The 1s will become the student leaders. If working with triads, the third students become 3s.
- The student leaders will read the left column (Prompt) in addition to managing the time and turn-taking if working with a triad.
- The 2s will explain the middle column of the chart (How to Respond). If working in triads, 3s take turns explaining the middle column.
- The 1s read the model in the right column (Model), and 2s and 3s restate the model as a question.
- All students should follow along with their pencil eraser while others are explaining the chart.
- Students must work from left to right, top to bottom in order to benefit from this activity.

Check for understanding by requesting an oral response to the following questions.

- If the prompt asks you to *clarify*, the response requires you to . . . (make a statement or situation less confusing).
- If the prompt asks you to *develop an argument*, the response requires you to . . . (work on a case over a period of time, during which it grows or changes).
- If the prompt asks you to *prove*, the response requires you to . . . (give evidence to show that it is true).
- If the prompt asks you to *support*, the response requires you to . . . (help it succeed).

Direct students to page 274 in their Student Books and read the instructions aloud. Let's read some prompts about a small section of the text before we expand to the entire text.

1. Clarify the author's claim that most of us "take for granted" our freedom to dress how we like.
2. Develop an argument against the author's claim that school uniforms stifle growth and creativity.
3. Use your personal clothing choices to prove the author's claim that our clothing sends a message.
4. Write a four-line poem to support the author's claim that dress codes are bad.

We are going to focus on the first section of the text. We will practice answering prompts with these new direction words. Having a good understanding of the text from the

Lesson 7 | Reading

Critical Understandings

Reread the first section of "Say Yes to Free Dress!" Respond to each prompt using complete sentences. Refer to the chart on pages 14 and 15 to determine how to respond to each prompt.

1. Clarify the author's claim that most of us "take for granted" our freedom to dress how we like.
   The author is saying that because many of us have always had the freedom to dress how we like, we do not appreciate it. People who are forced to dress in a certain way would likely have a greater appreciation for the freedom to dress to express.
2. Develop an argument against the author's claim that school uniforms stifle growth and creativity.
   School uniforms do not stifle growth and creativity. In fact, they do the opposite. When students are no longer allowed to express themselves through clothing (a very easy form of expression), they are forced to develop new methods of expression—increasing creativity and, thus, personal growth.
3. Use your personal clothing choices to prove the author's claim that our clothing sends a message.
   Answers will vary but should be about the way in which clothing choices express who students are and what they like and/or don't like.
4. Write a four-line poem to support the author's claim that dress codes are bad.
   Answers will vary. Possible answer:
   Who am I and what do I stand for?
   Instead of telling you, I would rather show you.
   In this polo and khaki pants I am silenced.
   How I long to express. How I long to express.

274 Unit 10

beginning will help build a foundation for understanding the rest of the te[xt and make] it feel less difficult.

Guided Practice

Let's practice answering questions that are written as prompts. Remember [to use the] chart as reference.

1. Clarify the author's claim that most of us "take for granted" our freed[om to] dress how we like.

How should we respond according to the chart? (If the prompt asks you to [clarify,] the response requires that you make a statement or situation less confusin[g.) Now,] turn the prompt into a question to confirm your understanding. Tell your [partner] the question. (What does the author mean when he or she says most of us [take for] granted" our freedom to dress how we like?)

While providing partner time, write the sentence starter on the board.

The author is saying ____________.

Have partners answer the question.

2. Develop an argument against the author's claim that school uniforms [stifle] growth and creativity.

How should we respond according to the chart? (If the prompt asks you to [develop] *an argument*, the response requires that you work on a case over a period [of time,] during which it grows or changes.) Now, turn the prompt into a question [to confirm] your understanding. Tell your partner the question. (What is the proof th[at school] uniforms do not stifle growth and creativity?) Because you are being aske[d to work on] a case over a period of time, you will need to pull in information from thin[gs you] learned in the past.

While providing partner time, write the sentence starter on the board.

School uniforms do not stifle growth and creativity. In fact, ____________

Have partners answer the question.

3. Use your personal clothing choices to prove the author's claim that o[ur] clothing sends a message.

How should we respond according to the chart? (If the prompt asks you to [prove,] the response requires that you give evidence to show that it is true.) Now, [turn the] prompt into a question to confirm your understanding. Tell your partner t[he question.] (What experiences from your personal clothing choices prove that our clo[thing sends] a message?) Remember, you are using personal clothing experiences as pr[oof] about this.

While providing partner time, write the sentence starter on the board.

Unit

Students are asked to provide evidence-based responses to develop conceptual understanding and strategic thinking. This carefully crafted learning progression teaches the key strategies needed to be successful on high-stakes assessments.

A strong grammar strand directly linked to the writing strand builds skilled writers.

Strategies and skills are explicitly taught using teacher modeling, guided practice, and student application.

ppositives

ou have learned that nouns have a variety of jobs in a sentence. What are some f the jobs that nouns can have in a sentence? (subject, direct object, or object of e preposition) Sometimes, we can use nouns to further identify or explain other ouns. Unlike adjectives that offer descriptive details, sometimes another noun helps e reader understand the *who* or *what* better. Nouns used in this way are called ppositives. What do you call nouns that serve to further identify other nouns? ppositives) Appositives offer us another way to vary the sentence structure while roviding more specific details about a noun in a sentence.

irect students to page 301 in their udent Books. Read the information bout appositives and the first set of xamples aloud.

Lesson 2 | Grammar

Appositives

An appositive:

- Is a noun, pronoun, or noun phrase that serves to explain or identify another noun or pronoun
- Immediately precedes or follows the noun that it is identifying
- Is set off by commas unless it is essential to the meaning of a sentence

Examples:
The old man, a widower, lives with his son.
Wang Lung, his only son, works hard to make a living on their farm.
The young farmer Wang Lung is soon to be married.

Read each sentence. Underline the appositive in each sentence and draw an arrow to the noun it modifies.

Example:
He had asked his male cousin, the young son of his uncle, to sup that night.

1. The young woman, a slave in the House of Hwang, would soon be his wife.
2. Wang Lung, a poor farmer, worked tirelessly to tend to his fields.
3. Wang Lung's father, an old and sickly man, expected his son's wife to take care of him.
4. Wang Lung's mother, a hardworking farmer's wife, had been dead for six years.
5. Wang Lung, an anxious and excited bridegroom, walked to town to meet his new wife.

Unit 11 301

lodel

ead the instructions for the activity.

isten as I read the example: *He had sked his male cousin, the young son of is uncle, to sup that night.*

he first thing I need to do is identify e appositive, or the noun phrase that enames or further identifies another oun in the sentence. Who or what is e sentence about? *He* is the subject. hat did he do? He *had asked*. ho did he ask? *His male cousin*. oes the sentence give me any more formation about who *he* is? No. Does give me any more information about e direct object *cousin*? Yes, it tells e he is the young son of his uncle. he phrase *the young son of his uncle* enames or further identifies the direct bject *cousin*. Because it is a noun phrase that further identifies another noun, it is an ppositive. I need to underline the phrase and then draw an arrow back to the noun at it renames. So, I draw an arrow back to *cousin*.

uided Practice

isten as I read #1: *The young woman, a slave in the House of Hwang, would soon be is wife.*

ho or what is the sentence about? (woman) Does the sentence give us details that entify her further? (yes) How does the sentence further explain her identity? (a ave in the House of Hwang) That's a noun phrase that adds information about the bject noun—an appositive. What is your next step? (underline the appositive) After nderlining the appositive, what's your last step? (draw an arrow from the phrase to *oman*)

Independent Practice

Have students complete the activity. Review the answers as a class.

Writing

Objectives

- Combine sentences using appositives.
- Use proper subject-verb agreement.

Appositives in Writing

Direct students to page 302 in their Student Books. Read the instructions aloud.

Using appositives when you write allows you to pack a lot of information into one sentence. It also allows you to add diversity and complexity to your sentence structure.

Lesson 2 | Writing

Appositives in Writing

Write one sentence that combines each pair of sentences by turning one sentence into an appositive. Remember to correctly punctuate each new sentence.

Example:
The stove is an earthen brick structure.
His grandfather built the stove with clay from his farm.
His grandfather built the stove, an earthen brick structure, with clay from his farm.

1. Wang Lung's father is a feeble old man.
   Wang Lung's father lives with him.
   Wang Lung's father, a feeble old man, lives with him.
2. Wang Lung's new wife is a slave in the House of Hwang.
   Wang Lung's new wife lives in town.
   Wang Lung's new wife, a slave in the House of Hwang, lives in town.
3. Wang Lung is a dutiful son.
   Wang Lung takes good care of his father.
   Wang Lung, a dutiful son, takes good care of his father.
4. Arranged marriages are a common practice in rural China.
   Arranged marriages are frowned upon in the Western world.
   Arranged marriages, a common practice in rural China, are frowned upon in the Western world.
5. Wang Lung's bride is a poor slave.
   The slave married Wang Lung for a chance for a better life.
   Wang Lung's bride, a poor slave, married Wang Lung for a chance at a better life.

302 Unit 11

Model

Listen as I read the example: *The stove is an earthen brick structure. His grandfather built the stove with clay from his farm.* What are both sentences about? They both give us information about the stove. We can further identify the stove by adding the phrase *earthen brick structure* to the second sentence. *His grandfather built the stove, an earthen brick structure, with clay from his farm.* What punctuation sets the phrase apart from the rest of the sentence? Commas before and after the phrase are needed to properly punctuate the sentence. The rewritten sentence is a good reminder to look for ways to expand any noun in a sentence, not just the subject noun. In this sentence, *stove* answers the *built what* question, making it the direct object.

Guided Practice

Listen as I read #1: *Wang Lung's father is a feeble old man. Wang Lung's father lives with him.* What are both sentences about? (Wang Lung's father) How can you combine the information about Wang Lung's father in the first sentence with the second sentence? Turn and tell your partner how you would combine the two sentences. Remember: our combined sentence needs to have a noun phrase that renames or further identifies one of the nouns in the sentence. What is the new sentence? (Wang Lung's father, a feeble old man, lives with him.) What punctuation do we need within the sentence? (commas before and after the phrase) Check your sentence to make sure you've written it correctly.

Requiring students to write their responses provides the handwriting practice students need to become more fluent writers.

Program Texts

Unit 1

Primary Texts
- Excerpt from *Holes*
- "The Science of Catching Criminals"

Independent Reading Texts
- The Kid and the Pen
- My Sis Beth

Fluency Text
- Our Dog King

Power Pass Text
- Clues

Unit 2

Primary Texts
- "Thank You, M'am"
- "If I Were in Charge of the World"
- "We Real Cool"

Independent Reading Texts
- Hope for Hugs
- A Boy Named Drew

Fluency Text
- Skills

Power Pass Text
- Vandal

Unit 3

Primary Texts
- Excerpt from *The Outsiders*
- Excerpt from *The Play of the Diary of Anne Frank*

Independent Reading Texts
- Help from an Outsider
- Things are Just Things

Fluency Text
- At the Zoo

Power Pass Text
- Teá Dobromir

Unit 4

Primary Texts
- "The Circuit"
- from *The Autobiography of Malcolm X*

Independent Reading Texts
- Read for Life
- War and Water

Fluency Text
- Camping in the Forest

Power Pass Text
- César Chávez

Unit 5

Primary Texts
- Excerpt from *Breaking Night*
- "From Homeless to Harvard"

Independent Reading Texts
- George Lopez
- A Family Man

Fluency Text
- Reba's Hero

Power Pass Text
- *StreetWise* magazine

Unit 6

Primary Texts
- "The Symbol of Freedom"
- "I Am Prepared to Die"

Independent Reading Texts
- Excerpt from *The Story of an African Farm*
- Excerpt from *A Rip Van Winkle of the Kalahari*

Fluency Text
- Chocolate Chip Bars

Power Pass Text
- Helpers and Heroes

Unit 7

Primary Texts
- Excerpt from *White Fang*
- "Return of the Wolves"

Independent Reading Texts
- Reading to Dogs
- Liak's Sled Dog

Fluency Text
- Snow Day

Power Pass Text
- Fenrir the Wolf

Unit 8

Primary Texts
- "The White Wolf of the Hartz Mountains"
- *Who Speaks for Wolf*

Independent Reading Texts
- A Dog's Talent
- How Smart Is that Animal?

Fluency Text
- A King's Domain

Power Pass Text
- Wolf Society

Unit 9

Primary Texts
- "The Mysterious Human Brain"
- Graphic Novel of *The Strange Case of Dr. Jekyll and Mr. Hyde*

Independent Reading Texts
- Hiding Out Through Surgery
- Dyeing to Help

Fluency Text
- The Bike and the Broken Arm

Power Pass Text
- A Wolf in Dark Glasses

Unit 10

Primary Texts
- North High School letter
- "Say Yes to Free Dress!"

Independent Reading Texts
- What Is a Culture?
- Colors Across Cultures

Fluency Text
- Rumors and Lies

Power Pass Text
- Must Be the Shoes

Unit 11

Primary Texts
- Excerpt from *The Good Earth*
- Excerpt from *Nectar in a Sieve*

Independent Reading Texts
- Excerpt from *Nectar in a Sieve*
- The Salt March

Fluency Text
- Seeing Stars

Power Pass Text
- Rising Giants

Unit 12

Primary Texts
- Part 1 of the Excerpt from *My Sister's Keeper*
- Part 2 of the Excerpt from *My Sister's Keeper*

Independent Reading Texts
- The Cancer Virus
- The Strange Case of the Separated Triplets

Fluency Text
- Sophie's Art

Power Pass Text
- To Clone or Not to Clone

Assessments

Effective Measurement Tools

LANGUAGE! Live Level 2 is designed for struggling students who read below grade level. To provide the highest quality of assessment information for placing and monitoring student progress, Cambium's assessment system includes the tools that have proved to be reliable and effective measures of reading.

LANGUAGE! Live Benchmark Assessments

Benchmark 1	Benchmark 2	Benchmark 3
PAR	PAR	PAR
TOSCRF	TOSCRF	TOSCRF
TWS-4	TWS-4	TWS-4

LANGUAGE! Live Benchmark Assessments consist of three norm-referenced assessments that measure students' literacy skills two to three times per calendar year. These assessments are taken online to provide immediate results. The three measures include:

Progress Assessment of Reading (PAR)

The Progress Assessment of Reading (PAR) assesses reading comprehension and yields a Lexile (L) score and is powered by The Lexile® Framework for Reading, a normed measurement system. These series of grade-level assessments monitors each student's reading level and matches text that presents the right degree of challenge to the reader. The Lexile scale ranges are based on grade-level expectations.

The grade-specific PAR consists of 40 questions. Students will need approximately 30 to 45 minutes to complete the PAR.

Test of Silent Contextual Reading Fluency (TOSCRF)

The Test of Silent Contextual Reading Fluency (TOSCRF) is a measure of silent contextual reading fluency. It measures the speed with which students can recognize the individual words in a series of printed passages that become progressively more difficult in their content, vocabulary, and grammar. This three-minute, norm-referenced test measures a wide variety of essential interrelated silent reading skills.

The Test of Written Spelling, 4th edition (TWS-4)

The Test of Written Spelling, 4th edition (TWS-4) is a norm-referenced test of spelling administered twice per year. It can be used to document the overall improvement in spelling as a result of intervention instruction. The test is administered using a dictated word format. The TWS-4 has consistently high reliability and a demonstrated high degree of validity.

Assessments

Ongoing Progress Monitoring

There are several means for progress monitoring within *LANGUAGE! Live* online and in print. The online progress monitoring assessments in Word Training are Unit Goals, Fluency Checks, and Power Pass text quizzes. In the Text Training component, additional opportunities are available to monitor fluency and comprehension through Content Mastery tests and writing samples.

Unit Goals

Unit Goals occur at the end of every Unit, and they assess students' level of mastery of critical elements taught within the Unit. They are composed of adaptive practice and reteach based on students' level of proficiency. The time to complete Goals varies by student since the program adapts based on each student's level of proficiency.

Each Goal is structured by individual goals; three in each Unit. The Unit Goals include Read Words, Spell Words, Sentence Completion, Syllable Stress, and Read Passages. These carefully scaffolded Unit Goals demonstrate a student's ability to read and spell words and build to fluency passages. A Fluency Check passage occurs at the end of each Unit that provides teachers a way to monitor students' fluency growth.

Goals by Unit

	Read Words	Spell Words	Read Passages	Syllable Stress	Sentence Completion	Fluency Check
Unit 1	•	•	•			
Unit 2	•	•	•			
Unit 3	•	•		•		•
Unit 4	•	•			•	•
Unit 5	•	•		•		•
Unit 6	•	•			•	•
Unit 7	•	•			•	•
Unit 8	•	•			•	•
Unit 9	•	•			•	•
Unit 10	•	•			•	•
Unit 11	•	•			•	•
Unit 12	•	•			•	•

Power Pass

Power Pass reading comprehension assessments are implemented at the end of every Unit. Each assessment comprises a short passage with 15 test items. Students answer multiple-choice questions—focusing on comprehension and vocabulary—as well as constructed responses. The assessment items are presented in a format similar to what students will see on a standardized test. These criterion-referenced assessments measure comprehension of text as well as contextual understanding of words and identification of evidence in support of answers. The online program alerts students when it is time to complete a Power Pass assessment at the discretion of the teacher.

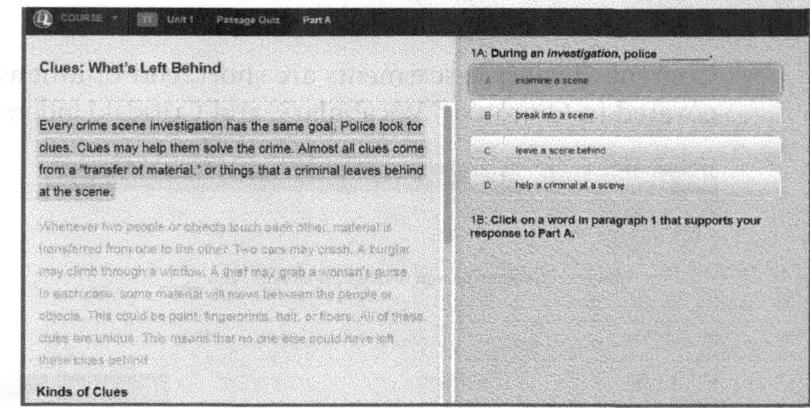

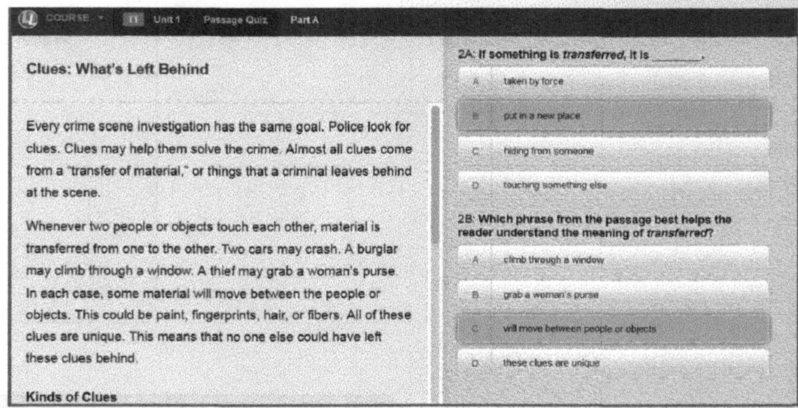

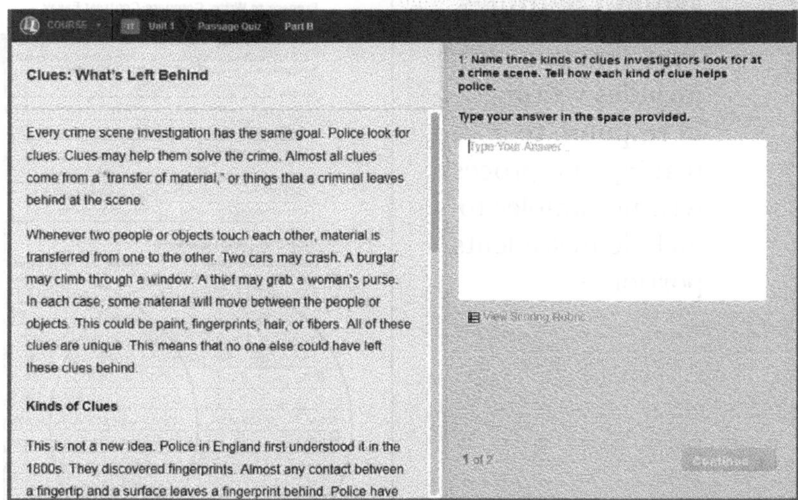

Assessments

Content Mastery

Content Mastery assessments are short, end-of-unit assessments on objectives covered in Grammar, Vocabulary, and Critical Understandings.

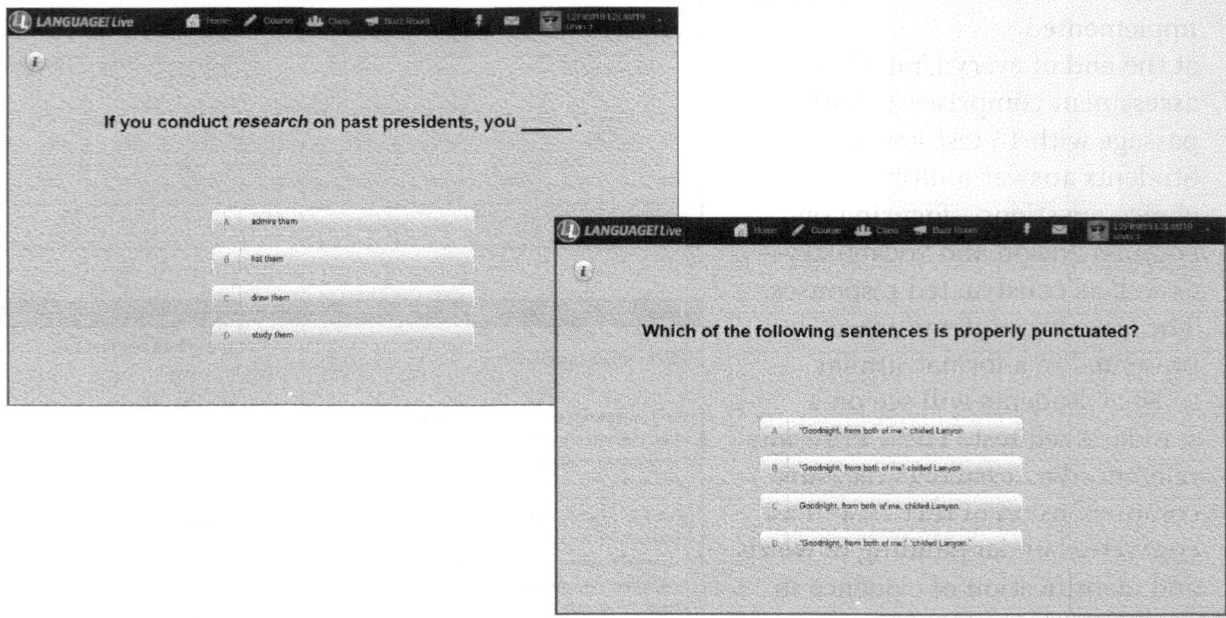

Writing Samples

Text Training also includes writing in response to reading and process writing samples to include in students' portfolios.

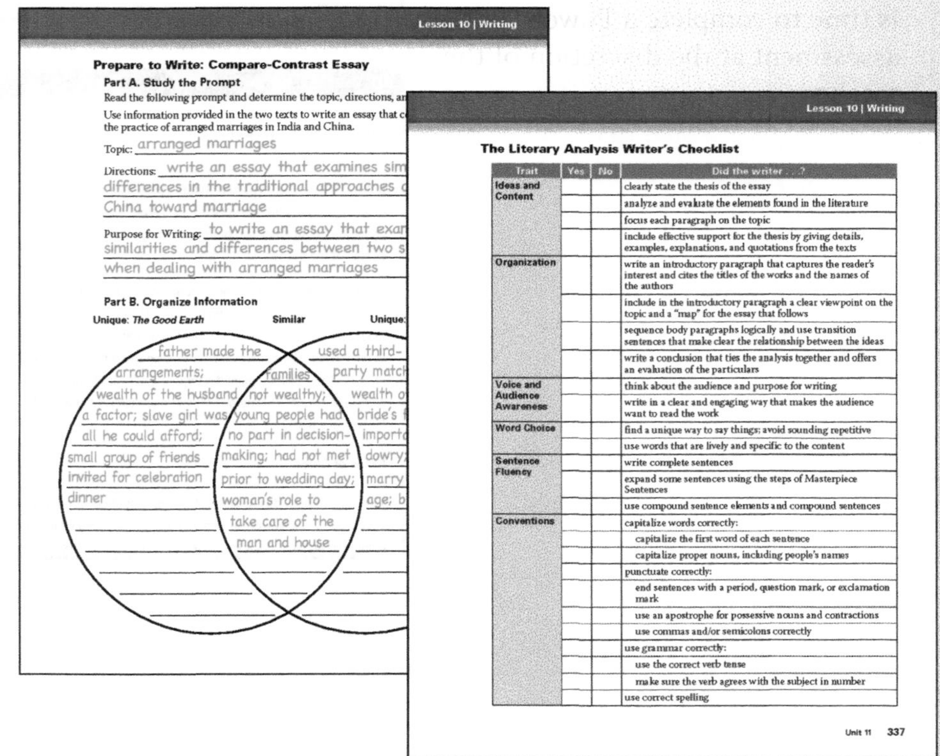

Lesson 10 | Writing

Prepare to Write: Compare-Contrast Essay

Part A. Study the Prompt

Read the following prompt and determine the topic, directions, an

Use information provided in the two texts to write an essay that c the practice of arranged marriages in India and China.

Topic: arranged marriages

Directions: write an essay that examines sim differences in the traditional approaches c China toward marriage

Purpose for Writing: to write an essay that exar similarities and differences between two s when dealing with arranged marriages

Part B. Organize Information

Unique: *The Good Earth* | Similar | Unique:

father made the arrangements; wealth of the husband a factor; slave girl was all he could afford; small group of friends invited for celebration dinner

families not wealthy; young people had no part in decision-making; had not met prior to wedding day; woman's role to take care of the man and house

used a third-party match wealth o bride's importa dowry; marry age; b

Lesson 10 | Writing

The Literary Analysis Writer's Checklist

Trait	Yes	No	Did the writer . . . ?
Ideas and Content			clearly state the thesis of the essay
			analyze and evaluate the elements found in the literature
			focus each paragraph on the topic
			include effective support for the thesis by giving details, examples, explanations, and quotations from the texts
Organization			write an introductory paragraph that captures the reader's interest and cites the titles of the works and the names of the authors
			include in the introductory paragraph a clear viewpoint on the topic and a "map" for the essay that follows
			sequence body paragraphs logically and use transition sentences that make clear the relationship between the ideas
			write a conclusion that ties the analysis together and offers an evaluation of the particulars
Voice and Audience Awareness			think about the audience and purpose for writing
			write in a clear and engaging way that makes the audience want to read the work
Word Choice			find a unique way to say things; avoid sounding repetitive
			use words that are lively and specific to the content
Sentence Fluency			write complete sentences
			expand some sentences using the steps of Masterpiece Sentences
			use compound sentence elements and compound sentences
Conventions			capitalize words correctly:
			capitalize the first word of each sentence
			capitalize proper nouns, including people's names
			punctuate correctly:
			end sentences with a period, question mark, or exclamation mark
			use an apostrophe for possessive nouns and contractions
			use commas and/or semicolons correctly
			use grammar correctly:
			use the correct verb tense
			make sure the verb agrees with the subject in number
			use correct spelling

Unit 11 337

Instructional Routines

Preteach Vocabulary

Key passage vocabulary should be mastered by end of unit. Students will benefit from multiple exposures to each word—orally, in reading, and in writing. Thus, students are not expected to achieve mastery of the words during Lessons 1 and 6. This procedure was designed to take five to ten minutes only and is an introduction to the words.

Research has proven that vocabulary is best learned when students represent their knowledge of words in linguistic and/or nonlinguistic ways. Thus, writing a definition in the vocabulary log can help students remember the meanings. However, this process is secondary to the conversation about the words. If your students would benefit from copying the definitions, please have them do so outside of instruction time. The definitions can be found in the margins of the passages.

Online Writing Projects

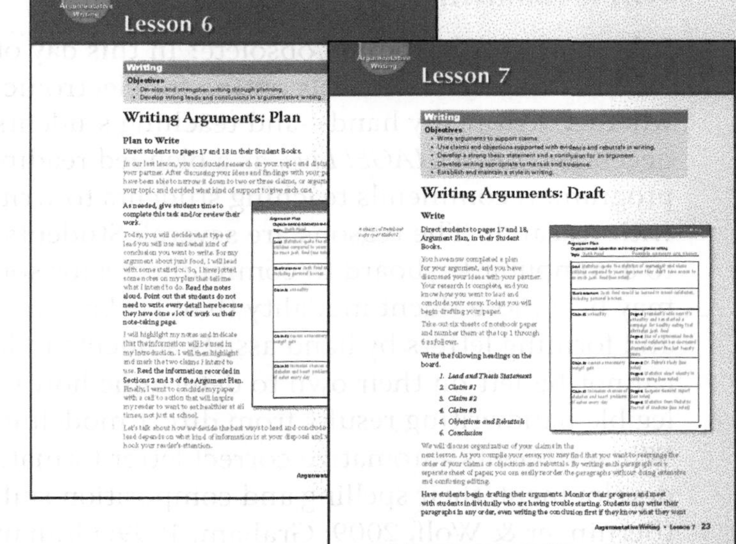
Lesson 6

Writing Arguments: Plan

Lesson 7

Writing Arguments: Draft

1. Lead and Thesis Statement
2. Claim #1
3. Claim #2
4. Claim #3
5. Objections and Rebuttals
6. Conclusion

Four major writing projects can be printed from the Teacher Resources online. The projects were developed to loosely coincide with the designated units in the Text Training, but completion of the units is not mandatory for completion of the projects.

Units 1–3: Informational Writing

Units 4–6: Argumentative Writing

Units 7–9: Compare and Contrast Writing

Units 10–12: Narrative Writing

Writing projects can be administered at the completion of three units of study in Text Training (roughly one per nine weeks) or as the teacher deems beneficial based on state assessment calendars. Each writing project is intended to take 8–10 class periods, and should be given ample time for student thoughts and writing to progressively develop. Students will work to master objectives, not only in writing within the specific genres, but also in analysis of text, peer collaboration, speaking and listening, research, use of technology, and presentation.

Facilitation of the writing projects, in conjunction with the Text Training and Word Training, will meet the necessary requirements for a full ELA curriculum.

Text Reading

Guiding Students Toward Independent Reading

It is important that students read as much and as often as they can. Assign readings that meet student needs, based on observations or data.

Options for reading text:

- Teacher read-aloud
- Teacher-led or student-led choral read
- Paired read or independent read

Handwriting Instruction

Why Is Handwriting Still Important?

Is handwriting becoming obsolete? In this day of texting and e-mail on mobile devices and schools opting for electronic textbooks, some question whether writing by hand—and teaching students to write by hand—is even necessary. *LANGUAGE! Live,* as a blended reading, writing, and language program, recommends teaching students to write by hand, in alignment with research. The reasons are several: Students will not always have access to a computer keyboard to communicate; for some students, handwriting may be a more fluent modality than keyboarding for written expression; and forming letters by hand assists students in learning to spell. Students cannot be left on their own to determine how to form the letters; rather, legible handwriting results from direct modeling, practice, and feedback. When students automatize correct letter formation early in writing development, their spelling and composition skills are likely to be stronger (Berninger & Wolf, 2009; Graham, 1999; Graham, Berninger, Abbott, Abbott, & Whitaker, 1997).

The goal of handwriting instruction is the development of graphomotor habits, or automatized sequences of pencil strokes for each letter, made in a specific direction, with size consistent with other letters. Letter formation is automatic when the component strokes are executed accurately without conscious effort. Letter formation requires more than hand-eye coordination. Letters are codes for speech sounds; thus, the motor habits that enable letter formation are connected neurologically to the language centers of the brain. The brain receives sensory feedback from the hand and directs the timing and direction of letter production; at the same time, however, letters are processed as symbols for speech. Therefore, recall is enhanced if students associate letter names with letter shapes and sounds.

Handwriting in *LANGUAGE! Live*

Measurable goals, based on research, can be referenced for alphabet writing and for sentence writing fluency (Beck, Conrad, & Anderson, 2009; Berninger & Richards, 2002). A fluent adult can produce the cursive alphabet in 20 to 30 seconds. A third-grade student should be able to produce the manuscript alphabet in well under a minute. Once students can copy connected text accurately from a model, fluency should improve with writing practice.

Until students master the fundamentals, handwriting deserves regular practice. When students learn to form the letters correctly and manage the directional, fine motor, and spatial requirements of handwriting, they are likely to write better-organized compositions that are more substantive and longer. As with reading, when students automatize lower-level writing skills, cognitive "desk space" is freed up for higher-level thinking about purpose, organization, audience, wording, and images.

During *LANGUAGE! Live* Text Training, teachers need to emphasize and reward accuracy and legibility during spelling, grammar, and writing instruction.

Additional lessons are available online in the Teacher Resources for students needing more support in handwriting. Some of these brief activities include the following:

- Letter formation manuscript and cursive
- Brief fluency drills
- Alphabet production
- Sentence copying and completion

Tips for Teaching Basic Letter Formation

- Teach lowercase manuscript first, then practice uppercase letters. Move to cursive later.
- Sequence the introduction of letters according to groups with similar basic strokes.
- Check student posture, pencil grip, and paper position. Accommodate left-handed students by tilting the paper toward the left.
- Name a letter, then demonstrate the letter's formation by verbally describing each stroke as you model writing the letter.
- Supply a modeled letter that uses numbered arrows to remind students of the order and direction of strokes.
- Ask students to imitate the motion with their whole arm, with index and middle fingers pointing, tracing in the air or on a rough surface.
- Ask students to trace on top of a well-formed letter on paper before they cover up the model and write the letter from memory. Always have students name the letter as they write it. (Berninger & Wolf, 2009)

Training and Support Services

Voyager Sopris Learning's Professional Development partnership is provided throughout the school year and integrates continuous training and implementation support with technical assistance and detailed reporting on student achievement.

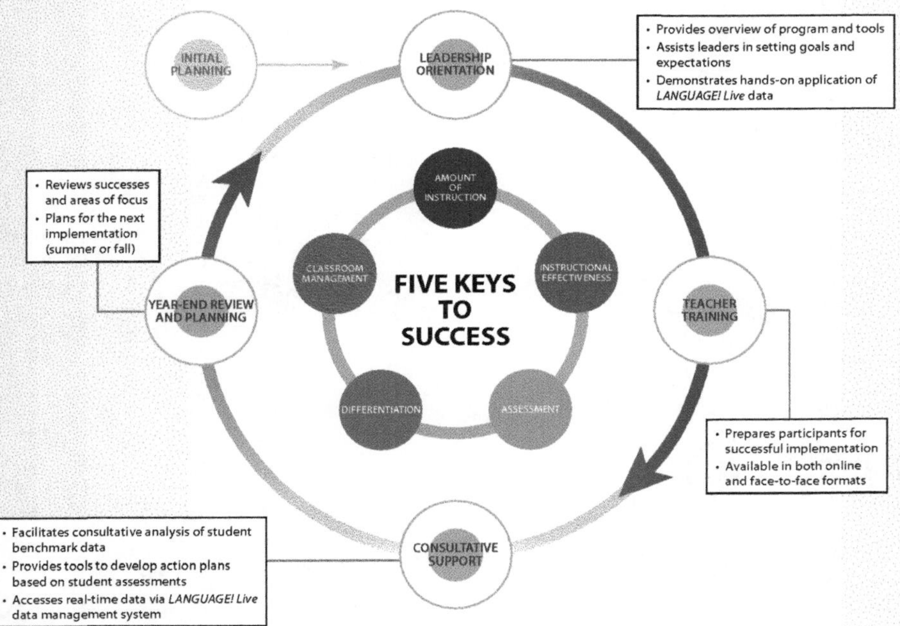

The framework is a cyclical model in which critical activities occur throughout the school year. From initial planning, to leadership and teacher training, to consultative support and year-end review, each step ensures that the implementation is positioned for success.

Initial Planning

Initial Planning is essential to the success of the program and provides an opportunity for the district leadership to articulate its goals for the program and for the team to tailor an implementation plan that addresses its unique needs. The planning sessions enable the team to address logistics, anticipate challenges, respond to questions, and clearly define roles and responsibilities.

Leadership Orientation

The Leadership Orientation is designed to ensure that site and district administrators understand the foundational principles of the curriculum and the resources and tools that are available to support teachers and monitor classroom implementation. The orientation also includes hands-on demonstrations of the *LANGUAGE! Live* data management system and an overview of the data and resources available within the system. Administrators also are provided guidance in setting goals and expectations.

Unit Plans and Lessons

Unit 7 2
Unit 8 78
Unit 9 186
Unit 10 274
Unit 11...364
Unit 12 450

Unit 7

Unit Plan

Primary Texts:

Excerpt from *White Fang*

by Jack London

Text type: literature

"Return of the Wolves"

Text type: informational

***LANGUAGE! Live* Online**

Grammar Practice

- Identify the function of phrases and clauses in sentences.
- Use conjunctions correctly.
- Use action verbs, linking verbs, helping verbs, and *to be* verbs correctly.

Vocabulary Practice

- Determine the meaning of words with multiple meanings.
- Determine the meaning of metaphors.

Content Mastery

- Demonstrate an understanding of . . .
  - word meaning by answering questions and using words in sentences.
  - phrases and clauses.
  - subordinating and coordinating conjunctions.

Word Study

- Blend, read, and spell multisyllabic words with vowel team syllables; prefixes con- and trans-; and suffixes -y and -ly.
- Identify noun and verb phrases.
- Add inflectional endings to words ending in -y.
- Read connected text to build fluency.

Lesson 1

Reading

- Determine and discuss the topic of a text.
- Determine and discuss the author's purpose.
- Use text features to preview text.

Vocabulary

- Evaluate word knowledge.
- Determine the meaning of key passage vocabulary.

Reading

- Read an excerpt from a novel.
- Monitor comprehension during text reading.
- Retell part of a story.
- Identify the plot of a story.
- Identify shifts in point of view from third-person omniscient to third-person limited.
- Analyze how parts of a story contribute to the plot.

Lesson 2

Vocabulary

- Review key passage vocabulary.

Grammar

- Distinguish between a phrase and a clause.
- Identify subordinating conjunctions and dependent clauses in sentences.
- Demonstrate understanding of the function of subordinate clauses.

Writing

- Use complex sentence structures through combining dependent and independent clauses.
- Use subordinating conjunctions correctly.

Lesson 6

Reading

- Determine and discuss the topic of a text.
- Determine and discuss the author's purpose.
- Use text features to preview text.

Vocabulary

- Evaluate word knowledge.
- Determine the meaning of key passage vocabulary.

Reading

- Read informational text.
- Monitor comprehension during text reading.

Lesson 7

Vocabulary

- Review key passage vocabulary.
- Distinguish among the connotations of words with similar denotations.
- Verify word knowledge using a dictionary.

Reading

- Determine how to respond to prompts.
- Use critical thinking skills to write responses to prompts about text.
- Support written answers with evidence from text.
- Use context to determine the meaning of words and phrases.
- Interpret information presented visually.

Writing Project, Units 7–9: Compare and Contrast Writing

Lesson 3	Lesson 4	Lesson 5
Reading • Establish a purpose for reading literary text. • Reread text for comprehension. • Use critical thinking skills to write responses to prompts about text. • Support written answers with evidence from text. • Objectively summarize literary text. • Identify the purpose and impact of a literary flashback. • Determine the plot of a story. • Identify the protagonist and antagonist of a story.	**Vocabulary** • Review key passage vocabulary. **Reading** • Read literature with purpose and understanding. • Answer questions to demonstrate comprehension of text. • Determine the meaning of personification, hyperboles, exaggerations, metaphors, similes, and idioms in text. • Determine the impact of the author's word choice on meaning, tone, and mood. • Monitor comprehension of text during reading. • Analyze an author's word choice used to create suspense. • Determine the meaning and purpose of conjunctive adverbs.	**Vocabulary** • Review key passage vocabulary. **Writing** • Use a plot summary to write coherent paragraphs in response to reading. • Write a narrative from an animal's point of view. **Reading** • Self-correct as comprehension of text deepens. • Answer questions to demonstrate comprehension of text. • Engage in class discussion. • Identify the enduring understandings from a piece of text.

Lesson 8	Lesson 9	Lesson 10
Reading • Establish a purpose for rereading informational text. • Monitor comprehension during text reading. • Use critical thinking skills to write responses to prompts about text. • Support written answers with evidence from text. • Interpret information from graphics to answer questions about text. • Identify evidence used by an author to support claims. • Objectively summarize informational text. • Analyze claims and counterclaims made in text.	**Vocabulary** • Review key passage vocabulary. **Reading** • Read informational text with purpose and understanding. • Answer questions to demonstrate comprehension of text. • Distinguish between text written from a subjective point of view and text written from an objective point of view. • Identify how an author distinguishes his or her positions on a topic from that of others. • Monitor comprehension of text during reading. • Track pronouns to their antecedents. • Strengthen word knowledge through use of synonyms and antonyms. • Determine the meaning of words with prefixes and suffixes. • Determine the meaning of figurative language.	**Vocabulary** • Review key passage vocabulary. **Writing** • Cite text in writing. • Use a process to write. • Write a persuasive argument. • Use a rubric to guide and evaluate writing. **Reading** • Self-correct as comprehension of text deepens. • Answer questions to demonstrate comprehension of text. • Engage in class discussion. • Identify the enduring understandings from a piece of text.

Unit 7

Lesson 1

Lesson Opener

Before the lesson, choose one of the following activities to write on the board or post on the *LANGUAGE! Live* Class Wall online.

- *Describe a time when you experienced bad luck.*
- *Write three sentences about being alone. Use a direct object in one, an object of the preposition in one, and a predicate noun in the last one.*
- *Write two sentences about your feelings toward a particular animal. Combine the sentences using a conjunction.*

Reading

Objectives

- Determine and discuss the topic of a text.
- Determine and discuss the author's purpose.
- Use text features to preview text.

Passage Introduction

Direct students to page 1 in their Student Books. Discuss the content focus.

Content Focus
survival; conditioning

What do you think you will read about? (Answers will vary.) What is the difference between a wolf and a dog? Have partners discuss.

Type of Text
literature—fiction

Literature can be divided into two categories. What are they? (fiction and nonfiction) Tell your partner the difference between fiction and nonfiction. Provide sharing time. Which one tells a story that isn't real? (fiction) What does *nonfiction* mean? (not fiction, not fake, true) We are going to read another piece of fiction; this one is written in third person where the author is not a character in the story.

Unit 7

Lesson 1 | Reading

Let's Focus: Excerpt from *White Fang*

Content Focus	Type of Text
survival; conditioning	literature—fiction

Author's Name Jack London

Author's Purpose to entertain, teach how environment influences behavior

Big Ideas
Consider the following Big Idea questions. Write your answer for each question.

Can good and evil be conditioned, or are people born that way?

______

Can a vicious beast be tamed in an environment of love and support?

______

Narrative Preview Checklist: The excerpt from *White Fang* on pages 5–9.

- ☐ Title: What clue does it provide about the passage?
- ☐ Pictures: What additional information is added here?
- ☐ Margin Information: What vocabulary is important to understand this story?

Enduring Understandings
After reading the text . . .

______

Unit 7 1

Author's Purpose

Have students glance at the text. Who is the author of the text? (Jack London) The author's purpose is the reason that he or she wrote the text. Authors write for different purposes. Most fiction pieces are written to entertain. *White Fang* is no different. In addition to entertaining you, the author wanted his readers to ponder how the environment influences behavior of humans and animals. Have students write the answers on the page.

Play the Unit 7 Text Training video found in the Teacher Resources online.

Before we read the excerpt from *White Fang,* we will watch a short video to help build our background knowledge. Play the Unit 7 Text Training video. Have partners discuss what they learned from the video.

Note: If you are unable to play the video, Background Information about wolves and dogs can be found in the Teacher Resources online.

Read the Big Idea questions aloud.

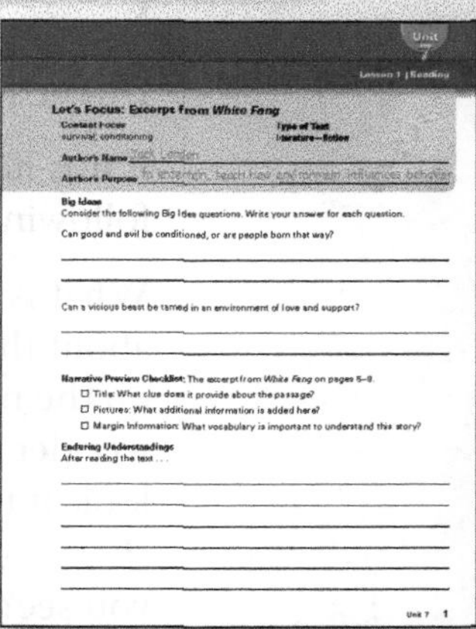

Big Ideas

Can good and evil be conditioned, or are people born that way?

Can a vicious beast be tamed in an environment of love and support?

As a class, consider the two Big Idea questions. After discussing each question, have students write an answer. We'll come back to these questions after we finish reading the text. You can add to your answers as you gain information and perspective.

Preview

Read the Preview Checklist on page 1. Follow the Preview Procedure outlined below.

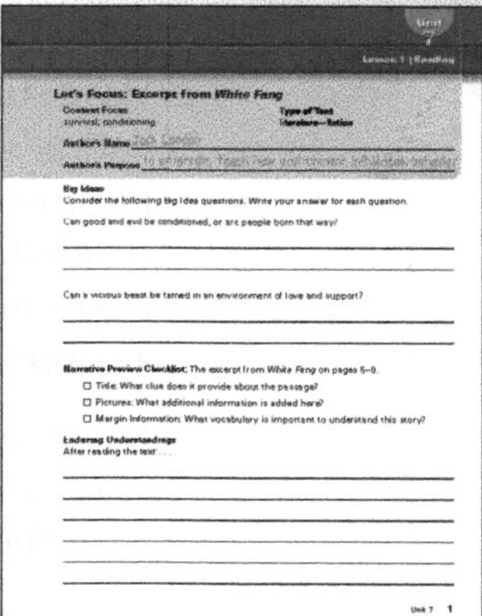

Preview Procedure

- Group students with partners or in triads.
- Have students count off as 1s or 2s. The 1s will become the student leaders. If working with triads, the third students become 3s.
- The student leaders will preview the text in addition to managing the checklist and pacing.
- The 2s and 3s will preview the text with 1s.
- Direct 1s to open their Student Books to page 1 and 2s and 3s to open their Student Books to page 5. This allows students to look at a few different pages at one time without turning back and forth.

Direct students to page 5. Have students preview the text.

If it is necessary, guide students in a short preview using the following talking points.

What is the title? (*White Fang*) What clue does the title provide about the passage? (Answers will vary.) Describe the graphic on the next page. (human footprints with blood drippings) I wonder what the footprints will have to do with the story. Let's look at the next picture. What do you see? (White Fang is sleeping in a quiet house.) Let's look at the next picture. What do you see? (White Fang is snarling like he's going to attack.) What might this have to do with the human footprints on page 6? Provide sharing time.

Vocabulary

Objectives

- Evaluate word knowledge.
- Determine the meaning of key passage vocabulary.

Rate Vocabulary Knowledge

Direct students to page 4 in their Student Books. Let's take a look at the vocabulary words from the excerpt from *White Fang*. I will say each word aloud. You will repeat the word and write it in the third column. Then, you will rate your knowledge of the word. Display the Vocabulary Rating Scale poster or write the information on the board. Review the meaning of each rating.

Lesson 1 | Vocabulary

Key Passage Vocabulary: Excerpt from *White Fang*

Read each word. Write the word in column 3. Then, circle a number to rate your knowledge of the word.

Vocabulary	Part of Speech	Write the Word	Knowledge Rating
restrain	(v)	restrain	0 1 2 3
encounter	(v)	encounter	0 1 2 3
pursue	(v)	pursue	0 1 2 3
vainly	(adv)	vainly	0 1 2 3
compel	(v)	compel	0 1 2 3
vengeance	(n)	vengeance	0 1 2 3
ignorant	(adj)	ignorant	0 1 2 3
promotion	(n)	promotion	0 1 2 3
advantage	(n)	advantage	0 1 2 3
ascent	(n)	ascent	0 1 2 3

4 Unit 7

Vocabulary Rating Scale

0—I have never heard the word before.

1—I have heard the word, but I'm not sure how to use it.

2—I am familiar with the word, but I'm not sure if I know the correct meaning.

3—I know the meaning of the word and can use it correctly in a sentence.

Remember, the points are there to help you know which words you need to focus on. By the end of this unit, you should be able to change all your ratings to a 3. That's the goal.

Read each word aloud and have students repeat it, write it, and rate it. Then, have volunteers who rated a word *2* or *3* use the word in an oral sentence.

Preteach Vocabulary

Explain that you will now take a closer look at the words. Follow the Preteach Procedure outlined below.

Preteach Procedure

This activity is intended to take only a short amount of time, so make it an oral exercise.

- Introduce each word as indicated on the word card.
- Read the definition and example sentences.
- Ask questions to clarify and deepen understanding.
- If time permits, allow students to share.

* If your students would benefit from copying the definitions, please have them do so in the vocabulary log in the back of the Student Books using the margin definitions in the passage selections. This should be done outside of instruction time.

restrain (v)

Let's read the first word together. *Restrain.*

Definition: *Restrain* means "to hold back." What means "to hold back"? (restrain)

Example 1: It is hard for me to *restrain* myself around ice cream; it's too tempting.

Example 2: When referees break up a fight during a game, they sometimes have to *restrain* the players involved.

Example 3: Dog owners should use leashes to *restrain* their dogs in public places.

Question 1: Could a mousetrap *restrain* a wolf? Yes or no? (no)

Question 2: Could a cage *restrain* a bird? Yes or no? (yes)

Pair Share: Turn to your partner and tell about a character in a movie or TV show that had to be *restrained.*

encounter (v)

Let's read the next word together. *Encounter.*

Definition: *Encounter* means "to meet; to come in contact with." What means "to meet; to come in contact with"? (encounter)

Example 1: You might *encounter* a snake in a grassy area near a lake or stream.

Example 2: I do not *encounter* many people on my early-morning walks.

Example 3: If you drive across Colorado in January, you are likely to *encounter* a snowstorm.

Question 1: You and a friend learn that you saw the same movie at the same theater but at different times. Did you *encounter* each other? Yes or no? (no)

Question 2: Would you be surprised to *encounter* a zebra at a bus stop? Yes or no? (yes)

Pair Share: Turn to your partner and tell about a time you *encountered* an animal or an insect that scared you.

pursue (v)

Let's read the next word together. *Pursue.*

Definition: *Pursue* means "to chase; to go after." What word means "to chase; to go after"? (pursue)

Example 1: In action movies, the "good guys" often *pursue* the "bad guys."

Example 2: Wolves and other predators *pursue* small animals in the hopes of catching a good meal.

Example 3: People who don't succeed at one career sometimes decide to *pursue* a different one.

Question 1: In the game of tag, does one person *pursue* the others? Yes or no? (yes)

Question 2: Someone drops a five-dollar bill on a crowded street and keeps walking. You pick it up and want to give it back. Do you *pursue* the person? Yes or no? (yes)

Pair Share: Turn to your partner and tell about a time someone you know forgot something and had to be *pursued*.

3

vainly (adv)

Let's read the next word together. *Vainly.*

Definition: If you do something *vainly*, you do it without success; you fail to achieve what you hoped to achieve. What word means "without success; not achieving what one hoped to"? (vainly)

Example 1: I often hunt *vainly* for a piece of chocolate in my desk.

Example 2: If your team is losing 49 to 0 in the third quarter, you might try *vainly* to come back and win.

Example 3: For years, scientists have been searching *vainly* for signs of intelligent life in outer space.

Question 1: You are locked out. You jiggle the doorknob, but it doesn't open. Are you *vainly* trying to open the door? Yes or no? (yes)

Question 2: You spend an hour looking for a lost bracelet and then find it in an unexpected place. Have you searched *vainly* for the bracelet? Yes or no? (no)

Pair Share: Turn to your partner and swap stories about something you *vainly* tried to do when you were younger.

compel (v)

Let's read the next word together. *Compel.*

Definition: *Compel* means "to make someone take a certain action." What word means "to make someone take a certain action"? (compel)

Example 1: The fear of accidents can *compel* cyclists to wear helmets.

Example 2: When a street is closed for repairs, drivers are *compelled* to take a detour.

Example 3: Freezing temperatures *compel* children to play indoors.

Question 1: The elevator is broken. You live on the fourth floor. Does this situation *compel* you to climb the stairs? Yes or no? (yes)

Question 2: The police arrested a suspect, handcuffed him, and took him to the police station. Did the police *compel* the suspect to go with them? Yes or no? (yes)

Pair Share: Turn to your partner and tell about a time when an injury or illness *compelled* you to miss out on something fun.

5

vengeance (n)

Let's read the next word together. *Vengeance.*

Definition: *Vengeance* is the act of repaying one hurtful deed with another. What means "the act of repaying one hurtful deed with another"? (vengeance)

Example 1: If you get hurt, you might feel like seeking *vengeance*, but acting on this feeling will only lead to trouble.

Example 2: If someone tickles me, I might take *vengeance* by tickling him or her back.

Example 3: Many of Shakespeare's plays involve people who seek *vengeance* on an enemy.

Question 1: You hear a strange noise outside and lock your window. Is this an act of *vengeance*? Yes or no? (no)

Question 2: Last year, a friend spread a rumor about you. This year, it's payback time. Are you aiming for *vengeance* by spreading a rumor about your friend? Yes or no? (yes)

Pair Share: Turn to your partner and tell why an act of *vengeance* can leave a person feeling worse than ever.

ignorant (adj)

Let's read the next word together. *Ignorant*.

Definition: *Ignorant* means "not knowing or having important information." What means "not knowing or having important information"? (ignorant)

Example 1: When someone is rude, I tell myself he or she may be having problems I am *ignorant* of.

Example 2: The fear of seeming *ignorant* can keep people from asking questions.

Example 3: Being *ignorant* of the rules does not give you an excuse to break them.

Question 1: You sign up for cross-country track even though you know workouts start at 5:00 a.m. Are you *ignorant* of the practice schedule? Yes or no? (no)

Question 2: You are planning a surprise party for a friend. The friend knows but hasn't let on. Are you *ignorant* of your friend's knowledge? Yes or no (yes)

Pair Share: Turn to your partner and tell about a time you felt *ignorant* about something and asked questions to learn more.

promotion (n)

Let's read the next word together. *Promotion*.

Definition: The *promotion* of something is an attempt to convince others that they should do, believe, or buy something. What word means "an attempt to convince others that they should do, believe, or buy something"? (promotion)

Example 1: In group work, the endless *promotion* of one's own ideas and opinions can be tiresome for the other members.

Example 2: On TV and in the media, the *promotion* of a product or service is called an ad.

Example 3: The *promotion* of a healthy lifestyle is best done through example; if people see you forming good habits, they will too.

Question 1: Everyone else wants to go swimming, but you argue that playing games would be more fun. Is this a *promotion* of your own opinion? Yes or no? (yes)

Question 2: You are running for class president. You hang posters of yourself all over the school. Is this an act of self-*promotion*? Yes or no? (yes)

Pair Share: Turn to your partner and name something you could devote your life to the *promotion* of.

advantage (n)

Let's read the next word together. *Advantage*.

Definition: An *advantage* is something that puts you in a better position than others. What means "something that puts you in a better position than others"? (advantage)

Example 1: If you are a basketball player, being tall is an *advantage*.

Example 2: On sale day, getting to a store early can be an *advantage*.

Example 3: One *advantage* of living on the top floor is that nobody bangs around above you.

Question 1: In a race, is getting a head start an *advantage*? Yes or no? (yes)

Question 2: You are on a walking tour of a big city, but you wore flip-flops and your feet hurt. Are your shoes an *advantage*? Yes or no? (no)

Pair Share: Turn to your partner and name a good habit of yours. Then tell why the habit is an *advantage*.

9

ascent (n)

Let's read the last word together. *Ascent*.

Definition: An *ascent* is an upward journey. What word means "an upward journey"? (ascent)

Example 1: A steep *ascent* on a bicycle can be challenging if you are not in shape.

Example 2: A rock climber uses special equipment to make his or her *ascent* safe.

Example 3: Airplane passengers prepare for *ascent* by buckling their seatbelts.

Question 1: A stream flows downhill. Does it make an *ascent*? Yes or no? (no)

Question 2: You hit a volleyball and it flies toward the rafters. Is it making an *ascent*? Yes or no? (yes)

Pair Share: Turn to your partner and tell about an *ascent* you have made or would like to make.

10

Reading

Objectives

- Read an excerpt from a novel.
- Monitor comprehension during text reading.
- Retell part of a story.
- Identify the plot of a story.
- Identify shifts in point of view from third-person omniscient to third-person limited.

Excerpt from *White Fang*

Direct students to pages 2 and 3 in their Student Books.

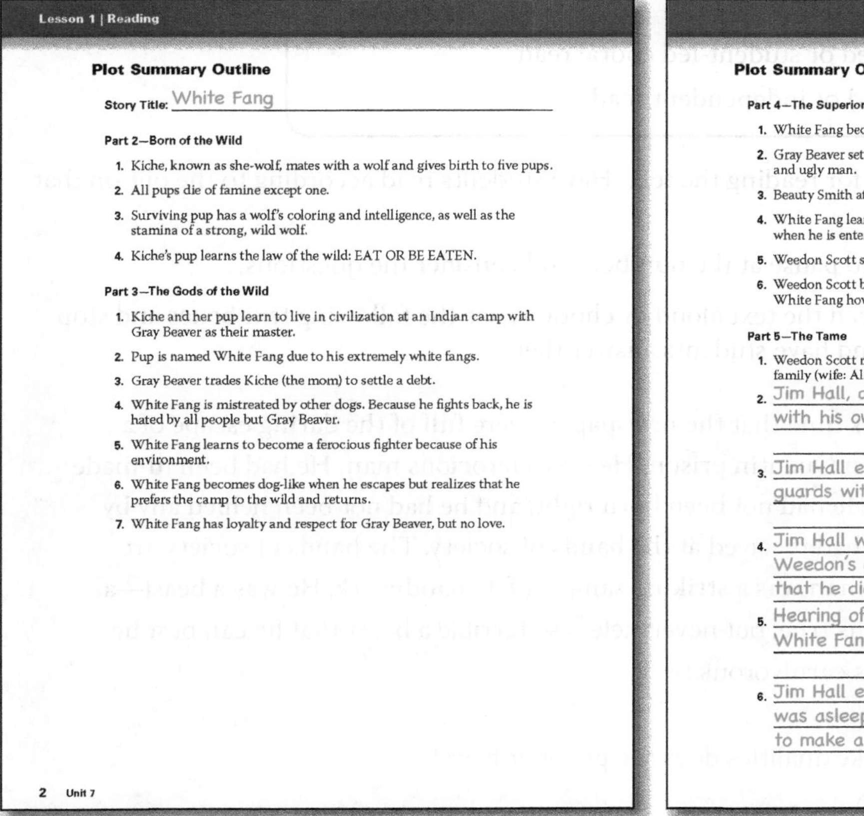

Lesson 1 | Reading

Plot Summary Outline

Story Title: White Fang

Part 2—Born of the Wild

1. Kiche, known as she-wolf, mates with a wolf and gives birth to five pups.
2. All pups die of famine except one.
3. Surviving pup has a wolf's coloring and intelligence, as well as the stamina of a strong, wild wolf.
4. Kiche's pup learns the law of the wild: EAT OR BE EATEN.

Part 3—The Gods of the Wild

1. Kiche and her pup learn to live in civilization at an Indian camp with Gray Beaver as their master.
2. Pup is named White Fang due to his extremely white fangs.
3. Gray Beaver trades Kiche (the mom) to settle a debt.
4. White Fang is mistreated by other dogs. Because he fights back, he is hated by all people but Gray Beaver.
5. White Fang learns to become a ferocious fighter because of his environment.
6. White Fang becomes dog-like when he escapes but realizes that he prefers the camp to the wild and returns.
7. White Fang has loyalty and respect for Gray Beaver, but no love.

2 Unit 7

Lesson 1 | Reading

Plot Summary Outline (*cont.*)

Part 4—The Superior Gods

1. White Fang becomes violent toward all other dogs.
2. Gray Beaver settles a debt by giving White Fang to Beauty Smith, a cruel, evil, and ugly man.
3. Beauty Smith attempts to tame White Fang with beatings and force.
4. White Fang learns to take out his hostility and hatred for Smith on other dogs when he is entered in dogfights. He becomes known as "The Fighting Wolf."
5. Weedon Scott saves White Fang from near death during a fight with a dog.
6. Weedon Scott becomes White Fang's new master and tries to teach White Fang how to experience love.

Part 5—The Tame

1. Weedon Scott returns to California with White Fang to live on his ranch with his family (wife: Alice, mom, and dad: Judge Scott).
2. Jim Hall, described as a human beast, killed a guard with his own teeth.
3. Jim Hall escaped from prison after killing two more guards with his own hands.
4. Jim Hall wanted revenge against Judge Scott, Weedon's dad, for sending him to jail for a crime that he did not commit.
5. Hearing of Hall's escape, Weedon's wife brought White Fang to sleep in the house at night.
6. Jim Hall entered the Scott home while the family was asleep. White Fang used his skills from the wild to make a surprise attack on this strange god.

Unit 7 3

Before reading the excerpt from *White Fang*, let's look at a plot summary outline of what has happened so far in the book. **Read and discuss the plot summary outline.** Retelling the story by using a plot summary outline will help build prior knowledge and enhance your ability to see how the chapters fit together as the plot unfolds. **Have students use the plot summary outline to retell the story with a partner. Have students take turns retelling parts 2–4.** Now, let's read *White Fang*, The Tame.

Direct students to page 5 in their Student Books.

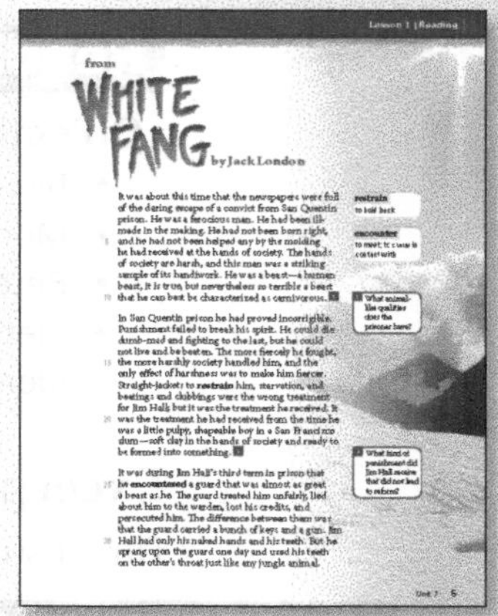

Guiding Students Toward Independent Reading

It is important that your students read as much and as often as they can. Assign readings that meet the needs of your students, based on your observations and data. This is a good opportunity to stretch your students. If students become frustrated, scaffold the reading with paired reading, choral reading, or a read-aloud.

Options for reading text:

- Teacher read-aloud
- Teacher-led or student-led choral read
- Paired read or independent read

Choose an option for reading the text. Have students read according to the option that you chose.

Remind students to pause at the numbers and consider the questions.

If you choose to read the text aloud or chorally, use the following text boxes and stop to ask questions and have students answer them.

SE p. 5, paragraph 1

It was about this time that the newspapers were full of the daring escape of a convict from San Quentin prison. He was a ferocious man. He had been ill-made in the making. He had not been born right, and he had not been helped any by the molding he had received at the hands of society. The hands of society are harsh, and this man was a striking sample of its handiwork. He was a beast—a human beast, it is true, but nevertheless so terrible a beast that he can best be characterized as carnivorous.

1. What animal-like qualities does the prisoner have?

SE p. 5, paragraph 2

In San Quentin prison he had proved incorrigible. Punishment failed to break his spirit. He could die dumb-mad and fighting to the last, but he could not live and be beaten. The more fiercely he fought, the more harshly society handled him, and the only effect of harshness was to make him fiercer. Straight-jackets to **restrain** him, starvation, and beatings and clubbings were the wrong treatment for Jim Hall; but it was the treatment he received. It was the treatment he had received from the time he was a little pulpy, shapeable boy in a San Francisco slum—soft clay in the hands of society and ready to be formed into something.

2. What kind of punishment did Jim Hall receive that did not lead to reform?

SE p. 5, paragraph 3

It was during Jim Hall's third term in prison that he **encountered** a guard that was almost as great a beast as he. The guard treated him unfairly, lied about him to the warden, lost his credits, and persecuted him. The difference between them was that the guard carried a bunch of keys and a gun. Jim Hall had only his naked hands and his teeth. But he sprang upon the guard one day and used his teeth on the other's throat just like any jungle animal.

SE p. 6, paragraph 1

After this, Jim Hall went to live in the incorrigible cell. He lived there three years. The cell was of iron, the floor, the walls, the roof. He never left this cell. He never saw the sky nor the sunshine. Day was a barely noticeable twilight and night was a black silence. He was in an iron tomb, buried alive. He saw no human face, spoke to no human thing. When his food was shoved in to him, he growled like a wild animal. He hated all things. For days and nights he bellowed his rage loudly at the universe. Then, for weeks and months he never made a sound, in the black silence eating his very soul. He was a man and a monstrosity, as fearful a thing of fear as ever imagined in the visions of a maddened brain.

3. What was life like for Jim Hall before his attack on the prison guard and after his attack on the prison guard?

SE p. 6, paragraphs 2–3

And then, one night, he escaped. The warders said it was impossible, but nevertheless the cell was empty, and half in half out of it lay the body of a slain guard. Two other dead guards marked his trail through the prison to the outer walls, and he had killed with his hands to avoid noise.

He was armed with the weapons of the slain guards—a live arsenal that fled through the hills **pursued** by the organized might of society. A heavy price of gold was upon his head. Greedy farmers hunted him with shotguns. His blood might pay off a loan or send a son to college. Public-spirited citizens took down their rifles and went out after him. A pack of bloodhounds followed the way of his bleeding feet. And the sleuth-hounds of the law, the paid fighting animals of society, with telephone, and telegraph, and special train, clung to his trail night and day.

4. Where did Jim Hall get his weapons?

SE p. 6, paragraph 4

> Sometimes they came upon him, and men faced him like heroes, or stampeded through barbed-wire fences to the delight of the people reading the account at the breakfast table. It was after such encounters that the dead and wounded were carted back to the towns, and their places filled by men eager for the manhunt.

SE p. 7, paragraph 1

> And then Jim Hall disappeared. The bloodhounds **vainly** quested for him on the lost trail. Inoffensive, ordinary ranchers in remote valleys were held up by armed men and **compelled** to identify themselves. While the remains of Jim Hall were discovered on a dozen mountainsides by greedy claimants for blood-money.

5. Why did so many men want to find Jim Hall?

SE p. 7, paragraphs 2–3

> In the meantime the newspapers were read at Sierra Vista, not so much with interest as with anxiety, or worry. The women were afraid. Judge Scott pooh-poohed and laughed, but not with reason, for it was in his last days on the bench that Jim Hall had stood before him and received sentence. And in open courtroom, before all men, Jim Hall had proclaimed that the day would come when he would wreak **vengeance** on the Judge that sentenced him.
>
> For once, Jim Hall was right. He was innocent of the crime for which he was sentenced. It was a case, in the language of thieves and police, of "railroading." Jim Hall was being "railroaded" to prison for a crime he had not committed. Because of the two prior convictions against him, Judge Scott imposed upon him a sentence of fifty years.

6. What is Jim Hall's connection to Judge Scott?

SE p. 7, paragraph 4

> Judge Scott did not know all things, and he did not know that he was party to a police conspiracy, that the evidence was hatched and falsified, that Jim Hall was guiltless of the crime charged. And Jim Hall, on the other hand, did not know that Judge Scott was merely **ignorant**. Jim Hall believed that the judge knew all about it and was hand in glove with the police in the **promotion** of the monstrous injustice. So it was, when the doom of fifty years of living death was uttered by Judge Scott, that Jim Hall, hating all things in the society that misused him, rose up and raged in the courtroom until dragged down by half a dozen of his blue-coated enemies. To him, Judge Scott was the keystone in the arch of injustice, and upon Judge Scott he emptied the vials of his wrath and hurled the angry threats of his revenge yet to come. Then Jim Hall went to his living death . . . and escaped.

7. In what ways are Jim Hall and Judge Scott both "falsely accused"?

SE p. 8, paragraph 1

Of all this White Fang knew nothing. But between him and Alice, the master's wife, there existed a secret. Each night, after Sierra Vista had gone to bed, she rose and let in White Fang to sleep in the big hall. Now White Fang was not a house dog, nor was he permitted to sleep in the house; so each morning, early, she slipped down and let him out before the family was awake.

8. Why do you think White Fang is introduced at this time?

SE p. 8, paragraphs 2–3

On one such night, while all the house slept, White Fang awoke and lay very quietly. And very quietly he smelled the air and read the message it bore of a strange god's presence. And to his ears came sounds of the strange god's movements. White Fang burst into no furious outcry. It was not his way. The strange god walked softly, but more softly walked White Fang, for he had no clothes to rub against the flesh of his body. He followed silently. In the Wild he had hunted live meat that was infinitely timid, and he knew the **advantage** of surprise.

The strange god paused at the foot of the great staircase and listened, and White Fang was as dead, so without movement was he as he watched and waited. Up that staircase the way led to the lovemaster and to the lovemaster's dearest possessions. White Fang bristled, but waited. The strange god's foot lifted. He was beginning the **ascent**.

9. Who is the strange god and the lovemaster?

SE p. 9, paragraph 1

Then it was that White Fang struck. He gave no warning, with no snarl anticipated his own action. Into the air he lifted his body in the spring that landed him on the strange god's back. White Fang clung with his forepaws to the man's shoulders, at the same time burying his fangs into the back of the man's neck. He clung on for a moment, long enough to drag the god over backward. Together they crashed to the floor. White Fang leaped clear, and, as the man struggled to rise, was in again with the slashing fangs.

10. How did White Fang complete the mission Alice had given him?

For confirmation of engagement, have partners share what they think will happen to Jim Hall and White Fang. Have volunteers share predictions with the class.

Point of View

Point of view has a major impact on text. Text can be written from the first-person point of view or the third-person point of view. If it is written by a character in the text, that is called first person. If it is written by a character outside the text, that is called third person.

Have volunteers share the pronouns typically seen in first-person text. (I, me, my, we, us, our).

Sometimes an author writing in third-person point of view seems to know the thoughts and feelings of all the characters. This is called *omniscient.* Other times, the author seems to only know the thoughts and feelings of one character and the story is told from his or her perspective.

This text is unique because both points of view are used.

Challenge students to find the place in the text when the story seems to be told from White Fang's point of view only. (Of all this White Fang knew nothing.)

Unit 7 Lesson 2

Lesson Opener

Before the lesson, choose one of the following activities to write on the board or post on the *LANGUAGE! Live* Class Wall online.

- *Describe a relationship you have had with a pet. How did that pet impact your life?*
- *Describe a time when you were wrongly accused of something. How did you feel? Underline the adjectives in your sentences.*
- *Write two compound sentences about wolves. Use a conjunction in each sentence, and don't forget the commas.*

Vocabulary

Objective

- Review key passage vocabulary.

Review Passage Vocabulary

Direct students to page 4 in their Student Books. Use the following questions to review the vocabulary words in the excerpt from *White Fang*. Have students answer each question using the vocabulary word or indicating its meaning in a complete sentence.

Lesson 1 | Vocabulary

Key Passage Vocabulary: Excerpt from *White Fang*

Read each word. Write the word in column 3. Then, circle a number to rate your knowledge of the word.

Vocabulary	Part of Speech	Write the Word	Knowledge Rating
restrain	(v)	restrain	0 1 2 3
encounter	(v)	encounter	0 1 2 3
pursue	(v)	pursue	0 1 2 3
vainly	(adv)	vainly	0 1 2 3
compel	(v)	compel	0 1 2 3
vengeance	(n)	vengeance	0 1 2 3
ignorant	(adj)	ignorant	0 1 2 3
promotion	(n)	promotion	0 1 2 3
advantage	(n)	advantage	0 1 2 3
ascent	(n)	ascent	0 1 2 3

4 Unit 7

- What was used in prison to *restrain* Jim Hall? (Straight-jackets were used to restrain him.) What was the effect of *restraining* him in this way? Did it break his spirit? (No, restraining him in this way did not break his spirit; it only made him more ferocious.)
- One day, Jim *encountered* a guard who treated him cruelly. What happened? (When Jim encountered the guard, he attacked him and sank his teeth into his throat like a wild animal.) For this offense, Jim was put in solitary confinement for three years. Did Jim *encounter* anybody during that time? (No, he didn't encounter anyone because he was alone.)
- Who *pursued* Jim after he escaped from prison? (Farmers, ordinary citizens, bloodhounds, and officers of the law all pursued him.) What else were many people *pursuing* in the race to catch Jim Hall? (They were pursuing the gold offered as a reward.)
- The bloodhounds *vainly* searched for him. Did they successfully search for him? (No; since they searched vainly, they searched without success.) Had Jim Hall *vainly* tried to escape from prison? (No, Jim Hall hadn't vainly tried to escape; he had successfully escaped.)

- After Jim Hall disappeared, ordinary ranchers were *compelled* to identify themselves.

Vocabulary Review Note: Remember, *identify* means "to say who or what something is."

Were the ranchers politely asked to identify themselves? (No; if the ranchers were compelled to identify themselves, they were forced to do so.) What would those who were searching for Jim finally be *compelled* to admit? (They would be compelled to admit that they couldn't find him.)

- On whom had Jim Hall sworn *vengeance* years ago, when he received a "guilty" sentence? (He had sworn vengeance on the judge.) Based on Jim Hall's behavior in prison, what kind of *vengeance* can readers guess he will take? (Readers can guess that Jim will take violent vengeance and kill the judge.)
- Of what had the judge been *ignorant*? (He had been ignorant of Jim's innocence.) Had the police been *ignorant* of the same thing? (No, the police had known Jim was innocent but conspired against him by creating false evidence.) Was Jim *ignorant* of the judge's *ignorance*? (*Ignorance* is the noun form of ignorant.) (Yes; Jim believed the judge knew all about the conspiracy. He was ignorant of the fact that the judge knew nothing.)
- The entire trial was a *promotion* of injustice, or unfairness. What does this mean? (If the trial was a promotion of injustice, it was set up to make an unfair ruling happen.) You could also say that the trial was a *promotion* of violence. How so? (The unjust ruling would cause Jim to express his rage through violence.)
- When Jim enters the judge's house, White Fang is at an *advantage*. Name at least two ways this is true. (White Fang is at an advantage because he has keen hearing, makes no noise as he moves, and knows how to surprise his victims.) Is Jim Hall's beastly strength an *advantage* against White Fang? (No, it isn't an advantage; White Fang acts so quickly, Jim doesn't have a chance to respond.)
- White Fang attacks Jim as he begins his *ascent*. Where does Jim intend for his *ascent* to take him? (He intends for his ascent to take him upstairs to the judge's bedroom.) Does he complete his *ascent*? Why or why not? (No, he doesn't complete his ascent because White Fang attacks him, pulls him to the floor, and slashes him with his fangs.)

Grammar

Objectives

- Distinguish between a phrase and a clause.
- Demonstrate understanding of subordinate conjunctions.
- Demonstrate understanding of the function of subordinate clauses.

Phrase vs. Clause

We've been working with several different kinds of phrases. A phrase is a group of words, but it is not a complete thought. It will not answer both the *who did it* and *did what* questions—it will not have a subject and a predicate.

A verb phrase is a helping verb plus the main verb: *is standing, was playing.* While a verb phrase may answer the *did what* question, it doesn't answer the *who did it* question. Turn to your partner and share an example of a verb phrase. **Provide sharing time.** A prepositional phrase is another type of phrase. A prepositional phrase always begins with a preposition and contains a noun or a pronoun. The prepositional phrase *in the morning* answers what question? (when) You have generated prepositional phrases that answer a variety of questions. Turn to your partner and share an example of a prepositional phrase. **Provide sharing time.**

A clause, on the other hand, will answer both key questions, *who or what did it* and *did what.* A clause has both a subject and a predicate. Listen to this group of words and decide if it's a phrase or a clause: *on one such night.* What is it? (phrase) It is only a phrase. What question does it answer? (when) Listen to this group of words: *He hated all things.* What is it? (a clause) Who did it? (He) Did what? (hated) Because you can answer both questions, it is a clause.

Direct students to page 10 in their Student Books and read the instructions aloud.

Model

Model the first two examples. Listen: *of the daring escape.* Is that a phrase or a clause? I have to ask myself if I can answer the *who did it* and *did what* question. I cannot answer either question, and it begins with the preposition *of.* I'm sure it's a phrase, so I put an X in the phrase column. Listen: *he was a ferocious man.* It doesn't begin with a preposition, and I can answer the *who did it* question. There isn't an action verb, but the linking verb *was* connects *he* with *ferocious man.* This group of words is a complete thought, so I put an X in the clause column.

Lesson 2 | Grammar

Phrase vs. Clause

Read the following groups of words and place an X in the proper column to identify them as a phrase or a clause.

	Phrase	Clause
Ex: of the daring escape	✗	
Ex: he was a ferocious man		✗
1. had been helped	✗	
2. punishment failed to break his spirit		✗
3. in the hands of society	✗	
4. during Jim Hall's third term in prison	✗	
5. the cell was of iron		✗
6. he saw no human face		✗
7. for weeks and months	✗	
8. in the visions of a maddened brain	✗	
9. he escaped		✗
10. Jim Hall disappeared		✗

10 Unit 7

Guided Practice

Look at #1: *had been helped.* What question does this group of words answer? (did what) Can we answer the *who did it* question? (no) What is it? (a phrase) It is a verb phrase, so put an X in the phrase column.

Look at #2: *punishment failed to break his spirit.* Think about the questions you can answer and then decide whether it's a phrase or a clause. Have students mark their responses and then orally review. What did it? (punishment) Did what? (failed) Because I can answer both questions, what is it? (a clause)

Independent Practice

Have students complete the activity. Review the answers as a class.

Subordinating Conjunctions

Write *conjunction* on the board and underline *junction.*

Conjunctions are words that join. The word *junction* helps us remember its function because a junction is where two things meet or come together.

Write *and, or,* and *but* on the board.

Let's review the meaning of these three conjunctions. What are they? (conjunctions) What do they do? (join words) Which conjunction would I use if I wanted to connect two similar ideas? (and) Which conjunction would I use if I need to signal a contrasting idea? (but) Which conjunction would I use to signal an alternative or a choice? (or) In each instance, the words that are joined are of equal value in the sentence. One is not dependent or more important than the other. This is not always the case.

Write the words *coordinating* and *subordinating* on the board.

The conjunctions we just reviewed are classified as coordinating conjunctions because they join two or more words, phrases, or clauses of equal weight or value. Have volunteers write sentences about the class on the board with compound subjects, compound objects, and compound predicates. Then, have volunteers write compound sentences on the board.

Examples of sentences:

Compound subject: Jim Hall and Judge Scott became enemies.
Compound predicate: Jim Hall could stay in prison or escape to find Judge Scott.
Compound object: Jim Hall hated people and animals.
Compound sentences: Jim Hall attempted to climb the stairs, but White Fang attacked.
Jim Hall entered the house, and White Fang detected an intruder.
Judge Scott would be killed, or White Fang would die to protect him.

Sometimes one idea is dependent on another, and even though it contains the answer to subject and predicate questions, it cannot stand alone. It depends on another clause to complete its meaning. Listen: *We stood in the rain.* Is that a complete thought or an independent clause? Is its meaning complete? (yes) Listen to how one word changes its meaning: *While we stood in the rain.* It still answers *who* and *what did we do* questions, but something happened while we stood in the rain. It is a clause, but it cannot stand alone. As readers, we need more information. Listen: *While we stood in the rain, others ran for cover. Others ran for cover* is a complete thought, so it can stand alone. Conjunctions that join a dependent clause to an independent clause are called *subordinating conjunctions*. When you hear the word *sub*, what do you think of? **Encourage students to respond and make the connection to *under*.** The clause that begins with one of these conjunctions is dependent on the rest of the sentence to complete it. It is *under* the independent clause.

Direct students to page 11 in their Student Books and read the chart of common subordinating conjunctions. Review the two jobs of subordinating conjunctions, and generate examples of dependent clauses that begin with a variety of subordinating conjunctions. Possible examples: *although I studied for the test; because we needed more time; before I came down for breakfast; since we had exhausted all of our options.*

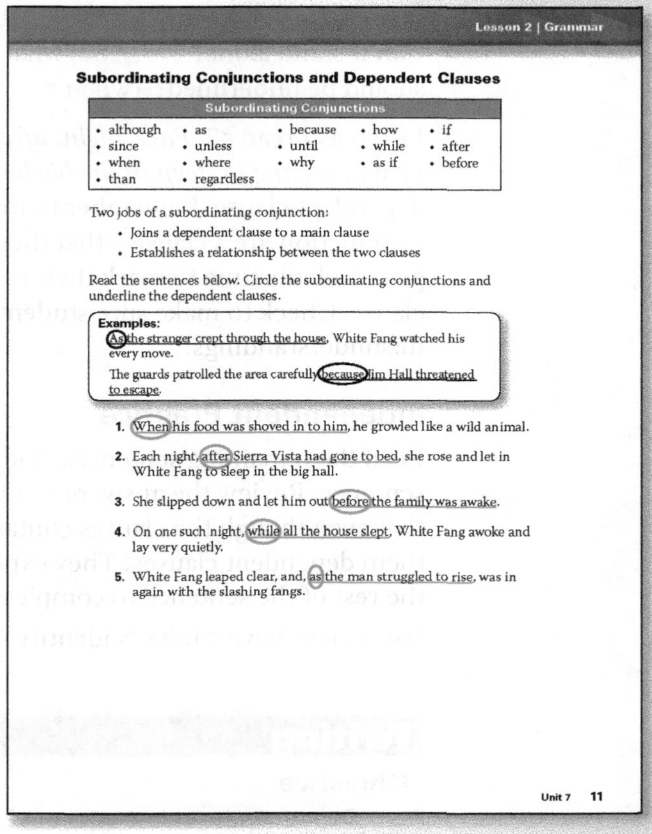
Lesson 2 | Grammar

Subordinating Conjunctions and Dependent Clauses

Subordinating Conjunctions				
• although	• as	• because	• how	• if
• since	• unless	• until	• while	• after
• when	• where	• why	• as if	• before
• than	• regardless			

Two jobs of a subordinating conjunction:

- Joins a dependent clause to a main clause
- Establishes a relationship between the two clauses

Read the sentences below. Circle the subordinating conjunctions and underline the dependent clauses.

Examples:
As the stranger crept through the house, White Fang watched his every move.
The guards patrolled the area carefully because Jim Hall threatened to escape.

1. When his food was shoved in to him, he growled like a wild animal.
2. Each night, after Sierra Vista had gone to bed, she rose and let in White Fang to sleep in the big hall.
3. She slipped down and let him out before the family was awake.
4. On one such night, while all the house slept, White Fang awoke and lay very quietly.
5. White Fang leaped clear, and, as the man struggled to rise, was in again with the slashing fangs.

Unit 7 11

Read the instructions for the activity.

Model

Listen as I read the first example: *As the stranger crept through the house, White Fang watched his every move.* The first thing I have to look for is a subordinating conjunction. If I can't remember them, I can look at the chart. The sentence begins with *as*, and I see *as* in the chart. I need to see if it begins a clause. *As* what? As the stranger crept through the house. That is a clause, but since it begins with a conjunction from the chart, it can't stand alone. It depends on the other clause to make it make sense. So, I circle *As* and underline *As the stranger crept through the house.*

Listen to the next example: *The guards patrolled the area carefully because Jim Hall threatened to escape.* I know the subject is *guards*. I know what the guards did—they patrolled. As I read further into the sentence, I see the conjunction *because.* It's a conjunction in the chart and it is followed by a *who*—Jim Hall—and a *did what*—threatened. Why did they patrol the area? *because Jim Hall threatened to escape.* I circle *because* and underline *because Jim Hall threatened to escape.* As you can see, dependent clauses can be in a variety of positions within a sentence.

Guided Practice

Let's look at #1: *When his food was shoved in to him, he growled like a wild animal.* Do you see a subordinating conjunction in this sentence? (when) Now, we have to determine if the group of words that follows contains a *who* or *what* and *did what.* Who or what? (food) Did what? (was shoved) What happened when his food was shoved in to him? (He growled like a wild animal.) Is that an independent clause? Can it stand alone? (yes) So, what word should be circled? (when) And what words should be underlined? (when his food was shoved in to him)

Listen as I read #2: *Each night, after Sierra Vista had gone to bed, she rose and let in White Fang to sleep in the big hall.* Identify the subordinate conjunction and dependent clause. Remember to make sure the words following the subordinate conjunction are a clause—that they contain a *who* or *what* and *did what.* Pause and give students time to mark their responses. Have volunteers share the conjunction and clause. Check to make sure students marked their sentence correctly, and clarify any misunderstandings.

Independent Practice

Read the remaining sentences, and have students mark their answers on each sentence. Review the answers as a class. Continue to help students focus on the idea that even though the clauses contain a subject noun and a verb, the conjunction makes them dependent clauses. They express an incomplete thought and are dependent on the rest of the sentence to complete their meaning.

For review, have students identify the phrases in numbers 2, 4, and 5.

Writing

Objective

- Demonstrate understanding of complex sentence structure through manipulation of dependent and independent clauses.

Sentences with Subordinating Conjunctions

Now that you practiced recognizing subordinate conjunctions and identifying dependent clauses, I want you to write your own dependent clauses. Write the following sentence frame on the board:

White Fang attacked Jim Hall because ________.

What words would complete the thought? Finish the sentence on the board with *he started to go up the stairs.* Read the entire sentence, and then ask students for other ways to finish the sentence. Make sure their responses are clauses.

Direct students to page 12 in their Student Books and read the instructions aloud. Each sentence frame contains a subordinating conjunction. Your job is to finish the dependent clause and make sure it makes sense in the sentence.

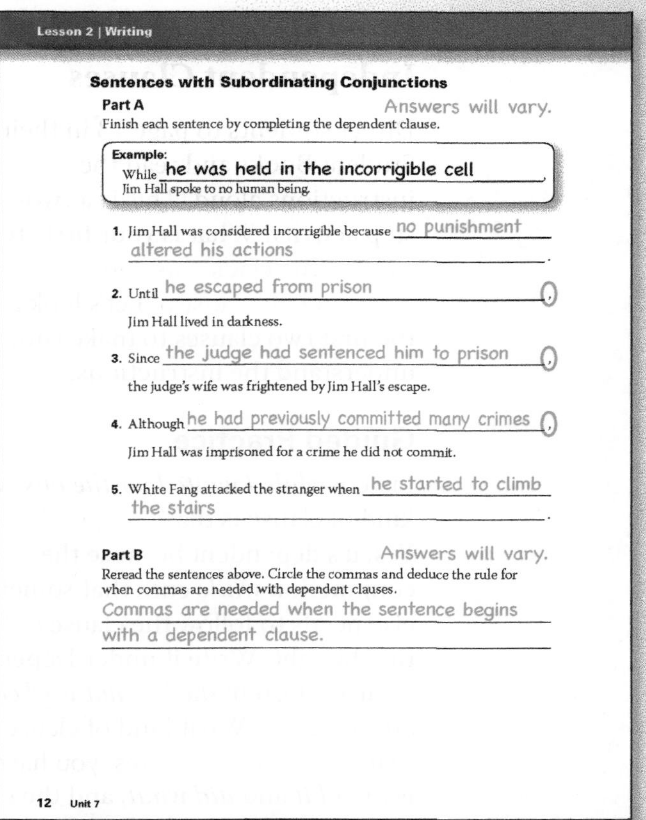

Lesson 2 | Writing

Sentences with Subordinating Conjunctions

Part A Answers will vary.

Finish each sentence by completing the dependent clause.

Example:
While he was held in the incorrigible cell,
Jim Hall spoke to no human being.

1. Jim Hall was considered incorrigible because no punishment altered his actions.
2. Until he escaped from prison,
Jim Hall lived in darkness.
3. Since the judge had sentenced him to prison,
the judge's wife was frightened by Jim Hall's escape.
4. Although he had previously committed many crimes,
Jim Hall was imprisoned for a crime he did not commit.
5. White Fang attacked the stranger when he started to climb the stairs.

Part B Answers will vary.

Reread the sentences above. Circle the commas and deduce the rule for when commas are needed with dependent clauses.

Commas are needed when the sentence begins with a dependent clause.

12 Unit 7

Model

Look at the example: *While ______________, Jim Hall spoke to no human being.* To complete this sentence, think about when Jim Hall would have been isolated from all of the other inmates. It was when he was in the special cell, the incorrigible cell. This clause makes sense: *While he was held in the incorrigible cell.* Another clause that would make sense would be: *While he was in solitary confinement.*

Guided Practice

Let's look at #1: *Jim Hall was considered incorrigible because . . .* Remember, *incorrigible* means he was beyond correcting or incapable of being reformed. How could you finish this sentence? Turn to your partner and share your thoughts. After a few minutes, call on several students to share their responses. If students need a model, consider finishing the sentence with *no punishment altered his actions.*

Independent Practice

Have partners complete the activity. Review the answers as a class.

Direct students to Part B. Punctuation impacts meaning. It helps us locate dependent clauses in written text. When you write sentences that contain dependent clauses, it is important that you use the proper punctuation. Have partners reread the sentences from Part A and circle all of the commas. Once you have circled the commas, analyze the pattern to determine the rule for punctuating dependent clauses.

Reinforce the idea that commas are needed after the clause when it begins the sentence, but not when it ends the sentence. While not illustrated in these sentences, commas are required before and after the clause when it lands within the sentence. An example can be found on page 11, numbers 2, 4, and 5.

Combining Dependent and Independent Clauses

Direct students to page 13 in their Student Books and read the instructions aloud. This is a two-step activity. What is your first step? (to sort the clauses as dependent or independent clauses) Let's look at the first two clauses to make sure you understand the instructions.

Guided Practice

Listen: *while I waited for the bus.* What kind of clause is that? (dependent) Yes, it's dependent because the conjunction *while* cues that something else needs to follow the clause to finish the thought. Write it under Dependent Clauses. Listen: *she has not worked out regularly.* What kind of clause is that? (independent) Yes, you have a *who did it* and *did what,* and the clause does not begin with a subordinate conjunction. It can stand alone.

Lesson 2 | Writing

Combining Dependent and Independent Clauses

Read the clauses and determine if they are dependent or independent clauses. Write them in the proper column in the chart. Then, create sentences by combining a dependent clause with an independent clause from the chart. Write the sentences on the lines below and remember to add commas when needed.

• while I waited for the bus • when wolves returned to Yellowstone Park • ranchers began to worry about their cattle and sheep	• she has not worked out regularly • because the storm brought heavy rains • the roads in the neighborhood were flooded	• I finished my homework • birds darted up and down the beach • as the young boy played in the sand • since the gym closed

Dependent Clauses	Independent Clauses
while I waited for the bus	ranchers began to worry about their cattle and sheep
when wolves returned to Yellowstone Park	she has not worked out regularly
because the storm brought heavy rains	the roads in the neighborhood were flooded
as the young boy played in the sand	I finished my homework
since the gym closed	birds darted up and down the beach

Answers will vary.

1. I finished my homework while I waited for the bus.
2. She has not worked out regularly since the gym closed.
3. Because the storm brought heavy rains, the roads in the neighborhood were flooded.
4. As the young boy played in the sand, birds darted up and down the beach.
5. When wolves returned to Yellowstone Park, ranchers began to worry about their cattle and sheep.

Unit 7 13

Independent Practice

Read the remaining clauses and have students sort them. Review the answers as a class.

Now that you have sorted the clauses, what is your next step? (to combine each dependent clause with an independent clause to create sentences) Look for meaning clues to help you create complex sentences that make sense. Remember, dependent clauses do not always have to begin the sentence. But if they do begin the sentence, remember how they should be punctuated.

Model the first sentence by reading the first dependent clause, *while I waited for the bus,* and then read each of the independent clauses. Ask students which combination makes sense. Model the process by reading the subordinate clause at the beginning of the sentence and then at the end of the sentence: *While I waited for the bus, I finished my homework. I finished my homework while I waited for the bus.* Allow students to decide which one they like the best, then write it for #1. Ask them if they used a comma, and if so, where they placed it. Have students work with a partner to complete the remaining sentences. Remind them to include correct punctuation for dependent clauses that begin a sentence. Have volunteers share their sentences. Prompt students to also share how they punctuated their sentences.

Unit 7 Lesson 3

Lesson Opener

Before the lesson, choose one of the following activities to write on the board or post on the *LANGUAGE! Live* Class Wall online.

- *What would you have done if you were Jim Hall and were treated unfairly by a guard?*
- *Write four sentences about a situation of injustice that you witnessed. Use a compound subject in two sentences and a compound predicate in two sentences.*
- *Write five sentences about the perfect pet for you. Use the future progressive tense in your sentences.*

Reading

Objectives

- Reread text for comprehension.
- Establish a purpose for reading text.
- Use critical thinking skills to write responses to prompts about text.
- Support written answers with evidence from text.
- Objectively summarize literary text.
- Identify the purpose and impact of a literary flashback.
- Determine the plot of a story.
- Identify the protagonist and antagonist of a story.

Reading for a Purpose: Excerpt from *White Fang*

This time, we will be reading for a specific purpose, which will help us pay attention to details that we may have missed the first time around. Let's read some questions about the text to provide a purpose for rereading.

Direct students to pages 16 and 17 in their Student Books. Have students read the prompts aloud with you.

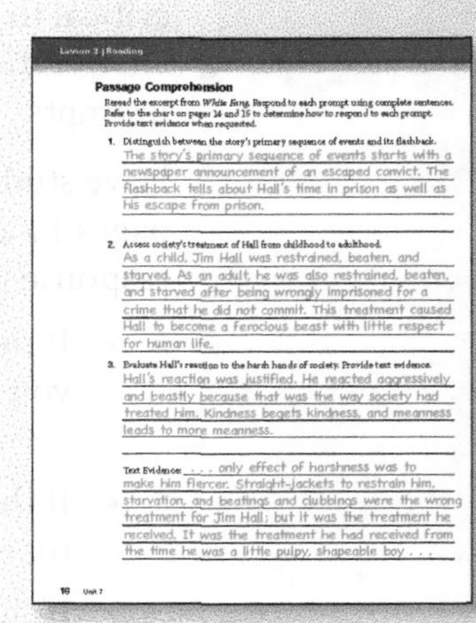
Lesson 3 | Reading

Passage Comprehension

Reread the excerpt from *White Fang*. Respond to each prompt using complete sentences. Refer to the chart on pages 14 and 15 to determine how to respond to each prompt. Provide text evidence when requested.

1. Distinguish between the story's primary sequence of events and its flashback.
   The story's primary sequence of events starts with a newspaper announcement of an escaped convict. The flashback tells about Hall's time in prison as well as his escape from prison.
2. Assess society's treatment of Hall from childhood to adulthood.
   As a child, Jim Hall was restrained, beaten, and starved. As an adult, he was also restrained, beaten, and starved after being wrongly imprisoned for a crime that he did not commit. This treatment caused Hall to become a ferocious beast with little respect for human life.
3. Evaluate Hall's reaction to the harsh hands of society. Provide text evidence.
   Hall's reaction was justified. He reacted aggressively and beastly because that was the way society had treated him. Kindness begets kindness, and meanness leads to more meanness.

   Text Evidence: . . . only effect of harshness was to make him fiercer. Straight-jackets to restrain him, starvation, and beatings and clubbings were the wrong treatment for Jim Hall; but it was the treatment he received. It was the treatment he had received from the time he was a little pulpy, shapeable boy . . .

16 Unit 7

1. Distinguish between the story's primary sequence of events and its flashback.
2. Assess society's treatment of Hall from childhood to adulthood.
3. Evaluate Hall's reaction to the harsh hands of society. Provide text evidence.
4. Distinguish between Judge Scott's and Jim Hall's missing information and explain how it led to the prisoner's revenge.
5. Use your summary plot outline to evaluate White Fang's perception of Weedon Scott.
6. Analyze Alice Scott's nightly routine.

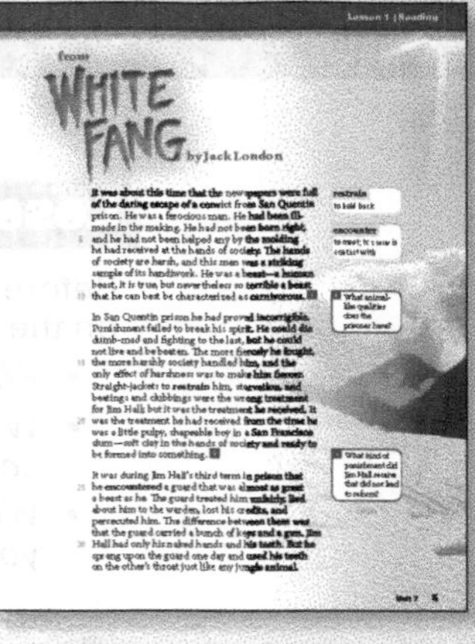

Direct students to page 5 in their Student Books or have them tear out the extra copy of the excerpt from the back of their book.

> **Note:** To minimize flipping back and forth between the pages, a copy of each text has been included in the back of the Student Books. Encourage students to tear this out and use it when working on activities that require the use of the text.

Pay attention to the flashback in the text. Remember that a flashback is used to insert an earlier event into the chronological order of a narrative. Flashbacks are used to provide a crucial back story necessary to understand the primary sequence of events.

Choose an option for reading text. Have students read the text according to the option that you chose.

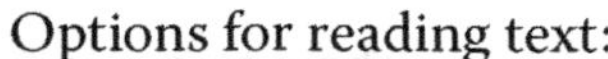

Options for reading text:

- Teacher read-aloud
- Teacher-led or student-led choral read
- Paired read or independent read with bold vocabulary words read aloud

Passage Comprehension

Write the words *analyze, assess, distinguish,* and *evaluate* on the board. Have students read the words aloud with you.

Direct students to pages 14 and 15 in their Student Books. It is critical to understand what the question is asking and how to answer it. Today, we will review four direction words used in prompts.

Have students review the words on the board in the chart on pages 14 and 15. Check for understanding by requesting an oral response to the following questions.

- If the prompt asks you to *analyze,* the response requires you to . . . (break down and evaluate or draw conclusions about the information).
- If the prompt asks you to *assess,* the response requires you to . . . (decide on the value, impact, or accuracy).
- If the prompt asks you to *distinguish,* the response requires you to . . . (recognize or explain the difference).
- If the prompt asks you to *evaluate,* the response requires you to . . . (think carefully to make a judgment; form a critical opinion of).

Direct students to pages 16 and 17 in their Student Books.

Passage Comprehension

Reread the excerpt from *White Fang*. Respond to each prompt using complete sentences. Refer to the chart on pages 14 and 15 to determine how to respond to each prompt. Provide text evidence when requested.

1. Distinguish between the story's primary sequence of events and its flashback.
   The story's primary sequence of events starts with a newspaper announcement of an escaped convict. The flashback tells about Hall's time in prison as well as his escape from prison.

2. Assess society's treatment of Hall from childhood to adulthood.
   As a child, Jim Hall was restrained, beaten, and starved. As an adult, he was also restrained, beaten, and starved after being wrongly imprisoned for a crime that he did not commit. This treatment caused Hall to become a ferocious beast with little respect for human life.

3. Evaluate Hall's reaction to the harsh hands of society. Provide text evidence.
   Hall's reaction was justified. He reacted aggressively and beastly because that was the way society had treated him. Kindness begets kindness, and meanness leads to more meanness.

   Text Evidence: . . . only effect of harshness was to make him fiercer. Straight-jackets to restrain him, starvation, and beatings and clubbings were the wrong treatment for Jim Hall; but it was the treatment he received. It was the treatment he had received from the time he was a little pulpy, shapeable boy . . .

Passage Comprehension (*cont.*)

4. Distinguish between Judge Scott's and Jim Hall's missing information and explain how it led to the prisoner's revenge.
   Judge Scott did not know that Jim Hall was a victim of false evidence and innocent of the crime, so he sentenced him to prison. Jim Hall did not know that Judge Scott was not part of the dishonest police work and was merely doing his job. Because Jim Hall thought that Judge Scott knowingly sentenced an innocent man, he planned his revenge.

5. Use your summary plot outline to evaluate White Fang's perception of Weedon Scott.
   White Fang perceived Weedon Scott as a savior. White Fang's life had been hard because he had been treated unkindly by humans. Weedon Scott not only saved his life, but also freed him from the vicious cycle of neglect and abuse.

6. Analyze Alice Scott's nightly routine.
   Each night, Alice Scott snuck White Fang in to sleep in the hall and woke up early to sneak him outside. This routine is proof that she believed there were reasons to feel threatened and afraid that Jim Hall would come for revenge on Judge Scott as he had promised. She trusted White Fang to protect them and keep them safe.

Let's practice answering questions that are written as prompts that require critical thinking.

Model

Listen as I model the first one for you.

1. Distinguish between the story's primary sequence of events and its flashback.

According to the chart, if the prompt asks me to *distinguish*, I need to recognize or explain the difference. In this case, I need to recognize the flashback so that I can comprehend the story better.

Now, I need to turn the prompt into a question to confirm my understanding.

What is the difference between the story's primary sequence of events and its flashback?

Remember that a flashback is like the backstory. First, I'll skim the first paragraph of text to remind myself that the story opens up by talking about a newspaper headline regarding an escaped convict. The next paragraph starts with a transition that answers *where: In San Quentin prison.* It sounds like the author is providing background on the escaped convict. The next two paragraphs tell about his time in prison, followed by four paragraphs about his escape. By the time I get to line 79, I'm back to the newspaper headlines. I think that the author is using the headline as an indicator that

I'm back to the main story. The backstory is all about Jim Hall's time in prison and his initial escape from prison.

With that said, let's see if I can write an answer to question 1.

The story's primary sequence of events starts with a newspaper announcement of an escaped convict. The flashback tells about Hall's time in prison as well as his escape from prison.

Guided Practice

2. Assess society's treatment of Hall from childhood to adulthood.

How should we respond according to the chart? (If the prompt asks you to *assess*, the response requires you to decide on its value, impact, or accuracy.) Now, turn the prompt into a question to confirm your understanding. Tell your partner the question. (What was the impact of society's treatment of Hall from childhood to adulthood?) Where was Jim Hall raised? (Jim Hall was raised in the slums of San Francisco.) How was Jim treated as a child? (As a child, he was restrained, beaten, and starved.) How was he treated as an adult? (As an adult, he was also restrained, beaten, and starved after being wrongly imprisoned for a crime that he did not commit.)

While providing partner time, write the sentence starters on the board.

As a child, Jim Hall was ______________________________.

As an adult, he was also ______________________________.
This treatment caused ______________________________.

Have partners answer the question.

Independent Practice

Have students respond to the remaining questions.

For students who need more assistance, provide the following alternative questions and sentence starters.

Alternative questions and sentence starters:

3. What is your opinion of Hall's reaction to mistreatment?

   Hall's reaction was ______________________.

   He reacted __________ *because* __________________.

4. What was the difference between Judge Scott's missing information and Jim Hall's missing information?

   Judge Scott did not know ______________________.

   Jim Hall did not know ______________________.

5. What was White Fang's perception of Weedon Scott? Why?

   White Fang perceived Weedon Scott as ______________________.

   White Fang's life ______________________.

   Weedon Scott ______________________.

6. What was Alice Scott's nightly routine? Why did she do this?

   Each night, Alice Scott ______________________.

   This routine is proof that ______________________.

Story Elements

Direct students back to the Plot Summary Outline on page 3 in their Student Books. Have partners complete the outline for Part 5.

When students have finished, review the common elements of a story. This story has many elements that make it a good tale. There is a protagonist and an antagonist, but these change as the point of view and time changes.

There are the conflicts of man vs. animal, man vs. man, and man vs. himself.

Have individual students identify each of the elements above.

Foreshadowing: Antagonist—Society/Judge Scott; Protagonist—Jim Hall
Other: Antagonist—Jim Hall; Protagonist—White Fang

Man vs. Animal: Jim Hall vs. White Fang
Man vs. Man: Jim Hall vs. Judge Scott
Man vs. Himself: Jim Hall vs. his thoughts in solitary confinement

Lesson 1 | Reading

Plot Summary Outline *(cont.)*

Part 4—The Superior Gods

1. White Fang becomes violent toward all other dogs.
2. Gray Beaver settles a debt by giving White Fang to Beauty Smith, a cruel, evil, and ugly man.
3. Beauty Smith attempts to tame White Fang with beatings and force.
4. White Fang learns to take out his hostility and hatred for Smith on other dogs when he is entered in dogfights. He becomes known as "The Fighting Wolf."
5. Weedon Scott saves White Fang from near death during a fight with a dog.
6. Weedon Scott becomes White Fang's new master and tries to teach White Fang how to experience love.

Part 5—The Tame

1. Weedon Scott returns to California with White Fang to live on his ranch with his family (wife: Alice, mom, and dad: Judge Scott).
2. Jim Hall, described as a human beast, killed a guard with his own teeth.
3. Jim Hall escaped from prison after killing two more guards with his own hands.
4. Jim Hall wanted revenge against Judge Scott, Weedon's dad, for sending him to jail for a crime that he did not commit.
5. Hearing of Hall's escape, Weedon's wife brought White Fang to sleep in the house at night.
6. Jim Hall entered the Scott home while the family was asleep. White Fang used his skills from the wild to make a surprise attack on this strange god.

Unit 7 3

Unit 7 Lesson 4

Lesson Opener

Before the lesson, choose one of the following activities to write on the board or post on the *LANGUAGE! Live* Class Wall online.

- *Dress your avatar as though you were about to seek revenge on someone who punished you unjustly. Explain your choices.*
- *Use the future tense to write five sentences about what happens after White Fang attacks Jim Hall.*
- *Make a list of adjectives describing Jim Hall. Make another list of adjectives describing Judge Scott.*

Reading

Objectives

- Read literature with purpose and understanding.
- Answer questions to demonstrate comprehension of text.
- Determine the meaning of personification, hyperboles, exaggerations, metaphors, similes, and idioms in text.
- Determine the impact of the author's word choice on meaning, tone, and mood.
- Monitor comprehension of text during reading.
- Analyze an author's word choice used to create suspense.
- Determine the meaning and purpose of conjunctive adverbs.

Close Reading of the Excerpt from *White Fang*

Highlighters or colored pencils

Let's reread the excerpt from *White Fang*. I will provide specific instructions on how to mark the text that will help with comprehension.

Have students get out a highlighter or colored pencil.

Direct students to pages 18–21 in their Student Books.

Draw a rectangle around the title, *White Fang*.

Circle the word that is an indication that this isn't the whole text. (from)

Now, let's read the vocabulary words aloud.

- What's the first bold vocabulary word? (restrain) *Restrain* means "to hold back." Seatbelts are used to *restrain* people in cars. Have partners use the word in a sentence.
- What's the next vocabulary word? (encountered) *Encountered* means "met; came in contact with." She *encountered* the attendance officer because she was tardy. Have partners use the word in a sentence.
- Next word? (pursued) *Pursued* means "chased; went after." My dad pursued his childhood sweetheart after college and married her. Have partners use the word in a sentence.
- Let's continue. (vainly) *Vainly* means "without success; not achieving what one hoped to." Though she had never won, she *vainly* played the lottery one more time. Have partners use the word in a sentence.

- Next word? (compelled) *Compelled* means "made someone take a certain action." The officers *compelled* the man to tell the truth. **Have partners use the word in a sentence.**
- Let's continue. (vengeance) *Vengeance* means "the act of repaying one hurtful deed with another." It is tempting to bring *vengeance* on someone who caused you harm. **Have partners use the word in a sentence.**
- Next word? (ignorant) *Ignorant* means "not knowing or having important information." The pet owner was *ignorant* about the difference between a dog and a wolf. **Have partners use the word in a sentence.**
- Let's continue. (promotion) *Promotion* means "an attempt to convince others that they should do, believe, or buy something." Teachers were not pleased with the *promotion* of cell phone use on the campus. **Have partners use the word in a sentence.**
- Next word? (advantage) *Advantage* means "something that puts you in a better position than others." Studying for a test gives you an *advantage* over those who don't study. **Have partners use the word in a sentence.**
- What is the last word? (ascent) *Ascent* means "an upward journey." The cabin pressure changed as the plane began its *ascent* toward the clouds. **Have partners use the word in a sentence.**

Talk with a partner about any vocabulary word that is still confusing for you to read consistently or understand its meaning.

You will read the excerpt from *White Fang* one section at a time. After each section, you will monitor your understanding by circling the check mark if you understand the text or the question mark if you don't understand the text. I also want you to draw a question mark over any confusing words, phrases, or sentences.

Options for reading text:

- Teacher read-aloud
- Teacher-led or student-led choral read
- Paired read or independent read with bold vocabulary words read aloud

Choose an option for reading text. Have students read lines 1–7 according to the option that you chose. Pay attention to the author's word choice. Mark any words used by the author to connect the human world to the animal world. (ferocious, harsh, beast, terrible, carnivorous)

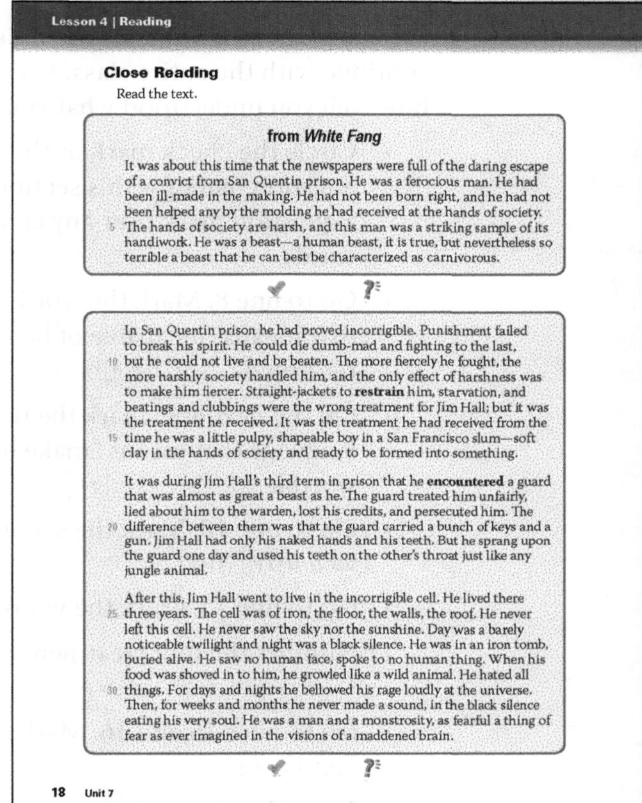

Lesson 4 | Reading

Close Reading

Read the text.

from *White Fang*

It was about this time that the newspapers were full of the daring escape of a convict from San Quentin prison. He was a ferocious man. He had been ill-made in the making. He had not been born right, and he had not been helped any by the molding he had received at the hands of society. The hands of society are harsh, and this man was a striking sample of its handiwork. He was a beast—a human beast, it is true, but nevertheless so terrible a beast that he can best be characterized as carnivorous.

In San Quentin prison he had proved incorrigible. Punishment failed to break his spirit. He could die dumb-mad and fighting to the last, but he could not live and be beaten. The more fiercely he fought, the more harshly society handled him, and the only effect of harshness was to make him fiercer. Straight-jackets to **restrain** him, starvation, and beatings and clubbings were the wrong treatment for Jim Hall; but it was the treatment he received. It was the treatment he had received from the time he was a little pulpy, shapeable boy in a San Francisco slum—soft clay in the hands of society and ready to be formed into something.

It was during Jim Hall's third term in prison that he **encountered** a guard that was almost as great a beast as he. The guard treated him unfairly, lied about him to the warden, lost his credits, and persecuted him. The difference between them was that the guard carried a bunch of keys and a gun. Jim Hall had only his naked hands and his teeth. But he sprang upon the guard one day and used his teeth on the other's throat just like any jungle animal.

After this, Jim Hall went to live in the incorrigible cell. He lived there three years. The cell was of iron, the floor, the walls, the roof. He never left this cell. He never saw the sky nor the sunshine. Day was a barely noticeable twilight and night was a black silence. He was in an iron tomb, buried alive. He saw no human face, spoke to no human thing. When his food was shoved in to him, he growled like a wild animal. He hated all things. For days and nights he bellowed his rage loudly at the universe. Then, for weeks and months he never made a sound, in the black silence eating his very soul. He was a man and a monstrosity, as fearful a thing of fear as ever imagined in the visions of a maddened brain.

18 Unit 7

When most of the students are finished, continue with the entire class. Let's see how well you understood what you read.

- Circle the check mark or the question mark for this section. Draw a question mark over any confusing words.
- Go to line 2. Use context to mark the synonym for *criminal.* (convict)
- On the same line, mark the synonym for *fierce.* (ferocious)
- On line 3, mark the evidence that Jim Hall had trouble his whole life. (had not been born right)
- Mark the clause that means "life is hard." (The hands of society are harsh)
- Go to line 7. Mark the word that means "meat eater." (carnivorous)

Have students read lines 8–33 according to the option that you chose. Mark any words used by the author to connect the human world with the animal world. (fiercely, fiercer, beast, sprang, jungle animal, growled, wild animal, bellowed, monstrosity)

When most of the students are finished, continue with the entire class. Let's see how well you understood what you read.

- Circle the check mark or the question mark for this section. Draw a question mark over any confusing words.
- Go to line 8. Mark the word that means "incapable of being reformed." (incorrigible)
- On the next line, mark the figurative language that means "make him feel worthless." (break his spirit)
- Go to line 10. Mark the synonym for *viciously.* (fiercely)
- Go to line 12. Mark the word that means "more fierce." (fiercer)
- Number the four treatments Jim Hall received that were the wrong treatments. (1. straight-jackets to restrain him; 2. starvation; 3. beatings; 4. clubbings)
- Go to lines 15 and 16. Mark the metaphor that describes Hall. (soft clay in the hands of society)
- Mark the name of the person the story has been about. (Jim Hall) Draw a line to the first noun used in the first paragraph to represent this person. (convict)
- Number the ways that the prison guard treated Hall unfairly. (1. lied about him to the warden; 2. lost his credits; 3. persecuted him)
- Go to line 19. Mark the synonym for *abused.* (persecuted)
- Go to lines 20 and 21. Mark the objects that distinguish Jim Hall from the guard. (keys; gun)
- On line 22, mark the word *other's.* Draw a line to whom this is referring. (guard)
- Go to line 24. Circle the pronoun *this.* Draw an arrow to show what *this* is referring to. (sprang upon the guard one day and used his teeth . . .)
- Mark Jim Hall's punishment for killing the guard. (the incorrigible cell) Mark the longevity of this punishment. (three years)
- On line 32, mark the example of personification that indicates solitary confinement was destroying anything good in Jim Hall. (eating his very soul)
- Mark the line that means "even crazy people can't imagine how scary of a man Jim Hall was." (as fearful of a thing of fear as ever imagined in the visions of a maddened brain)

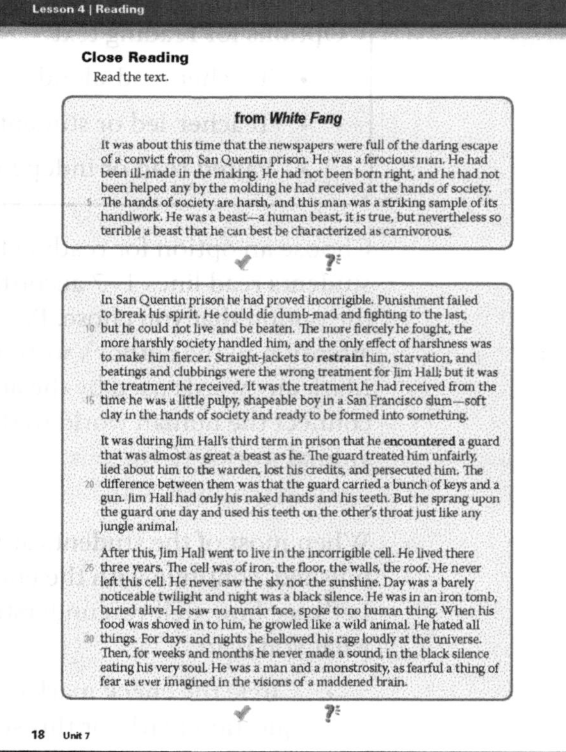

Lesson 4 | Reading

Close Reading

Read the text.

from *White Fang*

It was about this time that the newspapers were full of the daring escape of a convict from San Quentin prison. He was a ferocious man. He had been ill-made in the making. He had not been born right, and he had not been helped any by the molding he had received at the hands of society. The hands of society are harsh, and this man was a striking sample of its handiwork. He was a beast—a human beast, it is true, but nevertheless so terrible a beast that he can best be characterized as carnivorous.

In San Quentin prison he had proved incorrigible. Punishment failed to break his spirit. He could die dumb-mad and fighting to the last, but he could not live and be beaten. The more fiercely he fought, the more harshly society handled him, and the only effect of harshness was to make him fiercer. Straight-jackets to **restrain** him, starvation, and beatings and clubbings were the wrong treatment for Jim Hall; but it was the treatment he received. It was the treatment he had received from the time he was a little pulpy, shapeable boy in a San Francisco slum—soft clay in the hands of society and ready to be formed into something.

It was during Jim Hall's third term in prison that he **encountered** a guard that was almost as great a beast as he. The guard treated him unfairly, lied about him to the warden, lost his credits, and persecuted him. The difference between them was that the guard carried a bunch of keys and a gun. Jim Hall had only his naked hands and his teeth. But he sprang upon the guard one day and used his teeth on the other's throat just like any jungle animal.

After this, Jim Hall went to live in the incorrigible cell. He lived there three years. The cell was of iron, the floor, the walls, the roof. He never left this cell. He never saw the sky nor the sunshine. Day was a barely noticeable twilight and night was a black silence. He was in an iron tomb, buried alive. He saw no human face, spoke to no human thing. When his food was shoved in to him, he growled like a wild animal. He hated all things. For days and nights he bellowed his rage loudly at the universe. Then, for weeks and months he never made a sound, in the black silence eating his very soul. He was a man and a monstrosity, as fearful a thing of fear as ever imagined in the visions of a maddened brain.

18 Unit 7

Have students read lines 34–55 according to the option that you chose. Mark any words used by the author to connect the human world with the animal world. (hunted, bloodhounds, animals, trail, stampeded, manhunt)

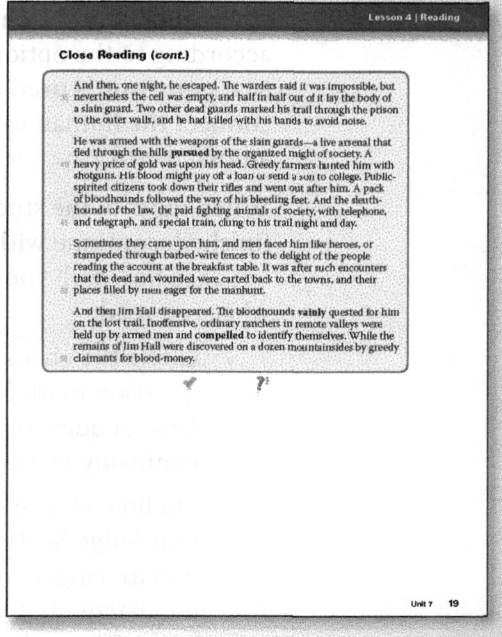

Lesson 4 | Reading

Close Reading (*cont.*)

And then, one night, he escaped. The warders said it was impossible, but nevertheless the cell was empty, and half in half out of it lay the body of a slain guard. Two other dead guards marked his trail through the prison to the outer walls, and he had killed with his hands to avoid noise.

He was armed with the weapons of the slain guards—a live arsenal that fled through the hills **pursued** by the organized might of society. A heavy price of gold was upon his head. Greedy farmers hunted him with shotguns. His blood might pay off a loan or send a son to college. Public-spirited citizens took down their rifles and went out after him. A pack of bloodhounds followed the way of his bleeding feet. And the sleuth-hounds of the law, the paid fighting animals of society, with telephone, and telegraph, and special train, clung to his trail night and day.

Sometimes they came upon him, and men faced him like heroes, or stampeded through barbed-wire fences to the delight of the people reading the account at the breakfast table. It was after such encounters that the dead and wounded were carted back to the towns, and their places filled by men eager for the manhunt.

And then Jim Hall disappeared. The bloodhounds **vainly** quested for him on the lost trail. Inoffensive, ordinary ranchers in remote valleys were held up by armed men and **compelled** to identify themselves. While the remains of Jim Hall were discovered on a dozen mountainsides by greedy claimants for blood-money.

Unit 7 19

When most of the students are finished, continue with the entire class. Let's see how well you understood what you read.

- Circle the check mark or the question mark for this section. Draw a question mark over any confusing words.
- Go to line 34. Circle the pronoun *he*. In the margin, write who *he* refers to. (Jim Hall)
- On the same line, mark the synonym for *guards*. (warders)
- On the same line, circle the pronoun *it*. Draw an arrow to show what *it* refers to. (escape)
- Go to line 35. Mark the conjunctive adverb that means "in spite of what has just been said" and is used to connect the two clauses. (nevertheless)
- Go to line 38. Mark the word that means "collection of weapons." (arsenal)
- In the same paragraph, mark the figurative language that means there was a reward offered for the capture of Jim Hall. (A heavy price of gold was upon his head.)
- Read the last sentence in that same paragraph again. Who does the author refer to as animals? Write your answer in the margin. (police/detectives)
- Go to lines 44 and 45. Number three strategies used to track Hall. (1. telephone; 2. telegraph; 3. special train)
- Go to line 48. Mark the synonym for *report*. (account)
- On the same line, mark the form of a vocabulary word that is used as a noun instead of a verb. (encounters)
- Go to line 49. Mark the outcome of the heroes who tracked Hall. (dead and wounded)
- Go to line 51. Mark the informal word for *detectives*. (bloodhounds)
- On the same line, mark the synonym for *searched*. (quested)
- Go to line 52. Mark the synonym for *harmless*. (inoffensive)
- On the same line, mark the word that means "far away." (remote)
- Go to lines 54 and 55. Mark the exaggeration that is an indication that the remains of Jim Hall weren't really found. (discovered on a dozen mountainsides by greedy claimants)
- Think about the words used by the author thus far. How have the words affected your feelings toward Jim Hall? How have they affected the mood of the text? Write your answer at the bottom of the page. (The use of "beastly" words has given a sinister/angry mood to the text; it has created a negative feeling toward Jim Hall.)

Have students read lines 56–86 according to the option that you chose. Mark any words used by the author to connect the human world with the animal world. (monstrous, wrath)

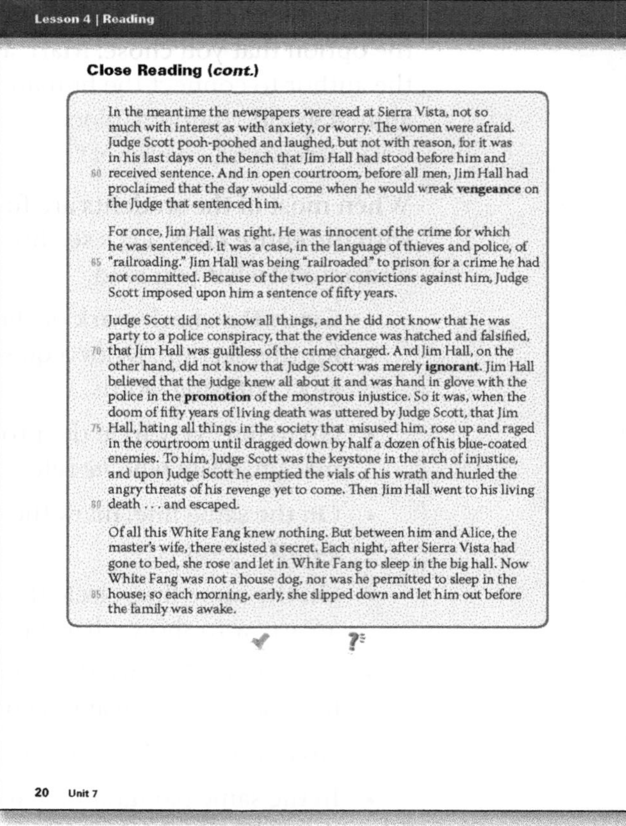

Lesson 4 | Reading

Close Reading (*cont.*)

In the meantime the newspapers were read at Sierra Vista, not so much with interest as with anxiety, or worry. The women were afraid. Judge Scott pooh-poohed and laughed, but not with reason, for it was in his last days on the bench that Jim Hall had stood before him and received sentence. And in open courtroom, before all men, Jim Hall had proclaimed that the day would come when he would wreak **vengeance** on the Judge that sentenced him.

For once, Jim Hall was right. He was innocent of the crime for which he was sentenced. It was a case, in the language of thieves and police, of "railroading." Jim Hall was being "railroaded" to prison for a crime he had not committed. Because of the two prior convictions against him, Judge Scott imposed upon him a sentence of fifty years.

Judge Scott did not know all things, and he did not know that he was party to a police conspiracy, that the evidence was hatched and falsified, that Jim Hall was guiltless of the crime charged. And Jim Hall, on the other hand, did not know that Judge Scott was merely **ignorant**. Jim Hall believed that the judge knew all about it and was hand in glove with the police in the **promotion** of the monstrous injustice. So it was, when the doom of fifty years of living death was uttered by Judge Scott, that Jim Hall, hating all things in the society that misused him, rose up and raged in the courtroom until dragged down by half a dozen of his blue-coated enemies. To him, Judge Scott was the keystone in the arch of injustice, and upon Judge Scott he emptied the vials of his wrath and hurled the angry threats of his revenge yet to come. Then Jim Hall went to his living death . . . and escaped.

Of all this White Fang knew nothing. But between him and Alice, the master's wife, there existed a secret. Each night, after Sierra Vista had gone to bed, she rose and let in White Fang to sleep in the big hall. Now White Fang was not a house dog, nor was he permitted to sleep in the house; so each morning, early, she slipped down and let him out before the family was awake.

20 Unit 7

When most of the students are finished, continue with the entire class. Let's see how well you understood what you read.

- Circle the check mark or the question mark for this section. Draw a question mark over any confusing words.
- On line 58, mark the evidence that Judge Scott didn't think he was in danger. (pooh-poohed and laughed) In the previous sentence, mark the evidence that his wife and daughter-in-law didn't agree. (The women were afraid.)
- On line 60, mark the words that mean "given his punishment." (received sentence)
- On the same line, mark the purposeful exaggeration. (before all men) A purposeful exaggeration is called a *hyperbole*. What do you think the author's purpose for this hyperbole is? (to make the reader understand the weight of Jim Hall's threat of vengeance)
- Go to line 61. Mark the word that means "bring about." (wreak)
- Go to line 63. Mark what Jim Hall was correct about. (innocent of the crime)
- Go to line 65. Mark the word that means "forced by unfair means." (railroaded)
- On line 67, mark the length of Jim Hall's prison term. (fifty years)
- Go to line 70. Mark the word that means "without guilt." (guiltless) Circle the suffix that means "without." (-less)
- Go to line 72. Mark the idiom that means "working together." (hand in glove)
- Go to line 74. Mark the oxymoron, or something that contradicts itself. (living death)
- On line 77, mark the metaphor that means "the most important piece." (the keystone in the arch)
- Go to lines 81 and 82. Mark the phrase that tells more about Alice. (the master's wife) Circle the punctuation meaning cues. (comma, comma)
- Go to line 83. Mark the secret that provided foreshadowing. (let in White Fang to sleep in the big hall)
- Go to line 84. Mark the word that means "allowed." (permitted)

Have students read from line 87 to the end according to the option that you chose. Mark any words used by the author to connect the human world with the animal world. (wild, hunted, struck, snarl)

When most of the students are finished, continue with the entire class. Let's see how well you understood what you read.

- Circle the check mark or the question mark for this section. Draw a question mark over any confusing words.
- In the first paragraph, mark the ways White Fang knew Jim Hall was in the house. (smelled the air and read the message it bore of a strange god's presence; sounds of the strange god's movements)
- On lines 93 and 94, mark what was different between White Fang's usual prey and Jim Hall. (live meat that was infinitely timid)
- In the second paragraph, mark the words that create suspense, which is the tension induced by fear of what will or will not happen. (The strange god paused; White Fang was as dead; he watched and waited; White Fang bristled, but waited; The strange god's foot lifted; beginning the ascent.)
- Go to line 98. Use context to mark the words that refer to family members. (dearest possessions)
- On the same line, mark the word that means "showed anger." (bristled)
- Go to line 99. Circle the subject. (strange god) In the margin, write the name of the strange god. (Jim Hall)
- Go to line 100. Circle the pronoun *he*. Draw an arrow to the noun that *he* represents. (White Fang)
- On the same line, mark the words that mean "surprise." (no warning)
- Go to lines 101 and 102. Mark the phrase that means "jumped." (lifted his body in the spring that landed him)
- Go to line 104. Mark the past tense of *cling*. (clung)
- At the end of the paragraph, mark the phrases that indicate White Fang is winning the struggle. (man struggled to rise, was in again with the slashing fangs)
- Based on the author's word choice to describe Jim Hall and White Fang, which does the author want you to see as a beast? Write your answer at the bottom of the page. (Jim Hall)

Have partners compare text markings and correct any errors.

Lesson 4 | Reading

Close Reading (*cont.*)

On one such night, while all the house slept, White Fang awoke and lay very quietly. And very quietly he smelled the air and read the message it bore of a strange god's presence. And to his ears came sounds of the strange god's movements. White Fang burst into no furious outcry. It was not his way. The strange god walked softly, but more softly walked White Fang, for he had no clothes to rub against the flesh of his body. He followed silently. In the Wild he had hunted live meat that was infinitely timid, and he knew the **advantage** of surprise.

The strange god paused at the foot of the great staircase and listened, and White Fang was as dead, so without movement was he as he watched and waited. Up that staircase the way led to the lovemaster and to the lovemaster's dearest possessions. White Fang bristled, but waited. The strange god's foot lifted. He was beginning the **ascent**.

Then it was that White Fang struck. He gave no warning, with no snarl anticipated his own action. Into the air he lifted his body in the spring that landed him on the strange god's back. White Fang clung with his forepaws to the man's shoulders, at the same time burying his fangs into the back of the man's neck. He clung on for a moment, long enough to drag the god over backward. Together they crashed to the floor. White Fang leaped clear, and, as the man struggled to rise, was in again with the slashing fangs.

✔ ?

Unit 7 21

Unit 7

Lesson 5

Lesson Opener

Before the lesson, choose one of the following activities to write on the board or post on the *LANGUAGE! Live* Class Wall online.

- *Write four sentences with at least two vocabulary words in each. Show you know the meanings. (restrain, encounter, pursue, vainly, compel, vengeance, ignorant, promotion, advantage, ascent)*
- *Write three sentences about Jim Hall's time in prison. Answer the following questions in your sentences. When? Where? How? Combine the three sentences into one Masterpiece Sentence.*
- *Label the following sentence parts as a phrase or a clause:*
  - *will be open*
  - *practice made him a better player*
  - *the school was made of brick*
  - *during seventh period*
  - *the work was tiring*

Vocabulary

Objective

- Review key passage vocabulary.

Recontextualize Passage Vocabulary

Direct students to page 4 in their Student Books. Use the following questions to review the vocabulary words from the excerpt from *White Fang*.

Lesson 1 | Vocabulary

Key Passage Vocabulary: Excerpt from *White Fang*

Read each word. Write the word in column 3. Then, circle a number to rate your knowledge of the word.

Vocabulary	Part of Speech	Write the Word	Knowledge Rating
restrain	(v)	restrain	0 1 2 3
encounter	(v)	encounter	0 1 2 3
pursue	(v)	pursue	0 1 2 3
vainly	(adv)	vainly	0 1 2 3
compel	(v)	compel	0 1 2 3
vengeance	(n)	vengeance	0 1 2 3
ignorant	(adj)	ignorant	0 1 2 3
promotion	(n)	promotion	0 1 2 3
advantage	(n)	advantage	0 1 2 3
ascent	(n)	ascent	0 1 2 3

4 Unit 7

- There's a thunderstorm brewing. You *vainly* call for your little brother to come inside. Does he hear you? (no) An ambulance turns on its sirens as it approaches an intersection. Cars move out of the way. Has it sounded its sirens *vainly*? (no) Every year, Max tries out for soccer, and every year, he doesn't make the team. He is trying out for soccer in what way? (vainly)
- On the way to school, your bike gets a flat. Have you *encountered* a problem? (yes) You start walking to school and hope someone you know drives by and offers you a ride. Nobody does. Have you *encountered* someone you know? (no) Oddly enough, you run into your next-door neighbor on the other side of town. What has happened? (You have encountered your neighbor.)
- At the end of the ride, the roller coaster swoops down into the station. Is the end of the ride an *ascent*? (no) The subway escalator is broken, and you must climb 82 steps to get to street level. Is this an *ascent*? (yes) In just two days, you've moved from the lowest to the highest rank on the leaderboard. This could be described as a rapid what? (ascent)

- Are you *pursuing* a high school diploma? (yes) Your three-year-old niece lets go of her balloon and it floats away. Is there any way to *pursue* it? (no) Someone you need to talk to passes by in the hallway. You get up and run after the person. What are you doing? (pursuing him or her)
- Your sister plays an embarrassing prank on you every April Fool's Day. This year, are you interested in *vengeance*? (yes) Your brother beats you big time at your favorite game. You don't want a rematch. Are you interested in *vengeance*? (no) Your football team's quarterback is sacked. As soon as the other team gets the ball, your team sacks their quarterback. This is an act of what? (vengeance)
- There's a TV crew in somebody's front yard down the street. You wonder what's going on. Are you *ignorant* of the circumstances? (yes) You're on your way to the pool. Little do you know that it has been closed for repairs. Are you *ignorant* of the closure? (yes) You walk in the front door and find your mom glaring at you. You have no idea why. What are you? (ignorant)
- Does a dam *restrain* water? (yes) Does a waterfall *restrain* water? (no) You are babysitting seven five-year-olds. They see the ice cream man coming down the street. What is it hard to do? (restrain them)
- You coax a scared kitten out from under the house with a bowl of milk. Have you *compelled* the cat to come out? (yes) You need $20 to pay a friend back by noon. The only way to earn the money is to help your uncle open his breakfast trailer at 6:00 a.m. Does this situation *compel* you to get up and help your uncle? (yes) You are trying to sleep, but a drip in the bathroom sink is keeping you awake. You are finally what? (compelled to get up and tighten the faucet)
- You've just moved to another country and don't speak the language. Is this an *advantage*? (no) You happen to know someone who will tutor you in the language every day after school. Is this an *advantage*? (yes) Your sister and you both want to apply for a job at your favorite store in the mall, but a person must be 16 to do so. You are 16, and your sister is 14. What do you have? (an advantage)
- You are going to be in a concert, but you haven't told anyone about it. Are you interested in self-*promotion*? (no) You're collecting canned food for the homeless and have spread the word with posters and flyers. You receive more food than your organization can store. Was your *promotion* of the food drive successful? (yes) Your aunt makes and sells jewelry. You wear it and tell all your friends about it. You are helping with what? (the promotion of her business)

Writing

Objectives

- Use a plot summary to write coherent paragraphs in response to reading.
- Write a narrative from an animal's point of view.

Quick Write in Response to Reading

Direct students to page 22 in their Student Books. Read the prompt. You have read several text selections that have been written from the first-person point of view. Remember to use pronouns such as *I, me, mine, we,* and *us*. You learned about White Fang's past and how he came to live at Sierra Vista. Use what you know and then add elaborations from White Fang's perspective.

Lesson 5 | Writing

Quick Write in Response to Reading Answers will vary.

Review the plot summary on pages 2 and 3. Think about how dramatically White Fang's life changed when he left the Yukon and came to live with the Scotts. Write a narrative from White Fang's point of view that describes this turning point. Use evidence from the plot summary in your writing. Consider using foreshadowing in your opening sentence to alert the reader of the big change that is coming.

As I watched the unfamiliar man walk up the street, I had no idea of how dramatically he was going to change my life. I remember a very long time ago, living with my mother in the wild. As a puppy, I learned the law of the wild: eat or be eaten. Beauty Smith forced me to be more than strong. He forced me to be a fearsome fighter. I became accustomed to his rough treatment.

There was a great deal of excitement as I was led into a small ring. Pain came with this excitement. Sharp fangs, claws, and biting would come soon. When my master gave the signal, I would become "The Fighting Wolf." I would weave and lunge, going for the bite that would still the other animal. I stopped wondering why my master wanted me to fight a creature I had never seen before.

Now in the ring, I saw the dog I was to fight. There was something very different about him, and as soon as we began lunging and snapping, I knew this fight would be different. I don't remember anything but searing pain and blackness. The noise from the crowd faded, and I became aware of my surroundings. The crowd was gone and in its place was the man I had seen walking up the street. He talked to me in tones I had never heard. Lyrical and soothing words were spoken to me. He gently stroked me and put warm liquid to my mouth. When I tried to stand, I felt immense pain and sank back down on a soft pallet. Once my wounds healed, we left the frozen, cold ground, and the life of the "The Fighting Wolf" was over.

22 Unit 7

Reading

Objectives

- Self-correct as comprehension of text deepens.
- Answer questions to demonstrate comprehension of text.
- Engage in class discussion.
- Identify the enduring understandings from a piece of text.

Revisit Passage Comprehension

Direct students back to pages 16 and 17 in their Student Books. Have students review their answers and make any necessary changes. Then, have partners share their answers and collaborate to perfect them.

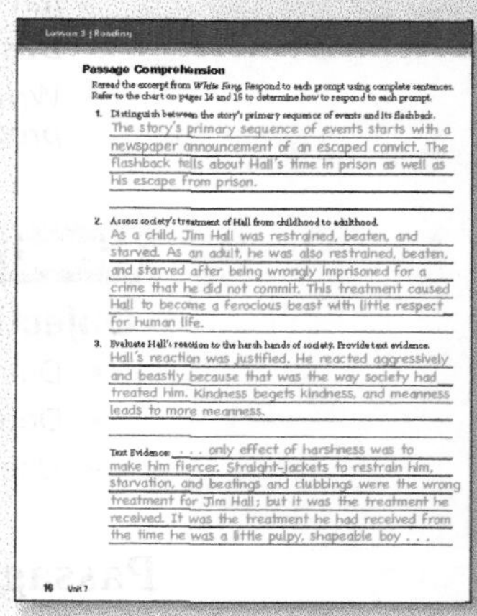

Passage Comprehension

Reread the excerpt from *White Fang*. Respond to each prompt using complete sentences. Refer to the chart on pages 14 and 15 to determine how to respond to each prompt.

1. Distinguish between the story's primary sequence of events and its flashback.
   The story's primary sequence of events starts with a newspaper announcement of an escaped convict. The flashback tells about Hall's time in prison as well as his escape from prison.
2. Assess society's treatment of Hall from childhood to adulthood.
   As a child, Jim Hall was restrained, beaten, and starved. As an adult, he was also restrained, beaten, and starved after being wrongly imprisoned for a crime that he did not commit. This treatment caused Hall to become a ferocious beast with little respect for human life.
3. Evaluate Hall's reaction to the harsh hands of society. Provide text evidence.
   Hall's reaction was justified. He reacted aggressively and beastly because that was the way society had treated him. Kindness begets kindness, and meanness leads to more meanness.

   Text Evidence: . . . only effect of harshness was to make him fiercer. Straight-jackets to restrain him, starvation, and beatings and clubbings were the wrong treatment for Jim Hall; but it was the treatment he received. It was the treatment he had received from the time he was a little pulpy, shapeable boy . . .

16 Unit 7

Enduring Understandings

Direct students back to page 1 in their Student Books. Reread the Big Idea questions.

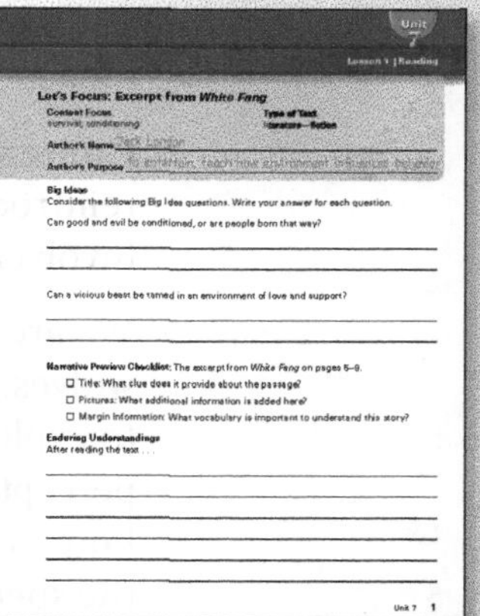

Unit 7

Let's Focus: Excerpt from *White Fang*

Content Focus
survival; conditioning

Type of Text
literature—fiction

Author's Name Jack London

Author's Purpose to entertain; teach how environment influences behavior

Big Ideas
Consider the following Big Idea questions. Write your answer for each question.

Can good and evil be conditioned, or are people born that way?

Can a vicious beast be tamed in an environment of love and support?

Narrative Preview Checklist: The excerpt from *White Fang* on pages 5–9.

- ☐ Title: What clue does it provide about the passage?
- ☐ Pictures: What additional information is added here?
- ☐ Margin Information: What vocabulary is important to understand this story?

Enduring Understandings
After reading the text . . .

Unit 7 1

Can good and evil be conditioned, or are people born that way?

Can a vicious beast be tamed in an environment of love and support?

Generate a class discussion about the questions and the answers students came up with in Lesson 1. Have them consider whether their answers have changed any after reading the text.

Use the following talking points to foster conversation. Then, have students write their enduring understandings from the unit.

- What if White Fang had stayed with Beauty Smith and never learned the love and affection of the Scott family? How would White Fang's personality have developed? Would White Fang have become like the human beast, Jim Hall, and become incorrigible? As demonstrated by White Fang, affection can reshape life despite hereditary traits and life experience.

What we read should make us think. Use our discussion and your thoughts about the text to determine what you will "walk away with." Has it made you think about a personal experience or someone you know? Has your perspective or opinion on a specific topic changed? Do you have any lingering thoughts or questions? Write these ideas as your enduring understandings. What will you take with you from this text?

Discuss the enduring understandings with the class. If time permits, have students post a personal response about their enduring understandings to the online class wall.

Remind students to consider why the author wrote the passage and whether he was successful.

Unit 7

Lesson 6

Lesson Opener

Before the lesson, choose one of the following activities to write on the board or post on the *LANGUAGE! Live* Class Wall online.

- *Write five sentences explaining what you would do to pass the time if you were in total darkness and isolation without the ability to leave or talk to other people. All you have is a concrete cell.*
- *Describe a time when you felt like you were mistreated. What did you do about it?*
- *Write four sentences about Jim Hall. Use him as a subject noun, direct object, predicate noun, and an object of the preposition.*

Reading

Objectives

- Determine and discuss the topic of a text.
- Determine and discuss the author's purpose.
- Use text features to preview text.

Passage Introduction

Direct students to page 23 in their Student Books. Discuss the content focus.

Content Focus
reintroduction of wolves; human involvement in the environment

We are about to learn more about wolves. Specifically, we are going to explore the environment and perceptions of wolves, as well as human involvement in the survival of the species.

Type of Text
informational—nonfiction

Text can be literature or informational. We are going to read an informational text called "Return of the Wolves." Let's discuss the meaning of *return* as used in this context. What do you think *return* means as it relates to wolves? Discuss possible meanings with students. Write *reappearance* on the board. *Return* in this context means "reappearance." What is the base word of *reappearance*? (appear) The prefix *re-* means "again." *Reappear* means "to appear again."

Lesson 6 | Reading

Let's Focus: "Return of the Wolves"

Content Focus
reintroduction of wolves; human involvement in the environment

Type of Text
informational—nonfiction

Author's Name unknown

Author's Purpose to teach about wolves in danger

Big Ideas
Consider the following Big Idea questions. Write your answer for each question.

How do stereotypes of wolves affect their image and perhaps even their existence?

Should humans interfere with nature? Explain.

Informational Preview Checklist: "Return of the Wolves" on pages 25–27.

- ☐ Title: What clue does it provide?
- ☐ Pictures: What additional information is added here?
- ☐ Margin Information: What vocabulary is important to understand this story?
- ☐ Features: What other features do you notice?

Enduring Understandings
After reading the text . . .

Unit 7 23

Write *reintroduction* on the board. What is the base word of *reintroduction*? (introduce) What does the prefix *re-* mean? (again) *Reintroduce* means "to introduce again."

So "Return of the Wolves" means the reappearance of wolves. The content focus is *reintroduction of wolves,* which means to introduce the wolves again. Why are they returning? Why do wolves need to be introduced back into the wild? **Discuss predictions.**

Author's Purpose

Have students glance at the text. Who is the author of the text? (unknown) This is the type of text you would read in a textbook. The information is factual, but there isn't an author's name attributed to it. It likely means that someone was paid to write this text for a publishing company but isn't necessarily considered an "author." We said that *White Fang* was written to entertain. "Return of the Wolves" is different. It is written to teach you about wolves so that you understand the issues surrounding wolves. You will likely learn something you didn't know. Maybe it will cause you to think differently about wolves.

> **Note:** Determine if students need Background Information pertaining to the gray wolf. This can be found in the Teacher Resources online.

Read the Big Idea questions aloud.

> ### Big Ideas
>
> How do stereotypes of wolves affect their image and perhaps even their existence?
>
> Should humans interfere with nature? Explain.

As a class, consider the two Big Idea questions. After discussing each question, have students write an answer. We'll come back to these questions after we finish reading the text. You can add to your answers as you gain information and perspective.

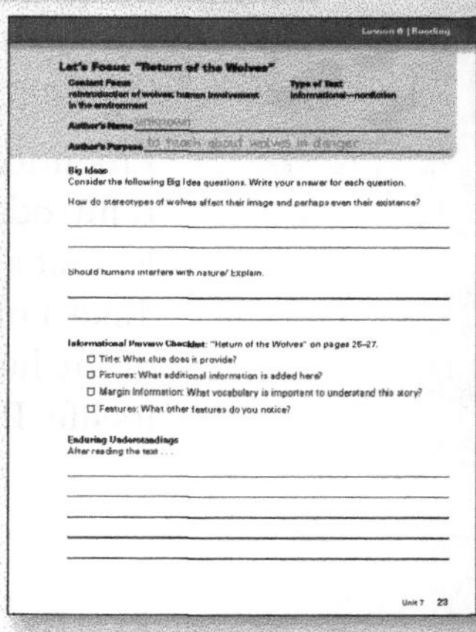

Lesson 6 | Reading

Let's Focus: "Return of the Wolves"

Content Focus
reintroduction of wolves; human involvement in the environment

Type of Text
informational—nonfiction

Author's Name unknown

Author's Purpose to teach about wolves in danger

Big Ideas
Consider the following Big Idea questions. Write your answer for each question.

How do stereotypes of wolves affect their image and perhaps even their existence?

Should humans interfere with nature? Explain.

Informational Preview Checklist: "Return of the Wolves" on pages 25–27.

- ☐ Title: What clue does it provide?
- ☐ Pictures: What additional information is added here?
- ☐ Margin Information: What vocabulary is important to understand this story?
- ☐ Features: What other features do you notice?

Enduring Understandings
After reading the text . . .

Unit 7 23

Preview

Read the Preview Checklist on page 23. Follow the Preview Procedure outlined below.

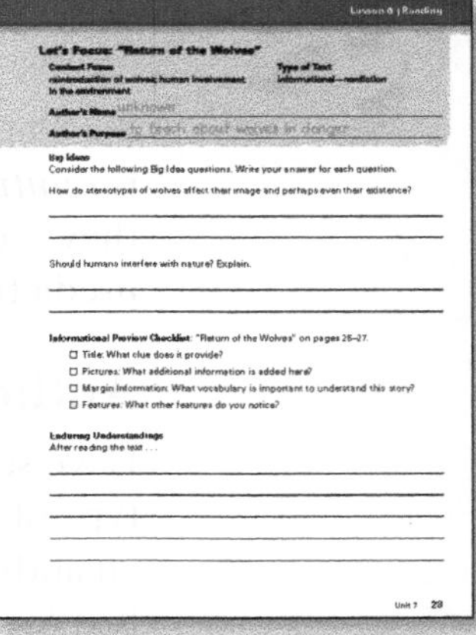

Preview Procedure

- Group students with partners or in triads.
- Have students count off as 1s or 2s. The 1s will become the student leaders. If working with triads, the third students become 3s.
- The student leaders will preview the text in addition to managing the checklist and pacing.
- The 2s and 3s will preview the text with 1s.
- Direct 1s to open their Student Books to page 23 and 2s and 3s to open their Student Books to page 25. This allows students to look at a few different pages at one time without turning back and forth.

Direct students to page 25.

If it is necessary, guide students in a short preview using the following talking points.

What is the title of the text? ("Return of the Wolves") Describe the graphic on the first page. (lone wolf with yellow eyes in the wild) Explain the picture on page 26. (A pack of four wolves is tracking an elk for food.)

I mentioned earlier that there are issues surrounding the reintroduction of wolves. Just as there is more than one way to look at a picture, there is more than one way to look at an issue. Take a moment and talk with your partner about the perspective of the hungry wolves and the perspective of the lone elk in fear of its life. Provide sharing time.

Vocabulary

Objectives

- Evaluate word knowledge.
- Determine the meaning of key passage vocabulary.

Rate Vocabulary Knowledge

Direct students to page 24 in their Student Books.

Before we read the text, let's take a look at the vocabulary words that appear in this text. Remind students that as you read each word in the first column aloud, they will write the word in the third column and then rate their knowledge of it. Display the Vocabulary Rating Scale poster or write the information on the board. Review the meaning of each rating.

Lesson 6 | Vocabulary

Key Passage Vocabulary: "Return of the Wolves"

Read each word. Write the word in column 3. Then, circle a number to rate your knowledge of the word.

Vocabulary	Part of Speech	Write the Word	Knowledge Rating
persistence	(n)	persistence	0 1 2 3
insecurity	(n)	insecurity	0 1 2 3
relocation	(n)	relocation	0 1 2 3
habitat	(n)	habitat	0 1 2 3
alter	(v)	alter	0 1 2 3
competition	(n)	competition	0 1 2 3
aspect	(n)	aspect	0 1 2 3
decline	(v)	decline	0 1 2 3
economy	(n)	economy	0 1 2 3
compromise	(n)	compromise	0 1 2 3

24 Unit 7

Vocabulary Rating Scale

0—I have never heard the word before.

1—I have heard the word, but I'm not sure how to use it.

2—I am familiar with the word, but I'm not sure if I know the correct meaning.

3—I know the meaning of the word and can use it correctly in a sentence.

The points are not a grade; they are just there to help you know which words you need to focus on. By the end of this unit, you should be able to change all your ratings to a 3. That's the goal.

Read each word aloud. Have students repeat it, write it, and rate it. Then, have volunteers who rated a word *2* or *3* use the word in an oral sentence.

Preteach Vocabulary

Let's take a closer look at the words. Follow the Preteach Procedure below.

Preteach Procedure

This activity is intended to take only a short amount of time, so make it an oral exercise.

- Introduce each word as indicated on the word card.
- Read the definition and example sentences.
- Ask questions to clarify and deepen understanding.
- If time permits, allow students to share.

* If your students would benefit from copying the definitions, please have them do so in the vocabulary log in the back of the Student Books using the margin definitions in the passage selections. This should be done outside of instruction time.

persistence (n)

Let's read the first word together. *Persistence.*

Definition: If you have *persistence*, you are able to keep doing something even though it is difficult. What word means "the ability to keep doing something even though it is difficult"? (persistence)

Example 1: It takes *persistence* to master the violin.

Example 2: To have *persistence,* you must be able to block out distractions and ignore even good reasons to quit.

Example 3: If you try to open a jar once and then give up, you lack *persistence.*

Question 1: If you pledge to learn one new word in a foreign language every day, but give up on day four, do you have *persistence*? Yes or no? (no)

Question 2: You're helping your dad build a shed. It's hot and you're tired, but you keep at it. Do you have *persistence*? Yes or no? (yes)

Pair Share: Turn to your partner and describe someone you know who has *persistence.*

insecurity (n)

Let's read the next word together. *Insecurity.*

Definition: *Insecurity* is the state of not feeling safe or steady. What is "the state of not feeling safe or steady"? (insecurity)

Example 1: People who lose their homes in natural disasters are often plagued by feelings of *insecurity* for years to come.

Example 2: My *insecurity* in the dark keeps me from staying out late.

Example 3: I feel *insecurity* in large, bustling cities I don't know well.

Question 1: Little Lulu cannot sleep at night unless she is surrounded by her stuffed animals. Does she have nighttime *insecurity*? Yes or no? (yes)

Question 2: You are comfortable in crowds and with groups of new people. Do you have social *insecurity*? Yes or no? (no)

Pair Share: You feel *insecurity* around deep water. Turn to your partner and tell whether you would like to go on a cruise, and why.

relocation (n)

Let's read the next word together. *Relocation.*

Definition: *Relocation* is the act of moving to a different place. What means "the act of moving to a different place"? (relocation)

Example 1: *Relocation* often happens when someone takes a job in a new city.

Example 2: The *relocation* of a lemon tree from Florida to Michigan would cause the tree to die.

Example 3: I was disappointed by the *relocation* of one of my favorite neighborhood stores.

Question 1: The students at one school are being moved to another. Is this an example of *relocation*? Yes or no? (yes)

Question 2: Your family has lived in the same town for generations. Is this an example of *relocation*? Yes or no? (no)

Pair Share: Turn to your partner and tell whether you hope to experience *relocation* someday, and why.

3

habitat (n)

Let's read the next word together. *Habitat.*

Definition: A *habitat* is the natural home of a plant or animal. What means "the natural home of a plant or animal"? (habitat)

Example 1: Oil spills disturb the *habitat* of many ocean creatures.

Example 2: I'm an outdoors person; I feel as if nature is my true *habitat.*

Example 3: Many zoos and aquariums try to re-create the *habitat* of the animals they house.

Question 1: Is the prairie a good *habitat* for a prairie dog? Yes or no? (yes)

Question 2: You catch a firefly in a jar. Is the firefly now in its *habitat*? Yes or no? (no)

Pair Share: Turn to your partner and describe the *habitat* of your favorite animal.

alter (v)

Let's read the next word together. *Alter.*

Definition: To *alter* something is to change it. What means "to change"? (alter)

Example 1: You can *alter* the length of a skirt by hemming it.

Example 2: I sometimes *alter* my route to school to keep from getting in a rut.

Example 3: If you have a schedule conflict, you may need to *alter* one or more classes.

Question 1: The dance captain has changed the routine. Has it been *altered*? Yes or no? (yes)

Question 2: A radio station uses the same playlist every afternoon, and you're getting bored with it. Do you want them to *alter* the playlist? Yes or no? (yes)

Pair Share: Turn to your partner and tell whether you would *alter* our school colors, and why.

5

competition (n)

Let's read the next word together. *Competition.*

Definition: *Competition* is the struggle between two or more people or groups who are trying to get the same thing. What means "the struggle between two or more people or groups who are trying to get the same thing"? (competition)

Example 1: *Competition* between grocery stores can keep prices low because each store is trying to get a limited number of customers to shop there.

Example 2: One bag of popcorn isn't enough for our family; we're always in *competition* for the last handful.

Example 3: People who thrive on *competition* enjoy the challenge of outsmarting their opponent.

Question 1: A club you belong to is selling school T-shirts. Another club starts selling very similar T-shirts for less. Is this a *competition*? Yes or no? (yes)

Question 2: Your two cats nudge each other out of the way to get to the food in the bowl. Is this a *competition*? Yes or no? (yes)

Pair Share: Turn to your partner and describe a *competition* you have seen on TV. Tell who was involved and what they were trying to get.

aspect (n)

Let's read the next word together. *Aspect.*

Definition: An *aspect* of something is one part, element, or angle of something. What word means "one part, element, or angle of something"? (aspect)

Example 1: If you are a farmer, the weather affects every *aspect* of your life.

Example 2: Cellular biologists study a single *aspect* of biology: cells.

Example 3: I have a friend who is a comedian, but her sense of humor is only one *aspect* of her personality.

Question 1: Your favorite thing about a movie was the music. Was the music the *aspect* you enjoyed most? Yes or no? (yes)

Question 2: You tend to make quick, rash decisions. Do you consider each *aspect* of both choices before you decide? Yes or no? (no)

Pair Share: Turn to your partner and discuss the two most important *aspects* of a good song.

decline (v)

Let's read the next word together. *Decline.*

Definition: *Decline* means "to grow smaller in size or strength." What word means "to grow smaller in size or strength"? (decline)

Example 1: Thankfully, violence in many U.S. cities continues to *decline.*

Example 2: Car sales have not *declined* even though gas prices are high.

Example 3: It is hard to watch the health of an older person you love slowly *decline.*

Question 1: The hailstorm is growing stronger. Is it *declining*? Yes or no? (no)

Question 2: Food trailers are popping up all over town. Are their numbers *declining*? Yes or no? (no)

Pair Share: What fashion trend do you hope will soon *decline*? Tell your partner.

8

economy (n)

Let's read the next word together. *Economy.*

Definition: An *economy* is the flow of money, goods, and services in a community. What word means "the flow of money, goods, and services in a community"? (economy)

Example 1: When everyone has a job, the *economy* is strong.

Example 2: In an agricultural *economy,* crops are the most important resource.

Example 3: In a just or fair *economy,* people working full-time make enough money to live on.

Question 1: You love to doodle. Does your doodling affect the *economy*? Yes or no? (no)

Question 2: Businesses in a small town are closing and people are moving away to find jobs. Is the *economy* strong? Yes or no? (no)

Pair Share: Turn to your partner and tell how a marble-based *economy* might work.

9

compromise (n)

Let's read the last word together. *Compromise.*

Definition: A *compromise* is a settlement reached when each side in an argument gives up a part of what it wants. What word means "the settlement reached when each side in an argument gives up a part of what it wants"? (compromise)

Example 1: If you want to stay out until 11:00 and your mom wants you home by 9:00, one *compromise* would be a 10:00 curfew.

Example 2: People who insist on having their way have not learned the art of *compromise.*

Example 3: I wanted hamburgers, but my friend wanted spinach pizza. Our *compromise* was hamburger pizza.

Question 1: You have great respect for other peoples' points of view. Does this help you when making a *compromise*? Yes or no? (yes)

Question 2: The student council asked the principal for a longer passing period. Instead, he made it shorter. Was this a *compromise*? Yes or no? (no)

Pair Share: You and your partner are buying a car together. Tell each other what kind of car you want and why. Then, come up with a *compromise.*

10

Reading

Objectives

- Read informational text.
- Monitor comprehension during text reading.

"Return of the Wolves"

Direct students to page 25 in their Student Books.

Now that we have previewed vocabulary, it's time to read. Unlike the first text in this unit, this is nonfiction text. The text features are different. We don't have characters and dialogue. Instead, we have facts, figures, and even graphs. It is important to pay attention to the text, the pictures, and the graphs because they each carry meaning and add to the author's message.

Guiding Students Toward Independent Reading

It is important that your students read as much and as often as they can. Assign readings that meet the needs of your students, based on your observations and data. This is a good opportunity to stretch your students. If students become frustrated, scaffold the reading with paired reading, choral reading, or a read-aloud.

Options for reading text:

- Teacher read-aloud
- Teacher-led or student-led choral read
- Paired read or independent read

Choose an option for reading text. Students read according to the option that you chose. Review the purpose of the numbered squares in the text and prompt students to stop periodically and check comprehension.

If you choose to read the text aloud or chorally, use the following text boxes and stop to ask questions and have students answer them.

SE p. 25, paragraph 1

The wolf has taken on many images over time. It has been known as both the noblest animal and the vilest animal. Native Americans respect the wolf for its bravery, intelligence, **persistence**, hunting skills, and love of family. However, authors and storytellers have made the wolf the villain of many stories like *Little Red Riding Hood* and *The Three Pigs*. And of course Hollywood has put its spin on the wolf by creating horror films to scare us. But the true image of the wolf in North America today is one of **insecurity**. It is trying to fit back into the land over which it once reigned king.

1. What is your image of wolves?

SE p. 25, paragraph 2

The wolf once ruled the West. Its spot at the top of the food chain was unchallenged for centuries. By the 1930s, however, this had changed. The wolf fell victim to overhunting and trapping. Laws did not protect it. By the early 1970s, the gray wolf had mostly vanished from the western United States. It was placed on the endangered species list. The federal government began a **relocation** project. Several dozen wolves were captured in Canada and released in Yellowstone National Park. This project was a great success. However, it created a division between people in the area. Some were for it. Others were against it.

2. How did the federal government protect wolves?

SE p. 26, paragraphs 1–2

There have been many good things about the relocation of wolves to Yellowstone. For one, tourists love wolves. People who like seeing wildlife have come to the park to see the wolf in its **habitat** and to take pictures. Naturalists have seen the relocation of the wolf as a victory in returning the West to the way it used to be. In addition, the people who visit the park to see the wolves have boosted the economy greatly.

The reintroduction of wolves into Yellowstone has helped bring the elk population under control. Wolves are natural carnivores. Because elk and deer are their favorite meal, the populations of these animals have decreased. This is a positive change because the elk had overpopulated Yellowstone.

3. How has the reintroduction been good for the area?

SE p. 26, paragraphs 3–4

Having too many elk had caused damage to aspen tree forests. This **altered** the beaver and bird populations. The flow of streams and rivers were changed as a result. The presence of wolves in the elk habitat creates what is called an "ecology of fear." Elk spend less time eating in one place. As a result, trees and shrubs grow back quicker. There's more variety in the plant life. In Yellowstone, researchers saw that open fields became more vegetated when they brought back wolves.

Because the wolf has returned, coyotes have been able to return to their natural habit of scavenging. Without wolves, coyotes had jumped up in the food chain. They could hunt animals without much **competition**. However, they struggled because they are not naturally good hunters. Having wolves in the area has provided more food for the coyotes. They feed on the remains of the wolves' kills.

4. How has the wolf's return affected elk, beavers, birds, coyotes, and aspen trees?

SE p. 27, paragraphs 1–2

There have also been negative **aspects** to reintroducing wolves. Ranchers believe that wolves pose a threat to the sheep and cattle industries of the areas surrounding Yellowstone. Wolves hunt as a pack. This makes herds of sheep and cattle surrounding the park vulnerable to their attacks. Ranchers have struggled to deal with the wolves' presence. According to ranchers, predatory livestock deaths have increased as the wolf population has increased. Because wolves are now protected by law, ranchers feel defenseless. However, the federal government pays the ranchers for the loss of their animals, and the actual losses of livestock to wolves have been relatively small.

Hunters, too, have been affected by the hunting skills of the wolf pack. The **declining** numbers of large-game animals such as elk and deer in the areas surrounding the park have made hunting tougher. It is estimated that in the surrounding areas, the elk population has been cut in half since the wolf's return to Yellowstone. Elk have fallen prey to the wolves, and they have moved to higher ground for safety. Hunters now have fewer animals for their own hunting activities. This in turn affects the **economy** of the surrounding areas because fewer hunters buy hunting permits.

5. How has the reintroduction of wolves been bad?

SE p. 27, paragraph 3

The battle of the wolf will rage on. Naturalists, ranchers, hunters, and people who want to see the wolf return to its historical home all have valuable viewpoints. The outcome must be a **compromise**. But for now, deep in the heart of Yellowstone National Park, there are wolves. Their lonesome howls can be heard on the darkest nights. Their shadowy images can be seen gliding through the aspen forests as they do what they do best—survive.

6. What is your viewpoint on the reintroduction of wolves?

For confirmation of engagement, have partners share their opinions of wolf reintroduction. Have volunteers share opinions with the class.

Unit 7

Lesson 7

Lesson Opener

Before the lesson, choose one of the following activities to write on the board or post on the *LANGUAGE! Live* Class Wall online.

- *Write a summary sentence about the issue regarding the reintroduction of wolves to Yellowstone.*
- *Make a list of benefits of the wolf's presence in Yellowstone.*
- *Identify the dependent clauses in the following sentences:*

  Because elk and deer are their favorite meal, the populations of these animals have decreased.

  In Yellowstone, researchers saw that open fields became more vegetated when they brought back wolves.

  Because wolves are now protected by law, ranchers feel defenseless.

  This in turn affects the economy of the areas because fewer hunters buy hunting permits.

Vocabulary

Objectives

- Review key passage vocabulary.
- Distinguish among the connotations of words with similar denotations.
- Verify word knowledge using a dictionary.

Review Passage Vocabulary

Direct students to page 24 in their Student Books. Use the following questions to review the vocabulary words from "Return of the Wolves." Have students answer each question using the vocabulary word or indicating its meaning in a complete sentence.

Lesson 6 | Vocabulary

Key Passage Vocabulary: "Return of the Wolves"

Read each word. Write the word in column 3. Then, circle a number to rate your knowledge of the word.

Vocabulary	Part of Speech	Write the Word	Knowledge Rating
persistence	(n)	persistence	0 1 2 3
insecurity	(n)	insecurity	0 1 2 3
relocation	(n)	relocation	0 1 2 3
habitat	(n)	habitat	0 1 2 3
alter	(v)	alter	0 1 2 3
competition	(n)	competition	0 1 2 3
aspect	(n)	aspect	0 1 2 3
decline	(v)	decline	0 1 2 3
economy	(n)	economy	0 1 2 3
compromise	(n)	compromise	0 1 2 3

24 Unit 7

- Native Americans respect the wolf for its *persistence*. Is the wolf likely to give up? (No; the wolf's persistence makes it able to survive difficult times.) Has the wolf shown *persistence* in recent years? (Yes, it has shown persistence; even though its numbers were dwindling in the West, it has made a comeback in Yellowstone National Park.)
- What put the wolf in a state of *insecurity* in the 1930s? (Overhunting and overtrapping put the wolf in a state of insecurity.) Species that are experiencing extreme *insecurity* are placed on what list? (Species that experience extreme insecurity are placed on the endangered species list.)
- Why did the federal government start a *relocation* project for the wolves? (It started a relocation project to move wolves to Yellowstone Park, where they would not be hunted or trapped.) What was one benefit of wolf *relocation*? (Possible responses: Relocation has given visitors to the park a glimpse of the wolf in its natural environment. It has also brought the elk population under control and strengthened the coyote population.)

- Is Yellowstone a good *habitat* for the wolf? Why or why not? (Yes, Yellowstone is a good habitat for the wolf. The wolf is thriving in its new environment and making the entire habitat healthy.) What other species thrive in the Yellowstone *habitat*? (Elk, deer, bears, birds, and coyotes thrive in the park's habitat.)
- Having too many elk in the Aspen forests damaged the trees. What did this *alter*? (Damaged trees altered the beaver and bird populations, which rely on trees.) How did the return of wolves *alter* this trend? (It reduced the elk population, which allowed the trees to thrive again.)
- When the wolves disappeared, coyotes could hunt without *competition*. What does this mean? (If coyotes could hunt without competition, they could hunt without another group trying to hunt the same prey.) Why was this lack of *competition* bad for the coyotes? (The lack of competition was bad for the coyotes because they are poor hunters and actually benefit from the wolves' kills; as scavengers, they eat the wolves' leftovers.)
- What are some negative *aspects* of moving wolves to Yellowstone? (One negative aspect is that sheep and cattle on nearby ranches are at risk; because the wolves are protected by law, the ranchers feel helpless. Another negative aspect is that the decreasing numbers of elk and deer have made hunting tougher, and hunting was an important business in the area.) Which *aspect* of the wolves' story interests you most? (Responses will vary, but should focus on one element of the wolves' plight, such as their original decline or their ability to adapt to their new home.)
- Did moving wolves to Yellowstone cause their numbers to *decline*? (No, it didn't cause their numbers to decline; it caused them to grow larger.) What populations did it cause to *decline*? Why? (It caused the elk and deer populations to decline because wolves hunt those animals.)
- How does the presence of wolves hurt the local *economy*? (It affects the economy by reducing the number of hunting permits sold and by putting the ranchers' main resource, their livestock, at risk.) How does the presence of wolves help the *economy*? (It draws curious tourists to the park.)
- Why must the outcome of this story involve a *compromise*? (People who support the presence of wolves in Yellowstone must reach a compromise, or settlement, with people who oppose the presence of wolves in Yellowstone.) What *compromise* do you suggest? (Responses will vary, but should specify how each side could give up a part of what it wants.)

Vocabulary Concept: Degrees of Meaning

Draw the following diagram on the board.

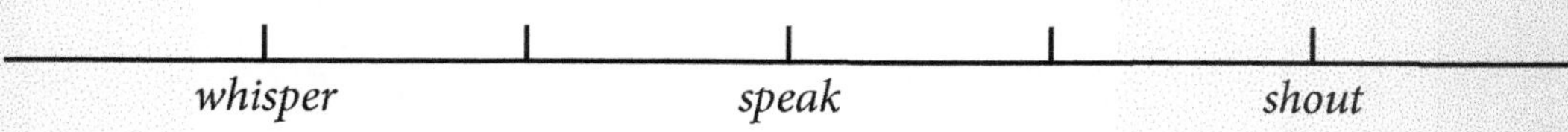

These three words are related. They name different ways of saying something out loud. But they have different degrees of meaning. Which word names the softest way of saying something out loud? (whisper) Which word names the loudest way of saying something out loud? (shout)

Write the words *declare* and *mumble* on the board. Where on the diagram would the word *declare* go? (between *speak* and *shout*) Where on the diagram would the word *mumble* go? (between *whisper* and *speak*)

Although these words are related, they are not interchangeable. You can't randomly use one in place of another. They are used differently in different sentences, or contexts, to communicate how a person is speaking. Write the following sentence frame on the board:

Little Theo ran toward the busy street. "STOP!" _____ his mother.

Tell students that the past tense form of one of the words on the diagram belongs on the blank. Ask them which it is. (shouted) Then, have students use the other words on the diagram in different contexts. (Sample responses: "The baby is finally asleep," *whispered* Mom; "I don't want to get up yet," *mumbled* the sleepy teen; "If you have something to say, please *speak*," said the principal; "I am no longer a baby!" *declared* the six-year-old.)

Direct students to page 28 in their Student Books. Read the instructions aloud.

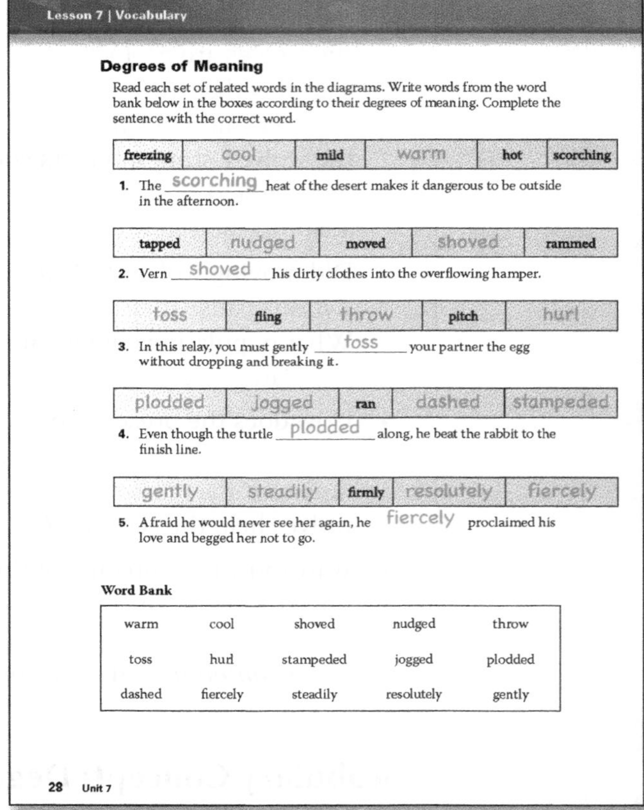

Lesson 7 | Vocabulary

Degrees of Meaning

Read each set of related words in the diagrams. Write words from the word bank below in the boxes according to their degrees of meaning. Complete the sentence with the correct word.

freezing	cool	mild	warm	hot	scorching

1. The scorching heat of the desert makes it dangerous to be outside in the afternoon.

tapped	nudged	moved	shoved	rammed

2. Vern shoved his dirty clothes into the overflowing hamper.

toss	fling	throw	pitch	hurl

3. In this relay, you must gently toss your partner the egg without dropping and breaking it.

plodded	jogged	ran	dashed	stampeded

4. Even though the turtle plodded along, he beat the rabbit to the finish line.

gently	steadily	firmly	resolutely	fiercely

5. Afraid he would never see her again, he fiercely proclaimed his love and begged her not to go.

Word Bank

warm	cool	shoved	nudged	throw
toss	hurl	stampeded	jogged	plodded
dashed	fiercely	steadily	resolutely	gently

28 Unit 7

Model

Dictionaries

Have students look at the first diagram. Model how to complete it.

- The words in the diagram are *freezing, mild, hot,* and *scorching.* All of these words are related to temperature.
- These words have different degrees of meaning, though. *Freezing* means "really, really cold"; *mild* means "pleasant," you know what *hot* means, and *scorching* means "really, really hot."
- *Warm* and *cool* are the words in the word bank that are related to temperature. They are the words I need to place in the boxes in the diagram.
- Something that is *warm* is not really, really hot, or *scorching*; but it's not *mild,* either. The word *warm* belongs in the box between *mild* and *hot.* Write *warm* where it belongs. **Pause to allow students to write the word.**
- Something that is *cool* is not really, really cold, or *freezing*; but it's not *mild,* either. The word *cool* belongs in the box between *freezing* and *mild.* Write *cool* where it belongs. **Pause to allow students to write the word.**
- **Read the sentence frame aloud.** I have to decide which of the words from the diagram belongs in this blank. The phrase *heat of the desert* and the word *dangerous* give me some clues. They tell me that I should choose a word with a strong degree of meaning—one that means "really, really hot." The word *scorching* belongs in this blank. Write it there. **Pause to allow students to write the word.**

Guided Practice

Let's do one together now.

- **Read the words in the second diagram aloud.** How are these words related? What do they all describe? (They describe the force with which someone moves something.)
- Which word on the diagram means "move with very little force"? (tapped)
- Which word on the diagram means "move with very great force"? (rammed)
- Which words in the word bank are related to the force with which we move something? Hint: pay attention to tense. (shoved, nudged)
- Which word belongs between *tapped* and *moved*? (nudged) **Have students write the answer on the page.**
- Which word belongs between *moved* and *rammed*? (shoved) **Have students write the answer on the page.**
- Which word completes the sentence? (shoved) **Have students write the answer on the page.**

Independent Practice

Assign online practice from the Text Training link on the left menu of your teacher dashboard.

Have students complete items 3–5. Have them verify their answers using a dictionary. Review the answers as a class.

Reading

Objectives

- Determine how to respond to prompts.
- Use critical thinking skills to write responses to prompts about text.
- Support written answers with evidence from text.

Critical Understandings: Direction Words *clarify, present, prove, synthesize*

We will respond to some prompts about our text. Remember, prompts are statements that require a constructed response, which can range from a list to a complete sentence to a paragraph or an essay.

Write the words *clarify, present, prove,* and *synthesize* on the board. Have students read the words aloud with you.

Direct students to pages 14 and 15 in their Student Books. It is critical to understand what the question is asking and how to answer it. Today, we will look at four direction words used in prompts.

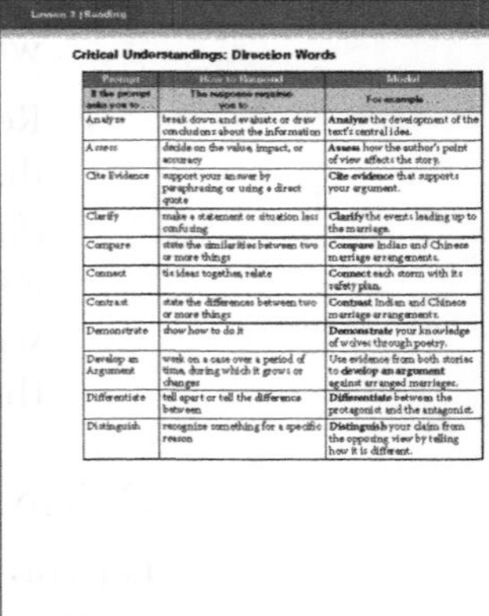
Lesson 7 | Reading

Critical Understandings: Direction Words

Prompt	How to Respond	Model
If the prompt asks you to . . .	The response requires you to . . .	For example . . .
Analyze	break down and evaluate or draw conclusions about the information	**Analyze** the development of the text's central idea.
Assess	decide on the value, impact, or accuracy	**Assess** how the author's point of view affects the story.
Cite Evidence	support your answer by paraphrasing or using a direct quote	**Cite evidence** that supports your argument.
Clarify	make a statement or situation less confusing	**Clarify** the events leading up to the marriage.
Compare	state the similarities between two or more things	**Compare** Indian and Chinese marriage arrangements.
Connect	tie ideas together, relate	**Connect** each storm with its safety plan.
Contrast	state the differences between two or more things	**Contrast** Indian and Chinese marriage arrangements.
Demonstrate	show how to do it	**Demonstrate** your knowledge of wolves through poetry.
Develop an Argument	work on a case over a period of time, during which it grows or changes	Use evidence from both stories to **develop an argument** against arranged marriages.
Differentiate	tell apart or tell the difference between	**Differentiate** between the protagonist and the antagonist.
Distinguish	recognize something for a specific reason	**Distinguish** your claim from the opposing view by telling how it is different.

14 Unit 7

Have students read about the four direction words in the chart with their partner.

Chart Reading Procedure

- Group students with partners or in triads.
- Have students count off as 1s or 2s. The 1s will become the student leaders. If working with triads, the third students become 3s.
- The student leaders will read the left column (Prompt) in addition to managing the time and turn-taking if working with a triad.
- The 2s will explain the middle column of the chart (How to Respond). If working in triads, 3s take turns explaining the middle column.
- The 1s read the model in the right column (Model), and 2s and 3s restate the model as a question.
- All students should follow along with their pencil eraser while others are explaining the chart.
- Students must work from left to right, top to bottom in order to benefit from this activity.

Check for understanding by requesting an oral response to the following questions.

- If the prompt asks you to *clarify*, the response requires you to . . . (explain it so that it is easy to understand).
- If the prompt asks you to *present*, the response requires you to . . . (deliver information).
- If the prompt asks you to *prove*, the response requires you to . . . (give evidence to show that it is true).
- If the prompt asks you to *synthesize*, the response requires you to . . . (combine information in a logical way).

Direct students to page 29 in their Student Books and read aloud the instructions. Let's read some prompts about a small section of the text before we expand to the entire text.

1. Synthesize the various images people have had of wolves over time and tell how these images have changed.
2. Clarify the meaning of *endangered* using context clues.
3. Present information from the Wolf and Elk Population graphs.
4. Prove that the reintroduction of wolves affected the elk population.

We are going to focus on the first two paragraphs of "Return of the Wolves." We will practice answering prompts with these new question words. Having a good understanding of the text from the beginning will help build a foundation for understanding the rest of the text and make it feel less difficult.

Lesson 7 | Reading

Critical Understandings

Reread lines 1–42 of "Return of the Wolves" and the graphs on page 27. Respond to each prompt using complete sentences. Refer to the chart on pages 14 and 15 to determine how to respond to each prompt. Provide text evidence when requested.

1. Synthesize the various images people have had of wolves over time and tell how these images have changed.

   Various images of wolves over time have been positive and negative. For example, Native Americans respect wolves as brave, intelligent, persistent, and caring. On the other hand, present-day media depicts wolves as vicious in horror films and tricky in fairy tales.

2. Clarify the meaning of *endangered* using context clues. List the context clues as text evidence.

   Endangered means that an animal has mostly vanished or is nearly extinct due to overhunting or trapping.

   Text Evidence: victim to overhunting and trapping; mostly vanished

3. Present information from the Wolf and Elk Population graphs.

   From 1995 to 2002, the wolf population in Northern Yellowstone increased from 20 to almost 100 wolves. During the same timeframe, the elk population decreased from about 19,000 to 9,000 in the park. In 2005, the wolf population decreased as the elk population increased. Both populations decreased from 2008 to 2012.

4. Prove that the reintroduction of wolves affected the elk population.

   The reintroduction of wolves has affected the elk population. Proof of this effect is that between 1995 and 2012, when the wolf population increased greatly, the elk population decreased greatly, and vice versa because wolves prey on elk.

Unit 7 29

Model

Let's practice answering questions that are written as prompts. Remember to use the chart as a reference. Listen as I model the first one for you.

> 1. **Synthesize the various images people have had of wolves over time and tell how these images have changed.**

According to the chart, if the prompt asks me to *synthesize*, the response requires that I combine information in a logical way. Now, I will turn the prompt into a question to confirm understanding. How have the images people have had of wolves changed over time? I am a little confused by the use of the word *image*. If I look up the definition of *image*, I will find that *image* can mean "opinion." Let's restate the question with that definition in mind. How have people changed their opinion of wolves over time? That makes more sense to me. For this answer, I will reread lines 1–21. **Have students read the text aloud.**

So, my answer would be:

Various images of wolves over time have been positive and negative. For example, Native Americans respect wolves as brave, intelligent, persistent, and caring. On the other hand, present-day media depicts wolves as vicious in horror films and tricky in fairy tales.

Guided Practice

Let's move on to the next prompt and question word.

> 2. **Clarify the meaning of *endangered* using context clues. List context clues as text evidence.**

How should we respond according to the chart? (If the prompt asks you to *clarify*, the response requires you to . . . explain it so that it is easy to understand.) Now, turn the prompt into a question to confirm your understanding. Tell your partner the question. (What does *endangered* mean in this context?)

Where is the word *endangered* in the text? (line 32) In order to use context clues and provide text evidence, I need to read around the word. I need to read what comes before the word and what comes after the word. Let's skim the text, starting at line 22, to determine what information is relevant to define *endangered*. Lines 22–26 are irrelevant, or unrelated to the definition of *endangered*. Line 27 provides some context clues. Raise your hand when you can find context clues that help us define *endangered*. (victim to overhunting and trapping) There is another clue in line 30. What is it? (mostly vanished) **Record context clues on the board.** Next, work with a partner to put part of the prompt in your answer and record your response.

While providing partner time, write the sentence starter on the board.

Endangered *means* ______________________________.

Have partners answer the question.

3. Present information from the Wolf and Elk Population graphs.

How should we respond according to the chart? (If the prompt asks you to *present*, the response requires you to deliver information.) The graphs show how the two populations changed over time. Turn the prompt into a question to confirm your understanding. Tell your partner the question. (What information is given in the population graphs?)

While providing partner time, write the sentence starters on the board.

From 1995 to 2002, the wolf population in Northern Yellowstone ________.

During the same timeframe, the elk population ____________________.

Have partners answer the question.

4. Prove that the reintroduction of wolves affected the elk population.

How should we respond according to the chart? (If the prompt asks you to *prove*, the response requires that you present evidence to show that it is true.) Now, turn the prompt into a question to confirm your understanding. Tell your partner the question. (What evidence proves that the reintroduction of wolves affected the elk population?) Will I get my information from the text, the graphs, or both? (both)

While providing partner time, write the sentence starters on the board.

The reintroduction of wolves has affected the elk population.

Proof of this effect is that between 1995 and 2012,

______________________________.

Have partners answer the question.

Unit 7

Lesson 8

Lesson Opener

Before the lesson, choose one of the following activities to write on the board or post on the *LANGUAGE! Live* Class Wall online.

- *Make a list of problems caused by the wolf's presence in Yellowstone.*
- *Write two sentences about the perception of wolves. Use a subordinating conjunction in your sentence.*
- *Elaborate one or more of these simple sentences, using the steps in Masterpiece Sentences.*

  Wolves hunt.

  Coyotes scavenge.

  Hunters leave the area.

  Tourists visit the park.

Reading

Objectives

- Establish a purpose for rereading text.
- Read informational text.
- Monitor comprehension during text reading.
- Use critical thinking skills to write responses to prompts about text.
- Support written answers with evidence from text.
- Interpret information from graphics to answer questions about text.
- Identify evidence used by an author to support claims.
- Objectively summarize informational text.

Reading for a Purpose: "Return of the Wolves"

We are going to reread "Return of the Wolves." Let's preview the prompts to provide a purpose for rereading the text.

Direct students to pages 30 and 31 in their Student Books. Have students read the prompts aloud with you.

1. Clarify the author's basic claim or focus of information in "Return of the Wolves."
2. Synthesize and explain the economic changes brought about by the wolf introduction.
3. Prove the theory that the author supports wolf reintroduction.
4. Clarify the counterclaim of ranchers.
5. Present data to prove that the ranchers' counterclaim is weak.
6. Synthesize and explain the author's recommendation regarding the reintroduction of wolves.

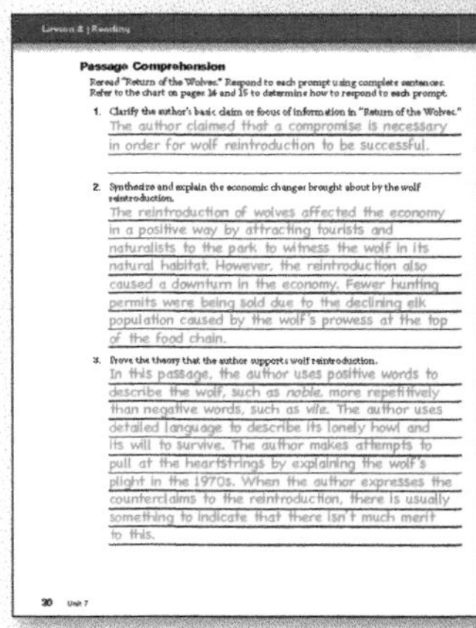

Lesson 8 | Reading

Passage Comprehension

Reread "Return of the Wolves." Respond to each prompt using complete sentences. Refer to the chart on pages 14 and 15 to determine how to respond to each prompt.

1. Clarify the author's basic claim or focus of information in "Return of the Wolves."
   The author claimed that a compromise is necessary in order for wolf reintroduction to be successful.
2. Synthesize and explain the economic changes brought about by the wolf reintroduction.
   The reintroduction of wolves affected the economy in a positive way by attracting tourists and naturalists to the park to witness the wolf in its natural habitat. However, the reintroduction also caused a downturn in the economy. Fewer hunting permits were being sold due to the declining elk population caused by the wolf's prowess at the top of the food chain.
3. Prove the theory that the author supports wolf reintroduction.
   In this passage, the author uses positive words to describe the wolf, such as *noble*, more repetitively than negative words, such as *vile*. The author uses detailed language to describe its lonely howl and its will to survive. The author makes attempts to pull at the heartstrings by explaining the wolf's plight in the 1970s. When the author expresses the counterclaims to the reintroduction, there is usually something to indicate that there isn't much merit to this.

30 Unit 7

It's time to revisit the text to help us answer critical thinking questions.

Choose an option for rereading text. Have students read the text according to the option that you chose.

Choose an option for rereading text.

- Teacher read-aloud
- Teacher-led or student-led choral read
- Paired read or independent read with bold vocabulary words read aloud

Direct students to page 25 in their Student Books or have them tear out the extra copy of the text from the back of their book.

Note: To minimize flipping back and forth between the pages, a copy of each text has been included in the back of the Student Books. Encourage students to tear this out and use it when working on activities that require the use of the text.

Have students read the text.

Passage Comprehension

Write the words *clarify, present, prove,* and *synthesize* on the board. Have students read the words aloud with you.

Direct students to pages 14 and 15 in their Student Books. It is critical to understand what the question is asking and how to answer it. Today, we will review four direction words used in prompts.

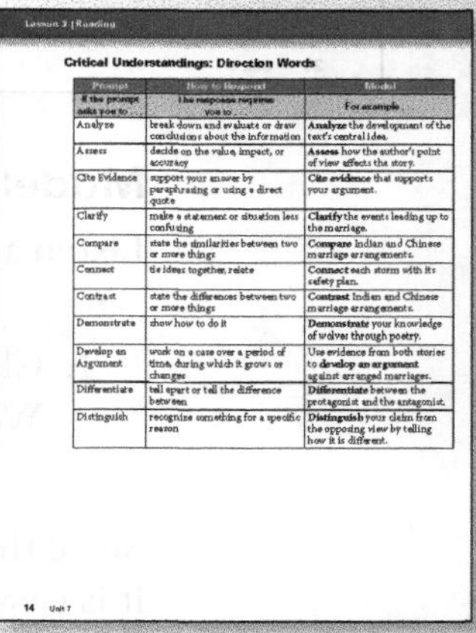

Have students read about the four words in the chart on pages 14 and 15 with their partner. Check for understanding by requesting an oral response to the following questions.

- If the prompt asks you to *clarify,* the response requires you to . . . (explain it so that it is easy to understand).
- If the prompt asks you to *present,* the response requires you to . . . (deliver information).
- If the prompt asks you to *prove,* the response requires you to . . . (give evidence to show that it is true).
- If the prompt asks you to *synthesize,* the response requires you to . . . (combine information in a logical way).

Let's practice answering questions that are written as prompts. Remember to use the chart as a reference. Don't forget, if the direction word is confusing, try to restate the prompt by using a question word.

Direct students to pages 30 and 31 in their Student Books.

Passage Comprehension

Reread "Return of the Wolves." Respond to each prompt using complete sentences. Refer to the chart on pages 14 and 15 to determine how to respond to each prompt.

1. Clarify the author's basic claim or focus of information in "Return of the Wolves."
   The author claimed that a compromise is necessary in order for wolf reintroduction to be successful.

2. Synthesize and explain the economic changes brought about by the wolf reintroduction.
   The reintroduction of wolves affected the economy in a positive way by attracting tourists and naturalists to the park to witness the wolf in its natural habitat. However, the reintroduction also caused a downturn in the economy. Fewer hunting permits were being sold due to the declining elk population caused by the wolf's prowess at the top of the food chain.

3. Prove the theory that the author supports wolf reintroduction.
   In this passage, the author uses positive words to describe the wolf, such as *noble*, more repetitively than negative words, such as *vile*. The author uses detailed language to describe its lonely howl and its will to survive. The author makes attempts to pull at the heartstrings by explaining the wolf's plight in the 1970s. When the author expresses the counterclaims to the reintroduction, there is usually something to indicate that there isn't much merit to this.

Passage Comprehension (*cont.*)

4. Clarify the counterclaim of ranchers.
   According to ranchers, wolves are responsible for the death of their sheep and cows, which is why they disagree with the reintroduction and with the government protection of wolves.

5. Present data to prove that the ranchers' counterclaim is weak.
   The counterclaim is weak because the government pays ranchers for any loss of wildlife caused by wolves, and the loss has been minimal. More data is needed to determine if the loss was due to wolves or other predators.

6. Synthesize and explain the author's recommendation regarding the reintroduction of wolves.
   The author recommends a compromise between supporters and dissenters be made because that is the only way in which the wolves will be allowed to thrive as king of the West and the ecosystem of Yellowstone will return to the way it should be.

Model

Listen as I model the first one for you.

1. Clarify the author's basic claim or focus of information in "Return of the Wolves."

Since the prompt is asking me to *clarify*, I know that I need to explain it so that it is easy to understand. Now, I will turn the prompt into a question to confirm understanding. What is the author's claim or focus of information in "Return of the Wolves"?

In order to proceed, I need to have an understanding of the word *claim* as it relates to persuasion or argument. A claim can be factual, asserting that something is true or not true. A claim could also be asserting that something is good or bad, more or less desirable. A claim can also relate to policy, asserting that one course of action is superior to another.

I need to understand the author's claim regarding the reintroduction of wolves. I think that the author made several types of claims. The author asserted that the elk population decreased as the wolf population increased. The author also seemed to claim that the reintroduction of wolves was a good thing, more desirable than undesirable. The course of action was undefined but recommended a compromise. Since most of the article was about different points of view, I think the compromise to make a successful reintroduction of wolves is my best answer. I will start by putting part of the question in my answer and then completing my sentence to finish my response.

The author claimed that a compromise is necessary in order for wolf reintroduction to be successful.

Guided Practice

2. Synthesize and explain the economic changes brought about by the wolf introduction.

How should we respond according to the chart? (If the prompt asks you to *synthesize*, the response requires you to combine information in a logical way.) Turn the prompt into a question to confirm your understanding. Tell your partner the question. (What information is presented about the economic changes caused by the wolf reintroduction? What does the information mean?)

While providing partner time, write the sentence starters on the board.

The reintroduction of wolves affected the economy ____________________.

However, the reintroduction also ____________________.

Have students answer the question.

Independent Practice

Have partners respond to the remaining prompts with text evidence. For students who need more assistance, provide the following alternative questions and sentence starters.

Alternative questions and sentence starters:

3. What evidence or examples support the theory that the author supports wolf reintroduction?

   In this passage, the author ______________________________, *which proves that he or she is in support of wolf reintroduction.*

4. What is the counterclaim of ranchers?

   According to ranchers, wolves are responsible for ____________________, *which is why* ______________________________.

5. What data proves that the ranchers' counterclaim is weak?

   The counterclaim is weak because ______________________________.

6. What is the author's recommendation regarding the reintroduction of wolves?

   The author recommends ____________________ *because* ____________________.

Summarization

We have been practicing summarizing text orally. For this unit, we are going to write our summary. Remember, we need to keep our opinions from popping up when we write our summary. When we summarize text, it is important to write an objective summary—one free from our own opinions. Do not include which side of the issue you agree with or who is wrong or right.

Your summary should include the main ideas of the text and the necessary supporting details.

Have students write an objective summary of "The Return of the Wolves" at the bottom of page 31. Then, have partners evaluate each other's summaries for accuracy and objectivity. The summaries should contain the overall meaning of the text as well as the main ideas and supporting details.

Unit 7

Lesson 9

Lesson Opener

Before the lesson, choose one of the following activities to write on the board or post on the *LANGUAGE! Live* Class Wall online.

- *Write three sentences to compare and contrast Yellowstone National Park before the reintroduction of wolves and after the reintroduction of wolves. Use a subordinating conjunction in each sentence.*
- *Complete the steps of Masterpiece Sentences to expand this base sentence: Wolves hunt in Yellowstone.*
- *Label the following sentence parts as dependent clauses or independent clauses.*

  while the wolves hunted
  the ecosystem was challenged
  because the wolves are predators
  the park returned to normal

Reading

Objectives

- Read with purpose and understanding.
- Answer questions to demonstrate comprehension of text.
- Distinguish between text written from a subjective point of view and text written from an objective point of view.
- Identify how an author distinguishes his or her positions on a topic from that of others.
- Monitor comprehension during text reading.

Close Reading of "Return of the Wolves"

Highlighters or colored pencils

Let's reread "Return of the Wolves." I will provide specific instructions on how to mark the text to help with comprehension.

Have students get out a highlighter or colored pencil.

Direct students to pages 32–34 in their Student Books.

Draw a rectangle around the title.

Now, let's read the vocabulary words aloud.

- What's the first bold vocabulary word? (persistence) *Persistence* means "the ability to keep doing something even though it is difficult." *Persistence* will pay off if you continue to work hard. Have partners use the word in a sentence.
- What's the next bold vocabulary word? (insecurity) *Insecurity* means "the state of not feeling safe or steady." The *insecurity* felt by animals separated from their mothers can be seen on their faces. Have partners use the word in a sentence.
- What's the next bold vocabulary word? (relocation) *Relocation* means "the act of moving to a different place." *Relocation* is difficult on immigrant families. Have partners use the word in a sentence.
- Let's continue. (habitat) *Habitat* means "the natural home of a plant or animal." A wolf's *habitat* is different from a dog's habitat. Have partners use the word in a sentence.

- Next word? (altered) *Altered* means "changed." Wolves *altered* the Yellowstone habitat. **Have partners use the word in a sentence.**
- Next word? (competition) *Competition* means "the struggle between two or more people or groups who are trying to get the same thing." The animals are in *competition* for food. **Have partners use the word in a sentence.**
- Next word? (aspects) *Aspects* means "parts, elements, or angles of something." All *aspects* of a person's personality are important. **Have partners use the word in a sentence.**
- Next word? (declining) *Declining* means "growing smaller in size or strength." Our school population is *declining* because people are leaving town to find jobs. **Have partners use the word in a sentence.**
- Next word? (economy) *Economy* means "the flow of money, goods, and services in a community." The *economy* is declining because businesses are being relocated overseas. **Have partners use the word in a sentence.**
- What's the last word? (compromise) *Compromise* means "the settlement reached when each side in an argument gives up a part of what it wants." A *compromise* is a good way to make both sides happy. **Have partners use the word in a sentence.**

Talk with a partner about any vocabulary word that is still confusing for you to read or understand.

As you read "Return of the Wolves," you will monitor your understanding by circling the check marks or the question marks. Please be sure to draw a question mark over any confusing words, phrases, or sentences.

Options for rereading text.

- **Teacher read-aloud**
- **Teacher-led or student-led choral read**
- **Paired read or independent read with bold vocabulary words read aloud**

Choose an option for reading text. Have students read lines 1–24 according to the option that you chose. While reading each section, pay attention to the varying points of view. If the position is pro-wolf, draw an up arrow in the margin. If the position is anti-wolf, draw a down arrow in the margin.

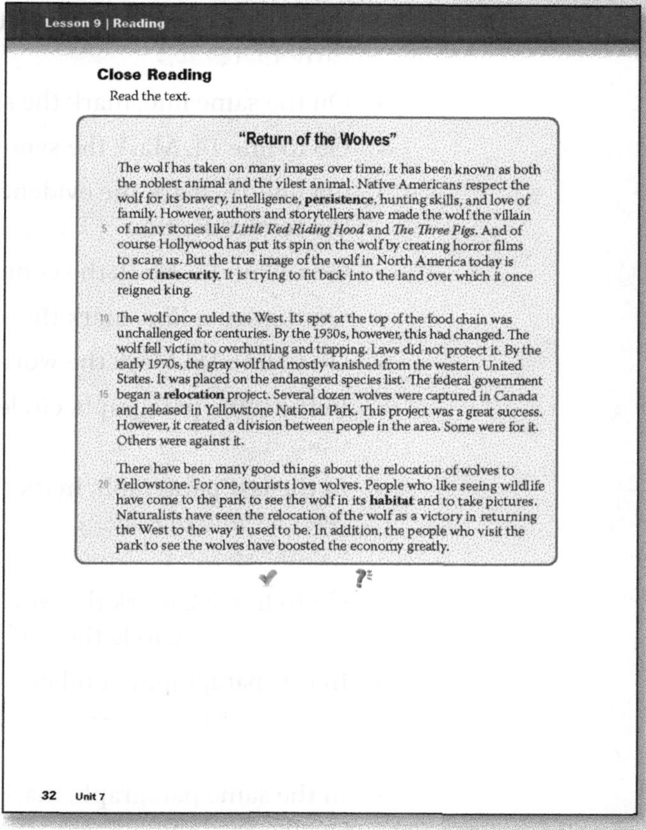

Lesson 9 | Reading

Close Reading

Read the text.

"Return of the Wolves"

The wolf has taken on many images over time. It has been known as both the noblest animal and the vilest animal. Native Americans respect the wolf for its bravery, intelligence, **persistence**, hunting skills, and love of family. However, authors and storytellers have made the wolf the villain of many stories like *Little Red Riding Hood* and *The Three Pigs*. And of course Hollywood has put its spin on the wolf by creating horror films to scare us. But the true image of the wolf in North America today is one of **insecurity**. It is trying to fit back into the land over which it once reigned king.

The wolf once ruled the West. Its spot at the top of the food chain was unchallenged for centuries. By the 1930s, however, this had changed. The wolf fell victim to overhunting and trapping. Laws did not protect it. By the early 1970s, the gray wolf had mostly vanished from the western United States. It was placed on the endangered species list. The federal government began a **relocation** project. Several dozen wolves were captured in Canada and released in Yellowstone National Park. This project was a great success. However, it created a division between people in the area. Some were for it. Others were against it.

There have been many good things about the relocation of wolves to Yellowstone. For one, tourists love wolves. People who like seeing wildlife have come to the park to see the wolf in its **habitat** and to take pictures. Naturalists have seen the relocation of the wolf as a victory in returning the West to the way it used to be. In addition, the people who visit the park to see the wolves have boosted the economy greatly.

32 Unit 7

When most of the students are finished, continue with the entire class. Let's see how well you understood what you read.

- Circle the check mark or the question mark for this section. Draw a question mark over any confusing words.
- Go to line 2. Mark the superlative adjective that compares wolves to several other animals with a strong positive connotation. (noblest) Circle the suffix. (-est)
- On the same line, mark the superlative adjective that compares wolves to several other animals with a strong negative connotation. (vilest) Circle the suffix. (-est)
- Number the Native Americans' view of the wolf. (1. bravery; 2. intelligence; 3. persistence; 4. hunting skills; 5. love of family)
- On line 4, mark the view of wolves for authors and storytellers. (villain)
- On lines 6 and 7, mark the view of wolves according to Hollywood. (horror, scare)
- On line 8, mark the word that is an indication that the wolf is no longer king. (once)
- On line 10, mark the term used to represent a specific region of the United States. (the West)
- On the same line, mark the evidence that the wolf was not hunted by other animals. (top of the food chain)
- Go to line 11. Mark the transition phrase that answers when. (By the 1930s)
- On the same line, mark the conjunction that shows a change of direction. (however) Mark the pronoun in the same sentence. (this) Draw an arrow to what the pronoun represents. (wolf once ruled the West)
- On line 12, mark what happened to the wolf. (overhunting, trapping) In the margin, write the name of the animal that finally challenged the wolf and removed it from the top of the food chain. (man)

- Go to lines 12 and 13. Mark the transition phrase that answers when. (By the early 1970s)
- On the same line, mark the synonym for *disappeared*. (vanished)
- Go to line 14. Mark the synonym for *dying*. (endangered)
- On line 16, mark the evidence the wolves grew in number in Yellowstone after the reintroduction. (This project was a great success.)
- Go to line 17. Mark the conjunction that means "but." (however)
- On the same line, mark the words that mean "pro." (for it)
- Go to line 18. Mark the words that mean "con." (against it)
- In the same paragraph, circle the pronouns used to replace *relocation project*. (this, it, it, it)
- In the last paragraph, mark the explanation that means that tourists love wolves. (People who like seeing wildlife have come to the park to see the wolf in its habitat and to take pictures.)
- Go to line 22. Mark the word that means "people who advocate for nature." (Naturalists) Circle the suffix. (-ist)
- In this paragraph, number the "good things" caused by the wolf reintroduction. (1. tourists love wolves; 2. returning the West to the way it used to be; 3. boosted the economy)
- In the same paragraph, mark the transition words used to indicate one of the "many good things." (For one; In addition)

Have students read lines 25–42 according to the option that you chose.

When most of the students are finished, continue with the entire class. Let's see how well you understood what you read.

- Circle the check mark or the question mark for this section. Draw a question mark over any confusing words.
- Go to line 25. Mark the word that means "act of introducing something again." (reintroduction) Circle the prefix that means "again." (re-)
- Go to line 26. Mark the word that means "meat eaters." (carnivores)
- Go to lines 26 and 27. Mark the explanation that supports that wolves are carnivores. (elk and deer are their favorite meal)
- Go to line 28. Mark the word that means "too many in one area." (overpopulated) Circle the prefix that means "too much or too many." (over-)
- In the second paragraph, number three problems caused by the overpopulation of elk. (1. damage to aspen tree forests; 2. altered the beaver and bird populations; 3. flow of streams and rivers were changed)
- Go to line 31. Mark the word that means "altered." (changed)
- Go to line 33. Mark the word that means "the relationship between living things and their environment." (ecology)
- In the same line, mark the sentence that supports that wolves create an ecology of fear for elk. (Elk spend less time eating in one place.)
- Go to line 34. Mark the transition words used to illustrate cause and effect. (as a result)
- Go to line 36. Mark the word that means "populated with plants and trees." (vegetated)
- Go to line 38. Mark the word that means "feeding on others' leftovers." (scavenging)
- Go to line 42. Mark the words that mean "scavenge." (feed on the remains of the wolves' kills)
- Number the five positive outcomes of wolf reintroduction on this page. (1. elk population under control; 2. trees and shrubs grow back quicker; 3. more variety in the plant life; 4. open fields are more vegetated; 5. more food for the coyotes)

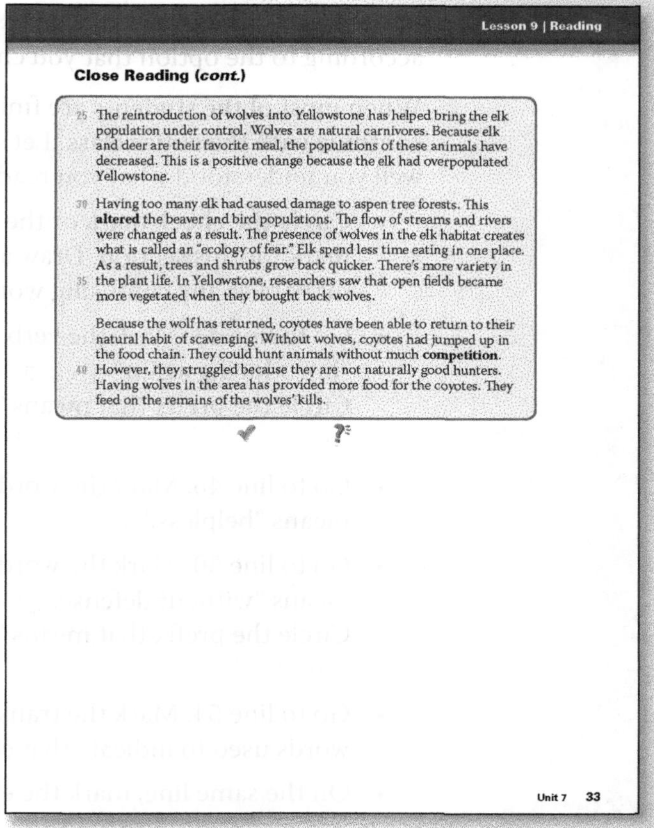
Lesson 9 | Reading

Close Reading (*cont.*)

The reintroduction of wolves into Yellowstone has helped bring the elk population under control. Wolves are natural carnivores. Because elk and deer are their favorite meal, the populations of these animals have decreased. This is a positive change because the elk had overpopulated Yellowstone.

Having too many elk had caused damage to aspen tree forests. This **altered** the beaver and bird populations. The flow of streams and rivers were changed as a result. The presence of wolves in the elk habitat creates what is called an "ecology of fear." Elk spend less time eating in one place. As a result, trees and shrubs grow back quicker. There's more variety in the plant life. In Yellowstone, researchers saw that open fields became more vegetated when they brought back wolves.

Because the wolf has returned, coyotes have been able to return to their natural habit of scavenging. Without wolves, coyotes had jumped up in the food chain. They could hunt animals without much **competition**. However, they struggled because they are not naturally good hunters. Having wolves in the area has provided more food for the coyotes. They feed on the remains of the wolves' kills.

Unit 7 33

Have students read from line 43 to the end according to the option that you chose.

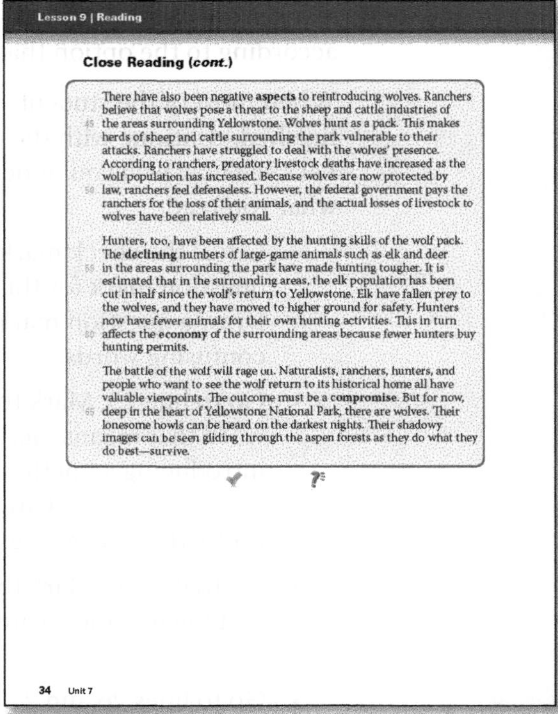

Lesson 9 | Reading

Close Reading (*cont.*)

There have also been negative **aspects** to reintroducing wolves. Ranchers believe that wolves pose a threat to the sheep and cattle industries of the areas surrounding Yellowstone. Wolves hunt as a pack. This makes herds of sheep and cattle surrounding the park vulnerable to their attacks. Ranchers have struggled to deal with the wolves' presence. According to ranchers, predatory livestock deaths have increased as the wolf population has increased. Because wolves are now protected by law, ranchers feel defenseless. However, the federal government pays the ranchers for the loss of their animals, and the actual losses of livestock to wolves have been relatively small.

Hunters, too, have been affected by the hunting skills of the wolf pack. The **declining** numbers of large-game animals such as elk and deer in the areas surrounding the park have made hunting tougher. It is estimated that in the surrounding areas, the elk population has been cut in half since the wolf's return to Yellowstone. Elk have fallen prey to the wolves, and they have moved to higher ground for safety. Hunters now have fewer animals for their own hunting activities. This in turn affects the **economy** of the surrounding areas because fewer hunters buy hunting permits.

The battle of the wolf will rage on. Naturalists, ranchers, hunters, and people who want to see the wolf return to its historical home all have valuable viewpoints. The outcome must be a **compromise**. But for now, deep in the heart of Yellowstone National Park, there are wolves. Their lonesome howls can be heard on the darkest nights. Their shadowy images can be seen gliding through the aspen forests as they do what they do best—survive.

34 Unit 7

When most of the students are finished, continue with the entire class. Let's see how well you understood what you read.

- Circle the check mark or the question mark for this section. Draw a question mark over any confusing words.
- Go to line 43. Mark the verb that means "introducing again." (reintroducing) Circle the prefix that means "again." (re-)
- Go to line 46. Mark the word that means "helpless." (vulnerable)
- Go to line 50. Mark the word that means "without defense." (defenseless) Circle the prefix that means "without." (-less)
- Go to line 54. Mark the transition words used to indicate that examples will follow. (such as)
- On the same line, mark the examples of large game animals. (elk and deer)
- Go to line 55. Mark the comparative adjective that compares two timeframes before and after reintroduction. (tougher) Circle the suffix. (-er)
- Go to line 64. Mark the compound word that means "opinions." (viewpoints)
- On the same line, mark the synonym for *result*. (outcome)
- On the same line, mark the words that mean "temporarily." (for now)
- Go to line 65. Mark the personification that means "center of." (heart of)
- Go to line 66. Mark the superlative adjective that compares several nights. (darkest)
- Go to line 68. Mark the punctuation used to indicate a pause and show emphasis of what follows. (em dash)
- On the same line, mark the word that shows what wolves do best. (survive)
- Number the three negative effects of wolf reintroduction on this page. (1. wolves pose a threat to the sheep and cattle industries; 2. declining numbers of large-game animals have made hunting tougher; 3. affects the economy of the area because fewer hunters buy hunting permits)
- Which group does the author agree with? Write your answer in the margin. (neither) Mark the evidence in the text that makes this known. (All have valuable viewpoints; the outcome must be a compromise.) Is this text objective or subjective? (objective)

Have partners compare text markings and correct any errors.

Lesson 10

Lesson Opener

Before the lesson, choose one of the following activities to write on the board or post on the *LANGUAGE! Live* Class Wall online.

- *Write four sentences with at least two vocabulary words in each. Show you know the meanings. (persistence, insecurity, relocation, habitat, alter, competition, aspect, decline, economy, compromise)*
- *Dress your avatar as though you were visiting Yellowstone National Park to watch the wolves. Explain your choices.*
- *Write a sentence about Yellowstone National Park. Include a dependent clause and an independent clause in the sentence. Identify both clauses.*

Vocabulary

Objective

- Review key passage vocabulary.

Recontextualize Passage Vocabulary

Direct students to page 24 in their Student Books. Use the following questions to review the vocabulary words in the excerpt from "Return of the Wolves."

Lesson 6 | Vocabulary

Key Passage Vocabulary: "Return of the Wolves"

Read each word. Write the word in column 3. Then, circle a number to rate your knowledge of the word.

Vocabulary	Part of Speech	Write the Word	Knowledge Rating
persistence	(n)	persistence	0 1 2 3
insecurity	(n)	insecurity	0 1 2 3
relocation	(n)	relocation	0 1 2 3
habitat	(n)	habitat	0 1 2 3
alter	(v)	alter	0 1 2 3
competition	(n)	competition	0 1 2 3
aspect	(n)	aspect	0 1 2 3
decline	(v)	decline	0 1 2 3
economy	(n)	economy	0 1 2 3
compromise	(n)	compromise	0 1 2 3

24 Unit 7

- Your dog digs and digs until he has tunneled under the fence. Does he have *persistence*? (yes) You want to make a piece of artwork by gluing hundreds of scraps of construction paper to a canvas. You give up after 20 scraps. Do you have *persistence*? (no) You have told yourself that if you do 100 sit-ups a day, Monday through Saturday, you can take Sunday off. What do you need to get through the week? (persistence)
- You are walking across a very high and very rickety bridge. Do you have a sense of *insecurity*? (yes) You're swimming in the ocean alone and think you see a shark fin. Do you feel a sense of *insecurity*? (yes) You dream that you're surrounded by tarantulas. What do you feel until you wake up? (insecurity)
- One of your teachers moves disruptive students to a desk right by hers. Does she use *relocation* to manage the classroom? (yes) People keep tripping over your backpack. Would the *relocation* of your backpack help? (yes) Your hometown baseball team is moving to another city. You hate this idea. What are you opposed to? (the team's relocation)
- You brought a new kitten home. She immediately curled up on the rug and went to sleep. Is she comfortable in her new *habitat*? (yes) Perry the Penguin lives in Kansas. Is this a good *habitat* for Perry? (no) The owner of your apartment complex covered an old garden with concrete. The garden snakes that lived there have nowhere to go. What did the snakes lose? (their habitat)
- Yesterday, you had long hair, but today, you are getting a very short haircut. Will this *alter* your appearance? (yes) If you *alter* the ingredients in a recipe, will the

dish taste different? (yes) A movie didn't end the way you hoped it would. What do you wish you could do to the ending? (alter it)

- Two athletes are trying to win the Olympic gold medal in the long jump. Is this a *competition*? (yes) An ice skater would also like to win a gold medal in her event. Is there *competition* between them? (no) There are two shaved ice stands near the park. Each keeps lowering its prices to draw business away from the other. What is happening between the two stands? (competition)
- You are looking at one side of a large sculpture in a museum. Your friend is looking at another side of it. Are you each looking at a different *aspect* of the sculpture? (yes) You like a local rap artist, but your sister doesn't. She can't say why; she just dislikes him in general. Is she criticizing a particular *aspect* of his music? (no) You've been asked to write an essay that describes all sides of a hot-button issue in your community. You have written about one side of the issue. What do you need to write about now? (the other aspects of it)
- People are moving away from a small town to a nearby city. Is the population of the city *declining*? (no) Monarch butterflies are migrating south for the winter. Are their numbers *declining* in northern areas? (yes) On a TV game show, players spin a giant wheel. The wheel spins quickly for a few seconds. Then what does its speed do? (declines)
- You have some backyard chickens that lay eggs. You sell the eggs to a nearby café. Are you involved in the local *economy*? (yes) A family friend has given up on society and moved to an isolated cabin in the wilderness. Is he participating in the *economy*? (no) Business slows down, and an employer lays off half her staff. She says she is forced to do this because of a weak what? (economy)
- You have plans, but your sister says you promised to take her shopping. You offer to cut your plans short and ask if you can shop a little later. She just pouts. Is she interested in a *compromise*? (no) There are plans to build an office building where a local park is. People in the surrounding neighborhood protest. In the end, half the land is used for the building and half remains a park. Did the groups reach a *compromise*? (yes) A couple on TV is arguing about the kind of house they want to buy. What do they need to come up with? (a compromise)

Writing

Objectives

- Cite text in writing.
- Use a process to write.
- Write a persuasive argument.
- Use a rubric to guide and evaluate writing.

Six Traits of Effective Writing

Direct students to page 35 in their Student Books. Reread the Six Traits of Effective Writing.

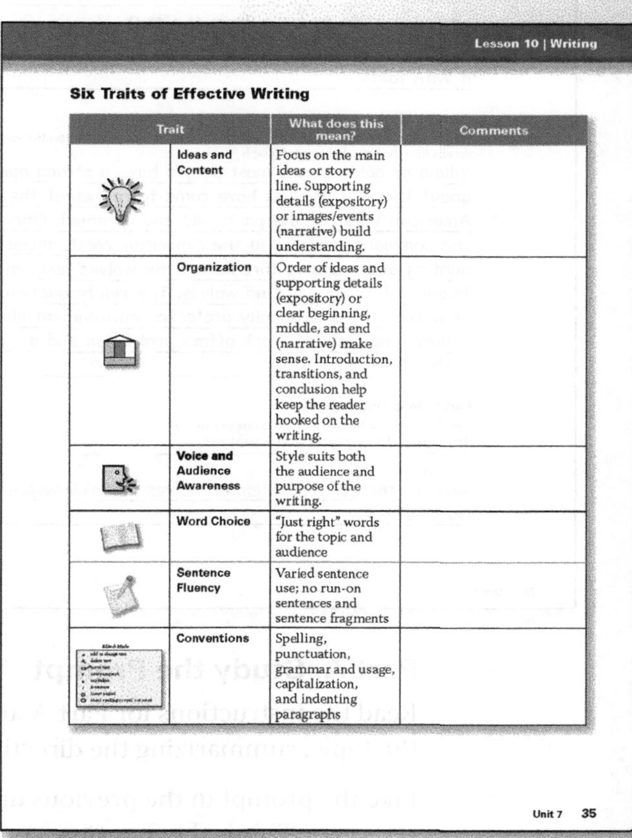

Lesson 10 | Writing

Six Traits of Effective Writing

Trait		What does this mean?	Comments
	Ideas and Content	Focus on the main ideas or story line. Supporting details (expository) or images/events (narrative) build understanding.	
	Organization	Order of ideas and supporting details (expository) or clear beginning, middle, and end (narrative) make sense. Introduction, transitions, and conclusion help keep the reader hooked on the writing.	
	Voice and Audience Awareness	Style suits both the audience and purpose of the writing.	
	Word Choice	"Just right" words for the topic and audience	
	Sentence Fluency	Varied sentence use; no run-on sentences and sentence fragments	
	Conventions	Spelling, punctuation, grammar and usage, capitalization, and indenting paragraphs	

Unit 7 35

In previous units, we have focused on sentence fluency, word choice, conventions, and organization. We have used varying sentence structures and descriptive language to keep our writing from sounding boring. We have used proper grammar, punctuation, and spelling to ensure the reader understands the text, and we have organized our paragraphs to include introductions, conclusions, and transitions. We have also made sure that our supporting details accurately support our main ideas/topic sentences and that the supporting details are backed up with elaborations, including evidence from the text.

Refer to the six traits as you are writing your multiparagraph essay, and be sure to address all six traits in your writing.

Prepare to Write: Argument Essay

Direct students to pages 36 and 37 in their Student Books.

Lesson 10 | Writing

Prepare to Write: Argument Essay Answers will vary.

Part A. Study the Prompt

Write an argument essay in which you take a position regarding the reintroduction of wolves into Yellowstone National Park. Present two reasons that support your position that are supported by evidence from the text.

Topic: reintroduction of wolves into Yellowstone National Park

Directions: write an argument essay that includes reasons and supporting evidence from the text

Purpose for writing: to take a position on a topic and support it with facts

Part B. Write an Introduction

Write a topic sentence that clearly states your position. Incorporate attention-getting details into the introductory paragraph.

Villain or noble beast, most people have a strong opinion about the wolf. Wolves have come to represent the American West of the past, wild and untamed. Once the dominant predator in the American West, unchecked hunting and trapping threatened the wolves' existence. Imagine if there were no wolves. The reintroduction of wolves into a nationally protected environment like Yellowstone National Park offers protection and a restoration of balance.

Part C. Map Your Argument

Get the reader's attention with an example/situation:
Imagine there were no wolves.

Statement of Position:
support the reintroduction of wolves into Yellowstone National Park

36 Unit 7

Lesson 10 | Writing

Prepare to Write: Argument Essay (*cont.*)

First reason:
restore ecological balance to the park

Evidence:
overpopulation of elk had a negative impact on the habitat for beaver and birds; put coyotes back in their natural role as scavenger as opposed to hunter

Second reason:
good for the park's economy

Evidence:
wolves are popular and their presence draws tourists; naturalists support restoring the park to the way it used to be

Anticipated objection:
threaten livestock

Response to objection:
Ranchers are reimbursed by the federal government for any loss due to wolf attacks, and the financial impact on ranchers has been relatively small.

Restate position:
Restoring the wolf population has been good for the ecology and economy of Yellowstone National Park.

Part D. Write a Conclusion That Defends Your Position

Restate your topic sentence and defend your position.

The reintroduction of wolves to Yellowstone has successfully restored balance in that environment. Wolves are thriving under the protective eye of the park service and helping other creatures within the park system thrive as well. The positive impact of the wolves' return far outweighs any negative impacts felt by local ranchers.

Unit 7 37

Part A. Study the Prompt

Read the instructions for Part A and the prompt. Guide students through identifying the topic, summarizing the directions, and understanding the purpose for writing.

Like the prompt in the previous unit, this assignment calls for a multiparagraph response. This is the first time you've been asked to develop a well-supported argument. You will have to take a position, for or against, the reintroduction of wolves into Yellowstone National Park and then find the evidence from the text to support your position.

Part B. Write an Introduction

Your introduction needs to state your position on wolves in Yellowstone National Park. Consider beginning with an attention-getting statement or scene, something that will make the reader want to continue reading. Mapping out your argument will help you construct an effective position statement and develop a scenario that illustrates your position. We will come back to write the introduction after you have completed your notes.

Part C. Map Your Argument

Work with students to come up with a scenario that dramatizes their position.

- Under the direst circumstances, what could the future look like?
- What if wolves became extinct?
- What if wolves began to roam the countryside in ferocious packs that were out of control?

Work through the map helping students identify reasons to support or criticize the wolves' return to the park. Prompt students to use their close reading from Lesson 9 to help them pull the evidence they need to support their position.

Now that you've mapped out your argument and spent some time thinking about how to open your argument essay, let's write the introduction. We will use the first two prompts of our map. Have students write a topic sentence and introduction.

Part D. Write a Conclusion That Defends Your Position

Consider ways you can restate your introduction that could serve as the conclusion of your essay. Your conclusion needs to summarize your arguments without sounding repetitive or redundant.

Write

Notebook paper

Have students consult the the Six Traits of Writing: Persuasion Rubric on page 552 as they write their essay. Encourage them to look closely at the rubric because this is a persuasive writing, and what is expected of them is slightly different.

Six Traits of Writing: Persuasion

	Ideas and Development	Organization	Voice and Audience Awareness	Word Choice	Sentence Fluency	Language Conventions
4	Clearly states a position on the issue. Fully develops main ideas with evidence, examples, and explanations that are compelling. No irrelevant information.	Introduction clearly states position. Ideas logically sequenced. Transition sentences link ideas. Conclusion ties essay together and gives reader something to think about. Follows required format.	Strong sense of person and purpose behind the words. Brings issue to life.	Words are specific, accurate, and vivid. Word choice enhances meaning and reader's enjoyment.	Writes complete sentences with varied sentence patterns and beginnings.	There are no major grammar errors. There are few errors in spelling, capitalization, or punctuation.
3	States a position on the issue. Develops main ideas adequately with some evidence, examples, and explanations. Limited irrelevant information.	Introduction states position. Ideas mostly logically sequenced. Some linkage among ideas. Conclusion ties essay together. Follows required format.	Some sense of person and purpose behind the words. Sense of commitment to the issue. Text may be too casual for the purpose.	Words are correctly used but may be somewhat general and unspecific.	Writes complete sentences with some expansion. Limited variety.	There are a few grammar errors. There are a few errors in spelling, capitalization, or punctuation.
2	Does not state a clear position on the issue and/or does not support main ideas with sufficient evidence, examples, and explanations. May be too repetitious or too much irrelevant information.	Introduction may not state a position. Ideas not logically sequenced. Transition sentences missing. Conclusion may be missing. Does not follow required format.	Little sense of person and purpose behind the words. Very little engagement with reader. Text may be too casual for the purpose.	Word choice limited. Words may be used inaccurately or repetitively.	Writes mostly simple and/or awkwardly constructed sentences. May include some run-ons and fragments.	There are many grammar or spelling errors. There are quite a few errors in capitalization and punctuation.
1	Does not address the prompt or does not develop a position. Elaboration lacking or unrelated to the issue.	Text has no evident structure. Lack of organization seriously interferes with meaning.	No sense of person or purpose behind the words. No sense of audience.	Extremely limited range of words. Restricted vocabulary impedes message.	Numerous run-ons and/or sentence fragments interfere with meaning.	There are many spelling and grammar errors. There are many errors in capitalization and punctuation.

Writing Rubric: Persuasion

552 Writing Rubric: Persuasion

Encourage students by reminding them that they've written the frames for the entire essay. If they struggle or need additional support in developing their essays, use the following essay as a model.

Sample Argument Essay

Villain or noble beast, most people have a strong opinion about the wolf. Wolves have come to represent the American West of the past, wild and untamed. Once the dominant predator in the American West, unchecked hunting and trapping threatened the wolves' existence. Imagine if there were no wolves. The reintroduction of wolves into a nationally protected environment like Yellowstone National Park offers protection and a restoration of balance.

First and foremost, the wolves' presence has restored the natural balance of the park's ecosystem. Without the wolves as a predator, the elk population soared. This had a negative impact on the habitat for beavers and birds. Coyotes have resumed their role as scavengers, surviving well off of the scraps from the wolves' hunting expeditions.

A secondary benefit has been an upswing in the economy of the area. Tourists like to watch the wolves in their natural environment. Naturalists have come to observe the wolf and note the advantages of restoring the park to the way it used to be. Increasing the number of park visitors has been good for the park's economy.

Though ranchers have claimed the wolves have threatened their livestock, this has had little effect on them. Few losses have actually been attributed to wolves. Plus, the federal government reimburses ranchers for any losses—eliminating a financial impact on the ranching industry.

The reintroduction of wolves to Yellowstone has successfully restored balance in that environment. Wolves are thriving under the protective eye of the park service and helping other creatures within the park system thrive as well. The positive impact of the wolves' return far outweighs any negative impacts felt by local ranchers.

Evaluate Writing

Direct students to page 38 in their Student Books and read the information in the checklist.

Notice that this checklist is different from the other checklists you have used. This checklist is a tool you can use to evaluate your persuasive writing and make sure you are using good technique. Have individuals quickly assess their writing, then have partners evaluate each other's writing based on the checklist.

Lesson 10 | Writing

The Persuasive Writer's Checklist

Trait	Yes	No	Did the writer . . . ?
Ideas and Content			clearly state a position on an issue
			focus the content of each paragraph on the topic
			include examples, evidence, and/or explanations that are logically, emotionally, or ethically compelling
			when necessary, include recent, relevant, reliable research to validate the position
			create a title
Organization			write an introductory paragraph that captures the reader's interest and contains a clear thesis statement that serves as a "map" for the essay
			sequence body paragraphs logically and use transition sentences that make clear the relationship between ideas
			write a concluding paragraph that restates the position and issues a call to action
Voice and Audience Awareness			write in a voice that is confident and reasonable
			write in a tone of voice that suits the audience and purpose for writing
			demonstrate that the beliefs and opinions that others might have on the topic have been considered
			acknowledge one or more objections that others may make
Word Choice			use words that are lively, accurate, specific to the content, and convey authority
			vary the words so that the writing does not sound repetitive
Sentence Fluency			write complete sentences
			use the steps of Masterpiece Sentences
			use compound sentence elements and compound sentences
Conventions			capitalize words correctly:
			capitalize the first word of each sentence
			capitalize proper nouns, including people's names
			punctuate correctly:
			put a period or question mark at the end of each sentence
			put an apostrophe before the s for a singular possessive noun
			use a comma after a long adverb phrase at the beginning of a sentence
			use grammar correctly:
			use the correct verb tense
			make sure the verb agrees with the subject in number
			use correct spelling

38 Unit 7

Note: Use Six Traits of Writing Scoring Rubric: Persuasion on page 547 of this book to assess students' writing. A printable version is located online in the Teacher Resources.

Six Traits of Writing: Persuasion

Reading

Objectives

- Self-correct as comprehension of text deepens.
- Answer questions to demonstrate comprehension of text.
- Engage in class discussion.
- Identify the enduring understandings from a piece of text.

Revisit Passage Comprehension

Direct students back to pages 30 and 31 in their Student Books. Have students review their answers and make any necessary changes. Then, have partners share their answers and collaborate to perfect them.

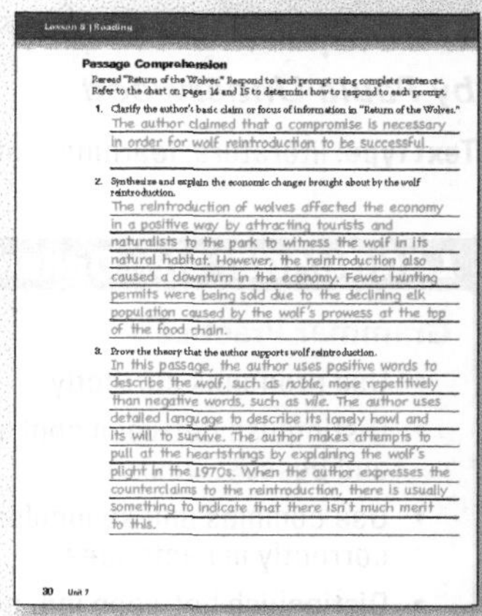

Passage Comprehension

Reread "Return of the Wolves." Respond to each prompt using complete sentences. Refer to the chart on pages 14 and 15 to determine how to respond to each prompt.

1. Clarify the author's basic claim or focus of information in "Return of the Wolves."
   The author claimed that a compromise is necessary in order for wolf reintroduction to be successful.
2. Synthesize and explain the economic changes brought about by the wolf reintroduction.
   The reintroduction of wolves affected the economy in a positive way by attracting tourists and naturalists to the park to witness the wolf in its natural habitat. However, the reintroduction also caused a downturn in the economy. Fewer hunting permits were being sold due to the declining elk population caused by the wolf's prowess at the top of the food chain.
3. Prove the theory that the author supports wolf reintroduction.
   In this passage, the author uses positive words to describe the wolf, such as *noble*, more repetitively than negative words, such as *vile*. The author uses detailed language to describe its lonely howl and its will to survive. The author makes attempts to pull at the heartstrings by explaining the wolf's plight in the 1970s. When the author expresses the counterclaims to the reintroduction, there is usually something to indicate that there isn't much merit to this.

Enduring Understandings

Direct students back to page 23 in their Student Books. Reread the Big Idea questions.

Let's Focus: "Return of the Wolves"

Content Focus
reintroduction of wolves; human involvement in the environment

Type of Text
informational—nonfiction

Author's Name unknown

Author's Purpose to teach about wolves in danger

Big Ideas
Consider the following Big Idea questions. Write your answer for each question.

How do stereotypes of wolves affect their image and perhaps even their existence?

Should humans interfere with nature? Explain.

Informational Preview Checklist: "Return of the Wolves" on pages 25–27.

- ☐ Title: What clue does it provide?
- ☐ Pictures: What additional information is added here?
- ☐ Margin Information: What vocabulary is important to understand this story?
- ☐ Features: What other features do you notice?

Enduring Understandings
After reading the text . . .

How do stereotypes of wolves affect their image and perhaps even their existence?

Should humans interfere with nature? Explain.

Generate a class discussion about the questions and answers students came up with in Lesson 6. Have them consider whether their answers have changed any after reading the text.

Use the following talking points to foster conversation. Then, have students write their enduring understandings from the unit.

- Wolves are shown as villains in storybooks and horror movies. In reality, wolves are insecure and at risk. It is important to educate ourselves beyond fiction, horror, and fairy tales in order to be knowledgeable about the issues that impact our ecology. It is also important to see past prejudices and understand that misconceptions exist among all species.
- Human interference impacts the ecosystem in ways that man did not fully realize. Is all human interference bad interference? Are humans at the top of the food chain? Are we simply following the natural order of life by interfering in animal habitats for our benefit? Or, is it possible that human interference can be positive, such as by bringing wolves out of jeopardy of extinction?

What we read should make us think. Use our discussion and your thoughts about the text to determine what you will "walk away with." Has it made you think about a personal experience or someone you know? Has your perspective or opinion on a specific topic changed? Do you have any lingering thoughts or questions? Write these ideas as your enduring understandings. What will you take with you from this text?

Assign online Unit 7 ***Content Mastery*** *quizzes and* ***Power Pass*** *from the Text Training link on the left menu of your teacher dashboard.*

Discuss the enduring understandings with the class. If time permits, have students post a personal response about their enduring understandings to the online class wall.

Remind students to consider why the author wrote the passage and whether he or she was successful.

Unit 8 Unit Plan

Primary Texts:
"The White Wolf of the Hartz Mountains"
by Captain Frederick Marryat

Text type: literature; short story

Who Speaks for Wolf
by Paula Underwood

Text type: literature; learning story

LANGUAGE! *Live* Online

Grammar Practice
- Use pronouns correctly.
- Distinguish between contractions and possessives.
- Use commas and semicolons correctly in sentences.
- Distinguish between independent and dependent clauses.
- Use indefinite pronouns correctly.
- Identify and correct vague and incorrect pronoun usage.
- Use conjunctions correctly.

Vocabulary Practice
- Determine the meaning of derivations of words.
- Increase depth of word knowledge through the use of analogies.

Content Mastery
- Demonstrate an understanding of . . .
  - word meaning by answering questions and using words in sentences.
  - relative pronouns and relative clauses.
  - apostrophe usage.

Word Study
- Blend, read, spell, and divide multisyllabic words with stable final syllable -cle.
- Add inflectional endings to words ending in -le .
- Identify homophones.
- Read connected text to build fluency.

Lesson 1

Reading
- Determine and discuss the topic of a text.
- Determine and discuss the author's purpose.
- Use text features to preview text.

Vocabulary
- Evaluate word knowledge.
- Determine the meaning of key passage vocabulary.

Reading
- Read a short story.
- Monitor comprehension during text reading.
- Identify first-person point of view.

Lesson 2

Vocabulary
- Review key passage vocabulary.

Grammar
- Distinguish between contractions and possessive nouns.
- Connect pronouns to their antecedents.
- Use pronouns correctly.
- Use and punctuate relative clauses correctly.

Writing
- Use relative clauses to create complex sentences.
- Use correct punctuation when writing sentences that contain relative clauses.

Lesson 6

Reading
- Determine and discuss the topic of a text.
- Determine and discuss the author's purpose.
- Use text features to preview text.

Vocabulary
- Evaluate word knowledge.
- Determine the meaning of key passage vocabulary.

Reading
- Read a legend.
- Monitor comprehension during text reading.
- Determine the point of view of literary text.
- Identify shifts in point of view.

Lesson 7

Vocabulary
- Review key passage vocabulary.

Reading
- Objectively summarize literary text.
- Identify the theme of a story.
- Contrast the themes of two myths about the same topic.
- Determine how to respond to prompts.
- Use critical thinking skills to write responses to prompts about text.
- Support written answers with evidence from text.

Writing Project, Units 7–9: Compare and Contrast Writing

Lesson 3	Lesson 4	Lesson 5
Reading • Establish a purpose for rereading literary text. • Use critical thinking skills to write responses to prompts about text. • Support written answers with evidence from text. • Identify the claims and counterclaims of characters in literature. • Cite evidence in support of a particular point.	**Vocabulary** • Review key passage vocabulary. **Reading** • Read literature with purpose and understanding. • Answer questions to demonstrate comprehension of text. • Monitor comprehension of text during reading. • Determine the impact of word choice. • Determine how differences in character point of view create suspense. • Identify leading questions and their intended purpose. • Identify shifts in mood. • Identify common religious or mythological themes in texts. • Determine the meaning and purpose of conjunctive adverbs. • Identify allusions to other texts in literature.	**Vocabulary** • Review key passage vocabulary. **Writing** • Write an analysis of the use of foreshadowing in "The White Wolf of the Hartz Mountains." • Identify how an author's choice of words is used to create suspense. **Reading** • Self-correct as comprehension of text deepens. • Engage in class discussion. • Identify the enduring understandings from a piece of text. • Objectively summarize literary text. • Determine the theme of a story. • Determine how the theme is developed over the course of a text. • Analyze the effect characters have on the theme. • Identify the author's point of view. • Identify common conventions of a tale.

Lesson 8	Lesson 9	Lesson 10
Reading • Establish a purpose for revisiting literature. • Listen to an audio version of a text. • Use information from text and media to answer questions. • Compare and contrast the experience of reading a story to listening to an audio version of the text. • Use critical thinking skills to write responses to prompts about text. • Support written answers with evidence from text. • Recognize a shift in character point of view in text. • Write objective summaries. • Evaluate the impact of an audio performance of a text.	**Vocabulary** • Review key passage vocabulary. **Reading** • Read literature with purpose and understanding. • Answer questions to demonstrate comprehension of text. • Identify and explain explicit details from text. • Monitor comprehension of text during reading. • Determine the impact of word choice, poetic style, and repetition. • Determine the meaning of proverbs, adages, and aphorisms. • Identify shifts in point of view. • Identify the use of the interrogative and conditional moods. • Identify foreshadowing in literature. • Determine the meaning and purpose of verbs in the past perfect tense.	**Vocabulary** • Review key passage vocabulary. **Writing** • Use multiple texts to write coherently. • Use a process to write. • Write a compare/contrast essay on cultural views of wolves. • Compare and contrast the treatment of similar topics in stories from different cultures. • Identify how an author's point of view influences the story. • Use a rubric to guide and evaluate writing. **Reading** • Self-correct as comprehension of text deepens. • Answer questions to demonstrate comprehension of text. • Engage in class discussion. • Identify the enduring understandings from a piece of text.

Unit 8 Lesson 1

Lesson Opener

Before the lesson, choose one of the following activities to write on the board or post on the *LANGUAGE! Live* Class Wall online.

- *Do you believe in werewolves? Why or why not?*
- *Write four sentences about your life. Use a different tense in each sentence.*
- *Write three sentences about wolves. Use action verbs, not linking or helping verbs.*

Reading

Objectives

- Determine and discuss the topic of a text.
- Determine and discuss the author's purpose.
- Use text features to preview text.

Passage Introduction

Direct students to page 39 in their Student Books. Discuss the content focus.

Content Focus
werewolves

In the last unit, we read about wolves. What do you think you will read about in this story? (Answers will vary.) What is the difference between a wolf and a werewolf? **Have partners discuss.**

Type of Text
literature—short story

Literature can be divided into two categories. What are they? (fiction and nonfiction) Turn to your neighbor and share the difference between fiction and nonfiction. **Provide sharing time.** Which one tells a story that isn't real? (fiction) What does *nonfiction* mean? (not fiction, not fake, real to life) We are going to read another piece of fiction. This short story is considered supernatural fiction and was written in first person, where the author is a character in the story.

Unit 8

Lesson 1 | Reading

Let's Focus: "The White Wolf of the Hartz Mountains"

Content Focus
werewolves

Type of Text
literature—short story

Author's Name Captain Frederick Marryat

Author's Purpose to entertain; to scare; to create suspense

Big Ideas
Consider the following Big Idea questions. Write your answer for each question.

To what degree is the proverb "love is blind" true? Explain.

Do humans have the ability to know things that cannot be known by normal use of the senses? Do animals? Explain.

Narrative Preview Checklist: "The White Wolf of the Hartz Mountains" on pages 41–50.

- ☐ Title: What clue does it provide about the passage?
- ☐ Pictures: What additional information is added here?
- ☐ Margin Information: What vocabulary is important to understand this story?

Enduring Understandings
After reading the text . . .

Unit 8 39

Author's Purpose

Have students glance at the text. Who is the author of this text? (Captain Frederick Marryat) The author's purpose is the reason that he or she wrote the text. Authors write for different purposes. They write to entertain, to persuade, or to inform or teach. Knowing an author's purpose can help a reader understand a text better. Most fiction pieces are written to entertain. Supernatural fiction, in addition to entertaining you, is meant to scare you or create suspense. **Have students write the answers on the page.**

Play the Unit 8 Text Training video found in the Teacher Resources online.

Before we read "The White Wolf of the Hartz Mountains," we will watch a short video to help build our background knowledge. **Play the Unit 8 Text Training video. Have partners discuss what they learned from the video.**

> **Note:** If you are unable to play the video, Background Information about werewolves can be found in the Teacher Resources online.

Read the Big Idea questions aloud.

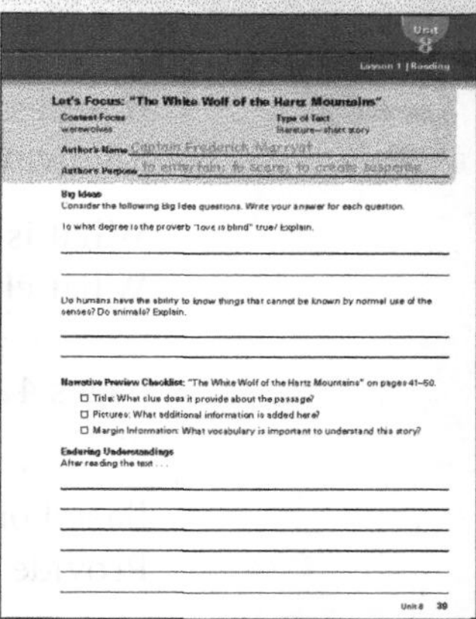
Unit 8
Lesson 1 | Reading

Let's Focus: "The White Wolf of the Hartz Mountains"

Content Focus
werewolves

Type of Text
literature—short story

Author's Name Captain Frederick Marryat

Author's Purpose to entertain; to scare; to create suspense

Big Ideas
Consider the following Big Idea questions. Write your answer for each question.

To what degree is the proverb "love is blind" true? Explain.

Do humans have the ability to know things that cannot be known by normal use of the senses? Do animals? Explain.

Narrative Preview Checklist: "The White Wolf of the Hartz Mountains" on pages 41–50.

- ☐ Title: What clue does it provide about the passage?
- ☐ Pictures: What additional information is added here?
- ☐ Margin Information: What vocabulary is important to understand this story?

Enduring Understandings
After reading the text . . .

Unit 8 39

Big Ideas

To what degree is the proverb "love is blind" true? Explain.

Do humans have the ability to know things that cannot be known by normal use of the senses? Do animals? Explain.

As a class, consider the two Big Idea questions. After discussing each question, have students write an answer. We'll come back to these questions after we finish reading the text. You can add to your answers as you gain information and perspective.

Preview

Read the Preview Checklist on page 39. Follow the Preview Procedure outlined below.

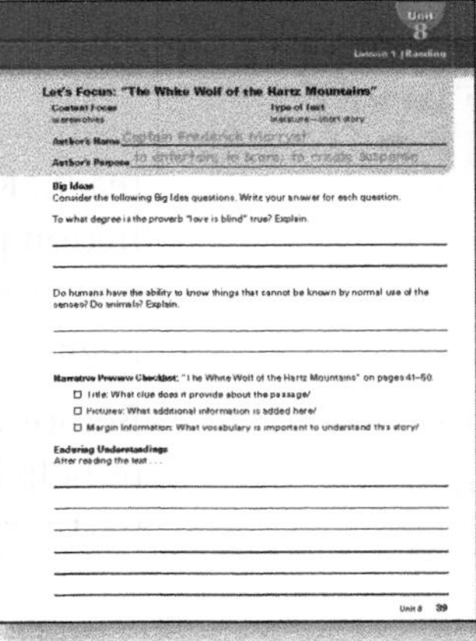

Preview Procedure

- Group students with partners or in triads.
- Have students count off as 1s or 2s. The 1s will become the student leaders. If working with triads, the third students become 3s.
- The student leaders will preview the text in addition to managing the checklist and pacing.
- The 2s and 3s will preview the text with 1s.
- Direct 1s to open their Student Books to page 39 and 2s and 3s to open their Student Books to page 41. This allows students to look at a few different pages at one time without turning back and forth.

Direct students to page 41.

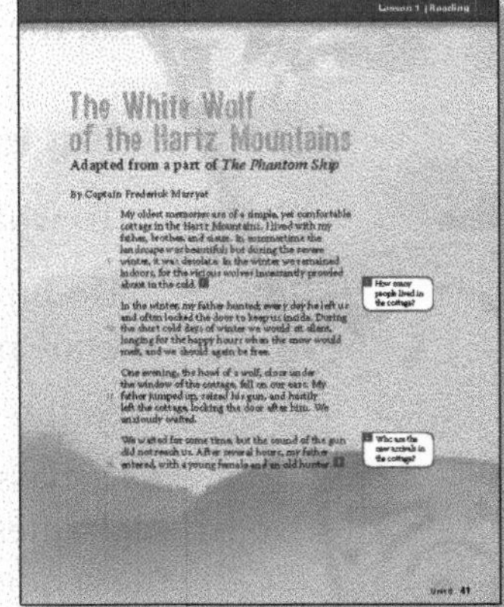

If necessary, guide students in a short preview using the following talking points.

What is the title? ("The White Wolf of the Hartz Mountains") What clue does the title provide about the passage? (Answers will vary.) Have students identify what they see by the cabin on pages 42, 44, 46, 48, and 50. (lady, grave, wolf, and lady and two graves)

Based on our preview, what is this story going to be about? Provide sharing time.

Vocabulary

Objectives

- Evaluate word knowledge.
- Determine the meaning of key passage vocabulary.

Rate Vocabulary Knowledge

Direct students to page 40 in their Student Books. We are about to read "The White Wolf of the Hartz Mountains." Before we read, let's take a look at the vocabulary words that appear in this text. Remind students that as you read each word in the first column aloud, they will write the word in the third column and then rate their knowledge of it in the fourth. Display the Vocabulary Rating Scale poster or write the information on the board. Review the meaning of each rating.

Vocabulary Rating Scale

0—I have never heard the word before.

1—I have heard the word, but I'm not sure how to use it.

2—I am familiar with the word, but I'm not sure if I know the correct meaning.

3—I know the meaning of the word and can use it correctly in a sentence.

Lesson 1 | Vocabulary

Key Passage Vocabulary: "The White Wolf of the Hartz Mountains"

Read each word. Write the word in column 3. Then, circle a number to rate your knowledge of the word.

Vocabulary	Part of Speech	Write the Word	Knowledge Rating
beckon	(v)	beckon	0 1 2 3
reside	(v)	reside	0 1 2 3
converse	(v)	converse	0 1 2 3
perish	(v)	perish	0 1 2 3
resolve	(v)	resolve	0 1 2 3
seldom	(adv)	seldom	0 1 2 3
rashness	(n)	rashness	0 1 2 3
implicated	(v)	implicated	0 1 2 3
restore	(v)	restore	0 1 2 3
penalty	(n)	penalty	0 1 2 3

40 Unit 8

Remember, the points are there to help you know which words you need to focus on. By the end of this unit, you should be able to change all your ratings to a 3. That's the goal.

Read each word aloud and have students repeat it, write it, and rate it. Then, have volunteers who rated a word *2* or *3* use the word in an oral sentence.

Preteach Vocabulary

Explain that you will now take a closer look at the words. Follow the Preteach Procedure outlined below.

Preteach Procedure

This activity is intended to take only a short amount of time. It is an oral exercise.

- Introduce each word as indicated on the word card.
- Read the definition and example sentences.
- Ask questions to clarify and deepen understanding.
- If time permits, allow students to share.

* If your students would benefit from copying the definitions, please have them do so in the vocabulary log in the back of the Student Books using the margin definitions in the passage selections. This should be done outside of instruction time.

beckon (v)

Let's read the first word together. *Beckon.*

Definition: *Beckon* means "to signal to someone to come to you." What means "to signal to someone to come to you"? (beckon)

Example 1: The coach *beckoned* the point guard to the sideline for a quick chat.

Example 2: If you have to *beckon* a waiter to get his attention, he's probably having a busy shift.

Example 3: Dogs do not usually respond if you *beckon*; you have to call, clap, or whistle instead.

Question 1: Would you *beckon* a newborn baby? Yes or no? (no)

Question 2: Can you *beckon* someone with your face? Yes or no? (no) Your head? Yes or no? (yes) Show me.

Pair Share: Turn to your partner and tell who you might *beckon* in a crowded stadium, and why.

reside (v)

Let's read the next word together. *Reside.*

Definition: *Reside* means "to live or stay in a place long-term." What means "to live or stay in a place long-term"? (reside)

Example 1: We *reside* in the state of _____.

Example 2: If you *reside* in a city, you can vote in its local elections.

Example 3: I have always wanted to *reside* in a mountain cabin.

Question 1: You are on a road trip. You stop overnight at a relative's house. Do you *reside* there? Yes or no? (no)

Question 2: Does the president *reside* in the White House? Yes or no? (yes)

Pair Share: Turn to your partner and tell whether you would like to *reside* on the top floor of a skyscraper, and why.

converse (v)

Let's read the next word together. *Converse.*

Definition: *Converse* means "to talk with one or more people." What word means "to talk with one or more people"? (converse)

Example 1: If you must *converse* in the library, please do so quietly.

Example 2: Some people would rather *converse* with a few good friends at home than chat with dozens of people at a big party.

Example 3: It's bothersome when you're trying to read or study and someone keeps trying to *converse* with you.

Question 1: Is it polite to *converse* loudly during a movie in a movie theater? Yes or no? (no)

Question 2: Late at night, your phone rings and wakes you from a deep sleep. Do you feel like *conversing*? Yes or no? (no)

Pair Share: Turn to your partner and *converse* briefly about the weather.

3

perish (v)

Let's read the word together. *Perish.*

Definition: To *perish* is to die. What word means "to die"? (perish)

Example 1: Thousands of people *perished* in the Indian Ocean tsunami of 2004.

Example 2: Pioneers heading west through the Rocky Mountains often *perished* from lack of food and water.

Example 3: I vividly remember the day seven American astronauts *perished* in the Space Shuttle Columbia disaster.

Question 1: You get to school and realize your shirt is on backward. Will you *perish*? Yes or no? (no)

Question 2: You swat a fly with a paperback book and your aim is good. Does the fly *perish*? Yes or no? (yes)

Pair Share: Turn to your partner and tell about a movie or TV show in which someone seems to *perish* but doesn't really.

resolve (v)

Let's read the next word together. *Resolve.*

Definition: If you *resolve* to do something, you make a firm decision to do it. What word means "to make a firm decision to do something"? (resolve)

Example 1: On New Year's Day, many people *resolve* to make a positive change in their life.

Example 2: When I want to tackle a big project, I *resolve* to do a small part of it each day.

Example 3: If you *resolve* "never" to do something again, you'll probably fail; "never" is a long time.

Question 1: You need to apologize to someone but feel nervous about it. Should you *resolve* to do it? Yes or no? (yes)

Question 2: You can't decide whether to spend all your money on a new pair of jeans. Have you *resolved* to buy the jeans? Yes or no? (no)

Pair Share: Turn to your partner and tell about something difficult you recently *resolved* to do—and did.

5

seldom (adv)

Let's read the next word together. *Seldom.*

Definition: *Seldom* means "rarely; not often." What means "rarely; not often"? (seldom)

Example 1: I *seldom* eat sushi; I don't care for raw fish.

Example 2: True friends are *seldom* rude but always honest.

Example 3: People who buy lottery tickets *seldom* win.

Question 1: You're an optimist. You always look on the bright side. Is it true that you *seldom* complain? Yes or no? (yes)

Question 2: Coyotes and foxes *seldom* wander into city neighborhoods. Do they wander into city neighborhoods often? Yes or no? (no)

Pair Share: Turn to your partner and tell about a game you played when you were little that you *seldom* play now.

6

rashness (n)

Let's read the next word together. *Rashness.*

Definition: *Rashness* is a tendency to act without thinking something through. What means "a tendency to act without thinking something through"? (rashness)

Example 1: People who have a problem with *rashness* make "impulse purchases" every time they go shopping.

Example 2: *Rashness* can run in a family; if parents act without thinking, their kids might also.

Example 3: I would rather suffer from *rashness* than be unable to act at all.

Question 1: You buy orange-and-blue striped pants because they are on sale. When you get home, they look funny on you. But since they were on sale, you can't return them. Do you regret your *rashness*? Yes or no? (yes)

Question 2: You've been planning how, when, and where you will start your own business for years. If your business is a success, will *rashness* be the cause? Yes or no? (no)

Pair Share: Turn to your partner and tell about a time *rashness* worked in your favor.

implicated (v)

Let's read the next word together. *Implicated.*

Definition: If you are *implicated* in something, people believe you are involved in it or guilty of it. What word means "thought to be involved in or guilty of something"? (implicated)

Example 1: If a person's fingerprints are all over a crime scene, that person is *implicated* in the crime.

Example 2: There are cookie crumbs on my shirt, and the cookies are all gone. I'm *implicated* in their disappearance.

Example 3: Insurance companies usually call all people who are *implicated* in a car wreck to get their sides of the story.

Question 1: Your favorite hoodie disappears in math class, and then you see a kid from that class wearing a similar one the next day. Is that person *implicated* in the disappearance of your hoodie? Yes or no? (yes)

Question 2: Somebody dumped the baked cauliflower in the trash. You are known for hating cauliflower. Are you *implicated* in the waste? Yes or no? (yes)

Pair Share: The front door was left unlocked overnight, and you are *implicated.* Tell your partner why.

restore (v)

Let's read the next word together. *Restore.*

Definition: To *restore* something is to bring it back or to return it to its usual state. What means "to bring back; to return something to its usual state"? (restore)

Example 1: When very old paintings are discovered, highly trained artists can *restore* them to their original condition.

Example 2: Some cars are just too beat up to *restore* and should be towed directly to the junkyard.

Example 3: Hearing aids can *restore* a person's ability to hear.

Question 1: A school gets a new fight song, and all the students love it. Should the old fight song be *restored*? Yes or no? (no)

Question 2: You're having fun with your friends. All of a sudden, one of them says something awkward and hurtful. Is it difficult to *restore* the earlier easygoing mood? Yes or no? (yes)

Pair Share: Turn to your partner and tell one way people can *restore* their health when they have a cold.

penalty (n)

Let's read the last word together. *Penalty.*

Definition: A *penalty* is the price you pay for breaking a rule or doing something wrong. What word means "the price you pay for breaking a rule or doing something wrong"? (penalty)

Example 1: When I was little, I received the *penalty* of a time-out if I did something wrong.

Example 2: A good *penalty* for painting graffiti is to spend a day cleaning up graffiti all over town.

Example 3: If people don't pay their taxes on time, they are charged interest as a *penalty.*

Question 1: You win the "most positive attitude" award. Is this a *penalty*? Yes or no? (no)

Question 2: You foul another player, and the coach takes you out of the game. Is being benched a *penalty*? Yes or no? (yes)

Pair Share: Turn to your partner and tell about a *penalty* you once received that you felt you did not deserve.

10

Reading

Objectives

- Read a short story.
- Monitor comprehension during text reading.
- Identify first-person point of view.

"The White Wolf of the Hartz Mountains"

Direct students to page 41 in their Student Books. Now that we have previewed vocabulary, it's time to read.

Guiding Students Toward Independent Reading

It is important that your students read as much and as often as they can. Assign readings that meet the needs of your students, based on your observations and data. This is a good opportunity to stretch your students. If students become frustrated, scaffold the reading with paired reading, choral reading, or a read-aloud.

Options for reading text:

- Teacher read-aloud
- Teacher-led or student-led choral read
- Paired read or independent read

Choose an option for reading the text. Have students read according to the option that you chose.

Remind students to pause at the numbers and consider the questions.

If you choose to read the text aloud or chorally, use the following text and stop to ask questions and have students answer them.

SE p. 41, paragraph 1

My oldest memories are of a simple, yet comfortable cottage in the Hartz Mountains. I lived with my father, brother, and sister. In summertime the landscape was beautiful; but during the severe winter, it was desolate. In the winter we remained indoors, for the vicious wolves incessantly prowled about in the cold.

1. How many people lived in the cottage?

SE p. 41, paragraphs 2–4

In the winter, my father hunted; every day he left us and often locked the door to keep us inside. During the short cold days of winter we would sit silent, longing for the happy hours when the snow would melt, and we should again be free.

One evening, the howl of a wolf, close under the window of the cottage, fell on our ears. My father jumped up, seized his gun, and hastily left the cottage, locking the door after him. We anxiously waited.

We waited for some time, but the sound of the gun did not reach us. After several hours, my father entered, with a young female and an old hunter.

2. Who are the new arrivals in the cottage?

SE p. 42, paragraphs 1–5

The female's features were very beautiful. Her hair was flaxen and bright as a mirror; her mouth, although somewhat large when it was open, showed the most brilliant teeth I have ever seen. But there was something about her eyes which made us children afraid; they were so restless, so sly; I could not at that time tell why, but I felt as if there was cruelty in her eyes; and when she **beckoned** us to come to her, we approached her with fear and trembling. Still she was beautiful, very beautiful. She spoke kindly to my brother and myself, patted our heads, and caressed us; but Marcella would not come near her; on the contrary, she slipped away and hid herself.

My father offered the young lady, whose name was Christina, his bed and he would remain at the fire, sitting up with her father. This arrangement was agreed to, and I and my brother crept into the other bed with Marcella, for we always slept together.

But we could not sleep; there was something so unusual, not only in seeing strange people, but in having those people sleep at the cottage, that we were bewildered. As for poor little Marcella, she was quiet but trembled and sobbed the whole night. My father and the hunter remained drinking and talking before the fire. Our curious ears were ready to catch the slightest whisper.

They filled their mugs to the brim, and drank to one another, in the German fashion. The conversation was then carried on in a low tone; all that we could collect from it was that our new guest and his daughter were to **reside** in our cottage, at least for the present. After an hour, they both fell back in their chairs and slept.

When we awoke the next morning, we found that the hunter's daughter had risen before us. She came up to little Marcella and caressed her; the child burst into tears and sobbed as if her heart would break.

3. Why didn't Marcella like Christina?

SE p. 43, paragraphs 1–4

The hunter and his daughter stayed in the cottage. My father and he went out hunting daily, leaving Christina with us. She performed all the household duties; was very kind to us children; and, gradually, we grew to like her—even Marcella. But a great change took place in my father; he was most attentive to Christina. Often, after her father and we were in bed, he would sit up with her, **conversing** in a low tone by the fire. After three weeks of this, my father asked for Christina's hand in marriage. Soon after, the wedding took place.

My father repeated his vows after the hunter. "I swear by all the spirits of the Hartz Mountains, by all their power for good or for evil, that I take Christina for my wedded wife; that I will protect her, cherish her, and love her; that my hand shall never be raised against her to harm her."

"And if I fail in this my vow, may all the vengeance of the spirits fall upon me and upon my children; may they **perish** by the vulture, by the wolf, or by other beasts of the forest; may their flesh be torn from their limbs, and their bones fade in the wilderness; all this I swear."

My father hesitated, as he repeated the last words; little Marcella could not restrain herself and burst into tears.

4. Why did Father hesitate?

SE p. 43, paragraphs 5–6

The next morning, the hunter mounted his horse and rode away.

Things went on much as before the marriage, except that our new stepmother did not show any kindness towards us; indeed, during my father's absence, she would often beat us, particularly little Marcella, and her eyes would flash fire as she looked eagerly upon the fair and lovely child.

SE p. 44, paragraphs 1–9

One night, my sister awoke me and my brother.

"What is the matter?" said Caesar.

"She has gone out," whispered Marcella.

"Gone out!"

"Yes, gone out the door, in her night-dress," replied the child. "I saw her."

What could bring her to leave the cottage, in such bitter wintry weather, was incomprehensible; we lay awake, and in about an hour we heard the growl of a wolf, close under the window.

"There is a wolf," said Caesar; "she will be torn to pieces."

A few minutes afterwards, our stepmother appeared; she was in her night-dress, as Marcella had stated. She let down the latch of the door, so as to make no noise, went to a pail of water, and washed her face and hands, and then slipped into the bed where my father lay.

We all three trembled, we hardly knew why, but we **resolved** to watch the next night. We did so—and many other nights as well, and always at about the same hour, would our stepmother rise from her bed, and leave the cottage—and after she was gone, we invariably heard the growl of a wolf under our window, and always saw her, on her return, wash herself before she retired to bed. We observed, also, that she **seldom** sat down to meals, and that when she did, she appeared to eat with dislike; but when the meat was being prepared, she would often put a raw piece into her mouth.

5. What do you know about Christina so far?

SE p. 45, paragraphs 1–2

My brother Caesar did not want to tell my father until he knew more. He resolved to follow her out and ascertain what she did. Marcella and I tried to dissuade him; but he would not be deterred, and the very next night he lay down in his clothes, and as soon as our stepmother left the cottage, he jumped up, took down my father's gun, and followed her.

Marcella and I waited in suspense. After a few minutes, we heard the sound of a gun. It did not awaken my father, and we lay trembling with anxiety. In a minute afterwards, we saw our stepmother enter the cottage—her dress was bloody. I put my hand to Marcella's mouth to prevent her crying out, although I was myself in great alarm. Our stepmother looked to see if our father was asleep, and then started a fire.

6. Who was shot?

SE p. 45, paragraphs 3–7

"Who is there?" said my father, waking up.

"Lie still, dearest," replied my stepmother, "it is only me; I have lighted the fire to warm some water; I am not quite well."

My father turned round and was soon asleep, but we watched our stepmother. She changed her clothes and threw the garments she had worn into the fire; and we then perceived that her right leg was bleeding, as if from a gun-shot wound. She bandaged it up and dressed herself.

Poor little Marcella, her heart beat quick as she pressed me to her side—so indeed did mine. Where was our brother, Caesar? How did my stepmother receive the wound unless from his gun? At last my father rose, and then, for the first time I spoke, saying, "Father, where is my brother, Caesar?"

"Your brother!" exclaimed he, "why, where can he be?"

SE p. 46, paragraph 1

"Merciful Heaven! I thought as I lay very restless last night," observed our stepmother, "that I heard somebody open the latch of the door; and dear husband, what has become of your gun?"

7. What does Christina want her husband to believe?

SE p. 46, paragraphs 2–6

My father cast his eyes up above the chimney, and perceived that his gun was missing. For a moment he looked perplexed, then seizing an axe, he went out of the cottage without saying another word.

He did not remain away from us long. In a few minutes he returned, bearing in his arms the mangled body of my poor brother; he laid it down and covered up his face.

My stepmother rose up and looked at the body, while Marcella and I threw ourselves by its side, wailing and sobbing bitterly.

"Go to bed again, children," said she sharply. "Husband, your boy must have taken the gun down to shoot a wolf, and the animal has been too powerful for him. Poor boy! He has paid dearly for his **rashness**."

My father made no reply; I wished to tell all, but Marcella, who saw my intention, held my arm and looked at me so imploringly that I stopped.

8. Why didn't Marcella want him to tell what he knew?

SE p. 46, paragraphs 7–8

My father, therefore, was deceived; but Marcella and I, although we could not comprehend it, knew that our stepmother was in some way connected with my brother's death.

That day, my father went out and dug a grave, and when he laid the body in the earth, he piled up stones over it, so that the villainous wolves should not be able to dig it up. The shock of this tragedy was severe for my father; for several days he did not hunt but uttered bitter vengeance against the wolves.

SE p. 47, paragraph 1

During this time of mourning, my stepmother's nocturnal wanderings continued with the same regularity as before.

9. What did Christina do on her nighttime wanderings?

SE p. 47, paragraphs 2–7

At last, my father took down his gun, and went hunting; but he soon returned and appeared bothered.

"Would you believe it, Christina, that the wolves—most evil of all animals—have actually dug up the body of my poor boy, and now there is nothing left of him but his bones?"

Marcella looked at me, and I saw in her intelligent eyes all she would have uttered.

"A wolf growls under our window every night, father," said I.

"Really?—why did you not tell me, boy?—wake me the next time you hear it."

I saw my stepmother turn away; her eyes flashed fire, and she gnashed her teeth.

10. Why is Christina upset?

SE p. 47, paragraphs 8–9

The spring finally came. The snow disappeared, and we were permitted to leave the cottage; but never would I leave, for one moment, my dear little sister, to whom, since the death of my brother, I was more attached than ever. I was afraid to leave her alone with my stepmother, who appeared to have a particular pleasure in ill-treating the child. My father was now working his little farm, and I was able to assist him.

Marcella used to sit by us while we were at work, leaving my stepmother alone in the cottage. As spring advanced, my stepmother decreased her nocturnal rambles, and we never heard the growl of the wolf under the window after I had spoken of it to my father.

SE p. 48, paragraph 1

One day, when my father and I were in the field, Marcella being with us, my stepmother came out, saying that she was going into the forest to collect some herbs my father wanted, and that Marcella must go to the cottage and watch the dinner. Marcella went, and my stepmother disappeared in the forest.

11. Predict what will happen next.

SE p. 48, paragraphs 2–4

About an hour afterwards, we were startled by shrieks from the cottage. "Marcella has burnt herself, father," said I, throwing down my spade. My father threw down his, and we both hastened to the cottage. Before we arrived, out darted a large white wolf. We rushed into the cottage and there saw poor little Marcella. Her body was extremely mangled, and the blood pouring from it had formed a large pool on the cottage floor. My father's first intention had been to seize his gun and pursue, but he was checked by this horrid spectacle; he knelt down by his dying child and burst into tears. Marcella looked kindly at us for a few seconds and then closed her eyes in death.

My father and I were still hovering over my sister's body when my stepmother came in. At the dreadful sight, she expressed much concern, but she did not appear to recoil from the sight of blood, as most women do.

"Poor child!" said she, "it must have been that great white wolf which passed me just now and frightened me so."

12. Where was Christina?

SE p. 48, paragraphs 5–6

My father cried in agony.

I thought my father would never recover from the effects of this second tragedy. He mourned over the body of his sweet daughter and for several days would not bury her. At last he dug a grave for her close by that of my poor brother and took every precaution that the wolves should not violate her remains.

SE p. 49, paragraphs 1–2

I was now really miserable, as I lay alone in the bed which I had formerly shared with my brother and sister. I could not help thinking that my stepmother was **implicated** in both their deaths, although I could not explain it. I no longer felt afraid of her; my heart was full of hatred and revenge.

The night after my sister was buried, as I lay awake, I saw my stepmother get up and go out of the cottage. I waited some time, then dressed myself, and looked out through the door. The moon shone bright, and I could see the spot where my brother and sister had been buried; and to my horror, I perceived my stepmother busily removing the stones from Marcella's grave.

13. What is Christina going to do?

SE p. 49, paragraphs 3–5

> She was in her white night-dress, and the moon shone full upon her. She was digging with her hands and throwing away the stones behind her with all the ferocity of a wild beast. At last, she raised the body to the side of the grave. I could bear it no longer; I ran to my father and awoke him.
>
> "Father! Father! Dress yourself, and get your gun."
>
> "What!" cried my father, "Is it the wolves?"

14. What does the narrator want to happen as indicated by the advice he has given his father?

SE p. 49, paragraphs 6–7

> He jumped out of bed, threw on his clothes, and in his anxiety did not notice the absence of his wife. I opened the door, he went out, and I followed him.
>
> Imagine his horror, when (unprepared as he was for such a sight) he beheld, as he advanced towards the grave, not a wolf, but his wife, in her night-dress, on her hands and knees, crouching by the body of my sister, and tearing off large pieces of the flesh and devouring them with the viciousness of a wolf. She was too busy to be aware of our approach. My father dropped his gun; he breathed heavily, and then his breath for a time stopped. I picked up the gun and put it into his hand. Suddenly he appeared as if rage had **restored** him to vigor; he leveled his piece, fired, and with a loud shriek, down fell the wretch whom he had married.

15. Why did Father drop his gun? Why did his son put the gun back in his hand?

SE p. 50, paragraphs 1–4

To our astonishment and horror, we found that instead of the dead body of my stepmother, we found the body of a large, white wolf.

For some time, my father remained in silence and deep thought. He then carefully lifted up the body of my sister, replaced it in the grave, and covered it over as before. Raving like a madman, he then struck the head of the wolf with the heel of his boot. He walked back to the cottage, shut the door, and threw himself on the bed; I did the same.

Shortly after, we left the cottage forever and headed for Holland. We had not been many days in Amsterdam before my father was seized with a fever and died raving mad.

Now the question remains whether I am to pay the **penalty** of the vow my father made on his wedding day? I am convinced that, in some way or another, I shall.

16. What is the narrator afraid of? Are his fears valid?

For confirmation of engagement, have partners share a connection with the treatment of the stepmother in this story and other fairy tales, such as "Cinderella." Have volunteers share connections with the class.

Point of View

Point of view has a major impact on text. Literature can be written from the first-person point of view or the third-person point of view. If it is written by a character in the text, that is called first person. If it is written by a character outside the text, that is called third person.

Have partners determine the point of view of "The White Wolf of the Hartz Mountains." (first person)

Unit 8 Lesson 2

Lesson Opener

Before the lesson, choose one of the following activities to write on the board or post on the *LANGUAGE! Live* Class Wall online.

- *Write five sentences about the Hartz Mountains with adverbs. Be sure to use the suffix -ly in your sentence.*
- *Write three sentences with a pair of homophones in each sentence.*
- *Write four sentences about werewolves. Use the passive voice (*to be *verbs) first, then rewrite each sentence with the active voice.*

Vocabulary

Objective

- Review key passage vocabulary.

Review Passage Vocabulary

Direct students to page 40 in their Student Books. Use the following questions to review the vocabulary words in "The White Wolf of the Hartz Mountains." Have students answer each question using the vocabulary word or indicating its meaning in a complete sentence.

Lesson 1 | Vocabulary

Key Passage Vocabulary: "The White Wolf of the Hartz Mountains"

Read each word. Write the word in column 3. Then, circle a number to rate your knowledge of the word.

Vocabulary	Part of Speech	Write the Word	Knowledge Rating
beckon	(v)	beckon	0 1 2 3
reside	(v)	reside	0 1 2 3
converse	(v)	converse	0 1 2 3
perish	(v)	perish	0 1 2 3
resolve	(v)	resolve	0 1 2 3
seldom	(adv)	seldom	0 1 2 3
rashness	(n)	rashness	0 1 2 3
implicated	(v)	implicated	0 1 2 3
restore	(v)	restore	0 1 2 3
penalty	(n)	penalty	0 1 2 3

40 Unit 8

- The father in this story brings home a beautiful young woman named Christina. Does the narrator—the boy who tells the story—like to see Christina *beckon* to him and his siblings? Why or why not? (No, he doesn't like to see her beckon to them because he sees cruelty in her eyes, and he and his siblings are afraid to approach her.) Does the father notice the cruel look in her eye when Christina *beckons*? How can you tell? (No, he must not notice because he falls in love with her and probably enjoys being beckoned by her.)
- How does Christina come to *reside* with the family on a permanent basis? (She resides with the family because she and the father are married.) Where does the family *reside*? (The family resides in a cottage in the Hartz Mountains.)
- The father *converses* with the old hunter by the fire every night for three weeks. What can we guess they are *conversing* about? (They are probably conversing about Christina and making plans for the father's marriage to her.) The father takes a dreadful vow by repeating after the old hunter. Are the two *conversing*? (No; to converse is not to repeat what someone else says, but to exchange ideas with one or more people.)
- The vow states that if the father ever raises his hand against his new wife, he and his children shall *perish*. What will he and his children do? (If they perish, they will die.) What will cause them to *perish*? (They will perish in violent attacks by vultures or other wild beasts.)

- The narrator and his siblings see their new stepmother leave the house stealthily, or sneakily, one night. After this, what do they *resolve* to do? (They resolve, or promise themselves, to keep watch the next night too.) After observing more strange behavior, what does the narrator's brother, Caesar, *resolve* to do? (He resolves to follow her.)
- When it comes to meals in the house, what does Christina *seldom* do? (She seldom sits down to eat them.) When it comes to her strange behavior, what does the father *seldom* do? (He seldom notices it.)
- Caesar is killed by a wild animal the night he follows Christina. She later blames it on his *rashness*. What does she mean? (She means he deserved to die because he tried to shoot a wolf in rashness, or without thinking it through first.) What could we say the father did out of *rashness*? (He married Christina out of rashness.)
- After his sister is killed too, who does the narrator feel is *implicated* in both deaths? (He believes Christina is implicated, or involved, in the deaths.) What evidence strongly suggests that she is *implicated*? (She is implicated by her late-night rambles, her bloody clothes, her preference for raw meat, her unkind behavior toward the children, and her quickness to blame them for their own misfortune.)
- When the father finally sees his wife devouring the body of his daughter, he becomes paralyzed. What *restores* him to action after a few moments? (Rage restores him, or returns him to action.) When she dies, Christina is *restored* to her earlier form. Explain. (She is restored to her true form, that of a wolf.)
- What *penalty* does the narrator now dread, and why? (He dreads the penalty of being ravaged by a wild beast because when his father shot Christina, he broke his vow.) How did his father pay the *penalty* promised in the vow? (He died of a fever, raving mad.)

Grammar

Objectives

- Distinguish between contractions and possessive nouns.
- Connect pronouns to their antecedents.
- Use pronouns correctly.
- Use and punctuate relative clauses correctly.

Apostrophes: Contraction or Possessive

As we read, it is important to notice punctuation marks and make sure we understand how they impact meaning. Just as nouns have different jobs, or functions, in a sentence, some punctuation marks have different functions or meanings. Apostrophes can have strikingly different meanings, impacting the overall meaning of a sentence. **Write the following sentences on the board and underline *Martha's*:**

Martha's dog was barking.

Martha's here.

What punctuation marks do you see? (apostrophes and periods) Let's focus on the apostrophe. You have learned two meanings for the apostrophe. It can show possession or a contraction, the omission of letters in a word. Look at the first sentence: *Martha's dog was barking.* What does the apostrophe mean in that sentence? Answer using the word *apostrophe*. (The apostrophe shows possession or ownership.) Whose dog is it? (Martha's) Listen to the next sentence: *Martha's here.* Does Martha own *here*? (no) What does the apostrophe signal in this sentence? (The apostrophe signals a contraction.) What two words are represented by the contraction? (Martha is)

Direct students to page 51 in their Student Books. Read the instructions aloud.

Lesson 2 | Grammar

Apostrophes: Contraction or Possessive

Circle words that contain apostrophes. Place a check mark in the proper column to identify its meaning. If it's a contraction, write the two words it represents. If it's a possessive, write what it possesses.

Sentence	Contraction	Possessive
Ex: You're not going on about the wolves again, are you?	✓ you are	
Ex: I believe that a wolf's life is important.		✓ life
I'm convinced I shall pay the penalty for his vow.	✓ I am	
I couldn't believe my eyes.	✓ could not	
When we awoke the next morning, we found that the hunter's daughter had risen before us.		✓ daughter
He's bound to believe me.	✓ he is	
My father and I were still hovering over my sister's body when my stepmother came in.		✓ body
The female's features were very beautiful.		✓ features
Lie still, dearest, it's only me.	✓ it is	

Unit 8 51

Model

Listen as I read the first example: *You're not going on about the wolves again, are you?* My first step is to circle the word that contains an apostrophe. I've circled *You're*. My next step is to decide if it's a contraction or if it shows possession. I know it's not a possessive because it doesn't end in 's. It's the contraction for *you are*. I've placed a check mark under Contraction and written *you are* below it. Listen to the next example: *I believe that a wolf's life is important.* My first step is to circle the word that contains an apostrophe. I've circled *wolf's*. My next step is to decide if it's a contraction or if it shows possession. If it's a possessive, something belongs to the wolf. Does it make sense for *life* to belong to the wolf? Yes, it does. It doesn't make sense to think it means *wolf is life*. I placed the check mark below Possessive and wrote *life* in the box below.

Guided Practice

Listen to the first sentence: *I'm convinced I shall pay the penalty for his vow.* What's the first step? (Circle the word with an apostrophe.) What word has an apostrophe? (I'm) Could that be a possessive? (no) If it's a contraction, what two words does *I'm* represent? (I am) Make sure you've placed a check mark in the proper column and written *I am* in the box below the check mark.

Independent Practice

Read the remaining sentences and have students enter their responses. Review the answers as a class.

Relative Pronouns

In the previous unit, we learned how to distinguish between a phrase, a dependent clause, and an independent clause. Let's review the difference between a phrase and a clause. I'm going to say a group of words, and I want you to tell me if it's a phrase or a clause. Remember, a clause has a subject and a verb, but a phrase does not.

Listen: *in the morning* (phrase); *by the boathouse on the river* (phrase); *outside the wind howled* (clause); *beneath the ocean's waves* (phrase); *when she wandered into the woods* (clause); *during the morning hours* (phrase); *although Beth thought the stew was good* (clause)

In thinking about the difference between a dependent clause and an independent clause, there's a hint in their names. **Write *independent* and *dependent* on the board.** A dependent clause depends on the rest of the sentence to complete the thought. While it has a subject and a predicate, it still needs to connect to something more in order for it to be complete. Listen again to this example of a dependent clause, and think about how you could complete the thought: *although Beth thought the stew was good.* Turn to your partner and share what you would add. **Have volunteers share their answers with the class.** (Possible response: she liked the chicken casserole better.)

The word at the beginning of the clause signals to us that something more is coming. *Although* is an example of a joining word, or a conjunction. We worked with this type of conjunction in the previous unit. It's a subordinating conjunction because it joins a dependent clause to the rest of the sentence. If a dependent clause depends on the rest of the sentence, what is an independent clause? (It can stand alone.) Yes, it even contains a prefix that you've worked with, in-. In- can mean "not," and in this case, it means "not dependent." **Underline *in-* to emphasize this application of prefix knowledge.**

Direct students to page 52 in their Student Books.

Guide students through the chart, introducing the relative pronouns, their functions, and each example. Review the bullets to more clearly define a relative pronoun and the subsequent relative clause.

Note: It is important to demonstrate that *that* can be used to refer to both people and things, while *who* and *whom* refer only to people. *Which* refers only to things, and *whose* is the only one of the five that reflects possession. *Which* can usually be set off by commas and can be taken out without changing the meaning of the sentence. *That* cannot.

Lesson 2 | Grammar

Relative Pronouns

Relative Pronoun	Function/Meaning	Example
who	subject or object pronoun for people	It was Marcella *who* feared Christina the most.
which	subject or object pronoun for animals and things; does not change the meaning of the sentence; set off with commas	The gun, *which* belonged to my father, was missing from the mantle.
whose	possessive pronoun for people, animals, and things	We wept for Caesar, *whose* death frightened us.
whom	object pronoun for people	It was Marcella for *whom* I felt the most responsible.
that	subject or object pronoun for people, animals, and things; changes the meaning of the sentence	Father grabbed the gun *that* hung above the fireplace.

All relative pronouns:

- Begin a relative clause—a type of dependent clause that modifies or describes a noun or noun phrase
- Follow the noun or noun phrase that it modifies
- Have a noun or pronoun as its antecedent

Circle the relative pronoun that correctly completes each sentence.

1. Christina is a woman ______ likes raw meat. (who, whom)
2. Christina removed the rocks ______ covered the body. (whose, that)
3. Christina, ______ mouth was large and filled with polished teeth, looked like a wolf. (whose, whom)
4. Christina, toward ______ I expressed my anger, showed no remorse. (whom, that)
5. Christina's clothes, ______ she burned, were covered in blood. (whom, which)

52 Unit 8

Guided Practice

Read the instructions aloud, and guide students in the completion of each sentence.

Relative Pronouns and Relative Clauses

We know that a relative pronoun begins a relative clause. A relative clause modifies or describes a noun or noun phrase. Sometimes it gives extra, nonessential information, and sometimes it gives essential (restrictive) information. Remember, commas set off the nonrestrictive or nonessential relative clauses—the ones that aren't necessary to understand the sentence.

Direct students to page 53 in their Student Books. Read the instructions aloud.

Lesson 2 | Grammar

Relative Pronouns and Relative Clauses

Read the sentences. Circle the relative pronoun and underline the relative clause. Draw an arrow from the relative clause to the noun or noun phrase it is describing.

Example:
The curse, which had already claimed the lives of Marcella and Caesar, haunted my thoughts.

1. My father offered the young lady, whose name was Christina, his bed and he would remain at the fire, sitting up with her father.
2. My father, who feared for our safety, hastily grabbed his gun and left the cottage.
3. Never would I leave my dear little sister to whom I was more attached than ever.
4. The sound, which sounded remarkably like a wolf howl, kept us from sleeping.
5. He took every precaution that the wolves should not violate her remains.
6. Marcella, who had reason to be afraid, cried when touched by Christina.
7. My father regretted making the vow, which sentenced us to death, on his wedding day.
8. The wolf that passed us looked familiar somehow.
9. The hunter, whose daughter was a werewolf, had cursed our family.
10. It was my father for whom I cried.

Unit 8 53

We actually have three steps to follow in order to complete this activity. What is the first step? (Circle the relative pronoun.) What is the second step? (Underline the relative clause.) What is the third step? (Draw an arrow from the relative clause to the noun or noun phrase it is describing.)

Model

Listen to the example: *The curse, which had already claimed the lives of Marcella and Caesar, haunted my thoughts.*

My first step is to find and circle the relative pronoun. The relative pronoun *which* has been used in this sentence, so I need to circle it. My second step is to identify and underline the relative clause. *Which had already claimed the lives of Marcella and Caesar* is the clause. It has a verb, *claimed*, and a subject. In this case, the subject is the pronoun *which. Which* is a pronoun used to take the place of the noun *curse*. This part of the sentence is underlined. My last step is to figure out what *which had already claimed the lives of Marcella and Caesar* is referencing. What claimed their lives? The curse claimed their lives, so an arrow is drawn from the clause back to *curse*. Is the relative clause essential? (no)

Guided Practice

Listen as I read #1: *My father offered the young lady, whose name was Christina, his bed and he would remain at the fire, sitting up with her father.*

What's our first step? (to find and circle the relative pronoun) What relative pronoun has been used in this sentence? (whose) Circle *whose*. What is the second step? (to identify and underline the relative clause) What words follow *whose* and complete the clause? (name was Christina) What is the clause you will underline? (*whose name was Christina*) What is the final step? (to draw an arrow from the relative clause to the noun or noun phrase that it describes) Whose name was Christina? (the young lady) So, the arrow goes from the clause back to the noun *lady*.

Notice the punctuation marks around this clause. The commas separate the clause from the rest of the sentence and help us identify the beginning and end of the clause. Commas are used to separate relative clauses when they are not essential to the meaning of the sentence. Listen as I read the sentence again without the clause and tell me if it still makes sense. *My father offered the young lady his bed, and he would remain at the fire, sitting up with her father.* (Yes, it still makes sense.)

Listen as I read #2: *My father, who feared for our safety, hastily grabbed his gun and left the cottage.* Complete the first step. What word did you circle? (who) What kind of word is that? (a relative pronoun) Complete the second step. What did you underline? (who feared for our safety) What is *who feared for our safety?* (a relative clause) As a relative clause, it modifies or describes a noun or noun phrase. Complete the third step. Who feared for our safety? (father) Your arrow should go from the clause back to *father*. Is the relative clause essential? (no)

Independent Practice

Have students complete the remaining sentences. Review the answers as a class.

> **Note:** In #3, clarify the use of *whom* vs. *who*. The pronoun is used as an object of the preposition *to*, which calls for *whom* rather than *who*.

Writing

Objectives

- Use relative clauses to create complex sentences.
- Use correct punctuation when writing sentences that contain relative clauses.

Using Relative Clauses

Understanding the job of relative clauses enables us to use them to create more variety in our sentence structure. Often, two short sentences can be effectively combined by creating a relative clause out of one of the sentences.

Direct students to page 54 in their Student Books. Read the instructions aloud. You have been given a relative pronoun to use in the new sentence. When combining the sentences, you must have one clause that can stand alone. What kind of clause can stand alone? (independent clause) Sentences that contain an independent clause and a dependent clause are called complex sentences.

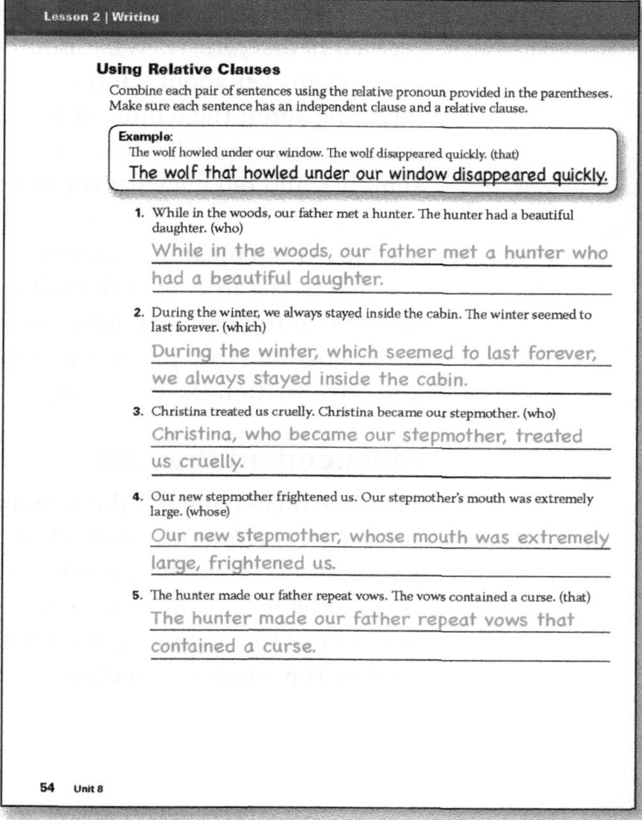
Lesson 2 | Writing

Using Relative Clauses

Combine each pair of sentences using the relative pronoun provided in the parentheses. Make sure each sentence has an independent clause and a relative clause.

Example:
The wolf howled under our window. The wolf disappeared quickly. (that)
The wolf that howled under our window disappeared quickly.

1. While in the woods, our father met a hunter. The hunter had a beautiful daughter. (who)
   While in the woods, our father met a hunter who had a beautiful daughter.
2. During the winter, we always stayed inside the cabin. The winter seemed to last forever. (which)
   During the winter, which seemed to last forever, we always stayed inside the cabin.
3. Christina treated us cruelly. Christina became our stepmother. (who)
   Christina, who became our stepmother, treated us cruelly.
4. Our new stepmother frightened us. Our stepmother's mouth was extremely large. (whose)
   Our new stepmother, whose mouth was extremely large, frightened us.
5. The hunter made our father repeat vows. The vows contained a curse. (that)
   The hunter made our father repeat vows that contained a curse.

54 Unit 8

Model

Listen as I read the example: *The wolf howled under our window. The wolf disappeared quickly.* We must use the relative pronoun *that* to join the two clauses and form a new complex sentence. I will think about how the sentences are related before I determine an effective way to combine them. If I think about the adjective questions, I can more readily determine how the two sentences are connected. Which wolf disappeared? The wolf that howled under our window is the wolf that disappeared. Using that question, I can combine the sentences to create: *The wolf that howled under our window disappeared quickly.* Only sentences that have a redundant *who* or *what* will work when trying to create a relative clause. When you are revising your writing, look for sentences that have the same subject, direct object, or object of the preposition. Those will be sentences that are candidates for this kind of combining.

Guided Practice

Listen as I read #1: *While in the woods, our father met a hunter. The hunter had a beautiful daughter.* What noun is in both sentences? (hunter) What do we know about the hunter? (Father met him in the woods, and he had a beautiful daughter.) We can answer the *Which one* question. Which hunter did Father meet in the woods? The hunter who had a beautiful daughter. How can we use this question to combine the two sentences? (While in the woods, our father met a hunter who had a beautiful daughter.) Is this information essential to the sentence? (yes) Because it is essential for meaning, we do not need a comma to separate the clause from the rest of the sentence. Make sure you have written the new complex sentence correctly.

Listen as I read #2: *During the winter, we always stayed inside the cabin. The winter seemed to last forever.* What noun is used in both sentences? (winter) What question can you answer about winter? (Which one?) The first sentence doesn't tell us anything about the winter. What clause can we add to the first sentence to explain the winter a little more? (which seemed to last forever) Now, put that clause with the first sentence and tell me what the new complex sentence is. (During the winter, which seemed to last forever, we always stayed inside the cabin.) Is this essential information for the overall meaning of the sentence? (no) We don't need to know that the winter seemed to last forever. It doesn't change the meaning of the sentence. The author included it to help the reader put him- or herself in the shoes of the character. Do we need a comma to separate the clause from the rest of the sentence? (yes) Make sure you have written the new complex sentence correctly.

Independent Practice

Have partners combine the remaining sentences. Remember to start by finding the noun that is referenced in both sentences and use the relative pronoun that is in the parentheses. Once the sentence is written, check your punctuation. If the information is essential for meaning, then you will not use commas. If it's just extra information not critical to meaning, use commas to separate it from the rest of the sentence. Review the answers as a class.

Unit 8

Lesson 3

Lesson Opener

Before the lesson, choose one of the following activities to write on the board or post on the *LANGUAGE! Live* Class Wall online.

- *Change the following verbs to adjectives (a word that answers the question* What kind?*) by adding a suffix. Then, write a sentence with each adjective.*

  froze, spoke, broke
- *Make a list of five celebrities. Write a sentence about each celebrity using a relative pronoun.*
- *Write five sentences about the portrayal of stepmothers in literature.*

Reading

Objectives

- Establish a purpose for reading literary text.
- Use critical thinking skills to write responses to prompts about text.
- Support written answers with evidence from text.
- Identify the claims and counterclaims of characters in literature.
- Cite evidence in support of a particular point.

Reading for a Purpose: "The White Wolf of the Hartz Mountains"

This time, we will be reading for a specific purpose, which will help us pay attention to details that we may have missed the first time around. Let's read some questions about the text to provide a purpose for rereading.

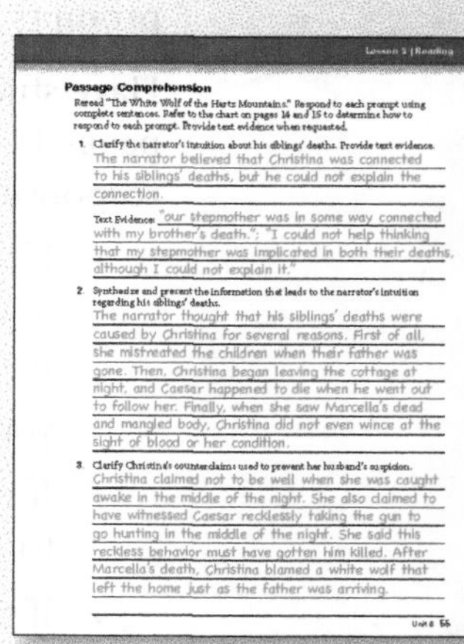

Lesson 3 | Reading

Passage Comprehension

Reread "The White Wolf of the Hartz Mountains." Respond to each prompt using complete sentences. Refer to the chart on pages 14 and 15 to determine how to respond to each prompt. Provide text evidence when requested.

1. Clarify the narrator's intuition about his siblings' deaths. Provide text evidence.
   The narrator believed that Christina was connected to his siblings' deaths, but he could not explain the connection.
   Text Evidence: "our stepmother was in some way connected with my brother's death."; "I could not help thinking that my stepmother was implicated in both their deaths, although I could not explain it."
2. Synthesize and present the information that leads to the narrator's intuition regarding his siblings' deaths.
   The narrator thought that his siblings' deaths were caused by Christina for several reasons. First of all, she mistreated the children when their father was gone. Then, Christina began leaving the cottage at night, and Caesar happened to die when he went out to follow her. Finally, when she saw Marcella's dead and mangled body, Christina did not even wince at the sight of blood or her condition.
3. Clarify Christina's counterclaims used to prevent her husband's suspicion.
   Christina claimed not to be well when she was caught awake in the middle of the night. She also claimed to have witnessed Caesar recklessly taking the gun to go hunting in the middle of the night. She said this reckless behavior must have gotten him killed. After Marcella's death, Christina blamed a white wolf that left the home just as the father was arriving.

Unit 8 55

Direct students to pages 55–57 in their Student Books. Have students read the prompts aloud with you.

1. Clarify the narrator's intuition about his siblings' deaths. Provide text evidence.
2. Synthesize and present the information that leads to the narrator's intuition regarding his siblings' deaths.
3. Clarify Christina's counterclaims used to prevent her husband's suspicion.
4. Present evidence to prove Christina's likeness to wolves.
5. Use the text to prove that werewolves exist.
6. Use the text to prove the narrator's fears at the end of the story are rational.

Direct students to page 41 in their Student Books or have them tear out the extra copy of the excerpt from the back of their book.

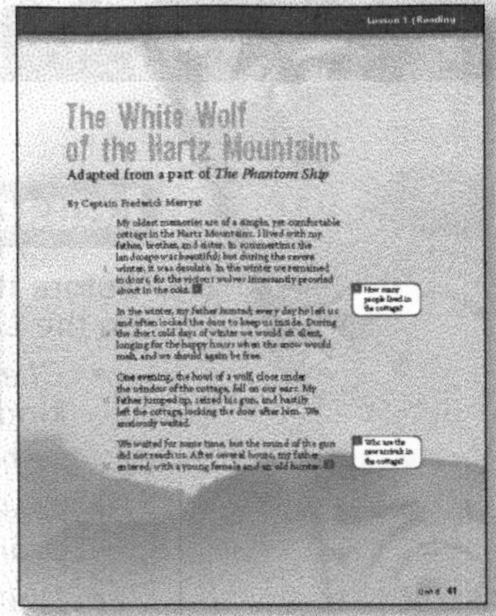
Lesson 1 | Reading

The White Wolf of the Hartz Mountains

Adapted from a part of *The Phantom Ship*

By Captain Frederick Marryat

My oldest memories are of a simple, yet comfortable cottage in the Hartz Mountains. I lived with my father, brother, and sister. In summertime the landscape was beautiful; but during the severe winter, it was desolate. In the winter we remained indoors, for the vicious wolves incessantly prowled about in the cold. 1

In the winter, my father hunted; every day he left us and often locked the door to keep us inside. During the short cold days of winter we would sit silent, longing for the happy hours when the snow would melt, and we should again be free.

One evening, the howl of a wolf, close under the window of the cottage, fell on our ears. My father jumped up, seized his gun, and hastily left the cottage, locking the door after him. We anxiously waited.

We waited for some time, but the sound of the gun did not reach us. After several hours, my father entered, with a young female and an old hunter. 2

1 How many people lived in the cottage?

2 Who are the new arrivals in the cottage?

Unit 8 41

Note: To minimize flipping back and forth between the pages, a copy of each text has been included in the back of the Student Books. Encourage students to tear this out and use it when working on activities that require the use of the text.

Choose an option for reading text. Have students read the text according to the option that you chose.

Options for reading text:

- Teacher read-aloud
- Teacher-led or student-led choral read
- Paired read or independent read with bold vocabulary words read aloud

Passage Comprehension

Write the words *clarify, present, prove,* and *synthesize* on the board. Have students read the words aloud with you.

Direct students to pages 14 and 15 in their Student Books. It is critical to understand what the question is asking and how to answer it. Today, we will review four direction words used in prompts.

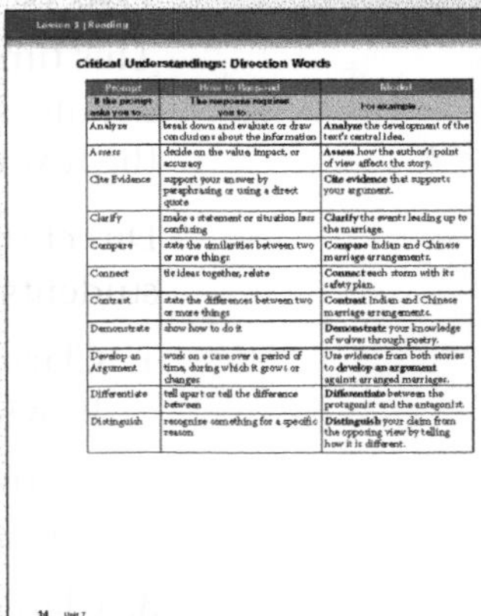
Lesson 3 | Reading

Critical Understandings: Direction Words

Prompt	How to Respond	Model
If the prompt asks you to . . .	The response requires you to . . .	For example . . .
Analyze	break down and evaluate or draw conclusions about the information	**Analyze** the development of the text's central idea.
Assess	decide on the value, impact, or accuracy	**Assess** how the author's point of view affects the story.
Cite Evidence	support your answer by paraphrasing or using a direct quote	**Cite evidence** that supports your argument.
Clarify	make a statement or situation less confusing	**Clarify** the events leading up to the marriage.
Compare	state the similarities between two or more things	**Compare** Indian and Chinese marriage arrangements.
Connect	tie ideas together, relate	**Connect** each storm with its safety plan.
Contrast	state the differences between two or more things	**Contrast** Indian and Chinese marriage arrangements.
Demonstrate	show how to do it	**Demonstrate** your knowledge of wolves through poetry.
Develop an Argument	work on a case over a period of time, during which it grows or changes	Use evidence from both stories to **develop an argument** against arranged marriages.
Differentiate	tell apart or tell the difference between	**Differentiate** between the protagonist and the antagonist.
Distinguish	recognize something for a specific reason	**Distinguish** your claim from the opposing view by telling how it is different.

14 Unit 7

Have students review the words on the board in the chart on pages 14 and 15. Check for understanding by requesting an oral response to the following questions.

- If the prompt asks you to *clarify,* the response requires you to . . . (explain it so that it is easy to understand).
- If the prompt asks you to *present,* the response requires you to . . . (deliver information).
- If the prompt asks you to *prove,* the response requires you to . . . (give evidence to show that it is true).
- If the prompt asks you to *synthesize,* the response requires you to . . . (combine information in a logical way).

Direct students to pages 55–57 in their Student Books.

Let's practice answering questions written as prompts that require critical thinking.

Lesson 3 | Reading

Passage Comprehension

Reread "The White Wolf of the Hartz Mountains." Respond to each prompt using complete sentences. Refer to the chart on pages 14 and 15 to determine how to respond to each prompt. Provide text evidence when requested.

1. Clarify the narrator's intuition about his siblings' deaths. Provide text evidence.
   The narrator believed that Christina was connected to his siblings' deaths, but he could not explain the connection.

   Text Evidence: "our stepmother was in some way connected with my brother's death."; "I could not help thinking that my stepmother was implicated in both their deaths, although I could not explain it."
2. Synthesize and present the information that leads to the narrator's intuition regarding his siblings' deaths.
   The narrator thought that his siblings' deaths were caused by Christina for several reasons. First of all, she mistreated the children when their father was gone. Then, Christina began leaving the cottage at night, and Caesar happened to die when he went out to follow her. Finally, when she saw Marcella's dead and mangled body, Christina did not even wince at the sight of blood or her condition.
3. Clarify Christina's counterclaims used to prevent her husband's suspicion.
   Christina claimed not to be well when she was caught awake in the middle of the night. She also claimed to have witnessed Caesar recklessly taking the gun to go hunting in the middle of the night. She said this reckless behavior must have gotten him killed. After Marcella's death, Christina blamed a white wolf that left the home just as the father was arriving.

Unit 8 55

Model

Listen as I model the first one for you.

1. Clarify the narrator's intuition about his siblings' deaths. Provide text evidence.

According to the chart, if the prompt asks me to *clarify,* I need to explain it so that it is easily understood.

Now, I need to turn the prompt into a question to confirm my understanding. But first, I need to figure out what *intuition* is because I am not familiar with the term. **Have a student look up the definition in a dictionary and share it with the class.**

Now that I know *intuition* means "something that is known or believed without proof," I will ask myself a basic question using the question word *what.* What did the narrator suspect that Christina was involved in?

Next, I need to look for text evidence. The text says ". . . our stepmother was in some way connected with my brother's death." and "I could not help thinking that my stepmother was implicated in both their deaths, although I could not explain it."

Write the answer on the board. Have students write the answer on their page as well as the text evidence.

The narrator believed that Christina was connected to his siblings' deaths, but he could not explain the connection.

Guided Practice

2. Synthesize and present the information that leads to the narrator's intuition regarding his siblings' deaths.

If the prompt asks you to *synthesize,* what should you do? (combine information in a logical way) And what do we do when we present? (deliver information) Let's turn the prompt into a question to confirm our understanding. If we change this to a question, what would it be? (What led to the narrator's intuition about Christina?)

Let's begin by framing our answer with some sentence starters. **Write the following sentence starters on the board.**

The narrator thought that his siblings' deaths were caused by ___________ ___________ for several reasons. First of all, ___________ ___________. Then, ___________.
Finally, ___________.

Let's take some time to find text evidence for each reason.

Lead students to the following evidence:

Line 90: "during my father's absence, she would often beat us"

Line 114: "and always at about the same hour, would our stepmother rise from her bed, and leave the cottage—and after she was gone, we invariably heard the growl of a wolf under our window, and always saw her, on her return, wash herself before she retired to bed."

Lines 129 and 166: "and as soon as our stepmother left the cottage, he jumped up, took down my father's gun, and followed her"; "In a few minutes he returned, bearing in his arms the mangled body of my poor brother"

Line 248: "but she did not appear to recoil from the sight of blood, as most women do."

Have partners answer the question.

Lesson 3 | Reading

Passage Comprehension (*cont.*)

4. Present evidence to prove Christina's likeness to wolves.

Christina had physical features like a wolf, such as a large mouth, brilliant teeth, and cruel-looking eyes. She was vicious like a wolf when she beat the kids, with eyes flashing fire, when their father was away. Christina exhibited wolf-like hunting behaviors when she left the cottage at night and snuck pieces of raw meat for her meals. During her nighttime wandering, the kids would hear a wolf howl outside their window.

5. Use the text to prove that werewolves exist.

The proof that werewolves exist is shown after Caesar went missing. Christina burned her nightclothes after returning with a gunshot wound to the leg. Christina continued to sneak out each winter night. During warmer weather, when Christina didn't sneak out, a wolf didn't growl under their window. The narrator and his father saw Christina removing stones from Marcella's grave and then eating her flesh. However, once the father shot Christina, a white wolf—not a human body—remained.

Or

Because the text is fiction, it does not provide proof of the existence of werewolves. The text is made up.

56 Unit 8

Lesson 3 | Reading

Passage Comprehension (*cont.*)

6. Use the text to prove the narrator's fears at the end of the story are rational.

The narrator's fears are rational because the father vowed that if he harmed Christina, his children would die ". . . by the vulture, by the wolf, or by other beasts of the forest." When the father killed her, the curse came to life. Marcella and Caesar had both been killed by a wolf, leaving the narrator alone to wait for his penalty.

Unit 8 57

Independent Practice

Have students respond to the remaining questions. For students who need more assistance, provide the following alternative questions and sentence starters.

Alternative questions and sentence starters:

3. What claims did Christina make to prevent her husband from getting suspicious?

   Christina claimed ____________________________________.

   She also claimed _____________________________________.

   After Marcella's death, Christina blamed ___________________________.

4. How is Christina similar to a wolf?

   Christina had physical features like a wolf, such as ________________________.

   Christina was vicious like a wolf when she ___________________________.

   Christina exhibited wolf-like hunting behaviors when she ____________________.

5. What evidence from the text supports that werewolves exist?

   The proof that werewolves exist is ___________________________________.

6. Why are the narrator's fears at the end of the story rational?

   The narrator's fears are rational because the father vowed ____.

   When the father ___________________________________, *the fear became real.*

   Marcella and Caesar had both _____________________________________, *leaving the narrator alone to wait for his penalty.*

Unit 8

Lesson 4

Lesson Opener

Before the lesson, choose one of the following activities to write on the board or post on the *LANGUAGE! Live* Class Wall online.

- *Dress your avatar as though you were hoping to convince someone to marry you. Explain your choices.*
- *Use conjunctions to write five sentences about how living in the woods is different from living in the city.*
- *Write two sentences about Christina. Combine the sentences using a relative pronoun and a relative clause.*

Reading

Objectives

- Read literature with purpose and understanding.
- Answer questions to demonstrate comprehension of text.
- Monitor comprehension of text during reading.
- Determine the impact of word choice.
- Determine how differences in character point of view create suspense.
- Identify leading questions and their intended purpose.
- Identify shifts in mood.
- Identify common religious or mythological themes in texts.
- Determine the meaning and purpose of conjunctive adverbs.
- Identify allusions to other texts in literature.

Close Reading of "The White Wolf of the Hartz Mountains"

Highlighters or colored pencils

Let's reread "The White Wolf of the Hartz Mountains." I will provide specific instructions on how to mark the text that will help with comprehension.

Have students get out a highlighter or colored pencil.

Direct students to pages 58–67 in their Student Books.

Draw a rectangle around the title, "The White Wolf of the Hartz Mountains."

Now, let's read the vocabulary words aloud.

- What's the first bold vocabulary word? (beckoned) *Beckoned* means "signaled to someone to come to you." I *beckoned* a student to come to my desk because he was misbehaving. Have partners use the word in a sentence.
- What's the next vocabulary word? (reside) *Reside* means "to live or stay in a place long-term." I *reside* in a house with my spouse and kids. Have partners use the word in a sentence.
- Next word? (conversing) *Conversing* means "talking with one or more people." Students are often late to class because they are *conversing* during passing periods. Have partners use the word in a sentence.
- Let's continue. (perish) *Perish* means "to die." The elk will *perish* when the pack of wolves arrives. Have partners use the word in a sentence.

- Next word? (resolved) *Resolved* means "made a firm decision to do something." I *resolved* to lose 10 pounds last year by exercising more often; I failed. **Have partners use the word in a sentence.**
- Let's continue. (seldom) *Seldom* means "rarely; not often." I *seldom* turn down pizza; it is my favorite food. **Have partners use the word in a sentence.**
- Next word? (rashness) *Rashness* means "a tendency to act without thinking something through." His *rashness* caused him to buy a car that he couldn't afford. **Have partners use the word in a sentence.**
- Let's continue. (implicated) *Implicated* means "thought to be involved in or guilty of something." The evidence *implicated* the stepmom of the crime. **Have partners use the word in a sentence.**
- Next word? (restored) *Restored* means "brought back; returned something to its usual state." Your recent good behavior *restored* my trust in you. **Have partners use the word in a sentence.**
- Last word. (penalty) *Penalty* means "the price you pay for breaking a rule or doing something wrong." A traffic ticket is a valid *penalty* for speeding. **Have partners use the word in a sentence.**

Talk with a partner about any vocabulary word that is still confusing for you to read consistently or understand its meaning.

You will reread "The White Wolf of the Hartz Mountains" one section at a time. After each section, you will monitor your understanding by circling the check mark if you understand the text or the question mark if you don't understand the text. I also want you to draw a question mark over any confusing words, phrases, or sentences.

Options for reading text:

- Teacher read-aloud
- Teacher-led or student-led choral read
- Paired read or independent read with bold vocabulary words read aloud

Choose an option for reading text. Have students read lines 1–12 according to the option that you chose.

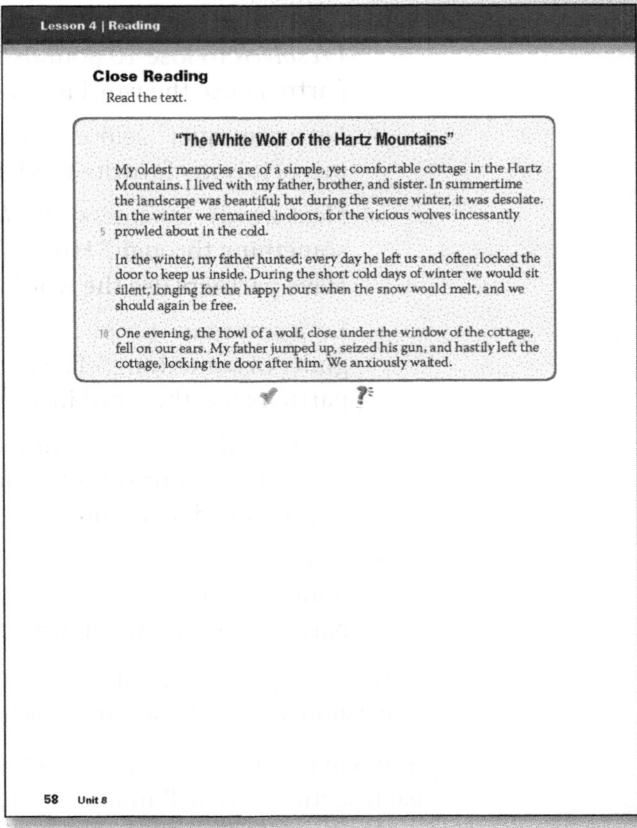

Lesson 4 | Reading

Close Reading

Read the text.

"The White Wolf of the Hartz Mountains"

My oldest memories are of a simple, yet comfortable cottage in the Hartz Mountains. I lived with my father, brother, and sister. In summertime the landscape was beautiful; but during the severe winter, it was desolate. In the winter we remained indoors, for the vicious wolves incessantly prowled about in the cold.

In the winter, my father hunted; every day he left us and often locked the door to keep us inside. During the short cold days of winter we would sit silent, longing for the happy hours when the snow would melt, and we should again be free.

One evening, the howl of a wolf, close under the window of the cottage, fell on our ears. My father jumped up, seized his gun, and hastily left the cottage, locking the door after him. We anxiously waited.

58 Unit 8

When most of the students are finished, continue with the entire class. Let's see how well you understood what you read.

- Circle the check mark or the question mark for this section. Draw a question mark over any confusing words.
- In the first paragraph, mark the words that describe the setting. (cottage, Hartz Mountains, summertime, landscape was beautiful, severe winter, desolate)
- Go to line 3. Circle the word that means "deserted; almost nothing there." (desolate)
- Go to line 4. Mark the word that means "worse than mean." (vicious)
- On the same line, mark the adverb that means "constantly, nonstop." Circle the common adverb suffix. (incessantly; -ly)
- Go to line 10. Find the word *window*. Mark what howled under the window. (wolf)
- Go to line 11. Mark the adverb that means "impulsively." (hastily) Circle the common adverb suffix. (-ly)
- Mark the evidence that the father was concerned for the safety of the children, and the children were concerned for the safety of the father. (locking the door after him; We anxiously waited.)
- Mark the words in this section that are used to describe wolves. (vicious; incessantly prowled; howl)

Have students read lines 13–40 according to the option that you chose. Pay attention to the descriptions of Christina. Mark the ways that she is beast-like when in human form. (mouth, although somewhat large; brilliant teeth; restless; sly; cruelty in her eyes)

When most of the students are finished, continue with the entire class. Let's see how well you understood what you read.

- Circle the check mark or the question mark for this section. Draw a question mark over any confusing words.
- Go to line 16. Mark the word that means "a yellowish color." (flaxen)
- In the same sentence, mark the simile that describes the female's hair. Circle the words being compared. (hair; mirror)
- Go to line 23. Mark the adverb that means "friendly." (kindly) Circle the common adverb suffix. (-ly)
- Go to line 24. Mark the transition phrase that changes directions and means "in contrast." (on the contrary)
- In the second paragraph, mark the indication that the children had a different point of view than the father. (made us children afraid; approached her with fear and trembling; Marcella would not come near her) In the margin, write why the author included this information. What mood is he trying to create? (suspense)
- In the fourth paragraph, mark the adjectives that tell why the kids were unable to sleep. (bewildered; curious)
- Go to line 32. In the margin, write a synonym for *bewildered*. (confused)
- Go to lines 34 and 35. Mark the example of personification. (Our curious ears were ready to catch the slightest whisper.)
- Go to line 37. Mark the word with the base word *converse*. (conversation)
- Mark the evidence in this section that Marcella had a sense that something wasn't right about Christina. (Marcella would not come near her; trembled and sobbed the whole night)

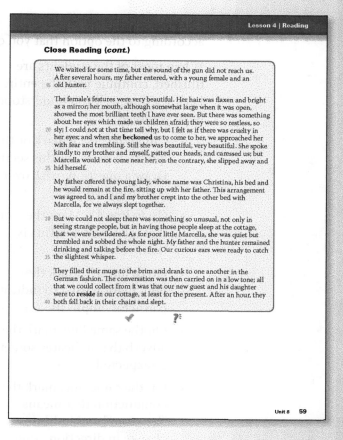

Close Reading (*cont.*)

We waited for some time, but the sound of the gun did not reach us. After several hours, my father entered, with a young female and an old hunter.

The female's features were very beautiful. Her hair was flaxen and bright as a mirror; her mouth, although somewhat large when it was open, showed the most brilliant teeth I have ever seen. But there was something about her eyes which made us children afraid; they were so restless, so sly; I could not at that time tell why, but I felt as if there was cruelty in her eyes; and when she **beckoned** us to come to her, we approached her with fear and trembling. Still she was beautiful, very beautiful. She spoke kindly to my brother and myself, patted our heads, and caressed us; but Marcella would not come near her; on the contrary, she slipped away and hid herself.

My father offered the young lady, whose name was Christina, his bed and he would remain at the fire, sitting up with her father. This arrangement was agreed to, and I and my brother crept into the other bed with Marcella, for we always slept together.

But we could not sleep; there was something so unusual, not only in seeing strange people, but in having those people sleep at the cottage, that we were bewildered. As for poor little Marcella, she was quiet but trembled and sobbed the whole night. My father and the hunter remained drinking and talking before the fire. Our curious ears were ready to catch the slightest whisper.

They filled their mugs to the brim and drank to one another in the German fashion. The conversation was then carried on in a low tone; all that we could collect from it was that our new guest and his daughter were to **reside** in our cottage, at least for the present. After an hour, they both fell back in their chairs and slept.

✔ ?

Have students read lines 41–62 according to the option that you chose.

When most of the students are finished, continue with the entire class. Let's see how well you understood what you read.

- Circle the check mark or the question mark for this section. Draw a question mark over any confusing words.
- Go to line 41. Mark the words that tell who Christina is. (hunter's daughter)
- Go to line 47. Mark the punctuation used to indicate a pause for emphasis. (em dash)
- On the same line, mark the adverb that indicates something unexpected. (even)
- On the same line, mark the conjunction that means "however" and indicates a change in direction. (but)
- Go to line 52. Mark the man who performed the marriage of Marcella's father. (hunter)
- Go to line 55. Mark the foreshadowing words in the marriage vows. (that my hand shall never be raised against her to harm her)
- Go to line 56. Mark the synonym for *revenge.* (vengeance)
- Go to line 57. Number the revengeful acts in the marriage vows. (1. perish; 2. flesh be torn; 3. bones fade in the wilderness)
- Go to line 61. Mark the synonym for *control.* (restrain)
- Go to line 62. Mark the action of Christina's father. (rode away)
- Mark the evidence in this section that Marcella had a sense that something wasn't right about Christina. (the child burst into tears and sobbed as if her heart would break; even Marcella; could not restrain herself and burst into tears)

Lesson 4 | Reading

Close Reading (*cont.*)

When we awoke the next morning, we found that the hunter's daughter had risen before us. She came up to little Marcella and caressed her; the child burst into tears and sobbed as if her heart would break.

The hunter and his daughter stayed in the cottage. My father and he went out hunting daily, leaving Christina with us. She performed all the household duties; was very kind to us children; and, gradually, we grew to like her—even Marcella. But a great change took place in my father; he was most attentive to Christina. Often, after her father and we were in bed, he would sit up with her, **conversing** in a low tone by the fire. After three weeks of this, my father asked for Christina's hand in marriage. Soon after, the wedding took place.

My father repeated his vows after the hunter. "I swear by all the spirits of the Hartz Mountains, by all their power for good or for evil, that I take Christina for my wedded wife; that I will protect her, cherish her, and love her; that my hand shall never be raised against her to harm her."

"And if I fail in this my vow, may all the vengeance of the spirits fall upon me and upon my children; may they **perish** by the vulture, by the wolf, or by other beasts of the forest; may their flesh be torn from their limbs, and their bones fade in the wilderness; all this I swear."

My father hesitated, as he repeated the last words; little Marcella could not restrain herself and burst into tears.

The next morning, the hunter mounted his horse, and rode away.

✔ ?

60 Unit 8

Have students read lines 63–89 according to the option that you chose. Pay attention to the descriptions of Christina. Mark the ways that she is beast-like when in human form. (did not show any kindness toward us; beat us; eyes would flash fire; growl; wash herself; leave the cottage; seldom sat down to meals; raw piece)

When most of the students are finished, continue with the entire class. Let's see how well you understood what you read.

- Circle the check mark or the question mark for this section. Draw a question mark over any confusing words.
- In the first paragraph, mark all the words that rename Christina. (stepmother, she, her, she)
- Go to line 64. Mark the conjunctive adverb that means "actually" and is used to connect the clauses. (indeed)
- Go to line 69. Circle *Caesar*. Draw an arrow to the word that shows his relation to Marcella. (brother)
- Go to line 74. Mark the word that literally means "not intelligible, or difficult to understand." (incomprehensible)
- Go to line 75. Mark the words that provide foreshadowing of danger. (growl of a wolf, close under the window)
- Go to line 84. Mark the adverb that means "always." (invariably) Circle the common adverb suffix. (-ly)
- Mark the two things that happened each time Christina left the cottage. (heard the growl of a wolf; washed herself)

Lesson 4 | Reading

Close Reading (*cont.*)

Things went on much as before the marriage, except that our new stepmother did not show any kindness towards us; indeed, during my father's absence, she would often beat us, particularly little Marcella, and her eyes would flash fire as she looked eagerly upon the fair and lovely child.

One night, my sister awoke me and my brother.

"What is the matter?" said Caesar.

"She has gone out," whispered Marcella.

"Gone out!"

"Yes, gone out the door, in her night-dress," replied the child. "I saw her."

What could bring her to leave the cottage, in such bitter wintry weather, was incomprehensible; we lay awake, and in about an hour we heard the growl of a wolf, close under the window.

"There is a wolf," said Caesar; "she will be torn to pieces."

A few minutes afterwards, our stepmother appeared; she was in her night-dress, as Marcella had stated. She let down the latch of the door, so as to make no noise, went to a pail of water, and washed her face and hands, and then slipped into the bed where my father lay.

We all three trembled, we hardly knew why, but we **resolved** to watch the next night. We did so—and many other nights as well, and always at about the same hour, would our stepmother rise from her bed, and leave the cottage—and after she was gone, we invariably heard the growl of a wolf under our window, and always saw her, on her return, wash herself before she retired to bed. We observed, also, that she **seldom** sat down to meals, and that when she did, she appeared to eat with dislike; but when the meat was being prepared, she would often put a raw piece into her mouth.

✔ ?

Unit 8 61

Have students read lines 90–119 according to the option that you chose.

When most of the students are finished, continue with the entire class. Let's see how well you understood what you read.

- Circle the check mark or the question mark for this section. Draw a question mark over any confusing words.
- Go to line 90. Mark the evidence that indicates Caesar didn't think their father would believe them. (My brother Caesar did not want to tell my father until he knew more.)
- Go to line 91. Mark the verb that means "figure out." (ascertain)
- Go to line 92. Mark the verb that means "discourage." (dissuade)
- On the same line, mark the word with a similar meaning. (deterred)
- Go to lines 102 and 103. Mark the lie. (I have lighted the fire to warm some water) In the margin, mark the real reason for the fire. (burn her clothes)
- Go to line 105. Mark the synonyms. (clothes, garments)
- Go to line 106. Mark the synonym for *noticed.* (perceived)
- In the next paragraph, mark the question that could be called a *leading question* because its intent is to make somebody take notice of something or think something specific. (Father, where is my brother, Caesar?) What does the narrator intend to do with this question? (get Christina caught)
- Go down a few lines and mark another leading question. (dear husband, what has become of your gun?) What does Christina intend to do with this question? (trick the father into thinking Caesar is to blame)
- Go to line 118. Mark the word that means "confused." (perplexed)

Lesson 4 | Reading

Close Reading (*cont.*)

My brother Caesar did not want to tell my father until he knew more. He resolved to follow her out and ascertain what she did. Marcella and I tried to dissuade him; but he would not be deterred, and the very next night he lay down in his clothes, and as soon as our stepmother left the cottage, he jumped up, took down my father's gun, and followed her.

Marcella and I waited in suspense. After a few minutes, we heard the sound of a gun. It did not awaken my father, and we lay trembling with anxiety. In a minute afterwards, we saw our stepmother enter the cottage—her dress was bloody. I put my hand to Marcella's mouth to prevent her crying out, although I was myself in great alarm. Our stepmother looked to see if our father was asleep, and then started a fire.

"Who is there?" said my father, waking up.

"Lie still, dearest," replied my stepmother, "it is only me; I have lighted the fire to warm some water; I am not quite well."

My father turned round and was soon asleep, but we watched our stepmother. She changed her clothes and threw the garments she had worn into the fire; and we then perceived that her right leg was bleeding, as if from a gun-shot wound. She bandaged it up and dressed herself.

Poor little Marcella, her heart beat quick as she pressed me to her side—so indeed did mine. Where was our brother, Caesar? How did my stepmother receive the wound unless from his gun? At last my father rose, and then, for the first time I spoke, saying, "Father, where is my brother, Caesar?"

"Your brother!" exclaimed he, "why, where can he be?"

"Merciful Heaven! I thought as I lay very restless last night," observed our stepmother, "that I heard somebody open the latch of the door; and dear husband, what has become of your gun?"

My father cast his eyes up above the chimney, and perceived that his gun was missing. For a moment he looked perplexed, then seizing an axe, he went out of the cottage without saying another word.

62 Unit 8

Have students read lines 120–141 according to the option that you chose.

When most of the students are finished, continue with the entire class. Let's see how well you understood what you read.

- Circle the check mark or the question mark for this section. Draw a question mark over any confusing words.
- Go to line 121. Mark the synonym for *carrying.* (bearing)
- Go to line 124. Circle "its side." Draw a line to show what *it* is referring to. (the body)
- On the same line, mark the adverb that means "with resentment." (bitterly) Circle the common adverb suffix. (-ly)
- Go to line 125. Mark the adverb that means "harshly." (sharply) Circle the common adverb suffix. (-ly)
- In the fourth paragraph, mark the evidence that Marcella is afraid of losing another brother. (I wished to tell all, but Marcella, who saw my intention, held my arm, and looked at me so imploringly, that I stopped.)
- Go to line 129. Circle the adverb that describes a desperate, begging way. (imploringly)
- Go to line 131. Mark the synonym for *understand.* (comprehend)
- Mark the word in this section that is used to describe wolves. (villainous)
- Go to line 138. Mark the word meaning "sadness" that is a homophone for a specific time of day. (mourning)
- On the same line, mark the adjective that is a synonym for *nighttime.* (nocturnal)

Lesson 4 | Reading

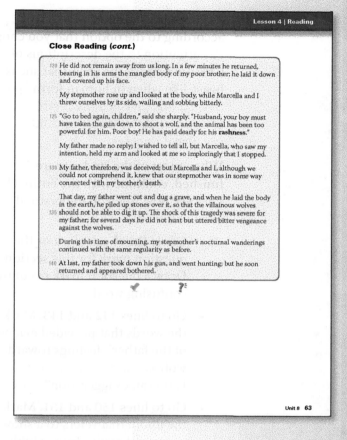

Close Reading (*cont.*)

He did not remain away from us long. In a few minutes he returned, bearing in his arms the mangled body of my poor brother; he laid it down and covered up his face.

My stepmother rose up and looked at the body, while Marcella and I threw ourselves by its side, wailing and sobbing bitterly.

"Go to bed again, children," said she sharply. "Husband, your boy must have taken the gun down to shoot a wolf, and the animal has been too powerful for him. Poor boy! He has paid dearly for his **rashness.**"

My father made no reply; I wished to tell all, but Marcella, who saw my intention, held my arm and looked at me so imploringly that I stopped.

My father, therefore, was deceived; but Marcella and I, although we could not comprehend it, knew that our stepmother was in some way connected with my brother's death.

That day, my father went out and dug a grave, and when he laid the body in the earth, he piled up stones over it, so that the villainous wolves should not be able to dig it up. The shock of this tragedy was severe for my father; for several days he did not hunt but uttered bitter vengeance against the wolves.

During this time of mourning, my stepmother's nocturnal wanderings continued with the same regularity as before.

At last, my father took down his gun, and went hunting; but he soon returned and appeared bothered.

✔ ?

Unit 8 63

Have students read lines 142–161 according to the option that you chose. Pay attention to the descriptions of Christina. Mark the ways that she is beast-like when in human form. (eyes flashed fire; gnashed her teeth; pleasure in ill-treating the child; nocturnal rambles)

When most of the students are finished, continue with the entire class. Let's see how well you understood what you read.

- Circle the check mark or the question mark for this section. Draw a question mark over any confusing words.
- Go to lines 142 and 143. Mark the words that provided evidence of the father's feelings toward wolves. (most evil of all animals) Is this an exaggeration? (yes)
- Go to lines 150 and 151. Mark the idiom that refers to a show of anger and comes from a biblical reference to evil. (gnashed her teeth)
- In the sixth paragraph, mark all the pronouns and references to Marcella. (my dear little sister; whom; her; the child) Write her name in the margin.
- Go to line 156. Mark the synonym for *abusing.* (ill-treating)
- Go to line 160. Mark the phrase that means "nighttime wanderings." (nocturnal rambles)

Lesson 4 | Reading

Close Reading (*cont.*)

"Would you believe it, Christina, that the wolves—most evil of all animals—have actually dug up the body of my poor boy, and now there is nothing left of him but his bones?"

Marcella looked at me, and I saw in her intelligent eyes all she would have uttered.

"A wolf growls under our window every night, father," said I.

"Really?—why did you not tell me, boy?—wake me the next time you hear it."

I saw my stepmother turn away; her eyes flashed fire, and she gnashed her teeth.

The spring finally came. The snow disappeared, and we were permitted to leave the cottage; but never would I leave, for one moment, my dear little sister, to whom, since the death of my brother, I was more attached than ever. I was afraid to leave her alone with my stepmother, who appeared to have a particular pleasure in ill-treating the child. My father was now working his little farm, and I was able to assist him.

Marcella used to sit by us while we were at work, leaving my stepmother alone in the cottage. As spring advanced, my stepmother decreased her nocturnal rambles, and we never heard the growl of the wolf under the window after I had spoken of it to my father.

✔ ?

64 Unit 8

Have students read lines 162–193 according to the option that you chose. Pay attention to the descriptions of Christina. Mark the way that she is beast-like when in human form. (did not appear to recoil from the sight of blood)

When most of the students are finished, continue with the entire class. Let's see how well you understood what you read.

- Circle the check mark or the question mark for this section. Draw a question mark over any confusing words.
- In the first paragraph, mark the way Christina was able to finally get Marcella alone. (saying that she was going into the forest to collect some herbs my father wanted, and that Marcella must go to the cottage and watch the dinner)

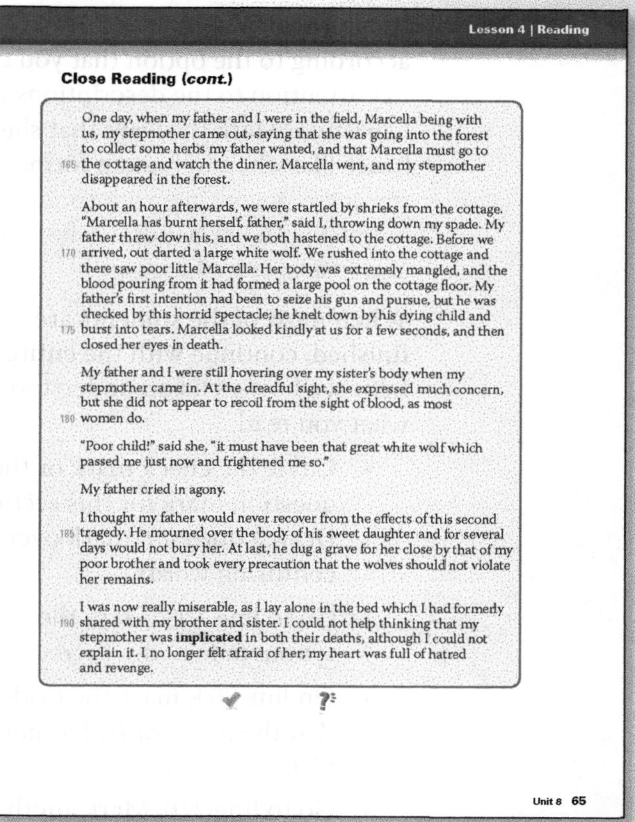

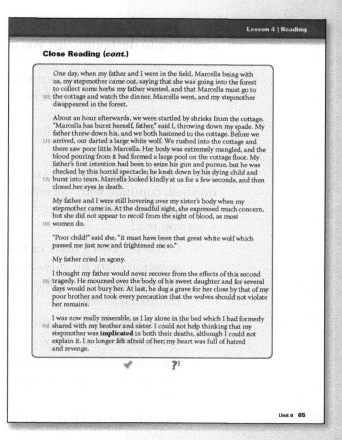

Close Reading (*cont.*)

One day, when my father and I were in the field, Marcella being with us, my stepmother came out, saying that she was going into the forest to collect some herbs my father wanted, and that Marcella must go to the cottage and watch the dinner. Marcella went, and my stepmother disappeared in the forest.

About an hour afterwards, we were startled by shrieks from the cottage. "Marcella has burnt herself, father," said I, throwing down my spade. My father threw down his, and we both hastened to the cottage. Before we arrived, out darted a large white wolf. We rushed into the cottage and there saw poor little Marcella. Her body was extremely mangled, and the blood pouring from it had formed a large pool on the cottage floor. My father's first intention had been to seize his gun and pursue, but he was checked by this horrid spectacle; he knelt down by his dying child and burst into tears. Marcella looked kindly at us for a few seconds, and then closed her eyes in death.

My father and I were still hovering over my sister's body when my stepmother came in. At the dreadful sight, she expressed much concern, but she did not appear to recoil from the sight of blood, as most women do.

"Poor child!" said she, "it must have been that great white wolf which passed me just now and frightened me so."

My father cried in agony.

I thought my father would never recover from the effects of this second tragedy. He mourned over the body of his sweet daughter and for several days would not bury her. At last, he dug a grave for her close by that of my poor brother and took every precaution that the wolves should not violate her remains.

I was now really miserable, as I lay alone in the bed which I had formerly shared with my brother and sister. I could not help thinking that my stepmother was **implicated** in both their deaths, although I could not explain it. I no longer felt afraid of her; my heart was full of hatred and revenge.

✔ ?

- Go to line 167. Mark the word that means "high-pitched screams." (shrieks)
- Go to line 168. Mark the reflexive pronoun used because the subject and direct object are the same. (herself)
- Go to line 169. Mark the synonym for *rushed.* (hastened)
- Go to line 170. Mark the proof that Christina was almost caught. (Before we arrived, out darted a large white wolf.)
- Go to line 171. Mark the two adjectives that are next to each other but not separated by a comma. (poor; little) If you insert *and* between these adjectives, the meaning would change. Therefore, they are not coordinate adjectives and do not require the use of a comma.
- Go to line 173. Mark the synonym for *chase.* (pursue)
- Go to line 174. Use context to mark the word that means "stopped." (checked)
- Go to line 179. Mark the synonym for *turn away.* (recoil)
- Go to line 183. Mark the synonym for *intense pain.* (agony)
- Go to line 187. Mark the word that means "action to avoid danger." (precaution) Circle the prefix that means "before." (pre-)
- On the same line, mark the word that means "bother or disrespect." (violate)

Have students read lines 194–217 according to the option that you chose.

Pay attention to the descriptions of Christina. Mark the ways that she is beast-like when in human form. (ferocity; devouring; viciousness; digging with her hands; on her hands and knees; crouching)

When most of the students are finished, continue with the entire class.

Let's see how well you understood what you read.

- Circle the check mark or the question mark for this section. Draw a question mark over any confusing words.
- Go to line 198. Mark the synonym for *saw.* (perceived)
- On line 204, mark the evidence that the narrator had a specific plan. (get your gun)
- Go to line 210. Mark another synonym for *saw.* (beheld)
- Go to line 213. Mark the word that means "ferocity." (viciousness)
- Go to line 216. Mark the synonym for *anger.* (rage)
- On the same line, mark the synonym for *liveliness.* (vigor)
- Go to line 217. Mark the word used in place of Christina. (wretch) Circle the winner, and mark an X through the loser. (he; the wretch) At this point in the story, a common mythological and religious theme occurs. What is that theme? (good triumphs over evil) Write the answer in the margin.
- Mark the single sentence on this page that is in the imperative (or commanding) mood. (Dress yourself, and get your gun.) Is the comma in this sentence necessary or unnecessary? (necessary) Why? (Both clauses can stand alone as complete sentences.) Because they are imperative sentences, or commands, they don't need a subject—the subject is implied. Therefore, each one has a subject and a verb.

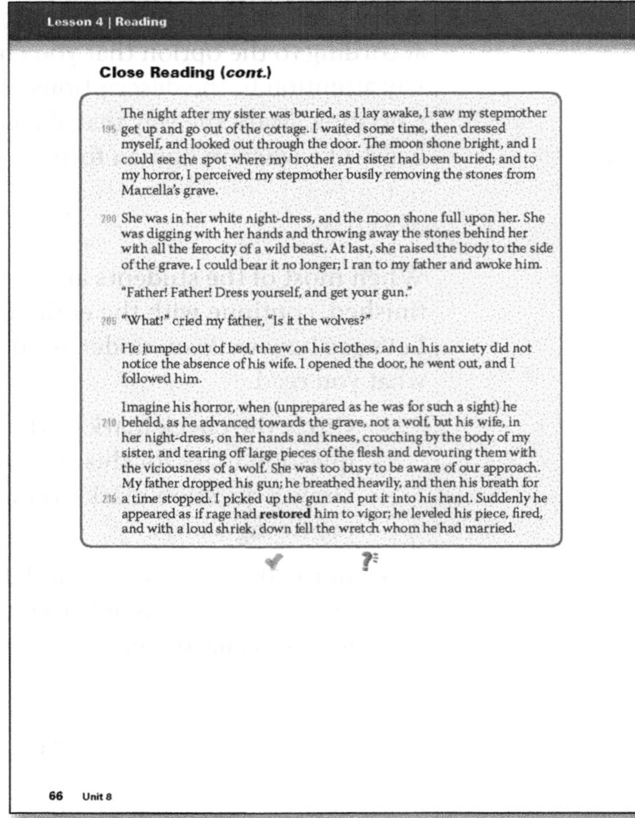

Lesson 4 | Reading

Close Reading (*cont.*)

The night after my sister was buried, as I lay awake, I saw my stepmother get up and go out of the cottage. I waited some time, then dressed myself, and looked out through the door. The moon shone bright, and I could see the spot where my brother and sister had been buried; and to my horror, I perceived my stepmother busily removing the stones from Marcella's grave.

She was in her white night-dress, and the moon shone full upon her. She was digging with her hands and throwing away the stones behind her with all the ferocity of a wild beast. At last, she raised the body to the side of the grave. I could bear it no longer; I ran to my father and awoke him.

"Father! Father! Dress yourself, and get your gun."

"What!" cried my father, "Is it the wolves?"

He jumped out of bed, threw on his clothes, and in his anxiety did not notice the absence of his wife. I opened the door, he went out, and I followed him.

Imagine his horror, when (unprepared as he was for such a sight) he beheld, as he advanced towards the grave, not a wolf, but his wife, in her night-dress, on her hands and knees, crouching by the body of my sister, and tearing off large pieces of the flesh and devouring them with the viciousness of a wolf. She was too busy to be aware of our approach. My father dropped his gun; he breathed heavily, and then his breath for a time stopped. I picked up the gun and put it into his hand. Suddenly he appeared as if rage had **restored** him to vigor; he leveled his piece, fired, and with a loud shriek, down fell the wretch whom he had married.

✔ ?

66 Unit 8

Have students read from line 218 to the end according to the option that you chose.

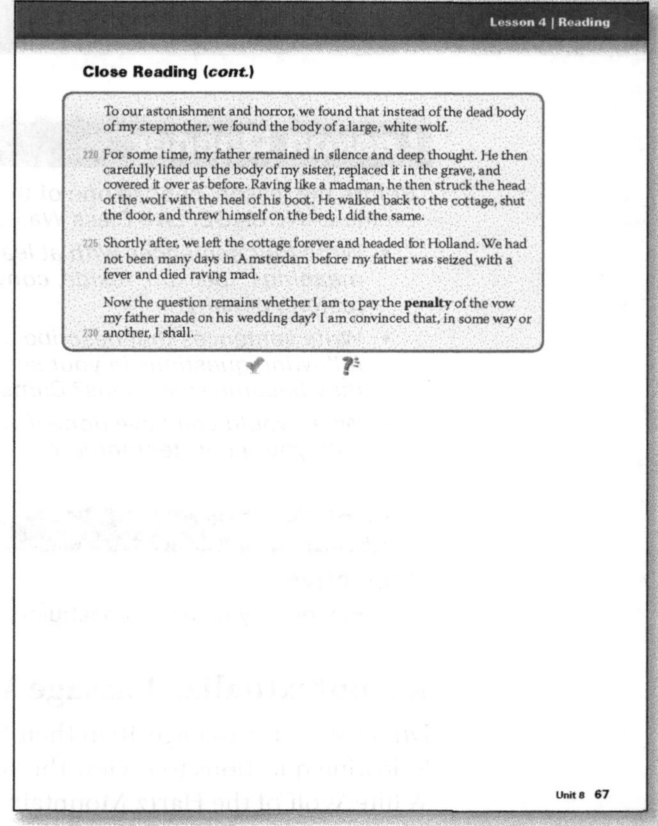

Lesson 4 | Reading

Close Reading (*cont.*)

To our astonishment and horror, we found that instead of the dead body of my stepmother, we found the body of a large, white wolf.

For some time, my father remained in silence and deep thought. He then carefully lifted up the body of my sister, replaced it in the grave, and covered it over as before. Raving like a madman, he then struck the head of the wolf with the heel of his boot. He walked back to the cottage, shut the door, and threw himself on the bed; I did the same.

Shortly after, we left the cottage forever and headed for Holland. We had not been many days in Amsterdam before my father was seized with a fever and died raving mad.

Now the question remains whether I am to pay the **penalty** of the vow my father made on his wedding day? I am convinced that, in some way or another, I shall.

Unit 8 67

When most of the students are finished, continue with the entire class. Let's see how well you understood what you read.

- Circle the check mark or the question mark for this section. Draw a question mark over any confusing words.
- Go to line 218. Mark the synonym for *bewilderment.* (astonishment)
- On the same line, mark the word that means "in its place." (instead)
- On lines 218 and 219, mark the keystone piece of evidence that the stepmother was indeed a werewolf. (instead of the dead body of my stepmother, we found the body of a large, white wolf) Circle the coordinate adjectives separated by a comma. (large; white) They equally modify the noun.
- Go to line 220. Mark the word that means "stayed." (remained)
- Go to lines 226 and 227. Mark the evidence that the father was cursed. (my father was seized with a fever and died raving mad)
- In the last two paragraphs, the mood shifts from the indicative, to the interrogative, to the subjunctive. This change in mood has been done with verb use. Underline a sentence that is in the indicative (or factual) mood. (. . . my father was seized with a fever and died raving mad) Underline a sentence that is in the interrogative (or questioning) mood. (. . . whether I am to pay the penalty of the vow my father made on his wedding day) Underline a sentence that is in the subjunctive (or hypothetical/imaginary) mood. (I am convinced that, in some way or another, I shall.)
- Based on the author's word choice to describe Christina, how do you think he felt about stepmothers in general? Do you think telling the story of the white wolf was for entertainment or to metaphorically describe all stepmothers? **Have students write their opinions in the margin.**
- Myths and epic tales often tell circle stories by circling back to a place from the beginning of the story at the end of the story. Mark the evidence that this is a circle story. (. . . the vow my father made)

Have partners compare text markings and correct any errors.

Unit 8

Lesson 5

Lesson Opener

Before the lesson, choose one of the following activities to write on the board or post on the *LANGUAGE! Live* Class Wall online.

- *Write four sentences with at least two vocabulary words in each. Show you know the meanings. (beckon, reside, converse, perish, resolve, seldom, rashness, implicated, restore, penalty)*
- *Write sentences that describe the children's suspicions of Christina. Answer the following questions in your sentences. When do they become suspicious? Why do they become suspicious? Combine the sentences into one Masterpiece Sentence.*
- *What would you have done if you were Marcella and sensed something was wrong with your new stepmother?*

Vocabulary

Objective

- Review key passage vocabulary.

Recontextualize Passage Vocabulary

Direct students to page 40 in their Student Books. Use the following questions to review the vocabulary words in "The White Wolf of the Hartz Mountains."

- Your sister accuses you of using her favorite lotion, Seascape. You do smell like a tropical breeze. Are you *implicated*? (yes) Someone dug a hole under the fence. Rover's paws are caked with dirt. Is Rover *implicated*? (yes) A group of students yarn-bomb the school. The knitting club is automatically what? (implicated)
- If a piece of silver jewelry is tarnished, you can use toothpaste to polish it. Will cleaning it with toothpaste *restore* its shine? (yes) You asked your cousin to dye your hair, but you hate the color. Will a quick shampoo *restore* your original color? (no) Some people make smoothies with leafy green vegetables and egg whites. They say these drinks boost their energy. What do the drinks do? (restore their energy)
- It takes you a week to decide whether you want to buy a friend's skateboard, but by then he's sold it to someone else. Is your *rashness* to blame? (no) You blurt out some gossip about a friend and then realize she's standing right behind you. The friendship ends. Is your *rashness* to blame? (yes) On the spur of the moment, you agree to help decorate the gym for a dance. When you arrive, you discover you're the only person on the decoration committee. What do you regret? (my rashness in agreeing to help)
- You live with your grandmother. Do you *reside* with her? (yes) You write a blog about places you hope to visit someday. Do you *reside* in those places? (no) Your dad insists that all the tools get stored in the toolbox when they aren't being used. If you asked him, he would say that the tools should what? (reside in the toolbox)

- Your friend is giving you a strange look from across the room. Is he *beckoning* you? (no) The crossing guard waves you forward across the street. Is she *beckoning* you? (yes) Beckon to a student. What am I doing to [name]? (beckoning him/her)
- You've overslept every day this week. Should you *resolve* to wake up on time tomorrow? (yes) You ask your sister to help pack the lunches, but she ignores you. Has she *resolved* to help? (no) You're tired of all the terrible shows on TV. You decide to become a producer and make better shows available. What do you do? (resolve to make better TV shows)
- You hang out in the front office because you like chatting with the secretary. Do you *converse* with her? (yes) When you see a certain person coming down the hallway, you turn and go the other direction. Do you want to *converse*? (no) Your friend likes someone from afar. What do you advise him to do before he decides if he really likes her? (converse with her)
- You can't walk by a piece of litter without picking it up and throwing it away. Do you *seldom* pass up a piece of trash? (yes) Your brother washes his hands 10 times a day. Does he *seldom* wash his hands? (no) Your mom makes her famous tamales only once a year. How often does she make them? (seldom)
- If you yell at the umpire on the baseball field, will you receive a *penalty*? (probably) If you help an elderly neighbor carry her groceries inside, will you receive a *penalty*? (no) If you don't e-mail an essay to your teacher by 4:00 p.m., it will be docked a letter grade. You e-mail your paper at 3:58. What have you narrowly avoided? (the penalty)
- You leave a potted plant on the front stoop overnight, and temperatures drop into the teens. Does the plant *perish*? (probably) If you say you want to get a tattoo and your mom says, "*Perish* the thought," what does she want you to do with that thought? (Let it die; stop having it.) You're playing a video game called Instant Death. What do you suppose will happen if you make a wrong move? (I will perish instantly.)

Writing

Objectives

- Write an analysis of the use of foreshadowing in "The White Wolf of the Hartz Mountains."
- Identify how an author's choice of words is used to create suspense.

Quick Write in Response to Reading

Direct students to page 68 in their Student Books. Read the prompt aloud. This selection has been written from the first-person point of view. The author uses the narrator to give us clues about Christina's true nature. Some details are obvious and others are more subtle, but authors rarely include random details. In this case, all of the details that have been provided paint a dark picture of the children's stepmother. Look at your close reading and pull out three details that you used as a reader to build your impression of Christina.

Have students complete the Quick Write in Response to Reading.

Lesson 5 | Writing

Quick Write in Response to Reading Answers will vary.

Authors often include clues about how the story will unfold and how characters will develop. In this text, the details provided by the narrator cause the reader to distrust Christina and suspect her true identity. Write a paragraph that describes three examples of foreshadowing and how that helped you determine Christina's true nature.

In "The White Wolf of the Hartz Mountains," the narrator shares details that lead the reader to suspect Christina's true nature. He includes descriptions of her physical appearance, deliberate actions, and unusual reactions. In describing her physical appearance, he speaks of her beauty but includes "her mouth, although somewhat large when it was open, showed the most brilliant teeth I have ever seen." In spite of her beauty, there was "something about her eyes which made us children afraid." Additionally, her actions make the reader suspicious. While the father remained oblivious to her behavior, we learn that she secretly ventured outside at night and returned unharmed by "vicious wolves" that prowled the forest. Also, her unusual eating habits kept her from enjoying traditionally prepared meals, but "when meat was being prepared, she would often put a raw piece in her mouth." In addition to her unusual behavior, her reactions to certain situations alarmed the narrator. Determined to find the wolf that was growling beneath their window, their father implored them to awaken him the next time they heard it. Christina's reactions showed her displeasure. The narrator saw her "turn away; her eyes flashed fire, and she gnashed her teeth." While Christina expressed concern over Marcella's gruesome death, "she did not appear to recoil from the sight of blood, as most women do." The foreshadowing in the text well prepares the reader for the eventual discovery of Christina's true identity and her inevitable death.

68 Unit 8

Reading

Objectives

- Self-correct as comprehension of text deepens.
- Engage in class discussion.
- Identify the enduring understandings from a piece of text.
- Objectively summarize literary text.
- Determine the theme of a story.
- Determine how the theme is developed over the course of a text.
- Analyze the effect characters have on the theme.
- Identify the author's point of view.
- Identify common conventions of a tale.

Revisit Passage Comprehension

Direct students back to pages 55–57 in their Student Books. Have students review their answers and make any necessary changes. Then, have partners share their answers and collaborate to perfect them.

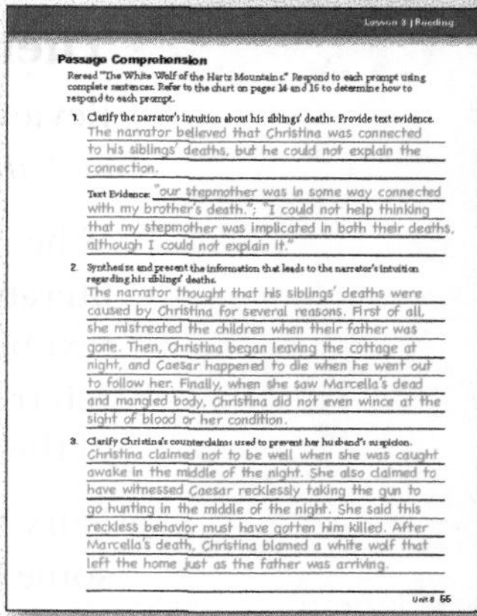

Enduring Understandings

Direct students back to page 39 in their Student Books. Reread the Big Idea questions.

To what degree is the proverb "love is blind" true? Explain.

Do humans have the ability to know things that cannot be known by normal use of the senses? Do animals? Explain.

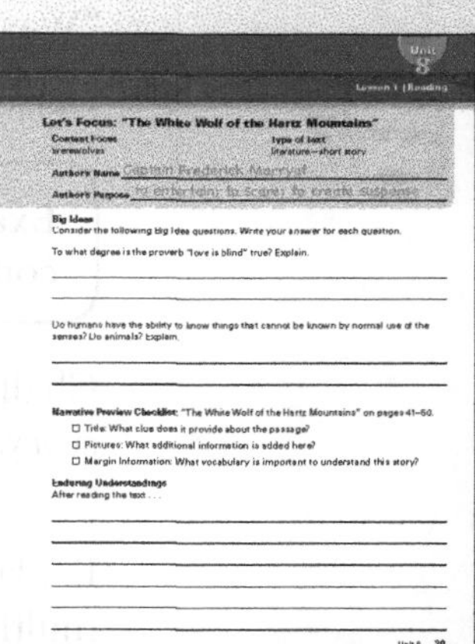

Generate a class discussion about the questions and the answers students came up with in Lesson 1. Have them consider whether their answers have changed any after reading the text.

Use the following talking points to foster conversation. Then, have students write their enduring understandings from the unit.

- Emotions play a huge role in our lives. An old proverb states that "love is blind." Some people are accused of wearing "rose-colored glasses" because they don't want to see the negative. Can emotions cloud our thinking and make it impossible for us to really "see"? Is that what happened to the father in this story?
- Some people believe in werewolves. Some people believe in metaphorical werewolves—or that people have the ability to transform (though not in the physical sense) when anger or other extreme emotions come into play. Is this possible?

- In the story, Marcella seemed to have a "gut feeling," or an intuition, about Christina. The father obviously didn't see it. Is it possible that humans are gifted with abilities such as these? What about animals?

What we read should make us think. Use our discussion and your thoughts about the text to determine what you will "walk away with." Has it made you think about a personal experience or someone you know? Has your perspective or opinion on a specific topic changed? Do you have any lingering thoughts or questions? Write these ideas as your enduring understandings. What will you take with you from this text?

Discuss the enduring understandings with the class. If time permits, have students post a personal response about their enduring understandings to the online class wall.

Remind students to consider why the author wrote the passage and whether he was successful.

Theme

Review the central ideas of "The Circuit" and the excerpts from *The Play of the Diary of Anne Frank, The Autobiography of Malcolm X,* and *Breaking Night.*

When we read informational text, we find the central idea, but when we read literature, we find the theme. *Theme* is similar to the central idea of an informational text because it can be applied to multiple texts and is universal. A theme is often referred to as the lesson or what the reader learns from reading the text (or the moral of the story)—especially in a fairy tale or a myth.

Fairy tales, fables, and many of the movies we watch have similar themes. What are some lessons that you have learned in stories or movies? Generate a class discussion of proverbs or general rules for life, such as "Treat others as you'd like to be treated," "Waste not, want not," etc.

Discuss the theme of a well-known fairy tale or story that students will relate to.

> **Example:** *The Tortoise and the Hare*—steady and consistent wins the race; pride comes before the fall.

Challenge students to look back at *Thank You, M'am* and determine the theme of the story. (Offering kindness to an undeserving person can have transforming results; everyone deserves a second chance; get to know someone before passing judgment.)

Explain that theme, like central idea, is often subjective, and one text can have multiple themes.

Draw a story map on the board.

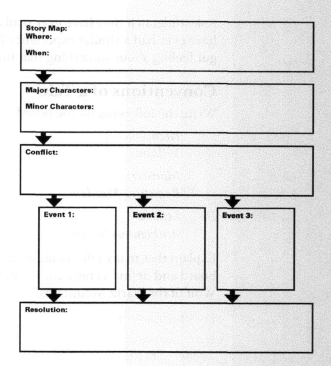

Story Map:		
Where:		
When:		
Major Characters:		
Minor Characters:		
Conflict:		
Event 1:	Event 2:	Event 3:
Resolution:		

As students answer the following questions, complete the map. Let's review the elements of literary text before we focus on theme. What are the elements of literary text? (characters, setting, problem and solution)

What is the setting of "The White Wolf of the Hartz Mountains"? (Germany, forest, cottage, Hartz Mountains)

Who are the main characters? (narrator; Marcella; Caesar; father; Christina; hunter)

What is the conflict? (the evil stepmother mistreats the children)

What is the resolution? (kill the werewolf stepmother)

Have students identify three major events that happened between the conflict and the resolution. Now, let's think about theme—or what we learned from the text. Remember, the theme is universal and can be applied to many other stories as well.

The theme usually develops over the course of a text. In fact, as you progress through a story, the theme will likely change as the plot changes. Sometimes the theme is easier to find if you summarize the passage. We will do that together—objectively.

As a class, summarize "The White Wolf of the Hartz Mountains" on the board. (A father and three children live alone in the woods. The father vows, under penalty of a curse, never to harm a strange woman when he makes her his wife. She mistreats his children and causes them to fear her. She exhibits behaviors known only to wild animals. The father remains ignorant of all this. After the mysterious deaths of two of his children, the father is made aware that the stepmother is the murderer. Upon killing the stepmother, he discovers she was indeed a werewolf. The father soon dies, as the curse stipulated, and the narrator is left wondering if he too will fall victim to the curse of the Hartz Mountains.)

As you can see, as the story progressed, the lesson or theme changed. It isn't until the end of the text that the father sees Christina for what she is and then dies himself. The theme can also be affected by the characters' traits. The father was seemingly lonely living without a wife in a desolate forest. He was unable to see the bad in Christina and married her after only a short time. Marcella distrusted her and was afraid of her from the moment she laid eyes on her. The father promised to never forsake Christina without even knowing her true self. What is the theme or lesson of this passage? (Impulsive decisions come back to bite you; trust your instincts; if it seems too good to be true, it probably is.) As you can see, both the father's and Marcella's character traits affected the theme.

Ask students if they have ever read a passage with a similar theme. Ask them if they have ever had a similar experience in which they made an impulsive decision or had a gut feeling about something that turned out to be correct.

Conventions of a Tale

Write the following on the board:

Hero:
Villain:

Monster:
Beautiful Maiden:

Lesson:
Ambiguous Setting:

Explain that many tales contain similar elements. Discuss each of the elements on the board and define as needed. Then, have students identify the elements in "The White Wolf of the Hartz Mountains."

Possible Answers:

Hero: narrator; father
Villain: Christina or her father

Monster: werewolf
Beautiful Maiden: Christina; Marcella

Lesson: Impulsive decisions come back to bite you; trust your instincts; never trust a beautiful woman
Ambiguous Setting: mountains; forest; seasons with no specified time

Point of View

We already talked about this text being written from the first-person point of view. That is one definition of point of view. Now, we are going to talk about another definition.

Every author has a purpose for writing. Sometimes an author's voice is neutral, and as a reader, you are not sure how the author feels about the topic. Most of the time, however, you can get a sense of the author's point of view. It expresses an opinion or offers an argument.

Authors use carefully chosen language to paint the picture they want the reader to "see." And they usually have a clear purpose for writing. Their point of view, or opinion, can often dictate how and what they write.

Based on what I've shared so far, how would you define "point of view"?

Write the following definition on the board:

Point of view: opinion or way of looking at something; in writing, it influences the way events are described and how characters act.

We are going to focus on the author's point of view of wolves. The author's point of view is readily apparent. Does he think wolves are good or bad? (bad) Use your Close Reading on pages 58–67 to determine the author's point of view of wolves. (evil, cruel, villainous) Keep this in mind as we continue the unit and read the second text.

Lesson 6

Lesson Opener

Before the lesson, choose one of the following activities to write on the board or post on the *LANGUAGE! Live* Class Wall online.

- *Make a list of five people you know at school. Write a sentence about each person using a relative pronoun.*
- *Describe a time when you were misunderstood. What did you do about it?*
- *Write one sentence about social studies class. Write one sentence about science class. Combine the sentences using a subordinating conjunction.*

Reading

Objectives

- Determine and discuss the topic of a text.
- Determine and discuss the author's purpose.
- Use text features to preview text.

Passage Introduction

Direct students to page 69 in their Student Books. Discuss the content focus.

Content Focus

man's impact on the environment
learning from nature, others, and mistakes

In this lesson, we will learn more about wolves. However, at a deeper level, we will learn about the importance of respecting nature without being selfish about our own needs. Finally, by digging deep, you will learn the importance of considering others' points of view before your own.

Type of Text

literature—legend

Text can be literature or informational. What are the two categories of literature? (fiction and nonfiction) What does *nonfiction* mean? (not fiction, not fake, real to life) What does *fiction* mean? (not true, made-up story) We will read a legend. Do you think it is fiction or nonfiction? First, we have to recall the meaning of *legend*. What is a legend? **Discuss responses.** A legend is considered fiction, but it is based in fact. The word *legend*, which literally means "to read," comes from Latin. The Latin word was originally limited to written stories. In English, a legend lives on in the stories that

Lesson 6 | Reading

Let's Focus: *Who Speaks for Wolf: A Native American Learning Story*

Content Focus
man's impact on the environment
learning from nature, others, mistakes

Type of Text
literature—fiction: legend, learning story

Author's Name Paula Underwood

Author's Purpose to teach others to respect the environment and learn from others

Big Ideas
Consider the following Big Idea questions. Write your answer for each question.

What impact do humans have on the environment?

What does "Just because you can, doesn't mean you should" mean to you?

Narrative Preview Checklist: *Who Speaks for Wolf* on pages 71–87.

- ☐ Title: What clue does it provide?
- ☐ Pictures: What additional information is added here?
- ☐ Margin Information: What vocabulary is important to understand this story?
- ☐ Features: What other text features do you notice?
- ☐ Form: What do you notice about the text's shape, layout, font, and punctuation?

Enduring Understandings
After reading the text . . .

Unit 8 69

people tell each other. Often times, a legend includes imaginative material that makes the story seem larger than life. So, what's a legend? Fiction or nonfiction? (fiction)

Author's Purpose

Have students glance at the text. Who is the author of the text? (Paula Underwood) Every author has a purpose for writing. Sometimes an author's voice is neutral, and as a reader, you are not sure how the author feels about the topic. Most of the time, however, you can get a sense of the author's point of view. It expresses an opinion or offers an argument. Authors use carefully chosen language to paint the picture they want the reader to "see." They usually have a clear purpose for writing. Their point of view, or opinion, can often dictate how and what they write. Based on what I've shared so far, how would you define "point of view"? **Provide sharing time. Have students fill in the Author's Purpose on their student page.**

Background Knowledge

Who Speaks for Wolf is subtitled *A Native American Learning Story.* The author cited her ancestors as believing ". . . learning is so valuable . . . that it is therefore sacred." This story has been told year after year, generation after generation. This story is ageless and can be read or retold on multiple levels. This book was designed to make you think, understand, consider, and remember, regardless of your age. Each time you read this authentic story, you may think of different questions or reveal new meanings. Eventually, you will see that asking the question "Who speaks for Wolf?" can be used as a springboard to look for new ways to solve a variety of problems.

Big Ideas

Read the Big Idea questions aloud.

> **Big Ideas**
>
> What impact do humans have on the environment?
>
> What does "Just because you can, doesn't mean you should" mean to you?

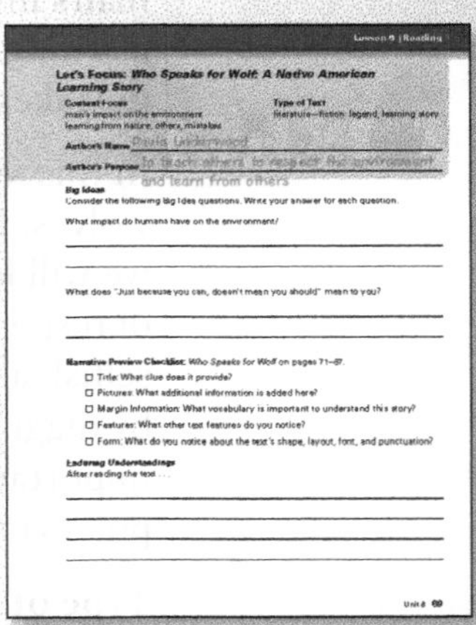

Let's Focus: *Who Speaks for Wolf: A Native American Learning Story*

Content Focus
man's impact on the environment
learning from nature, others, mistakes

Type of Text
literature—fiction: legend, learning story

Author's Name Paula Underwood

Author's Purpose to teach others to respect the environment and learn from others

Big Ideas
Consider the following Big Idea questions. Write your answer for each question.

What impact do humans have on the environment?

What does "Just because you can, doesn't mean you should" mean to you?

Narrative Preview Checklist: *Who Speaks for Wolf* on pages 71–87.

- ☐ Title: What clue does it provide?
- ☐ Pictures: What additional information is added here?
- ☐ Margin Information: What vocabulary is important to understand this story?
- ☐ Features: What other text features do you notice?
- ☐ Form: What do you notice about the text's shape, layout, font, and punctuation?

Enduring Understandings
After reading the text . . .

As a class, consider the two Big Idea questions. After discussing each question, have students write an answer. We'll come back to these questions after we finish reading the text. You can add to your answers as you gain information and perspective.

Preview

Read the Preview Checklist on page 69. Follow the Preview Procedure outlined below.

Preview Procedure

- Group students with partners or in triads.
- Have students count off as 1s or 2s. The 1s will become the student leaders. If working with triads, the third students become 3s.
- The student leaders will preview the text in addition to managing the checklist and pacing.
- The 2s and 3s will preview the text with 1s.
- Direct 1s to open their Student Books to page 69 and 2s and 3s to open their Student Books to page 71. This allows students to look at a few different pages at one time without turning back and forth.

Direct students to page 71.

If necessary, guide students in a short preview using the following talking points.

What is the title of the text? (*Who Speaks for Wolf: A Native American Learning Story*) Describe the photograph on the first page. (elderly Native American man who looks serious or unhappy as he stares into his smoky surroundings, possibly near a fire) How does the photograph compare to the picture on pages 72 and 73? (Instead of one older man, we can see an entire community of Native American adults and children.) How does the photograph compare to the picture on page 87? (The last page shows a picture of a large wolf in the background looking toward the Native American village.) While looking at the graphics, did you notice anything about the print that was unusual? (Some of the text is written in paragraphs; some of the text is written in verse.) The verse represents a chant that Grandfather is singing to his grandson. A chant is a type of song with a simple rhythm and a lot of repetition. What do you notice about the first line of every section in Grandfather's chant? (The first line of every section is written with all capital letters and italicized.) Why do you think capital letters are used in the first line of each verse? What does writing in all caps mean in today's social media and texting? (All caps means shouting.) When we're reading, let's pay close attention to the words in capital letters and see if they mean shouting.

Vocabulary

Objectives

- Evaluate word knowledge.
- Determine the meaning of key passage vocabulary.

Rate Vocabulary Knowledge

Direct students to page 70 in their Student Books.

Before we read the text, let's take a look at the vocabulary words that appear in this text. Remind students that as you read each word in the first column aloud, they will write the word in the third column and then rate their knowledge of it. Display the Vocabulary Rating Scale poster or write the information on the board. Review the meaning of each rating.

Vocabulary Rating Scale

0—I have never heard the word before.

1—I have heard the word, but I'm not sure how to use it.

2—I am familiar with the word, but I'm not sure if I know the correct meaning.

3—I know the meaning of the word and can use it correctly in a sentence.

Lesson 6 | Vocabulary

Key Passage Vocabulary: *Who Speaks for Wolf*

Read each word. Write the word in column 3. Then, circle a number to rate your knowledge of the word.

Vocabulary	Part of Speech	Write the Word	Knowledge Rating
immobile	(adj)	immobile	0 1 2 3
sought	(v)	sought	0 1 2 3
counsel	(v)	counsel	0 1 2 3
reconsider	(v)	reconsider	0 1 2 3
apparent	(adj)	apparent	0 1 2 3
devise	(v)	devise	0 1 2 3
course	(n)	course	0 1 2 3
maintain	(v)	maintain	0 1 2 3
cherish	(v)	cherish	0 1 2 3
omission	(n)	omission	0 1 2 3

70 Unit 8

The points are not a grade; they are just there to help you know which words you need to focus on. By the end of this unit, you should be able to change all your ratings to a 3. That's the goal.

Read each word aloud. Have students repeat it, write it, and rate it. Then, have volunteers who rated a word *2* or *3* use the word in an oral sentence.

Preteach Vocabulary

Let's take a closer look at the words. Follow the Preteach Procedure below.

Preteach Procedure

This activity is intended to take only a short amount of time, so make it an oral exercise.

- Introduce each word as indicated on the word card.
- Read the definition and example sentences.
- Ask questions to clarify and deepen understanding.
- If time permits, allow students to share.

* If your students would benefit from copying the definitions, please have them do so in the vocabulary log in the back of the Student Books using the margin definitions in the passage selections. This should be done outside of instruction time.

immobile (adj)

Let's read the first word together. *Immobile.*

Definition: If something is *immobile*, it is completely still. What means "completely still"? (immobile)

Example 1: When you are posing for school pictures, the photographer expects you to remain *immobile.*

Example 2: During really scary scenes of a movie, I become *immobile.*

Example 3: On most nights, the moon appears *immobile*, but it's actually moving slowly across the sky.

Question 1: The music ends, and the dance team strikes a final pose. Are the dancers *immobile*? Yes or no? (yes)

Question 2: A flag is billowing in the breeze. Is it *immobile*? Yes or no? (no)

Pair Share: Turn to your partner and describe a task or game in which someone or something must be *immobile.* (If students need suggestions, provide these: threading a needle, face-painting, removing a splinter, and building a human pyramid)

sought (v)

Let's read the next word together. *Sought.*

Definition: *Sought* is the past tense of the verb *seek.* If you *sought* to do something, you tried to do, find, or get it. What means "tried to do, find, or get something"? (sought)

Example 1: If you tried to get a school rule changed, you *sought* to change the rule.

Example 2: Some of the most effective leaders in history *sought* to make peace, not war.

Example 3: The first European settlers in North America *sought* to adapt to the land, not change it.

Question 1: You have tried every way you can think of to make up with a friend. Have you *sought* to make up? Yes or no? (yes)

Question 2: You have worked hard outside of volleyball practice to improve your serve. Have you *sought* to improve your serve? Yes or no? (yes)

Pair Share: Turn to your partner and tell about a time when you were a child and *sought* to do something and succeeded.

counsel (v)

Let's read the next word together. *Counsel.*

Definition: To *counsel* is to give advice or support to someone. What means "to give advice or support to someone"? (counsel)

Example 1: Older sisters often *counsel* younger sisters about their social lives.

Example 2: When older relatives try to *counsel* you, listen patiently; they usually have wisdom to share.

Example 3: In strong friendships, both parties *counsel* each other at different times; in weak friendships, one person always tells the other what to do.

Question 1: Your little brother asks for help with math, but you tell him you're busy. Have you *counseled* him? Yes or no? (no)

Question 2: Your aunt always has great advice about dating. Do you like it when she *counsels* you? Yes or no? (yes)

Pair Share: Turn to your partner and tell from whom you ask *counsel* when you are struggling with a problem, and why.

3

reconsider (v)

Let's read the next word together. *Reconsider.*

Definition: To *reconsider* is to think about whether a past action or decision should be changed. What means "to think about whether a past action or decision should be changed"? (reconsider)

Example 1: Sometimes after drafting an e-mail, I *reconsider* the way I've said something and change it.

Example 2: A good coach is always willing to *reconsider* a strategy if it doesn't work.

Example 3: People sometimes accept a responsibility but then *reconsider* when they realize how much work it involves.

Question 1: You agree to join a club and then learn there's a $100 membership fee. Do you *reconsider* joining? Yes or no? (yes)

Question 2: You're about to do laundry when a friend calls and says she has a free ticket to the water park. Do you *reconsider* doing laundry? Yes or no? (yes)

Pair Share: Turn to your partner and name two things that might make you *reconsider* your decision to attend a party.

apparent (adj)

Let's read the next word together. *Apparent.*

Definition: If something is *apparent*, it is easy to see or understand. What means "easy to see or understand"? (apparent)

Example 1: If you fall asleep in all your morning classes, it's *apparent* you didn't get enough rest.

Example 2: The kindness of people in this school building is *apparent* when they hold doors open for others.

Example 3: When a girl puts on a raincoat and rain boots and grabs an umbrella, it is *apparent* that she is headed outside into the rain.

Question 1: What makes it *apparent* that someone just guzzled a glass of milk? (a milk mustache)

Question 2: Is the meaning of a poem or an artwork always *apparent*? Yes or no? (no)

Pair Share: Turn to your partner and tell what you could do to make it *apparent* that you are unhappy.

devise (v)

Let's read the next word together. *Devise.*

Definition: To *devise* is to plan or invent something. What word means "to plan or invent something"? (devise)

Example 1: I have *devised* a method to reuse rainwater to water my plants.

Example 2: The Wright brothers *devised* a machine for human flight.

Example 3: People who need to stay busy are always *devising* complicated social plans for the weekend.

Question 1: If you just go along with others' ideas, have you *devised* a plan of your own? Yes or no? (no)

Question 2: The light switch is across the room from your bed. You figure out how to turn off the light without getting up. Have you *devised* a method for staying in bed? Yes or no? (yes)

Pair Share: If I asked you to *devise* a plan for learning ten new vocabulary words a day, how would you do it? Tell your partner.

6

course (n)

Let's read the next word together. *Course.*

Definition: *Course* means "the path or direction that someone or something moves along." What word means "the path or direction that someone or something moves along"? (course)

Example 1: War has the power to change the *course* of history; so do you.

Example 2: In some video games, a player moves an avatar along a *course* full of obstacles.

Example 3: The team took a roundabout *course* to the championship, but they finally made it.

Question 1: You can't decide whether you want to be a firefighter or join the army after high school. Are you on a particular *course* toward the future? Yes or no? (no)

Question 2: You're playing a board game. If you draw four penalty cards, you're out of the game. You've drawn three. Are you on a *course* to elimination? Yes or no? (yes)

Pair Share: Turn to your partner and tell what *course* a person should follow if he or she wants to be happy in old age.

7

maintain (v)

Let's read the next word together. *Maintain.*

Definition: To *maintain* something is to continue having or doing it. What word means "to continue having or doing something"? (maintain)

Example 1: If you want to *maintain* good posture, you have to remember to hold your shoulders back and suck in your tummy. Try it.

Example 2: To *maintain* good dental health, I brush and floss twice a day.

Example 3: Some people put a lot of time and energy into *maintaining* an up-to-date wardrobe.

Question 1: My neighbor's yard is a big weed patch. Does she *maintain* her yard? Yes or no? (no)

Question 2: You decide to teach yourself how to play the guitar. You practice three days in a row, but then forget for a week. Have you *maintained* your practice schedule? Yes or no? (no)

Pair Share: Turn to your partner and tell what a person should do to *maintain* a friendship.

8

cherish (v)

Let's read the next word together. *Cherish.*

Definition: *Cherish* means to treat with love or care; to hold dear. What word means "to treat with love or care; to hold dear"? (cherish)

Example 1: I *cherish* memories of my grandmother, who recently passed away.

Example 2: Some people *cherish* their pets but treat their friends and relatives poorly.

Example 3: If you love your cousins but only see them occasionally, you probably *cherish* your time together.

Question 1: You *cherish* a medal your grandfather left to you. Do you take good care of it? Yes or no? (yes)

Question 2: If you *cherish* a friend, do you ignore him or her? Yes or no? (no)

Pair Share: Turn to your partner and describe an object in your home that you *cherish.*

9

omission (n)

Let's read the last word together. *Omission.*

Definition: An *omission* is the act of leaving something out or leaving it undone. What word means "the act of leaving something out or undone"? (omission)

Example 1: I forgot to invite a friend to a party. This *omission* upset her greatly.

Example 2: The assembly ended early due to the *omission* of announcements.

Example 3: The *omission* of an important word in a sentence may make your meaning unclear.

Question 1: The yearbook editors forgot to include blank pages for classmates' notes and signatures. Was this an *omission*? Yes or no? (yes)

Question 2: Three of my friends share the same birthday, and on that day, I call each and every one of them and sing the birthday song. Do I make an *omission*? Yes or no? (no)

Pair Share: Tell your partner what *omission* and what addition you would like to see in your schedule.

10

Reading

Objectives

- Read a legend.
- Monitor comprehension during text reading.
- Determine the point of view of literary text.
- Identify shifts in point of view.

Who Speaks for Wolf: A Native American Learning Story

Direct students to page 71 in their Student Books.

Now that we have previewed vocabulary, it's time to read.

Guiding Students Toward Independent Reading

It is important that your students read as much and as often as they can. Assign readings that meet the needs of your students, based on your observations and data. This is a good opportunity to stretch your students. If students become frustrated, scaffold the reading with paired reading, choral reading, or a read-aloud.

Options for reading text:

- Teacher read-aloud
- Teacher-led or student-led choral read
- Paired read or independent read

Choose an option for reading text. Students read according to the option that you chose. Review the purpose of the numbered squares in the text, and prompt students to stop periodically and check comprehension.

If you choose to read the text aloud or chorally, use the text on the following pages and stop to ask questions and have students answer them.

SE p. 72, paragraphs 1–7

Almost at the edge of the circle of light cast by Central Fire—Wolf was standing. His eyes reflected the fire's warmth with a colder light. Wolf stood there, staring at the fire.

A boy of eight winters was watching Wolf—as **immobile** as Wolf—as fascinated. Finally, the boy turned to Grandfather, warming his old bones from winter's first chill.

"Why does Wolf stand there and only watch the fire?"

"Why do you?" Grandfather replied.

And then the boy remembered that he had sat there, ever since the fire was lit, watching the flames—until Wolf came. Now, instead, he watched Wolf. He saw that it was because Wolf was so different from him, yet also watched the fire, and that there seemed no fear in Wolf. It was this the boy did not understand.

Beyond where Wolf was standing there was a hill—still so close to the Central Fire that the boy was surprised to see the dim outline of another Wolf face. This one was looking at the moon.

Moon-Looking-Wolf began to sing her song. More and more joined her until at last even Wolf-Looks-at-Fire chortled in his throat the beginnings of a song. They sang for the Moon, and for each other, and for any who might listen. They sang of how Earth was a good place to be, of how much beauty surrounds us, and of how all this is sometimes most easily seen in Moon and Fire.

1. Why do the wolves sing?

SE p. 73, paragraphs 1–6

The boy listened and—and wanted to do nothing else with his life but listen to Wolf singing.

After a long and particularly beautiful song, Moon-Looking-Wolf quieted, and one by one her brothers joined her in silence, until even the most distant—crying "I am here! Don't forget me!"—made space for the night and watched—and waited. Wolf-Looks-at-Fire turned and left the clearing, joining his brothers near the hill.

"But I still don't understand," the boy continued. "Why does Wolf look at Fire? Why does he feel at home so close to our living space? Why does Wolf Woman begin her song on a hill so close to us who are not Wolf?"

"We have known each other for a long time," the old man answered. "We have learned to live with one another."

The boy still looked puzzled. Within himself he saw only the edges of understanding.

Grandfather was silent for a time—and then began at last the slow cadences of a chant. The boy knew with satisfaction that soon he would understand—would know Wolf better than before—would learn how it had been between us.

2. What is the boy hoping that his grandfather will teach him? How will the grandfather teach him?

SE p. 73, paragraphs 7–8

LONG AGO . . . LONG AGO . . . LONG AGO . . .

Grandfather chanted, the rhythm taking its place with Wolf's song as something appropriate for the forest.

SE p. 74, paragraphs 1–2

LONG AGO
Our People grew in number so that where we were
was no longer enough
Many young men
were sent out from among us
to seek a new place
where the People might be who-they-were
They searched
and they returned
each with a place selected
each determined his place was best

3. Why did the People need to move?

SE p. 74, paragraph 3

AND SO IT WAS
That the People had a decision to make:
which of the many was most appropriate

SE p. 75, paragraphs 1–2

NOW, AT THAT TIME
There was one among the People
to whom Wolf was brother
He was so much Wolf's brother
that he would sing their song to them
and they would answer him
He was so much Wolf's brother
that their young
would sometimes follow him through the forest
and it seemed they meant to learn from him

SO IT WAS, AT THIS TIME
That the People gave That One a special name
They called him WOLF'S BROTHER
and if any ***sought*** *to learn about Wolf*
if any were curious
or wanted to learn to sing Wolf's song
they would sit beside him
and describe their curiosity
hoping for a reply

4. Why was Wolf's Brother important?

SE p. 76, paragraphs 1–8

"Has it been since that time that we sing to Wolf?" the boy asked eagerly. "Was it he who taught us how?" He clapped his hands over his mouth to stop the tumble of words. He knew he had interrupted Grandfather's Song.

The old man smiled, and the crinkles around his eyes spoke of other boys—and other times.

"Yes, even he!" he answered. "For since that time it has pleased many of our people to sing to Wolf and to learn to understand him."

Encouraged, the boy asked, "And ever since our hunters go to learn to sing to Wolf?"

"Many people go, not only hunters. Many people go, not only men," Grandfather chided. "For was it not Wolf Woman who began the song tonight? Would it then be appropriate if only the men among us replied?"

The boy looked crestfallen. He wanted so much to be a hunter—to learn Wolf's song, but he knew there was wisdom in Grandfather's words. Not only hunters learn from Wolf.

"But you have led me down a different path," the Old One was saying. "It would please me to finish my first song."

The boy settled back and waited to learn.

5. Why was the boy disappointed? What gave the boy hope?

SE p. 77, paragraph 1

AS I HAVE SAID
The people sought a new place in the forest
They listened closely to each of the young men
as they spoke of hills and trees
of clearings and running water
of deer and squirrels and berries
They listened to hear which place
might be drier in rain
more protected in winter
and where our Three Sisters
Corn, Beans, and Squash
might find a place to their liking

6. Who are the Three Sisters? Why are crops referred to in familial terms?

SE p. 77, paragraph 2

They listened
and they chose
Before they chose
they listened to each young man
Before they chose
they listened to each among them
he who understood the flow of waters
she who understood Long House construction
he who understood the storms of winter
she who understood Three Sisters
to each of these they listened
until they reached agreement
and the Eldest among them
finally rose and said:
"SO BE IT—
FOR SO IT IS"

SE p. 78, paragraph 1

"BUT WAIT"
Someone cautioned—
"Where is Wolf's Brother?
WHO, THEN, SPEAKS FOR WOLF?"

7. Explain the attributes of the land they were seeking.

SE p. 78, paragraphs 2–3

BUT
THE PEOPLE WERE DECIDED
and their mind was firm
and the first people were sent
to choose a site for the first Long House
to clear a space for our Three Sisters
to mold the land so that water
would run away from our dwelling
so that all would be secure within

AND THEN WOLF'S BROTHER RETURNED
He asked about the New Place
and said at once that we must choose another
"You have chosen the Center Place
for a great community of Wolf"

8. What is the problem?

SE p. 78, paragraph 4

But we answered him
that many had already gone
and that it could not wisely be changed
and that surely Wolf could make way for us
as we sometimes make way for Wolf
But Wolf's Brother ***counseled***—
"I think that you will find
that it is too small a place for both
and that it will require more work then—
than change would presently require"

9. What caution does Wolf's Brother share with his Native American people?

SE p. 79, paragraphs 1–3

BUT
THE PEOPLE CLOSED THEIR EARS
and would not ***reconsider***
When the New Place was ready
all the People rose up as one
and took those things they found of value
and looked at last upon their new home

NOW CONSIDER HOW IT WAS FOR THEM
This New Place
had cool summers and winter protection
and fast-moving streams
and forests around us
filled with deer and squirrel
there was room even for our Three Beloved Sisters

AND THE PEOPLE SAW THAT THIS WAS GOOD
AND DID NOT SEE
WOLF WATCHING FROM THE SHADOWS!

10. What problem has been caused because they didn't listen to Wolf's Brother?

SE p. 80, paragraphs 1–4

BUT AS TIME PASSED
They began to see—
for someone would bring deer or squirrel
and hang him from a tree
and go for something to contain the meat
but would return
to find nothing hanging from the tree
AND WOLF BEYOND

AT FIRST
This seemed to us an appropriate exchange—
some food for a place to live

BUT
It soon became **apparent** *that it was more than this—*
for Wolf would sometimes walk between the dwellings
that we had fashioned for ourselves
and the women grew concerned
for the safety of the little ones
Thinking of this
they devised for a while an agreement with Wolf
whereby the women would gather together
at the edge of our village
and put out food for Wolf and his brothers

SE p. 81, paragraph 1

BUT IT WAS SOON APPARENT
That this meant too much food
and also Wolf grew bolder
coming in to look for food
so that it was worse than before

SE p. 81, paragraphs 2–4

WE HAD NO WISH TO TAME WOLF
AND SO
    Hearing the wailing of the women
        the men ***devised*** *a system*
            whereby some ones among them
                were always alert to drive off Wolf
AND WOLF WAS SOON HIS OLD UNTAMED SELF

BUT
    They soon discovered
        that this required so much energy
            that there was little left for winter preparations
        and the Long Cold began to look longer and colder
            with each passing day

THEN
    The men counseled together
        to choose a different ***course***

11. What changes happened with Wolf after the People moved into his territory?

SE p. 82, paragraphs 1–6

THEY SAW
That neither providing Wolf with food
nor driving him off
gave the People a life that was pleasing

THEY SAW
That Wolf and the People
could not live comfortably together
in such a small space

THEY SAW
That it was possible
to hunt down this Wolf People
until they were no more

BUT THEY ALSO SAW
That this would require much energy over many years

THEY SAW, TOO,
That such a task would change the People:
they would become Wolf Killers
A People who took life only to sustain their own
would become a People who took life
rather than move a little

IT DID NOT SEEM TO THEM
THAT THEY WANTED TO BECOME SUCH A PEOPLE

12. How did the People want to change?

SE p. 83, paragraphs 1–4

AT LAST
One of the Eldest of the People
spoke what was in every mind:
"It would seem
that Wolf's Brother's vision
was sharper than our own
To live here indeed requires more work now
than change would have made necessary

Grandfather paused, making his knee a drum on which to **maintain** the rhythm of the chant, and then went on.

NOW THIS WOULD BE A SIMPLE TELLING
OF A PEOPLE WHO DECIDED TO MOVE
ONCE WINTER WAS PAST

EXCEPT
THAT FROM THIS
THE PEOPLE LEARNED A GREAT LESSON

IT IS A LESSON
WE HAVE NEVER FORGOTTEN

SE p. 84, paragraphs 1–2

FOR
At the end of their Council
one of the Eldest rose again and said:
"Let us learn from this
so that not again
need the People build only to move
Let us not again think we will gain energy
only to lose more than we gain
We have learned to choose a place
where winter storms are less
rather than rebuild
We have learned to choose a place
where water does not stand
rather than sustain sickness

LET US NOW LEARN TO CONSIDER WOLF!"

13. What is the lesson learned?

SE p. 85, paragraphs 1–4

AND SO IT WAS
That the People devised among themselves
a way of asking each other questions
whenever a decision was to be made
on a New Place or a New Way
We sought to perceive the flow of energy
through each new possibility
and how much was enough
and how much was too much

UNTIL AT LAST
Someone would rise
and ask the old, old question
to remind us of things
we do not yet see clearly enough to remember

"TELL ME NOW MY BROTHERS
TELL ME NOW MY SISTERS
WHO SPEAKS FOR WOLF?"

14. What does the question really mean?

SE p. 86, paragraphs 1–5

And so Grandfather's Song ended . . . and my father's voice grew still.

"Did the boy learn to sing with Wolf?" I asked.

"All may," my father answered.

"And did the People always remember to ask Wolf's Question?"

My father smiled. "They remembered for a long time . . . a long time. And when the wooden ships came, bringing a new People, they looked at them and saw that what we accomplish by much thought and considering the needs of all, they accomplish by building tools and changing the earth, with much thought of winter and little of tomorrow. We could not teach them to ask Wolf's question. They did not understand he was their brother. We knew how long it had taken us to listen to Wolf's voice. It seemed to us that These Ones could also learn. And so we **cherished** them . . . when we could . . . and held them off . . . when we must . . . and gave them time to learn."

15. Who are the new People?

SE p. 86, paragraphs 6–7

"Will they learn, do you think, my father? Will they learn?"

"Sometimes wisdom comes only after great foolishness. We still hope they will learn. I do not know even if our own People still ask their question. I only know that at the last Great Council when we talked about the Small Ones in their wooden ships and decided that their way and our way might exist side by side—and decided, therefore, to let them live . . . I only know that someone rose to remind them of the things we had not yet learned about these Pale Ones."

SE p. 87, paragraphs 1–2

"He rose and he reminded us of what we had already learned, of how these New Ones believed that only one way was Right and all others Wrong. He wondered out loud whether they would be as patient with us—once they were strong—as we were now with them. He wondered what else might be true for them that we did not yet see. He wondered how all these things—seen and unseen—might affect our lives and the lives of our children's children's children. Then to remind us of the great difficulties that may arise from the simple **omission** of something we forgot to consider, he gazed slowly around the Council Circle and asked the ancient question:

"TELL ME NOW MY BROTHERS
TELL ME NOW MY SISTERS
WHO SPEAKS FOR WOLF?"

16. Who is *Wolf* referring to now?

For confirmation of engagement, have partners share a valuable lesson learned in the story.

Point of View

Point of view has a major impact on text. Literature can be written from the first-person point of view or the third-person point of view. If it is written by a character in the text, that is called first person. If it is written by a character outside the text, that is called third person.

Direct students to pages 72 and 73. Have them identify the point of view at this point in the tale. (third-person limited)

If students struggle, point out that in paragraph 5, the words "there seemed no fear in Wolf" is an indication that the narrator is not "all knowing," and therefore is not omniscient. Then, direct them to paragraph 7. Generate a class discussion about why some people may consider this to be omniscient. (he knows why the wolves sing)

Direct students to pages 86 and 87 and have them identify the point of view at this point in the story. (first person) Have students speculate why it changes, but do not answer the question. This will be answered in Lesson 8.

Unit 8 Lesson 7

Lesson Opener

Before the lesson, choose one of the following activities to write on the board or post on the *LANGUAGE! Live* Class Wall online.

- *Write a summary sentence about the lesson the People learned.*
- *Make a list of adjectives describing Wolf after the people moved to his territory.*
- *Identify the following as a phrase or a clause.*
  - *the white wolf's brother*
  - *who lived outside*
  - *running fast through the woods*
  - *she felt alive once more*
  - *a wolf in disguise*
  - *was looking at me with hatred*

Vocabulary

Objective

- Review key passage vocabulary.

Review Passage Vocabulary

Direct students to page 70 in their Student Books. Use the following questions to review the vocabulary words in *Who Speaks for Wolf*. Have students answer each question using the vocabulary word or indicating its meaning in a complete sentence.

Lesson 8 | Vocabulary

Key Passage Vocabulary: *Who Speaks for Wolf*

Read each word. Write the word in column 3. Then, circle a number to rate your knowledge of the word.

[illegible]	[illegible]	[illegible]	[illegible]
immobile	(adj)	immobile	0 1 2 3
sought	(v)	sought	0 1 2 3
counsel	(v)	counsel	0 1 2 3
reconsider	(v)	reconsider	0 1 2 3
apparent	(adj)	apparent	0 1 2 3
devise	(v)	devise	0 1 2 3
course	(n)	course	0 1 2 3
maintain	(v)	maintain	0 1 2 3
cherish	(v)	cherish	0 1 2 3
omission	(n)	omission	0 1 2 3

70 Unit 8

- Wolf stares at the fire and the boy watches Wolf; both are *immobile*. Are they moving? (No; if they are immobile, they are perfectly still.) Why does Wolf's behavior make the boy *immobile*? (It makes him immobile because he is fascinated; Wolf doesn't seem afraid of anything.)
- Grandfather sings the story of the shared history between Wolf and the people. One of the people was known as Wolf's Brother. People who *sought* what would go to him? (People who sought knowledge of Wolf would go to Wolf's Brother.) When the People outgrew the place where they lived, what did they *seek*? (They sought a new place to live.)
- The People chose a new place without being *counseled* by Wolf's Brother. Did they ask Wolf's Brother his opinion? (No; if they chose a new place without his counseling, they chose it without getting his opinion.) When Wolf's Brother learned of the new choice, what did he *counsel* his people to do? Why? (He counseled them to choose a different place because they would not be able to coexist with Wolf in the place they had chosen.)
- Once they learned Wolf's Brother's opinion, did the People *reconsider* their choice? Why or why not? (No, they did not reconsider because they had already started the work of settling in the new place.) As time passed, what events caused them to begin to *reconsider*? (They began to reconsider when their food began to disappear and when Wolf began to walk among their dwellings.)

- The women started putting out food for Wolf at the edge of the village, but what soon became *apparent*? (It soon became apparent that this would be too big a drain on the food supply.) What else made the problems with this plan *apparent*? (The problems with this plan became more apparent when Wolf grew bolder and began coming into the village to look for food.)
- What strategy did the men *devise* in response? (They devised a strategy to protect the village by standing guard and driving Wolf away if needed.) This strategy used up all their energy. What other plan did they *devise* but not put into action? (They devised but did not follow through with a plan to kill all the wolves.)
- What did the People realize would happen to them if they followed such a *course*? (They realized that if they followed such a course, they would become Wolf Killers, people who took other creatures' lives to sustain their own.) What did one of the Elders realize about the *course* Wolf's Brother had recommended? (He realized that the course Wolf's Brother had recommended was the wiser course—that in the end, it would have required less time and energy.)
- When Grandfather pauses in his story, how does he *maintain* the rhythm of the chant? (He maintains rhythm by tapping his knee in time.) When he resumes the story, he tells how the people realized their mistake and vowed to *maintain* a new way of life. What new way of life do they vow to *maintain*? (They vow to maintain a way of life in which they thoroughly discuss any new decision and think through all the possible ways energy might flow through each course of action.)
- When the new People came on wooden ships, did they *cherish* Wolf as Grandfather's people had learned to do? (No, they did not cherish Wolf; they did not understand that he was their brother.) How do Grandfather's people show that they *cherish* the new People, even though the new People are foolish? (They show they cherish the new People by giving them time to learn and by maintaining hope that they will change as they grow strong.)

Assign online practice from the Text Training link on the left menu of your teacher dashboard.

- The story ends by pointing out an *omission* in the conversation between Grandfather's people and the new People. What is this *omission*? (The omission is that nobody seems to be speaking for Wolf.) Think of Wolf as a symbol of nature. What *omissions* or actions in our day and age show that nobody is speaking for Wolf? (Possible responses: We are using nature and killing parts of it for our own advancement. We pass few laws to protect nature. We fail to control pollution in many forms. We build on any open space without thinking of the consequences for other species. All of these omissions or forms of neglect show that nobody is speaking for Wolf.)

Reading

Objectives

- Objectively summarize literary text.
- Identify the theme of a story.
- Contrast the themes of two myths about the same topic.
- Determine how to respond to prompts.
- Use critical thinking skills to write responses to prompts about text.
- Support written answers with evidence from text.

Theme

What are the elements of literary text? (characters, setting, problem and solution) What is the setting of *Who Speaks for Wolf*? (outdoors; campfire; Native American village) Who are the main characters? (Boy; Grandfather; Father; Wolf)

What is the moral of a story or the lesson learned called? (theme)

Review the theme of "The White Wolf of the Hartz Mountains."

(Impulsive decisions come back to bite you; trust your instincts; if it seems too good to be true, it probably is.)

Remember, the theme is easier to find if you objectively summarize the passage.

As a class, summarize *Who Speaks for Wolf* on the board. (The People ran out of room and moved to a new place without considering the impact it would have on Wolf. They tried to live side-by-side with Wolf, but it took more energy and effort to do this than it would take to move to a new area. The People moved to a new place and always remembered to consider Wolf in all they did.)

The People wanted to move to an area that would be best for them. They did not consider how their move would affect Wolf. Even though they were warned, they did not heed the advice. Through much trial, they learned that they must consider the impact of their actions on all involved. When the white people moved in, what did they do? (They did not consider others.) What is the theme or lesson of this passage? Remember, there can be more than one theme. The lesson you learned from the text may be different from the lesson I learned from the text. Our past experiences usually guide our idea of theme. (Be considerate of other people and animals; consider all the consequences when making a decision; in all decisions, consider the impact on others; all nature's creatures are as important as humans.)

Ask students if they have ever read a passage with a similar theme. Ask them if they have ever had a similar experience in which they did not consider the impact a decision would have on someone or something else.

Have partners contrast the themes in both texts.

Critical Understandings: Direction Words *evaluate, integrate, summarize, trace*

Let's review the difference between a question and prompt. Prompts are statements that require a constructed response, which can range from a list to a complete sentence to a paragraph or an essay.

Write the words *evaluate, integrate, summarize,* and *trace* on the board. Have students read the words aloud with you.

Direct students to pages 14 and 15 in their Student Books. It is critical to understand what the question is asking and how to answer it. Today, we will look at four direction words used in prompts.

Have students read about the four direction words in the chart with their partner.

Lesson 3 | Reading

Critical Understandings: Direction Words

Prompt	How to Respond	Model
If the prompt asks you to . . .	The response requires you to . . .	For example . . .
Analyze	break down and evaluate or draw conclusions about the information	**Analyze** the development of the text's central idea.
Assess	decide on the value, impact, or accuracy	**Assess** how the author's point of view affects the story.
Cite Evidence	support your answer by paraphrasing or using a direct quote	**Cite evidence** that supports your argument.
Clarify	make a statement or situation less confusing	**Clarify** the events leading up to the marriage.
Compare	state the similarities between two or more things	**Compare** Indian and Chinese marriage arrangements.
Connect	tie ideas together, relate	**Connect** each storm with its safety plan.
Contrast	state the differences between two or more things	**Contrast** Indian and Chinese marriage arrangements.
Demonstrate	show how to do it	**Demonstrate** your knowledge of wolves through poetry.
Develop an Argument	work on a case over a period of time, during which it grows or changes	Use evidence from both stories to **develop an argument** against arranged marriages.
Differentiate	tell apart or tell the difference between	**Differentiate** between the protagonist and the antagonist.
Distinguish	recognize something for a specific reason	**Distinguish** your claim from the opposing view by telling how it is different.

14 Unit 7

Chart Reading Procedure

- Group students with partners or in triads.
- Have students count off as 1s or 2s. The 1s will become the student leaders. If working with triads, the third students become 3s.
- The student leaders will read the left column (Prompt) in addition to managing the time and turn-taking if working with a triad.
- The 2s will explain the middle column of the chart (How to Respond). If working in triads, 3s take turns explaining the middle column.
- The 1s read the model in the right column (Model), and 2s and 3s restate the model as a question.
- All students should follow along with their pencil eraser while others are explaining the chart.
- Students must work from left to right, top to bottom in order to benefit from this activity.

Check for understanding by requesting an oral response to the following questions.

- If the prompt asks you to *evaluate,* the response requires you to . . . (think carefully to make a judgment; form a critical opinion of).
- If the prompt asks you to *integrate,* the response requires you to . . . (combine different kinds of information to form a complete whole).
- If the prompt asks you to *summarize,* the response requires you to . . . (tell the most important ideas or concepts).
- If the prompt asks you to *trace,* the response requires you to . . . (follow information closely).

Direct students to pages 88 and 89 in their Student Books and read the instructions aloud. Let's read some prompts about the text.

1. Integrate information learned from the campfire discussion with content from Grandfather's Song to determine why Wolf felt comfortable with the People. Provide text evidence.
2. Trace the decision-making process that the People used before deciding where to move. Who and what was omitted from the decision-making process?
3. Evaluate the People's move to the Center Place for a great community of Wolf from Wolf's Brother's perspective.
4. Summarize the lesson learned when the People failed to consider Wolf.

Critical Understandings

Read the prompts and respond using complete sentences. Refer to the chart on pages 14 and 15 to determine how to respond. Provide text evidence when requested.

1. Integrate information learned from the campfire discussion with content from Grandfather's Song to determine why Wolf felt comfortable with the People. Provide text evidence.
   Wolf felt comfortable with the People because they went through many trials learning that they cannot live in the same space and compete for the same food. When they each had their own space, they learned to communicate and respect each other—forging a friendship of sorts.
   Text Evidence from the campfire discussion: "We have known each other for a long time," the old man answered. "We have learned to live with one another."
   Text Evidence from the chant: "'You have chosen the Center Place for a great community of Wolf.' But we answered him that many had already gone and that it could not wisely be changed and that surely Wolf could make way for us as we sometimes make way for Wolf."
2. Trace the decision-making process that the People used before deciding where to move. Who and what was omitted from the decision-making process?
   First, the People took turns listening to each other about their needs for running water, farming land, good weather, and plentiful hunting options until they reached an agreement. Next, they chose a location. Unfortunately, they omitted Wolf's Brother from the decision-making process, which meant that that they did not consider Wolf.

Model

Let's practice responding to prompts with the new direction words. Remember to use the chart on pages 14 and 15 as a reference. Listen as I model the first one for you.

1. Integrate information learned from the campfire discussion with content from Grandfather's Song to determine why Wolf felt comfortable with the People. Provide text evidence.

Since the prompt is asking me to *integrate,* I know that I need to combine different kinds of information to form a complete whole. Now, I will turn the prompt into a question to confirm understanding. *Why did Wolf feel comfortable with the People?* I have to remember that *the People* refers to the Native American people.

Will I get my information from Grandfather's campfire discussion or from his chant or both? (both) I can tell the difference between Grandfather's discussion and Grandfather's chant by referring to text features that we discussed earlier. The campfire discussion is written in regular font. The chant is written in verse using italics and some words in capital letters.

Direct students to the following evidence in the text:

Text Evidence from campfire discussion: Line 45, "We have known each other for a long time," the old man answered. "We have learned to live with one another."

Text Evidence from chant: Lines 161 and 163, "You have chosen the Center Place for a great community of Wolf." But we answered him that many had already gone and that it could not wisely be changed and that surely Wolf could make way for us as we sometimes make way for Wolf.

I will combine information from the discussion and the chant to form my answer. From the discussion, I learned that Wolf felt comfortable with the People because they had known each other for a long time. From the chant, I learned that they tried to live in Wolf's habitat but eventually had to leave out of fear.

Write the answer on the board and have students write it on the page.

> *Wolf felt comfortable with the People because they went through many trials learning that they cannot live in the same space and compete for the same food. When they each had their own space, they learned to communicate and respect each other—forging a friendship of sorts.*

Guided Practice

Let's move on to the next prompt.

2. Trace the decision-making process that the People used before deciding where to move. Who and what was omitted from the decision-making process?

How will you start your answer? First, tell your partner how to respond according to the chart. (If the prompt asks you to *trace*, the response requires you to follow information closely.) Turn the prompt into a question to confirm understanding. (How did the People decide where to move? What did they leave out?)

I cannot start writing my answer until I trace information in the text. First, find evidence of decision making in the chant. (lines 119–144) Which words are repeated for emphasis? (they listened; they chose) What was the first step of the decision-making process? (they listened) What was the next step of the decision-making process? (they chose) Who/what was left out the decision-making process? (They omitted Wolf's Brother from the decision-making process.) Why was that a big deal? (Omitting Wolf's Brother meant that they did not consider Wolf when making their decision.)

Write the following sentence frames on the board:

> *First, the People took turns listening to each other about* ______________.
>
> *Next, they* ______________________________________.
>
> *Unfortunately, they omitted* ______________*, which meant that they did not consider* ______________________________________.

Have partners answer the question.

3. Evaluate the People's move to the Center Place for a great community of Wolf from Wolf's Brother's perspective.

Tell your partner how to respond according to the chart. (If the prompt asks you to *evaluate*, the response requires you to think carefully to make a judgment; form a critical opinion of) Turn the prompt into a question to confirm understanding. (What did Wolf's Brother think of the People's move to the Center Place for a great community of Wolf?) Will you get your information from the discussion or the chant or both? (chant)

Write the following sentence starter on the board.

> *Wolf's Brother (agreed/disagreed) with the People's move into a Wolf community because ______ ____________________.*

Have partners answer the question.

Lesson 7 | Reading

Critical Understandings (*cont.*)

3. Evaluate the People's move to the Center Place for a great community of Wolf from Wolf's Brother's perspective.
Wolf's Brother disagreed with the People's move into a Wolf community because it would be easier to relocate to a separate area than to try to live in territory already inhabited by wolves.

4. Summarize the lesson learned when the People failed to consider Wolf.
The People failed to consider Wolf when they moved to a place with more space and better resources, knowing that it belonged to wolves. They tried to live with the wolves, but they eventually realized that it was taking more energy to live with them and making them a people they didn't want to be. Thus, they learned to consider the impact of their decisions on all living creatures before taking action.

Unit 8 89

4. Summarize the lesson learned when the People failed to consider Wolf.

Tell your partner how to respond according to the chart. (If the prompt asks you to *summarize*, the response requires you to tell the most important ideas or concepts.) Turn the prompt into a question to confirm understanding. (What are the most important things that happened when the People failed to consider wolf?)

Write the following sentence starters on the board.

> *The People failed to consider Wolf when they ____________________. They tried to ______________, but they eventually realized ________ ____________________. Thus, they learned to ______________ ____________________.*

Have partners answer the question.

Unit 8 Lesson 8

Lesson Opener

Before the lesson, choose one of the following activities to write on the board or post on the *LANGUAGE! Live* Class Wall online.

- *Write five sentences explaining what you would do if you knew something you were doing to make your life better was negatively affecting other people.*
- *Write the dialogue of a conversation you think the People may have had with the new People. Don't forget the correct punctuation.*
- *Expand on one or more of these simple sentences, using the steps in Masterpiece Sentences.*

  Christina wandered.

  Marcella cried.

  The hunter cursed him.

  Father was blind.

Reading

Objectives

- Establish a purpose for revisiting literature.
- Listen to an audio version of a text.
- Use information from text and media to answer questions.
- Compare and contrast the experience of reading a story to listening to an audio version of the text.
- Use critical thinking skills to write responses to prompts about text.
- Support written answers with evidence from text.
- Recognize a shift in character point of view in text.
- Write objective summaries.
- Evaluate the impact of an audio performance of a text.

Reading for a Purpose: *Who Speaks for Wolf*

We are going to revisit *Who Speaks for Wolf.* Let's preview the prompts to provide a purpose for returning to the text.

Direct students to pages 90–92 in their Student Books. Have students read the prompts aloud with you.

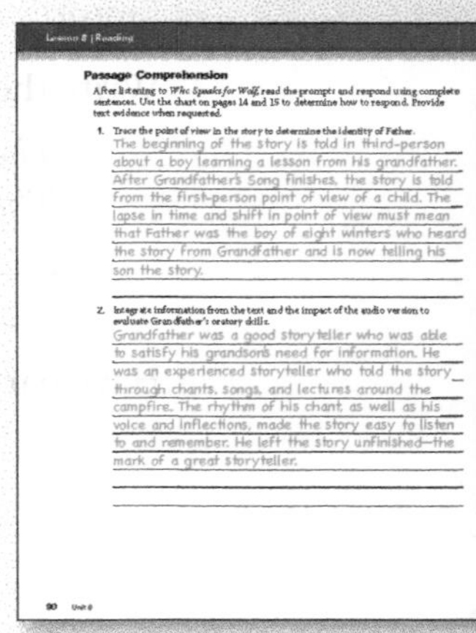

Lesson 8 | Reading

Passage Comprehension

After listening to *Who Speaks for Wolf,* read the prompts and respond using complete sentences. Use the chart on pages 14 and 15 to determine how to respond. Provide text evidence when requested.

1. Trace the point of view in the story to determine the identity of Father.

   The beginning of the story is told in third-person about a boy learning a lesson from his grandfather. After Grandfather's Song finishes, the story is told from the first-person point of view of a child. The lapse in time and shift in point of view must mean that Father was the boy of eight winters who heard the story from Grandfather and is now telling his son the story.

2. Integrate information from the text and the impact of the audio version to evaluate Grandfather's oratory skills.

   Grandfather was a good storyteller who was able to satisfy his grandson's need for information. He was an experienced storyteller who told the story through chants, songs, and lectures around the campfire. The rhythm of his chant, as well as his voice and inflections, made the story easy to listen to and remember. He left the story unfinished—the mark of a great storyteller.

90 Unit 8

1. Trace the point of view in the story to determine the identity of Father.
2. Integrate information from the text and the impact of the audio version to evaluate Grandfather's oratory skills.
3. Trace and evaluate how the wolves' points of view changed regarding living with the People. Provide text evidence.
4. Evaluate the impact of hearing Grandfather's Song the way it was intended.
5. Summarize human interaction with the environment from the People's point of view.
6. Summarize human interaction with the environment from the new People's point of view.

It's time to revisit the text. This time, we will listen to the text. Sometimes it is beneficial to hear a text the way it was intended. We can often understand what we read, but not "feel" it as the author intended. This is a story passed down over generations. It was intended to be "told."

Play the audio version of Who Speaks for Wolf, *which can be found in the Teacher Resources online.*

Play the audio version of *Who Speaks for Wolf,* which can be found in the Teacher Resources online.

Have students listen to the text.

Generate a class discussion about what students understood from the text during the audio version that they did not understand while reading. Ask specific/leading questions to generate the discussion.

Passage Comprehension

Write the words *evaluate, integrate, summarize,* and *trace* on the board. Have students read the words aloud with you.

Direct students to pages 14 and 15 in their Student Books. It is critical to understand what the question is asking and how to answer it. Today, we will review four direction words used in prompts.

Lesson 3 | Reading

Critical Understandings: Direction Words (*cont.*)

Prompt	How to Respond	Model
If the prompt asks you to . . .	The response requires you to . . .	For example . . .
Evaluate	think carefully to make a judgment; form a critical opinion of	**Evaluate** the impact of the character's personality traits.
Illustrate	use examples to demonstrate or prove	**Illustrate** the internal battle between good and evil through Dr. Jekyll's research and explanations.
Integrate	combine different kinds of information to form a complete whole	**Integrate** information from several sources to write a report.
Present	deliver information	**Present** the benefits of wolf reintroduction.
Prove	give evidence to show that it is true	**Prove** that arranged marriages can work.
Relate	explain the connection between ideas or concepts	**Relate** Mr. Hyde to Jim Hall.
Summarize	tell the most important ideas or concepts	**Summarize** the passage.
Support	help it succeed	**Support** the statement that people have two selves.
Synthesize	combine information in a logical way	**Synthesize** information from both texts to explain the impact of anger.
Trace	follow information closely	**Trace** the boy's bad decisions.

Unit 7 15

Have students read about the four words in the chart on page 15 with their partner. Check for understanding by requesting an oral response to the following questions.

- If the prompt asks you to *evaluate,* the response requires you to . . . (think carefully to make a judgment; form a critical opinion of).
- If the prompt asks you to *integrate,* the response requires you to . . . (combine different kinds of information to form a complete whole).
- If the prompt asks you to *summarize,* the response requires you to . . . (tell the most important ideas or concepts).
- If the prompt asks you to *trace,* the response requires you to . . . (follow information closely).

Let's practice answering questions that are written as prompts. Remember to use the chart as a reference. Don't forget, if the direction word is confusing, try to restate the prompt by using a question word.

Direct students to pages 90–92 in their Student Books.

Model

Listen as I model the first one for you.

1. Trace the point of view in the story to determine the identity of Father.

Lesson 8 | Reading

Passage Comprehension

After listening to *Who Speaks for Wolf*, read the prompts and respond using complete sentences. Use the chart on pages 14 and 15 to determine how to respond. Provide text evidence when requested.

1. Trace the point of view in the story to determine the identity of Father.
The beginning of the story is told in third-person about a boy learning a lesson from his grandfather. After Grandfather's Song finishes, the story is told from the first-person point of view of a child. The lapse in time and shift in point of view must mean that Father was the boy of eight winters who heard the story from Grandfather and is now telling his son the story.

2. Integrate information from the text and the impact of the audio version to evaluate Grandfather's oratory skills.
Grandfather was a good storyteller who was able to satisfy his grandson's need for information. He was an experienced storyteller who told the story through chants, songs, and lectures around the campfire. The rhythm of his chant, as well as his voice and inflections, made the story easy to listen to and remember. He left the story unfinished—the mark of a great storyteller.

90 Unit 8

According to the chart, if the prompt asks you to *trace*, the response requires you to follow information closely. Now, I will turn the prompt into a question to confirm understanding. Who is Father? How does the point of view lead to this answer?

I cannot start writing my answer until I trace information in the text.

Let's look at lines 1–18. What first-person pronouns do you see? (none) In the text, it refers to "the boy" and "the grandfather," but I do not see *I* or *me*.

From that information, I can start formulating my answer.

At first, the story is told in third-person point of view, following a boy and his grandfather.

Next, let's look at lines 305–325. What pronouns do you see? (I, my) Who is involved in the story now? (father, son)

From that information, I can add to my answer.

Later, the story is told from the first-person point of view of a young boy. The dialogue is between him and his father, but no grandfather.

Now, let's look at lines 311 and 312. I notice that "a long time" has passed.

From that information, what is the answer? **Have students try to explain what happens in the story before offering the answer.**

The beginning of the story is told in third-person about a boy learning a lesson from his grandfather. After Grandfather's Song finishes, the story is told from the first-person point of view of a child. The lapse in time and shift in point of view must mean that Father was the boy of eight winters who heard the story from Grandfather and is now telling his son the story.

Have students write the answer on the page.

Guided Practice

2. Integrate information from the text and the impact of the audio version to evaluate Grandfather's oratory skills.

How will I start my answer? This particular prompt has two direction words. Tell your partner how to respond according to the chart. (If the prompt asks you to *integrate*, the response requires that you combine different kinds of information. If the prompt asks you to *evaluate*, the response requires that you think carefully to make a judgment; form a critical opinion of) Will I use information from the text or audio? (both) Turn the prompt into a question to confirm understanding. (Is Grandfather a good speaker, chanter, storyteller in your opinion?) Now, let's find evidence in the conversation between grandfather and the boy.

If needed, guide students to lines 51 and 97 and 98.

The boy knew with satisfaction that soon he would understand . . . Line 51

. . . the crinkles around his eyes spoke of other boys—and other times. Lines 97 and 98

Have students think about the sound of Grandfather's voice and the dramatization of his words. Write the following sentence frames on the board.

Grandfather was a good/bad storyteller who ____________________.
He is an experienced/inexperienced storyteller who ____________.
When hearing the chant, ____________________________________
____.

Lesson 8 | Reading

Passage Comprehension (*cont.*)

3. Trace and evaluate how the wolves' points of view changed regarding living with the People. Provide text evidence.

At first, the wolves felt comfortable and merely watched the People from afar. When the People moved into the center of their habitat, the wolves changed, grew bold, and appeared savage because man and wolf were competing for the same food resources. There were no longer any boundaries.

Text Evidence: "But I still don't understand," the boy continued. "Why does Wolf look at Fire? Why does he feel at home so close to our living space? Why does Wolf Woman begin her song on a hill so close to us who are not Wolf?"; "We have known each other for a long time," the old man answered. "We have learned to live with one another."; *"and also Wolf grew bolder coming in to look for food so that it was worse than before WE HAD NO WISH TO TAME WOLF"*

4. Evaluate the impact of hearing Grandfather's Song the way it was intended.

Reading the chant allows the reader to understand the content of the lesson and know how the People came to learn from Wolf. However, hearing the chant as told by Grandfather allows the listener to understand the rhythm of the chant and commit the lesson to memory in a more successful way.

Unit 8 91

Lesson 8 | Reading

Passage Comprehension (*cont.*)

5. Summarize human interaction with the environment from the People's point of view.

The wolves wanted to live in peace with the People (Native Americans) at a distance, but the People moved into their habitat and used up their resources. So, the wolves treated the People like the enemy instead of their neighbor. After making this mistake, the People believed that human interaction with the environment should be one of reciprocation and empathy. In the end, the People learned to consider every aspect of the environment and how their actions would affect the environment and those inhabiting it.

6. Summarize human interaction with the environment from the new People's point of view.

The new People believed that human interaction with the environment should be to use what is needed, when it is needed, in the manner that it is needed, without regard to other living beings. The new People sailed to the new land and wanted to do things their way—the way they believed was right. Even though the People wanted them to learn from their mistakes and consider the future of the environment and all living things, they did not listen. The new People used the land and resources in the ways that benefited them the most, with little regard for others. This made the Native Americans wonder about the future of the land and their people and whether the new People would ever learn to consider "Wolf."

92 Unit 8

Independent Practice

Have partners respond to the remaining prompts with text evidence when requested. For students who need more assistance, provide the following alternative questions and sentence starters.

Alternative questions and sentence starters:

3. How did the wolves' point of view change regarding living with the People?

   At first, ______.

   When the People moved into the center of their habitat, ______.

4. What is the impact of hearing Grandfather's chant the way it was intended?

   Reading the chant allows the reader ______.

   However, hearing the chant as told by Grandfather allows the listener ______.

5. What is the most important information about human interaction with the environment from the People's point of view?

   The wolves wanted to live in peace with the people at a distance, but the People ______.

   So, the wolves treated the People ______.

   After making a mistake, the People believed that human interaction with the environment ______.

   In the end, the People learned ______.

6. What is the most important information about human interaction with the environment from the new People's point of view?

   The new People believed that human interaction with the environment should be ______.

   The new People sailed to the new land and wanted ______.

   Even though the People wanted them to learn from their mistakes and consider ______, *they* ______.

   The new People ______.

Unit 8

Lesson 9

Lesson Opener

Before the lesson, choose one of the following activities to write on the board or post on the *LANGUAGE! Live* Class Wall online.

- *Answer the following question in one paragraph. How do you speak for Wolf?*
- *Write one sentence about the beliefs of the People and one sentence about the beliefs of the new People. Combine them using a subordinating conjunction.*
- *Identify the following as dependent clauses or independent clauses.*
  - *within himself he saw*
  - *joining his brothers near the hill*
  - *beyond where Wolf was standing*
  - *they sang for the moon*
  - *the boy listened*
  - *to seek a new place*

Reading

Objectives

- Read literature with purpose and understanding.
- Answer questions to demonstrate comprehension of text.
- Identify and explain explicit details from text.
- Monitor comprehension of text during reading.
- Determine the impact of word choice, poetic style, and repetition.
- Determine the meaning of proverbs, adages, and aphorisms.
- Identify shifts in point of view.
- Identify the use of the interrogative and conditional moods.
- Identify foreshadowing in literature.
- Determine the meaning and purpose of verbs in the past perfect tense.

Close Reading of *Who Speaks for Wolf*

Highlighters or colored pencils

Let's reread *Who Speaks for Wolf.* I will provide specific instructions on how to mark the text to help with comprehension.

Have students get out a highlighter or colored pencil.

Direct students to pages 93–105 in their Student Books.

Draw a rectangle around the title.

Draw a star at the beginning of the chant. How do you know where the chant begins? (capital letters; italics)

Now, let's read the vocabulary words aloud.

- What's the first bold vocabulary word? (immobile) *Immobile* means "completely still." My broken arm will be *immobile* after the doctor puts it in a cast. **Have partners use the word in a sentence.**
- What's the next bold vocabulary word? (sought) *Sought* means "tried to do, find, or get something." I *sought* the perfect schedule for my senior year but ended up still having seven classes. **Have partners use the word in a sentence.**

- Let's continue. (counseled) *Counseled* means "gave advice or support to someone." My friends *counseled* me on how to handle the pressures of studying and playing sports in college. **Have partners use the word in a sentence.**
- Next word? (reconsider) *Reconsider* means "to think about whether a past action or decision should be changed." Your parents may *reconsider* their decision to let you drive to school if you get a speeding ticket. **Have partners use the word in a sentence.**
- Next word? (apparent) *Apparent* means "easy to see or understand." Working hard in school makes it *apparent* that you care about your future. **Have partners use the word in a sentence.**
- Next word? (devised) *Devised* means "planned or invented something." In my dream, I *devised* a way to make money while lying on a beach and doing nothing. **Have partners use the word in a sentence.**
- Next word? (course) *Course* means "the path or direction that someone or something moves along." The *course* of the river winds through the mountains. **Have partners use the word in a sentence.**
- Let's continue. (maintain) *Maintain* means "to continue having or doing something." Develop good study habits to *maintain* good grades. **Have partners use the word in a sentence.**
- Next word? (cherished) *Cherished* means "treated with love or care; held dear." When I was your age, teens *cherished* their opportunities to talk on the telephone; now, teens *cherish* their opportunities to text and IM. **Have partners use the word in a sentence.**
- Last word? (omission) *Omission* means "the act of leaving something out or undone." The *omission* of standardized tests would make many students happy. **Have partners use the word in a sentence.**

Talk with a partner about any vocabulary word that is still confusing for you to read or understand.

As you read the story, you will monitor your understanding by circling the check marks or the question marks. Please be sure to draw a question mark over any confusing words, phrases, or sentences.

Options for rereading text.

- Teacher read-aloud
- Teacher-led or student-led choral read
- Paired read or independent read with bold vocabulary words read aloud

Choose an option for reading text. Have students read lines 1–24 according to the option that you chose.

When most of the students are finished, continue with the entire class. Let's see how well you understood what you read.

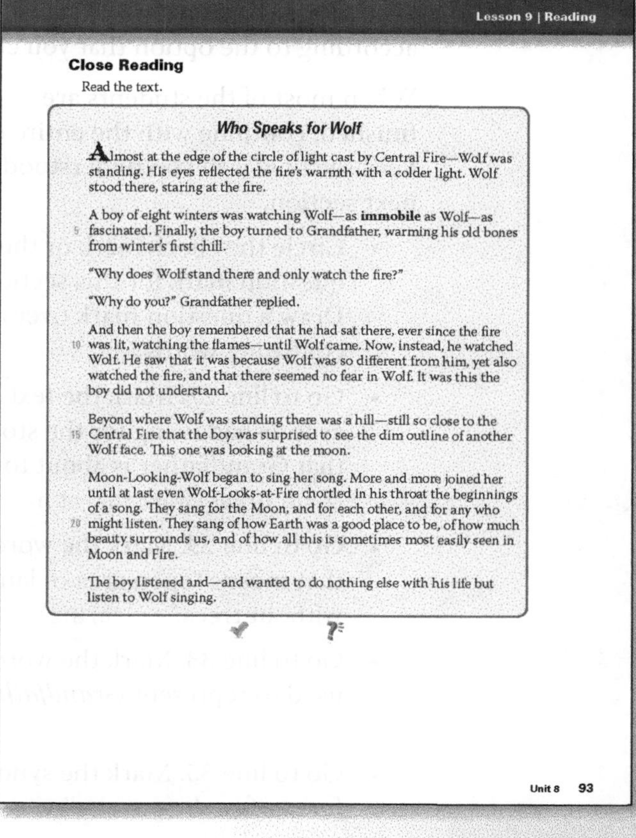

Lesson 9 | Reading

Close Reading

Read the text.

Who Speaks for Wolf

Almost at the edge of the circle of light cast by Central Fire—Wolf was standing. His eyes reflected the fire's warmth with a colder light. Wolf stood there, staring at the fire.

A boy of eight winters was watching Wolf—as **immobile** as Wolf—as fascinated. Finally, the boy turned to Grandfather, warming his old bones from winter's first chill.

"Why does Wolf stand there and only watch the fire?"

"Why do you?" Grandfather replied.

And then the boy remembered that he had sat there, ever since the fire was lit, watching the flames—until Wolf came. Now, instead, he watched Wolf. He saw that it was because Wolf was so different from him, yet also watched the fire, and that there seemed no fear in Wolf. It was this the boy did not understand.

Beyond where Wolf was standing there was a hill—still so close to the Central Fire that the boy was surprised to see the dim outline of another Wolf face. This one was looking at the moon.

Moon-Looking-Wolf began to sing her song. More and more joined her until at last even Wolf-Looks-at-Fire chortled in his throat the beginnings of a song. They sang for the Moon, and for each other, and for any who might listen. They sang of how Earth was a good place to be, of how much beauty surrounds us, and of how all this is sometimes most easily seen in Moon and Fire.

The boy listened and—and wanted to do nothing else with his life but listen to Wolf singing.

Unit 8 93

- Circle the check mark or the question mark for this section. Draw a question mark over any confusing words.
- Go to line 1. Mark the word that means "to shine, throw, or give off." (cast)
- On the same line, mark the word for *center.* (Central)
- Go to line 4. Mark the age of the boy. (eight winters)
- Go to line 12. Mark what the boy believed to be true of Wolf. (there seemed no fear in Wolf)
- On the same line, circle the pronoun *this.* Draw an arrow to the phrase that *this* refers to. (no fear in Wolf)
- Go to line 18. Mark the synonym for *laughed.* (chortled)

Have students read lines 25–40 according to the option that you chose.

When most of the students are finished, continue with the entire class. Let's see how well you understood the next section.

- Circle the check mark or the question mark for this section. Draw a question mark over any confusing words.
- Go to line 27. Mark the text used as foreshadowing for the story that Grandfather is about to tell. (I am here! Don't forget me!)
- Go to line 29. Mark the word that means "open area of land without trees." (clearing)
- Go to line 33. Mark the words used to represent *Grandfather*. (old man)
- Go to line 35. Mark the synonym for *confused*. (puzzled)
- In the next sentence, mark the phrase that provides evidence that the boy still had many questions. (saw only the edges of understanding)
- Go to line 38. Mark the word that means "regular beats or rhythm." (cadences)
- Mark the evidence that shows the boy believes Grandfather is wise. (The boy knew with satisfaction that soon he would understand.)

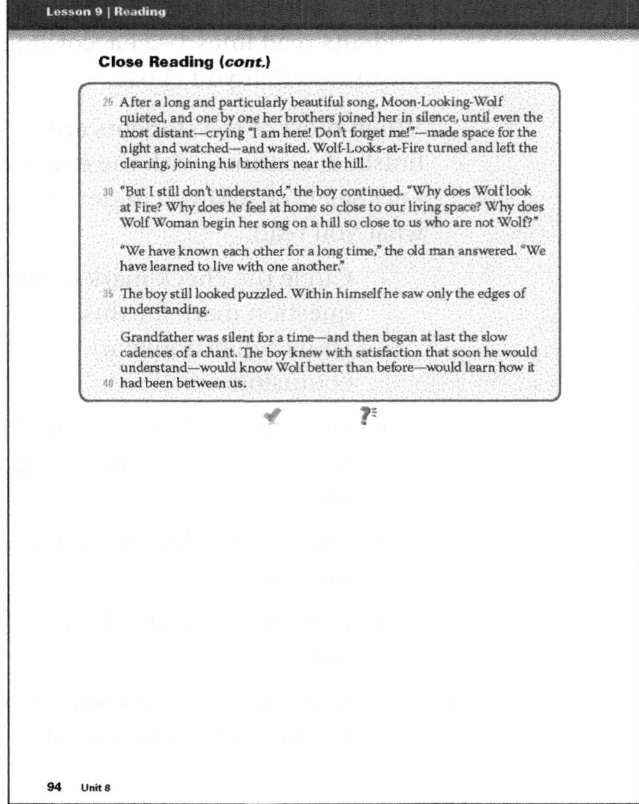
Lesson 9 | Reading

Close Reading (*cont.*)

After a long and particularly beautiful song, Moon-Looking-Wolf quieted, and one by one her brothers joined her in silence, until even the most distant—crying "I am here! Don't forget me!"—made space for the night and watched—and waited. Wolf-Looks-at-Fire turned and left the clearing, joining his brothers near the hill.

"But I still don't understand," the boy continued. "Why does Wolf look at Fire? Why does he feel at home so close to our living space? Why does Wolf Woman begin her song on a hill so close to us who are not Wolf?"

"We have known each other for a long time," the old man answered. "We have learned to live with one another."

The boy still looked puzzled. Within himself he saw only the edges of understanding.

Grandfather was silent for a time—and then began at last the slow cadences of a chant. The boy knew with satisfaction that soon he would understand—would know Wolf better than before—would learn how it had been between us.

94 Unit 8

Have students read lines 41–67 according to the option that you chose.

When most of the students are finished, continue with the entire class. Let's see how well you understood what you read.

- Circle the check mark or the question mark for this section. Draw a question mark over any confusing words.
- Go to line 42. Mark the person who is telling the story. (Grandfather)
- Go to lines 45 and 46. Mark the evidence that the People needed more space. (where we were was no longer enough)
- Go to line 49. Mark the present tense of a vocabulary word meaning "to look for." (seek)
- Go to line 53. Mark the synonym for *chosen*. (selected)
- Go to line 54. Mark the evidence of competition among the People. (each determined his place was best)
- Mark the words under *Long Ago* that use past tense to convey time. (grew, sent, searched, returned, selected, determined)
- Go to line 61. Mark the person who understood and was trusted by the wolves. (Wolf's brother)
- Mark the words under *Now, At That Time* that are evidence that the wolves trusted Wolf's brother. (he would sing their song; they would answer him; their young would follow him; they meant to learn from him)
- Go to line 60. Mark the word *Wolf*. In the margin, write what "Wolf" represents. (wolves)

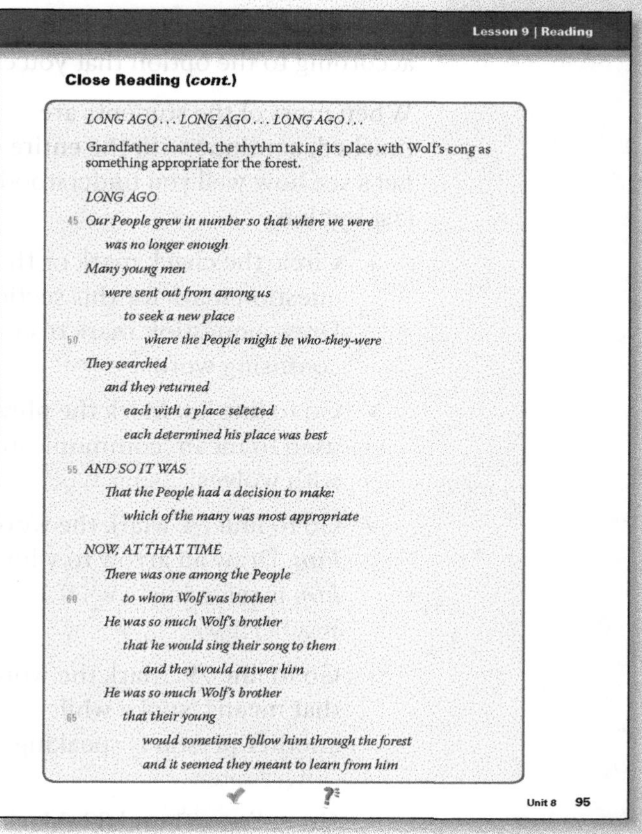

Lesson 9 | Reading

Close Reading (*cont.*)

LONG AGO . . . LONG AGO . . . LONG AGO . . .

Grandfather chanted, the rhythm taking its place with Wolf's song as something appropriate for the forest.

LONG AGO
Our People grew in number so that where we were
was no longer enough
Many young men
were sent out from among us
to seek a new place
where the People might be who-they-were
They searched
and they returned
each with a place selected
each determined his place was best
AND SO IT WAS
That the People had a decision to make:
which of the many was most appropriate
NOW, AT THAT TIME
There was one among the People
to whom Wolf was brother
He was so much Wolf's brother
that he would sing their song to them
and they would answer him
He was so much Wolf's brother
that their young
would sometimes follow him through the forest
and it seemed they meant to learn from him

✓ ?

Unit 8 95

Have students read lines 68–95 according to the option that you chose.

When most of the students are finished, continue with the entire class. Let's see how well you understood the last section.

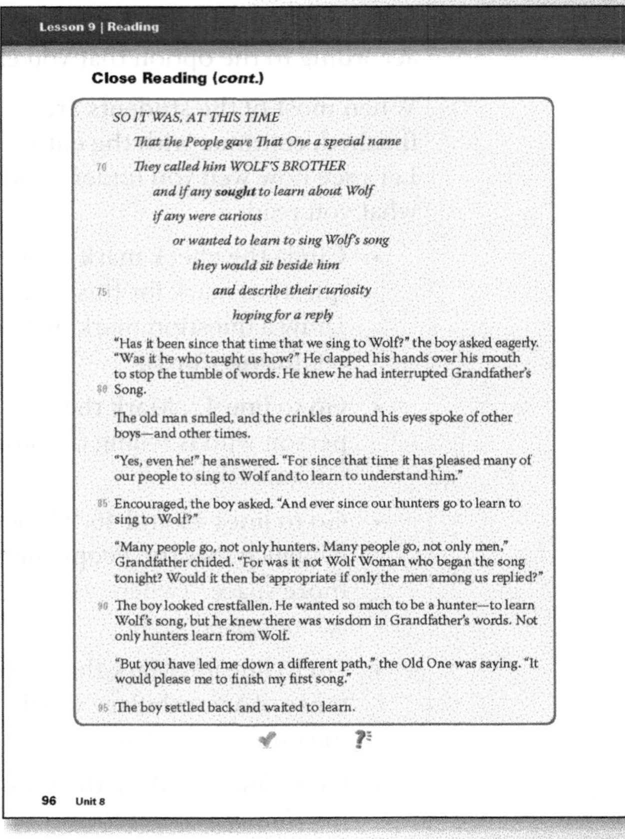

Lesson 9 | Reading

Close Reading (*cont.*)

SO IT WAS, AT THIS TIME
That the People gave That One a special name
They called him WOLF'S BROTHER
and if any ***sought*** *to learn about Wolf*
if any were curious
or wanted to learn to sing Wolf's song
they would sit beside him
and describe their curiosity
hoping for a reply

"Has it been since that time that we sing to Wolf?" the boy asked eagerly. "Was it he who taught us how?" He clapped his hands over his mouth to stop the tumble of words. He knew he had interrupted Grandfather's Song.

The old man smiled, and the crinkles around his eyes spoke of other boys—and other times.

"Yes, even he!" he answered. "For since that time it has pleased many of our people to sing to Wolf and to learn to understand him."

Encouraged, the boy asked, "And ever since our hunters go to learn to sing to Wolf?"

"Many people go, not only hunters. Many people go, not only men," Grandfather chided. "For was it not Wolf Woman who began the song tonight? Would it then be appropriate if only the men among us replied?"

The boy looked crestfallen. He wanted so much to be a hunter—to learn Wolf's song, but he knew there was wisdom in Grandfather's words. Not only hunters learn from Wolf.

"But you have led me down a different path," the Old One was saying. "It would please me to finish my first song."

The boy settled back and waited to learn.

96 Unit 8

- Circle the check mark or the question mark for this section. Draw a question mark over any confusing words.
- Go to line 73. Mark the phrase used to mean "communicate with wolves." (sing Wolf's song)
- Go to line 74. Mark the word *him*. Draw an arrow to whom *him* is referring. (WOLF'S BROTHER)
- Go to line 79. Mark the word that means "spoke while another person is speaking." (interrupted)
- Go to lines 81 and 82. Mark the evidence that Grandfather is used to telling stories. (crinkles around his eyes spoke of other boys—and other times)
- Go to line 88. Mark the word that means "lectured or scolded." (chided)
- Go to line 90. Mark the word that means "disappointed." (crestfallen)
- On lines 90–92, mark the evidence that the tribe learned to stalk prey from the Wolf. (He wanted so much to be a hunter—to learn Wolf's song; Not only hunters learn from Wolf)
- Go to line 93. Mark the synonym for *course*. (path)
- On the same line, mark the reference to Grandfather. (the Old One)
- Look carefully at the different types of text on the page. The top part is Grandfather's chant. The bottom half is written text about the dialogue between the boy and his grandfather. Why do you think the author chose to write the "chant" in a poetic form? (Answers will vary.) What is the impact of this decision? In the margin, explain the difference between the two texts and how you interpret the decision to make them appear so different.

Have students read lines 96–123 according to the option that you chose.

When most of the students are finished, continue with the entire class. Let's see how well you understood this section.

- Circle the check mark or the question mark for this section. Draw a question mark over any confusing words.
- In this section, mark the repetitive phrases that the author uses for emphasis. (they listened, they chose, he/she who understood)
- Go to line 106. Mark what are defined as the Three Sisters. (Corn, Beans, and Squash)
- Go to line 107. Mark the phrase that Grandfather uses to express the need for fertile soil. (might find a place to their liking)
- Go to line 108. Mark the word *They*. In the margin, write who *They* is referring to. (the People)
- Mark the reference to the person who knew the landscape. (he who understood the flow of waters)
- Mark the reference to the person who knew about building material and geology. (she who understood Long House construction)
- Mark the reference to the person who knew weather patterns. (he who understood the storms of winter)
- Mark the reference to the person who knew about agriculture. (she who understood Three Sisters)
- Go to line 120. Mark the word that means "oldest." (Eldest)
- Mark the statement indicating a decision was made. (SO BE IT—FOR SO IT IS)

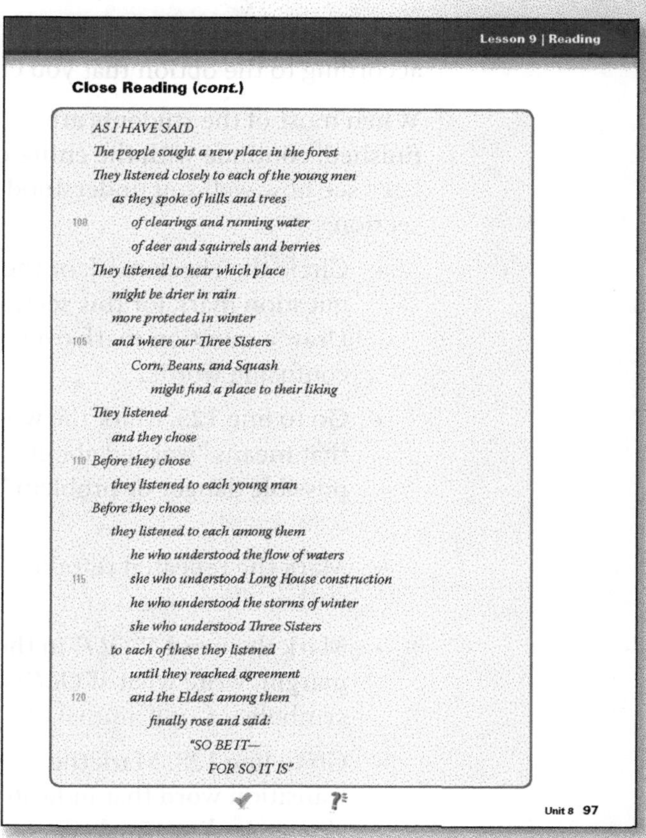

Lesson 9 | Reading

Close Reading (*cont.*)

AS I HAVE SAID
The people sought a new place in the forest
They listened closely to each of the young men
as they spoke of hills and trees
of clearings and running water
of deer and squirrels and berries
They listened to hear which place
might be drier in rain
more protected in winter
and where our Three Sisters
Corn, Beans, and Squash
might find a place to their liking
They listened
and they chose
Before they chose
they listened to each young man
Before they chose
they listened to each among them
he who understood the flow of waters
she who understood Long House construction
he who understood the storms of winter
she who understood Three Sisters
to each of these they listened
until they reached agreement
and the Eldest among them
finally rose and said:
"SO BE IT—
FOR SO IT IS"

Unit 8 97

Have students read lines 124–151 according to the option that you chose.

When most of the students are finished, continue with the entire class. Let's see how well you understood this section.

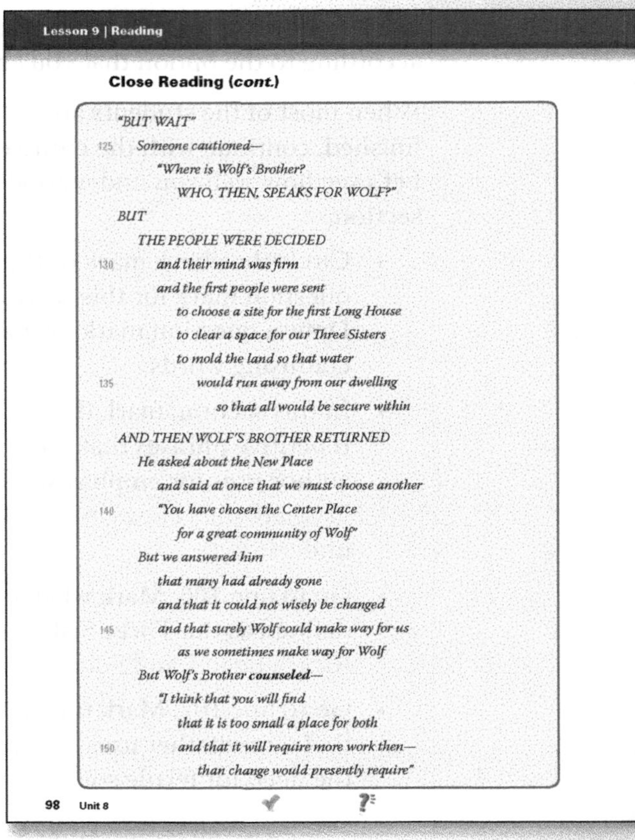

Lesson 9 | Reading

Close Reading (*cont.*)

"BUT WAIT"
Someone cautioned—
"Where is Wolf's Brother?
WHO, THEN, SPEAKS FOR WOLF?"
BUT
THE PEOPLE WERE DECIDED
and their mind was firm
and the first people were sent
to choose a site for the first Long House
to clear a space for our Three Sisters
to mold the land so that water
would run away from our dwelling
so that all would be secure within
AND THEN WOLF'S BROTHER RETURNED
He asked about the New Place
and said at once that we must choose another
"You have chosen the Center Place
for a great community of Wolf"
But we answered him
that many had already gone
and that it could not wisely be changed
and that surely Wolf could make way for us
as we sometimes make way for Wolf
*But Wolf's Brother **counseled**—*
"I think that you will find
that it is too small a place for both
and that it will require more work then—
than change would presently require"

98 Unit 8

- Circle the check mark or the question mark for this section. Draw a question mark over any confusing words.
- Go to line 125. Mark the word that means "warned about possible danger or problem." (cautioned)
- Mark the repeated refrain. (Who, Then, Speaks for Wolf?)
- Mark the word *WOLF.* In the margin, write what *WOLF* is symbolic of. (all animal life)
- Go to line 128. Mark the transition word that indicates a change in direction. (BUT)
- Go to line 130. Mark the evidence that the People could not be persuaded. (their mind was firm)
- Go to line 136. Mark the word that means "free from danger or risk; safe." (secure)
- Go to lines 140 and 141. Mark the evidence that indicates that the People are moving into an animal habitat. (You have chosen the Center Place for a great community of Wolf)
- Go to line 145. Mark the evidence that the People believe that Wolf is capable of rational thinking. (surely Wolf could make way for us)
- Go to lines 150 and 151. Mark the line in which Wolf's Brother is encouraging the People to prevent problems instead of react to them. (and that it would require more work then—than change would presently require)
- Go to line 151. Circle the word that is used to compare *work* and *change.* (than)

Have students read lines 152–176 according to the option that you chose.

When most of the students are finished, continue with the entire class. Let's see how well you understood this section.

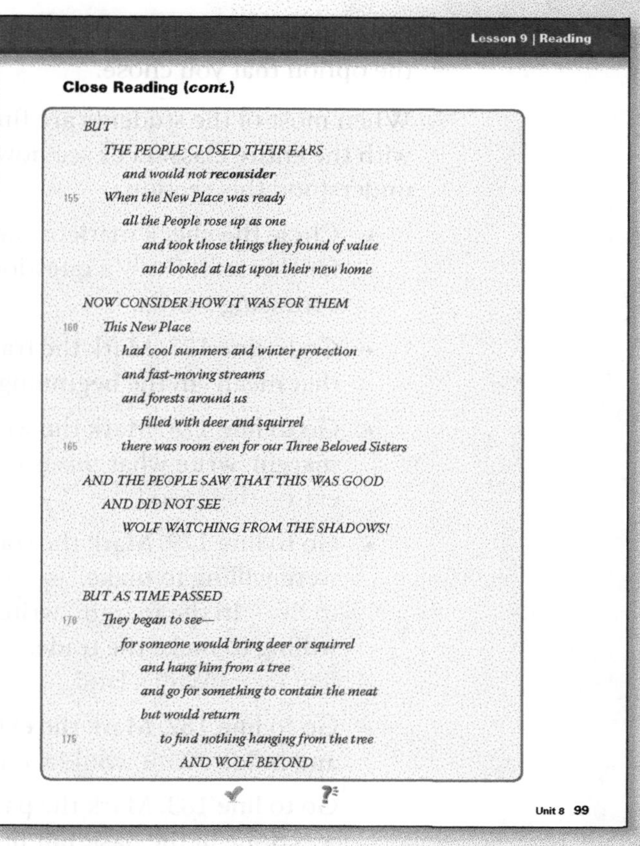

Lesson 9 | Reading

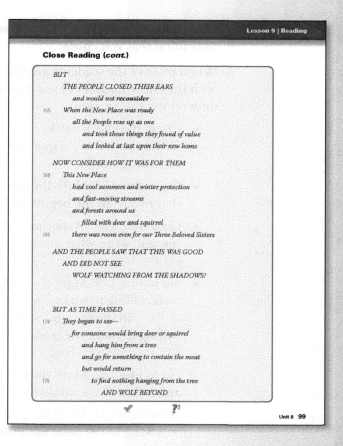

Close Reading (*cont.*)

BUT
THE PEOPLE CLOSED THEIR EARS
and would not ***reconsider***
When the New Place was ready
all the People rose up as one
and took those things they found of value
and looked at last upon their new home

NOW CONSIDER HOW IT WAS FOR THEM
This New Place
had cool summers and winter protection
and fast-moving streams
and forests around us
filled with deer and squirrel
there was room even for our Three Beloved Sisters

AND THE PEOPLE SAW THAT THIS WAS GOOD
AND DID NOT SEE
WOLF WATCHING FROM THE SHADOWS!

BUT AS TIME PASSED
They began to see—
for someone would bring deer or squirrel
and hang him from a tree
and go for something to contain the meat
but would return
to find nothing hanging from the tree
AND WOLF BEYOND

✓ ?

Unit 8 99

- Circle the check mark or the question mark for this section. Draw a question mark over any confusing words.
- Mark the words under *BUT* that provide evidence that the People ignored Wolf's Brother. (THE PEOPLE CLOSED THEIR EARS and would not reconsider)
- Go to line 157. Mark the word that means "usefulness or importance." (value)
- Number the attributes of the new place under *This New Place.* (1. cool summers and winter protection 2. fast-moving streams 3. forests filled with deer and squirrel 4. room for our Three Beloved Sisters)
- Go to line 168. Mark the line that foreshadows danger. (WOLF WATCHING FROM THE SHADOWS) Which character is the author using to produce suspense? (Wolf)
- Go to line 175. Mark the evidence that Wolf was stealing their food. (to find nothing hanging from the tree AND WOLF BEYOND)

Have students read lines 177–202 according to the option that you chose.

When most of the students are finished, continue with the entire class. Let's see how well you understood this section.

Lesson 9 | Reading

Close Reading (*cont.*)

AT FIRST
This seemed to us an appropriate exchange—
some food for a place to live

BUT
*It soon became **apparent** that it was more than this—*
for Wolf would sometimes walk between the dwellings
that we had fashioned for ourselves
and the women grew concerned
for the safety of the little ones
Thinking of this
they devised for a while an agreement with Wolf
whereby the women would gather together
at the edge of our village
and put out food for Wolf and his brothers

BUT IT WAS SOON APPARENT
That this meant too much food
and also Wolf grew bolder
coming in to look for food
so that it was worse than before
WE HAD NO WISH TO TAME WOLF

AND SO
Hearing the wailing of the women
*the men **devised** a system*
whereby some ones among them
were always alert to drive off Wolf

AND WOLF WAS SOON HIS OLD UNTAMED SELF

100 Unit 8

- Circle the check mark or the question mark for this text. Draw a question mark over any confusing words.
- Go to line 177. Mark the transition words that mean "In the beginning." (AT FIRST)
- Go to line 178. Mark the word *This*. In the margin, write what *this* is referring to. (Wolf eating their food)
- Go to line 179. Mark the trade that people were willing to make. (some food for a place to live) In the margin, write why they were willing to make the trade. (they knew they had taken Wolf's land)
- Go to line 182. Mark the evidence that Wolf was becoming more comfortable and bold. (Wolf would sometimes walk between the dwellings)
- Go to line 183. Mark the past perfect verb phrase indicating that the action was done in the past, but prior to Wolf walking between the dwellings. (had fashioned)
- Go to line 184. Mark the evidence that the women were afraid. (the women grew concerned) In the margin, write what they were afraid would happen. (Wolf would harm their children)
- Go to lines 188–190. Mark the plan devised to keep wolf from coming near their homes and children. (women would gather together at the edge of our village and put out food for Wolf and his brothers)
- Go to line 192. Mark the evidence that people couldn't afford to continue feeding Wolf. (this meant too much food)
- Go to line 193. Mark the comparative adjective that means "more unafraid of danger." (bolder)
- On line 194, mark the way the bolder Wolf got food. (coming in to look for food) In the margin, write what we know about the wolf's eating habits that would make the people scared of him looking for food in the village. (predator; hunter)
- Go to line 195. Mark the word *it*. In the margin, write what *it* refers to. (Wolf's presence in the village)
- Go to line 196. Mark the word that means "to make less wild." (TAME)
- Go to lines 200 and 201. Mark the new plan to take care of the wolf problem. (some ones among them were always alert to drive off Wolf)
- Go to line 202. Mark the evidence that the attempt to tame Wolf was a failure. (AND WOLF WAS SOON HIS OLD UNTAMED SELF) Circle the prefix that means "not." (un-)

Have students read lines 203–225 according to the option that you chose.

When most of the students are finished, continue with the entire class. Let's see how well you understood this section.

- Circle the check mark or the question mark for this text. Draw a question mark over any confusing words.
- Go to line 205. Mark the evidence that the People were working too hard to keep themselves safe from Wolf. (that this required so much energy) Did Wolf's Brother's prediction come true? Write your answer in the margin. (yes)
- Go to line 207. Mark the words used to represent winter. (the Long Cold)
- Mark the words under *THEY SAW* that are proof that the People realized that the extra work wasn't worth the benefits of the new place. (neither providing Wolf with food nor driving him off gave the People a life that was pleasing)
- Go to line 222. Mark evidence that the People knew how to solve the problem. (hunt down this Wolf People until they were no more)
- What words are repeated four times in this section? (They Saw)

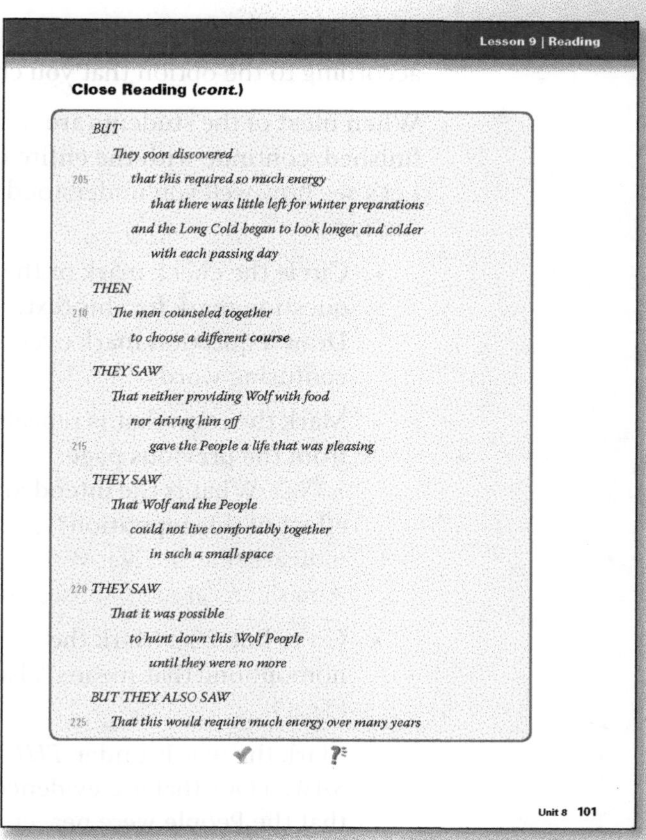
Lesson 9 | Reading

Close Reading (*cont.*)

BUT
They soon discovered
that this required so much energy
that there was little left for winter preparations
and the Long Cold began to look longer and colder
with each passing day

THEN
The men counseled together
to choose a different course

THEY SAW
That neither providing Wolf with food
nor driving him off
gave the People a life that was pleasing

THEY SAW
That Wolf and the People
could not live comfortably together
in such a small space

THEY SAW
That it was possible
to hunt down this Wolf People
until they were no more

BUT THEY ALSO SAW
That this would require much energy over many years

Unit 8 101

Have students read lines 226–249 according to the option that you chose.

When most of the students are finished, continue with the entire class. Let's see how well you understood this section.

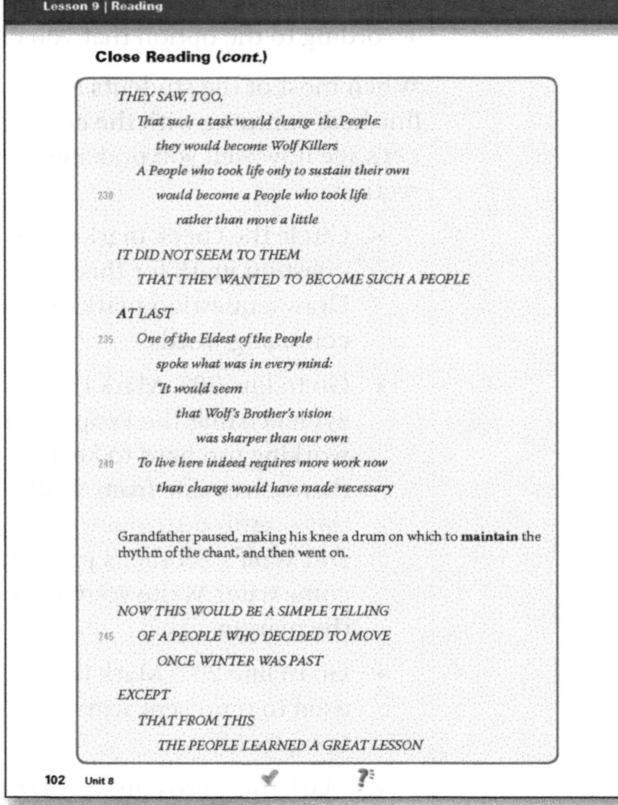
Lesson 9 | Reading

Close Reading (*cont.*)

THEY SAW, TOO,
That such a task would change the People:
they would become Wolf Killers
A People who took life only to sustain their own
would become a People who took life
rather than move a little

IT DID NOT SEEM TO THEM
THAT THEY WANTED TO BECOME SUCH A PEOPLE

AT LAST
One of the Eldest of the People
spoke what was in every mind:
"It would seem
that Wolf's Brother's vision
was sharper than our own
To live here indeed requires more work now
than change would have made necessary

Grandfather paused, making his knee a drum on which to **maintain** the rhythm of the chant, and then went on.

NOW THIS WOULD BE A SIMPLE TELLING
OF A PEOPLE WHO DECIDED TO MOVE
ONCE WINTER WAS PAST
EXCEPT
THAT FROM THIS
THE PEOPLE LEARNED A GREAT LESSON

102 Unit 8

- Circle the check mark or the question mark for this text. Draw a question mark over any confusing words.
- Mark the term that is repeated from the previous page. (THEY SAW) What is the intended effect of this repetition? (to indicate that the Native Americans are very observant)
- Go to line 226. Mark the homophone that means "also." (TOO)
- Mark the words under *THEY SAW, TOO,* that are evidence that the People were peaceful. (they would become Wolf Killers)
- In the same section, mark the line that indicates they were a people who only killed animals for food. (a People who took life only to sustain their own)
- Go to line 231. Mark the phrase that means "instead of." (rather than)
- Go to line 234. Mark the transition words that mean "finally." (AT LAST)
- Go to line 247. Mark the transition word that indicates a change of direction and means "but." (EXCEPT)
- Go to line 249. Mark what was learned. (A GREAT LESSON) In the margin, write what the People learned. (It is not only important to choose a place that gives you what you need, but it is important to choose a place that does not disrupt the quality of life of other beings.)

Have students read lines 250–266 according to the option that you chose.

When most of the students are finished, continue with the entire class. Let's see how well you understand this section.

- Circle the check mark or the question mark for this text. Draw a question mark over any confusing words.
- Go to line 253. Mark the word that means "a group that makes decisions." (Council) In the margin, write the vocabulary word that is a homophone for this word. (counsel)
- Go to line 261. Mark what destroys houses and forces them to rebuild. (winter storms)
- Go to line 264. Mark the words that mean "running water." (water does not stand)
- Mark what is caused by standing water. (sickness)
- Go to line 266. Mark the word of Latin origin that literally means "to look closely." (CONSIDER)
- In the margin, mark what Wolf is representing now. (all living beings)

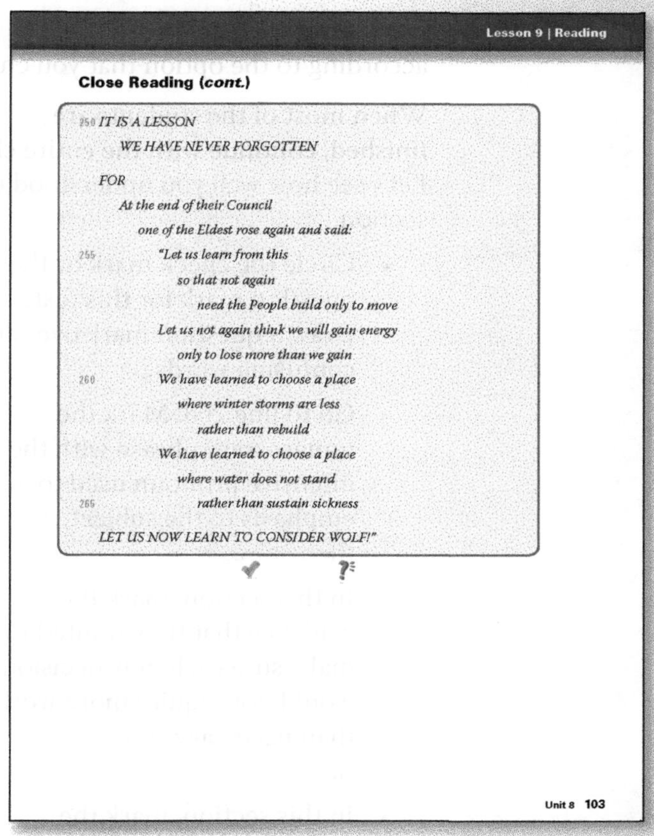
Lesson 9 | Reading

Close Reading (*cont.*)

IT IS A LESSON
WE HAVE NEVER FORGOTTEN
FOR
At the end of their Council
one of the Eldest rose again and said:
"Let us learn from this
so that not again
need the People build only to move
Let us not again think we will gain energy
only to lose more than we gain
We have learned to choose a place
where winter storms are less
rather than rebuild
We have learned to choose a place
where water does not stand
rather than sustain sickness
LET US NOW LEARN TO CONSIDER WOLF!"

Unit 8 103

Have students read lines 267–283 according to the option that you chose.

When most of the students are finished, continue with the entire class. Let's see how well you understood this section.

- Circle the check mark or the question mark for this text. Draw a question mark over any confusing words.
- Go to line 268. Mark the unnecessary phrase with the intensive pronoun used to add emphasis to the subject. (among themselves)
- In this section, mark the evidence that they wanted to make sure each new decision would not require more work than necessary. (perceive the flow of energy)
- In this section, mark the evidence that the People did not want to live in excess. (how much was too much)
- In this section, mark the words used to indicate that sometimes people do not understand and, therefore, cannot remember. (to remind us of things we do not yet see clearly enough to remember)

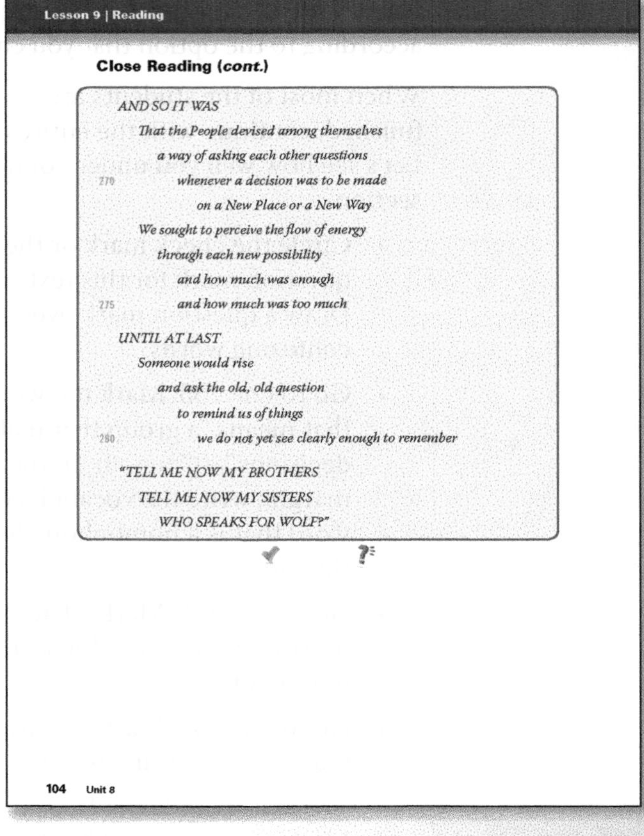

Close Reading (*cont.*)

AND SO IT WAS
That the People devised among themselves
a way of asking each other questions
whenever a decision was to be made
on a New Place or a New Way
We sought to perceive the flow of energy
through each new possibility
and how much was enough
and how much was too much

UNTIL AT LAST
Someone would rise
and ask the old, old question
to remind us of things
we do not yet see clearly enough to remember

"TELL ME NOW MY BROTHERS
TELL ME NOW MY SISTERS
WHO SPEAKS FOR WOLF?"

Have students read from line 284 to the end according to the option that you chose.

When most of the students are finished, continue with the entire class. Let's see how well you understood this section.

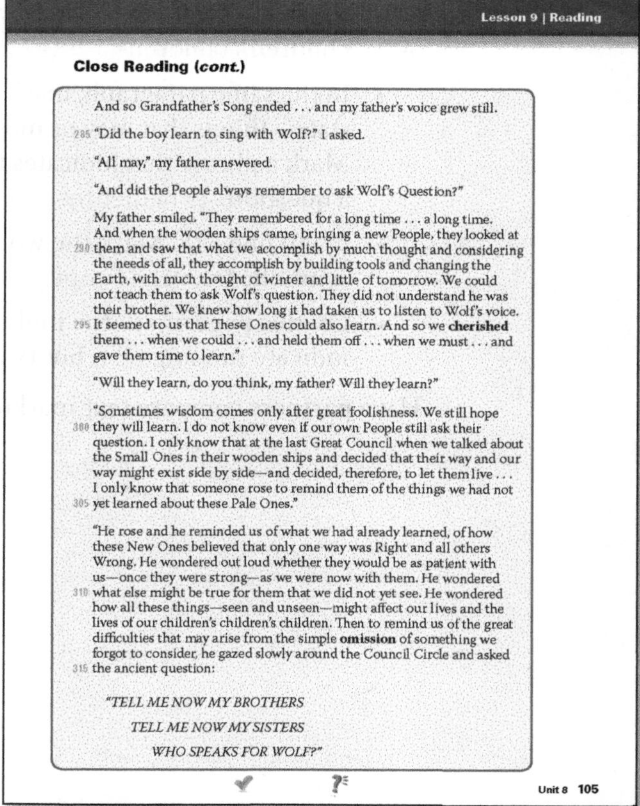

Lesson 9 | Reading

Close Reading (*cont.*)

And so Grandfather's Song ended . . . and my father's voice grew still.

"Did the boy learn to sing with Wolf?" I asked.

"All may," my father answered.

"And did the People always remember to ask Wolf's Question?"

My father smiled. "They remembered for a long time . . . a long time. And when the wooden ships came, bringing a new People, they looked at them and saw that what we accomplish by much thought and considering the needs of all, they accomplish by building tools and changing the Earth, with much thought of winter and little of tomorrow. We could not teach them to ask Wolf's question. They did not understand he was their brother. We knew how long it had taken us to listen to Wolf's voice. It seemed to us that These Ones could also learn. And so we **cherished** them . . . when we could . . . and held them off . . . when we must . . . and gave them time to learn."

"Will they learn, do you think, my father? Will they learn?"

"Sometimes wisdom comes only after great foolishness. We still hope they will learn. I do not know even if our own People still ask their question. I only know that at the last Great Council when we talked about the Small Ones in their wooden ships and decided that their way and our way might exist side by side—and decided, therefore, to let them live . . . I only know that someone rose to remind them of the things we had not yet learned about these Pale Ones."

"He rose and he reminded us of what we had already learned, of how these New Ones believed that only one way was Right and all others Wrong. He wondered out loud whether they would be as patient with us—once they were strong—as we were now with them. He wondered what else might be true for them that we did not yet see. He wondered how all these things—seen and unseen—might affect our lives and the lives of our children's children's children. Then to remind us of the great difficulties that may arise from the simple **omission** of something we forgot to consider, he gazed slowly around the Council Circle and asked the ancient question:

"TELL ME NOW MY BROTHERS

TELL ME NOW MY SISTERS

WHO SPEAKS FOR WOLF?"

Unit 8 105

- Circle the check mark or the question mark for this text. Draw a question mark over any confusing words.
- Mark the evidence that Father was singing the chant, not Grandfather. (my father's voice grew still)
- On this page, there is a change in point of view. Circle the first pronoun used to indicate it is now first person. (my)
- Go to line 289. Mark the words used to mean "Europeans." (a new People)
- Go to line 290. Mark the word that means "succeed in doing." (accomplish)
- Go to line 292. Mark the words that prove that the white people failed to think about the effects of their actions. (. . . with much thought of winter and little of tomorrow)
- On lines 293 and 294, mark the evidence that proves the Europeans did not respect other beings. (They did not understand he was their brother.)
- Go to line 295. Mark the words used to rename the European explorers. (These Ones)
- Go to lines 299 and 300. Mark the line indicating that the white people still haven't learned to think of all other beings. (We still hope they will learn.)
- Go to line 302. Mark the words used to rename the European explorers. (Small Ones)
- Circle the word that indicates that European explorers didn't get it. (small)
- Go to line 303. Mark the synonym for *live.* (exist)
- Go to line 305. Mark the words used to rename the European explorers. (Pale Ones)
- In the same paragraph, mark the age-old wisdom that can be applied to many other situations. (. . . wisdom comes only after great foolishness)
- Go to lines 307 and 308. Mark the evidence that it would be hard to live with the New Ones. (believed that only one way was Right and all others Wrong)

- Go to line 312. Mark the words that mean "great grandchildren." (children's children's children)
- In the same paragraph, mark phrases that indicate future tense in the conditional state—things that may or may not happen. (might be, might affect, may arise) Mark a phrase that indicates future tense in the interrogative state—things that are a question. (whether they would be)
- Go to line 318. Mark the word *WOLF.* In the margin, write what *WOLF* is symbolic for. (the People)
- On this page, mark the multiple uses of a punctuation mark that is often used to indicate missing text, but that is used here to show hesitation. (ellipses)

Have partners compare text markings and correct any errors.

Unit 8 Lesson 10

Lesson Opener

Before the lesson, choose one of the following activities to write on the board or post on the *LANGUAGE! Live* Class Wall online.

- *Write four sentences with at least two vocabulary words in each. Show you know the meanings. (immobile, sought, counsel, reconsider, apparent, devise, course, maintain, cherish, omission)*
- *Dress your avatar as though he or she were sitting around a campfire and listening to stories. Describe his clothing and why it is appropriate.*
- *Knowing the perceptions of wolves across cultures, what is your perception of wolves? Write one paragraph providing evidence in support of your position.*

Vocabulary

Objective

- Review key passage vocabulary.

Recontextualize Passage Vocabulary

Direct students to page 70 in their Student Books. Use the following questions to review the vocabulary words from *Who Speaks for Wolf*?

Key Passage Vocabulary: *Who Speaks for Wolf*

Read each word. Write the word in column 3. Then, circle a number to rate your knowledge of the word.

[illegible]	[illegible]	[illegible]	[illegible]
immobile	(adj)	immobile	0 1 2 3
sought	(v)	sought	0 1 2 3
counsel	(v)	counsel	0 1 2 3
reconsider	(v)	reconsider	0 1 2 3
apparent	(adj)	apparent	0 1 2 3
devise	(v)	devise	0 1 2 3
course	(n)	course	0 1 2 3
maintain	(v)	maintain	0 1 2 3
cherish	(v)	cherish	0 1 2 3
omission	(n)	omission	0 1 2 3

70 Unit 8

- You solved the algebra problem but forgot to write your answer on the homework sheet. Was this an *omission*? (yes) Your dad left you a list of chores to do. You did them all well, but you did the last one extra well. Was this an *omission*? (no) You are writing a song, but it isn't working. You take some of the most complicated parts out, and now it sounds perfect. What helped make the song better? (the omissions I made)
- The librarian spots you sitting quietly, but without any books, and she asks if you need help. Would it make sense for you to answer, "No, I just *sought* peace and quiet"? (yes) "Where did you get those shoes?" your mother asks. Would it make sense for you to answer, "I *sought* them"? (no) The grocery store gives stickers, and if you collect a thousand of them, you can cash them in for a beach towel. You saved stickers for an entire year and then got your beach towel. It would make sense to say that you desperately what? (sought a new beach towel)
- You are a trainer, and you're trying to wrap an athlete's ankle, but she keeps tapping her foot to music. Is her ankle *immobile*? (no) If you wrap it properly, will it be *immobile*? (yes) Your four-year-old niece asks you to paint her fingernails. Why is this a challenging task? (She can't stay immobile.)
- You decide to go for a jog, but when you look outside, it's raining. Do you *reconsider*? (yes) You get a job at the pizza place. On day one, you learn that you get unlimited pizza for free. Do you *reconsider* accepting the job? (no) You decide to wear a white suit or dress to a dance. Then, you learn that the dance theme is "The Dark Side." Do you stick to your original choice of outfit? (No, I reconsider.)

- Spinach lasagna was served in the cafeteria today. Your friend has a giant green glob stuck in his front teeth. Is it *apparent* that he had the lasagna? (yes) The restaurant is dark, and the parking lot is empty. Is it *apparent* that the restaurant is closed? (yes) Your buddy Red wears only red shirts. Red is his favorite color. This is what? (apparent)
- You wish there was a way to get flies out of the house without killing them. Have you *devised* a way? (no) You figure out how to tie your shoes without bending over. Have you *devised* a way to do so? (yes) Your friend lives next door. The two of you have come up with a way to communicate without texting. What have you done? (devised a way of communicating)
- You are about to buy the blue sweater, and your friend comments that she has a sweater just like it. Is she *counseling* you? (no) You need help in geometry, and your teacher tells you to come in early the next day for a review. Is he *counseling* you? (yes) You want to try out for the jazz band, but the rehearsal schedule conflicts with your karate lessons. A friend in the jazz band tells you how you can make it work. What is the friend doing? (counseling me)
- In your hardest class, your average has gone up and down. Have you been *maintaining* a high average? (no) Is it the job of a police officer to *maintain* law and order? (yes) When singing, you can hold a note for longer than any other member of the choir. What can you do to the note? (maintain it)
- A small community theater in your neighborhood may have to relocate because the rent for their space has gone up. The neighborhood comes together and raises money for the theater group. Does the neighborhood *cherish* the group? (yes) Your uncle spent many difficult years in a foreign country as a child. He doesn't like to talk about those times. Does he *cherish* the memories? (no) When you were in kindergarten, you appeared in the newspaper for winning a contest. You keep the newspaper clipping in a very safe place. How do you feel about the clipping? (I cherish it.)
- A stream flows from the top of a mountain into a valley. Does it follow a *course*? (yes) The prisoner was not released early because he had not made positive changes in his life. Was he on a new *course*? (no) You pick up a pamphlet titled "How to Stop Biting Your Nails in Six Easy Steps." The pamphlet describes a what? (a course of action for breaking the habit)

Writing

Objectives

- Use multiple texts to write coherently.
- Use a process to write.
- Write a compare/contrast essay on cultural views of wolves.
- Compare and contrast the treatment of similar topics in stories from different cultures.
- Identify how an author's point of view influences the story.
- Use a rubric to guide and assess writing.

Six Traits of Effective Writing

Direct students back to page 35 in their Student Books. Reread the Six Traits of Effective Writing.

We will continue to focus on writing with all six traits.

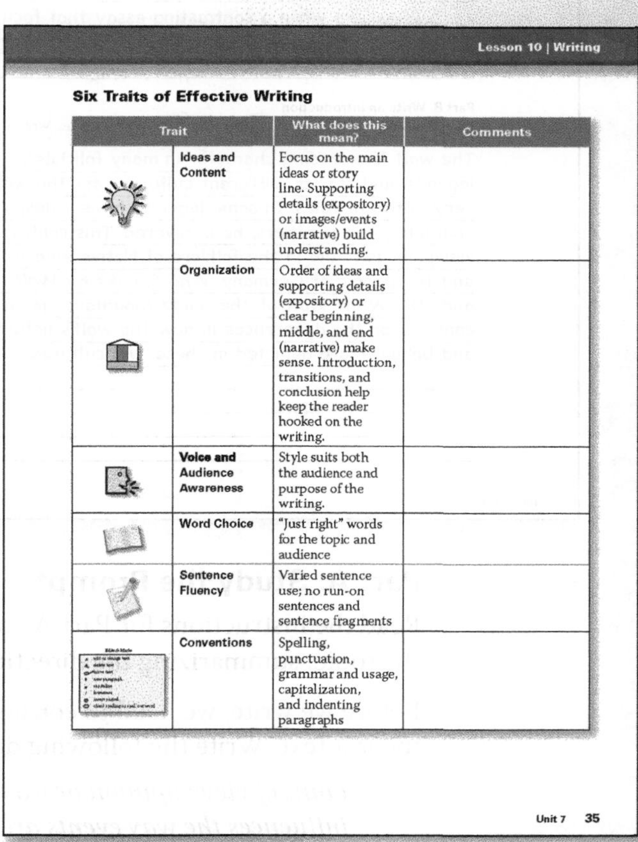

Lesson 10 | Writing

Six Traits of Effective Writing

Trait		What does this mean?	Comments
	Ideas and Content	Focus on the main ideas or story line. Supporting details (expository) or images/events (narrative) build understanding.	
	Organization	Order of ideas and supporting details (expository) or clear beginning, middle, and end (narrative) make sense. Introduction, transitions, and conclusion help keep the reader hooked on the writing.	
	Voice and Audience Awareness	Style suits both the audience and purpose of the writing.	
	Word Choice	"Just right" words for the topic and audience	
	Sentence Fluency	Varied sentence use; no run-on sentences and sentence fragments	
	Conventions	Spelling, punctuation, grammar and usage, capitalization, and indenting paragraphs	

Unit 7 35

Prepare to Write: Contrast Essay

Direct students to pages 106–108 in their Student Books.

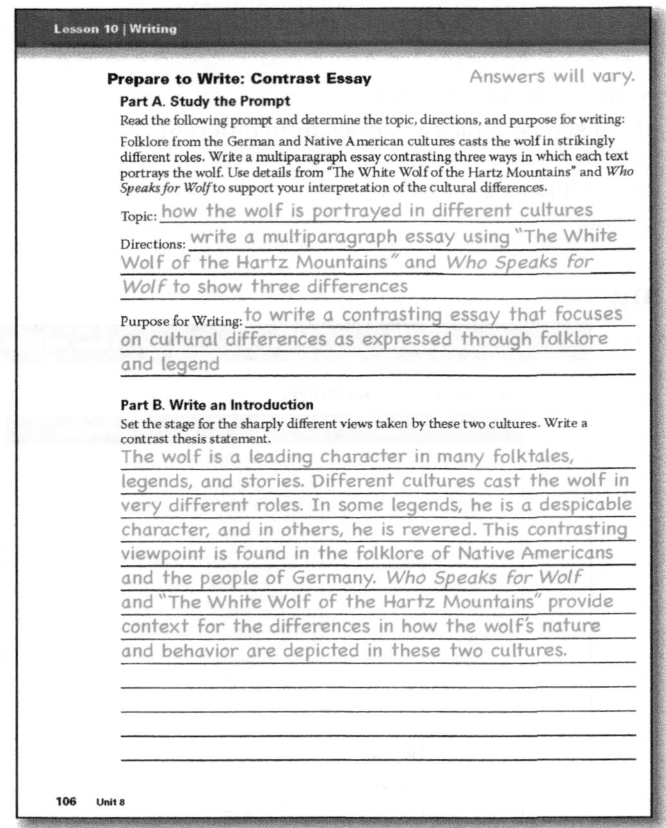

Lesson 10 | Writing

Prepare to Write: Contrast Essay Answers will vary.

Part A. Study the Prompt

Read the following prompt and determine the topic, directions, and purpose for writing:

Folklore from the German and Native American cultures casts the wolf in strikingly different roles. Write a multiparagraph essay contrasting three ways in which each text portrays the wolf. Use details from "The White Wolf of the Hartz Mountains" and *Who Speaks for Wolf* to support your interpretation of the cultural differences.

Topic: how the wolf is portrayed in different cultures

Directions: write a multiparagraph essay using "The White Wolf of the Hartz Mountains" and *Who Speaks for Wolf* to show three differences

Purpose for Writing: to write a contrasting essay that focuses on cultural differences as expressed through folklore and legend

Part B. Write an Introduction

Set the stage for the sharply different views taken by these two cultures. Write a contrast thesis statement.

The wolf is a leading character in many folktales, legends, and stories. Different cultures cast the wolf in very different roles. In some legends, he is a despicable character, and in others, he is revered. This contrasting viewpoint is found in the folklore of Native Americans and the people of Germany. *Who Speaks for Wolf* and "The White Wolf of the Hartz Mountains" provide context for the differences in how the wolf's nature and behavior are depicted in these two cultures.

106 Unit 8

Lesson 10 | Writing

Prepare to Write: Contrast Essay (*cont.*)

Part C. Map Your Argument

"The White Wolf of the Hartz Mountains"	
Characteristic	**Text Evidence**
fierce	"we remained indoors, for the vicious wolves incessantly prowled about in the cold" "throwing stones behind her with all the ferocity of a wild beast." ". . . tearing off large pieces of the flesh, and devouring them with the viciousness of a wolf."
untrustworthy	"sly"; "but Marcella would not come near her" ". . . did not show any kindness towards us; indeed, during my father's absence, she would often beat us," "I was afraid to leave her alone with my stepmother . . . appeared to have a particular pleasure in ill-treating the child"
evil/cursed	"wolves—most evil of all animals" "vengeance of the spirits fall upon me and upon my children; may they perish by . . . the wolf" "whether I am to pay the penalty of the vow my father made on his wedding day?"

Unit 8 107

Part A. Study the Prompt

Read the instructions for Part A and the prompt. Guide students through identifying the topic, summarizing the directions, and understanding the purpose for writing.

Before we write, we need to consider the author's point of view of wolves as we did for the last text. Write the following definition on the board:

> *Point of view: opinion or way of looking at something; in writing it influences the way events are described and how characters act.*

This passage is referred to as "A Native American Learning Story." The author obviously wants you to learn from the story. The author's point of view is readily apparent. What is the author's point of view of wolves? (Wolves are noble, intelligent creatures who should be respected.)

Now, we can focus on the writing. Like the prompt in the previous unit, this assignment calls for a multiparagraph response. Your introductory paragraph will establish the direction and content of your essay, and it will include your thesis or position statement. This means that each paragraph will have its own topic sentence.

Part B. Write an Introduction

Your introduction needs to state your position. In writing the introduction, consider the Big Idea of cultural values and differences. This will help you build an interesting hook for your reader. We will come back to write the introduction after you have chosen the ways in which you will contrast the view of the wolf and taken some notes.

Lesson 10 | Writing

Prepare to Write: Contrast Essay (*cont.*)

Who Speaks for Wolf	
Characteristic	**Text Evidence**
gentle	wolves singing at the moon "the boy listened and—and wanted to do nothing else with his life but listen to Wolf singing." "Why does he feel at home so close to our living space?"
trustworthy	"we have known each other for a long time . . . we have learned to live with one another" "it has pleased many of our people to sing to Wolf and to learn to understand him"
worth protecting	"you must choose another" "You have chosen the Center Place for a great community of Wolf" "let us now learn to consider Wolf" learned about honoring other living beings from the wolf

Part D. Write a Conclusion

Summarize your key points without being redundant.

The wolf of Native American folklore sang to the moon, sang of nature's beauty, and possessed wisdom worth pursuing. In sharp contrast, the wolf of Germany was a monster, vile and vicious. The characterization of the wolf in these legends reveals starkly contrasting views of the natural world in which these cultures resided.

108 Unit 8

Part C. Map Your Argument

Work with students to pull information from their Close Readings of both texts. Guide them to consider how the details cluster around bigger contrasting character traits. The sample map provides some examples, but students may come up with other equally valid character traits to use in contrasting the two texts' treatment of the wolf.

Now that you've determined the traits upon which you will focus, it will be easier to write your introduction. Work for a few minutes on your ideas for a thesis statement and general introductory paragraph. Then, share your ideas with your partner. Using their feedback, write your introduction on the lines provided. **Give students time to reflect, collaborate, and then write their introductions. Once they have completed their introductions, move their attention to writing a conclusion.**

Part D. Write a Conclusion

Reread your introduction. Consider your Big Ideas by looking back at your map. How can you summarize your position without sounding repetitive or redundant? Change your sentence structure and consider the message you want readers to take away from your essay. Reflect for a few minutes and then turn and share your ideas with your partners. Use their feedback to formalize your conclusion. **Again, give students time to reflect, collaborate, and then write their conclusions. Call on several students to share their introductions and then their conclusions. Help students see this is a good strategy for ensuring their conclusions restate the Big Ideas of their introduction without repeating themselves.**

Write

Notebook paper

Have students consult the the Six Traits of Writing: Literary Analysis Rubric on page 553 as they write their essay on a piece of notebook paper.

Encourage students by reminding them that they've written the frames for the entire essay. If they struggle or need additional support in developing their paragraph, use the following paragraph as a model.

Six Traits of Writing: Literary Analysis

	Ideas and Development	Organization	Voice and Audience Awareness	Word Choice	Sentence Fluency	Language Conventions
4	States thesis clearly. Develops main ideas fully with elaborations. Direct quotations from text support ideas. All information pertinent to thesis.	Introduction contains thesis statement and cites title, author of work. Ideas logically sequenced. Transition sentences link ideas. Conclusion offers some evaluation of the work.	Strong sense of person and purpose behind the words. Brings topic to life.	Words are specific, accurate, and vivid. Word choice enhances meaning and reader's enjoyment.	Writes complete sentences with varied sentence patterns and beginnings.	There are no major grammar errors. There are few errors in spelling, capitalization, or punctuation.
3	States thesis clearly. Develops main ideas with some elaboration. May lack direct quotations from text to support ideas. Limited amount of irrelevant information.	Introduction contains thesis statement and cites title, author of work. Ideas mostly logically sequenced. Some linkage of main ideas. Formulaic conclusion may not offer evaluation of the work.	Some sense of person and purpose behind the words. Sense of commitment to the topic. Text may be too casual for purpose.	Words are correctly used but may be somewhat general and unspecific.	Writes complete sentences with some expansion. Limited variety.	There are a few grammar errors. There are a few errors in spelling, capitalization, or punctuation.
2	Does not state thesis clearly and/or minimal development of main ideas. No direct quotations to support ideas. Too repetitious or too much irrelevant information.	Introduction may not have clear thesis. Ideas not logically sequenced. Transitions may be missing. May lack conclusion, or conclusion is formulaic with no evaluation of the work.	Little sense of person and purpose behind the words. Very little engagement with the reader. Text may be too casual for purpose.	Word choice limited. Words may be used inaccurately or repetitively.	Writes mostly simple and/or awkwardly constructed sentences. May include some run-ons and fragments.	There are many grammar or spelling errors. There are quite a few errors in capitalization and punctuation.
1	Does not address the prompt or does not develop a thesis. Elaboration lacking or unrelated to a thesis.	No evident structure. Lack of organization seriously interferes with meaning.	No sense of person or purpose behind the words. No sense of audience.	Extremely limited range of words. Restricted vocabulary impedes message.	Numerous run-ons and/or sentence fragments interfere with meaning.	There are many spelling and grammar errors. There are many errors in capitalization and punctuation.

Writing Rubric: Persuasion 553

Writing Rubric: Persuasion

Sample Contrast Essay:

The wolf is a leading character in many folktales, legends, and stories. Different cultures cast the wolf in very different roles. In some legends, he is a despicable character, and in others, he is revered. This contrasting viewpoint is found in the folklore of Native Americans and the people of Eastern Europe. Who Speaks for Wolf *and "The White Wolf of the Hartz Mountains" provide context for the differences in how the wolf's nature and behavior are depicted in these two cultures.*

The wolves of the Hartz Mountains were fierce and vicious creatures. The children "remained indoors, for the vicious wolves incessantly prowled about in the cold." Actions as simple as digging were characterized as "throwing stones . . . with all the ferocity of a wild beast." Even the act of eating was frenzied and crazed: "tearing off large pieces of the flesh and devouring them with the viciousness of a wolf." On the other hand, the wolf of Native American legend stood pensively by the fire, close to the Native Americans. Neither the wolf nor the Native American were afraid. The wolves sang beautifully to the moon and of nature. So beautiful was their song that "the boy listened and—and wanted to do nothing else with his life but listen to Wolf singing."

Additionally, the wolves of the Hartz Mountains, when characterized in Christina the werewolf, were portrayed as untrustworthy, something to be feared. While the boys were cautious around Christina, "Marcella would not come near her." Christina's demeanor changed once she married the children's father. According to the narrator, she "did not show any kindness towards us, indeed during my father's absence, she would often beat us." Because of the way she treated Marcella, the narrator confesses "I was afraid to leave her alone with my stepmother" because she "appeared to have a particular pleasure in ill-treating the child." Thus, the story is implying that wolves are menacing around children. In sharp contrast, the Native Americans take pride in saying "we have known each other for a long time" and "we have learned to live with one another." The needs of the wolf became as important as their own needs and people wanted "to sing to Wolf and to learn to understand him."

The most striking difference is the sense of innate evil that the Hartz Mountain wolves possessed. Wolves were considered the "most evil of all animals." They were associated with evil spirits, spells, and curses; curses that would "fall upon me and my children, may they perish by . . . the wolf." To the Native American, the wolf was worth protecting and respecting. In not respecting the wolves and their needs, the Native Americans upset the natural balance of energy and security. They were finally able to say "let us now learn to consider Wolf." They learned about honoring other living beings from the wolf.

The wolf of Native American folklore sang to the moon, sang of nature's beauty, and possessed wisdom worth pursuing. In sharp contrast, the wolf of Eastern Europe was a monster, vile and vicious. The characterization of the wolf in these legends reveals starkly contrasting views of the natural world in which these cultures lived.

Evaluate Writing

Direct students to page 109 in their Student Books and read the information in the checklist.

We are analyzing literature, so you have a new checklist to evaluate your writing and make sure you are using good technique. Have individuals quickly assess their writing, then have partners evaluate each other's writing based on the checklist.

Note: Use Six Traits of Writing Scoring Rubric: Literary Analysis on page 548 of this book to assess students' writing. A printable version is located online in the Teacher Resources.

Writing Rubric: Literary Analysis

Six Traits of Writing: Literary Analysis

	Ideas and Development	Organization	Voice and Audience Awareness	Word Choice	Sentence Fluency	Language Conventions
4	States thesis clearly. Develops main ideas fully with elaborations. Direct quotations from text support ideas. All information pertinent to thesis.	Introduction contains thesis statement and cites title, author of work. Ideas logically sequenced. Transition sentences link ideas. Conclusion offers some evaluation of the work.	Strong sense of person and purpose behind the words. Brings topic to life.	Words are specific, accurate, and vivid. Word choice enhances meaning and reader's enjoyment.	Writes complete sentences with varied sentence patterns and beginnings.	*Capitalization & Punctuation* No errors. Indents paragraphs. *Grammar/Usage* 0–1 error *Spelling* 0–1 error
3	States thesis clearly. Develops main ideas with some elaboration. May lack direct quotations from text to support ideas. Limited amount of irrelevant information.	Introduction contains thesis statement and cites title, author of work. Ideas mostly logically sequenced. Some linkage of main ideas. Formulaic conclusion may not offer evaluation of the work.	Some sense of person and purpose behind the words. Sense of commitment to the issue. Text may be too casual for purpose.	Words are correctly used but may be somewhat general and unspecific.	Writes complete sentences with some expansion. Limited variety.	*Capitalization & Punctuation* 1 error. Indents paragraphs. *Grammar/Usage* 2 errors *Spelling* 2 errors
2	Does not state thesis clearly and/or minimal development of main ideas. No direct quotations to support ideas. Too repetitive or too much irrelevant information.	Introduction may not have clear thesis. Ideas not logically sequenced. Transitions may be missing. May lack conclusion, or conclusion is formulaic with no evaluation of the work.	Little sense of person and purpose behind the words. Very little engagement with the reader. Text may be too casual for purpose.	Word choice limited. Words may be used inaccurately or repetitively.	Writes mostly simple and/or awkwardly constructed sentences. May include some run-ons and fragments.	*Capitalization & Punctuation* 2 errors. May not indent paragraphs. *Grammar/Usage* 3 errors *Spelling* 3 errors
1	Does not address the prompt OR does not develop a thesis. Elaboration lacking or unrelated to a thesis.	No evident structure. Lack of organization seriously interferes with meaning.	No sense of person or purpose behind the words. No sense of audience.	Extremely limited range of words. Restricted vocabulary impedes message.	Numerous run-ons and/or sentence fragments interfere with meaning.	*Capitalization & Punctuation* 3+ errors. May not indent paragraphs. *Grammar/Usage* 4+ errors interfere with meaning *Spelling* 4+ errors
Value						

Comments ________________________________

548 LANGUAGE! Live

Lesson 10 | Writing

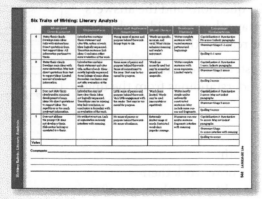

The Literary Analysis Writer's Checklist

Trait	Yes	No	Did the writer . . .?
Ideas and Content			clearly state the thesis of the essay
			analyze and evaluate the elements found in the literature
			focus each paragraph on the topic
			include effective support for the thesis by giving details, examples, explanations, and quotations from the texts
Organization			write an introductory paragraph that captures the reader's interest and cites the titles of the works and the names of the authors
			include in the introductory paragraph a clear viewpoint on the topic and a "map" for the essay that follows
			sequence body paragraphs logically and use transition sentences that make clear the relationship between the ideas
			write a conclusion that ties the analysis together and offers an evaluation of the particulars
Voice and Audience Awareness			think about the audience and purpose for writing
			write in a clear and engaging way that makes the audience want to read the work
Word Choice			find a unique way to say things; avoid sounding repetitive
			use words that are lively and specific to the content
Sentence Fluency			write complete sentences
			expand some sentences using the steps of Masterpiece Sentences
			use compound sentence elements and compound sentences
Conventions			capitalize words correctly:
			capitalize the first word of each sentence
			capitalize proper nouns, including people's names
			punctuate correctly:
			end sentences with a period, question mark, or exclamation mark
			use an apostrophe for possessive nouns and contractions
			use commas and/or semicolons correctly
			use grammar correctly:
			use the correct verb tense
			make sure the verb agrees with the subject in number
			use correct spelling

Unit 8 109

Reading

Objectives

- Self-correct as comprehension of text deepens.
- Answer questions to demonstrate comprehension of text.
- Engage in class discussion.
- Identify the enduring understandings from a piece of text.

Revisit Passage Comprehension

Direct students to pages 90–92 in their Student Books. Have students review their answers and make any necessary changes. Then, have partners share their answers and collaborate to perfect them.

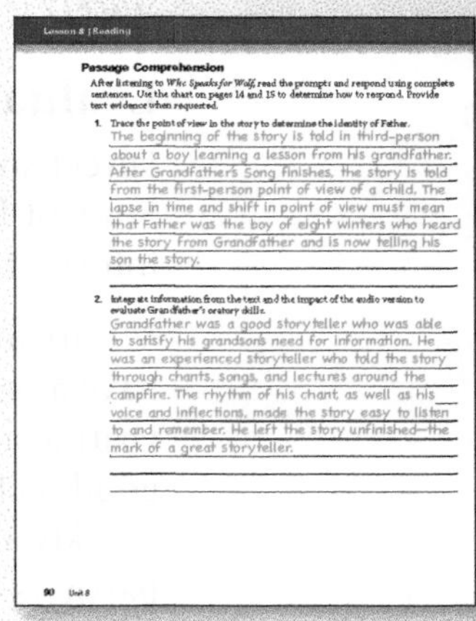
Lesson 8 | Reading

Passage Comprehension

After listening to *Who Speaks for Wolf*, read the prompts and respond using complete sentences. Use the chart on pages 14 and 15 to determine how to respond. Provide text evidence when requested.

1. Trace the point of view in the story to determine the identity of Father.
The beginning of the story is told in third-person about a boy learning a lesson from his grandfather. After Grandfather's Song finishes, the story is told from the first-person point of view of a child. The lapse in time and shift in point of view must mean that Father was the boy of eight winters who heard the story from Grandfather and is now telling his son the story.

2. Integrate information from the text and the impact of the audio version to evaluate Grandfather's oratory skills.
Grandfather was a good storyteller who was able to satisfy his grandson's need for information. He was an experienced storyteller who told the story through chants, songs, and lectures around the campfire. The rhythm of his chant, as well as his voice and inflections, made the story easy to listen to and remember. He left the story unfinished—the mark of a great storyteller.

90 Unit 8

Enduring Understandings

Direct students back to page 69 in their Student Books. Reread the Big Idea questions.

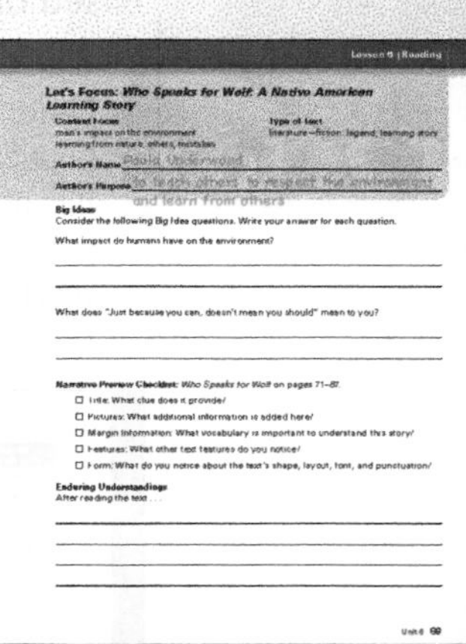
Lesson 6 | Reading

Let's Focus: *Who Speaks for Wolf: A Native American Learning Story*

Author's Name David Underwood

Author's Purpose to teach others to respect the environment and learn from others

Big Ideas

Consider the following Big Idea questions. Write your answer for each question.

What impact do humans have on the environment?

What does "Just because you can, doesn't mean you should" mean to you?

Narrative Preview Checklist: *Who Speaks for Wolf* on pages 71–87.

- ☐ Pictures: What additional information is added here?
- ☐ Margin Information: What vocabulary is important to understand this story?
- ☐ Features: What other text features do you notice?
- ☐ Form: What do you notice about the text's shape, layout, font, and punctuation?

Enduring Understandings

After reading the text . . .

Unit 8 69

What impact do humans have on the environment?

What does "Just because you can, doesn't mean you should" mean to you?

Generate a class discussion about the questions and the answers students came up with in Lesson 6. Have them consider whether their answers have changed any after reading the text.

Use the following talking points to foster conversation. Then, have students write their enduring understandings from the unit.

Consider this quote:

"I think that you will find
that it is too small a place for both
and that it will require more work then—
than change would presently require."

- Wolf's Brother tried to teach his people to respect nature rather than make selfish choices for today. He tried to teach his people to consider that their decisions would cause more work in the long run because they were not respecting nature.
- Are all creatures of equal importance? Consider man and animal—is one more important than the other? Now consider people. Are all people of equal importance? How would society change if everyone believed this?

What we read should make us think. Use our discussion and your thoughts about the text to determine what you will "walk away with." Has it made you think about a personal experience or someone you know? Has your perspective or opinion on a specific topic changed? Do you have any lingering thoughts or questions? Write these ideas as your enduring understandings. What will you take with you from this text?

Discuss the enduring understandings with the class. If time permits, have students post a personal response about one of the enduring understandings to the online class wall.

Assign online Unit 8 ***Content Mastery*** *quizzes and* ***Power Pass*** *from the Text Training link on the left menu of your teacher dashboard.*

Remind students to consider why the author wrote the passage and whether she was successful.

Unit 9

Unit Plan

Primary Texts:
"The Mysterious Human Brain"

Text type: informational

Graphic Novel of *The Strange Case of Dr. Jekyll and Mr. Hyde*
by Robert L. Stevenson; Carl Bowen

Text type: graphic novel

LANGUAGE! Live Online

Grammar Practice

- Identify the function of clauses in sentences.
- Distinguish between active and passive voice.
- Distinguish between uses of the apostrophe.
- Identify sentence fragments.
- Determine the meaning of punctuation.

Vocabulary Practice

- Determine the meaning of derivations of words.
- Determine the meaning of idioms, proverbs, and adages.

Content Mastery

- Demonstrate an understanding of . . .
  - word meaning by answering questions and using words in sentences.
  - punctuation used when writing dialogue.
  - the function of relative clauses.

Word Study

- Blend, read, and spell multisyllabic words with Anglo-Saxon suffixes -hood, -ful, -less, -ness, -ish, and -ship; and Latin suffixes -able, -ible, -al, -ment, -ion, and -ic.
- Discuss Latin morphemes.
- Read connected text to build fluency.

Lesson 1	Lesson 2
Reading • Determine and discuss the topic of a text. • Determine and discuss the author's purpose. • Use text features to preview text. **Vocabulary** • Evaluate word knowledge. • Determine the meaning of key passage vocabulary. **Reading** • Read informational text. • Monitor comprehension during text reading.	**Vocabulary** • Review key passage vocabulary. **Grammar** • Identify relative clauses and their function. • Differentiate between noun, adjective, and adverb clauses. **Writing** • Distinguish between active and passive voice.

Lesson 6	Lesson 7
Reading • Determine and discuss the topic of a text. • Determine and discuss the author's purpose. • Use text features to preview text. • Analyze an artist's visual interpretation of text. **Vocabulary** • Evaluate word knowledge. • Determine the meaning of key passage vocabulary. **Reading** • Read a graphic novel. • Monitor comprehension during text reading.	**Vocabulary** • Review key passage vocabulary. **Writing** • Use correct punctuation when writing dialogue. **Reading** • Determine how to respond to prompts. • Use critical thinking skills to write responses to prompts about text. • Support written answers with evidence from text. • Determine the purpose of a literary flashback. • Make connections between characters from multiple texts. • Determine variations in meaning of the same words and phrases. • Analyze how differing text structures contribute to meaning and style.

Writing Project, Units 7–9: Compare and Contrast Writing

Lesson 3	Lesson 4	Lesson 5
Reading • Establish a purpose for rereading informational text. • Use critical thinking skills to write responses to prompts about text. • Support written answers with evidence from text. • Objectively summarize informational text. • Use information found in text features to answer questions. • Trace the claims made in a text. • Establish an opinion on an issue and use text evidence to support this opinion. • Evaluate an author's point of view of a topic.	**Vocabulary** • Review key passage vocabulary. **Reading** • Read informational text with purpose and understanding. • Answer questions to demonstrate comprehension of text. • Identify and explain explicit details from text. • Monitor comprehension of text during reading. • Analyze connections made between individuals within a text. • Analyze how sections of informational text contribute to the overall purpose of the text. • Determine the meaning of idioms and proverbs. • Evaluate the author's use of an epigraph. ** See pg. 216 for additional lesson objectives.*	**Vocabulary** • Review key passage vocabulary. **Writing** • Use text to write coherent paragraphs in response to reading. • Demonstrate understanding of the constructs of argumentation through writing. • Write persuasive text. **Reading** • Self-correct as comprehension of text deepens. • Answer questions to demonstrate comprehension of text. • Engage in class discussion. • Identify the enduring understandings from a piece of text.

Lesson 8	Lesson 9	Lesson 10
Reading • Establish a purpose for rereading a graphic novel. • Monitor comprehension during text reading. • Use critical thinking skills to write responses to prompts about text. • Support written answers with evidence from text. • Analyze how visual elements contribute to character development. • Analyze how an adapted work of fiction stays true to the original version. • Assess the strength and validity of claims and counterclaims made by characters. • Integrate information from both literary and informational text on the same topic to answer questions. • Compare literary character development to biographical information in other texts.	**Vocabulary** • Review key passage vocabulary. **Reading** • Read a graphic novel with purpose and understanding. • Answer questions to demonstrate comprehension of text. • Identify and explain explicit details from text. • Monitor comprehension of text during reading. • Identify a sequential structure used to organize text. • Analyze how dialogue or incidents propel the action and reveal character traits. • Analyze the way in which character point of view creates suspense. • Identify the protagonist and antagonist in literature. • Determine the meaning of idioms. • Identify common religious themes in literature. • Analyze an author's unique approach to a common theme. ** See pg. 252 for additional lesson objectives.*	**Vocabulary** • Review key passage vocabulary. **Writing** • Use multiple texts to write coherently. • Use a process to write. • Rewrite a scene from a graphic novel as a narrative, using proper punctuation and accurate word choice. • Use a rubric to guide and evaluate writing. **Reading** • Self-correct as comprehension of text deepens. • Answer questions to demonstrate comprehension of text. • Engage in class discussion. • Identify the enduring understandings from a piece of text. • Determine the effect of shifting point of view and flashbacks in literature. • Analyze the way in which an author creates suspense.

Unit 9 Lesson 1

Lesson Opener

Before the lesson, choose one of the following activities to write on the board or post on the *LANGUAGE! Live* Class Wall online.

- *Describe a time when you didn't have the courage to do something. Is there someone else you know who would have done it with no problem? Explain.*
- *Write two sentences about your favorite teacher. Use a relative pronoun in each and identify the dependent clauses.*
- *Write two sentences about your day. Use a subordinating conjunction in each and identify the dependent clauses.*

Reading

Objectives

- Determine and discuss the topic of a text.
- Determine and discuss the author's purpose.
- Use text features to preview text.

Passage Introduction

Direct students to page 111 in their Student Books. Discuss the content focus.

Content Focus
mental health

What do you think you will read about in this text? (Answers will vary.) What does it mean to be in good health? Have partners discuss.

If necessary, write the following sentence frames on the board for students to use during discussion:

I am in good health when ______ ______.

Good health includes ______ ______.

Listen to see if their explanations are about their physical health or mental health. Use their explanations to elaborate on the next question.

Unit 9
Lesson 1 | Reading

Let's Focus: "The Mysterious Human Brain"

Content Focus mental health
Type of Text informational
Author's Name unknown
Author's Purpose to inform others about mental health issues

Big Ideas
Consider the following Big Ideas. Write your answer for each question.

Is it possible for a person to have multiple selves?

______

Should people be held responsible for their actions regardless of their mental health condition?

______

Informational Preview Checklist: "The Mysterious Human Brain" on pages 113–120.

- ☐ Title: What clue does it provide about the passage?
- ☐ Pictures and captions: What additional information is added here?
- ☐ Headings: How is the information organized?
- ☐ Illustrations: What information is in charts, graphs, or other illustrations?

Enduring Understandings
After reading the text . . .

______

Unit 9 111

What is the difference between mental health and physical health? Provide discussion time. We will learn more about mental health in this unit.

Type of Text

Text can be divided into two categories: informational and literature. **Discuss the differences.** In the last unit, we read two literary fiction pieces involving wolves. Did we read real-life stories or ones that were made up? (made up) Which genre tells real information, not made-up stories? (nonfiction or informational) What does *nonfiction* mean? (not fiction, not fake; real to life) Look at the first page of the text and determine what type of text this is. Write your answer on the page.

Author's Purpose

Have students glance at the text. Who is the author of the text? (unknown) This text is the type of text you would read in a textbook. The information is factual, but there isn't an author's name attributed to it. It likely means that someone was paid to write this text for a publishing company but isn't necessarily considered an "author." Beginning in this unit, you will be determining the author's purpose on your own. Prior to reading, make an educated guess as to what the author's purpose for writing is. After you finish, you will return to this section and revise your answers if you need to. **Have students write the answers on the page.**

Play the Unit 9 Text Training video found in the Teacher Resources online.

Before we read "The Mysterious Human Brain," we will watch a short video to help build our background knowledge. **Play the Unit 9 Text Training video. Have partners discuss what they learned from the video.**

Note: If you are unable to play the video, Background Information about mental health can be found in the Teacher Resources online.

Read the Big Idea questions aloud.

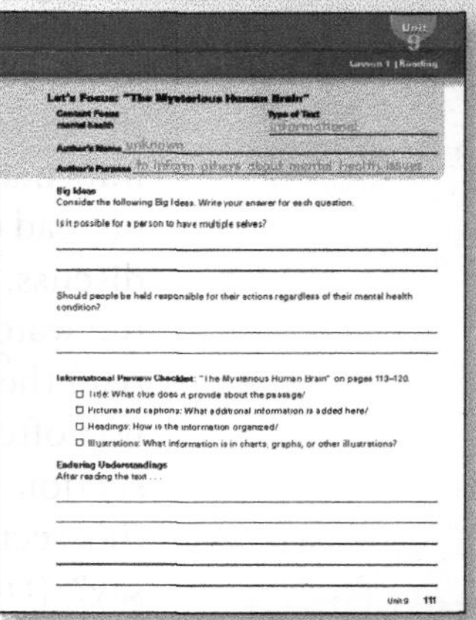

Big Ideas

Is it possible for a person to have multiple selves?

Should people be held responsible for their actions regardless of their mental health condition?

As a class, consider the two Big Idea questions. After discussing each question, have students write an answer. We'll come back to these questions after we finish reading the text. You can add to your answers as you gain information and perspective.

Preview

Read the Preview Checklist on page 111. Follow the Preview Procedure outlined below.

Preview Procedure

- Group students with partners or in triads.
- Have students count off as 1s or 2s. The 1s will become the student leaders. If working with triads, the third students become 3s.
- The student leaders will preview the text in addition to managing the checklist and pacing.
- The 2s and 3s will preview the text with 1s.
- Direct 1s to open their Student Books to page 111 and 2s and 3s to open their Student Books to page 113. This allows students to look at a few different pages at one time without turning back and forth.

Direct students to page 113. Have students preview the text.

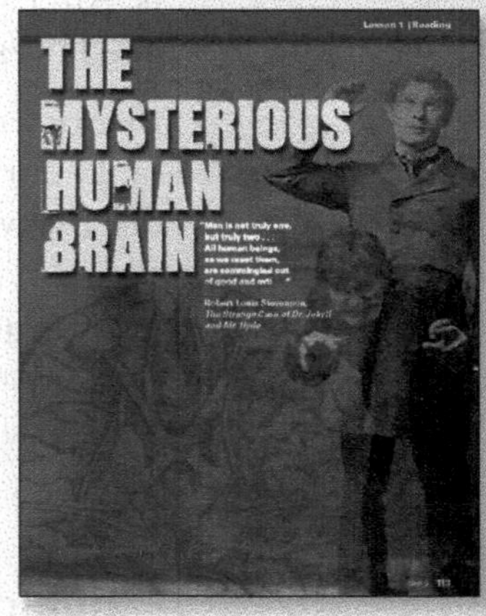

If necessary, guide students in a short preview using the following talking points.

What is the title? ("The Mysterious Human Brain") What clue does the title provide about the passage? (Answers will vary.) What does *mysterious* mean? (not explained or understood) Describe the first graphic. (one man turning into a different man) Describe the subsequent graphics on each page. Students may recognize Beyoncé, the Hulk, Superman, and professional football player Herschel Walker. What do you notice under the three pictures on page 119? (captions) Captions contain information that is not in the primary text. Captions need to be read carefully because they explain pictures. Have students read the captions and discuss. Look closely at each page. A watermark is a light shadow of a graphic. What is the watermark on each page? (brain) Now that we have looked at all the graphics and read the captions, there are more text features that we need to consider. Nonfiction text often has headings. Headings organize text and provide a clue about what each section will be about. Let me read the first heading to you: Alter Egos? What will this section be about? Have students share predictions. What does the next heading say? (Dissociative Identity Disorder) What will that section be about? Have students share predictions. What is the next heading? (The Debate) What will that section be about? Have students share predictions. What is the next heading? (In the Court of Law) What will that section be about? Have students share predictions. What two text features did we miss? (quotes and schizophrenia chart) What do you think the link between the chart and the text will be? (similar diseases) Let's read and discuss the first two quotes. Read and discuss quotes.

Have students predict what they will learn about in the text.

Vocabulary

Objectives

- Evaluate word knowledge.
- Determine the meaning of key passage vocabulary.

Rate Vocabulary Knowledge

Direct students to page 112 in their Student Books. Let's take a look at the vocabulary words from "The Mysterious Human Brain." I will say each word aloud. You will repeat the word and write it in the third column. Then, you will rate your knowledge of the word. Display the Vocabulary Rating Scale poster or write the information on the board. Review the meaning of each rating.

Lesson 1 | Vocabulary

Key Passage Vocabulary: "The Mysterious Human Brain"

Read each word. Write the word in column 3. Then, circle a number to rate your knowledge of the word.

Vocabulary	Part of Speech	Write the Word	Rate the Word
inhibition	(n)	inhibition	0 1 2 3
distinct	(adj)	distinct	0 1 2 3
controversial	(adj)	controversial	0 1 2 3
prone (to)	(adj)	prone (to)	0 1 2 3
media	(n)	media	0 1 2 3
standard	(n)	standard	0 1 2 3
previously	(adv)	previously	0 1 2 3
transport	(v)	transport	0 1 2 3
image	(n)	image	0 1 2 3
implement	(v)	implement	0 1 2 3

112 Unit 9

Vocabulary Rating Scale

0—I have never heard the word before.

1—I have heard the word, but I'm not sure how to use it.

2—I am familiar with the word, but I'm not sure if I know the correct meaning.

3—I know the meaning of the word and can use it correctly in a sentence.

Remember, the points are there to help you know which words you need to focus on. By the end of this unit, you should be able to change all your ratings to a 3. That's the goal.

Read each word aloud and have students repeat it, write it, and rate it. Then, have volunteers who rated a word *2* or *3* use the word in an oral sentence.

Preteach Vocabulary

Explain that you will now take a closer look at the words. Follow the Preteach Procedure outlined below.

Preteach Procedure

This activity is intended to take only a short amount of time, so make it an oral exercise.

- Introduce each word as indicated on the word card.
- Read the definition and example sentences.
- Ask questions to clarify and deepen understanding.
- If time permits, allow students to share.

* If your students would benefit from copying the definitions, please have them do so in the vocabulary log in the back of the Student Books using the margin definitions in the passage selections. This should be done outside of instruction time.

inhibition (n)

Let's read the first word together. *Inhibition.*

Definition: An *inhibition* is a feeling of fear or embarrassment that keeps you from doing something. What means "a feeling of fear or embarrassment that keeps you from doing something"? (inhibition)

Example 1: When I was a student, my *inhibitions* sometimes kept me from speaking up in class.

Example 2: People who suffer from social *inhibitions* may feel uncomfortable at parties and meetings.

Example 3: Very outspoken people seem to have few *inhibitions* when it comes to sharing their opinions.

Question 1: A friend asks you to dance, but you say "no" because you feel like everyone will be watching you. Do you have *inhibitions* about dancing? Yes or no? (yes)

Question 2: The talent show is coming up. You, your sister, and your brother are looking forward to performing a cultural dance you learned as kids. Do you have *inhibitions* about performing? Yes or no? (no)

Pair Share: Turn to your partner. Name an *inhibition* it would be good to overcome, and tell why.

1

distinct (adj)

Let's read the next word together. *Distinct.*

Definition: If something is *distinct*, it is separate or different. What means "separate; different"? (distinct)

Example 1: Twins often resemble each other but have *distinct* personalities.

Example 2: Spanish and Russian are two *distinct* languages.

Example 3: From a distance, the trees on the hillside are not *distinct*; instead, they blend together into a blanket of green.

Question 1: You are in biology class. Two blobs of gel look exactly alike until you put them under the microscope. Do they look *distinct* under the microscope? Yes or no? (yes)

Question 2: Your mother's side of the family comes from Africa, and your father's side of the family comes from Indonesia. Are the two branches of the family *distinct*? Yes or no? (yes)

Pair Share: Turn to your partner and describe two *distinct* types of movies.

controversial (adj)

Let's read the next word together. *Controversial.*

Definition: If something is *controversial*, it stirs up disagreement or debate. What means "stirring up disagreement or debate"? (controversial)

Example 1: Books about *controversial* subjects are sometimes banned from school libraries to prevent students from reading them.

Example 2: When it was first passed, the seat belt law was very *controversial*; some people thought it was a good idea and others thought it violated their freedom.

Example 3: Fewer than 100 years ago, the idea that women should have the right to vote was extremely *controversial*.

Question 1: Critics and viewers alike agree: a new movie about outer space is fantastic. Is the movie *controversial*? Yes or no? (no)

Question 2: People are outraged that a one-sided movie about racism won a major award. Is the movie *controversial*? Yes or no? (yes)

Pair Share: Turn to your partner. Name a *controversial* issue in the news right now.

3

prone (to) (adj)

Let's read the next word together. *Prone.*

Definition: The word *prone* is often used with the preposition *to*: prone to. If you are *prone* to do something, you tend to do it or you do it naturally. What means "tending to do something or doing it naturally"? (prone)

Example 1: People with vertigo are *prone* to getting dizzy when they look down from a steep height.

Example 2: Sensitive people are *prone* to having their feelings hurt.

Example 3: I am *prone* to sleeping a little later on weekends.

Question 1: When you wear a certain pair of shoes, you trip a lot. Do the shoes make you *prone* to tripping? Yes or no? (yes)

Question 2: You feel the need to check your appearance every time you pass a mirror or a window. Are you *prone* to checking your appearance? Yes or no? (yes)

Pair Share: Turn to your partner and name two things you are *prone* to doing when you are very nervous about something.

4

media (n)

Let's read the next word together. *Media.*

Definition: *Media* is a plural noun. It refers to forms of communication, such as TV, radio, newspapers, and the Internet, as a group. What means "TV, radio, newspapers, the Internet, and other forms of communication as a group"? (media) One of these on its own, by the way, is called a *medium*: TV is one medium of communication, and radio is another.

Example 1: When something tragic happens, the *media* covers every possible angle of the event; but when something good happens, they tend to ignore it.

Example 2: Some experts believe that tuning into the *media* at all times of the day is unhealthy.

Example 3: *Media* coverage of an approaching storm can help people know when and how to take cover.

Question 1: Your uncle is planning to run for public office, but only your family knows. Has the story been covered by the *media*? Yes or no? (no)

Question 2: You want to learn more about the ancient Aztecs. What form of *media* would you go to for information? (Internet)

Pair Share: Turn to your partner and tell which *medium* you use most often when you want to know what is going on in the world.

standard (n)

Let's read the next word together. *Standard.*

Definition: A *standard* is something used to judge, measure, or define something else. What is "something used to judge, measure, or define something else"? (a standard)

Example 1: Educational *standards* help teachers know what they should teach their students.

Example 2: The goods a factory produces must meet certain *standards* before they are approved for sale on the market.

Example 3: Great coaches set high *standards* of achievement for their players.

Question 1: You never know whether your teacher is going to like your work or not. Are your teacher's *standards* clear? Yes or no? (no)

Question 2: Everything has to be "just so" in your grandmother's apartment. Does she have high *standards* for neatness? Yes or no? (yes)

Pair Share: You are president of the "Random Acts of Kindness" club. What is the *standard* for membership? Turn and tell your partner.

previously (adv)

Let's read the next word together. *Previously.*

Definition: *Previously* means "earlier" or "before." What word means "earlier" or "before"? (previously)

Example 1: *Previously* this year, we read a chapter from the novel *White Fang.*

Example 2: At the beginning of a TV show episode, viewers are sometimes given reminders about what happened *previously.*

Example 3: People usually return to a restaurant they *previously* visited and enjoyed.

Question 1: When you were in elementary school, you were the teacher's pet. Were you the teacher's pet *previously*? Yes or no? (yes)

Question 2: Tomorrow you will drive a car for the first time. Have you driven *previously*? Yes or no? (no)

Pair Share: Turn to your partner and name something you did *previously* but won't do again.

7

transport (v)

Let's read the next word together. *Transport.*

Definition: To *transport* something is to move it from one place to another, usually in a vehicle of some sort. What means "to move something from one place to another"? (transport)

Example 1: Eighteen-wheelers *transport* goods from one region to another.

Example 2: Ski lifts *transport* skiers from the bottom of a mountain to the top.

Example 3: It can be tricky to *transport* large animals from one zoo to another.

Question 1: You walk to school. Does the school bus *transport* you? Yes or no? (no)

Question 2: Your parents own a moving company. Do they help *transport* people's belongings? Yes or no? (yes)

Pair Share: With your partner, name two ways letters and packages might be *transported* to a distant country.

image (n)

Let's read the next word together. *Image.*

Definition: An *image* is a picture of something in your mind. What word means "a picture in the mind"? (image)

Example 1: The *image* I had of the Grand Canyon was nothing like the real thing.

Example 2: Some people say it is difficult to meditate. This is because when you close your eyes and try to get quiet, dozens of thoughts and *images* instantly spring to life.

Example 3: Some people avoid horror movies because they don't want certain *images* trapped in their minds forever.

Question 1: You saw a shirt at the mall and really liked it. When you went back to buy it, though, it wasn't anything like you remembered. Did you have a clear *image* of it? Yes or no? (no)

Question 2: You're looking at the most beautiful flower you've ever seen. Is the flower an *image*? Yes or no? (no)

Pair Share: Turn to your partner and describe your *image* of a car in the distant future.

9

implement (v)

Let's read the last word together. *Implement.*

Definition: *Implement* means "to put something into action or put it to use." What word means "to put something into action or put it to use"? (implement)

Example 1: I would like to see the leaders of our town *implement* a plan for creating more green space.

Example 2: It is wise for young adults to *implement* a savings plan for retirement.

Example 3: The government recently *implemented* a new health care law.

Question 1: The neighborhood group canceled plans to help homeless people in the area. Did the group *implement* the plan? Yes or no? (no)

Question 2: The community college decided to ask senior citizens to teach classes in their skill areas. This year, six of the school's instructors are senior citizens. Has the school *implemented* the plan? Yes or no? (yes)

Pair Share: Turn to your partner and describe how students could *implement* a plan to beautify the school building.

Reading

Objectives

- Read informational text.
- Monitor comprehension during text reading.

"The Mysterious Human Brain"

Direct students to page 113 in their Student Books. Now that we have previewed vocabulary, it's time to read.

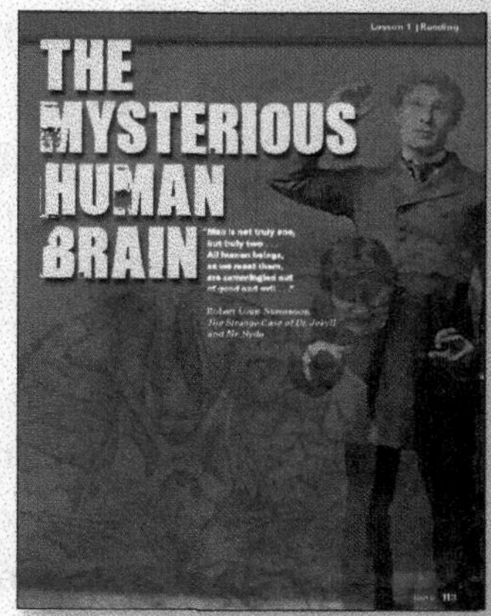

Guiding Students Toward Independent Reading

It is important that your students read as much and as often as they can. Assign readings that meet the needs of your students, based on your observations and data. This is a good opportunity to stretch your students. If students become frustrated, scaffold the reading with paired reading, choral reading, or a read-aloud.

Options for reading text:

- Teacher read-aloud
- Teacher-led or student-led choral read
- Paired read or independent read

Choose an option for reading the text. Have students read according to the option that you chose.

Remind students to pause at the numbers and consider the questions.

If you choose to read the text aloud or chorally, use the following text boxes and stop to ask questions and have students answer them.

SE p. 113, epigraph

"Man is not truly one, but truly two . . . All human beings, as we meet them, are commingled out of good and evil . . ."

Robert Louis Stevenson,
The Strange Case of Dr. Jekyll and Mr. Hyde

Alter Egos?

SE p. 114, paragraph 1

The comic book character Clark Kent, who sees a crime happening, rushes into a phone booth and emerges as Superman. Bruce Banner loses control of his anger and transforms into a green version of himself: the Incredible Hulk. Dr. Jekyll exits his laboratory void of **inhibitions** as the villainous Edward Hyde. All of these fictitious characters have another "self" that they become when the need arises. We hear people talk about them, watch superheroes turn into them, and read about them in literature. These alter egos entertain audiences in the world of fantasy. But are alter egos a part of our real world?

1. What is an alter ego?

SE p. 114, paragraph 2

The answer is yes. Many of us daydream that we are someone else—someone smarter, richer, or more famous. Some of us, like Beyoncé, take on different personalities around different people and in different situations. Some of us love costume parties. These are typical kinds of "alter egos." They express our imagination and help us explore who we are. But a person whose alter egos are too "real" may have a mental illness called dissociative identity disorder. All-Pro running back Herschel Walker is one of these people. He was diagnosed with this disorder shortly after he retired from the NFL.

2. How is Herschel Walker different from many of us?

Dissociative Identity Disorder

SE p. 115, paragraph 1

Dissociative identity disorder (DID) is a condition in which a single person has more than one **distinct** identity or self. People with DID switch their identities when under stress. Some psychologists believe the condition to be most common among survivors of traumatic events. The condition seems to begin when a child copes with trauma by convincing him- or herself that it is happening to someone else. The child tries to dissociate him- or herself from the experience. This creates a trigger that causes the child to create alternate personalities called "alters" who take over. The alters can carry over into adulthood. A person can lose control over when the personalities "switch" and may not remember what happens to them while they are switched. In fact, many people with the disorder tell tales of memory loss and blackouts.

3. What does DID stand for?

SE p. 115, paragraph 2

page break

Many people often mistakenly confuse DID with schizophrenia. Schizophrenia is a mental disorder in which sufferers have difficulty telling the difference between what is real and what | is not real. (See the chart below for more information on this disorder.) However, there are distinct characteristics of DID that distinguish it from schizophrenia. Sufferers of DID don't often see or hear things that are not real, but instead have serious gaps in memory. In addition, their alters usually have recognizable personality types. They might be protectors, frightened children, or even animals. The average number of alters in a person with DID is 10. Some victims claim to have many more. At one DID conference, a woman by the name of Cassandra claimed to have more than 180 of them.

4. What are the attributes of DID?

SE p. 116, paragraphs 1–2

The Debate

Formerly known as multiple personality disorder, DID is one of the most **controversial** mental disorders. Mental health professionals have studied this illness for years. They disagree on the causes and its treatments. They even disagree on whether it exists.

page break

Many believers consider the disorder a legitimate defense mechanism of children who have been traumatized. Psychologists explain that traumatized children can create another "self" to endure the suffering in their place. Young children have brains | that are still growing and underdeveloped personalities. This makes them **prone** to "splitting" their personality into "alters." Alters have their own memories and attitudes. These come into play when an alter controls the body and brain of the person with the disorder. The person may not be aware of the disorder until much later in life. Instead, he or she might only feel a sense of forgetfulness or time lapse.

5. How do believers defend DID?

SE p. 117, paragraph 1

Doubters of the disorder do not believe that multiple personalities can exist within a person. Their thinking goes like this. They agree that most sufferers have probably been abused, which leads them to therapy. But, patients' mental instability makes them vulnerable to suggestions by therapists. The therapists might suggest there are hidden memories. Patients feel as though their behavior is rationalized, or explained, and they embrace the diagnosis.

6. How do doubters of DID defend their position?

SE p. 117, paragraphs 2–3

Other doubters argue that the definition of an alter personality is unclear. Some doctors refer to the symptoms as a form of post-traumatic stress disorder (PTSD) instead of DID.

Most cases of DID have been reported in the United States and Canada. This has led people to question the integrity of the disorder and the influence of **media**. Few reports of multiple personality disorder existed until the book and movie *Sybil* were released in the 1970s. After this account of a woman with 16 alters, based on a true story, became known to the public, diagnoses of the disorder significantly increased. Doubters say this is proof it is an imagined disorder. However, believers say it is proof that therapists were simply misguided and undereducated about the disorder before the release. Having been educated, they knew what to look for and how to diagnose, which created a natural increase in cases.

7. How did the movie *Sybil* change things?

SE p. 117, paragraph 4

In the Court of Law

Can someone with DID be held responsible for crimes committed by the alters? Each state in the United States has its own **standard** for determining whether a person was legally insane, and therefore not responsible, at the time his or her crime was committed. A defendant may be found not guilty by reason of insanity if "at the time of committing the act, he was laboring under such a defect of reason from disease of the mind as not to know the nature and quality of the act he was doing, or if he did know it, that he did not know what he was doing was wrong." | With DID, however, insanity is a complicated concept. If the alter knows what he or she is doing and knows that it is wrong, is the person guilty or not guilty? Take a look at a couple of DID court cases.

page break

8. Why is insanity a complicated concept for people diagnosed with DID?

SE p. 118, paragraph 1

Robin Grimsley learned she might have cancer. This psychological trauma, according to Grimsley, caused her alternate personality, Jennifer, to emerge. Grimsley described Jennifer as impulsive, angry, fearful, and anxious, and as having a drinking problem. On one occasion, Grimsley drove after drinking and subsequently was charged with driving under the influence of alcohol. In her defense, Grimsley said that when Jennifer, her alternate personality, is in control, Robin, her primary personality, is not aware of what is going on and cannot control Jennifer's actions. Though Grimsley had **previously** been diagnosed with DID, the court found her guilty of the crime. According to the court, an individual's criminal responsibility rests on the mental state of the alter in control at the time of the crime. The court concluded that because the alter personality—Jennifer—was not unconscious at the time of the drunken driving, Grimsley as a whole should be held criminally accountable.

9. Why was Grimsley found guilty?

SE p. 118, paragraph 2

Bridget Denny-Shaffer disguised herself as a medical student, entered a hospital nursery, took a newborn baby, and **transported** the baby to another state, telling her ex-boyfriend that she had given birth. Once captured, Denny-Shaffer was charged with kidnapping and transporting the infant across state lines. Her defense was that she was unconscious and not aware of the kidnapping for all or part of those weeks. In fact, it was shown in court that at least two alter personalities, Rina and Mother Superior, were in control. Denny-Shaffer was found not guilty. The court could not prove that the host personality was mentally aware of the goings on, and thus she couldn't be held responsible for the actions of the alter egos. The host personality—rather than the alter in control—is the person on trial. If the host personality isn't aware of what is happening, then by reason of insanity, the person is not responsible.

10. Why was Denny-Shaffer found not guilty?

SE p. 118, paragraph 3
page break

Denny-Shaffer, like most criminals found not guilty by reason of insanity, was sentenced to time in a mental | institution. According to the American Psychiatric Association, persons found not guilty by reason of insanity are likely to spend the same amount of time or more in a psychiatric institution as they would have in prison if found guilty of the crime. However, mentally ill people are often found guilty and sent to prison because treatments are offered within prison walls. Are the treatments equal? How are people found to be mentally ill treated in the United States?

11. What is the typical sentence for many mentally ill criminals?

SE p. 119, paragraph 1

page break

SE p. 120, paragraphs 1–2

SE p. 120, paragraphs 3–4

Society's Treatment of the Mentally Ill

People who suffered from mental illness during the 17th and 18th centuries were treated horribly. Those judged insane were frequently admitted to madhouses, workhouses, poorhouses, and jails. Those thought to be particularly dangerous were put in restraints and sentenced to confinement. By the end of the 17th century, the prevailing **image** of the mentally ill was that of uncontrollable, wild animals. | Harsh treatment and restraint with chains was thought to be needed therapy to suppress the animal instincts. Treatment in public asylums was similar to prison life. The most notorious of these was Bedlam in England. It is said that at one time, spectators could pay to watch the patients there as a form of entertainment. Today, the word *bedlam* is a common noun that means "a state of total confusion."

By the end of the 18th century, a moral treatment movement developed. This movement **implemented** more humane and personalized approaches to treatment of the mentally ill. The following century saw a growth in the number and size of insane asylums. Laws were introduced that allowed authorities to deal with those deemed insane. Unfortunately, the institutions became overburdened with large numbers of people, leading to very few therapeutic activities.

The turn of the 20th century saw even more changes. Advocates worked to improve the conditions in asylums, which were now known as hospitals. New treatments used drugs to control symptoms. More and more patients were released from institutions. The public began to understand that a mental illness is a disease, just like a physical illness.

12. How has the treatment of people with mental illness changed over time?

Remaining Questions

The debate over DID will likely not be resolved anytime soon. People will continue to debate whether a person can have multiple personalities and whether DID is misdiagnosed. Juries and judges will continue to argue whether all persons should be held accountable for their actions, regardless of their mental state. Among the lingering questions, one fact remains. Since 1999, the Department of Justice has found that more than half of the people in the nation's prisons are mentally ill—and far less than half of those receive any mental health treatment.

Should people be imprisoned for crimes committed by alter egos? You decide.

13. Why is DID controversial?

For confirmation of engagement, have partners share two things they learned about DID.

Unit 9 Lesson 2

Lesson Opener

Before the lesson, choose one of the following activities to write on the board or post on the *LANGUAGE! Live* Class Wall online.

- *Describe a relationship you have had with a mentor or trusted guide. How did that person help you to become a better version of yourself?*
- *All of us can quickly think of our 10 worst qualities, or things we would like to change about ourselves. Thinking of the good things is much more difficult. Make a list of your 10 best qualities.*
- *Write five questions you would ask someone who suffers from DID.*

Vocabulary

Objective

- Review key passage vocabulary.

Review Passage Vocabulary

Direct students to page 112 in their Student Books. Use the following questions to review the vocabulary words from "The Mysterious Human Brain." Have students answer each question using the vocabulary word or indicating its meaning in a complete sentence.

Lesson 1 | Vocabulary

Key Passage Vocabulary: "The Mysterious Human Brain"

Read each word. Write the word in column 3. Then, circle a number to rate your knowledge of the word.

[illegible]	[illegible]	[illegible]	[illegible]
inhibition	(n)	inhibition	0 1 2 3
distinct	(adj)	distinct	0 1 2 3
controversial	(adj)	controversial	0 1 2 3
prone (to)	(adj)	prone (to)	0 1 2 3
media	(n)	media	0 1 2 3
standard	(n)	standard	0 1 2 3
previously	(adv)	previously	0 1 2 3
transport	(v)	transport	0 1 2 3
image	(n)	image	0 1 2 3
implement	(v)	implement	0 1 2 3

112 Unit 9

- If Dr. Jekyll loses his *inhibitions* when he becomes Mr. Hyde, what happens to his fears and embarrassments? (If he loses his inhibitions, he loses his fears and embarrassments.) What would happen if we all suddenly lost our *inhibitions* all at once? (Possible response: If we all suddenly lost our inhibitions, we would all start acting in bold, surprising, and even outrageous ways.)
- If a person has dissociative identity disorder, he or she has two or more *distinct* what? (People with DID have two or more distinct selves or identities.) What makes two selves or identities *distinct*? (Distinct identities are totally different. They have different characteristics and ways of interacting with others.)
- Why is DID *controversial*? (DID is controversial because professionals disagree on what causes it and how to treat it.) Why are things that are hard to measure or track more *controversial* than others? (They are more controversial because they can't be proven.)
- Some experts say that when young children experience trauma, they are *prone* to what? (They are prone to "splitting," or creating alternate personalities.) If they are *prone* to "splitting," are they likely to do it? (Yes, they are likely to split.) After splitting, what are people with DID *prone* to do in difficult situations? (They are prone to switching personalities.)
- According to doubters of DID, what role does the *media* play? (The media plants the idea for the condition in people's minds.) What example of this is given in the article? (After the book and movie *Sybil* came out in the '70s, diagnoses of DID skyrocketed.)

- What *standard* has been set in the United States for determining whether someone was legally insane at the time of a crime? (The standard is that if a person did not know what he or she was doing or that it was wrong, he or she was legally insane.) How is this *standard* complicated in cases involving DID? (The standard is complicated because one identity of a person with DID might be sane while another identity is legally insane.)
- Robin Grimsley was convicted of driving under the influence of alcohol. She had been *previously* diagnosed with DID. When was she diagnosed? (She was diagnosed before the conviction.) Why did the court decide that being *previously* diagnosed did not make her innocent? (The court decided that her earlier diagnosis was irrelevant because criminal responsibility rests on the alter in control at the time, and at the time of the crime, the alter, Jennifer, was not legally insane.)
- Bridget Denny-Shaffer *transported* a kidnapped baby. What did she do to the baby? (When she transported the baby, she moved her across state lines.) Whom did Bridget claim actually *transported* the baby? (She claimed that two alters, Rina and Mother Superior, transported the baby.)
- During the 20th century, mental health professionals tried to change the *image* people had of "insane asylums." What did they try to change? (They tried to change the picture people had in their minds of the places where mentally ill people were treated.) Did they succeed? What *image* do you have of mental hospitals today? (Possible response: They have succeeded. The image I have of a mental hospital is much like a regular hospital—plain, sterile rooms; a regular schedule; and doctors and other health care workers in attendance.)
- Denny-Shaffer was found not guilty because the court said she was not responsible for the actions of her alters. In the 17th and 18th centuries, people like Bridget Denny-Shaffer spent their lives in madhouses, workhouses, poorhouses, and jails. What was *implemented* in the 19th century to change the fates of people like Denny-Shaffer? (More humane ways of treating mentally ill people were implemented.) Once these new, more humane treatments were *implemented*, what problem arose? (Once the more humane treatments were implemented, the institutions became overcrowded.)

Grammar

Objectives

- Identify relative clauses and their function.
- Differentiate between noun, adjective, and adverb clauses.

Relative Clauses as Adjectives

In the previous unit, we learned how to distinguish between a phrase, a dependent clause, and an independent clause. Which one of these groups of words is not a complete thought? (phrase) Which one of these groups of words is a complete thought that can stand alone? (independent clause) Which one, even though it has a subject and a predicate, cannot stand alone? (dependent clause) We've worked with two different kinds of dependent clauses. When a subordinating conjunction joins two clauses, one clause is dependent on the other. This dependent clause answers the *when, where, why,* and *how* questions. The clause functions like an adverb and is called a relative clause.

Write the following sentences (without underlines) on the board and have students identify the subordinating conjunctions and relative clauses.

- *When children are abused, they often create alters to deal with the pain.*
- *There is often a history of abuse before the alters emerge.*
- *Although there have been many documented cases of DID, the disorder remains controversial.*
- *As the movie* Sybil *gained popularity, the cases of DID increased dramatically.*
- *Some people believe a criminal is guilty regardless of which alter ego was in control at the time of the crime.*
- *During the 17th century, before people were well educated on mental health, the mentally ill were put in jail.*

Another type of clause begins with a relative pronoun and answers the *which one, what kind,* or *how many* questions. How does this dependent clause function? (It functions like an adjective.) This other dependent clause is also a relative clause but can be referred to as an adjective clause. As an adjective clause, it provides more information about a noun or pronoun in the sentence.

Direct students to page 121 in their Student Books. Read the information in the chart, emphasizing the new words *where* and *when*. Read the instructions aloud.

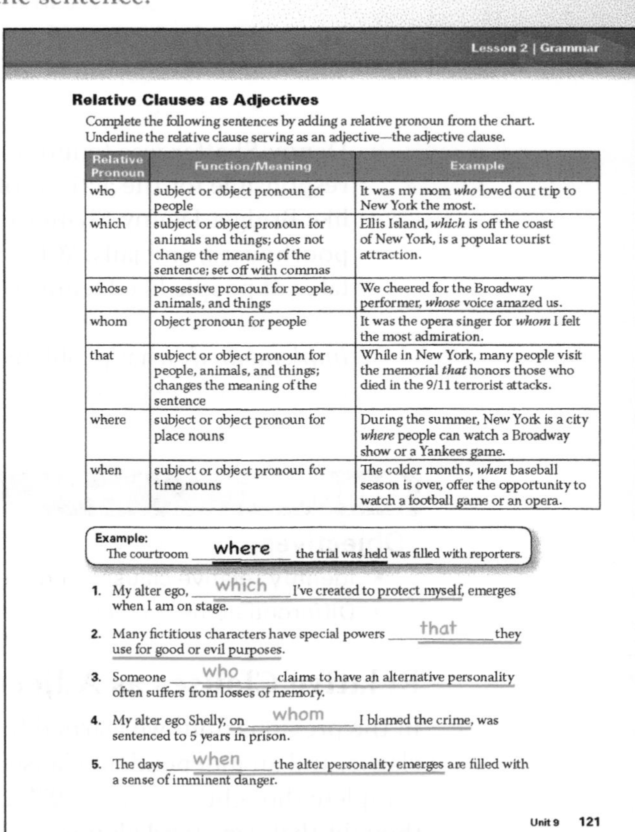

Lesson 2 | Grammar

Relative Clauses as Adjectives

Complete the following sentences by adding a relative pronoun from the chart. Underline the relative clause serving as an adjective—the adjective clause.

Relative Pronoun	Function/Meaning	Example
who	subject or object pronoun for people	It was my mom *who* loved our trip to New York the most.
which	subject or object pronoun for animals and things; does not change the meaning of the sentence; set off with commas	Ellis Island, *which* is off the coast of New York, is a popular tourist attraction.
whose	possessive pronoun for people, animals, and things	We cheered for the Broadway performer, *whose* voice amazed us.
whom	object pronoun for people	It was the opera singer for *whom* I felt the most admiration.
that	subject or object pronoun for people, animals, and things; changes the meaning of the sentence	While in New York, many people visit the memorial *that* honors those who died in the 9/11 terrorist attacks.
where	subject or object pronoun for place nouns	During the summer, New York is a city *where* people can watch a Broadway show or a Yankees game.
when	subject or object pronoun for time nouns	The colder months, *when* baseball season is over, offer the opportunity to watch a football game or an opera.

Example:
The courtroom ___where___ the trial was held was filled with reporters.

1. My alter ego, ___which___ I've created to protect myself, emerges when I am on stage.
2. Many fictitious characters have special powers ___that___ they use for good or evil purposes.
3. Someone ___who___ claims to have an alternative personality often suffers from losses of memory.
4. My alter ego Shelly, on ___whom___ I blamed the crime, was sentenced to 5 years in prison.
5. The days ___when___ the alter personality emerges are filled with a sense of imminent danger.

Unit 9 121

Model

Listen as I read the example: *The courtroom ______ the trial was held was filled with reporters.* In this case, I want to explain the courtroom and answer the *which one* question. Which courtroom was filled with reporters? *Courtroom* is a thing and also a place. My options for relative pronouns would be *which, that,* and *where.* Read the sentence with each one and have students choose the one that sounds correct. My adjective clause is *where the trial was held.* I have to check to make sure my dependent clause contains a subject and a verb. *Trial* is the subject of the clause and *was held* is the verb. So I have underlined a clause that answers the *which one* question. It is functioning as an adjective.

Guided Practice

Listen as I read #1: *My alter ego,* _____ *I've created to protect myself, emerges when I am on stage.* In this case, I want to explain the alter ego and answer the *which one* question. Which alter ego emerges when I am on stage? (*the one I've created to protect myself*) *Alter ego* is a thing. My options for relative pronouns would be *which* and *that.* We need to find out if the clause changes the meaning of the sentence or if it just helps the reader understand what the writer is thinking. Does it change the meaning? (no) Because it doesn't change the meaning, which pronoun should we use? (which) What other clue helps us know that the pronoun should be *which*? (commas)

What is the dependent clause? (which I've created to protect myself) What is the subject? (I) What is the verb? (have created) **Explain the division of the contraction for the purpose of identifying the subject and the verb.**

Independent Practice

Have students complete the activity. Review the answers as a class.

Relative Clauses as Nouns

We've learned that clauses can function as adjectives and adverbs. Clauses can also function as a noun in a sentence. Let's review the jobs of nouns. One job a noun can have in a sentence is to be the subject. What are the other jobs a noun can have in a sentence? (direct object, object of the preposition, predicate noun) **If students struggle with the answers, write the following examples on the board:**

Jaime eats chips. (direct object)

Jaime likes to eat dip with the chips. (object of the preposition)

Jaime's favorite food is chips. (predicate noun)

Direct students to page 122 in their Student Books. Read the information about noun clauses aloud.

By focusing on the question a clause answers, you can more easily determine its function. Thinking about the questions also helps you write more sophisticated sentences. When you look at the words that begin noun clauses, you should see some very familiar words. *That, which, who,* and *whom* are used in adjective clauses as well as noun clauses. Because clauses have multiple functions, we have to always question how the clause is being used as opposed to jumping to a conclusion. Let's practice recognizing noun clauses when we're reading.

Read the instructions for the activity.

Lesson 2 | Grammar

Relative Clauses as Nouns

- Have a subject and a predicate but cannot stand alone
- Take the place of a noun: subject or object
- Answer the *who* or *what* question
- Begin with: *that, what, whatever, which, whichever, who, whoever, whom, whomever, whose*

Read each sentence and determine whether the underlined group of words is a noun clause. Place an X in the appropriate column.

	Noun Clause	Other
Ex: I would say that we wear different hats in different situations.	✗	
1. Psychologists explain that when children under the age of 6 are traumatized, they create another "self" to endure the suffering in their place.	✗	
2. He was diagnosed with a mental illness called dissociative identity disorder.		✗
3. They agree that most sufferers have probably been abused.	✗	
4. All of these fictitious characters have another "self" that they become when the need arises.		✗
5. Laws were introduced that allowed authorities to deal with those deemed insane.		✗
6. The criminal forgot which alter was in control but knew it wasn't her.	✗	
7. Multiple personalities that conflict with each other are often created during childhood.		✗
8. According to the jury, whoever was in control at the time of the crime is the guilty party.	✗	

122 Unit 9

Model

Listen as I read the example: *I would say that we wear different hats in different situations.* First, I need to focus on the underlined words and determine if they are a clause. Is there a subject and a verb in the words that are underlined? If so, I need to figure out what question the clause answers. For it to function as a noun, it needs to answer the *who* or *what* question. The underlined words include a subject, *we*, and a verb, *wear*. It's a clause, and it provides the answer to the *say what* question. Because it is a clause that answers a *what* question, it's functioning as a noun clause. I put an X in the Noun Clause column.

Guided Practice

Listen as I read #1: *Psychologists explain that when children under the age of 6 are traumatized, they create another "self" to endure the suffering in their place.* What words are underlined? (that when children under the age of 6 are traumatized) Is it a clause? (yes) What is the subject of the clause? (children) What is the verb? (are traumatized) Does the clause tell us any information about which psychologist or what kind of psychologist? (no) Does it tell us what the psychologists explain? (yes) Because it answers the *explain what* question, how is this clause functioning in this sentence? (It is functioning as the direct object.) Where will you put your X? (under Noun Clause)

Listen as I read #2: *He was diagnosed with a mental illness called dissociative identity disorder.* What words are underlined? (with a mental illness) Is that a clause? (no) Why not? (It doesn't have a subject and a verb.) It's just a phrase, a prepositional phrase. Where will you place your X? (under Other)

Independent Practice

Have students complete the activity. Review the answers as a class.

Adjective, Adverb, and Noun Clauses

Write the following sentences on the board (without underlines), and have students identify the dependent clause and whether it is an adjective clause, an adverb clause, or a noun clause.

- *Students who eat a good breakfast are more successful during the day.* (adjective clause)
- *Good students know which peer will be a good choice for group work.* (noun clause)
- *After the final bell rings, good students continue learning.* (adverb clause)

Direct students to page 123 in their Student Books. Read the instructions aloud.

This activity will help you cement your understanding of the differences between adjective, adverb, and noun clauses.

Model

Listen as I read #1: *People who suffered from mental illness during the 17th and 18th centuries were treated horribly. Who suffered from mental illness during the 17th and 18th centuries* is the clause. It follows *people* and tells me which people were treated horribly. Because it answers the *which one* question, I know it's functioning as an adjective. I need to write the clause in the chart under Adjective Clause.

Lesson 2 | Grammar

Adjective, Adverb, and Noun Clauses

Read each sentence and determine the function of the underlined clause. Sort them appropriately in the chart.

1. People who suffered from mental illness during the 17th and 18th centuries were treated horribly.
2. Since 1999, the Department of Justice has found that more than half of the people in the nation's prisons are mentally ill.
3. He was diagnosed with this disorder shortly after he retired from the NFL.
4. The comic book character Clark Kent, who sees a crime happening, rushes into a phone booth and emerges as Superman.
5. The condition seems to begin when a child copes with trauma by convincing him- or herself that it is happening to someone else.
6. This creates a trigger that causes a child to create alternate personalities called "alters" who take over.
7. This creates a trigger that causes a child to create alternate personalities called "alters" who take over.
8. A person can lose control over when the personalities "switch" and may not remember what happens to them while they are switched.
9. Having been educated, they knew what to look for and how to diagnose, which created a natural increase in cases.
10. The person may not be aware of the disorder until much later in life because it usually only appears during trauma.

Adjective Clause	Adverb Clause	Noun Clause
who suffered from mental illness during the 17th and 18th centuries	shortly after he retired	that more than half of the people in the nation's prisons are mentally ill
who sees a crime happening	while they are switched	that it is happening to someone else
that causes a child to create alternate personalities called "alters"	because it usually only appears during trauma	what to look for and how to diagnose
who take over		

Unit 9 123

Guided Practice

Listen as I read #2: *Since 1999, the Department of Justice has found* *<u>that more than half of the people in the nation's prisons are mentally ill</u>*. What is the clause? (that more than half of the people in the nation's prisons are mentally ill) Think for a minute about the question that clause answers. Is it telling us something about the subject by answering the *which one* or *what kind* question? (no) Is it telling us something about the verb by answering the *when, where,* or *how* question? (no) Is it answering a *who* or *what* question? (yes) Because this clause tells us what the Department of Justice found, it is functioning as the direct object. Where will you write this clause? (under Noun Clause)

Independent Practice

Have students complete the activity. Review the answers as a class.

Writing

Objective

- Distinguish between active and passive voice.

Active and Passive Voice

Think about what you've learned about verbs. They are the driving force of a sentence. When working with the stages in Masterpiece Sentences, you paint the verb by answering questions about the verb. As you prepare the canvas, you ask the *what did they do it to* question about the verb. If this question can be answered, the sentence contains a direct object.

Write the following sentence on the board: *Beth kicked the ball.*

What is the verb in this sentence? (kicked) Who kicked? (Beth) Kicked what? (ball) What is the function of the noun, *ball*, in this sentence? (direct object)

Write the following sentence under the first sentence on the board: *The ball was kicked by Beth.*

What is the verb in this sentence? (was kicked) What is the subject? (ball) In the first sentence, the subject, *Beth*, does the action, *kicked*. In the second sentence, the subject actually receives the action. This sentence is considered passive voice because the subject is passive. It is not doing anything. In the second sentence, what words follow *kicked*? (by Beth) Instead of a direct object, the verb is followed by a prepositional phrase. While there may be some occasions where passive voice is an effective choice, most of the time you should try to write using active voice. You can recognize passive voice by two features. First, the verb will always have a helping verb. What is the verb phrase in the second sentence? (was kicked) This one feature is not enough to guarantee the sentence has been written in passive voice. The other significant clue is that the subject is *receiving* the action as opposed to *doing* the action. When you find both of these features in a sentence, you've probably found a sentence written in passive voice.

Write the following sentence pairs on the board, and have students identify which one in each set is active and which one is passive.

- *The test was taken by all 9th grade students.* (passive)
- *All 9th grade students took the test.* (active)
- *Fifty challenging questions were answered by the thorough test takers.* (passive)
- *The thorough test takers answered fifty challenging questions.* (active)

Direct students to page 124 in their Student Books. Read the instructions aloud. Because you should use passive voice sparingly, this activity focuses on revising the sentence structure and using active voice.

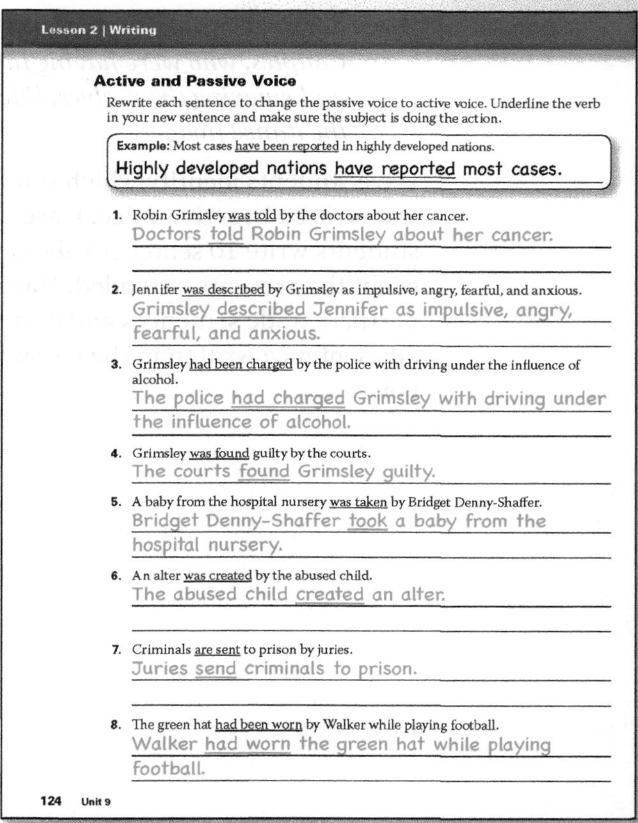

Lesson 2 | Writing

Active and Passive Voice

Rewrite each sentence to change the passive voice to active voice. Underline the verb in your new sentence and make sure the subject is doing the action.

Example: Most cases have been reported in highly developed nations.
Highly developed nations have reported most cases.

1. Robin Grimsley was told by the doctors about her cancer.
   Doctors told Robin Grimsley about her cancer.
2. Jennifer was described by Grimsley as impulsive, angry, fearful, and anxious.
   Grimsley described Jennifer as impulsive, angry, fearful, and anxious.
3. Grimsley had been charged by the police with driving under the influence of alcohol.
   The police had charged Grimsley with driving under the influence of alcohol.
4. Grimsley was found guilty by the courts.
   The courts found Grimsley guilty.
5. A baby from the hospital nursery was taken by Bridget Denny-Shaffer.
   Bridget Denny-Shaffer took a baby from the hospital nursery.
6. An alter was created by the abused child.
   The abused child created an alter.
7. Criminals are sent to prison by juries.
   Juries send criminals to prison.
8. The green hat had been worn by Walker while playing football.
   Walker had worn the green hat while playing football.

124 Unit 9

Model

Listen as I read the example: *Most cases have been reported in highly developed nations.* I notice the verb phrase contains two helping verbs: *have* and *been*. *Cases* did not report. Who did the reporting? Highly developed nations did the reporting. What did they report? They reported cases. To write this sentence in active voice, I need to make *highly developed nations* my subject and *most cases* needs to become my direct object. My new sentence is: *Highly developed nations have reported most cases.* In this sentence, my subject did the action. I no longer need to use the helping verb *been*.

Guided Practice

Listen as I read #1: *Robin Grimsley was told by the doctors about her cancer.* Who told Robin Grimsley about her cancer? (the doctors) Let's rewrite this sentence and make the doctors the subject. We can use *doctors* or *the doctors* as our subject. What did they do? (told) What is the complete sentence? (Doctors told Robin Grimsley about her cancer.) We no longer need the helping verb *was,* and our verb is followed by a direct object instead of a prepositional phrase.

Independent Practice

Have students rewrite the remaining sentences. Review the answers as a class.

Active Voice Optional Activity

Direct students to page 125 in their Student Books. Read the instructions aloud.

Write the following sentences on the board to use as modeling.

> *The dance floor was filled with couples having fun and enjoying themselves.*
>
> *Couples, who were having fun and enjoying themselves, filled the dance floor.*

Have students identify which sentence was written in active voice. Have students write 10 sentences about an event they recently attended. Have partners trade sentences and correct any sentence written in the passive voice.

Lesson 2 | Writing

Active Voice Optional Activity

Write 10 sentences about an event you recently attended. Use the active voice in your sentences.

1. Answers will vary.
2.
3.
4.
5.
6.
7.
8.
9.
10.

Unit 9 125

Unit 9

Lesson 3

Lesson Opener

Before the lesson, choose one of the following activities to write on the board or post on the *LANGUAGE! Live* Class Wall online.

- *Write five compound sentences about this class using subordinating conjunctions.*
- *Describe something that is mysterious to you.*
- *Write five sentences about an alter ego you would like to have. What situations would the alter come out in? Use an adjective clause, an adverb clause, or a noun clause in each sentence.*

Reading

Objectives

- Establish a purpose for rereading informational text.
- Use critical thinking skills to write responses to prompts about text.
- Support written answers with evidence from text.
- Objectively summarize informational text.
- Use information found in text features to answer questions.
- Trace the claims made in a text.
- Establish an opinion on an issue and use text evidence to support this opinion.
- Evaluate an author's point of view of a topic.

Reading for a Purpose: "The Mysterious Human Brain"

It is time to answer some more specific questions. Because critical understanding requires active participation, we are going to read the text again. This time, we will be reading for a specific purpose, which will help us pay attention to details that we may have missed the first time around.

Let's read some questions about the text to provide a purpose for rereading.

Direct students to pages 126–128 in their Student Books. Have students read the prompts aloud with you.

1. Objectively summarize dissociative identity disorder.
2. Integrate information from the primary text and text features (bulleted text box) to contrast schizophrenia and DID.
3. Trace the doubters' claims that DID is an "imagined disorder." Provide text evidence.
4. Evaluate the merit of DID. Provide text evidence to support your evaluation.
5. Summarize and evaluate the outcomes of the DID court cases.
6. Evaluate the author's point of view regarding society's treatment of the mentally ill.

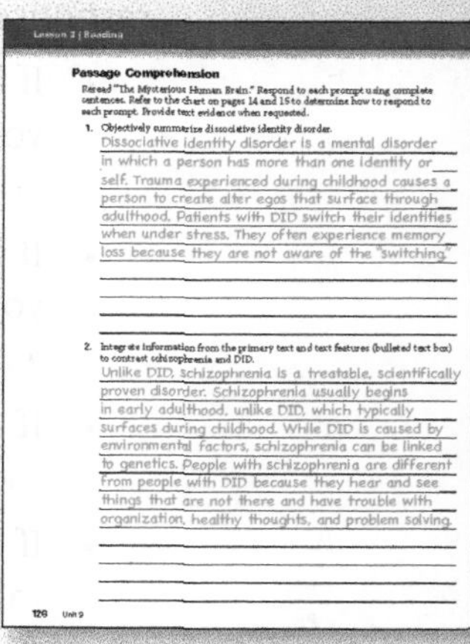

Lesson 3 | Reading

Passage Comprehension

Reread "The Mysterious Human Brain." Respond to each prompt using complete sentences. Refer to the chart on pages 14 and 15 to determine how to respond to each prompt. Provide text evidence when requested.

1. Objectively summarize dissociative identity disorder.

   Dissociative identity disorder is a mental disorder in which a person has more than one identity or self. Trauma experienced during childhood causes a person to create alter egos that surface through adulthood. Patients with DID switch their identities when under stress. They often experience memory loss because they are not aware of the "switching."

2. Integrate information from the primary text and text features (bulleted text box) to contrast schizophrenia and DID.

   Unlike DID, schizophrenia is a treatable, scientifically proven disorder. Schizophrenia usually begins in early adulthood, unlike DID, which typically surfaces during childhood. While DID is caused by environmental factors, schizophrenia can be linked to genetics. People with schizophrenia are different from people with DID because they hear and see things that are not there and have trouble with organization, healthy thoughts, and problem solving.

126 Unit 9

Direct students to page 113 in their Student Books or have them tear out the extra copy of the text from the back of their book.

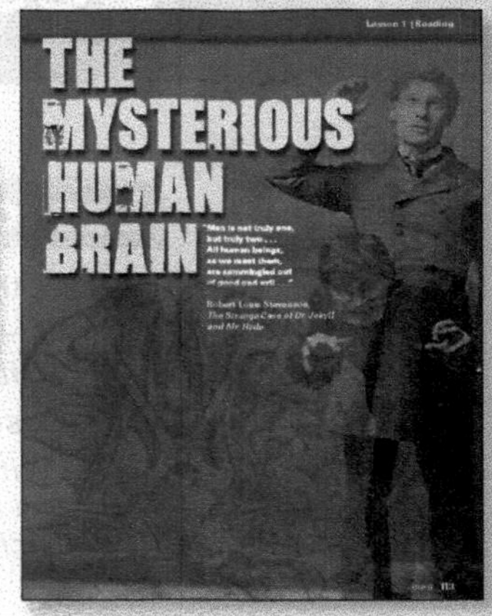

Note: To minimize flipping back and forth between the pages, a copy of each text has been included in the back of the Student Books. Encourage students to tear this out and use it when working on activities that require the use of the text.

Choose an option for reading text. Have students read the text according to the option that you chose.

Options for reading text:

- Teacher read-aloud
- Teacher-led or student-led choral read
- Paired read or independent read with bold vocabulary words read aloud

Passage Comprehension

Write the words *evaluate, integrate, summarize,* and *trace* on the board. Have students read the words aloud with you.

Direct students to pages 14 and 15 in their Student Books. It is critical to understand what the question is asking and how to answer it. Today, we will review four direction words used in prompts.

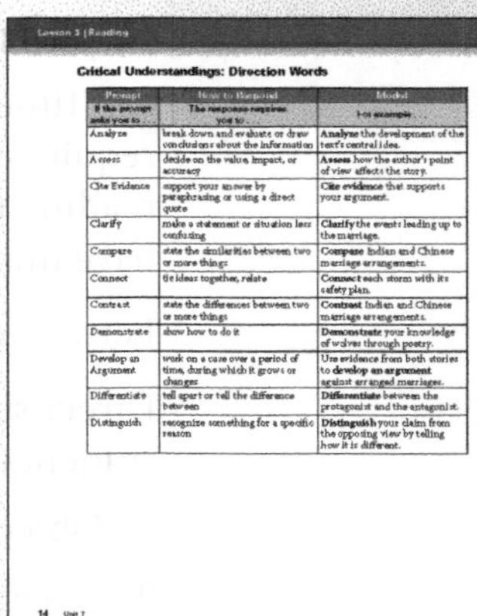

Lesson 3 | Reading

Critical Understandings: Direction Words

Prompt	How to Respond	Model
If the prompt asks you to . . .	The response requires you to . . .	For example . . .
Analyze	break down and evaluate or draw conclusions about the information	**Analyze** the development of the text's central idea.
Assess	decide on the value, impact, or accuracy	**Assess** how the author's point of view affects the story.
Cite Evidence	support your answer by paraphrasing or using a direct quote	**Cite evidence** that supports your argument.
Clarify	make a statement or situation less confusing	**Clarify** the events leading up to the marriage.
Compare	state the similarities between two or more things	**Compare** Indian and Chinese marriage arrangements.
Connect	tie ideas together, relate	**Connect** each storm with its safety plan.
Contrast	state the differences between two or more things	**Contrast** Indian and Chinese marriage arrangements.
Demonstrate	show how to do it	**Demonstrate** your knowledge of wolves through poetry.
Develop an Argument	work on a case over a period of time, during which it grows or changes	Use evidence from both stories to **develop an argument** against arranged marriages.
Differentiate	tell apart or tell the difference between	**Differentiate** between the protagonist and the antagonist.
Distinguish	recognize something for a specific reason	**Distinguish** your claim from the opposing view by telling *how it is different.*

Have students review the words on the board in the chart on pages 14 and 15. Check for understanding by requesting an oral response to the following questions.

- If the prompt asks you to *evaluate,* the response requires you to . . . (think carefully to make a judgment; form a critical opinion of).
- If the prompt asks you to *integrate,* the response requires you to . . . (combine different kinds of information to form a complete whole).
- If the prompt asks you to *summarize,* the response requires you to . . . (tell the most important ideas or concepts).
- If the prompt asks you to *trace,* the response requires you to . . . (follow information closely).

Direct students to pages 126–128 in their Student Books.

Lesson 3 | Reading

Passage Comprehension

Reread "The Mysterious Human Brain." Respond to each prompt using complete sentences. Refer to the chart on pages 14 and 15 to determine how to respond to each prompt. Provide text evidence when requested.

1. Objectively summarize dissociative identity disorder.

Dissociative identity disorder is a mental disorder in which a person has more than one identity or self. Trauma experienced during childhood causes a person to create alter egos that surface through adulthood. Patients with DID switch their identities when under stress. They often experience memory loss because they are not aware of the "switching."

2. Integrate information from the primary text and text features (bulleted text box) to contrast schizophrenia and DID.

Unlike DID, schizophrenia is a treatable, scientifically proven disorder. Schizophrenia usually begins in early adulthood, unlike DID, which typically surfaces during childhood. While DID is caused by environmental factors, schizophrenia can be linked to genetics. People with schizophrenia are different from people with DID because they hear and see things that are not there and have trouble with organization, healthy thoughts, and problem solving.

126 Unit 9

Lesson 3 | Reading

Passage Comprehension (*cont.*)

3. Trace the doubters' claims that DID is an "imagined disorder." Provide text evidence.

People who believe that DID is an imagined disorder claim that therapy leads patients to believe a diagnosis about multiple personalities that the patient was unaware of. Doubters also claim that media exposure increased the diagnosis of this controversial mental illness, proving that it isn't based in science, but based on trends.

Text Evidence: Therapy leads to embracing the diagnosis; Media has influenced the increased diagnosis of DID since 1970.

4. Evaluate the merit of DID. Provide text evidence to support your evaluation.

Based on text evidence, I am a believer/doubter because (answers will vary but should support either believers or doubters).

Text Evidence: For believers: personality splits into many alters due to abuse prior to the age of 6 when brains are developing. Doubters agree that patients have probably been abused. Media attention based on a real woman's story increased education on the topic including symptoms and how to diagnose, which increased the number of patients with this diagnosis.

For doubters: therapy leads to embracing the diagnosis. Media has influenced the increased diagnoses of DID since 1970.

Unit 9 127

Let's practice answering questions written as prompts that require critical thinking.

Model

Listen as I model the first one for you.

1. Objectively summarize dissociative identity disorder.

First, I have to understand what *objectively* means. It means I have to write a summary that is based in fact and not give my opinion about it. In order to be objective, I have to be impartial or neutral on the topic. According to the chart, if the prompt asks me to *summarize*, I need to tell the most important ideas or concepts.

Now, we need to turn the prompt into a question to confirm our understanding.

Lesson 3 | Reading

Passage Comprehension (*cont.*)

5. Summarize and evaluate the outcomes of the DID court cases.

Grimsley was found guilty of drunk driving because her alter personality was not insane.
Denny-Shaffer was found not guilty of kidnapping, by reason of insanity, because she was unaware of her alter egos' actions.
I agree/disagree with the outcome of the Grimsley case because (answers will vary but should include a rationale based on reading).
I agree/disagree with the outcome of the Denny-Shaffer case because (answers will vary but should include a rationale based on reading).

6. Evaluate the author's point of view regarding society's treatment of the mentally ill.

The author feels that the treatment of people with mental illness has improved over the centuries. In the 17th and 18th centuries, people were treated horribly. The author disagrees with harsh treatments that included restraining sufferers with chains like wild animals. By the end of the 18th century, they were treated better. Instead of jails, hospitals were built and laws were created to deal with insane people. By the 20th century, the public finally began to realize that mental illness is a disease, which led to better conditions in hospitals and appropriate treatments for the sufferers.

128 Unit 9

For this prompt, we will ask ourselves basic questions that will help to determine the most important ideas related to DID. Answers to these questions guide our summary.

Write the following questions and answers on the board.

> *What is DID? mental disorder in which a person has more than one identity or self*
>
> *What does someone with DID do? switches identities when under stress; forgets what happened; experiences memory loss*
>
> *What is the cause of DID? surviving childhood trauma*

From here, I can use my answers to write complete sentences that form a summary. I have to keep my opinion about DID to myself in order to provide an objective summary. I have to avoid information about other disorders, like schizophrenia, since that is irrelevant and unrelated to DID. Read the following sentences aloud while writing the summary on the board.

> *Dissociative identity disorder is a mental disorder in which a person has more than one identity or self. Trauma experienced during childhood causes a person to create alter egos that surface through adulthood. Patients with DID switch their identities when under stress. They often experience memory loss because they are not aware of the "switching."*

Guided Practice

2. Integrate information from the primary text and text features (bulleted text box) to contrast schizophrenia and DID.

If the prompt asks you to *integrate*, what should you do? (combine different kinds of information to form a complete whole) And we know, without needing the chart, that if a prompt asks us to *contrast*, we need to tell the differences between two things. Let's turn the prompt into a question to confirm our understanding. If we change this to a question, what would it be? (How is schizophrenia different from DID? Use the text and text features.)

The good news is that the answer to the first prompt provides information from the text about DID. We can combine text information with information in the chart to learn more about schizophrenia.

Let's ask ourselves some questions. Answers to these questions inform our response.

- Is schizophrenia controversial or scientific? (scientific)
- Is it treatable? (yes)
- When does it begin? (early adulthood)
- Is it caused by a person's environment, by his or her genetics, or both? (both)
- What else do we know? (Schizophrenics have trouble with organization, healthy thoughts, and problem solving. They see and hear things that aren't there.)

From here, you can use your answers to write complete sentences that contrast the two disorders. Be sure to include transition words that show differences. Some transition words might include: *unlike, in contrast, on the other hand,* etc.

Have partners respond to the prompt.

Independent Practice

Have students respond to the remaining questions. For students who need more assistance, provide the following alternative questions and sentence starters.

Alternative questions and sentence starters:

3. What evidence has led to the claims that DID is an "imagined disorder"? Provide text evidence.

   People who believe that DID is an imagined disorder claim that ____.

   Doubters also claim that ____________________.

4. Is DID a valid disorder?

   I am a believer/doubter that DID is a valid disorder because ____________________.

5. What are the most important ideas of the Grimsley case? What are the most important ideas of the Denny-Shaffer case? What is your opinion of each outcome?

   Grimsley was found guilty/not guilty __________ *because* ____________________.

   Denny-Shaffer was guilty/not guilty __________ *because* ____________________.

   I agree/disagree with the outcome of the Grimsley case because ____________________.

   I agree/disagree with the outcome of the Denny-Shaffer case because ____________________.

6. In your opinion, what is the author's point of view of society's treatment of the mentally ill?

   The author feels that the treatment of people with mental illness ____________________.

   In the 17th and 18th centuries, ____________________.

   By the 20th century, ____________________.

Unit 9

Lesson 4

Lesson Opener

Before the lesson, choose one of the following activities to write on the board or post on the *LANGUAGE! Live* Class Wall online.

- *Dress your avatar as though he or she just transformed into an alter ego. Explain your choices.*
- *Use passive voice to write five sentences about the behavior of a person with DID. Edit each sentence to the active voice.*
- *Identify the dependent clause in each sentence and label it as a noun clause, adjective clause, or adverb clause.*

  People who have alter egos can be treated.

  DID patients claim that they are not in control of the alter egos.

  People with DID experience temporary memory loss after an alter ego has taken control.

Reading

Objectives

- Read informational text with purpose and understanding.
- Answer questions to demonstrate comprehension of text.
- Identify and explain explicit details from text.
- Monitor comprehension of text during reading.
- Analyze connections made between individuals within a text.
- Analyze how sections of informational text contribute to the overall purpose of the text.
- Determine the meaning of idioms and proverbs.
- Evaluate the author's use of an epigraph.
- Determine the meaning of punctuation (ellipses).
- Identify the function of pronouns.
- Analyze connections made between ideas within a text.
- Identify verbs in the imperative mood.
- Determine the meaning of abbreviations used in text.
- Identify the purpose of indefinite pronouns.

Close Reading of "The Mysterious Human Brain"

Highlighters or colored pencils

Let's reread "The Mysterious Human Brain." I will provide specific instructions on how to mark the text that will help with comprehension.

Have students get out a highlighter or colored pencil.

Direct students to pages 129–135 in their Student Books.

Draw a rectangle around the title, "The Mysterious Human Brain."

Circle each heading.

Draw a star next to the epigraph.

Now, let's read the vocabulary words aloud.

- What's the first bold vocabulary word? (inhibitions) *Inhibitions* means "feelings of fear or embarrassment that keep you from doing something." Alter egos behave with a lack of *inhibitions*. Have partners use the word in a sentence.

- What's the next vocabulary word? (distinct) *Distinct* means "separate; different." Every sport has a *distinct* way of scoring. **Have partners use the word in a sentence.**
- Next word? (controversial) *Controversial* means "stirring up disagreement or debate." *Controversial* movies gain a lot of media attention. **Have partners use the word in a sentence.**
- Let's continue. (prone) *Prone* means "tending to do something or doing it naturally." Athletes are *prone* to injuries. **Have partners use the word in a sentence.**
- Next word? (media) *Media* means "TV, radio, newspapers, the Internet, and other forms of communication as a group." Beyoncé exposed her alter ego to the *media*. **Have partners use the word in a sentence.**
- Let's continue. (standard) *Standard* means "something used to judge, measure, or define something else." Each school has its own *standard* for behavior. **Have partners use the word in a sentence.**
- Next word? (previously) *Previously* means "earlier; before." The game was *previously* aired on live television. **Have partners use the word in a sentence.**
- Let's continue. (transported) *Transported* means "moved something from one place to another." The bus *transported* you to and from school yesterday. **Have partners use the word in a sentence.**
- Next word? (image) *Image* means "a picture in the mind." The *image* of my grandmother that I conjure up most often is one of her laughing. **Have partners use the word in a sentence.**
- Last word. (implemented) *Implemented* means "put something into action or put it to use." Our school *implemented* a new cell phone policy. **Have partners use the word in a sentence.**

Talk with a partner about any vocabulary word that is still confusing for you to read consistently or to understand its meaning.

You will read "The Mysterious Human Brain" one section at a time. After each section, you will monitor your understanding by circling the check mark if you understand the text or the question mark if you don't understand the text. I also want you to draw a question mark over any confusing words, phrases, or sentences.

Options for reading text:

- Teacher read-aloud
- Teacher-led or student-led choral read
- Paired read or independent read with bold vocabulary words read aloud

Choose an option for reading text. Have students read the epigraph and the section Alter Egos? according to the option that you chose.

When most of the students are finished, continue with the entire class. Let's see how well you understood what you read.

- Circle the check mark or the question mark for this section. Draw a question mark over any confusing words.
- Go to the epigraph. An epigraph is a quotation at the beginning of a text that sets forth the theme or central idea. In the margin, write the central idea of the text based on your understanding of the epigraph. (Every person has two personalities: one good and one evil.)
- Mark the punctuation used in the epigraph to indicate that there are missing words. (ellipses)

Close Reading

Read the text.

"The Mysterious Human Brain"

"Man is not truly one, but truly two . . . All human beings, as we meet them, are commingled out of good and evil . . ."

Robert Louis Stevenson, *The Strange Case of Dr. Jekyll and Mr. Hyde*

Alter Egos?

The comic book character Clark Kent, who sees a crime happening, rushes into a phone booth and emerges as Superman. Bruce Banner loses control of his anger and transforms into a green version of himself: the Incredible Hulk. Dr. Jekyll exits his laboratory void of **inhibitions** as the villainous Edward Hyde. All of these fictitious characters have another "self" that they become when the need arises. We hear people talk about them, watch superheroes turn into them, and read about them in literature. These alter egos entertain audiences in the world of fantasy. But are alter egos a part of our real world?

The answer is yes. Many of us daydream that we are someone else—someone smarter, richer, or more famous. Some of us, like Beyoncé, take on different personalities around different people and in different situations. Some of us love costume parties. These are typical kinds of "alter egos." They express our imagination and help us explore who we are. But a person whose alter egos are too "real" may have a mental illness called dissociative identity disorder. All-Pro running back Herschel Walker is one of these people. He was diagnosed with this disorder shortly after he retired from the NFL.

✔ ?

- Go to line 7. Mark the phrase that means "without." (void of)
- Go to line 8. Mark the word used to describe Superman, the Incredible Hulk, and Edward Hyde. (fictitious)
- Go to line 9. Mark the word *they*. Draw a line to the noun that the pronoun is referencing. (characters)
- In the next sentence, mark the repeated word. (them) Draw a line from each instance to the noun that the pronoun is referencing. (another "self")
- Circle the term in line 11 that means the same thing as another "self." (alter egos) Draw a line connecting the two.
- On the same line, mark the purpose of stories about alter egos. (entertain audiences)
- In the first paragraph, number the fictitious characters that act as alter egos. (1. Superman; 2. the Incredible Hulk; 3. Edward Hyde)
- An indefinite pronoun does not refer to any specific person, thing, or amount. It is "not definite." In the second paragraph, mark the indefinite pronouns. (many, someone, someone, some, some, one)
- Go to line 13. Mark what many of us do. (daydream that we are someone else)
- Go to lines 17 and 18. Mark what a typical "alter ego" allows us to do. (express our imagination; explore who we are)

- Go to line 19. Mark the name of Walker's mental illness. (dissociative identity disorder)
- The author of the text wants the reader to see a connection, as well as a distinction, between Beyoncé and Herschel Walker. In the margin, write the connection and the distinction. (connection: alter egos; distinction: Beyoncé takes on different personalities in different situations, while Walker has a disorder that he cannot control.)
- Headings are used to organize text. Each section of text contributes to the overall message or purpose of the text. How does the section Alter Egos? contribute to the whole text? Write your answer below the section. (It explains the difference between everyday "alter egos" and those that are brought on by DID.)

Have students read the Dissociative Identity Disorder section according to the option that you chose.

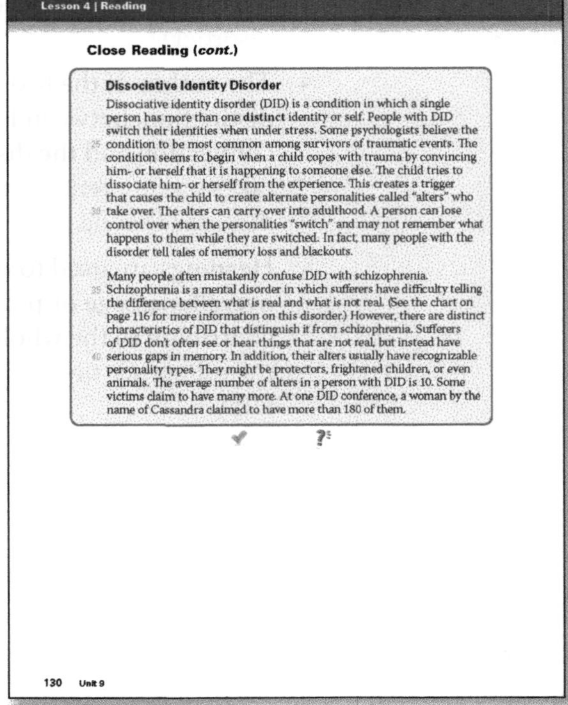

Lesson 4 | Reading

Close Reading (*cont.*)

Dissociative Identity Disorder

Dissociative identity disorder (DID) is a condition in which a single person has more than one **distinct** identity or self. People with DID switch their identities when under stress. Some psychologists believe the condition to be most common among survivors of traumatic events. The condition seems to begin when a child copes with trauma by convincing him- or herself that it is happening to someone else. The child tries to dissociate him- or herself from the experience. This creates a trigger that causes the child to create alternate personalities called "alters" who take over. The alters can carry over into adulthood. A person can lose control over when the personalities "switch" and may not remember what happens to them while they are switched. In fact, many people with the disorder tell tales of memory loss and blackouts.

Many people often mistakenly confuse DID with schizophrenia. Schizophrenia is a mental disorder in which sufferers have difficulty telling the difference between what is real and what is not real. (See the chart on page 116 for more information on this disorder.) However, there are distinct characteristics of DID that distinguish it from schizophrenia. Sufferers of DID don't often see or hear things that are not real, but instead have serious gaps in memory. In addition, their alters usually have recognizable personality types. They might be protectors, frightened children, or even animals. The average number of alters in a person with DID is 10. Some victims claim to have many more. At one DID conference, a woman by the name of Cassandra claimed to have more than 180 of them.

✓ ?

130 Unit 9

When most of the students are finished, continue with the entire class. Let's see how well you understood what you read.

- Circle the check mark or the question mark for this section. Draw a question mark over any confusing words.
- Authors and speakers often use abbreviations for ease of writing and speaking. An initial abbreviation is when the first letter of each word is read. Go to line 22. Mark the abbreviation for dissociative identity disorder. (DID)
- On the same line, mark the synonym of *illness.* (condition)
- Go to lines 26 and 27. Mark what some children do to cope with abuse. (convincing him- or herself that it is happening to someone else)
- Go to line 28. Mark the antonym of *associate.* (dissociate) Circle the prefix that means "not." (dis-)
- In the same sentence, mark the hyphenated reflexive pronouns used because the subject and direct object are the same person. (him- or herself) In the margin, explain why the hyphenated version of the pronoun is used. (The noun *child* is not gender-specific.)
- In the same line, mark the word that means "something that sets a person off." (trigger)
- Go to line 29. Mark the word *alters.* Circle the context clue. (called) Draw an arrow to the definition of *alters.* (alternate personalities)
- Go to line 34. Mark the disorder that is often confused with DID. (schizophrenia) Draw an arrow to the definition of *schizophrenia.* (a mental disorder in which sufferers have difficulty telling the difference between what is real and what is not real)
- Go to line 37. Mark the transition word that changes direction and means "but." (however)
- Number the common personality types of alters. (1. protectors; 2. frightened children; 3. animals)
- Go to line 42. Mark the average number of personalities. (10)
- Go to line 44. Mark the extreme number of personalities of Cassandra. (more than 180) In the margin, write whether you believe this could happen or doubt this could happen.
- How does the section Dissociative Identity Disorder contribute to the whole text? Write your answer below the section. (It explains the basics of DID.)

Have students read the section The Debate according to the option that you chose.

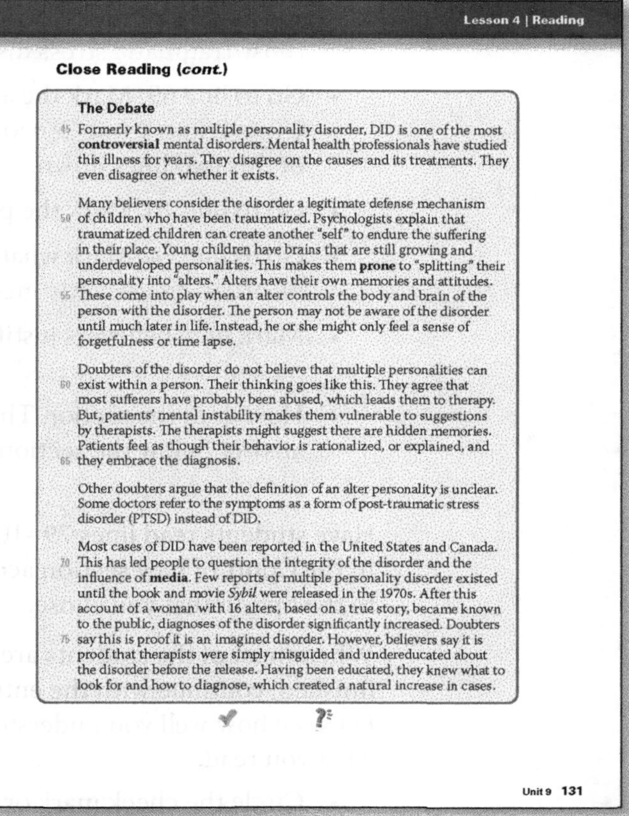

Lesson 4 | Reading

Close Reading (*cont.*)

The Debate

Formerly known as multiple personality disorder, DID is one of the most **controversial** mental disorders. Mental health professionals have studied this illness for years. They disagree on the causes and its treatments. They even disagree on whether it exists.

Many believers consider the disorder a legitimate defense mechanism of children who have been traumatized. Psychologists explain that traumatized children can create another "self" to endure the suffering in their place. Young children have brains that are still growing and underdeveloped personalities. This makes them **prone** to "splitting" their personality into "alters." Alters have their own memories and attitudes. These come into play when an alter controls the body and brain of the person with the disorder. The person may not be aware of the disorder until much later in life. Instead, he or she might only feel a sense of forgetfulness or time lapse.

Doubters of the disorder do not believe that multiple personalities can exist within a person. Their thinking goes like this. They agree that most sufferers have probably been abused, which leads them to therapy. But, patients' mental instability makes them vulnerable to suggestions by therapists. The therapists might suggest there are hidden memories. Patients feel as though their behavior is rationalized, or explained, and they embrace the diagnosis.

Other doubters argue that the definition of an alter personality is unclear. Some doctors refer to the symptoms as a form of post-traumatic stress disorder (PTSD) instead of DID.

Most cases of DID have been reported in the United States and Canada. This has led people to question the integrity of the disorder and the influence of **media**. Few reports of multiple personality disorder existed until the book and movie *Sybil* were released in the 1970s. After this account of a woman with 16 alters, based on a true story, became known to the public, diagnoses of the disorder significantly increased. Doubters say this is proof it is an imagined disorder. However, believers say it is proof that therapists were simply misguided and undereducated about the disorder before the release. Having been educated, they knew what to look for and how to diagnose, which created a natural increase in cases.

Unit 9 131

When most of the students are finished, continue with the entire class. Let's see how well you understood what you read.

- Circle the check mark or the question mark for this section. Draw a question mark over any confusing words.
- Go to lines 47 and 48. Number three disagreements that make DID controversial. (1. causes; 2. treatments; 3. whether it exists)
- Go to line 49. Mark the word that means "people who believe." (believers) Circle the suffix that means "people who." (-ers)
- Mark the synonym of *valid.* (legitimate)
- Go to line 51. Mark the word that means "shocked as a result of a disturbing or painful experience." (traumatized)
- On the same line, mark the words that mean "alters" or "alter egos." (another "self")
- Go to lines 52 and 53. Number the reasons children are prone to developing alters. (1. brains that are still growing; 2. underdeveloped personalities)
- Go to line 53. Underline the word used to mean "the creation of alter egos." (splitting)
- Mark the sentence that is rationale for why people with DID suffer from memory loss. (Alters have their own memories and attitudes.)
- Go to line 55. Mark the word *these.* Draw an arrow to what *these* is referring to. (their own memories and attitudes)
- Go to lines 57 and 58. Mark why people don't realize they have the disorder until later in life. (only feel a sense of forgetfulness or time lapse)
- Go to line 59. Mark the antonym of *believers.* (doubters)
- Go to line 62. Mark the words that mean "an imbalance of the brain." (mental instability) Draw a line to the cause of the imbalance. (abused)
- On the same line, mark the word that means "easy to persuade." (vulnerable)
- Go to line 64. Mark the reason patients embrace the diagnosis of DID. (behavior is rationalized) Circle a synonym for *rationalized.* (explained)

- Go to lines 67 and 68. Mark the disorder that doctors diagnose in place of DID. (post-traumatic stress disorder) Circle the initial abbreviation. (PTSD)
- Go to line 69. Mark the areas in which most DID cases can be found. (The United States and Canada) Draw an arrow to what doubters believe is the cause of this two lines down. (media)
- Go to line 70. Mark the phrase that means "doubt." (question the integrity)
- Go to line 74. Mark what happened after *Sybil* was released. (diagnoses of the disorder significantly increased)
- Mark how believers justify the increase in diagnoses. (therapists were simply misguided and undereducated about the disorder before the release)
- How does the section The Debate contribute to the whole text? Write your answer below the section. (It shows that not everyone believes DID is a valid disorder.)

Have students read lines 79–103 of the In the Court of Law section according to the option that you chose.

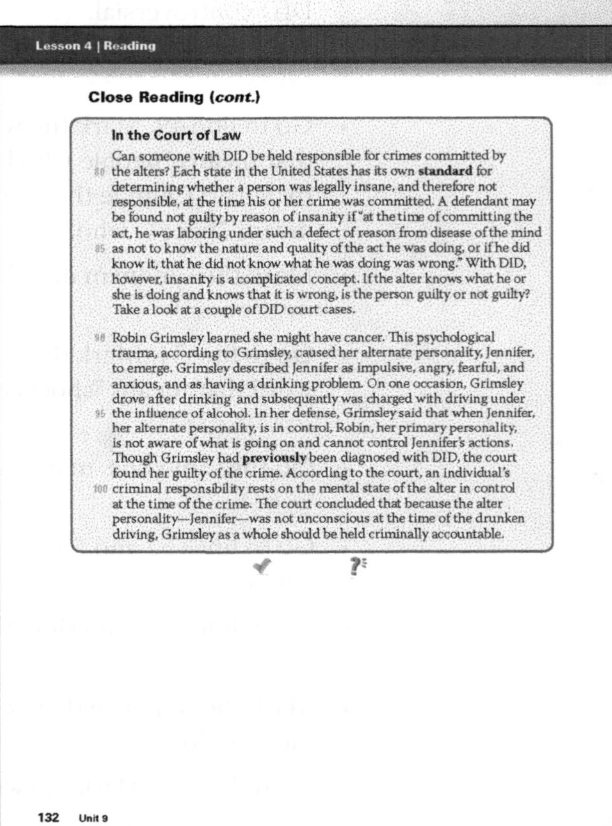

Lesson 4 | Reading

Close Reading (*cont.*)

In the Court of Law

Can someone with DID be held responsible for crimes committed by the alters? Each state in the United States has its own **standard** for determining whether a person was legally insane, and therefore not responsible, at the time his or her crime was committed. A defendant may be found not guilty by reason of insanity if "at the time of committing the act, he was laboring under such a defect of reason from disease of the mind as not to know the nature and quality of the act he was doing, or if he did know it, that he did not know what he was doing was wrong." With DID, however, insanity is a complicated concept. If the alter knows what he or she is doing and knows that it is wrong, is the person guilty or not guilty? Take a look at a couple of DID court cases.

Robin Grimsley learned she might have cancer. This psychological trauma, according to Grimsley, caused her alternate personality, Jennifer, to emerge. Grimsley described Jennifer as impulsive, angry, fearful, and anxious, and as having a drinking problem. On one occasion, Grimsley drove after drinking and subsequently was charged with driving under the influence of alcohol. In her defense, Grimsley said that when Jennifer, her alternate personality, is in control, Robin, her primary personality, is not aware of what is going on and cannot control Jennifer's actions. Though Grimsley had **previously** been diagnosed with DID, the court found her guilty of the crime. According to the court, an individual's criminal responsibility rests on the mental state of the alter in control at the time of the crime. The court concluded that because the alter personality—Jennifer—was not unconscious at the time of the drunken driving, Grimsley as a whole should be held criminally accountable.

132 Unit 9

When most of the students are finished, continue with the entire class. Let's see how well you understood what you read.

- Circle the check mark or the question mark for this section. Draw a question mark over any confusing words.
- Go to line 81. Mark the word that means "mentally ill." (insane)
- Go to line 87. Mark how DID changes the idea of insanity. (complicated)
- Go to line 90. Mark the trauma Robin Grimsley experienced. (learned she might have cancer)
- Go to line 92. Mark the synonym of *appear.* (emerge)
- On the same line, mark the word that means "acting without thinking." (impulsive)
- Go to line 94. Mark the synonym of *later.* (subsequently)
- On the same line, mark the synonym of *accused.* (charged)
- Go to line 96. Mark the word with the base word *alter.* (alternate)
- Go to line 100. Mark where criminal responsibility rests. (mental state of the alter in control)

Have students read lines 104–124 of the In the Court of Law section according to the option that you chose.

When most of the students are finished, continue with the entire class. Let's see how well you understood what you read.

- Circle the check mark or the question mark for this section. Draw a question mark over any confusing words.
- Go to line 109. Mark the phrase that means "actually." (in fact)
- Go to line 112. Mark the word that means "primary." (host)
- Go to line 113. Mark the transition word that means "therefore." (thus)
- Go to line 118. Because Denny-Shaffer was not guilty by reason of insanity, where did she "do time?" Mark the answer. (mental institution)
- Go to line 121. Mark where mentally ill people who are found guilty "do time." (prison)
- Go to line 123. Mark what they receive while in prison. (treatments)
- Mark the question the next section will likely answer. (How are people found to be mentally ill treated in the United States?)
- How does the section In the Court of Law contribute to the whole text? Write your answer below the section. (It explains the details of court cases in which a person claimed to be not guilty of a crime because of DID.)

Lesson 4 | Reading

Close Reading (*cont.*)

Bridget Denny-Shaffer disguised herself as a medical student, entered a hospital nursery, took a newborn baby, and **transported** the baby to another state, telling her ex-boyfriend that she had given birth. Once captured, Denny-Shaffer was charged with kidnapping and transporting the infant across state lines. Her defense was that she was unconscious and not aware of the kidnapping for all or part of those weeks. In fact, it was shown in court that at least two alter personalities, Rina and Mother Superior, were in control. Denny-Shaffer was found not guilty. The court could not prove that the host personality was mentally aware of the goings on, and thus she couldn't be held responsible for the actions of the alter egos. The host personality—rather than the alter in control—is the person on trial. If the host personality isn't aware of what is happening, then by reason of insanity, the person is not responsible.

Denny-Shaffer, like most criminals found not guilty by reason of insanity, was sentenced to time in a mental institution. According to the American Psychiatric Association, persons found not guilty by reason of insanity are likely to spend the same amount of time or more in a psychiatric institution as they would have in prison if found guilty of the crime. However, mentally ill people are often found guilty and sent to prison because treatments are offered within prison walls. Are the treatments equal? How are people found to be mentally ill treated in the United States?

✔ ?

Unit 9 133

Have students read the Society's Treatment of the Mentally Ill section according to the option that you chose.

When most of the students are finished, continue with the entire class. Let's see how well you understood what you read.

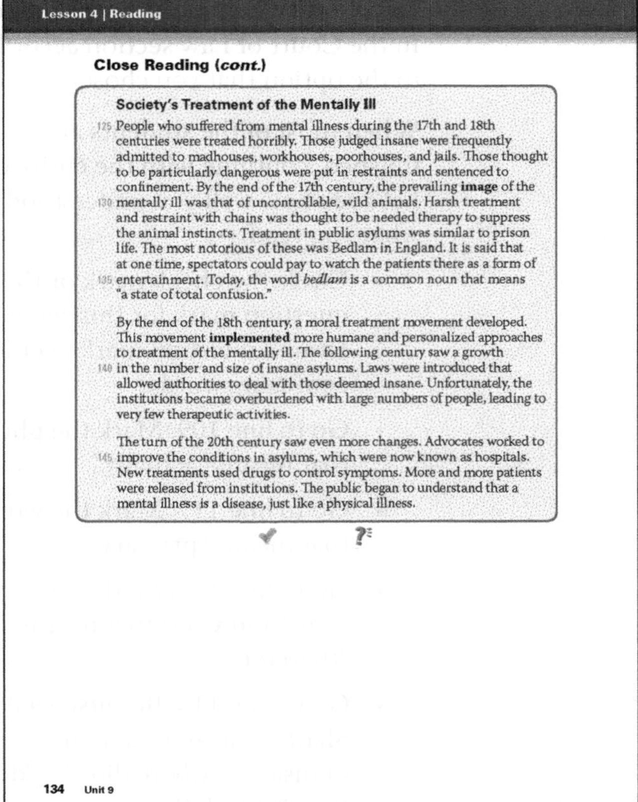

Lesson 4 | Reading

Close Reading (*cont.*)

Society's Treatment of the Mentally Ill

People who suffered from mental illness during the 17th and 18th centuries were treated horribly. Those judged insane were frequently admitted to madhouses, workhouses, poorhouses, and jails. Those thought to be particularly dangerous were put in restraints and sentenced to confinement. By the end of the 17th century, the prevailing **image** of the mentally ill was that of uncontrollable, wild animals. Harsh treatment and restraint with chains was thought to be needed therapy to suppress the animal instincts. Treatment in public asylums was similar to prison life. The most notorious of these was Bedlam in England. It is said that at one time, spectators could pay to watch the patients there as a form of entertainment. Today, the word *bedlam* is a common noun that means "a state of total confusion."

By the end of the 18th century, a moral treatment movement developed. This movement **implemented** more humane and personalized approaches to treatment of the mentally ill. The following century saw a growth in the number and size of insane asylums. Laws were introduced that allowed authorities to deal with those deemed insane. Unfortunately, the institutions became overburdened with large numbers of people, leading to very few therapeutic activities.

The turn of the 20th century saw even more changes. Advocates worked to improve the conditions in asylums, which were now known as hospitals. New treatments used drugs to control symptoms. More and more patients were released from institutions. The public began to understand that a mental illness is a disease, just like a physical illness.

134 Unit 9

- Circle the check mark or the question mark for this section. Draw a question mark over any confusing words.
- Go to line 126. Mark the word that means "thought to be." (judged)
- Go to lines 130 and 131. Mark what was used to control the mentally ill. (harsh treatments; restraint with chains)
- Go to line 131. Mark the word that means "put an end to something by force." (suppress)
- In the same sentence, mark the word that means "natural responses." (instincts)
- Go to line 132. Mark the word that means "hospitals for people with mental illness." (asylums)
- On the next line, mark the word that means "famous" but has a negative connotation meaning "wicked and well known." (notorious)
- Go to lines 132–135. Use context to mark the origin of the common noun *bedlam*. (public asylum, Bedlam in England, people who pay to watch the ill)
- Go to line 138. Mark the word that indicates the new treatment would be compassionate. (humane)
- Go to line 143. Mark the synonym of *beneficial*. (therapeutic)
- In the last paragraph, mark what was used to control symptoms and continues to be used today. (drugs)
- Mark the wording used by the author to connect physical illness and mental illness. (mental illness is a disease, just like a physical illness)
- How does the section Society's Treatment of the Mentally Ill contribute to the whole text? Write your answer below the section. (It explains the history of treatment of mentally ill patients and convicts.)

Have students read the Remaining Questions section according to the option that you chose.

When most of the students are finished, continue with the entire class. Let's see how well you understood what you read.

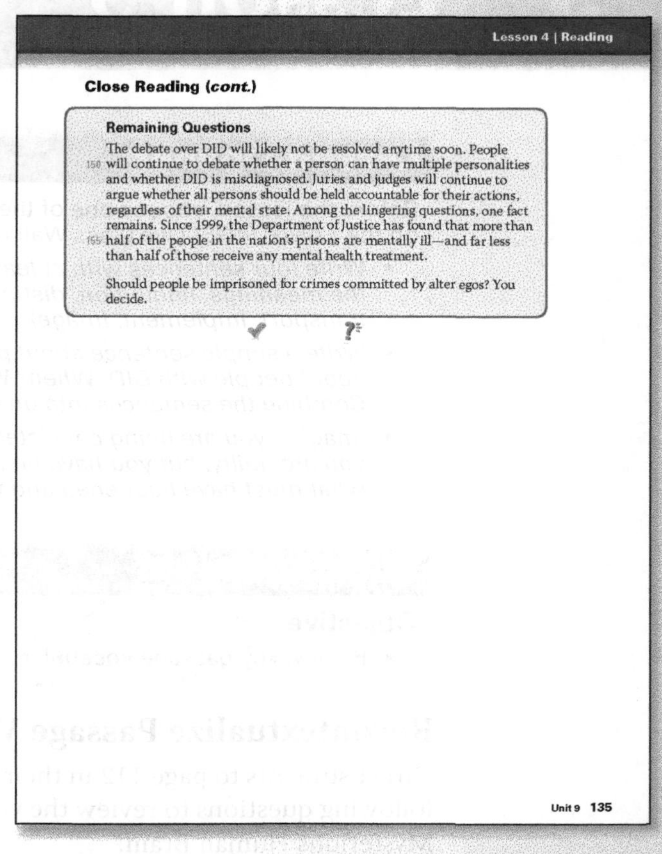
Lesson 4 | Reading

Close Reading (*cont.*)

Remaining Questions

The debate over DID will likely not be resolved anytime soon. People will continue to debate whether a person can have multiple personalities and whether DID is misdiagnosed. Juries and judges will continue to argue whether all persons should be held accountable for their actions, regardless of their mental state. Among the lingering questions, one fact remains. Since 1999, the Department of Justice has found that more than half of the people in the nation's prisons are mentally ill—and far less than half of those receive any mental health treatment.

Should people be imprisoned for crimes committed by alter egos? You decide.

✔ ?

Unit 9 135

- Circle the check mark or the question mark for this section. Draw a question mark over any confusing words.
- Go to line 149. Mark the synonym of *argument*. (debate)
- Go to line 151. Mark the word that means "identified wrongly." (misdiagnosed) Mark the prefix that means "wrong." (mis-)
- Go to line 153. Mark the synonym of *enduring*. (lingering)
- In the same paragraph, mark the problem in today's treatment of the mentally ill. (more than half of the people in the nation's prisons are mentally ill—and far less than half of those receive any mental health treatment)
- Mark the imperative statement that is giving you, the reader, a command. (You decide.)
- How does the section Remaining Questions contribute to the whole text? Write your answer below the section. (It poses questions for the reader to think about regarding DID and crimes committed by sufferers of the disease.)

Have partners compare text markings and correct any errors.

Unit 9

Lesson 5

Lesson Opener

Before the lesson, choose one of the following activities to write on the board or post on the *LANGUAGE! Live* Class Wall online.

- *Write four sentences with at least two vocabulary words in each. Show you know the meanings. (inhibition, distinct, controversial, prone, media, standard, previously, transport, implement, image)*
- *Write a simple sentence about people with DID. Then, answer the following questions about people with DID. When? Where? How? Which one? What kind? How many? Combine the sentences into one Masterpiece Sentence.*
- *Imagine you are being convicted of a crime, and there is video evidence proving that you are guilty, but you have no memory of the crime. Write five sentences to explain what must have happened and why you can't be held accountable for the crime.*

Vocabulary

Objective

- Review key passage vocabulary.

Recontextualize Passage Vocabulary

Direct students to page 112 in their Student Books. Use the following questions to review the vocabulary words in "The Mysterious Human Brain."

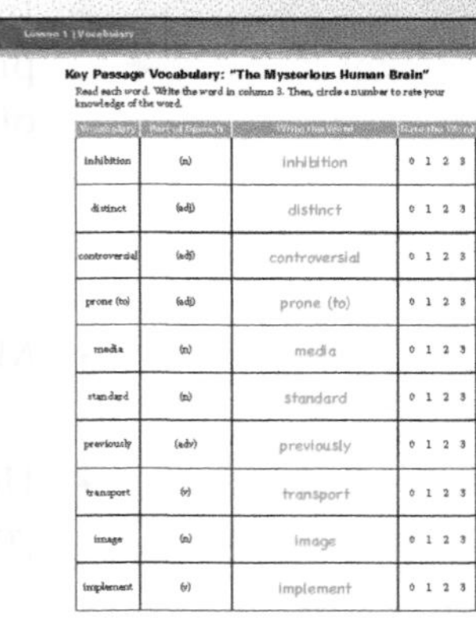
Lesson 1 | Vocabulary

Key Passage Vocabulary: "The Mysterious Human Brain"

Read each word. Write the word in column 3. Then, circle a number to rate your knowledge of the word.

Vocabulary	Part of Speech	Write the Word	Rate the Word
inhibition	(n)	inhibition	0 1 2 3
distinct	(adj)	distinct	0 1 2 3
controversial	(adj)	controversial	0 1 2 3
prone (to)	(adj)	prone (to)	0 1 2 3
media	(n)	media	0 1 2 3
standard	(n)	standard	0 1 2 3
previously	(adv)	previously	0 1 2 3
transport	(v)	transport	0 1 2 3
image	(n)	image	0 1 2 3
implement	(v)	implement	0 1 2 3

112 Unit 9

- The Milky Way looks like a faint smear of white in the night sky because the stars that make it up are too far away to see separately. Are the stars that make up the Milky Way *distinct*? (no) Above all the voices in the choir, one voice rises clear, sharp, and high. Is the voice *distinct*? (yes) From a distance, I can't tell if you are laughing or crying. Up close, what does the expression on your face become? (distinct)
- It's spring again, and every time you step outdoors, you sneeze. Are you *prone* to allergies? (yes) You have a superhuman resistance to tickling. It rarely makes you laugh. Are you *prone* to laughing when tickled? (no) Gloomy weather tends to put you in a gloomy mood. What are you during gloomy weather? (prone to being in a gloomy mood)
- You and a friend are swimming at a neighborhood pool. He keeps doing daredevil, show-off jumps from the diving board. Does he have swimming *inhibitions*? (no) You've been asked to sing the national anthem at the next basketball game because you have a lovely voice, but the idea paralyzes you. Do you have an *inhibition*? (yes) There are assigned seats on the bus for the field trip. You're sitting next to a kid you hardly know, and you feel awkward. If you want to start a conversation, what will you have to overcome? (my inhibitions)

- There's a plan to fill the entire school courtyard with gravel. The administration says it will cut down on watering expenses, but students are upset because it will make the courtyard hot and uncomfortable. Is the gravel plan *controversial*? (yes) Another plan proposes that the courtyard be "carpeted" with a soft green turf. Everyone likes this plan. Is it *controversial*? (no) Half your town wants to raise taxes to create bike lanes and jogging paths, but the other half does not. What would you call the tax increase? (controversial)
- You've read all about karate but have yet to start practicing it. Have you *implemented* what you learned? (no) Part of your plan to stay organized is to write your assignments on a calendar. You've recorded your assignments all week long. Are you *implementing* your plan? (yes) Next year, flip-flops will not be allowed in school. For the first week, teachers will be at the doors checking shoes. What will the teachers be doing? (implementing the new rule)
- When you were very small, you lived in a different home. Now, you can hardly remember what it was like. Do you have a clear *image* of the place? (no) It's a hot summer day, and you've been supervising day-camp kids on the playground all morning. You are dreaming of a cold glass of lemonade. Do you have a clear *image* of the lemonade? (yes) When you feel down, you close your eyes and think of your favorite place in the world. Do this now. **Pause.** What do you have in your mind? (an image of the place)
- You have heard good things about a new TV show and are looking forward to watching it. Have you seen it *previously*? (no) Your friend offers you her yogurt, but it's a flavor you tried before and didn't like. Did you try it *previously*? (yes) You had a goldfish when you were little, but now you want a lizard. When did you have a goldfish? (previously)
- The librarian asks you to load some dictionaries on a cart and move them to a closet down the hall. Is he asking you to *transport* the books? (yes) After you move the books, the librarian asks you to water the plants on the ledge by the window. Is he asking you to *transport* the plants? (no) Your cousin got a job driving a cart that carries people from gate to gate at the airport. What does the cart do? (It transports passengers.)
- You write all of your private thoughts in a diary that you keep under your mattress. Are your private thoughts in the *media*? (no) You return a wallet containing $500 to its owner. The story travels fast and is soon on local TV and radio and also in the newspapers. Is the story being covered by the *media*? (yes) Someday, you would like to work as a TV reporter. You hope to have a career in what? (Possible responses: the media; the medium of TV)
- One of your friends is always perfectly dressed. You measure everyone else's outfits—including your own—against what this friend is wearing. Does the friend set a fashion *standard* for you? (yes) To enter the art contest, your painting must be no larger than 12 inches by 12 inches, and it must be painted with oils on canvas. Your painting is 14 by 14 and is painted with watercolors on fabric. Does it meet the contest *standards*? (no) As captain of the team, you are expected to be a role model for young players. You are expected to set what for behavior? (the standard)

Writing

Objectives

- Use text to write coherent paragraphs in response to reading.
- Demonstrate understanding of the constructs of argumentation through writing.
- Write persuasive text.

Quick Write in Response to Reading

Direct students to page 136 in their Student Books. Read the prompt aloud. To complete this assignment, you will need to consider what you learned from the text regarding dissociative identity disorder. What information is contained within the text that could be used in the defense of someone suffering from DID and being accused of a crime? A good closing argument will need an introduction that grabs the attention of the reader and a powerful conclusion that calls for action.

Lesson 5 | Writing

Quick Write in Response to Reading Answers will vary.

Juries evaluate the evidence and decide who is guilty or innocent. Closing arguments of the lawyers are often the last thing a jury hears and, thus, have the power to convince the jury of a person's guilt or innocence.

Imagine you are the defense attorney for a person with DID who is on trial for attacking a complete stranger. Your client claims that an "alter" identity took charge because he or she felt threatened. Write a closing argument in defense of your client, explaining why he or she should not be punished for this crime.
Note: Lawyers use facts, reason, and **emotions** to convince the jury.

Imagine waking up and finding yourself covered with mud and blood. You are frightened and confused. You have no idea how you got that way. Your last memory is of walking home from the bus stop after work. This could actually happen to you if you suffer from dissociative identity disorder. Belinda knows this fear and confusion because she lives with this disorder. People who suffer from this disorder need treatment as opposed to punishment.

A history of child abuse explains Belinda's need to create Martha, a protective alter ego. Experts agree that child abuse creates mental as well as physical scars. Her irrational attack of a perfect stranger provides evidence of her mental scarring and her desperate need for help. Society is well served by an investment in therapy for Belinda as it will do more to prevent this incident from recurring than time in prison. Belinda already lives in a prison of her mind's own making. Please do not sentence her to a harsh and punitive environment that is sure to prompt Martha's reemergence.

136 Unit 9

Reading

Objectives

- Self-correct as comprehension of text deepens.
- Answer questions to demonstrate comprehension of text.
- Engage in class discussion.
- Identify the enduring understandings from a piece of text.

Revisit Passage Comprehension

Direct students back to pages 126–128 in their Student Books. Have students review their answers and make any necessary changes. Then, have partners share their answers and collaborate to perfect them.

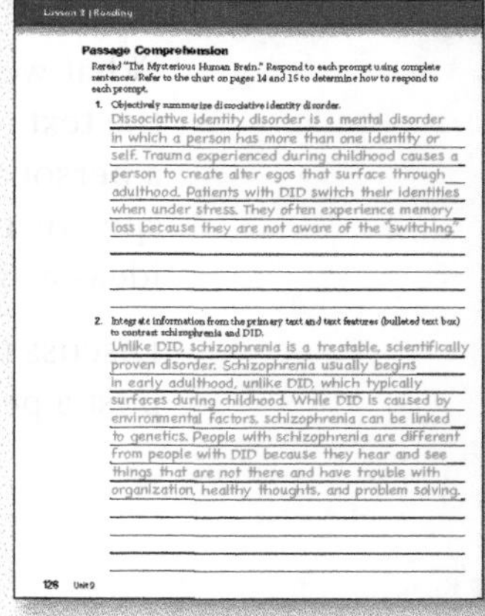

Author's Purpose

Direct students back to page 111 in their Student Books. We have finished studying a nonfiction selection about mental health. Before discussing our enduring understandings, let's talk about the author's purpose. Why did this author write the text? **Have students share ideas with a partner and then share in whole group. If necessary, elaborate or clarify their responses.** (The author's purpose is the reason that he or she wrote the text. Authors write for different purposes. They write to entertain, to persuade, or to inform or teach. Knowing an author's purpose can help a reader understand a text better. Most nonfiction text is written to inform. Since the author is not a character in the story, facts are presented in a more objective way without much emotion in a less casual tone. This informational text was written to teach about a controversial mental illness.) **Have students correct their answer on their page as necessary.**

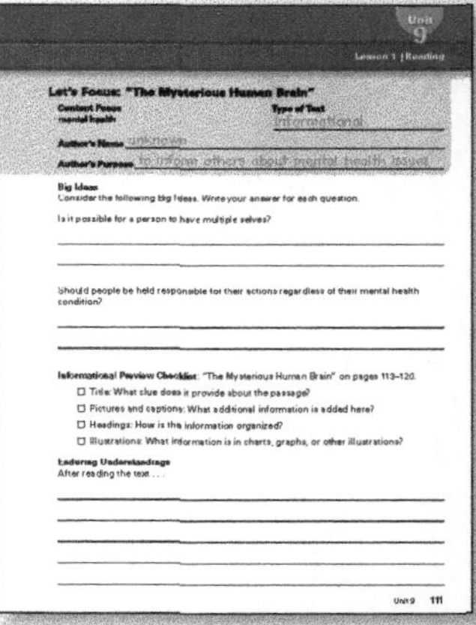

Enduring Understandings

Reread the Big Idea questions.

Is it possible for a person to have multiple selves?

Should people be held responsible for their actions regardless of their mental health condition?

Generate a class discussion about the questions and the answers students came up with in Lesson 1. Have them consider whether their answers have changed any after reading the text.

Use the following talking points to foster conversation. Then, have students write their enduring understandings from the unit.

- We learned that there is more than one type of multiple personality disorder. We also learned that DID is controversial. Where do you stand? Are you a believer or a doubter? Which side did you identify with most readily?
- We also read about two court cases. One person was found not guilty by reason of insanity, and one person was found guilty. What if you were the person who was hurt, or it was someone you loved? Would you want the person to go to prison?

What we read should make us think. Use our discussion and your thoughts about the text to determine what you will "walk away with." Has it made you think about a personal experience or someone you know? Has your perspective or opinion on a specific topic changed? Do you have any lingering thoughts or questions? Write these ideas as your enduring understandings. What will you take with you from this text?

Discuss the enduring understandings with the class. If time permits, have students post a personal response about their enduring understandings to the online class wall.

Unit 9

Lesson 6

Lesson Opener

Before the lesson, choose one of the following activities to write on the board or post on the *LANGUAGE! Live* Class Wall online.

- *Imagine someone you loved hurt you, but that person didn't realize it. What would you do?*
- *Describe a time when you became very angry and had a difficult time controlling your actions.*
- *Write three sentences about a person you trust using relative pronouns.*

Reading

Objectives

- Determine and discuss the topic of a text.
- Determine and discuss the author's purpose.
- Use text features to preview text.
- Analyze an artist's visual interpretation of text.

Passage Introduction

Direct students to page 137 in their Student Books. Discuss the content focus.

Content Focus

multiple personalities; good and evil

We are about to learn more about multiple personalities. However, this text was written before there was a name for such a thing. What do you think you will read about in this text? (Answers will vary.)

Type of Text

Text can be divided into two categories: informational and literary. **Discuss the differences.** What are the two categories of literature? (fiction and nonfiction) What does *nonfiction* mean? (not fiction, not fake, or real to life) What does *fiction* mean? (not true, made-up story) We are about to read a graphic novel with few words. The pictures will tell the majority of the story. Do you think that is fiction or nonfiction? (fiction) The story we're about to read was adapted from a gothic novel written more than 120 years ago. A gothic novel is a genre of fiction that includes mystery and supernatural horror. What is *supernatural*? (paranormal, eerie) Write the text type on the page.

Let's Focus: Graphic Novel of *The Strange Case of Dr. Jekyll and Mr. Hyde*

Content Focus
multiple personalities
good and evil

Type of Text Gothic fiction; graphic novel

Authors' Names Robert L. Stevenson; Carl Bowen

Authors' Purpose to entertain; to scare

Big Ideas
Consider the following Big Idea questions. Write your answer for each question.

Can people control their thoughts? Explain.

____

____

To what degree do our thoughts influence our actions? Explain.

____

____

Graphic Novel Preview Checklist: the graphic novel of *The Strange Case of Dr. Jekyll and Mr. Hyde* on pages 139–199.

- ☐ Title: What clue does it provide?
- ☐ Characters: What information is added here?
- ☐ Artwork: What do you notice at quick glance?
- ☐ Features: What other text features do you notice? Find the following:
  - Narrative Box: page 142
  - Dialogue Balloon: page 142
  - Sound Effect: page 158
  - Thought Balloon: page 190
  - Panel: page 142

Point of View
Chapters 1–4: Utterson Chapter 5: Jekyll

Enduring Understandings
After reading the text . . .

____

____

Author's Purpose

Have students glance at the text. Who are the authors of the text? (Robert L. Stevenson; Carl Bowen) Explain that the original story was written by Robert Louis Stevenson, but this retelling was written by Carl Bowen.

Prior to reading, make an educated guess as to what the author's purpose is for writing. After we finish, you will return to this section and revise your answer if necessary. Have students write the answer on the page.

> **Note:** Determine if students need Background Information pertaining to the internal struggle between good and evil. This can be found in the Teacher Resources online.

Big Ideas

Read the Big Idea questions aloud.

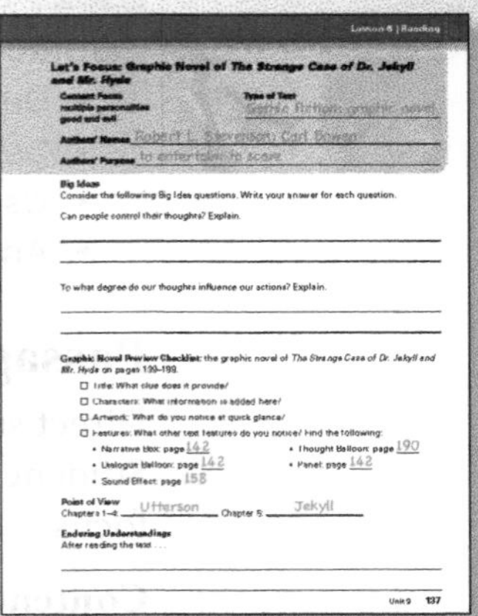

Lesson 6 | Reading

Let's Focus: Graphic Novel of *The Strange Case of Dr. Jekyll and Mr. Hyde*

Content Focus: multiple personalities; good and evil

Type of Text: graphic fiction; graphic novel

Authors' Names: Robert L. Stevenson; Carl Bowen

Authors' Purpose: to entertain; to scare

Big Ideas

Consider the following Big Idea questions. Write your answer for each question.

Can people control their thoughts? Explain.

To what degree do our thoughts influence our actions? Explain.

Graphic Novel Preview Checklist: the graphic novel of *The Strange Case of Dr. Jekyll and Mr. Hyde* on pages 130–199.

- ☐ Title: What clue does it provide?
- ☐ Characters: What information is added here?
- ☐ Artwork: What do you notice at quick glance?
- ☐ Features: What other text features do you notice? Find the following:
  - Narrative Box: page 142
  - Dialogue Balloon: page 142
  - Sound Effect: page 158
  - Thought Balloon: page 190
  - Panel: page 142

Point of View

Chapters 1–4: Utterson Chapter 5: Jekyll

Enduring Understandings

After reading the text . . .

Unit 9 137

> ### Big Ideas
>
> Can people control their thoughts? Explain.
>
> To what degree do our thoughts influence our actions? Explain.

As a class, consider the two Big Idea questions. After discussing each question, have students write an answer. We'll come back to these questions after we finish reading the text. You can add to your answers as you gain information and perspective.

Before we preview the text, I want you to close your eyes and listen to this description. This is from the original book, *The Strange Case of Dr. Jekyll and Mr. Hyde*. Try to picture Edward Hyde in your mind.

" . . . Edward Hyde was so much smaller, slighter, and younger than Henry Jekyll . . . evil was written broadly and plainly on the face . . . Evil . . . had left on that body an imprint of deformity and decay."

In your mind, what does Edward Hyde look like? Let's turn the page and see how the artist of the graphic novel interpreted the story. Have students discuss the discrepancies between their image and the artist's image.

Preview

Read the Preview Checklist on page 137. Follow the Preview Procedure outlined below.

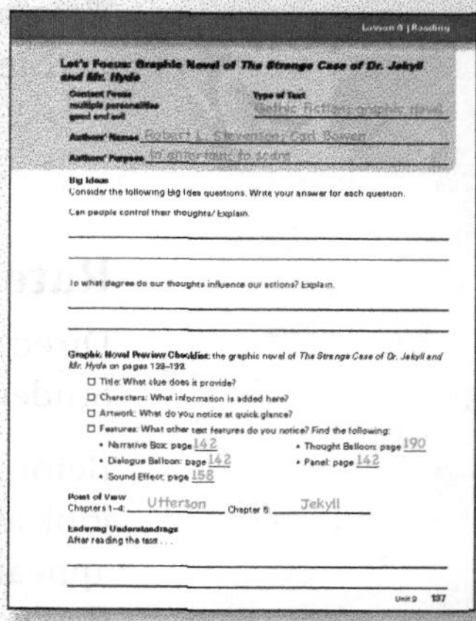

Lesson 6 | Reading

Let's Focus: Graphic Novel of *The Strange Case of Dr. Jekyll and Mr. Hyde*

Content Focus multiple personalities; good and evil

Type of Text Gothic fiction; graphic novel

Authors' Names Robert L. Stevenson; Carl Bowen

Authors' Purpose to entertain; to scare

Big Ideas
Consider the following Big Idea questions. Write your answer for each question.

Can people control their thoughts? Explain.

To what degree do our thoughts influence our actions? Explain.

Graphic Novel Preview Checklist: the graphic novel of *The Strange Case of Dr. Jekyll and Mr. Hyde* on pages 129–192.

- ☐ Title: What clue does it provide?
- ☐ Characters: What information is added here?
- ☐ Artwork: What do you notice at quick glance?
- ☐ Features: What other text features do you notice? Find the following:
  - Narrative Box: page 142
  - Thought Balloon: page 190
  - Dialogue Balloon: page 142
  - Panel: page 142
  - Sound Effect: page 158

Point of View
Chapters 1–4: Utterson Chapter 5: Jekyll

Ordering Understandings
After reading the text . . .

Unit 9 137

Preview Procedure

- Group students with partners or in triads.
- Have students count off as 1s or 2s. The 1s will become the student leaders. If working with triads, the third students become 3s.
- The student leaders will preview the text in addition to managing the checklist and pacing.
- The 2s and 3s will preview the text with 1s.
- Direct 1s to open their Student Books to page 137 and 2s and 3s to open their Student Books to page 139. This allows students to look at a few different pages at one time without turning back and forth.

Direct students to page 139. Have students preview the text.

If necessary, guide students in a short preview using the following talking points.

What is the title of the text? (*The Strange Case of Dr. Jekyll and Mr. Hyde*) Describe the graphic on the title page. (a male split into two people holding a green potion bottle) Turn to your partner and describe one side of the character on the title page. **Provide sharing time.** Switch roles. The listener should describe the other side of the character on the title page. **Provide sharing time. Go through the checklist and point out specific examples of each text feature (dialogue balloon, thought balloon, narrative box, panel). Note that there are several examples of each text feature. Students only have to find one of each. A few text features may require more explanation.** What is the difference between a dialogue balloon and a thought balloon? (One shares what the character says, and one shares what the character thinks.) Which text feature gives plot or background information? (narrative box) Which text feature is similar to a paragraph in a print story? (a panel) Understanding text features of graphic novels will help you comprehend this comic-style book.

Vocabulary

Objectives

- Evaluate word knowledge.
- Determine the meaning of key passage vocabulary.

Rate Vocabulary Knowledge

Direct students to page 138 in their Student Books.

Before we read the text, let's take a look at the vocabulary words that appear in this text. Remind students that as you read each word in the first column aloud, they will write the word in the third column and then rate their knowledge of it. Display the Vocabulary Rating Scale poster or write the information on the board. Review the meaning of each rating.

Lesson 6 | Vocabulary

Key Passage Vocabulary: Graphic Novel of *The Strange Case of Dr. Jekyll and Mr. Hyde*

Read each word. Write it in column 3. Then, circle a number to rate your knowledge of the word.

Vocabulary	Part of Speech	Write the Word	Rate the Word
attend	(v)	attend	0 1 2 3
involved	(adj)	involved	0 1 2 3
incident	(n)	incident	0 1 2 3
conflict	(n)	conflict	0 1 2 3
challenge	(n)	challenge	0 1 2 3
formula	(n)	formula	0 1 2 3
urge	(n)	urge	0 1 2 3
reaction	(n)	reaction	0 1 2 3
research	(n)	research	0 1 2 3
obtain	(v)	obtain	0 1 2 3

138 Unit 9

Vocabulary Rating Scale

0—I have never heard the word before.

1—I have heard the word, but I'm not sure how to use it.

2—I am familiar with the word, but I'm not sure if I know the correct meaning.

3—I know the meaning of the word and can use it correctly in a sentence.

The points are not a grade; they are just there to help you know which words you need to focus on. By the end of this unit, you should be able to change all your ratings to a 3. That's the goal.

Read each word aloud. Have students repeat it, write it, and rate it. Then, have volunteers who rated a word *2* or *3* use the word in an oral sentence.

Preteach Vocabulary

Let's take a closer look at the words. Follow the Preteach Procedure below.

Preteach Procedure

This activity is intended to take only a short amount of time, so make it an oral exercise.

- Introduce each word as indicated on the word card.
- Read the definition and example sentences.
- Ask questions to clarify and deepen understanding.
- If time permits, allow students to share.

* If your students would benefit from copying the definitions, please have them do so in the vocabulary log in the back of the Student Books using the margin definitions in the passage selections. This should be done outside of instruction time.

attend (v)

Let's read the first word together. *Attend.*

Definition: If you *attend* to someone or something, you take care of the person or thing. What means "to take care of someone or something"? (attend)

Example 1: When a child gets sick, a parent must stay home from work and *attend* to him or her.

Example 2: If your car won't start, you might *attend* to the problem by calling a mechanic.

Example 3: Hotel staff members should *attend* promptly to guests' needs.

Question 1: You cut your finger and immediately put a bandage on it. Have you *attended* to it? Yes or no? (yes)

Question 2: You really need to organize your binder for a binder check but keep putting it off. Have you *attended* to your binder? Yes or no? (no)

Pair Share: You are *attending* to supper because your mom is working late. Turn to your partner and act out what you are doing.

1

involved (adj)

Let's read the next word together. *Involved.*

Definition: If you are *involved* in something, you are connected with it or mixed up in it. What word means "connected with; mixed up with"? (involved)

Example 1: Being overly *involved* in a disagreement between friends can make the problem worse.

Example 2: People who are *involved* in politics often donate time and money to election campaigns.

Example 3: Doctors are trained not to get *involved* in their patients' personal lives.

Question 1: Your friend invites you to "invest" in his new laundry business by providing the washing machine. You say "No, thanks." Are you getting *involved*? Yes or no? (no)

Question 2: You hear a big crash in the classroom next door and go to investigate. Two hours later, you're still helping the teacher organize the supply shelves. Did you get *involved*? Yes or no? (yes)

Pair Share: Turn to your partner and tell each other what kind of career you would like to have. Then, tell your partner what sorts of groups or activities he or she could get *involved* with now to improve his or her chances at success later on.

2

incident (n)

Let's read the next word together. *Incident.*

Definition: An *incident* is an event or a happening that is noticed or creates a stir. What word means "an event or happening that is noticed or creates a stir"? (incident)

Example 1: A shift supervisor must report all unusual *incidents* to his or her manager.

Example 2: After several *incidents* of car theft in our neighborhood, we started a neighborhood watch program.

Example 3: In some schools, a single *incident* of cheating will get you suspended.

Question 1: You just ate a sandwich. Was this an *incident*? Yes or no? (no)

Question 2: Three times this week, someone has drawn emoticons on the front doors of the school with toothpaste. Would you call this a series of related *incidents*? Yes or no? (yes)

Pair Share: Turn to your partner and describe an amusing *incident* that happened recently.

3

conflict (n)

Let's read the next word together. *Conflict.*

Definition: A *conflict* is a clash or struggle between two sides or forces. What word means "a clash or struggle between two sides or forces"? (conflict)

Example 1: Inner *conflict* happens when one part of us wants something and the other part knows we shouldn't have it.

Example 2: Many of the greatest stories and movies deal with the *conflict* between good and evil.

Example 3: The best way to solve a *conflict* with a friend is to sit down and listen to him or her with an open heart and mind.

Question 1: You and your cousin decide to plant a vegetable garden in the empty lot down the street. Is this a *conflict*? Yes or no? (no)

Question 2: The person who owns the lot comes along and accuses you of trespassing. You ask why you can't use the property for your garden as long as it isn't being used for anything else. The owner threatens to take you to court. Is this a *conflict*? Yes or no? (yes)

Pair Share: Turn to your partner and describe a *conflict* you recently saw on TV or read about in a book.

4

challenge (n)

Let's read the next word together. *Challenge.*

Definition: A *challenge* is a problem or question that takes effort to solve. What word means "a problem or question that takes effort to solve"? (challenge)

Example 1: It can be a *challenge* to eat a healthy meal in a fast-food restaurant.

Example 2: When four people share one bathroom, getting ready in the morning is a *challenge.*

Example 3: People who love mathematical *challenges* often become engineers.

Question 1: You run five miles every weekend to stay fit. To get an A in PE, you must be able to run one mile. Is it a *challenge* for you to get an A? Yes or no? (no)

Question 2: You are on a cooking show. You must make a tasty meal with these ingredients: snails, gummy bears, and ketchup. Will it be a *challenge* to make a tasty meal? Yes or no? (yes)

Pair Share: Turn to your partner and tell about a *challenge* you successfully faced as a younger kid.

5

formula (n)

Let's read the next word together. *Formula.*

Definition: A *formula* is a mixture or a recipe for a mixture. What means "a mixture; a recipe"? (formula)

Example 1: Hot tea, milk, and honey is a good *formula* for soothing a sore throat.

Example 2: Hard work plus a willingness to take risks is one *formula* for success.

Example 3: My uncle Leonard made the best lemonade I've ever tasted, but he never would reveal his secret *formula.*

Question 1: You ask your aunt how to get a spaghetti stain out of your shirt and she says "lemon juice." Is this a *formula*? Yes or no? (no)

Question 2: To clean jewelry, you can mix a teaspoon of baking soda with three drops of water. Is this a *formula*? Yes or no? (yes)

Pair Share: Turn to your partner and tell your *formula* for happiness. Include at least three ingredients.

6

urge (n)

Let's read the next word together. *Urge.*

Definition: An *urge* is a strong need or drive to do something. What means "a strong need or drive to do something"? (urge)

Example 1: If you have an itch, you probably have an *urge* to scratch it.

Example 2: After a couple of hours in a car, I feel an *urge* to get out and stretch my legs.

Example 3: People who are addicted to their phones feel a constant *urge* to check for messages.

Question 1: You see a pizza commercial and then feel as if you must have pizza. Has the commercial created an *urge*? Yes or no? (yes)

Question 2: You can't stand it when the whiteboard is not erased thoroughly. The teacher erases it in a hurry, and you can still see marks. Do you have an *urge* to get up and erase the board? Yes or no? (yes)

Pair Share: You know you shouldn't text someone, but you are about to do it anyway. Tell your partner two strategies for dealing with this *urge*.

7

reaction (n)

Let's read the next word together. *Reaction.*

Definition: A *reaction* is what someone feels, says, or does in response to something else. What word means "what someone feels, says, or does in response to something else"? (reaction)

Example 1: If you say "Boo!" to someone, his or her *reaction* will probably be to flinch.

Example 2: When someone sneezes, your first *reaction* might be to say "Bless you."

Example 3: When the alarm goes off, my *reaction* is to hit the snooze button.

Question 1: You hear really good news and smile. Is your smile a *reaction*? Yes or no? (yes)

Question 2: It starts raining. Next, your phone rings. Does the phone ring in *reaction* to the rain? Yes or no? (no)

Pair Share: You just won a million dollars. Show or tell your partner your *reaction*.

research (n)

Let's read the next word together. *Research.*

Definition: *Research* is the act of studying something or gathering information about it. What means "the act of studying something or gathering information about it"? (research)

Example 1: When I want to make fun weekend plans, I go online to do *research* on various possibilities.

Example 2: Scientists are doing *research* to discover the causes of climate change.

Example 3: A *research* paper would require you to find information about a topic in several different sources.

Question 1: You want to buy a particular pair of sunglasses. You Google local stores that sell them. Are you doing *research*? Yes or no? (yes)

Question 2: You want to take drum lessons. You borrow your cousin's drum set. Have you done *research*? Yes or no? (no)

Pair Share: Tell your partner about something you have recently done *research* on and what you learned in the process.

9

obtain (v)

Let's read the last word together. *Obtain.*

Definition: If you *obtain* something, you get it or gain it. What word means "to get; to gain"? (obtain)

Example 1: Before you have a garage sale, you must *obtain* a permit from the city.

Example 2: At my favorite coffee shop, they stamp a card every time I buy a cup of coffee. When I *obtain* 10 stamps, I get a free cup.

Example 3: To *obtain* a friend's forgiveness, ask for it.

Question 1: You need 20 extra-credit points to get a B. You have 18. Have you *obtained* a B? Yes or no? (no)

Question 2: You need a passport to travel to another country. Your passport came in the mail today. Have you *obtained* it? Yes or no? (yes)

Pair Share: Turn to your partner and name a project that needs doing around your home. Then, tell what supplies need to be *obtained* before the project can be undertaken.

10

Reading

Objectives

- Read a graphic novel.
- Monitor comprehension during text reading.

Graphic Novel of *The Strange Case of Dr. Jekyll and Mr. Hyde*

Direct students to page 139 in their Student Books.

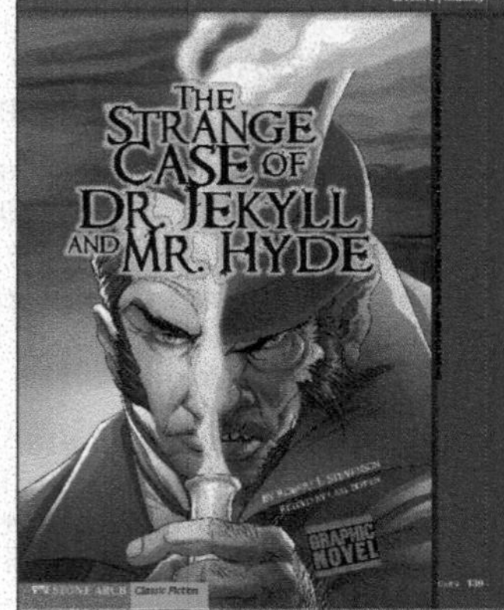

Now that we have previewed vocabulary, it's time to read.

Guiding Students Toward Independent Reading

It is important that your students read as much and as often as they can. Assign readings that meet the needs of your students, based on your observations and data. This is a good opportunity to stretch your students. If students become frustrated, scaffold the reading with paired reading, choral reading, or a read-aloud.

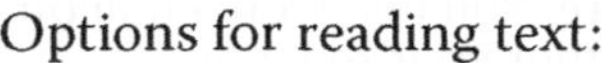

Options for reading text:

- Teacher read-aloud
- Teacher-led or student-led choral read
- Paired read or independent read

Choose an option for reading text. Students read according to the option that you chose.

Review the purpose of the numbered squares in the text and prompt students to stop periodically and check comprehension.

Point out the difference between the text in the yellow narrative boxes (part of the story, but not being said by someone on the page) and the white speech balloons (thoughts and dialogue of the characters on the page).

Because of the nature of this text, if you choose to read the text aloud or chorally, you will need to use a Student Edition in order to be able to see the graphics as well as the text. When students have finished reading, confirm engagement by having students share the difference between Dr. Jekyll and Mr. Hyde.

Unit 9

Lesson 7

Lesson Opener

Before the lesson, choose one of the following activities to write on the board or post on the *LANGUAGE! Live* Class Wall online.

- *Write a summary of* The Strange Case of Dr. Jekyll and Mr. Hyde.
- *Make a list of adjectives describing Henry Jekyll. Make a list of adjectives describing Edward Hyde. Write three compound sentences comparing the men.*
- *Imagine that by drinking a potion, you could become a different person, then return to your usual self. Write five sentences describing the person you would become.*

Vocabulary

Objective

- Review key passage vocabulary.

Review Passage Vocabulary

Direct students to page 138 in their Student Books. Use the following questions to review the vocabulary words from the graphic novel of *The Strange Case of Dr. Jekyll and Mr. Hyde.* Have students answer each question using the vocabulary word or indicating its meaning in a complete sentence.

- In the first scene of the story, why does a doctor need to *attend* to a young girl? (A doctor must attend to the young girl because she has been struck down by a stranger who then fled the scene. The girl is probably hurt.) What might *attending* to the girl involve? (Attending to her would probably involve checking for injuries, treating them, giving the girl medicine if needed, and trying to make her comfortable.)
- When Mr. Utterson meets Mr. Hyde, he wonders why Dr. Jekyll ever got *involved* with such an unpleasant person. What is he wondering? Put it in your own words. (He is wondering how Dr. Jekyll got connected with such a person or tangled up with him.) Would you say Mr. Utterson himself is getting *involved* with Mr. Hyde? Why or why not? (Yes, he is getting involved with Mr. Hyde. His curiosity is leading him to try to discover Hyde's connection with Dr. Jekyll.)
- After being reassured by Dr. Jekyll, Mr. Utterson hears nothing from either Hyde or Jekyll for several months. What *incident* in Soho brings Jekyll back to mind? (A man named Hastie Lanyon is murdered. A young lady sees the entire incident.) How does Dr. Jekyll respond when Utterson tells him about the *incident*? (When he learns about the incident, he is upset. He states that he is through with Hyde, and then admits he had been foolish to think he could control him.) What later *incident* proves that Jekyll and Hyde are still connected? (Hyde is found dead in Jekyll's laboratory, and Jekyll has disappeared.)

- In his confession, what *conflict* does Jekyll say he discovered within the mind of every person? (He discovers the conflict between the "high mind," which seeks goodness, and the "low mind," which seeks only what it wants.) What plan does Jekyll come up with to resolve the *conflict*? (To resolve the conflict, he plans to separate the two minds from each other.)
- Jekyll admits the plan was a *challenge*. What does he mean by this? (He means it was very difficult.) What ingredient was a *challenge* to get, and why? (A certain rare salt was a challenge to get because it was only available halfway around the world.)
- The salt went into a special *formula*. Was it the only thing in the formula? How do you know? (The salt was not the only thing in the formula because a formula is a mixture of different ingredients.) Once Jekyll had perfected the *formula*, what did he do with it? (Once he had perfected the formula, he tested it by drinking it.) Did the *formula* work as expected? Why or why not? (No, the formula didn't work as expected. Instead, it created a body for his "low mind" only.)
- Once it had its own body, Jekyll's "low mind" had evil *urges*. What does this mean? (It means it felt driven to do evil, wicked, violent things.) When he drank the formula again, did it create a body with only good *urges*? (No; it returned him to his former self.) If the formula *had* produced a body that had only good *urges*, what might some of these *urges* be? (Good urges might include acts of kindness and generosity.)
- When Dr. Jekyll shared his "accomplishment" with his friend Lanyon, what was Lanyon's *reaction*? (Lanyon's reaction was one of horror. He grew upset and made Jekyll leave.) Jekyll vowed not to take the formula again. But what was the *reaction* of his "low mind" to this decision? (The reaction of the low mind was to turn into Mr. Hyde without the formula.) What was Jekyll's *reaction* to this unexpected event? (His reaction was to dash to the laboratory, mix some formula, drink it, and hope it worked.)
- Why did Jekyll begin to conduct new *research*? (He conducted new research because he wanted to find a way to keep Hyde from returning.) Why did Hyde destroy the *research*? (He destroyed the research because he did not want Jekyll to succeed in learning how to get rid of him.)
- After he lost his research, Jekyll came up with a new plan. First, he tossed out the rare salt. Did he plan to *obtain* more? (No, he did not want to obtain, or get, any more.) He also changed his will in order to keep Hyde from *obtaining* what? (He changed his will to keep Hyde from obtaining Jekyll's money and property.) Finally, Hyde killed himself—and Jekyll too. Learning this, what does Utterson decide no one else should ever *obtain*? (He decides no one should ever obtain information about the strange case of Dr. Jekyll and Mr. Hyde.)

Assign online practice from the Text Training link on the left menu of your teacher dashboard.

Writing

Objective

- Use correct punctuation when writing dialogue.

Dialogue

An upcoming writing assignment will ask you to write some of the dialogue from *The Strange Case of Dr. Jekyll and Mr. Hyde.* In order to complete the task, you will need to know what punctuation marks are required. In addition to punctuation, you need to give some thought to how you identify the speakers.

Direct students to page 201 in their Student Books.

Lesson 7 | Writing

Dialogue

To rewrite dialogue, identify the speaker and include correct punctuation.

Example:

"Say, Utterson," asked Richard Enfield, "you see this property here?"

"Yes," responded Utterson, "we walk past it once a week, cousin."

Enfield continued, "Not long ago, a most remarkable event led me here. I'm surprised I've never told you."

"Then tell me now," implored Utterson.

Rewrite the following dialogue. Remember to identify the speaker, vary the verb, and include proper punctuation.

Answers will vary.

"Horrible!" exclaimed Utterson. "You didn't let him get away with it?" "Indeed not," insisted Enfield, "while a doctor attended the girl, I chased the villain down!"

Unit 9 201

Look at the dialogue balloons in these two panels from the text. A narrative box identifies the two men who are walking down the street. Stems from the balloons are used in the graphic novel to show who is talking. When we write dialogue in narrative text, we typically identify the speaker by name. When writers choose not to include the names, the reader has to work doubly hard to track the dialogue.

Listen as I read the first dialogue balloon: *Say, Utterson, you see this property here?* Who is speaking? (Richard Enfield) Look at the rewritten dialogue. He is asking Utterson a question, so the dialogue identifies the speaker along with the verb *asked*. What words have been placed inside the first set of quotation marks? (Say, Utterson) What words have been placed inside the second set of quotation marks? (you see this property here?) Are the words *asked Richard Enfield* placed inside quotation marks? (no) So, the quotation marks are only placed around the actual words that were spoken. How does Utterson respond? (Yes, we walk past it once a week, cousin.) Where have the quotation marks been placed in the narrative version? (around *Yes* and around *we walk past it once a week, cousin*) Do the quotation marks include *responded Utterson*? (no) What punctuation mark is used to separate the speaker's identity from the words that were spoken? (commas) Notice that the commas have been placed within the quotation marks before the verb and then again after the speaker's name.

One of the challenges of writing effective dialogue is to vary the words you use for *said* and *asked*. Richard *asked* and Utterson *responded*. Notice the verb choices for the next panel. Because the conversation is ongoing, Enfield *continued*. He has gotten Utterson's attention, so Utterson *implored,* which means he strongly urged his cousin to tell the story. In this frame, the speaker is identified at the beginning and at the end of the dialogue, and a comma is used again to separate the verb from the spoken words. It is inside the quotation marks if the spoken words come first.

Direct students' attention to the activity and read the instructions aloud. Have students work with their partners to brainstorm verbs to use instead of *said*. After providing time to rewrite the dialogue, have volunteers share their responses. Check to make sure the dialogue is punctuated correctly.

Reading

Objectives

- Determine how to respond to prompts.
- Use critical thinking skills to write responses to prompts about text.
- Support written answers with evidence from text.
- Determine the purpose of a literary flashback.
- Make connections between characters from multiple texts.
- Determine variations in meaning of the same words and phrases.
- Analyze how differing text structures contribute to meaning and style.

Critical Understandings: Direction Words *analyze, assess, differentiate, relate*

Let's review some prompts.

Write the words *analyze, assess, differentiate,* and *relate* on the board. Have students read the words aloud with you.

Direct students to pages 14 and 15 in their Student Books.

Have students read about the four direction words in the chart with their partner.

Lesson 3 | Reading

Critical Understandings: Direction Words

Prompt	How to Respond	Model
If the prompt asks you to . . .	The response requires you to . . .	For example . . .
Analyze	break down and evaluate or draw conclusions about the information	**Analyze** the development of the text's central idea.
Assess	decide on the value, impact, or accuracy	**Assess** how the author's point of view affects the story.
Cite Evidence	support your answer by paraphrasing or using a direct quote	**Cite evidence** that supports your argument.
Clarify	make a statement or situation less confusing	**Clarify** the events leading up to the marriage.
Compare	state the similarities between two or more things	**Compare** Indian and Chinese marriage arrangements.
Connect	tie ideas together, relate	**Connect** each storm with its safety plan.
Contrast	state the differences between two or more things	**Contrast** Indian and Chinese marriage arrangements.
Demonstrate	show how to do it	**Demonstrate** your knowledge of wolves through poetry.
Develop an Argument	work on a case over a period of time, during which it grows or changes	Use evidence from both stories to **develop an argument** against arranged marriages.
Differentiate	tell apart or tell the difference between	**Differentiate** between the protagonist and the antagonist.
Distinguish	recognize something for a specific reason	**Distinguish** your claim from the opposing view by telling how it is different.

14 Unit 7

Chart Reading Procedure

- Group students with partners or in triads.
- Have students count off as 1s or 2s. The 1s will become the student leaders. If working with triads, the third students become 3s.
- The student leaders will read the left column (Prompt) in addition to managing the time and turn-taking if working with a triad.
- The 2s will explain the middle column of the chart (How to Respond). If working in triads, 3s take turns explaining the middle column.
- The 1s read the model in the right column (Model), and 2s and 3s restate the model as a question.
- All students should follow along with their pencil eraser while others are explaining the chart.
- Students must work from left to right, top to bottom in order to benefit from this activity.

Check for understanding by requesting an oral response to the following questions.

- If the prompt asks you to *analyze*, the response requires you to . . . (break down and evaluate or draw conclusions about the information).
- If the prompt asks you to *assess*, the response requires you to . . . (decide on the value, impact, or accuracy).
- If the prompt asks you to *differentiate*, the response requires you to . . . (tell apart or tell the difference between).
- If the prompt asks you to *relate*, the response requires you to . . . (explain the connection between ideas or concepts).

Direct students to pages 202 and 203 in their Student Books and read aloud the instructions. Let's read some prompts about the first three chapters of the graphic novel.

1. Analyze the graphic treatment of the flashback on page 143.
2. Relate the role Hastie Lanyon plays in the life of Edward Hyde to the role Judge Scott plays in the life of Jim Hall.
3. Differentiate between Hyde's use of "I must have you for dinner some night" and Jekyll's use of the same statement.
4. Assess the content in Dr. Jekyll's will.

We will focus on Chapters 1–3 as we practice answering prompts with these direction words.

Lesson 7 | Reading

Critical Understandings

Refer to Chapters 1–3 of the graphic novel of *The Strange Case of Dr. Jekyll and Mr. Hyde.* Respond to each prompt using complete sentences. Refer to the chart on pages 14 and 15 to determine how to respond to each prompt.

1. Analyze the graphic treatment of the flashback on page 143.

   Panels 1 and 2 on page 143 are slightly more golden in color, which illustrates an event from the past. The narrative boxes tell the story that happened in the past. The slight variation in color does not make it clear that the event happened in the past. However, the text in the narrative boxes does.

2. Relate the role Hastie Lanyon plays in the life of Edward Hyde to the role Judge Scott plays in the life of Jim Hall.

   Hastie Lanyon and Judge Scott played similar roles by engaging in behavior that led to the creation of a beastly man with little regard for human life and no inhibitions. Judge Scott faultily sent Jim Hall to prison, which turned him into the beast that he became, seeking vengeance upon the judge. Hastie Lanyon angered Dr. Jekyll by laughing at his theory, which made the doctor more committed to proving the theory. Lanyon then expressed horror when the theory was proven. This mockery and disapproval of a friend led to Hyde becoming a more permanent fixture who sought vengeance on the doubting friend.

202 Unit 9

Guided Practice

Now, let's practice answering questions that are written as prompts. Remember to use the chart as reference.

1. Analyze the graphic treatment of the flashback on page 143.

How do we respond according to the chart? (If the prompt asks you to *analyze*, the response requires you to break down and evaluate or draw conclusions about the information.) Turn the prompt into a question to confirm understanding. (How is a flashback represented graphically, and what do you think about the graphic treatment of the flashback?)

We cannot start writing our answer until we study the illustrations on pages 142 and 143. We also have to remember that a flashback is a literary device that interjects a scene that takes the story back in time from the current point. **Have students discuss the differences they see in the graphic treatments.**

Now we are ready to start our answer.

Write the following sentence frames on the board.

Panels ___________ on page 143 are ________________, which illustrate an event from the past. The narrative boxes ____________________ ___________. The ______________ does/doesn't make it clear that ________________________.

Generate a class discussion about the variances in the graphics and whether students think the flashback is evident. Then, answer the question as a class based on the discussion.

Let's move on to the next prompt.

2. Relate the role Hastie Lanyon plays in the life of Edward Hyde to the role Judge Scott plays in the life of Jim Hall.

How do we respond according to the chart? (If the prompt asks you to *relate*, the response requires you to explain the connection between ideas or concepts.) Turn the prompt into a question to confirm understanding. (How is the role of Hastie Lanyon connected to the role of Judge Scott?)

We need to think back to the excerpt from *White Fang*. What role did Judge Scott play in the life of Jim Hall? **Generate a class discussion about Judge Scott wrongly sending Jim Hall to prison, which turned him into the beast that he became, seeking vengeance upon the judge.** Next, we need to think about the role that Hastie Lanyon played in Edward Hyde's life. **Generate a class discussion about Hastie Lanyon angering Dr. Jekyll by laughing at his theory, then expressing horror when his theory was proven. This mockery and disapproval of a friend led to Hyde becoming a more permanent fixture and seeking vengeance on the doubting friend.**

Have partners discuss the connection and search the texts for the answer. While providing partner time, write the following sentence starters on the board.

Hastie Lanyon and Judge Scott played similar roles by ________________.

Judge Scott ____.

Hastie Lanyon ____.

Have partners answer the question. Discuss possible answers.

3. Differentiate between Hyde's use of "I must have you for dinner some night" and Jekyll's use of the same statement.

Lesson 7 | Reading

Critical Understandings (*cont.*)

3. Differentiate between Hyde's use of "I must have you for dinner some night" and Jekyll's use of the same statement.

When Mr. Hyde said "I must have you for dinner some night," he was threatening Utterson's life. When Dr. Jekyll said the same thing, he was legitimately inviting Utterson to dinner in a friendly manner.

4. Assess the content in Dr. Jekyll's will.

Dr. Jekyll's will says "In the event of my death or disappearance, I, Dr. Henry Jekyll, leave all my money and property to Mister Edward Hyde." Because Dr. Jekyll includes Mr. Hyde in his will, he allows Utterson to believe there is a possible link between the two men. Utterson fears that the evil Mr. Hyde has some power over Jekyll. He speaks to both men about it, which leads to connection, suspicion, and discovery.

Unit 9 203

How do we respond according to the chart? (If the prompt asks you to *differentiate*, the response requires you to tell apart or tell the difference between.) Turn the prompt into a question to confirm understanding. (What is the difference between the two uses of "I must have you for dinner some night"?) Use your prior knowledge of what having someone for dinner means. To do this, you need to consider the multiple meanings of the word *have*. Sometimes we say, "I will have pizza for dinner." In this usage, what is *have* synonymous for? (eat) Have partners discuss the other meaning of *have* and search the text for the answer to the question. While providing partner time, write the following sentence starters on the board.

When Mr. Hyde said "I must have you for dinner some night," he was ______ ____. *When Dr. Jekyll said the same thing, he was* ________________________________.

Have partners answer the question. Discuss possible answers.

4. Assess the content in Dr. Jekyll's will.

How do we respond according to the chart? (If the prompt asks you to *assess*, the response requires you to decide on the value, impact, or accuracy.) Turn the prompt into a question to confirm understanding. (What is the impact of the content of Dr. Jekyll's will?) Have partners search the text for the answer. While providing partner time, write the following sentence starters on the board.

*Dr. Jekyll's will says*________________________*. Because Dr. Jekyll includes Mr. Hyde in his will,* _______________________*. Utterson fears that the evil Mr. Hyde*___________________*. He speaks to both men about it, which leads to* _______________________________________.

Have partners answer the question. Discuss possible answers.

Text Structure and Literary Meaning and Style

Carl Bowen reworked a classic piece of literature. The original version was 144 pages of text. Bowen's version was less than 60 pages of graphics with very little text. What is the effect of this change?

Ask the following questions to generate conversation.

1. Do you think the graphics make the story easier to understand?
2. Do you think the audience changed with the introduction of the graphic novel?
3. Does the addition of graphics make the reader less likely to use his or her imagination?
4. Are the theme and central ideas of the story still the same?

Have partners discuss which version they would prefer to read and why. Then, ask them to discuss why some people would prefer to read the text version.

Many people like the opportunity to create images in their own minds and not let someone else interpret the text for them. Do you think Bowen interpreted the text, or did he simply draw exactly what the text described?

Note: The full text of Robert Louis Stevenson's version of the story can be found online in ReadingScape. Students can read the original version and determine the extent to which Bowen stayed true to the story.

Unit 9

Lesson 8

Lesson Opener

Before the lesson, choose one of the following activities to write on the board or post on the *LANGUAGE! Live* Class Wall online.

- *Write three sentences about Edward Hyde using relative pronouns.*
- *Write the dialogue of a conversation between Edward Hyde and the lady who answered the door at his house.*
- *Expand one or more of these simple sentences, using the steps in Masterpiece Sentences.*

  Edward Hyde emerges.

  Dr. Jekyll drinks a potion.

  Mr. Utterson sees Edward Hyde.

  Dr. Jekyll studied.

Reading

Objectives

- Establish a purpose for rereading a graphic novel.
- Monitor comprehension during text reading.
- Use critical thinking skills to write responses to prompts about text.
- Support written answers with evidence from text.
- Analyze how visual elements contribute to character development.
- Analyze how an adapted work of fiction stays true to the original version.
- Assess the strength and validity of claims and counterclaims made by characters.
- Integrate information from both literary and informational text on the same topic to answer questions.
- Compare literary character development to biographical information in other texts.

Reading for a Purpose: The Graphic Novel of *The Strange Case of Dr. Jekyll and Mr. Hyde*

Good readers read text more than once to gain understanding. Nothing is wrong with you if you don't understand the text after the first read. Difficult text requires you to reread the text or parts of the text, especially when the vocabulary words are difficult or unfamiliar.

Let's preview the prompts to provide a purpose for rereading the text. You should recognize the question words that we practiced in the last lesson.

Direct students to pages 204–206 in their Student Books. Have students read the prompts aloud with you.

1. Relate the visual image of Mr. Hyde to his character.
2. Differentiate between the low mind and the high mind.
3. Use the following excerpt from the text version of the story to assess the degree to which Bowen's graphic novel retelling stayed true to Stevenson's original novel.
4. Utterson claims that Hyde has some hold over Jekyll. Assess the strength of Dr. Jekyll's counterclaim that he has a hold

over Hyde. Is his reasoning sound with sufficient, relevant evidence to support his claim?

5. Analyze the connection between Dr. Jekyll and Mr. Hyde and dissociative identity disorder.
6. Relate Dr. Jekyll to Robin Grimsley and the outcome of her trial.

It's time to revisit the text.

Choose an option for reading text. Have students read the text according to the option that you chose.

Options for reading text:

- Teacher read-aloud
- Teacher-led or student-led choral read
- Paired read or independent read with bold vocabulary words read aloud

Direct students to page 139 in their Student Books or have them tear out the extra copy of the text from the back of their book.

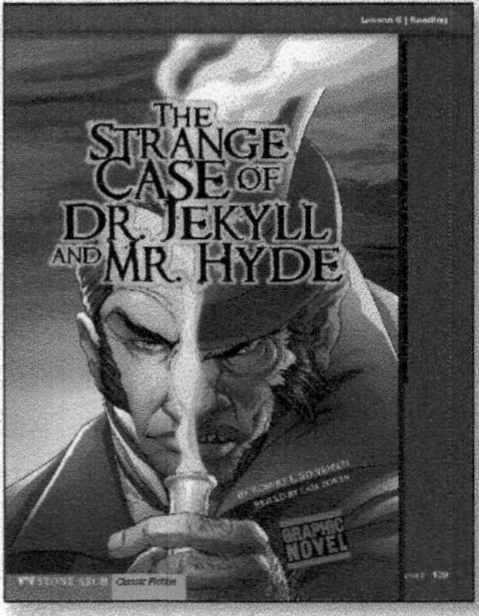

Note: To minimize flipping back and forth between the pages, a copy of each text has been included in the back of the Student Books. Encourage students to tear this out and use it when working on activities that require the use of the text.

Have students read the text.

Passage Comprehension

Write the words *analyze, assess, differentiate,* and *relate* on the board. Have students read the words aloud with you.

Direct students to pages 14 and 15 in their Student Books. It is critical to understand what the question is asking and how to answer it. Today, we will review four direction words used in prompts.

Have students read the chart with their partner. Check for understanding by requesting an oral response to the following questions.

- If the prompt asks you to *analyze,* the response requires you to . . . (break down and evaluate or draw conclusions about the information).
- If the prompt asks you to *assess,* the response requires you to . . . (decide on the value, impact, or accuracy).
- If the prompt asks you to *differentiate,* the response requires you to . . . (tell apart or tell the difference between).
- If the prompt asks you to *relate,* the response requires you to . . . (explain the connection between ideas or concepts).

Lesson 3 | Reading

Critical Understandings: Direction Words

Prompt	How to Respond	Model
If the prompt asks you to . . .	**The response requires you to . . .**	**For example . . .**
Analyze	break down and evaluate or draw conclusions about the information	**Analyze** the development of the text's central idea.
Assess	decide on the value, impact, or accuracy	**Assess** how the author's point of view affects the story.
Cite Evidence	support your answer by paraphrasing or using a direct quote	**Cite evidence** that supports your argument.
Clarify	make a statement or situation less confusing	**Clarify** the events leading up to the marriage.
Compare	state the similarities between two or more things	**Compare** Indian and Chinese marriage arrangements.
Connect	tie ideas together, relate	**Connect** each storm with its safety plan.
Contrast	state the differences between two or more things	**Contrast** Indian and Chinese marriage arrangements.
Demonstrate	show how to do it	**Demonstrate** your knowledge of wolves through poetry.
Develop an Argument	work on a case over a period of time, during which it grows or changes	Use evidence from both stories to **develop an argument** against arranged marriages.
Differentiate	tell apart or tell the difference between	**Differentiate** between the protagonist and the antagonist.
Distinguish	recognize something for a specific reason	**Distinguish** your claim from the opposing view by telling how it is different.

14 Unit 7

Let's practice answering questions that are written as prompts. Remember to use the chart as reference. Don't forget; if the direction word is confusing, try to restate the prompt by using a question word.

Direct students to pages 204–206 in their Student Books.

Passage Comprehension

Reread the graphic novel of *The Strange Case of Dr. Jekyll and Mr. Hyde*. Respond to each prompt using complete sentences. Refer to the chart on pages 14 and 15 to determine how to respond to each prompt.

1. Relate the visual image of Mr. Hyde to his character.

Mr. Hyde's image seems to be an accurate portrayal of his character. Mr. Hyde is short and hunched over, making him appear small and weak. He wears a dark cape as if he has something to hide, and he looks suspicious and predatory. Mr. Hyde's face is discolored and wrinkled with bulging eyes and a pointed nose. These monster-like features depict the evil with which Dr. Jekyll describes him. Hyde is often shouting with rage depicted on his face, which further exemplifies his wicked character. His large hands and vicious wolf-like teeth have similarities to that of beasts, as he was described by Utterson. The two descriptions of the low mind, vain and greedy, aren't readily evident in the image of Hyde.

2. Differentiate between the low mind and the high mind.

The low mind is "vain and greedy, seeking only what's best for itself," while the high mind "seeks only beauty and goodness in life."

Passage Comprehension (*cont.*)

3. Use the following excerpt from the text version of the story to assess the degree to which Bowen's graphic novel retelling stayed true to Stevenson's original novel.

"My provision of the salt, which had never been renewed since the date of the first experiment, began to run low. I sent out for a fresh supply, and mixed the draught; the ebullition followed, and the first change of colour, not the second; I drank it and it was without efficiency. You will learn from Poole how I have had London ransacked; it was in vain; and I am now persuaded that my first supply was impure, and that it was that unknown impurity which lent efficacy to the draught.

About a week has passed, and I am now finishing this statement under the influence of the last of the old powders. This, then, is the last time, short of a miracle, that Henry Jekyll can think his own thoughts or see his own face (now how sadly altered!) in the glass."

Bowen's graphic novel retelling did not stay completely true to the original novel. While both versions indicate that the rare salt was the magic ingredient in the formula, the graphic novel indicates that Jekyll dumped the salt to keep from continuing the cycle. However, in the novel, Jekyll didn't dump the salt, but simply wasn't able to get the same salt anymore because of an unknown impurity in the first batch. This alters the story because it changes it to a conscious decision of never using the potion again from one of being unable to use it again due to outside circumstances.

4. Utterson claims that Hyde has some hold over Jekyll. Assess the strength of Dr. Jekyll's counterclaim that he has a hold over Hyde. Is his reasoning sound with sufficient, relevant evidence to support his claim?

Dr. Jekyll's counterclaim that he has a hold over Hyde is not accurate. Jekyll's counterclaim is not sound because he admitted losing control of Hyde when he murdered Lanyon. Eventually Jekyll began changing into Hyde without cause and without the formula, which indicates that he does not have control. Jekyll had to hide things from Hyde and dispose of the salt because he was in fact out of control.

Guided Practice

1. Relate the visual image of Mr. Hyde to his character.

How do we respond according to the chart? (If the prompt asks you to *relate*, the response requires that you explain the connection between ideas or concepts.) Turn the prompt into a question to confirm understanding. (What is the connection between Hyde's visual image and his character?)

We cannot start writing our answer until we understand Hyde's character. **Have students search the narrative boxes and dialogue balloons for words describing Hyde or the low mind.** (awful, villain, beast, monster, vain, greedy, small, weak, evil, wicked)

We need to look at multiple pictures of Hyde and determine if these pictures

Passage Comprehension (*cont.*)

5. Analyze the connection between Dr. Jekyll and Mr. Hyde and dissociative identity disorder.

Dissociative identity disorder is a condition in which a single person has more than one distinct identity or self, just like Dr. Jekyll. The host personality is Jekyll. Eventually, Jekyll named his alter Hyde because he acted like a completely different person. People with DID have high IQs and serious gaps in memory—both of which are evident in Dr. Jekyll's life. Jekyll was a brilliant scientist who did well in school and created a potion to alter his self. According to Jekyll, "I changed for no reason, and I wasn't fully aware of my actions." This is a symptom of DID.

6. Relate Dr. Jekyll to Robin Grimsley and the outcome of her trial.

Dr. Jekyll has no control over the actions of Mr. Hyde, just as Grimsley did not have control of her alter. Both alters—Hyde and Jennifer—were impulsive and angry. Because Jekyll willingly brought Hyde into the world through a potion, and Hyde knew what he was doing when he killed Lanyon, I believe Jekyll should be sentenced like Robin Grimsley and found guilty of the crime because the whole person should be held criminally accountable.

match the descriptions. Direct students to page 152; page 159, frame 4; pages 182 and 183, and page 192, frame 3. Write the following sentence starters on the board while students study the graphics.

> *Mr. Hyde's image seems to be an accurate/inaccurate portrayal of his character. Mr. Hyde is __________, making him appear small and weak.*
>
> *Mr. Hyde's face is __________________, which ____________.*
>
> *His _____________ have similarities to that of__________ as he was described by Utterson.*

Independent Practice

Have partners respond to the remaining prompts. For students who need more assistance, provide the following alternative questions and sentence starters.

Alternative questions and sentence starters:

2. What is the difference between the low mind and the high mind?

   The low mind is ____________________, while the high mind ______________ ____.

3. How accurate is Bowen's retelling?

   Bowen's graphic novel retelling did/did not stay completely true to the original novel.

   While both versions indicate ____________________, the graphic novel indicates ________________________________.

   However, in the novel,________________________________.

4. How accurate is Dr. Jekyll's counterclaim that he has a hold over Hyde? Is there evidence to suggest that Dr. Jekyll is correct?

   Dr. Jekyll's counterclaim that he has a hold over Hyde is/is not accurate. Jekyll's counterclaim is/is not correct because ______________________.

5. What is the link between Dr. Jekyll and Mr. Hyde and dissociative identity disorder?

   Dissociative identity disorder is a condition in which _____________, just like ________________________. People with DID have _______________.

6. How is Dr. Jekyll connected to Robin Grimsley and the outcome of her trial?

   Dr. Jekyll has ____________________, just as Grimsley _____________ ____________________. Both alters______________________.

   Because Jekyll ________________________________.

Unit 9

Lesson 9

Lesson Opener

Before the lesson, choose one of the following activities to write on the board or post on the *LANGUAGE! Live* Class Wall online.

- *Write three sentences about Dr. Henry Jekyll using relative pronouns.*
- *Write the dialogue of a conversation between Dr. Jekyll and the girl who was attacked by Edward Hyde.*
- *Write five compound sentences about the story of Dr. Jekyll and Mr. Hyde using subordinating conjunctions.*

Reading

Objectives

- Read a graphic novel with purpose and understanding.
- Answer questions to demonstrate comprehension of text.
- Identify and explain explicit details from text.
- Monitor comprehension during text reading.
- Identify a sequential structure used to organize text.
- Analyze how dialogue or incidents propel the action and reveal character traits.
- Analyze the way in which character point of view creates suspense.
- Identify the protagonist and antagonist in literature.
- Determine the meaning of idioms.
- Identify common religious themes in literature.
- Analyze an author's unique approach to a common theme.
- Identify the denouement/resolution of a plot.

Close Reading: The Graphic Novel of *The Strange Case of Dr. Jekyll and Mr. Hyde*

Highlighters or colored pencils

Let's reread the graphic novel of *The Strange Case of Dr. Jekyll and Mr. Hyde*. I will provide specific instructions on how to mark the text to help with comprehension.

Have students get out a highlighter or colored pencil.

Direct students to pages 207–237 in their Student Books.

> **Note:** If students have difficulty reading the text on the Close Reading pages, project the pages, which can be found in the Teacher Resources online.

Draw a rectangle around the title.

Circle the names of the characters.

Skim Chapters 1–4, paying attention to the first narrative box on each page. In the margin, write the transition words that tell time. Remember, transition words that tell time answer the question *When*?

(Page 209, panel 1 of bottom page: some months ago
Page 211, panel 1 of bottom page: Later that evening
Page 212, panel 1 of top page: the next day

Page 212, panel 1 of bottom page: Hours later . . .
Page 215, Panel 1 of top page: Early the next day . . .
Page 217, Panel 1 of top page: A few months passed
Page 218, Panel 1 of top page: The next morning
Page 218, Panel 1 of bottom page: Later,
Page 220, panel 1 of top page: A short time later . . .
Page 221, Panel 1 of top page: Weeks later,
Page 224, Panel 1 of top page: The next day . . .)

Skim Chapter 4, paying attention to the first narrative box on each page. In the margin, write the prepositional phrases that name a place. Remember, prepositional phrases that name a place answer the question *Where*?

(Page 218, Panel 1 of bottom page: at the morgue . . .
Page 221, Panel 1 of top page: at Utterson's house . . .
Page 221, Panel 1 of bottom page: At Dr. Jekyll's house . . .
Page 224, Panel 1 of bottom page: Back at Utterson's house . . .)

Now, let's read the vocabulary words aloud.

- What's the first bold vocabulary word? (attended) *Attended* means "took care of someone or something." You *attended* to your homework in the evenings and so maintained a good grade. **Have partners use the word in a sentence.**
- What's the next vocabulary word? (involved) *Involved* means "connected with; mixed up with." Many students are *involved* in extracurricular activities. **Have partners use the word in a sentence.**
- Next word? (incident) *Incident* means "an event or happening that is noticed or creates a stir." The bullying *incident* caused parents to meet with the principal. **Have partners use the word in a sentence.**
- Let's continue. (conflict) *Conflict* means "a clash or struggle between two sides or forces." The *conflict* can be remediated with counseling. **Have partners use the word in a sentence.**
- Next word? (challenge) *Challenge* means "a problem or question that takes effort to solve." The *challenge* of working in a group is getting everyone to participate equally. **Have partners use the word in a sentence.**
- Let's continue. (formula) *Formula* means "a mixture; a recipe." Texting and driving is a *formula* for disaster. **Have partners use the word in a sentence.**
- Next word? (urges) *Urges* means "strong needs or drives to do something." She overcame her *urges* to eat junk food by going for walks instead. **Have partners use the word in a sentence.**
- Let's continue. (reaction) *Reaction* means "what someone feels, says, or does in response to something else." My *reaction* to the news of the crash was disbelief and sadness. **Have partners use the word in a sentence.**
- Next word? (research) *Research* means "the act of studying something or gathering information about it." To write our paper, we will need to go to the library and do *research*. **Have partners use the word in a sentence.**
- Last word. (obtained) *Obtained* means "got; gained." You *obtained* your driver's permit on the very first attempt. **Have partners use the word in a sentence.**

Talk with a partner about any vocabulary word that is still confusing for you to read or understand.

As you reread the graphic novel, you will monitor your understanding by circling the check marks or the question marks. Please be sure to draw a question mark over any confusing words, phrases, or sentences.

Options for rereading text.

- Teacher read-aloud
- Teacher-led or student-led choral read
- Paired read or independent read with bold vocabulary words read aloud

Choose an option for reading text. Have students read through Chapter 1 according to the option that you chose.

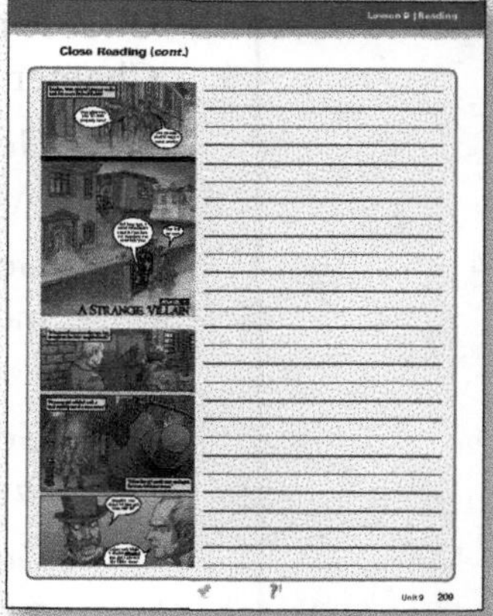

- Look at the introduction of the characters. What can you determine about the story based on the illustrator's choice of expressions? Write your answer on the lines. (The story is serious and dark.)
- Look at page 209. Write the title of the chapter. (A Strange Villain) In parentheses, indicate who the villain is. (Hyde)
- Look at panel 1. Write the setting. (London, 1885)
- Look at panel 2. Write the word that means "extraordinary" or "unusual." (remarkable)

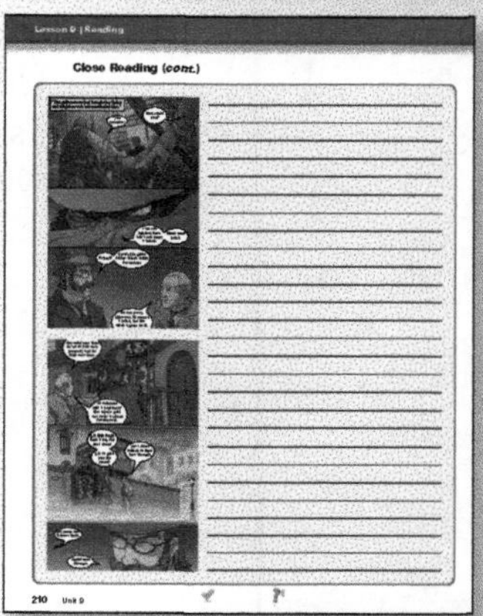

- Go to page 210, panel 2. Write the word that means "without help." (helpless) Circle the suffix that means "without." (-less)
- Go to page 211, panel 2. Write the word that means "someone who pays for services." (client)
- A proverb is a popular saying that gives advice about how to live. Look at the next panel. Write the proverb used to show that nothing good can come from continuing the conversation. (The less said, the better.)
- Go to page 212, panel 2. Write the adverb that means "at some later time; in the end." (eventually)
- Look at the next panel. Write the words spoken by Utterson that create suspense—the feeling of excitement about what may happen. (when you do, I'll be waiting)

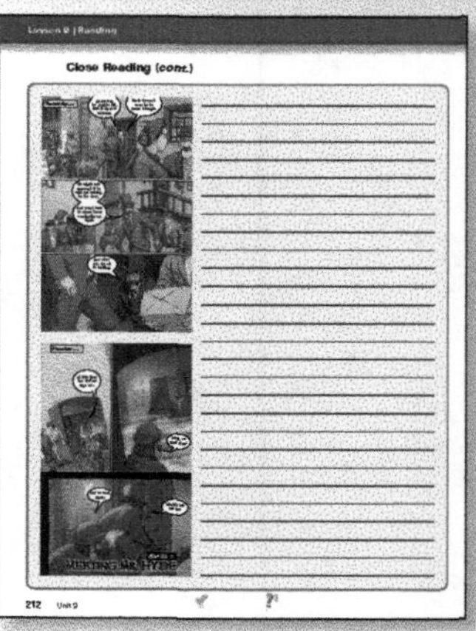

Choose an option for reading text. Have students read Chapter 2 according to the option that you chose.

- Go to page 212. Write the title of Chapter 2. (Meeting Mr. Hyde)
- Go to panel 4. Draw the punctuation that indicates that Utterson's thought was interrupted. (—; em dash)
- Go to page 213, panel 1. Write the synonym of *lawyer*. (attorney)
- Go to page 214, panel 5. Write the third-person pronoun. (him) Next to the pronoun, write the name of the person the pronoun is referencing. (Jekyll) Write the question Utterson will be asking Jekyll. (How did Jekyll ever get involved with such a beast?)

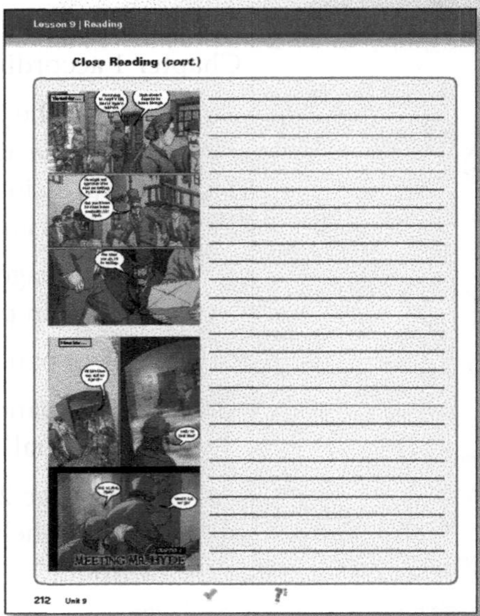
Lesson 9 | Reading

Close Reading (cont.)

212 Unit 9

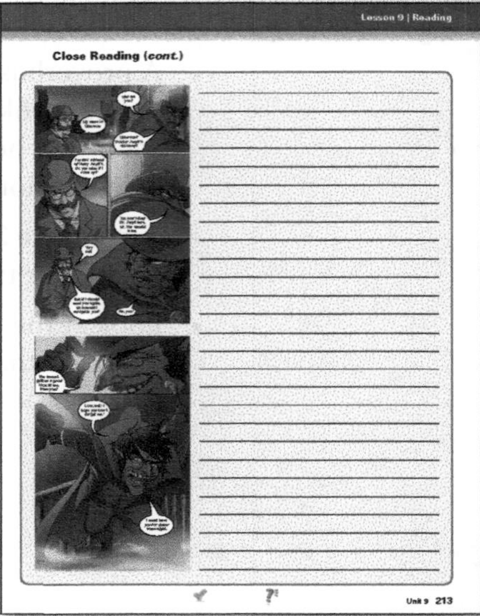
Lesson 9 | Reading

Close Reading (cont.)

Unit 9 213

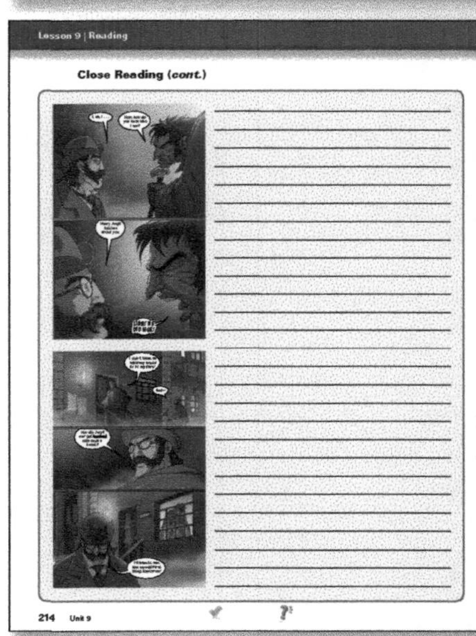
Lesson 9 | Reading

Close Reading (cont.)

214 Unit 9

Choose an option for reading text. Have students read Chapter 3 according to the option that you chose.

- Go to page 215. Write the title of Chapter 3. (Dr. Henry Jekyll) Find the first picture of Dr. Jekyll. Star the picture.
- In the same panel, write the words that indicate Jekyll is happy to see Utterson. (pleasant surprise)
- Go to panel 3. Write the lie being told and the name of the liar. (Jekyll is not surprised to see Utterson.)
- Go to panel 6. Write the word that means "place where experiments happen." (laboratory)
- Go to panel 7. Write the word that means "control." (hold)
- In the same panel, write all three pronouns from the second dialogue balloon in the margin. Write the name of the person each pronoun is referring to. (I—Utterson; he—Hyde; you—Jekyll)
- Go to page 216, panel 1. Dr. Jekyll seems to be very confident. Why would the author include this in the story? Write the answer on the lines. (to establish the primary character trait of Dr. Jekyll—in control)
- Go to panel 2. Write the idiom that means "believe you." (take your word for it)
- Go to panel 5. Notice the quotation marks around the first sentence. Write the reason it is in quotation marks. (He is repeating something Jekyll said.)
- What do we now know about Utterson's character that could make Jekyll nervous? Write your answer in the margin. (He pays attention to details; he is inquisitive.)

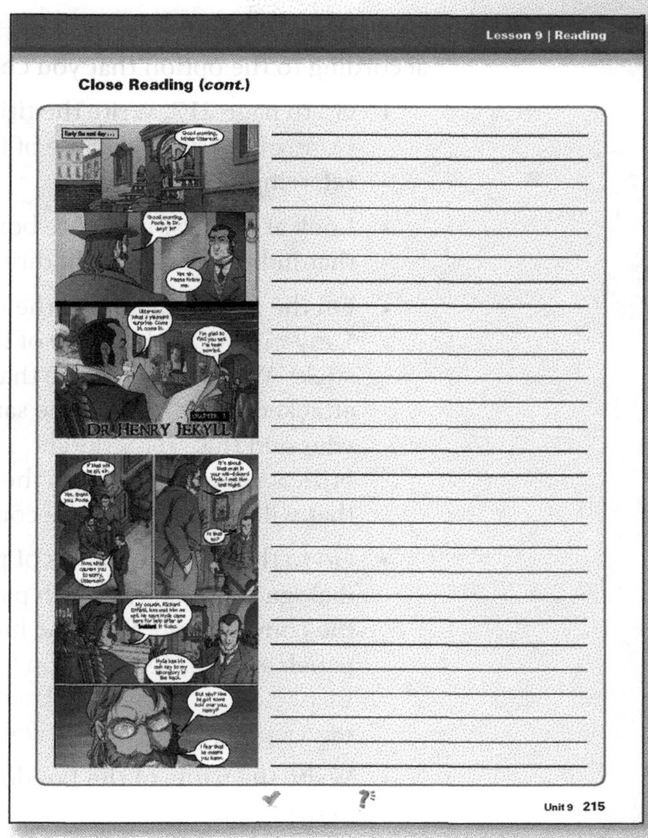
Lesson 9 | Reading

Close Reading (*cont.*)

DR. HENRY JEKYLL

Unit 9 215

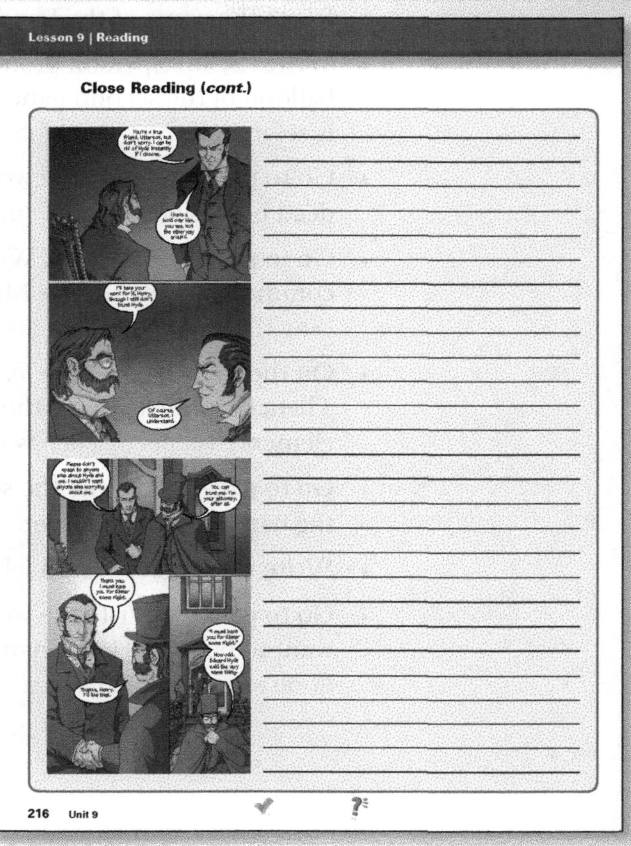
Lesson 9 | Reading

Close Reading (*cont.*)

216 Unit 9

Choose an option for reading text. Have students read Chapter 4 according to the option that you chose.

- Go to page 217. Write the title of the chapter. (Out of Control) Write the name of the person to whom the title is referring. (Hyde)
- Look at the first narrative box. Write the transition words that indicate a change in direction. (But then . . .)
- On the same page, write the name of the victim. (Hastie Lanyon) Write the name of the weapon. (cane or walking stick) Write the evidence that Lanyon recognized his attacker. (You!) Write the sarcastic comment, and indicate who said this. (Goodnight, Lanyon! From both of me!—Hyde said it.) What does the author include on this page that will likely change the course of the story? (a witness)
- Go to the first two panels of page 218. Number the dialogue balloons for each panel to show the order of the conversation. Start the numbering over with each panel. (1. Gabriel Utterson?, 2. What's this about? 3. I am Inspector . . . ; 1. There's been a murder . . . , 2. Who was the victim?, 3. We hoped you could tell us.)
- Write the name of the London police force. (Scotland Yard)
- Write the name of the London neighborhood. (Soho)
- Write the first-person pronoun used in the third dialogue balloon of the second panel, and indicate who the pronoun is referencing. (we; members of Scotland Yard)
- Go to panel 3. Write the word that means "place where dead bodies are stored." (morgue)
- Go to page 219, panel 2. Write what you think the comment "Come to take Mister Hyde away, I hope" means. (She thinks he has been doing something illegal.)
- On the same page, write *foreshadowing* in the margin. Then, draw an arrow to the panel that displays this literary element. (panel 6, There's someone else . . .)
- Go to page 220. Write the setting. (Jekyll's house) Write the name of Jekyll's butler. (Poole)
- Write what likely scared Jekyll. (the killing of his friend)
- Go to panel 5. Write the words that prove Jekyll does not want to become Hyde anymore. (I'm through with him! I hope to never see his face again.)

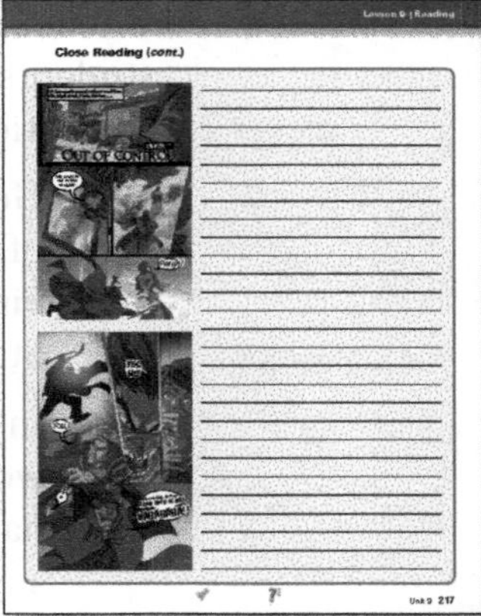

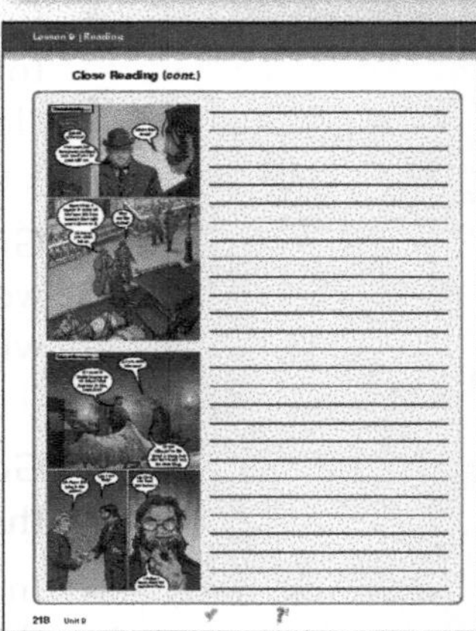

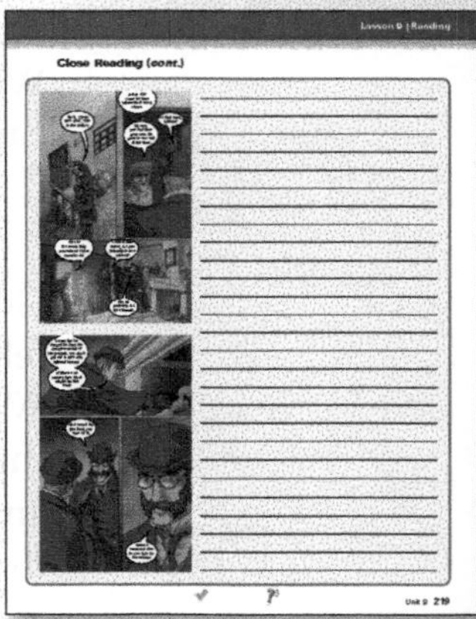

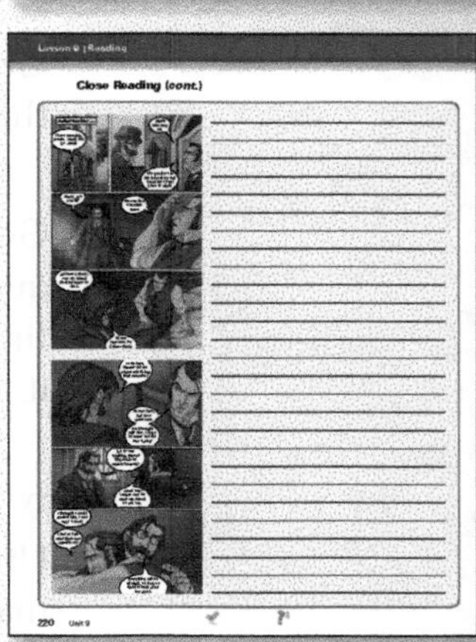

- Go to page 221, panel 1. Write the setting. (Utterson's house)
- Go to panel 4. Write the setting. (Dr. Jekyll's house)
- Go to page 222, panel 1. Write the setting. (laboratory) Write the evidence that Poole doesn't want Jekyll to know Utterson is with him. (don't make a sound)
- On the same page, write the bolded dialogue that indicates anger. (get rid of him) Write the words and visual element that indicate that Utterson is shocked. (My God!; hand over mouth)
- Go to page 223. Write the visual evidence that backs Utterson's claim that Hyde killed himself. (test tube bottle, unconscious Hyde, chaotic surroundings)
- Go to page 224, panel 3. Who is talking about the envelope? (Inspector Newcomen)
- Go to panels 4 and 5. Write the evidence that Utterson is surprised. (What?) Write the context clues that help infer the meaning *confess*. (you've done something wrong)

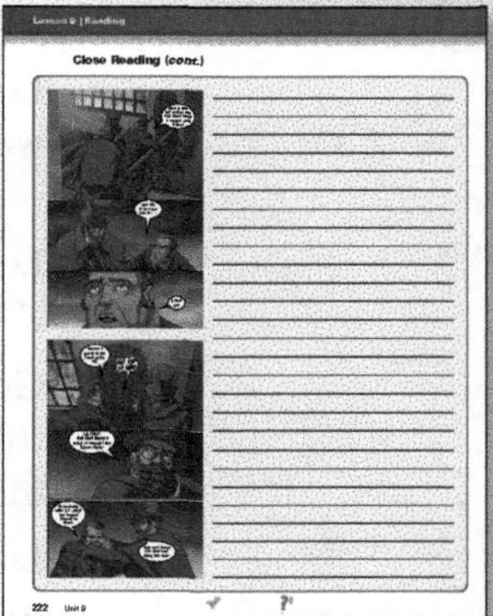

Choose an option for reading text. Have students read Chapter 5 according to the option that you chose.

- Go to page 225. Write the title of Chapter 5. (Jekyll's Confession)
- Go to panels 2 and 3. Circle the punctuation marks that indicate the text is direct quotes from Jekyll's letter. (quotation marks) Circle the picture of young Jekyll in each panel.
- Go to panel 4. Write the names of the three friends depicted in the panel. (Jekyll, Utterson, Lanyon)
- Go to page 226, panel 1. Label the character in panel 1. (Jekyll)
- Look at panel 2. Write the scientific questions Jekyll wanted answers to. (Why are some men smarter than others? Why are some men good and others evil?)
- Look at panel 3. Write the answer to Jekyll's questions. (Every man has two minds within a single body!)
- Go to panel 4. Write the descriptions of the two minds. (high mind: seeks only beauty and goodness in life; low mind: vain and greedy, seeking only what's best for itself)
- Look at panel 5. Write the reason Jekyll was motivated to find his low mind. (every unhappiness in my life was caused by the conflict between the low mind and the high mind)
- In panels 4 and 5, what graphic element is used by the artist to indicate the separation between the two "selves"? (shadowing)
- Go to page 227. Write the three pieces of evidence that Lanyon rejected Jekyll's claim regarding his low mind/high mind. (1. A neat idea, but not worth anything; 2. It's not like you can give those minds their own separate bodies; 3. "He didn't take me seriously.")
- In the margin, write how Lanyon's rejection propelled the action in the story. (It fueled Jekyll to figure out how to separate the high and the low mind.)
- Write the quote that Hyde uses later to prove that Jekyll never forgave Lanyon for rejecting his claim. ("Goodnight, Lanyon! From both of me! Ha ha ha!")
- Go to panel 4. Write the words used to indicate that Jekyll started working on the formula right away. (at once) Write the main ingredient to Jekyll's scientific experiment. (rare salt) Write the person used to test Jekyll's formula. (Jekyll)

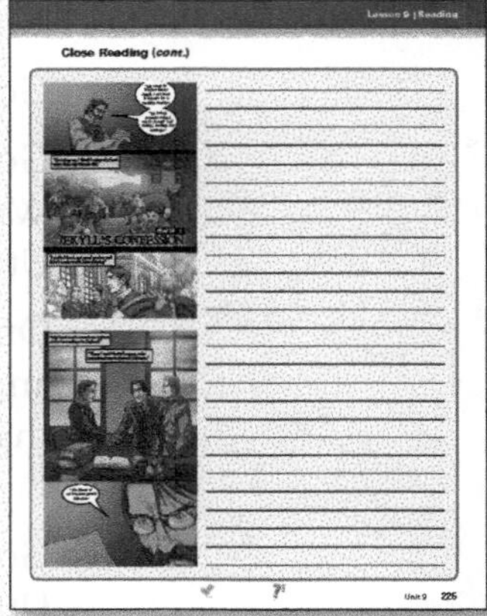

- Go to page 228. Analyze the visual elements of this two-page spread. How did the organization change to increase the drama of the story? (no panel outlines; The two pages are treated as one.) Number the panels. Circle the panel that is an interruption of chronological sequence. (panel 3) Write an adjective to describe Utterson in panel 3. (shocked)
- Go to page 229. Write the evidence that Jekyll's results did not align with his hypothesis. (My formula hadn't worked as I expected. I hadn't been split into two. I had created a body for my low mind alone!) Write the reason for Hyde being small and weak. (I always ignored my low mind) Think about that statement. If it is true, what will likely happen to Hyde as he gets more and more attention? (He will get larger and stronger.) What is the author creating here? (suspense)
- Go to panel 3. Write what Hyde wanted to do. (evil things)
- Go to page 230. Write a description of the visual elements that show that Jekyll was in pain. (sweating/crying, eyes rolled back, facial expression appears to be screaming in pain, size of graphic compared to others)
- Go to panel 3. Write the evidence that Jekyll was satisfied with his results even though the formula didn't work as expected. (But that was good enough for me.)
- Go to page 231. Write the name of the person Hyde approached to show the effect of the formula. (Lanyon) Write Lanyon's reaction. (horror)
- Go to page 232. Write Lanyon's emotion. (upset) Write what Lanyon's reaction convinced Jekyll to do. (set aside my formula) Was that an effective step? (no)

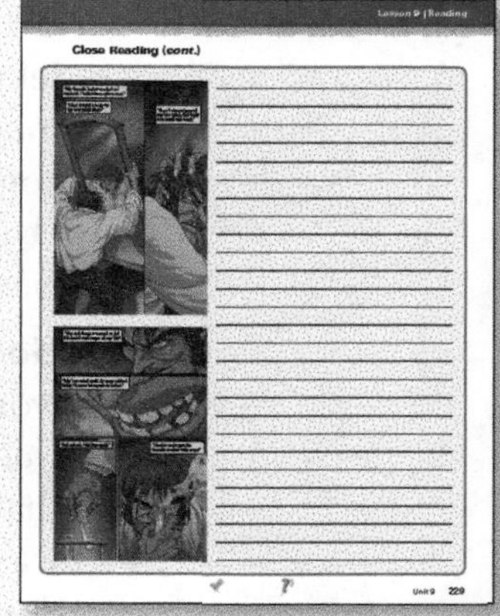

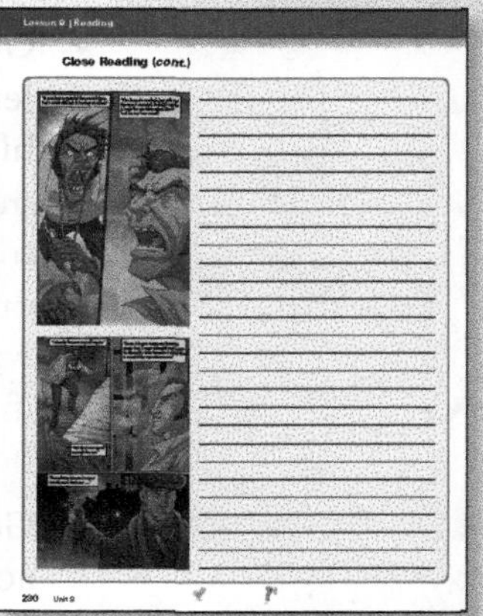

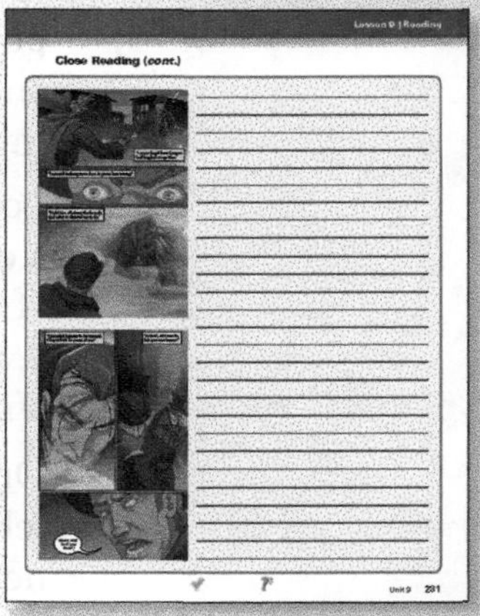

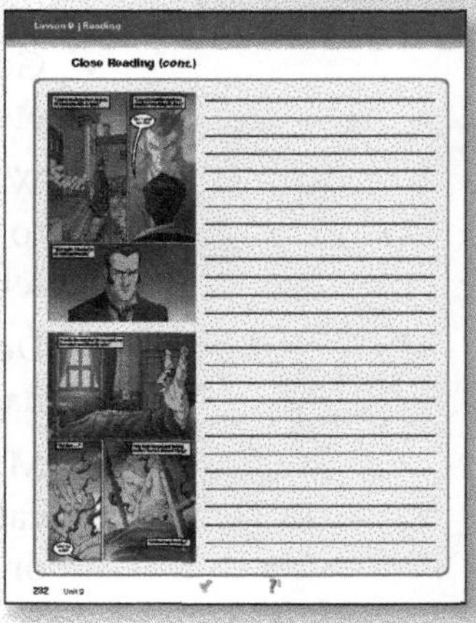

- Go to page 233. Summarize Jekyll's problem. (His low mind was fighting him for control. He now, often, changed for no reason and wasn't aware of his actions.)
- Go to page 234. Write the word that means "make fun of." (mock) Write the evidence that Jekyll was resurfacing and was remorseful. (What have I done!)
- Go to page 235. Summarize Jekyll's attempted solution to his problem. (He wanted to make his formula stronger to keep Hyde from returning or develop an antidote. He wanted to isolate his high mind instead—in essence, return to normal.)
- Go to panel 4. Write the actions Hyde took to keep Jekyll from minimizing his power. (found my new notes and destroyed them; burned my original research notes)
- Look at page 236. Write the steps to Jekyll's plan. (1. disposed of rare salt; 2. wrote a new will; 3. finished writing the confession)
- On the same page, write what Jekyll intended to happen the next time Hyde took control. (face justice for his crimes) 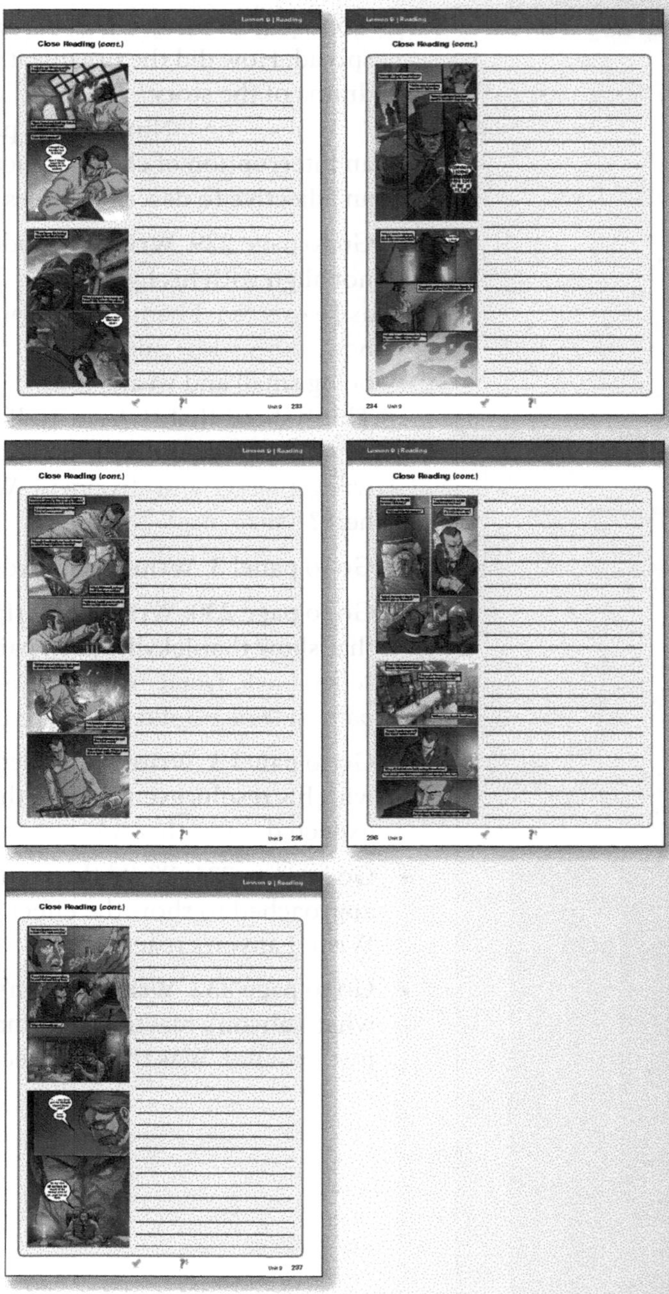
- Go to page 237. Write the evidence that Utterson felt sorry for Jekyll. (Poor Henry)
- What promise is made by Utterson that serves as the denouement or resolution to the story? (No one else will ever learn the secret of the strange case of Dr. Jekyll and Mr. Hyde.)
- Describe the visual element that reflects the theory behind DID. (a face that is half one person and half the alter)
- Many stories contain a main character who is the "good" person in the story, called the protagonist, as well as a secondary character who is the "bad" person, or antagonist. *The Strange Case of Dr. Jekyll and Mr. Hyde* is one of these stories.

Write the name of each in the margin. (Dr. Jekyll: protagonist; Mr. Hyde: antagonist) Explain the irony in this. (They are the same person.)

- What is the common theme addressed in this story? (good vs. evil) How is the treatment of the theme of this story different from many stories that share the same theme? (The struggle between good and evil exists in all people and is internal—not external.)

Have partners compare text markings and correct any errors.

Lesson 10

Lesson Opener

Before the lesson, choose one of the following activities to write on the board or post on the *LANGUAGE! Live* Class Wall online.

- *Write four sentences with at least two vocabulary words in each. Show you know the meanings. (attend, involved, incident, conflict, challenge, formula, urge, reaction, research, obtain)*
- *Dress your avatar as though it was your last day on Earth. How would you want to be remembered? Explain your choices.*
- *Knowing the consequences of allowing your low mind to take control by drinking a potion, would you drink the potion if given the opportunity? Why or why not?*

Vocabulary

Objective

- Review key passage vocabulary.

Recontextualize Passage Vocabulary

Direct students to page 138 in their Student Books. Use the following questions to review the vocabulary words from the graphic novel of *The Strange Case of Dr. Jekyll and Mr. Hyde.*

- You're about to put your hand on a doorknob. A loud voice yells "STOP!" and you do. Was this a *reaction*? (yes) You're in the car with your dad. The car in front of you slams on its breaks, and your dad slams on his. Was this a *reaction*? (yes) A spotlight shines straight into your eyes and you squint. Your squinting is a what? (reaction)
- Two children are arguing over something in the yard next door. You go over to see if you can help straighten things out. Are you now *involved*? (yes) The cheerleaders need someone tall to help them hang posters. You are tall. You slip out the back door. Do you want to get *involved*? (no) You happen to walk through the kitchen while your sister is making marshmallow treats. "Quick, hold the pot while I scrape the candy onto the pan!" she cries. You do. What are you? (involved)
- You're riding bikes with a friend. He wipes out. You stop to see if he's okay. Are you *attending* to him? (yes) Your little brother trips, falls, and cries. You tell him to shake it off. Are you *attending* to him? (no) Your dog has a thorn in his paw. You remove it, scratch him behind the ears, and give him a new bone to chew on. What are you doing? (attending to him)
- Your friend wants you to go to a concert, but you dislike the music. No part of you wants to go. Are you in *conflict* over whether to go? (no) You insist it's your sister's turn to take out the trash, but she insists it's yours. Are you having a *conflict*? (yes) Tara's mother will not let her get her nose pierced. Tara doesn't understand what the big deal is. They argue about it constantly. What are they having? (a conflict)

- You watch a gorgeous sunset from the rooftop of your building. Does this involve *research*? (no) You have to write about 10 countries of South America and their capitals for geography homework. Will this involve *research*? (yes) Your mom is putting together a genealogy, or history of her family. She spends a lot of time reading old letters and calling distant relatives. What is she doing? (research)
- Football workouts have begun. You haven't lifted a weight in six months. Are the workouts a *challenge*? (yes) You expect the test to be hard, but it's easy. Is it a *challenge*? (no) Your mom's car isn't working. You've been looking under the hood for 30 minutes and can't figure out what's wrong. Her car problem is what? (a challenge)
- Before the movie starts, a giant carton of popcorn appears on the screen. You're hungry. Do you suddenly have an *urge* to buy popcorn? (yes) After nine hours of sleep, you wake up feeling refreshed and energized. Do you feel an *urge* to go back to bed? (no) You're talking with a friend, and she yawns long and loud. What might you suddenly have? (an urge to yawn)
- You want to make a bracelet for your friend but don't have the right beads. Do you need to *obtain* them? (yes) You want to take banjo lessons. Luckily, there's a banjo in the closet that no one ever uses. Do you need to *obtain* a banjo? (no) To be excused from class, you must get a parent's signature. What must you do? (obtain a parent's signature)
- You are a papier-mâché artist. You've discovered how to make the perfect paste using certain amounts of flour and water. Have you found the perfect *formula* for paste? (yes) Your favorite number is 13. Is this a *formula*? (no) Your brother mixes ketchup, mustard, and mayo to make a sauce for his fries. He calls this his "gourmet" what? (formula)
- The couple upstairs is having another loud party. Is this an unpleasant *incident*? (yes) Time drags in your least favorite class. Is this an *incident*? (no) Three times in a row, someone has taken your sports drink from the fridge. You decide to question your brother about these what? (incidents)

Writing

Objectives

- Use multiple texts to write coherently.
- Use a process to write.
- Rewrite a scene from a graphic novel as a narrative, using proper punctuation and accurate word choice.
- Use a rubric to guide and evaluate writing.

Six Traits of Effective Writing

Direct students back to page 35 in their Student Books. Reread the Six Traits of Effective Writing.

While we will continue to utilize all six traits, we will focus our attention on word choice and conventions in this unit. Because we are converting images to words, it is imperative that we use descriptive language to "explain" what is currently being said with pictures. Our narrative will include dialogue, so we will also need to focus on formatting and punctuation.

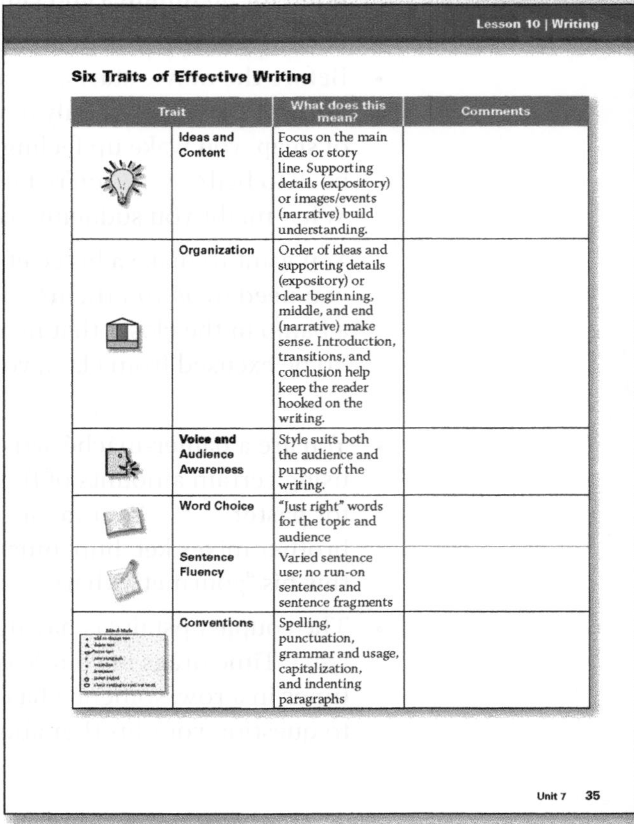

Lesson 10 | Writing

Six Traits of Effective Writing

Trait		What does this mean?	Comments
	Ideas and Content	Focus on the main ideas or story line. Supporting details (expository) or images/events (narrative) build understanding.	
	Organization	Order of ideas and supporting details (expository) or clear beginning, middle, and end (narrative) make sense. Introduction, transitions, and conclusion help keep the reader hooked on the writing.	
	Voice and Audience Awareness	Style suits both the audience and purpose of the writing.	
	Word Choice	"Just right" words for the topic and audience	
	Sentence Fluency	Varied sentence use; no run-on sentences and sentence fragments	
	Conventions	Spelling, punctuation, grammar and usage, capitalization, and indenting paragraphs	

Unit 7 35

Prepare to Write: Narrative

Direct students to page 238 in their Student Books. Read the instructions for Part A and the prompt.

Part A. Study the Prompt

Guide students through identifying the topic, summarizing the directions, and understanding the purpose for writing.

Part B. Introduce the Scene

Have a student read the instructions aloud for Part B. Look back at the text and choose the page you want to convert to narrative text. Once you've selected your page, tell your partner the story being told on your page of the novel. Provide choosing and retelling time.

Lesson 10 | Writing

Prepare to Write: Narrative

Part A. Study the Prompt Answers will vary.

Read the prompt and identify the topic, directions, and purpose for writing.

Choose one page from the graphic novel of *The Strange Case of Dr. Jekyll and Mr. Hyde* and rewrite it in third-person narrative.

Include the dialogue from the scene and identify the speakers.
Use descriptive words to paint the scenes shown in pictures in the text.

Topic: the graphic novel of *The Strange Case of Dr. Jekyll and Mr. Hyde*

Directions: choose one page from *The Strange Case of Dr. Jekyll and Mr. Hyde* and rewrite it in third-person narrative

Purpose for writing: transform a graphic novel into a narrative text

Part B. Introduce the Scene

After selecting a page, write an introduction that sets up the action in the scene and helps the reader understand how the scene is connected to what has previously happened in the story.

Setting: dark streets of London, 1885

Characters: Richard Enfield and Gabriel Utterson

What led up to this? N/A

Introduction: The year is 1885. Gabriel Utterson and his cousin Richard Enfield walk along the dimly lit streets of London. Deep in conversation, their path is illuminated by a few windows and the pale glow of the streetlamps. The streets are empty and as they pass by a particular house, their conversation turns to a tale of horror. Terrible secrets lie hidden in the dark London streets.

238 Unit 9

I'll model how you might complete Part B. Let's look back at the first page of the story. **Have students turn to page 142 in their Student Books.**

I will need to introduce or set up the action taking place in the frames. My opening basically sets up the story. In this case, I don't know what happened before, as this is the beginning of the story. What is the setting? (London, 1885) Who are the characters? (Enfield; Utterson)

Write the following paragraph on the board.

> *The year is 1885. Gabriel Utterson and his cousin Richard Enfield walk along the dimly lit streets of London. Deep in conversation, their path is illuminated by a few windows and the pale glow of the streetlamps. The streets are empty and as they pass by a particular house, their conversation turns to a tale of horror. Terrible secrets lie hidden in the dark London streets.*

Notice how my introductory paragraph establishes the setting and introduces the two characters. Of what significance is the year? (tells the reader it happened a long time ago; very little technology for communication, tracking people, or gathering evidence) Take a minute and consider the setting and the characters that are in the frames on your selected page. Write these details on your page. Then, write your introduction to the scene.

Part C. Map Your Scene

Now, we will look at our scene and map what we see. **Have students explain the events on the page.** (Utterson and Enfield are walking down the street. Enfield tells Utterson of a tragic event that happened at a particular house.) **Then, have students describe the scene in each panel.** (dark; cobblestone streets; men dressed in suits and hats; fancy buildings; nice house with gated entrance) **Have students identify the dialogue of each character.** (Enfield: "Say, Utterson, you see this property here?" "Not long ago, a most remarkable event led me here. I'm surprised I've never told you." Utterson: "Yes, we walk past it once a week, cousin." "Then tell me now.")

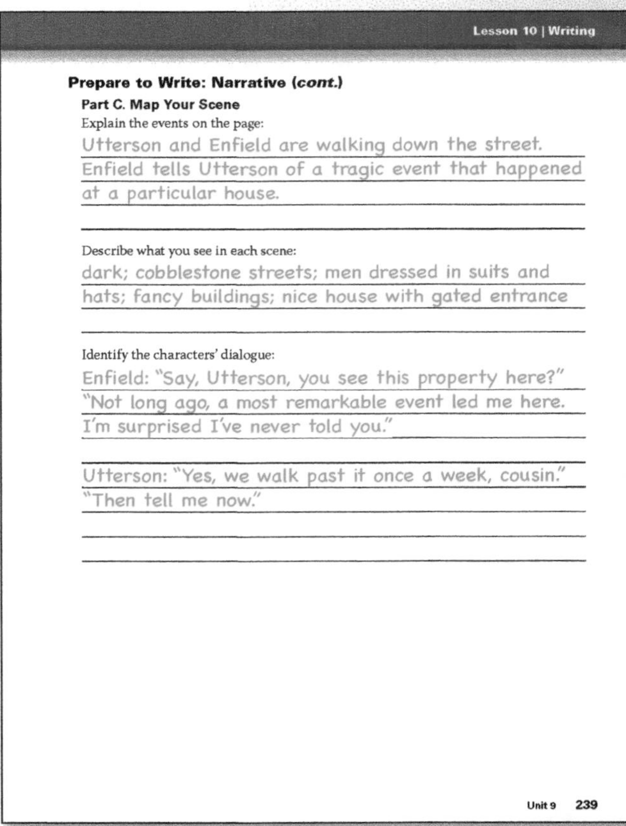

Lesson 10 | Writing

Prepare to Write: Narrative (*cont.*)

Part C. Map Your Scene

Explain the events on the page:

Utterson and Enfield are walking down the street. Enfield tells Utterson of a tragic event that happened at a particular house.

Describe what you see in each scene:

dark; cobblestone streets; men dressed in suits and hats; fancy buildings; nice house with gated entrance

Identify the characters' dialogue:

Enfield: "Say, Utterson, you see this property here?" "Not long ago, a most remarkable event led me here. I'm surprised I've never told you."

Utterson: "Yes, we walk past it once a week, cousin." "Then tell me now."

Unit 9 239

Have students complete the three steps on their page. As they do this, write the following dialogue on the board.

> *"Say, Utterson," asked Richard Enfield, "you see this property here?"*

"Yes," responded Utterson, "we walk past it once a week, cousin."

Enfield continued, "Not long ago, a most remarkable event led me here. I'm surprised I've never told you."

"Then tell me now," implored Utterson.

Part D. Upgrade the Dialogue

Direct students to the dialogue upgrade chart and review the word choices. Think about the work we've done in Masterpiece Sentences to upgrade word choices. To add variety and dimension to the dialogue, reference the chart to paint the verbs used in identifying speakers.

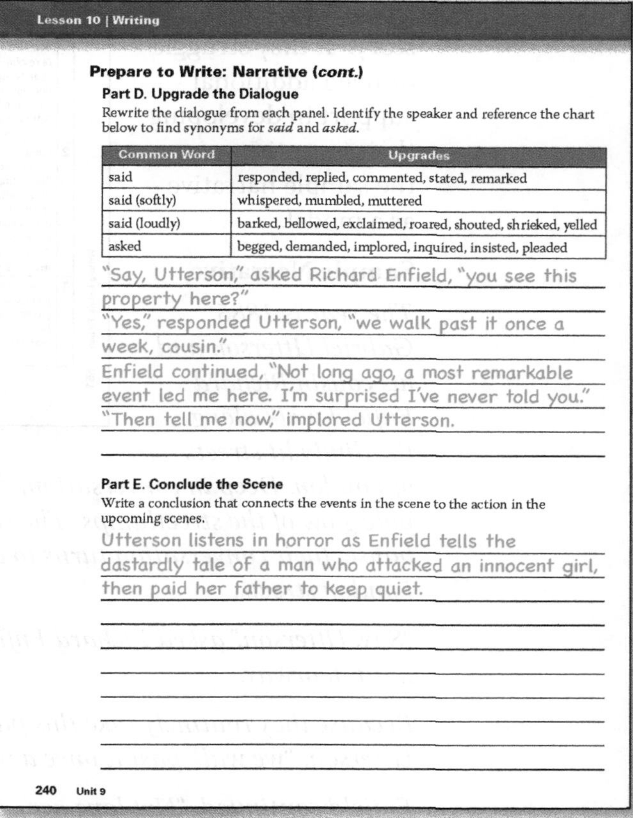

Lesson 10 | Writing

Prepare to Write: Narrative (*cont.*)

Part D. Upgrade the Dialogue

Rewrite the dialogue from each panel. Identify the speaker and reference the chart below to find synonyms for *said* and *asked*.

Common Word	Upgrades
said	responded, replied, commented, stated, remarked
said (softly)	whispered, mumbled, muttered
said (loudly)	barked, bellowed, exclaimed, roared, shouted, shrieked, yelled
asked	begged, demanded, implored, inquired, insisted, pleaded

"Say, Utterson," asked Richard Enfield, "you see this property here?"

"Yes," responded Utterson, "we walk past it once a week, cousin."

Enfield continued, "Not long ago, a most remarkable event led me here. I'm surprised I've never told you."

"Then tell me now," implored Utterson.

Part E. Conclude the Scene

Write a conclusion that connects the events in the scene to the action in the upcoming scenes.

Utterson listens in horror as Enfield tells the dastardly tale of a man who attacked an innocent girl, then paid her father to keep quiet.

240 Unit 9

Have students write the dialogue for their page. Have volunteers share their dialogue. Compare the verb choices made by the students, reinforcing the power of *painting* those verbs.

Part E. Conclude the Scene

To conclude the scene, we will need to connect what is happening on this page with what happens on the next one or two pages.

Verbally conclude your narrative by directing students to the second page in the novel.

Utterson listens in horror as Enfield tells the dastardly tale of a man who attacked an innocent girl, then paid her father to keep quiet.

Have students write their conclusion.

Write

Have students consult the Six Traits of Writing: Fiction Rubric on page 551 as they write their story. If they struggle or need additional support in developing their narrative, use the sample narrative as a model.

Six Traits of Writing: Fiction

	Ideas and Development	Organization	Voice and Audience Awareness	Word Choice	Sentence Fluency	Language Conventions
4	Clear plot events, as well as a readily identifiable conflict/problem and setting. The climax and resolution are clear. Rich details and sensory description make characters come to life. No irrelevant material.	Beginning grabs reader's attention. Logically sequenced plot. Story transitions link events. Conclusion caps off story and does not leave the reader hanging.	Strong sense of person and purpose behind the words. Brings story to life.	Words are specific, accurate, and vivid. Word choice enhances meaning and reader's enjoyment.	Writes complete sentences with varied sentence patterns and beginnings.	There are no major grammar errors. There are few errors in spelling, capitalization, or punctuation.
3	Identifiable plot events. Conflict/problem may not be entirely clear. The climax or resolution may not be clear. Some details/sensory description. Characters present but may not be fully developed. Setting may be missing. Limited irrelevant material.	Beginning interests reader. Plot somewhat logically sequenced but may lack one story element such as climax or satisfying conclusion. Story transitions link some events.	Some sense of person and purpose behind the words.	Words are correctly used but may be somewhat general and unspecific.	Writes complete sentences with some expansion. Limited variety.	There are a few grammar errors. There are a few errors in spelling, capitalization, or punctuation.
2	Limited plot and/or the conflict/problem is not clear. The setting, climax, and/or resolution may not be apparent. There are insufficient details and description. Characterization is weak. Too repetitious or too much irrelevant material.	Beginning does not capture reader's interest. Plot underdeveloped and two or more story elements (setting, initiating event, climax, resolution) missing. Story transitions missing.	Little sense of person and purpose behind the words.	Word choice limited. Words may be used inaccurately or repetitively.	Writes mostly simple and/or awkwardly constructed sentences. May include some run-ons and fragments.	There are many grammar or spelling errors. There are quite a few errors in capitalization and punctuation.
1	Does not address the prompt or the plot, conflict/problem are not discernible. Description, details, and characterization are missing.	Text has no evident structure. Lack of organization seriously interferes with meaning.	No sense of person or purpose behind the words.	Extremely limited range of words. Restricted vocabulary impedes message.	Numerous run-ons and/or sentence fragments interfere with meaning.	There are many spelling and grammar errors. There are many errors in capitalization and punctuation.

Writing Rubric: Fiction 551

Writing Rubric: Fiction

Sample Narrative

The year is 1885. Gabriel Utterson and his cousin Richard Enfield walk along the dimly lit streets of London. Deep in conversation, their path is illuminated by a few windows and the pale glow of the streetlamps. The streets are empty, and as they pass by a particular house, their conversation turns to a tale of horror. Terrible secrets lie hidden in the dark London streets.

"Say, Utterson," asked Richard Enfield, "you see this property here?" Enfield points to an unlit doorway.

Because they routinely take this path, the doorway is a familiar one. "Yes," responded Utterson, "we walk past it once a week, cousin."

Enfield continued, "Not long ago, a most remarkable event led me here. I'm surprised I've never told you." The two gentlemen stop walking to linger in the dark street. Utterson studies the expression on Enfield's face as his cousin's thoughts return to the horrific event. He has Utterson's undivided attention.

"Then tell me now," implored Utterson.

Utterson listens in horror as Enfield tells the dastardly tale of a man who attacked an innocent girl, then paid her father to keep quiet.

Evaluate Writing

Direct students to page 241 in their Student Books and read the information in the checklist. Notice that this checklist is different than the previous checklists. This checklist is specifically for narrative writing. It is a tool you can use to evaluate your writing and make sure you are using good technique. Have individuals quickly assess their writing, then have partners evaluate each other's writing based on the checklist.

Note: Use Six Traits of Writing Scoring Rubric: Fiction on page 546 of this book to assess students' writing. A printable version is located online in the Teacher Resources.

Six Traits of Writing: Fiction

Lesson 10 | Writing

The Narrative Writer's Checklist

Trait	Yes	No	Did the writer . . .?
Ideas and Content			include characters, setting, plot
			create an opening that grabs the reader's attention
			include enough description so that the reader can picture the characters and setting
			include dialogue between characters
Organization			create an initiating event, conflict (or rising action), and climax
			include a resolution, as well as a conclusion that ties everything up
			create a clear sequence of events
Voice and Audience Awareness			think about the audience and purpose for writing
			write in a clear and engaging way that makes the audience want to read the work; select a point of view (1st or 3rd person) and maintain it consistently
Word Choice			find a unique way to say things
			use words that are lively and specific to the content
Sentence Fluency			write complete sentences
			expand some sentences using the steps of Masterpiece Sentences
			use compound sentence elements and compound sentences
Conventions			capitalize words correctly:
			capitalize the first word of each sentence
			capitalize proper nouns, including people's names
			punctuate correctly:
			end sentences with a period, question mark, or exclamation mark
			use an apostrophe for possessive nouns and contractions
			use commas and/or semicolons correctly
			use grammar correctly:
			use the correct verb tense
			make sure the verb agrees with the subject in number
			use correct spelling

Unit 9 241

Reading

Objectives

- Self-correct as comprehension of text deepens.
- Answer questions to demonstrate comprehension of text.
- Engage in class discussion.
- Identify the enduring understandings from a piece of text.
- Determine the effect of shifting point of view and flashbacks in literature.
- Analyze the way in which an author creates suspense.

Revisit Passage Comprehension

Direct students back to pages 204–206 in their Student Books. Have students review their answers and make any necessary changes. Then, have partners share their answers and collaborate to perfect them.

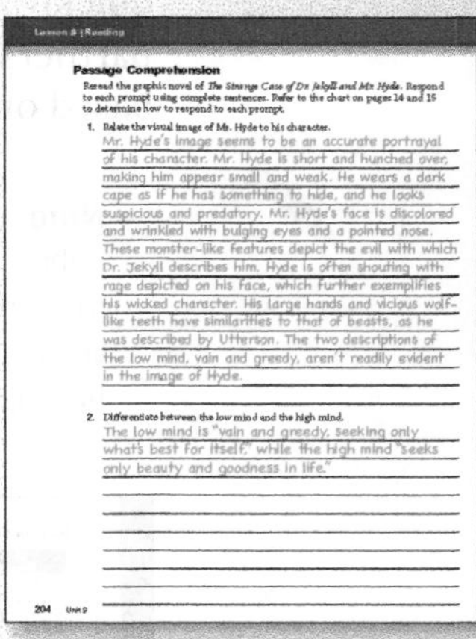

Lesson 8 | Reading

Passage Comprehension

Reread the graphic novel of *The Strange Case of Dr Jekyll and Mr Hyde*. Respond to each prompt using complete sentences. Refer to the chart on pages 14 and 15 to determine how to respond to each prompt.

1. Relate the visual image of Mr. Hyde to his character.
   Mr. Hyde's image seems to be an accurate portrayal of his character. Mr. Hyde is short and hunched over, making him appear small and weak. He wears a dark cape as if he has something to hide, and he looks suspicious and predatory. Mr. Hyde's face is discolored and wrinkled with bulging eyes and a pointed nose. These monster-like features depict the evil with which Dr. Jekyll describes him. Hyde is often shouting with rage depicted on his face, which further exemplifies his wicked character. His large hands and vicious wolf-like teeth have similarities to that of beasts, as he was described by Utterson. The two descriptions of the low mind, vain and greedy, aren't readily evident in the image of Hyde.
2. Differentiate between the low mind and the high mind.
   The low mind is "vain and greedy, seeking only what's best for itself," while the high mind "seeks only beauty and goodness in life."

204 Unit 9

Author's Purpose

Direct students back to page 137 in their Student Books. Let's review. What type of text is the story of Dr. Jekyll and Mr. Hyde? Fiction or nonfiction? (fiction)

Every author has a purpose for writing. Why did the author write this fiction graphic novel? What was his purpose? (The author wants to entertain and maybe even scare us.) Record your answers.

Point of View

Let's review point of view. Consider Chapters 1–4. From whose point of view is the story told? (Utterson) How does point of view change in Chapter 5? (The letter of confession is written from Jekyll's point of view.) Record your answers.

Have partners discuss the author's purpose for the change in point of view. Use the following questions to lead students toward the idea that the author used the particular sequencing and point of view to create suspense.

1. Why didn't the author tell the entire story chronologically from Jekyll's point of view?
2. Why are flashbacks used frequently?

Enduring Understandings

Reread the Big Idea questions.

Can people control their thoughts? Explain.

To what degree do our thoughts influence our actions? Explain.

Generate a class discussion about the questions and the answers students came up with in Lesson 6. Have them consider whether their answers have changed any after reading the text.

Use the following talking points to foster conversation. Then, have students write their enduring understandings from the unit.

- Consider this quote by Mahatma Gandhi: "Your beliefs become your thoughts, your thoughts become your words, your words become your actions, your actions become your habits, your habits become your values, your values become your destiny."
- Dr. Jekyll's thoughts got out of control. Those thoughts turned into spoken and written words, which later turned into aggressive and violent actions. Soon, Dr. Jekyll wasn't able to control the thoughts or actions of the evil Mr. Hyde, which caused more than one death. Over time, Dr. Jekyll's reputation changed among his friends and his staff. Dr. Jekyll's thoughts influenced his actions, which changed his reputation or the way that people thought of him.

What we read should make us think. Use our discussion and your thoughts about the text to determine what you will "walk away with." Has it made you think about a personal experience or someone you know? Has your perspective or opinion on a specific topic changed? Do you have any lingering thoughts or questions? Write these ideas as your enduring understandings. What will you take with you from this text?

*Assign online Unit 9 **Content Mastery** quizzes and **Power Pass** from the Text Training link on the left menu of your teacher dashboard.*

Discuss the enduring understandings with the class. If time permits, have students post a personal response from their enduring understandings to the online class wall.

Unit 10 Unit Plan

Primary Texts:
North High School letter

Text type: letter; persuasive

"Say Yes to Free Dress!"

Text type: persuasive

***LANGUAGE! Live* Online**

Grammar Practice
- Use gerunds correctly.
- Use present and past participles correctly.
- Distinguish between transitive and intransitive verbs.
- Identify and correct passive voice.
- Determine the meaning of punctuation.
- Identify and correct sentence fragments in writing.
- Identify and understand the function of noncount nouns.

Vocabulary Practice
- Determine the meaning of derivations of words.
- Increase depth of word knowledge through the use of analogies.

Content Mastery
- Demonstrate an understanding of . . .
  - word meaning by answering questions and using words in sentences.
  - gerunds and participles.
  - transitive and intransitive verbs.

Word Study
- Blend, read, and spell multisyllabic words with Latin suffixes -ous, -ive, -or, -age, -ure, -ant, -ent, -ance, -ence, -ist, and -ian; and more than one suffix.
- Read connected text to build fluency.

Lesson 1	Lesson 2
Reading • Determine and discuss the topic of a text. • Determine and discuss the author's purpose. • Use text features to preview text. **Vocabulary** • Evaluate word knowledge. • Determine the meaning of key passage vocabulary. **Reading** • Read a letter and formal policy. • Monitor comprehension during text reading.	**Vocabulary** • Review key passage vocabulary. **Grammar** • Identify the function and purpose of gerunds. • Identify the functions and purpose of participles. • Identify multiple functions of words. **Writing** • Distinguish between transitive and intransitive verbs.

Lesson 6	Lesson 7
Reading • Determine and discuss the topic of a text. • Determine and discuss the author's purpose. • Use text features to preview text. **Vocabulary** • Evaluate word knowledge. • Determine the meaning of key passage vocabulary. **Reading** • Read persuasive text. • Monitor comprehension during text reading.	**Vocabulary** • Review key passage vocabulary. **Reading** • Determine how to respond to prompts. • Use critical thinking skills to write responses to prompts about text. • Support written answers with evidence from text. • Use personal knowledge as evidence in support of an author's claim. • Develop counterclaims against an author based on personal experience. **Writing** • Identify story elements for writing.

Writing Project, Units 10–12: Narrative Writing

Lesson 3	Lesson 4	Lesson 5
Reading • Reread persuasive text for comprehension. • Establish a purpose for reading text. • Use critical thinking skills to write responses to prompts about text. • Support written answers with evidence from text. • Make personal connections to text.	**Vocabulary** • Review key passage vocabulary. **Reading** • Read persuasive text with purpose and understanding. • Answer questions to demonstrate comprehension of text. • Identify and explain explicit details from text. • Monitor comprehension of text during reading. • Identify and determine the meaning of puns used by an author. • Analyze the claims made by an author and determine if they are accurate and supported with evidence. • Identify rhetorical fallacies in persuasive text. • Identify the antecedents of pronouns in writing.	**Vocabulary** • Review key passage vocabulary. **Writing** • Use text to write coherent paragraphs in response to reading. • Demonstrate understanding the constructs of argumentation through writing. • Write a persuasive letter. **Reading** • Self-correct as comprehension of text deepens. • Answer questions to demonstrate comprehension of text. • Engage in class discussion. • Identify the enduring understandings from a piece of text.

Lesson 8	Lesson 9	Lesson 10
Reading • Establish a purpose for rereading persuasive text. • Monitor comprehension during text reading. • Use critical thinking skills to write responses to prompts about text. • Support written answers with evidence from text. • Use personal knowledge as evidence in support of an author's claim. • Develop counterclaims against an author based on personal experience. • Use multiple texts to develop counterclaims against an argument.	**Vocabulary** • Review key passage vocabulary. **Reading** • Read persuasive text with purpose and understanding. • Answer questions to demonstrate comprehension of text. • Identify and explain explicit details from text. • Monitor comprehension of text during reading. • Objectively summarize text. • Analyze a summary for accuracy and content. • Analyze how an author distinguishes position from that of others. • Analyze an author's response to conflicting viewpoints. • Analyze the presentation of differing viewpoints on the same issue. • Identify where texts disagree. • Identify rhetorical fallacies in text. • Determine the validity of an author's claims and counterclaims. ** See pg. 342 for additional lesson objectives.*	**Vocabulary** • Review key passage vocabulary. **Writing** • Use multiple texts to write coherently. • Use a process to write. • Write a short story that contains the requisite story elements. • Use a rubric to guide and evaluate writing. **Reading** • Self-correct as comprehension of text deepens. • Answer questions to demonstrate comprehension of text. • Engage in class discussion. • Identify the enduring understandings from a piece of text.

Unit 10

Lesson 1

Lesson Opener

Before the lesson, choose one of the following activities to write on the board or post on the *LANGUAGE! Live* Class Wall online.

- *List five pros and five cons of school uniforms.*
- *Write two sentences about rules in this school that you would change if you could. Use the relative pronouns* that *or* which *in each sentence.*
- *Write three sentences about your weekend. Use an adjective clause in one sentence, an adverb clause in one sentence, and a noun clause in one sentence. Identify the clauses.*

Reading

Objectives

- Determine and discuss the topic of a text.
- Determine and discuss the author's purpose.
- Use text features to preview text.

Passage Introduction

Direct students to page 243 in their Student Books. Discuss the content focus.

Content Focus

dress code

What do you think you will read about in this text? (Answers will vary.) What does it mean to have a dress code? Provide sharing time.

Type of Text

Text can be divided into two categories: informational and literature. Discuss the differences. In the last unit, we read one nonfiction and one fiction piece on DID. In this unit, we are going to read about dress codes. Look at the first page of the text and determine what type of text it is. Write your answer on the page.

Unit 10

Lesson 1 | Reading

Let's Focus: North High School letter

Content Focus
dress code

Type of Text
letter; persuasive; policy

Author's Name Principal Dogan

Author's Purpose to inform others about a new dress code policy and persuade them of the need

Big Ideas
Consider the following Big Ideas. Write your answer for each question.

Is a person's success in life affected by the way he or she dresses? Explain.

Are people treated differently based on their appearance? Explain.

Informational Preview Checklist: North High School letter on pages 245–252.

- ☐ Title: What clue does it provide about the passage?
- ☐ Pictures and Captions: What additional information is added here?
- ☐ Headings: How is the information organized?
- ☐ Features: What other text features do you notice?

Enduring Understandings
After reading the text . . .

Unit 10 243

Author's Purpose

Have students glance at the text. Who is the author of the text? (Principal Dogan) Prior to reading, make an educated guess as to what the author's purpose for writing is. After you finish, you will return to this section and revise your answer if you need to. Have students write the answers on the page.

Play the Unit 10 Text Training video found in the Teacher Resources online.

Before we read the North High School letter, we will watch a short video to help build our background knowledge. Play the Unit 10 Text Training video. Have partners discuss what they learned from the video.

> **Note:** If you are unable to play the video, Background Information about compulsory education and dress codes can be found in the Teacher Resources online.

Read the Big Idea questions aloud.

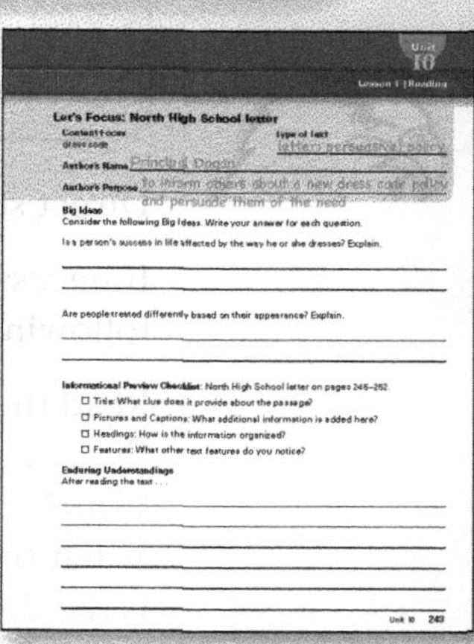

Unit 10
Lesson 1 | Reading

Let's Focus: North High School letter

Content Focus: dress code

Type of Text: letter; persuasive; policy

Author's Name: Principal Dogan

Author's Purpose: to inform others about a new dress code policy and persuade them of the need

Big Ideas
Consider the following Big Ideas. Write your answer for each question.

Is a person's success in life affected by the way he or she dresses? Explain.

Are people treated differently based on their appearance? Explain.

Informational Preview Checklist: North High School letter on pages 245–252.

- ☐ Title: What clue does it provide about the passage?
- ☐ Pictures and Captions: What additional information is added here?
- ☐ Headings: How is the information organized?
- ☐ Features: What other text features do you notice?

Enduring Understandings
After reading the text . . .

Unit 10 243

Big Ideas

Is a person's success in life affected by the way he or she dresses? Explain.

Are people treated differently based on their appearance? Explain.

As a class, consider the two Big Idea questions. After discussing each question, have students write an answer. We'll come back to these questions after we finish reading the text. You can add to your answers as you gain information and perspective.

Preview

Read the Preview Checklist on page 243. Follow the Preview Procedure outlined below.

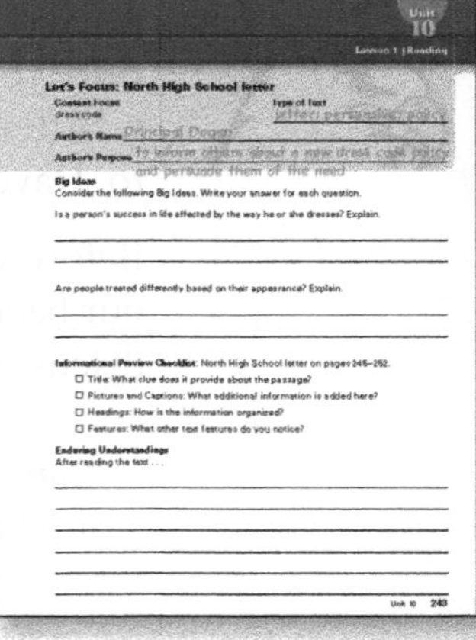

Preview Procedure

- Group students with partners or in triads.
- Have students count off as 1s or 2s. The 1s will become the student leaders. If working with triads, the third students become 3s.
- The student leaders will preview the text in addition to managing the checklist and pacing.
- The 2s and 3s will preview the text with 1s.
- Direct 1s to open their Student Books to page 243 and 2s and 3s to open their Student Books to page 245. This allows students to look at a few different pages at one time without turning back and forth.

Direct students to page 245. Have students preview the text.

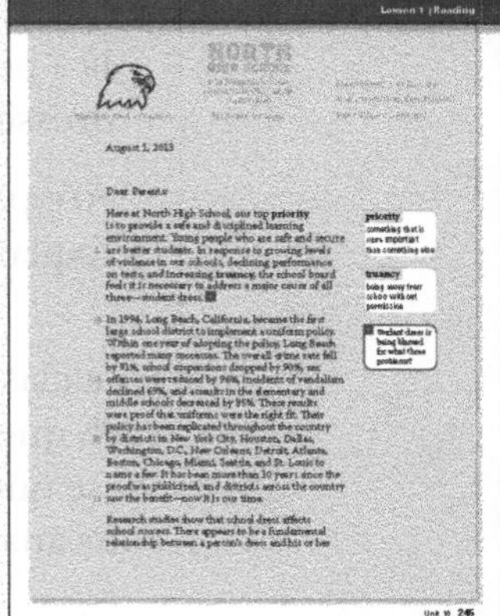

If necessary, guide students in a short preview using the following talking points.

Read the letterhead to determine where the letter is from. (North High School in Pleasantville, Ohio) Who is the letter from? (Principal Dogan) Read the last paragraph of the letter. What time of year do you think this letter was sent? (fall) What is the difference between a policy and a letter? (A policy is a plan of action written by a person or a team of people. A letter is a communication to someone from someone else.)

Have partners predict what kind of dress code the students will be asked to follow.

Vocabulary

Objectives

- Evaluate word knowledge.
- Determine the meaning of key passage vocabulary.

Rate Vocabulary Knowledge

Direct students to page 244 in their Student Books. Let's take a look at the vocabulary words from the North High School letter. I am going to say each word aloud. You will repeat the word and write it in the third column. Then, you will rate your knowledge of the word. **Display the Vocabulary Rating Scale poster or write the information on the board. Review the meaning of each rating.**

Lesson 1 | Vocabulary

Key Passage Vocabulary: North High School letter

Read each word. Write the word in column 3. Then, circle a number to rate your knowledge of the word.

Read the Word	Part of Speech	Write the Word	Rate the Word
priority	(n)	priority	0 1 2 3
truancy	(n)	truancy	0 1 2 3
enforce	(v)	enforce	0 1 2 3
enhance	(v)	enhance	0 1 2 3
distracted	(adj)	distracted	0 1 2 3
principle	(n)	principle	0 1 2 3
resist	(v)	resist	0 1 2 3
appropriate	(adj)	appropriate	0 1 2 3
restrictive	(adj)	restrictive	0 1 2 3
consultation	(n)	consultation	0 1 2 3

244 Unit 10

Vocabulary Rating Scale

0—I have never heard the word before.

1—I have heard the word, but I'm not sure how to use it.

2—I am familiar with the word, but I'm not sure if I know the correct meaning.

3—I know the meaning of the word and can use it correctly in a sentence.

Remember, the points are there to help you know which words you need to focus on. By the end of this unit, you should be able to change all your ratings to a 3. That's the goal.

Read each word aloud and have students repeat it, write it, and rate it. Then, have volunteers who rated a word *2* or *3* use the word in an oral sentence.

Preteach Vocabulary

Explain that you will now take a closer look at the words. Follow the Preteach Procedure outlined below.

Preteach Procedure

This activity is intended to take only a short amount of time, so make it an oral exercise.

- Introduce each word as indicated on the word card.
- Read the definition and example sentences.
- Ask questions to clarify and deepen understanding.
- If time permits, allow students to share.

* If your students would benefit from copying the definitions, please have them do so in the vocabulary log in the back of the Student Books using the margin definitions in the passage selections. This should be done outside of instruction time.

priority (n)

Let's read the first word together. *Priority.*

Definition: If something is a *priority*, it is more important than something else. What means "something that is more important than something else"? (priority)

Example 1: Helping you develop strong reading skills is my top *priority.*

Example 2: Making sure our planet is healthy should be this generation's first *priority.*

Example 3: A *priority* for many teenagers is socializing.

Question 1: You need to write a paper for social studies, but you also want to watch a movie. Is watching the movie a *priority*? Yes or no? (no)

Question 2: A state government wants wind energy to become the state's top energy source. Is building wind turbines a *priority* of the state? Yes or no? (yes)

Pair Share: Turn to your partner and discuss what *priorities* each of you has today.

truancy (n)

Let's read the next word together. *Truancy.*

Definition: *Truancy* means "being away from school without permission." What means "being away from school without permission"? (truancy)

Example 1: Many schools take *truancy* very seriously and suspend students who have too many unexcused absences.

Example 2: *Truancy* is rarely a problem in classes that are interesting and enjoyable.

Example 3: Some people refer to *truancy* as "playing hooky."

Question 1: Rick leaves school for lunch and decides to skip his afternoon classes. Is this an example of *truancy*? Yes or no? (yes)

Question 2: You miss your first class because of a doctor's appointment. The doctor's office gives you a note that says you were there. Is this an example of *truancy*? Yes or no? (no)

Pair Share: Turn to your partner and discuss what you know about the *truancy* rules at our school.

2

enforce (v)

Let's read the next word together. *Enforce.*

Definition: To *enforce* a rule or a law is to make sure it is obeyed. What means "to make sure a rule or law is obeyed"? (enforce)

Example 1: In neighborhoods with a lot of dogs, it can be difficult to *enforce* leash laws.

Example 2: When I was growing up, my mom *enforced* a strict bedtime.

Example 3: Referees and umpires sometimes *enforce* good sportsmanship rules by throwing angry coaches out of a game.

Question 1: A teacher sees a student chewing gum but does nothing about it. Has the teacher *enforced* the school's "no gum" policy? Yes or no? (no)

Question 2: A cop pulls your older brother over for speeding. Has the cop *enforced* the speed limit? Yes or no? (yes)

Pair Share: Turn to your partner. Name a rule one of your teachers loves to *enforce.*

3

enhance (v)

Let's read the next word together. *Enhance.*

Definition: If you *enhance* something, you improve it. What means "to improve something"? (enhance)

Example 1: Polishing old silver can *enhance* its beauty.

Example 2: Taking the time to style your hair and wash your face will *enhance* your appearance.

Example 3: Adding just the right amount of salt to soup *enhances* its flavor.

Question 1: Does a well-tended flower garden *enhance* the "curb appeal" of a house? Yes or no? (yes)

Question 2: Right before a game, an athlete has an argument with her boyfriend. Will the argument *enhance* her performance? Yes or no? (no)

Pair Share: Turn to your partner and name something that would *enhance* this classroom.

distracted (adj)

Let's read the next word together. *Distracted.*

Definition: If you are *distracted*, you are not focused on what you should be focused on. What means "not focused on what you should be focused on"? (distracted)

Example 1: I get *distracted* when I'm trying to work and someone is playing loud music.

Example 2: People who are easily *distracted* take a long time to complete a task.

Example 3: If you tend to be *distracted* by digital devices, you should put them in another room before sitting down to study.

Question 1: You're trying to read but keep gazing out the window instead. Are you *distracted*? Yes or no? (yes)

Question 2: Your dad is sanding a table in the backyard. You have to call to him three times before he realizes you want his attention. Is he easily *distracted*? Yes or no? (no)

Pair Share: Turn to your partner and describe a situation in which you are easily *distracted.*

principle (n)

Let's read the next word together. *Principle.*

Definition: A *principle* is a belief about what is important or how you should act. What is "a belief about what is important or how you should act"? (a principle) The leader of a school is also called a *principal*. However, that word is spelled differently. It ends with the letters *-pal* instead of the letters *-ple*. Write the two words on the board and make sure students understand their different meanings.

Example 1: It is a *principle* of mine to count to 10 before saying something in anger.

Example 2: Children learn basic *principles*—such as loving your neighbor and doing your best—from their parents.

Example 3: A democracy is built on the *principles* of individual freedom and group responsibility.

Question 1: Pirates hijack ships and steal cargo. Do they have high moral *principles*? Yes or no? (no)

Question 2: Your mother expects you to be polite with older adults. Has she passed an important *principle* on to you? Yes or no? (yes)

Pair Share: Turn to your partner and name a *principle* you live by.

resist (v)

Let's read the next word together. *Resist.*

Definition: If you *resist* something, you want it but say "no" to it anyway. What word means "to say 'no' to something you want but shouldn't have"? (resist)

Example 1: It is impossible for me to *resist* the smell of hot, fresh popcorn in a movie theater.

Example 2: When someone says something hurtful, it's best to *resist* saying something hurtful in return; you might regret it later on.

Example 3: Financial advisers say it's best to *resist* buying something with credit and to pay cash for it instead.

Question 1: You have a cookie, and then you have another. Have you *resisted* the second cookie? Yes or no? (no)

Question 2: A friend calls with a tempting invitation, but you've promised to help your mom with a chore. You say "no thanks" and stay home with your mom. Have you *resisted* the outing with your friend? Yes or no? (yes)

Pair Share: Turn to your partner and name a movie or show that's hard for you to *resist* if you enter a room and see it on TV.

7

appropriate (adj)

Let's read the next word together. *Appropriate.*

Definition: If something is *appropriate*, it's fitting, or right for a certain time and place. What means "fitting; right for a certain time and place"? (appropriate)

Example 1: It is usually *appropriate* to wear a dark color to a funeral.

Example 2: It is not *appropriate* to answer a phone call in the middle of class.

Example 3: Until the mid-1900s, shorts were not considered *appropriate* clothing for women.

Question 1: Would it be *appropriate* to wear a monster costume to a Halloween party? Yes or no? (yes)

Question 2: Would it be *appropriate* to wear a monster costume to a job interview? Yes or no? (no)

Pair Share: With your partner, discuss two things it would be *appropriate* to say to someone who just won an award you were hoping to receive.

restrictive (adj)

Let's read the next word together. *Restrictive.*

Definition: If something is *restrictive*, it is limiting and keeps you from having full freedom. What word means "limiting; keeping someone from having full freedom"? (restrictive)

Example 1: Teenagers often find early curfews too *restrictive*.

Example 2: In the 1800s, women in high society wore *restrictive* corsets that were tightly laced to make their waistlines smaller.

Example 3: Rules relating to the use of free time are very *restrictive* in high-security prisons.

Question 1: Your aunt lets your cousins do whatever they want, whenever they want. Does your aunt have a *restrictive* parenting style? Yes or no? (no)

Question 2: You have to ride in a very small backseat with your two brothers for three hours. Is this *restrictive*? Yes or no? (yes)

Pair Share: Turn to your partner and describe a situation that a long-distance runner might find *restrictive*.

consultation (n)

Let's read the last word together. *Consultation.*

Definition: *Consultation* means "discussion" or "conversation." What word means "discussion; conversation"? (consultation)

Example 1: I usually make important decisions only after *consultation* with trusted friends.

Example 2: Students can change their schedules only through *consultation* with a school counselor.

Example 3: Women who think they want a certain haircut sometimes change their minds after a *consultation* with their stylist.

Question 1: You buy an expensive gadget without discussing the pros and cons of the purchase with anyone. Did you seek *consultation*? Yes or no? (no)

Question 2: You want to take an advanced music class but aren't sure you qualify. Would *consultation* with the teacher be a good idea? Yes or no? (yes)

Pair Share: Turn to your partner and describe a situation in which a person might seek *consultation* with a doctor.

10

Reading

Objectives

- Read a letter and formal policy.
- Monitor comprehension during text reading.

North High School Letter

Direct students to page 245 in their Student Books. Now that we have previewed vocabulary, it's time to read.

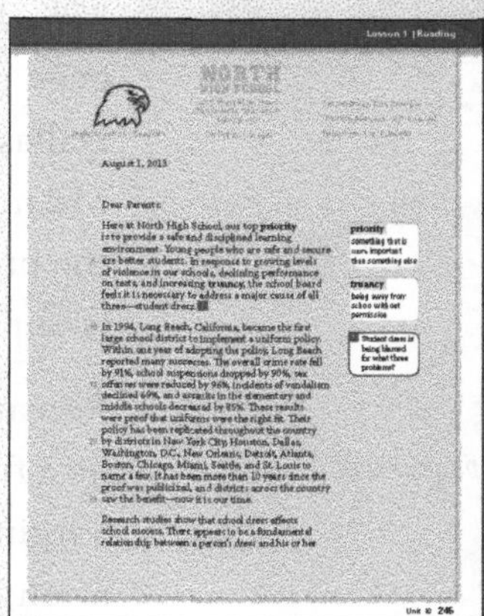

Lesson 1 | Reading

August 1, 2013

Dear Parents:

Here at North High School, our top **priority** is to provide a safe and disciplined learning environment. Young people who are safe and secure are better students. In response to growing levels of violence in our schools, declining performance on tests, and increasing **truancy**, the school board feels it is necessary to address a major cause of all three—student dress.

priority something that is more important than something else

truancy being away from school without permission

Student dress is being blamed for what three problems?

Unit 10 245

Guiding Students Toward Independent Reading

It is important that your students read as much and as often as they can. Assign readings that meet the needs of your students, based on your observations and data. This is a good opportunity to stretch your students. If students become frustrated, scaffold the reading with paired reading, choral reading, or a read-aloud.

Options for reading text:

- Teacher read-aloud
- Teacher-led or student-led choral read
- Paired read or independent read

Choose an option for reading the text. Have students read according to the option that you chose.

Remind students to pause at the numbers and consider the questions.

If you choose to read the text aloud or chorally, use the following text boxes and stop to ask questions and have students answer them.

SE p. 245, paragraph 1

August 1, 2013

Dear Parents:

Here at North High School, our top **priority** is to provide a safe and disciplined learning environment. Young people who are safe and secure are better students. In response to growing levels of violence in our schools, declining performance on tests, and increasing **truancy**, the school board feels it is necessary to address a major cause of all three—student dress.

1. Student dress is being blamed for what three problems?

SE p. 245, paragraphs 2-3

In 1994, Long Beach, California, became the first large school district to implement a uniform policy. Within one year of adopting the policy, Long Beach reported many successes. The overall crime rate fell by 91%, school suspensions dropped by 90%, sex offenses were reduced by 96%, incidents of vandalism declined 69%, and assaults in the elementary and middle schools decreased by 85%. These results were proof that uniforms were the right fit. Their policy has been replicated throughout the country by districts in New York City, Houston, Dallas, Washington, D.C., New Orleans, Detroit, Atlanta, Boston, Chicago, Miami, Seattle, and St. Louis to name a few. It has been more than 10 years since the proof was publicized, and districts across the country saw the benefit—now it is our time.

page break

Research studies show that school dress affects school success. There appears to be a fundamental relationship between a person's dress and his or her | behavior. Virginia Draa, an assistant professor at Youngstown State University, reviewed attendance rates, as well as graduation and proficiency pass rates, at 64 public high schools in Ohio. Her study concluded that those schools with uniform policies improved in attendance, graduation, and suspension rates.

2. What impact did uniforms have on Ohio high schools?

SE p. 246, paragraphs 1–3

Our dress is material. It affects our performance and motivation. People who work out of their home feel their workday is more productive when they are dressed professionally. They feel better about themselves, which makes them feel as though what they are producing is of higher value.

We have had a dress code across the district for many years. However, enforcing the dress code by sending violators to the office has been a problem. They call home and wait for clothes to be brought to school. Sometimes, they get an in-school suspension. All this has only accomplished one thing—less time actively engaged in learning.

Rather than rewriting a dress code that is difficult to **enforce**, the school board has adopted a uniform policy for all grade levels across the district. Even former President Bill Clinton said in a radio address, "If it means teenagers will stop killing each other over designer jackets, then our public schools should be able to require their students to wear school uniforms." The adoption of this school uniform policy will promote school safety, increase learning time, and **enhance** the learning environment—putting North High School on the path to academic excellence.

3. What option was considered prior to establishing a uniform policy?

SE p. 246, paragraph 4

The uniform policy will eliminate a lot of problems we have had in the past with school dress. Students' choice of dress has caused other students to feel threatened, intimidated, and even **distracted**. | Baggy pants, clothing of certain colors, bandannas, and an emphasis on one side of the body (e.g., one pant leg pulled up) can be interpreted as gang dress. Dressing as a gang member intimidates other students and spreads fear. This makes an environment focused on academic success nearly impossible to achieve.

page break

SE p. 247, paragraphs 1–4

Pants with large pockets, coats, purses, and backpacks can hold a weapon or drugs. Students are unable to feel safe and at ease in their classrooms when they are worried about the contents of another student's pockets or bags.

Though most offenders disagree on the definition of "seductive," seductive clothing *is* a great distraction. Bare midriffs, shoulders, backs, and legs, as well as overly tight garments, visible underwear, and clothes that draw attention to the bosom or buttocks (i.e., V-neck shirts and pants with words on the backside) cause students to lose their focus and think about other things.

Clothing advertising cigarettes or alcohol may persuade other students to try these controlled substances. Television has restricted the advertisement of cigarettes and alcohol when minors are typically watching TV, so it doesn't make sense to allow students to advertise these things in school—a gathering place for minors. Clothing that depicts violence or foul language may also persuade students to act in the same manner.

Name-brand and designer labels cause problems as well. Some students have missed school because they didn't have fashionable clothes to wear or the one pair of designer jeans was being laundered. If students are not distracted by the distinction | between the "haves" and the "have nots," they will be able to zero in on what is truly important—learning and growing.

page break

4. In what ways are clothes a distraction during school?

SE p. 248, paragraphs 1–2

When a child feels safe and unthreatened in school, he or she makes better grades and is a much happier person. Students are excited to come to school when they are dressed well, and they will embrace better moral **principles**. The potential benefits of school uniforms include:

- improving attendance;
- decreasing economic discrimination;
- decreasing violence and theft;
- decreasing gang violence;
- improving self-discipline;
- helping parents and students **resist** peer pressure;
- helping students concentrate on their schoolwork; and
- helping staff recognize intruders who come to the school.

Thank you for taking the time to read this letter. I thank you in advance for your cooperation in making our new uniform policy a success. Please read the uniform policy on the following pages, and prepare your child for the upcoming school year.

Sincerely,

Principal Dogan

5. How does a child need to feel while in school to make good grades and be happy?

SE p. 249, paragraphs 1–3

Uniform Policy

School Uniforms

You are required to wear a school uniform at all times while attending school or any school-sponsored activity (unless special permission is given).

A. Basic Uniforms

Girls: The basic uniform for girls is a long- or short-sleeved gray polo shirt with plain solid-colored brown pants or skorts of cotton fabric. Dresses may be worn but must be solid brown with short or long sleeves and follow the other requirements of this policy. If skorts or a dress is worn, legs must be covered in nude-colored full-length panty hose. Wear brown leather shoes that tie or buckle.

Boys: The basic uniform for boys is a long- or short-sleeved gray polo shirt with plain solid-colored brown pants of cotton fabric with a brown leather belt. Wear brown leather shoes that tie or buckle.

6. What is the difference between acceptable dress for boys and acceptable dress for girls?

SE p. 249, paragraphs 4–5

Clothing must be the **appropriate** size for you, not oversized or undersized. The waist of the garment shall be worn so that the waistband is at the waist and not below the waist. You may not wear baggy/saggy pants.

Shirts must cover the midriff, back, and sides at all times; should be fastened with no visible cleavage or undergarments; and may not have a visible manufacturer's logo.

SE p. 250, paragraph 1

Skorts and dresses shall be worn no shorter than "mid-thigh." Mid-thigh is determined by placing your student ID at the top of the knee. The garment must touch the ID (using normal posture).

7. What body parts can be visible?

SE p. 250, paragraphs 2–7

B. Alternatives

In addition to the above basic uniform, the principal may designate:

1. school-sponsored T-shirts with a crew neck; and
2. more **restrictive** dress code requirements, if approved by the school's administration.

Each school will provide students/parents with a copy of the school's dress code.

C. Exceptions

If you enter the school district after the start of the school year, you will have a grace period of ten (10) school days before being required to wear the school uniform.

You may wear special clothing necessary for a school-sponsored activity, as permitted by the principal.

If you are enrolled in a career academy, you may wear the uniform of that program.

The superintendent, in **consultation** with the principal, may waive the school uniform policy on a case-by-case basis for reasons such as, but not limited to, medical necessity or sincerely held religious belief.

8. What are the exceptions to the rule?

SE p. 251, paragraphs 1–2

D. Outer Garments

You may wear coats, jackets, sweatshirts, sweaters, or other appropriate outer garments when necessary due to weather conditions or for other legitimate reasons. The outer garments must be of the appropriate size for you and shall not be overly baggy or violate any other provisions of the dress code.

All backpacks and purses must be see-through.

9. Why do bags need to be see-through? Could this ever be embarrassing?

SE p. 251, paragraph 3

You may not wear:

1. clothing that is not properly fastened;
2. clothing that is torn or has holes, or pants that are frayed;
3. visible undergarments, sleepwear, or outer garments traditionally designed as undergarments such as boxer shorts or bras;
4. outer garments or accessories (such as backpacks, jewelry, and purses) that have slogans, signs, images, or symbols that:
   - promote drugs, alcohol, tobacco, gang identification, weapons, or inappropriate behavior, or
   - denigrate or promote discrimination for or against an individual or group.
5. hats, headgear, or other head coverings, except when approved by office staff;
6. body-piercing jewelry, except for earrings on the ears; all other body-piercings must be removed or concealed;
7. jewelry or accessories that may be used as weapons, such as chains, spiked jewelry, or arm bands;
8. unnatural hair coloring (colors other than blonde, brown, black, or auburn);
9. combs, curlers, or hair picks; or
10. sunglasses inside the school building.

10. What accessories CAN be worn?

SE p. 252, paragraphs 1–2

E. Discipline

The principal or designee has the authority to decide whether your clothing complies with school board policy.

If the principal determines that your clothing does not comply with school board policy, your parent/guardian may be asked to bring an appropriate change of clothes to school or you may be asked to leave an after-school activity. You may also receive a disciplinary consequence for violating the school's dress code policy. Repeated violations may result in progressively more serious consequences.

11. What are the consequences for failing to comply with the dress code?

For confirmation of engagement, have partners share two things about the dress code that they like and two things that they don't like.

Lesson 2

Lesson Opener

Before the lesson, choose one of the following activities to write on the board or post on the *LANGUAGE! Live* Class Wall online.

- *List five things in the NHS dress code policy that you think are unreasonable.*
- *Write five sentences about the way students dress in your school. Use a semicolon in each sentence. Remember that both sides of the semicolon can stand alone.*
- *Change the following sentences to active voice.*

  The student was told by the principal to change his shirt.

  Jeff was taken to the office by his teacher for refusing to tuck in his shirt.

  A weapon was found in the student's see-through backpack by his first period teacher.

  The teachers were instructed to follow the dress code policy by the superintendent.

Vocabulary

Objective

- Review key passage vocabulary.

Review Passage Vocabulary

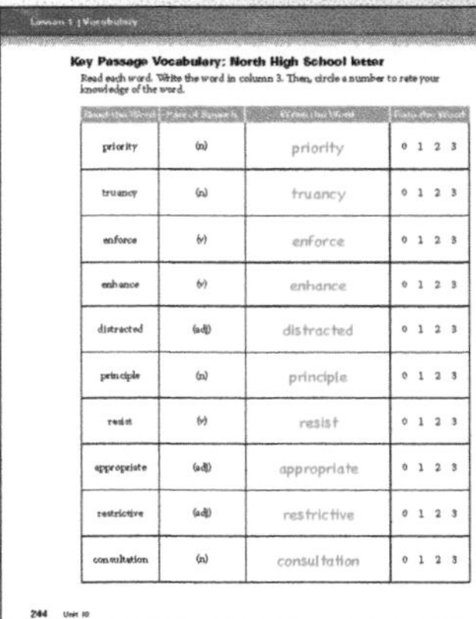
Lesson 1 | Vocabulary

Key Passage Vocabulary: North High School letter

Read each word. Write the word in column 3. Then, circle a number to rate your knowledge of the word.

Read the Word	Part of Speech	Write the Word	Rate the Word
priority	(n)	priority	0 1 2 3
truancy	(n)	truancy	0 1 2 3
enforce	(v)	enforce	0 1 2 3
enhance	(v)	enhance	0 1 2 3
distracted	(adj)	distracted	0 1 2 3
principle	(n)	principle	0 1 2 3
resist	(v)	resist	0 1 2 3
appropriate	(adj)	appropriate	0 1 2 3
restrictive	(adj)	restrictive	0 1 2 3
consultation	(n)	consultation	0 1 2 3

244 Unit 10

Direct students to page 244 in their Student Books. Use the following questions to review the vocabulary words in the North High School letter. Have students answer each question using the vocabulary word or indicating its meaning in a complete sentence.

- If a safe, disciplined environment is the top *priority* at North High, what is it? (If it's a priority, it's one of the most important things.) After a safe environment, what should be the top *priority* of a high school, in your opinion? (Possible response: Another top priority should be inspiring students to do their best.)
- In the letter, the principal admits that *truancy* levels are on the rise. What is happening more often? (If truancy levels are on the rise, students are skipping class without permission more often.) What does the principal say will help solve the *truancy* problem, and why? (She says that uniforms will help solve the truancy problem because there is a relationship between how a person dresses and how he or she acts.)
- According to the principal, does sending dress code violators to the office *enforce* the dress code in a useful way? Why or why not? (No, it doesn't enforce the dress code, or make students follow it, because the violators sit in the office and wait for clothes to be brought to them or are suspended—both of which mean less time learning.) Why might a uniform policy be easier to *enforce*? (A uniform policy would be easier to enforce because violations would be more obvious, which in turn would prompt students to violate the uniform policy less often.)

- According to the principal, does skimpy dress *enhance* the learning environment or make it worse? (No, it doesn't enhance the learning environment.) What type of clothing might *enhance* the learning environment? (Answers will vary, but should include the word *enhance*.)
- The principal claims that choice of dress can make students *distracted*. In other words, it can make students what? (Distracted students are unable to concentrate on learning.) Why might gang-related clothing make other students *distracted*? (It might make them distracted by causing them to worry about their own safety or to think about the activities of gangs.)
- If students come to school well dressed, the principal writes, their moral *principles* will improve. What does she mean? (She means that if students are well dressed, they will act better.) Does the principal hope parents share her *principles*? Why or why not? (She does hope parents share her principles, or beliefs, about clothing because she wants everyone to support the new uniform policy.)
- What does the principal say uniforms will help students *resist*? (She says uniforms will help students resist peer pressure.) If you *resist* peer pressure, what do you do? Give an example. (If you resist peer pressure, you say "no" to what your peers are pressuring you to do. Possible examples include drinking, using drugs, skipping school, and bullying others.)
- According to the new uniform policy, students' clothing must be of an *appropriate* size. Appropriately sized clothing is not too what? (Appropriately sized clothing is not too small or too large.) What would be an *appropriate* outer garment on a very cold day? (On a very cold day, an appropriate outer garment would be a coat.)
- The principal reserves the right to put more *restrictive* dress code requirements in place, if necessary. What kind of dress code requirements would these be? (More restrictive dress code requirements would be those that gave students even less freedom with their clothing choices.) Would you find a dress code that allowed students to wear only polka dots *restrictive*? Why or why not? (Yes, such a dress code would be restrictive because it's not easy to find clothes that have only polka dots and such a code severely limits students' dress options.)
- According to the new policy, the superintendent, in *consultation* with the principal, may decide that the policy does not apply to certain students in certain situations. What do the superintendent and the principal do when they are in *consultation* about the dress code? (When they are in consultation about the dress code, they discuss it.) Before making the decision to implement the dress code, what other people or groups do you think the principal may have been in *consultation* with? (Possible response: She may have been in consultation with parents, teachers, other principals, and education experts.)

Grammar

Objectives

- Identify the function and purpose of gerunds.
- Identify the functions and purpose of participles.
- Identify multiple functions of words.

Gerunds: Verbs as Nouns

You have learned that many words in the English language have multiple meanings and multiple functions. You cannot simply use their form to determine meaning. One way to make a word plural is to add an -s, but not every word that ends in -s is a plural noun. Their meaning and function is determined by the way the words are used in sentences. We're going to work with words that look like verbs, but they don't function as verbs in sentences.

When you want to express an ongoing action, you add -ing to a verb. Think about the word *dance* as a verb. She is dancing in this show. What is she doing? (dancing) Adding the -ing suffix means the action continues to happen. You cannot, however, assume that every word ending in -ing is a verb. Listen to the way I use *dancing* in this sentence: Dancing is my favorite way to exercise. Who or what is this sentence about? (dancing) We must focus on the way words are being used in each sentence. We think about the questions that the words or phrases answer to make sure we understand what we are reading.

Direct students to page 253 in their Student Books. Read the information on gerunds aloud. Instead of providing an action, a gerund names an activity.

Read the instructions for the activity and model the examples to clarify understanding.

Lesson 2 | Grammar

Gerunds: Verbs as Nouns

A verb form that ends in -ing and functions as a noun is called a gerund.
A gerund answers the *who* or *what* question.

Function: swim + -ing	Examples
Verb	She is **swimming** laps in the pool.
Gerund	**Swimming** is good exercise.
Gerund phrase	**Swimming** ***with goggles*** protects your eyes from the chlorine.

Read each sentence and determine if the underlined word is functioning as a verb or as a gerund. Place an X in the proper column to identify its function.

	Gerund	Verb
Examples: The dress code is changing soon.		✗
Changing the dress code will improve student behavior.	✗	
1. Dressing as a gang member intimidates other students and spreads fear.	✗	
2. They are waiting in the office for more appropriate clothes.		✗
3. Dressing seductively is a great distraction to the opposite sex.	✗	
4. However, enforcing the dress code by sending violators to the office has been a problem.	✗	
5. Rewriting the dress code was a task for the school board.	✗	
6. The school board is adopting a school uniform policy that promotes school safety.		✗
7. The uniform policy is eliminating a lot of the problems that we have had in the past with school dress.		✗
8. A safe environment promotes student learning.	✗	
9. Her clothes are distracting others and keeping them form learning.		✗
10. Advertising for cigarettes is no longer allowed on television.	✗	

Unit 10 253

Model

Listen as I read the first example: *The dress code is changing soon.* What is underlined? *Changing* is underlined. To figure out if it's functioning as a verb or as a noun, I need to determine what question it answers. Who or what is this sentence about? *Dress code* is the subject. What did it do? *Is changing* is my verb, so I put an X in the Verb column.

Listen as I read the second example: *Changing the dress code will improve student behavior. Changing* is underlined, so I need to figure out its function in this sentence. One thing I notice is the absence of a helping verb. I wonder if this is a clue as to how it's being used in this sentence. Who or what is the sentence about? I see the words *dress code*, but something happening to the dress code is the subject of this sentence. Finding the verb should help me clarify the subject. Did what? *Will improve* is my verb. What will improve student behavior? The activity of changing the dress code will improve student behavior, so this sentence actually has a gerund phrase as its subject. I put an X in the Gerund column.

Guided Practice

Listen as I read #1: *Dressing as a gang member intimidates other students and spreads fear.* What is underlined? (Dressing) Our next step is to determine what question it answers. Who or what is this sentence about? I see the words *gang member.* A member is a person, so it's a noun. Is that the subject? (no) Those words are part of a phrase, *as a gang member,* that tells us more about the word *dressing.* Finding the verb will help us clarify the subject. Did or does what? (intimidates) What intimidates? (dressing as a gang member) *Dressing* is functioning as what? (a gerund) Where does the X belong? (under the Gerund column) Like one of the examples, this sentence contains a gerund phrase.

Independent Practice

Have students complete the activity. Review the answers as a class.

Participles: Verbs as Adjectives

We're going to continue our focus on verb forms that are functioning as something other than a verb. When a verb form ends in -ing and functions as a noun, what is it called? (a gerund) Verbs can also function as adjectives. They answer the *what kind* or *which one* question. To introduce the concept of a verb functioning as a noun, I used the verb form *dancing.* What if I paired the word *dancing* with another naming word?

Write the following sentence on the board:

The dancing bear entertained the children.

Who or what is this sentence about? (bear) What kind of bear? (dancing) In this sentence, *dancing* is not a verb nor is it a noun; it is functioning as an adjective.

Verb forms ending in -ed can also function as adjectives. Think about the word *learned.* I learned a new move in karate class. What did I do? (learned) *Learned* is functioning as a past tense verb. *The newly learned move helped me win my practice round.* Is *learned* functioning as the verb in this sentence? No, it is telling me more about *move,* the subject of the sentence. What kind of move? (newly learned)

These verb forms are called participles. A participle is simply a form of a verb that is used to show past or present action *and* that can also be used like an adjective. What is the term for a verb form that shows past or present action and can also be used like an adjective? (participle) When you see a word ending in -ing or -ed, you cannot afford to make any assumptions about its function. How can you determine its function? (by figuring out which question it answers)

Direct students to page 254 in their Student Books. Read the information about participles. Read the instructions for Part A aloud.

Lesson 2 | Grammar

Participles: Verbs as Adjectives

Present and past participles can be used to describe nouns. They answer the adjective questions *which one* or *what kind.*

Participles as Adjectives	Examples
Present participle	The dress code enhances the **learning** environment.
Past participle	Her **shredded** jeans violated the dress code.
Participial phrase • Set off by commas	His T-shirt, **covered with vulgar language**, was not appropriate for school.

Part A

Read each sentence and determine if the underlined word is functioning as a verb or as an adjective. Place an X in the proper column to identify its function.

	Adjective	Verb
Examples: Students are fleeing the school to avoid wearing uniforms.		✗
The fleeing students will be arrested for truancy.	✗	
1. Here at North High School, our top priority is to provide a safe and disciplined learning environment.	✗	
2. In response to growing levels of violence in our schools, declining performance on tests, and increasing truancy, the school board feels it is necessary to address the problem.	✗	
3. Her study concluded that those schools with uniform policies improved in attendance, graduation, and suspension rates.		✗
4. Intimidated students have a hard time concentrating on school tasks.	✗	
5. They called home and waited for clothes to be brought to school.		✗
6. The blouse, advertising an alcoholic beverage, violated the dress code.	✗	
7. The new dress code prohibits sagging pants.	✗	
8. Attending school excited students once they felt safe.		✗
9. The benefits of school uniforms included better attendance and less economic discrimination.		✗
10. Because of the new school uniform policy, our classrooms are filled with neatly dressed students.	✗	

254 Unit 10

Model

Listen as I read the first example: *Students are fleeing the school to avoid wearing uniforms.* The word *fleeing* is underlined. I have to determine if it's functioning as a verb or as an adjective. I see several clues that lead me to think this is functioning as a verb. I see the helping verb *are.* Who or what is this sentence about? *Students* is the *who* or the subject of this sentence. What are the students doing? They are fleeing. *Fleeing* is a verb. My X belongs in the Verb column.

Listen as I read the second example: *The fleeing students will be arrested for truancy.* Again, *fleeing* is the underlined word. Is it functioning as the verb or as an adjective? I see the verb phrase *will be arrested.* Who will be arrested? Students will be arrested. Which students? Fleeing students. Because *fleeing* answers the *which one* question, I placed my X in the Adjective column.

Guided Practice

Let's look at #1: *Here at North High School, our top priority is to provide a safe and disciplined learning environment.* What is the underlined word? (disciplined) Does it answer the *did what* question? (no) This sentence has a linking verb, *is.* Does *disciplined* answer the *what kind* question? (yes) It is telling us what kind of environment the school wants to provide. Where does the X belong? (Adjective column) While it's not underlined, *learning* is also a present participle functioning as an adjective. Both participles describe *environment.*

Let's look at #2: *In response to growing levels of violence in our schools, declining performance on tests, and increasing truancy, the school board feels it is necessary to address the problem.* What is the underlined word? (increasing) Think about the question it answers. If it answers the *did what* question, it's functioning as the verb. If it answers the *what kind* question, it's functioning as an adjective. What kind of truancy? (increasing) Because it answers the *what kind* question, where should you place the X? (Adjective column) Have students find the other participles in the sentence. (growing, declining)

Independent Practice

Have students complete the activity. Review the answers as a class.

Direct students to Part B on page 255 and read the instructions. Now, I want you to apply your understanding of participles by generating sentences. Write two sentences with each participle. Use the participle first as an adjective and then as a verb. Remember to think about the questions they need to answer to function as an adjective or as a verb. Have students write their sentences. Then, have volunteers share their sentences for each participle. Have the other students determine if the participle has been used correctly as an adjective or as a verb.

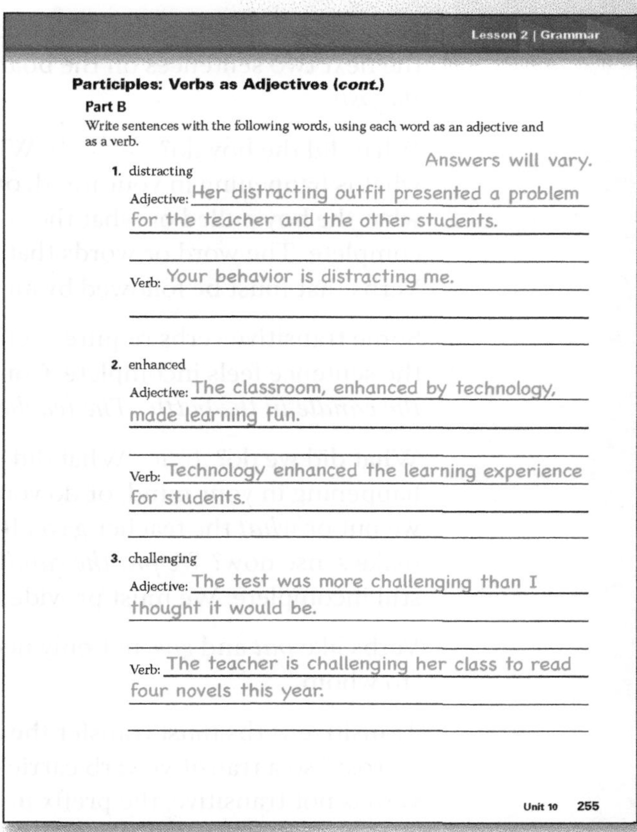
Lesson 2 | Grammar

Participles: Verbs as Adjectives (*cont.*)

Part B

Write sentences with the following words, using each word as an adjective and as a verb.

Answers will vary.

1. distracting

Adjective: Her distracting outfit presented a problem for the teacher and the other students.

Verb: Your behavior is distracting me.

2. enhanced

Adjective: The classroom, enhanced by technology, made learning fun.

Verb: Technology enhanced the learning experience for students.

3. challenging

Adjective: The test was more challenging than I thought it would be.

Verb: The teacher is challenging her class to read four novels this year.

Unit 10 255

Writing

Objective

- Distinguish between transitive and intransitive verbs.

Properties of Verbs

Write the following sentences on the board and underline the verb in each sentence:

The sad boy cried.

The baby slept.

The boy pulled his sister's scarf.

The cook broiled the fish.

We put the candle in the bottle.

The teacher gave extra time to the student.

We are going to continue to focus on verbs. If we know a verb well, we know whether certain kinds of words must go with it. Some verbs can stand alone and make sense with just a subject noun. Consider the first two sentences on the board: *The sad boy cried. The baby slept.*

What did the boy do? (cried) What did the baby do? (slept) These are called intransitive verbs. They don't have to be followed by an object. They provide enough information for us to know what is going on.

Some other verbs must be followed by an object to complete their meaning. Consider the next two sentences on the board: *The boy pulled his sister's scarf. The cook broiled the fish.*

What did the boy do? (pulled) What did the cook do? (broiled) Can you picture what is happening in your mind, or do you need more information? You have to know what the boy pulled or what the cook broiled for the sentences to make sense and be complete. The word or words that explain *to what* are the objects, like *scarf* and *fish*. Verbs that must be followed by an object are called transitive verbs.

Some transitive verbs require even more information, and unless it is in the sentence, the sentence feels incomplete. Consider the last two sentences on the board: *We put the candle in the bottle. The teacher gave extra time to the student.*

What did we do? (put) What did the teacher do? (gave) Can you picture what is happening in your mind, or do you need more information? You have to know *what* we put or *what* the teacher gave. If we include the direct objects, do the sentences make sense now? *We put the candle. The teacher gave extra time.* The sentences are still incomplete. We must provide more information like where and to whom.

Verbs like *put* and *give* not only need a "to what" but also a phrase to say "where" or "to whom."

Transitive verbs must transfer the action to an object. Trans- is a prefix meaning "across," so a transitive verb carries the action across to a direct object. An intransitive verb is not transitive; the prefix in- means "not." You might hear these terms as you study language in the future. The important idea is that some verbs are content to be alone in a sentence and others are very grabby; they must have other words, such as direct objects, with them.

Direct students to page 256 in their Student Books. Read the information in the chart aloud. Then, read the instructions for the activity.

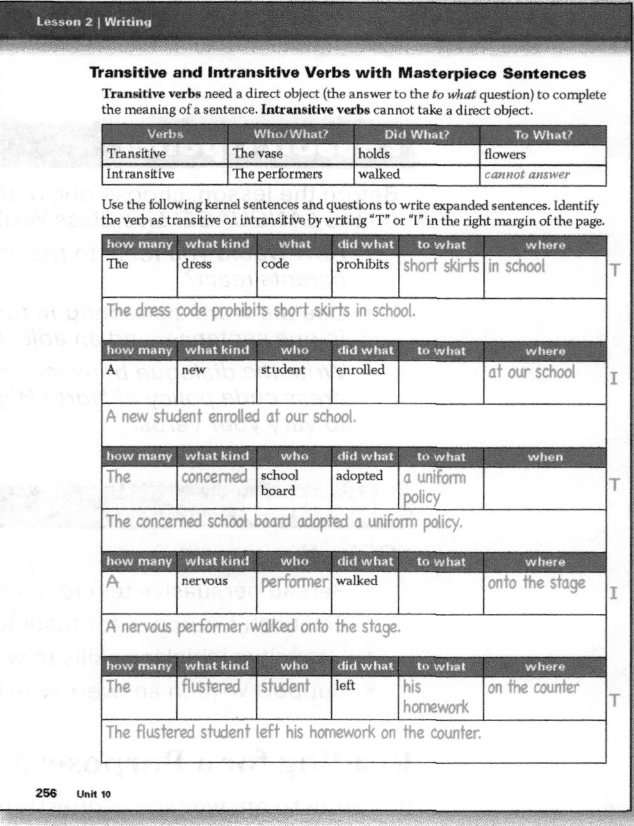

Lesson 2 | Writing

Transitive and Intransitive Verbs with Masterpiece Sentences

Transitive verbs need a direct object (the answer to the *to what* question) to complete the meaning of a sentence. **Intransitive verbs** cannot take a direct object.

Verbs	Who/What?	Did What?	To What?
Transitive	The vase	holds	flowers
Intransitive	The performers	walked	*cannot answer*

Use the following kernel sentences and questions to write expanded sentences. Identify the verb as transitive or intransitive by writing "T" or "I" in the right margin of the page.

how many	what kind	what	did what	to what	where	
The	dress	code	prohibits	short skirts	in school	T

The dress code prohibits short skirts in school.

how many	what kind	who	did what	to what	where	
A	new	student	enrolled		at our school	I

A new student enrolled at our school.

how many	what kind	who	did what	to what	when	
The	concerned	school board	adopted	a uniform policy		T

The concerned school board adopted a uniform policy.

how many	what kind	who	did what	to what	where	
A	nervous	performer	walked		onto the stage	I

A nervous performer walked onto the stage.

how many	what kind	who	did what	to what	where	
The	flustered	student	left	his homework	on the counter	T

The flustered student left his homework on the counter.

256 Unit 10

Guided Practice

Questions help us determine how words are functioning in a sentence, and they also help us expand our own sentences. Let's focus on the main *what* and *did what* questions in the first sentence. *Code prohibits.* What kind of code? *Dress code* prohibits. How many codes? *The* dress code prohibits. Is that enough information? (no) What does it prohibit? **Have volunteers share possibilities and write the possible sentences on the board.** Once we have answered all of the questions, we need to write our expanded sentence. Write the sentence in the blank provided. Because we were able to answer the *to what* question, we know our verb is transitive. **Have students write "T" in the right margin of the page.**

Independent Practice

Have students complete the activity. Review the answers as a class.

Unit 10 Lesson 3

Lesson Opener

Before the lesson, choose one of the following activities to write on the board or post on the *LANGUAGE! Live* Class Wall online.

- *How would you react to the dress code policy at North High School? How would your parents react?*
- *Use the word* distracting *in three sentences. Use it as a verb in one sentence, a noun in one sentence, and an adjective in another sentence.*
- *Write the dialogue between you and the principal if you were asked to follow the dress code policy of North High School. Don't forget the appropriate punctuation and to vary your verbs.*

Reading

Objectives

- Reread persuasive text for comprehension.
- Establish a purpose for reading text.
- Use critical thinking skills to write responses to prompts about text.
- Support written answers with evidence from text.

Reading for a Purpose: North High School Letter

It is time to answer some questions. Because critical understanding requires active participation, we are going to read the text again. This time, we will be reading for a specific purpose, which will help us pay attention to details that we may have missed the first time around.

Let's read some questions about the text to provide a purpose for rereading.

Direct students to pages 257–259 in their Student Books. Have students read the prompts aloud with you.

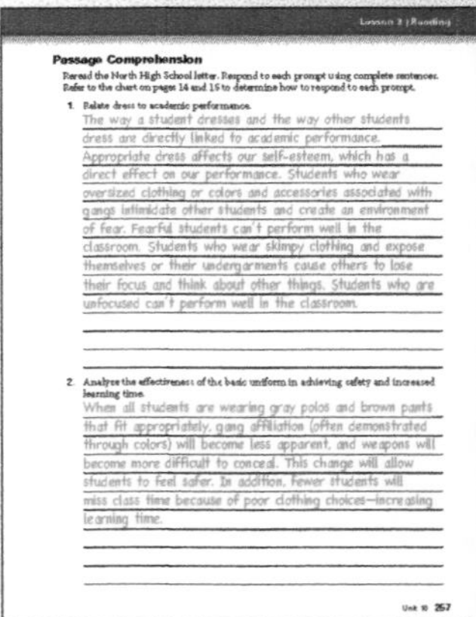

Lesson 3 | Reading

Passage Comprehension

Reread the North High School letter. Respond to each prompt using complete sentences. Refer to the chart on pages 14 and 15 to determine how to respond to each prompt.

1. Relate dress to academic performance.

   The way a student dresses and the way other students dress are directly linked to academic performance. Appropriate dress affects our self-esteem, which has a direct effect on our performance. Students who wear oversized clothing or colors and accessories associated with gangs intimidate other students and create an environment of fear. Fearful students can't perform well in the classroom. Students who wear skimpy clothing and expose themselves or their undergarments cause others to lose their focus and think about other things. Students who are unfocused can't perform well in the classroom.

2. Analyze the effectiveness of the basic uniform in achieving safety and increased learning time.

   When all students are wearing gray polos and brown pants that fit appropriately, gang affiliation (often demonstrated through colors) will become less apparent, and weapons will become more difficult to conceal. This change will allow students to feel safer. In addition, fewer students will miss class time because of poor clothing choices—increasing learning time.

Unit 10 257

1. Relate dress to academic performance.
2. Analyze the effectiveness of the basic uniform in achieving safety and increased learning time.
3. Analyze the decision to adopt a uniform policy at North High School rather than rewrite the current dress code policy.
4. Using your own experiences, assess the claim that "There appears to be a fundamental relationship between a person's dress and his or her behavior." Provide examples.
5. Use the information in the policy to differentiate between appropriate and inappropriate dress for boys.
6. Differentiate between North High School's uniform and the required clothing at your school.

Direct students to page 245 in their Student Books or have them tear out the extra copy of the letter from the back of their book.

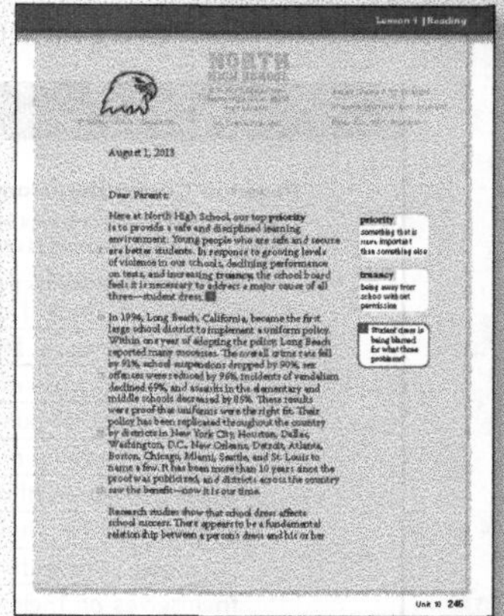

Lesson 1 | Reading

NORTH HIGH SCHOOL

August 1, 2013

Dear Parents:

Here at North High School, our top **priority** is to provide a safe and disciplined learning environment. Young people who are safe and secure are better students. In response to growing levels of violence in our schools, declining performance on tests, and increasing **truancy**, the school board feels it is necessary to address a major cause of all three—student dress.

In 1994, Long Beach, California, became the first large school district to implement a uniform policy. Within one year of adopting the policy, Long Beach reported many successes. The overall crime rate fell by 91%, school suspensions dropped by 90%, sex offenses were reduced by 96%, incidents of vandalism declined 69%, and assaults in the elementary and middle schools decreased by 85%. These results were proof that uniforms were the right fit. Their policy has been replicated throughout the country by districts in New York City, Houston, Dallas, Washington, D.C., New Orleans, Detroit, Atlanta, Boston, Chicago, Miami, Seattle, and St. Louis to name a few. It has been more than 10 years since the proof was publicized, and districts across the country saw the benefit—now it is our time.

Research studies show that school dress affects school success. There appears to be a fundamental relationship between a person's dress and his or her

priority something that is more important than something else

truancy being away from school without permission

Student dress is being blamed for what three problems?

Unit 10 245

> **Note:** To minimize flipping back and forth between the pages, a copy of each text has been included in the back of the Student Books. Encourage students to tear this out and use it when working on activities that require the use of the text.

Choose an option for reading text. Have students read the text according to the option that you chose.

Options for reading text:

- Teacher read-aloud
- Teacher-led or student-led choral read
- Paired read or independent read with bold vocabulary words read aloud

Passage Comprehension

Write the words *analyze, assess, differentiate,* and *relate* on the board. Have students read the words aloud with you.

Direct students to pages 14 and 15 in their Student Books. It is critical to understand what the question is asking and how to answer it. Today, we will review four direction words used in prompts.

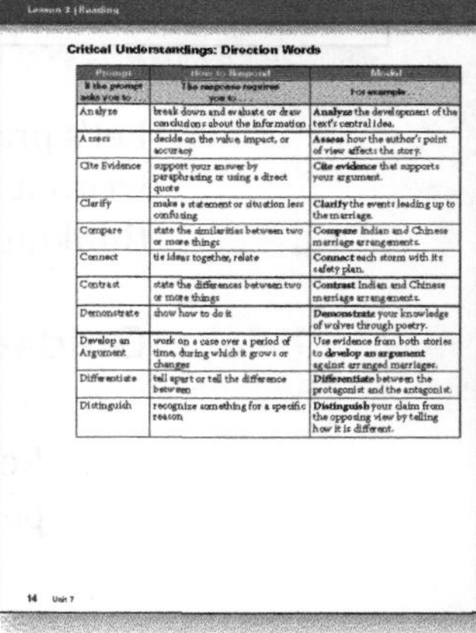

Lesson 3 | Reading

Critical Understandings: Direction Words

Prompt	How to Respond	Model
If the prompt asks you to . . .	The response requires you to . . .	For example . . .
Analyze	break down and evaluate or draw conclusions about the information	**Analyze** the development of the text's central idea.
Assess	decide on the value, impact, or accuracy	**Assess** how the author's point of view affects the story.
Cite Evidence	support your answer by paraphrasing or using a direct quote	**Cite evidence** that supports your argument.
Clarify	make a statement or situation less confusing	**Clarify** the events leading up to the marriage.
Compare	state the similarities between two or more things	**Compare** Indian and Chinese marriage arrangements.
Connect	tie ideas together, relate	**Connect** each storm with its safety plan.
Contrast	state the differences between two or more things	**Contrast** Indian and Chinese marriage arrangements.
Demonstrate	show how to do it	**Demonstrate** your knowledge of wolves through poetry.
Develop an Argument	work on a case over a period of time, during which it grows or changes	Use evidence from both stories to **develop an argument** against arranged marriages.
Differentiate	tell apart or tell the difference between	**Differentiate** between the protagonist and the antagonist.
Distinguish	recognize something for a specific reason	**Distinguish** your claim from the opposing view by telling how it is different.

14 Unit 7

Have students review the words on the board in the chart on pages 14 and 15. Check for understanding by requesting an oral response to the following questions.

- If the prompt asks you to *analyze,* the response requires you to . . . (break down and evaluate or draw conclusions about the information).
- If the prompt asks you to *assess,* the response requires you to . . . (decide on the value, impact, or accuracy).
- If the prompt asks you to *differentiate,* the response requires you to . . . (tell apart or tell the difference between).
- If the prompt asks you to *relate,* the response requires you to . . . (explain the connection between ideas or concepts).

Direct students to pages 257–259 in their Student Books.

Passage Comprehension

Reread the North High School letter. Respond to each prompt using complete sentences. Refer to the chart on pages 14 and 15 to determine how to respond to each prompt.

1. Relate dress to academic performance.

The way a student dresses and the way other students dress are directly linked to academic performance. Appropriate dress affects our self-esteem, which has a direct effect on our performance. Students who wear oversized clothing or colors and accessories associated with gangs intimidate other students and create an environment of fear. Fearful students can't perform well in the classroom. Students who wear skimpy clothing and expose themselves or their undergarments cause others to lose their focus and think about other things. Students who are unfocused can't perform well in the classroom.

2. Analyze the effectiveness of the basic uniform in achieving safety and increased learning time.

When all students are wearing gray polos and brown pants that fit appropriately, gang affiliation (often demonstrated through colors) will become less apparent, and weapons will become more difficult to conceal. This change will allow students to feel safer. In addition, fewer students will miss class time because of poor clothing choices—increasing learning time.

Passage Comprehension (*cont.*)

3. Analyze the decision to adopt a uniform policy at North High School rather than rewrite the current dress code policy.

North High School adopted a uniform policy instead of rewriting the current dress code policy because dress code policies are difficult to enforce. While attempting to enforce the dress code policy, violators miss class time, which greatly affects academic success. Uniforms, on the other hand, "promote school safety, increase learning time, and enhance the learning environment."

4. Using your own experiences, assess the claim that "There appears to be a fundamental relationship between a person's dress and his or her behavior." Provide examples.

Answers will vary but should offer examples in support or dissent of the statement.

Let's practice answering questions written as prompts that require critical thinking.

Guided Practice

1. Relate dress to academic performance.

If the prompt asks you to *relate*, what should you do? (Explain the connection between ideas or concepts.) Let's turn the prompt into a question to confirm our understanding. If we change this to a question, what would it be? (How is dress connected to academic performance?) Will we answer this prompt by using the letter, the policy, or both? (the letter)

Let's create a sentence starter together.

Passage Comprehension (*cont.*)

5. Use the information in the policy to differentiate between appropriate and inappropriate dress for boys.

Appropriate dress for boys consists of appropriately sized, hole-free brown pants that sit at the waist and are secured by a brown leather belt. A gray polo shirt and brown leather shoes complete the appropriate outfit. However, inappropriate dress consists of clothing with holes, visible undergarments, garments with non-positive messages, hats, piercings, hair utensils, and sunglasses.

6. Differentiate between North High School's uniform and the required clothing at your school.

Answers will vary but should include how North High School's dress code is different from their dress code policy.

Have students offer suggestions and write them on the board. One possibility includes:

The way a student dresses and the way other students dress is directly linked to academic performance. Appropriate dress _______________. Students who wear ______________________________.

Have partners answer the question.

2. Analyze the effectiveness of the basic uniform in achieving safety and increased learning time.

If the prompt asks you to *analyze,* what should you do? (Break down and evaluate or draw conclusions about the information.) Let's turn the prompt into a question to confirm our understanding. If we change this to a question, what would it be? (Is the basic uniform effective in achieving safety and increased learning time? Why?)

Let's create a sentence starter together.

Have students offer suggestions and write them on the board. One possibility includes:

When all students are wearing gray polos and brown pants that fit appropriately, __________________. In addition, ______________________________.

Have partners answer the question.

Independent Practice

Have students respond to the remaining questions. For students who need more assistance, provide the following alternative questions.

Alternative questions:

3. Why did North High School adopt a uniform policy instead of rewriting or enforcing their current dress code policy?
4. Is it accurate to say "There appears to be a fundamental relationship between a person's dress and his or her behavior."?
5. What is the difference between appropriate and inappropriate dress for boys?
6. What is the difference between the uniforms at North High School and the required clothing at your school?

Unit 10

Lesson 4

Lesson Opener

Before the lesson, choose one of the following activities to write on the board or post on the *LANGUAGE! Live* Class Wall online.

- *Dress your avatar as though he or she were attending North High School. Explain your choices.*
- *Use transitive verbs to write five sentences about why uniforms are a good idea.*
- *Use the word* advertising *in three sentences. Use it as a verb in one sentence, a noun in one sentence, and an adjective in another sentence.*

Reading

Objectives

- Read with purpose and understanding.
- Answer questions to demonstrate comprehension of text.
- Identify and explain explicit details from text.
- Monitor comprehension of text during reading.
- Identify and determine the meaning of puns used by an author.
- Analyze the claims made by an author and determine if they are accurate and supported with evidence.
- Identify rhetorical fallacies in persuasive text.
- Identify the antecedents of pronouns in writing.

Close Reading of the North High School Letter

Copy of school dress code

Let's reread the North High School letter and policy. I will provide specific instructions on how to mark the text that will help with comprehension.

Highlighters or colored pencils

Have students get out a highlighter or colored pencil.

Direct students to pages 260–265 in their Student Books.

Circle the principal's signature.

Star the place where the text transitions from letter to policy.

Now, let's read the vocabulary words aloud.

- What's the first bold vocabulary word? (priority) *Priority* means "something that is more important than something else." Reading proficiency is my *priority*, and I hope that it is yours. **Have partners use the word in a sentence.**
- What's the next vocabulary word? (truancy) *Truancy* means "being away from school without permission." In some nations, *truancy* isn't a problem because going to school is a privilege and students are honored to have the opportunity. **Have partners use the word in a sentence.**
- Next word? (enforce) *Enforce* means "to make sure a rule or law is obeyed." Because I have put my hand on someone's chewed gum sticking under a desk, I will *enforce* the "no gum" rule in this classroom. **Have partners use the word in a sentence.**

- Let's continue. (enhance) *Enhance* means "to improve something." Food coloring is used to *enhance* the look of many foods. **Have partners use the word in a sentence.**
- Next word? (distracted) *Distracted* means "not focused on what you should be focused on." Some students are *distracted* by their cell phones. **Have partners use the word in a sentence.**
- Let's continue. (principles) *Principles* means "beliefs about what is important or how you should act." In a school, it is important that we adhere to a shared set of *principles*. **Have partners use the word in a sentence.**
- Next word? (resist) *Resist* means "to say 'no' to something you want but shouldn't have." Even though I know they aren't healthy, donuts are difficult to *resist*. **Have partners use the word in a sentence.**
- Let's continue. (appropriate) *Appropriate* means "fitting; right for a certain time and place." The language you use in this classroom must be *appropriate* for school. **Have partners use the word in a sentence.**
- Next word? (restrictive) *Restrictive* means "limiting; keeping someone from having full freedom." Though they are *restrictive*, most rules are intended to protect you. **Have partners use the word in a sentence.**
- Last word. (consultation) *Consultation* means "discussion; conversation." A *consultation* with your counselor is helpful prior to scheduling classes. **Have partners use the word in a sentence.**

Talk with a partner about any vocabulary word that is still confusing for you to read consistently or to understand its meaning.

You will read the North High School letter one section at a time. After each section, you will monitor your understanding by circling the check mark if you understand the text or the question mark if you don't understand the text. I also want you to draw a question mark over any confusing words, phrases, or sentences.

Options for reading text:

- Teacher read-aloud
- Teacher-led or student-led choral read
- Paired read or independent read with bold vocabulary words read aloud

Choose an option for reading text. Have students read lines 1–34 according to the option that you chose. The principal's letter is an attempt to convince students and parents of the need for a uniform policy. Listen for facts that support the change as well as unsupported claims by the principal.

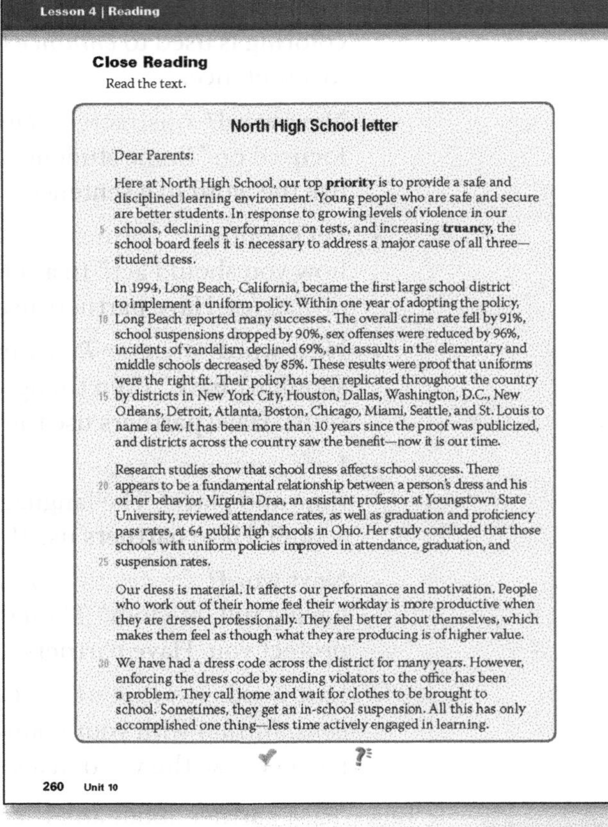

Lesson 4 | Reading

Close Reading

Read the text.

North High School letter

Dear Parents:

Here at North High School, our top **priority** is to provide a safe and disciplined learning environment. Young people who are safe and secure are better students. In response to growing levels of violence in our schools, declining performance on tests, and increasing **truancy,** the school board feels it is necessary to address a major cause of all three—student dress.

In 1994, Long Beach, California, became the first large school district to implement a uniform policy. Within one year of adopting the policy, Long Beach reported many successes. The overall crime rate fell by 91%, school suspensions dropped by 90%, sex offenses were reduced by 96%, incidents of vandalism declined 69%, and assaults in the elementary and middle schools decreased by 85%. These results were proof that uniforms were the right fit. Their policy has been replicated throughout the country by districts in New York City, Houston, Dallas, Washington, D.C., New Orleans, Detroit, Atlanta, Boston, Chicago, Miami, Seattle, and St. Louis to name a few. It has been more than 10 years since the proof was publicized, and districts across the country saw the benefit—now it is our time.

Research studies show that school dress affects school success. There appears to be a fundamental relationship between a person's dress and his or her behavior. Virginia Draa, an assistant professor at Youngstown State University, reviewed attendance rates, as well as graduation and proficiency pass rates, at 64 public high schools in Ohio. Her study concluded that those schools with uniform policies improved in attendance, graduation, and suspension rates.

Our dress is material. It affects our performance and motivation. People who work out of their home feel their workday is more productive when they are dressed professionally. They feel better about themselves, which makes them feel as though what they are producing is of higher value.

We have had a dress code across the district for many years. However, enforcing the dress code by sending violators to the office has been a problem. They call home and wait for clothes to be brought to school. Sometimes, they get an in-school suspension. All this has only accomplished one thing—less time actively engaged in learning.

260 Unit 10

When most of the students are finished, continue with the entire class. Let's see how well you understood what you read.

- Circle the check mark or the question mark for this section. Draw a question mark over any confusing words.
- Go to line 3. Mark the synonym of *controlled*. (disciplined)
- On the same line, mark the synonym of *protected*. (secure)
- Go to line 5. Mark the antonym pair. (declining/increasing)
- In the first paragraph, number the problems at the school. (1. growing levels of violence in our schools; 2. declining performance on tests; 3. increasing truancy) Draw a line from each one to the major cause. (student dress)
- Go to line 8. Mark the first large school district to implement a uniform policy. (Long Beach, California)
- In the same paragraph, number the five problems that became less frequent because of the uniform policy. (1. crime rate; 2. school suspensions; 3. sex offenses; 4. vandalism; 5. assaults)
- In the same paragraph, mark the statement that is funny because of the multiple meanings of words. This play on words is called a *pun*. (uniforms were the right fit)
- Go to line 14. Mark the word that means "copied." (replicated)
- In the margin next to this paragraph, write the reason the writer uses the statistics of the Long Beach school district. (proof of the impact of this change)
- Go to line 19. Mark the verb that means "has an impact on." (affects)
- Go to line 22. Mark the word that means *competence* but not *expertise*. (proficiency)
- Go to lines 24 and 25. Number the three improvements brought about by the uniform policies in Ohio. (1. attendance; 2. graduation; 3. suspension rates)

- In the next paragraph, mark the pun, or play on words because of multiple meanings. (Our dress is material.) Circle the word with multiple meanings in the pun. (material) In the margin, write the definition of the word as it is being used here. (important)
- In the last sentence of the same paragraph, mark the pronouns, including the reflexive pronoun that is used because the subject and object of the preposition are the same. (They, themselves, them, they) Draw an arrow from each one to what they are referencing. (People who work out of their home)
- In the margin, write *proven* if the principal has provided evidence to back up this claim or *overgeneralization* if you think she is just using the thoughts of some as evidence of the thoughts of others. (overgeneralization)
- Mark how long the district has had a dress code. (many years)
- Go to line 32. Mark the pronoun *they*. Draw a line to the noun that *they* refers to. (violators)
- Mark the problem with enforcing the current dress code. (less time actively engaged in learning)
- Return to the first paragraph. Look at the three consequences of student dress. Now, look at the evidence cited from Long Beach and Virginia Draa. Does the evidence support all three claims? (no) Circle the supposed consequence that is not supported. (declining performance on tests) In the margin, identify this as a fallacy.

Have students read lines 35–67 according to the option that you chose. Pay attention to the claims made by the principal and the board in the letter. Draw a star in the margin if you have had an experience similar to the one being described.

When most of the students are finished, continue with the entire class. Let's see how well you understood what you read.

Close Reading (*cont.*)

Rather than rewriting a dress code that is difficult to **enforce**, the school board has adopted a uniform policy for all grade levels across the district. Even former President Bill Clinton said in a radio address, "If it means teenagers will stop killing each other over designer jackets, then our public schools should be able to require their students to wear school uniforms." The adoption of this school uniform policy will promote school safety, increase learning time, and **enhance** the learning environment—putting North High School on the path to academic excellence.

The uniform policy will eliminate a lot of problems we have had in the past with school dress. Students' sloppy dress has caused other students to feel threatened, intimidated, and even **distracted**. Baggy pants, clothing of certain colors, bandannas, and an emphasis on one side of the body (e.g., one pant leg pulled up) can be interpreted as gang dress. Dressing as a gang member intimidates other students and spreads fear. This makes an environment focused on academic success nearly impossible to achieve.

Pants with large pockets, coats, purses, and backpacks can hold a weapon or drugs. Students are unable to feel safe and at ease in their classrooms when they are worried about the contents of another student's pockets or bags.

Though most offenders disagree on the definition of "seductive," seductive clothing *is* a great distraction. Bare midriffs, shoulders, backs, and legs, as well as overly tight garments, visible underwear, and clothes that draw attention to the bosom or buttocks (i.e., V-neck shirts and pants with words on the backside) cause students to lose their focus and think about other things.

Clothing advertising cigarettes or alcohol may persuade other students to try these controlled substances. Television has restricted the advertisement of cigarettes and alcohol when minors are typically watching TV, so it doesn't make sense to allow students to advertise these things in school—a gathering place for minors. Clothing that depicts violence or foul language may also persuade students to act in the same manner.

✔ ?

- Circle the check mark or the question mark for this section. Draw a question mark over any confusing words.
- Go to line 35. Mark the reason they don't want to rewrite a dress code. (difficult to enforce)
- Go to line 38. Mark the pronoun *it*. Draw a line to what *it* represents. (school uniforms) In the margin, write a sentence inferring what had happened prior to Clinton's radio address. (A teen was killed over clothes. Parents fought against uniform policies.)
- Go to line 41. Mark the synonym of *encourage*. (promote)
- Go to line 42. Mark the claim that is not supported by evidence or Clinton's quote. (enhance the learning environment)
- Go to line 44. Mark the word that means "to get rid of." (eliminate)
- Go to line 45. Mark the subjective word used to describe clothing students wear. (sloppy)
- Go to line 47. Mark the phrase that means "calling attention to." (an emphasis on)
- Go to line 48. Circle the Latin abbreviation that means an example is coming. (e.g.)
- Go to line 49. Mark the synonym of *threatens*. (intimidates)
- Reread the next paragraph. Is the second sentence fact or an exaggeration? Write your answer in the margin. (exaggeration)
- Go to line 55. Mark the word used to refer to "people who break the rule." (offenders)
- Go to line 57. Mark the synonym of *clothing*. (garments)
- Number the items considered to be seductive. (1. bare midriffs; 2. bare shoulders; 3. bare backs; 4. bare legs; 5. overly tight garments; 6. visible underwear; 7. clothes that draw attention to the bosom or buttocks) Mark the effects of such things. (lose their focus; think about other things)

- Circle the Latin abbreviation that means a clarification is coming. (i.e.)
- Go to line 61. Mark the synonym of *encourage.* (persuade)
- Go to line 62. Mark *these substances.* Draw an arrow to what *these substances* is referring to. (cigarettes, alcohol)
- In the same line, mark the synonym of *limited.* (restricted)
- Go to line 65. Mark the punctuation used to indicate a pause for added emphasis. (em dash)
- In the same paragraph, mark the subjunctive statement indicating that something is a possibility, but not a guarantee. (Clothing that depicts violence or foul language may also persuade students to act in the same manner.)

Have students read lines 68–90 according to the option that you chose. Pay attention to the claims made by the principal and the board in the letter. Draw a star in the margin if you have had an experience similar to the one being described.

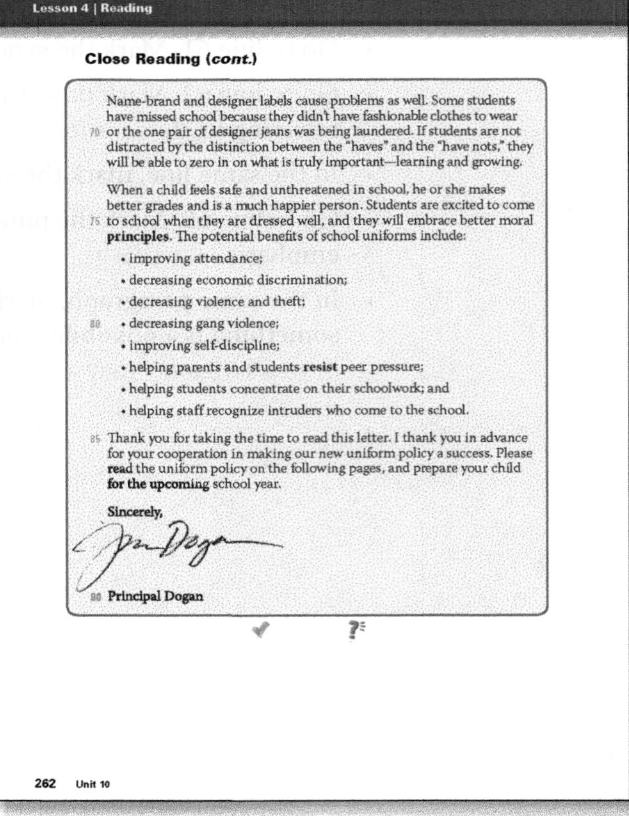

Lesson 4 | Reading

Close Reading (*cont.*)

Name-brand and designer labels cause problems as well. Some students have missed school because they didn't have fashionable clothes to wear or the one pair of designer jeans was being laundered. If students are not distracted by the distinction between the "haves" and the "have nots," they will be able to zero in on what is truly important—learning and growing.

When a child feels safe and unthreatened in school, he or she makes better grades and is a much happier person. Students are excited to come to school when they are dressed well, and they will embrace better moral **principles**. The potential benefits of school uniforms include:

- improving attendance;
- decreasing economic discrimination;
- decreasing violence and theft;
- decreasing gang violence;
- improving self-discipline;
- helping parents and students **resist** peer pressure;
- helping students concentrate on their schoolwork; and
- helping staff recognize intruders who come to the school.

Thank you for taking the time to read this letter. I thank you in advance for your cooperation in making our new uniform policy a success. Please **read** the uniform policy on the following pages, and prepare your child **for the upcoming** school year.

Sincerely,

Principal Dogan

?

262 Unit 10

When most of the students are finished, continue with the entire class. Let's see how well you understood what you read.

- Circle the check mark or the question mark for this section. Draw a question mark over any confusing words.
- In the first paragraph, number the problems that designer labels cause. (1. students have missed school; 2. students are distracted)
- Draw a dollar sign over the title given to people with money. ("haves") Circle the title given to people without money. ("have nots")
- Go to line 72. Mark the idiom used to mean "focus." (zero in)
- Number the effects of feeling safe in school. (1. better grades; 2. happier)
- Go to line 76. Mark the word that is a homophone for the leaders of schools. (principles)
- In the same line, mark the word that indicates this is not a guarantee. (potential)
- In the same paragraph, circle the claims that are subjective, or based on opinion instead of fact. (happier person; excited to come to school; embrace better moral principles)
- Go to line 82. Mark the word that means "someone at your own level." (peer)
- Go to lines 85 and 86. Number two things that the principal is thanking parents for. (1. read this letter; 2. cooperation in making our new uniform policy a success)
- Number two things the principal is asking parents to do. (1. read the uniform policy; 2. prepare child)

Have students read lines 91–114 according to the option that you chose.
Pay attention to the policy specifics. Draw an asterisk in the margin if you think the demand is unreasonable.

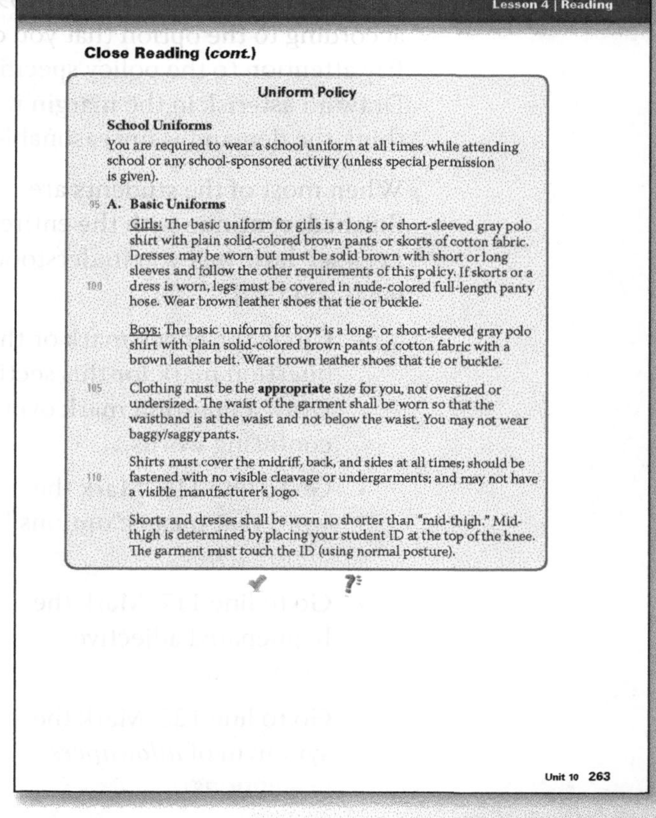
Lesson 4 | Reading

Close Reading (*cont.*)

Uniform Policy

School Uniforms

You are required to wear a school uniform at all times while attending school or any school-sponsored activity (unless special permission is given).

A. Basic Uniforms

Girls: The basic uniform for girls is a long- or short-sleeved gray polo shirt with plain solid-colored brown pants or skorts of cotton fabric. Dresses may be worn but must be solid brown with short or long sleeves and follow the other requirements of this policy. If skorts or a dress is worn, legs must be covered in nude-colored full-length panty hose. Wear brown leather shoes that tie or buckle.

Boys: The basic uniform for boys is a long- or short-sleeved gray polo shirt with plain solid-colored brown pants of cotton fabric with a brown leather belt. Wear brown leather shoes that tie or buckle.

Clothing must be the **appropriate** size for you, not oversized or undersized. The waist of the garment shall be worn so that the waistband is at the waist and not below the waist. You may not wear baggy/saggy pants.

Shirts must cover the midriff, back, and sides at all times; should be fastened with no visible cleavage or undergarments; and may not have a visible manufacturer's logo.

Skorts and dresses shall be worn no shorter than "mid-thigh." Mid-thigh is determined by placing your student ID at the top of the knee. The garment must touch the ID (using normal posture).

Unit 10 263

When most of the students are finished, continue with the entire class.
Let's see how well you understood what you read.

- Circle the check mark or the question mark for this section. Draw a question mark over any confusing words.
- Go to lines 93 and 94. Mark the punctuation mark used to show a clarification. (parentheses)
- Underline what is needed for a student to be noncompliant. (special permission)
- In the second paragraph, mark the hyphenated adjectives. (long- /short-sleeved, solid-colored, nude-colored, full-length)
- Go to lines 105 and 106. Mark the *nonexamples* of appropriate size. (oversized; undersized)
- On line 111, mark the word that means "company that makes something." (manufacturer's) In the margin, list some examples.
- On the same line, mark the synonym of *symbol.* (logo)
- Go to line 112. Mark the prefix that means "in the middle." (mid) In the margin, write *correct* if you think the principal's definition is correct or *incorrect* if you think it is wrong.
- Go to line 113. Mark the synonym of *decided.* (determined)
- Go to line 114. Mark the word that means "sitting or standing position." (posture)

Have students read lines 115–139 according to the option that you chose. Pay attention to the policy specifics. Draw an asterisk in the margin if you think the demand is unreasonable.

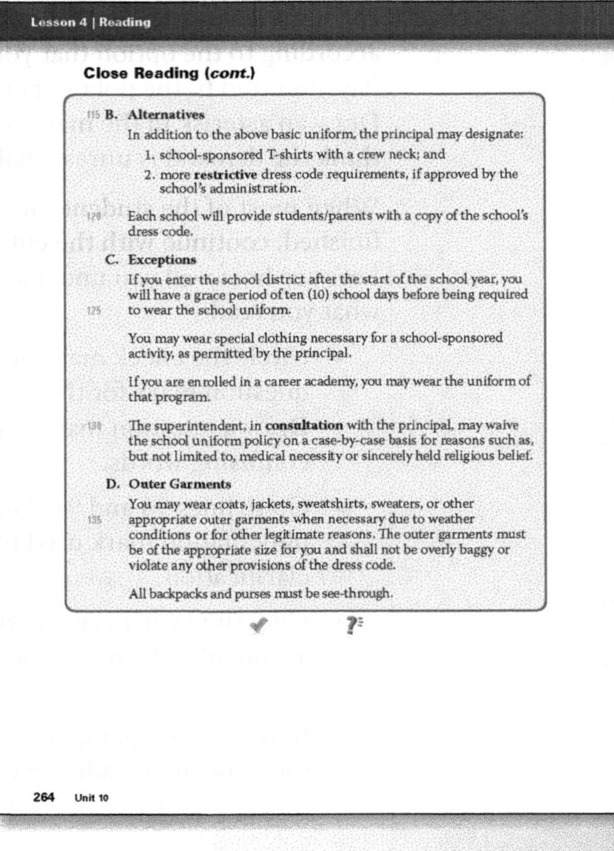

Close Reading (*cont.*)

B. Alternatives

In addition to the above basic uniform, the principal may designate:

1. school-sponsored T-shirts with a crew neck; and
2. more **restrictive** dress code requirements, if approved by the school's administration.

Each school will provide students/parents with a copy of the school's dress code.

C. Exceptions

If you enter the school district after the start of the school year, you will have a grace period of ten (10) school days before being required to wear the school uniform.

You may wear special clothing necessary for a school-sponsored activity, as permitted by the principal.

If you are enrolled in a career academy, you may wear the uniform of that program.

The superintendent, in **consultation** with the principal, may waive the school uniform policy on a case-by-case basis for reasons such as, but not limited to, medical necessity or sincerely held religious belief.

D. Outer Garments

You may wear coats, jackets, sweatshirts, sweaters, or other appropriate outer garments when necessary due to weather conditions or for other legitimate reasons. The outer garments must be of the appropriate size for you and shall not be overly baggy or violate any other provisions of the dress code.

All backpacks and purses must be see-through.

When most of the students are finished, continue with the entire class. Let's see how well you understood what you read.

- Circle the check mark or the question mark for this section. Draw a question mark over any confusing words.
- Go to line 115. Mark the word that means "options." (alternatives)
- Go to line 117. Mark the hyphenated adjective. (school-sponsored)
- Go to line 122. Mark the synonym of *allowances.* (exceptions)
- On line 124, mark the word that means "forgiveness." (grace)
- Go to line 127. Mark the synonym of *allowed.* (permitted)
- Go to line 130. Mark the word that means "officially ignore." (waive)
- Number two reasons for a waiver. (1. medical necessity; 2. religious belief)
- Mark the words that indicate there are other possibilities not mentioned. (but not limited to)
- Go to line 138. Mark the synonym of *requirements.* (provisions)
- On line 139, mark the hyphenated adjective that means "clear." (see-through)

Have students read from line 140 to the end according to the option that you chose. Pay attention to the policy specifics. Draw an asterisk in the margin if you think the demand is unreasonable.

When most of the students are finished, continue with the entire class. Let's see how well you understood what you read.

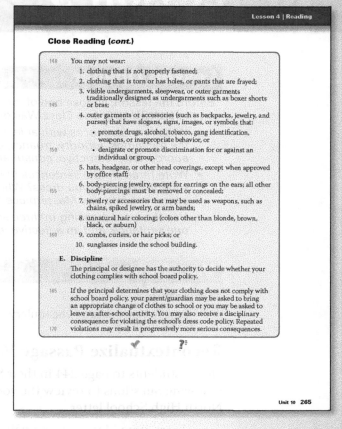

- Circle the check mark or the question mark for this section. Draw a question mark over any confusing words.
- Go to the numbered list. Underline the adjective clauses used to describe clothing and accessories that may not be worn. (that is not properly fastened; that is torn or has holes; that are frayed; that have slogans, signs, images, or symbols; that may be used as weapons)
- Go to line 142. Mark the word that means "threadbare." (frayed)
- Go to line 150. Mark the word that means "say bad things." (denigrate)
- On the same line, mark the synonym of *bias*. (discrimination)
- On line 155, mark the word that means "hidden." (concealed)
- On line 164, mark the word that means "obeys." (complies)
- Go to line 170. Mark the synonym of *increasingly*. (progressively)

Have partners compare text markings and correct any errors.

Lesson 4 | Reading

Close Reading (*cont.*)

You may not wear:

1. clothing that is not properly fastened;
2. clothing that is torn or has holes, or pants that are frayed;
3. visible undergarments, sleepwear, or outer garments traditionally designed as undergarments such as boxer shorts or bras;
4. outer garments or accessories (such as backpacks, jewelry, and purses) that have slogans, signs, images, or symbols that:
   - promote drugs, alcohol, tobacco, gang identification, weapons, or inappropriate behavior, or
   - denigrate or promote discrimination for or against an individual or group.
5. hats, headgear, or other head coverings, except when approved by office staff;
6. body-piercing jewelry, except for earrings on the ears; all other body-piercings must be removed or concealed;
7. jewelry or accessories that may be used as weapons, such as chains, spiked jewelry, or arm bands;
8. unnatural hair coloring; (colors other than blonde, brown, black, or auburn)
9. combs, curlers, or hair picks; or
10. sunglasses inside the school building.

E. Discipline

The principal or designee has the authority to decide whether your clothing complies with school board policy.

If the principal determines that your clothing does not comply with school board policy, your parent/guardian may be asked to bring an appropriate change of clothes to school or you may be asked to leave an after-school activity. You may also receive a disciplinary consequence for violating the school's dress code policy. Repeated violations may result in progressively more serious consequences.

✓ ?

Unit 10 265

Unit 10

Lesson 5

Lesson Opener

Before the lesson, choose one of the following activities to write on the board or post on the *LANGUAGE! Live* Class Wall online.

- *Write four sentences with at least two vocabulary words in each. Show you know the meanings. (priority, truancy, enforce, enhance, distracted, principle, resist, appropriate, restrictive, consultation)*
- *Write three simple sentences that describe the way you dress when you are not in school. When do you dress? Where do you go? How do you dress? Combine the three sentences into one Masterpiece Sentence.*
- *Use the word* dressing *in three sentences. Use it as a verb in one sentence, a noun in one sentence, and an adjective in another sentence.*

Vocabulary

Objective

- Review key passage vocabulary.

Recontextualize Passage Vocabulary

Direct students to page 244 in their Student Books. Use the following questions to review the vocabulary words from the North High School letter.

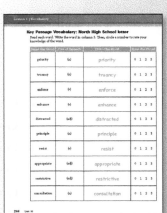

- Every time Marcus sees a pair of jeans he likes, he buys them. Can he *resist* a great pair of jeans? (no) Your uncle is the "grammar police." He corrects anyone and everyone who says something the wrong way. Can he *resist* correcting people? (no) Maria loves lip gloss. Whenever her favorite brand puts out a new color, she has to buy it. Maria has a hard time doing what? (resisting new shades of lip gloss)
- You trip in the hallway, and it makes you five seconds late to class. Is this an example of *truancy*? (no) Walter decides to play video games all morning instead of going to school. Is he guilty of *truancy*? (yes) At a struggling school, only half of the students show up for class. What problem does this school need to address? (truancy)
- You and your science tutor decide you are totally prepared for the test. Have you decided this in *consultation* with your tutor? (yes) You wear a shirt your mother hates. You slip out of the house before she can see you. Have you chosen the shirt in *consultation* with your mother? (no) Before you ask someone out, you talk to that person's best friend to see if she thinks it would be a good idea. She says it would be. You are glad you had the what? (consultation)
- Nina's algebra teacher asks to meet with her after school, but Nina blows it off. Is meeting with her algebra teacher a *priority* for Nina? (no) More than anything else in the world, you want to get into art school after graduation. To do that, your GPA has to be 3.5 when you apply. Is getting a 3.5 GPA a *priority* for you? (yes) You spend every Saturday afternoon working at a soup kitchen. For you, helping people in need is a what? (priority)

- One dating *principle* of yours is that you and your date should always split the bill. Do you believe you and your date should split the bill? (yes) The girl who sits next to you in biology class tries to copy your homework. Would you say she has strong ethical *principles*? (no) You believe that a person learns more by failing an assignment than by cheating on it. You have high what? (principles)
- Your little sister has asked you to help her stop biting her nails. You see her biting her nails and say nothing. Are you helping *enforce* her new policy? (no) You aren't supposed to wear T-shirts with writing on them to school. You do. A teacher stops you in the hallway, gives you a large white T-shirt, and tells you to change. Is he *enforcing* the dress code? (yes) You work the gate at the neighborhood pool. Kids under 13 aren't allowed in the pool area without a parent. Two 10-year-olds come to the gate. What should you do? (enforce the rules)
- You go to a fancy wedding in jeans and an old shirt with rips and stains. Is your clothing *appropriate*? (no) A friend says you look nice today, and you shove her out of the way. Is your action *appropriate*? (no) Even though you don't like the birthday gift you received from your great aunt, you write her a thank-you note. You do this because writing a thank-you note is what? (appropriate)
- You want to *enhance* your image as a friendly person. You say "hi" to everyone you see. Does this help? (yes) You want to *enhance* your brown eyes. Does wearing sunglasses help? (no) In children's books, pictures do what? (enhance the story)
- It's "wear your pajamas to school" day. You wear a loose top and your flannel PJ bottoms. Is your outfit *restrictive*? (no) After surgery, patients are sometimes limited to a diet of gelatin, broth, and water. Is such a diet *restrictive*? (yes) You usually watch a couple of hours of TV every day. Suddenly, your mom says you can only watch TV on weekends. You find this new rule what? (restrictive)
- You are trying to keep an eye on your baby niece, but a friend keeps texting you. Are you *distracted*? (yes) You know texting while babysitting is not a good idea, so you silence your phone and put it in your bag. Are you *distracted* now? (no) Your niece needs to go to bed, but her new puppy keeps jumping on the bed and making her giggle. What is she? (distracted)

Writing

Objectives

- Use text to write coherent paragraphs in response to reading.
- Demonstrate understanding of the constructs of argumentation through writing.
- Write a persuasive letter.

Quick Write in Response to Reading

Direct students to pages 266 and 267 in their Student Books. Read the prompt.

Lesson 5 | Writing

Quick Write in Response to Reading Answers will vary.

Write a letter in response to Ms. Dogan, principal of North High School. Express your support or criticism of the new dress code. Make sure your letter responds directly to specific arguments used to justify the adoption of a school uniform policy.

Arguments needing a response:

1. school dress affects school success
2. enforcing old policy kept students out of classrooms
3. uniform policy promotes school safety

Dear Ms. Dogan,

As a student at North High School, I have a great stake in the implementation of the new uniform policy. It seems to me that you presented some very serious problems plaguing our school system, but your solution appears to be overly simplistic. Changing the way we dress will not solve these serious problems.

You claim school dress affects school success and cite Virginia Draa's research to substantiate your claim. I find myself wondering what else besides a uniform policy sets the stage for improvements in attendance, graduation, and suspension rates. Other factors like school leadership, curriculum choices, community involvement, and student voice could have played a part in their successes.

Another justification for changing the dress code focused on the problems encountered when trying to enforce the code. Students lingered in the office and missed valuable instruction time. Instead of moving to a uniform policy, schools could have simply changed the way they enforced the dress code. What will happen to students who do not wear the proper uniform? Will

266 Unit 10

Lesson 5 | Writing

Quick Write in Response to Reading (*cont.*)

they also be sent to the office to wait for proper attire?

Additionally, you claim the uniform policy will promote school safety. Changing the way we dress will not eliminate the reasons students fight or seek to disrupt the school environment. By not addressing the underlying problems, students will simply find more creative ways to bring contraband to school.

Our schools are facing serious problems, and students who want to learn are negatively impacted by these issues. District leadership needs to examine the underlying causes and seek solutions that significantly and positively impact our learning landscape. I believe the most important part of those solutions will come from empowering the student voice, not silencing it.

Bring us into the discussion and allow us to work with the leadership in this district to bring exciting changes to our classrooms. Please don't take away our individuality and our voice.

Thank you,

A concerned North High student

Unit 10 267

Before you begin to compose your letter, consider the points you want to make. Look at your Close Reading of the letter on pages 260–265 and write down three things you want to address. These can be points with which you agree or points with which you disagree. Once you've decided the position you want to take and the issues you want to address, then you can begin writing your response. **Have students write the letter.**

Reading

Objectives

- Self-correct as comprehension of text deepens.
- Answer questions to demonstrate comprehension of text.
- Engage in class discussion.
- Identify the enduring understandings from a piece of text.

Revisit Passage Comprehension

Direct students back to pages 257–259 in their Student Books. Have students review their answers and make any necessary changes. Then, have partners share their answers and collaborate to perfect them.

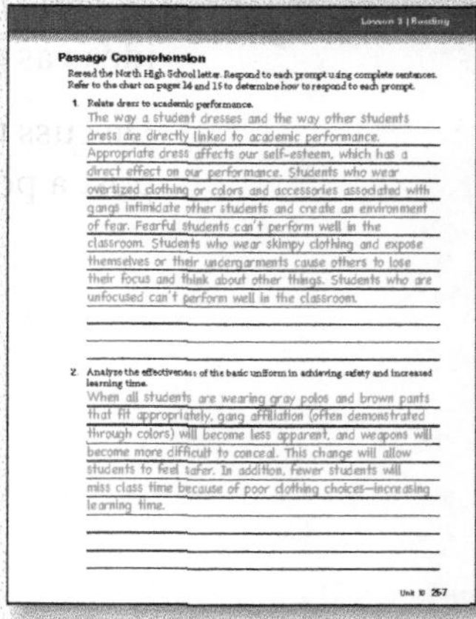

Lesson 3 | Reading

Passage Comprehension

Reread the North High School letter. Respond to each prompt using complete sentences. Refer to the chart on pages 14 and 15 to determine how to respond to each prompt.

1. Relate dress to academic performance.
   The way a student dresses and the way other students dress are directly linked to academic performance. Appropriate dress affects our self-esteem, which has a direct effect on our performance. Students who wear oversized clothing or colors and accessories associated with gangs intimidate other students and create an environment of fear. Fearful students can't perform well in the classroom. Students who wear skimpy clothing and expose themselves or their undergarments cause others to lose their focus and think about other things. Students who are unfocused can't perform well in the classroom.

2. Analyze the effectiveness of the basic uniform in achieving safety and increased learning time.
   When all students are wearing gray polos and brown pants that fit appropriately, gang affiliation (often demonstrated through colors) will become less apparent, and weapons will become more difficult to conceal. This change will allow students to feel safer. In addition, fewer students will miss class time because of poor clothing choices—increasing learning time.

Unit 10 257

Author's Purpose

Direct students back to page 243 in their Student Books. We just finished studying a nonfiction selection about dress code. Before discussing our enduring understandings, let's talk about the author's purpose. Why did this author write the text? Have students share ideas with a partner and then the whole group. If necessary, elaborate on or clarify their responses. (The author's purpose is the reason that he or she wrote the text. Authors write for different purposes. The principal clearly wrote the policy to inform the students and parents of the new dress code. However, the information in the letter seems to not only be an attempt to inform, but also an attempt to persuade them of the need for the dress code.) Have students correct the answer on the page if necessary.

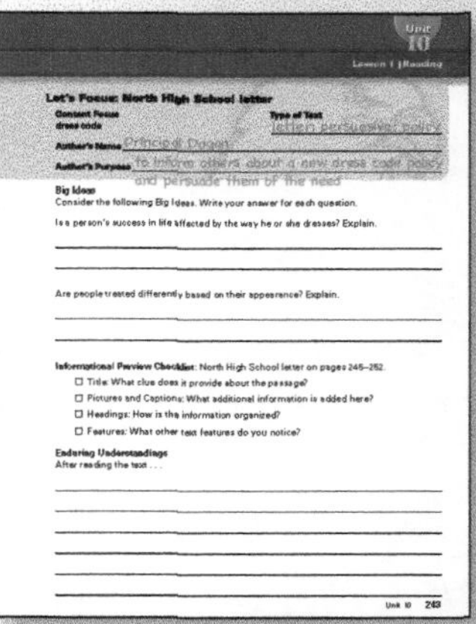

Unit 10

Lesson 1 | Reading

Let's Focus: North High School letter

Content Focus: dress code

Type of Text: letter, persuasive, policy

Author's Name: Principal Dagan

Author's Purpose: to inform others about a new dress code policy and persuade them of the need

Big Ideas

Consider the following Big Ideas. Write your answer for each question.

Is a person's success in life affected by the way he or she dresses? Explain.

Are people treated differently based on their appearance? Explain.

Informational Preview Checklist: North High School letter on pages 245–252.

- ☐ Title: What clue does it provide about the passage?
- ☐ Pictures and Captions: What additional information is added here?
- ☐ Headings: How is the information organized?
- ☐ Features: What other text features do you notice?

Enduring Understandings

After reading the text . . .

Unit 10 243

Enduring Understandings

Reread the Big Idea questions.

Is a person's success in life affected by the way he or she dresses?

Are people treated differently based on their appearance?

Generate a class discussion about the questions and the answers students came up with in Lesson 1. Have them consider whether their answers have changed any after reading the text.

Use the following talking points to foster conversation. Then, have students write their enduring understandings from the unit.

- Do you judge people by the way they dress? Do people judge you by the way you dress? What does the clothing you wear say about you? Is it the message you want to send?

- Often, people with more power than us make rules and laws intended to protect us. Is the benefit of protection always worth the loss of freedom? What is more important: freedom or security? If you don't agree with a law or a rule, what can you do about it? Can youth be heard?

What we read should make us think. Use our discussion and your thoughts about the text to determine what you will "walk away with." Has it made you think about a personal experience or someone you know? Has your perspective or opinion on a specific topic changed? Do you have any lingering thoughts or questions? Write these ideas as your enduring understandings. What will you take with you from this text?

Discuss the enduring understandings with the class. If time permits, have students post a personal response about their enduring understandings to the online class wall.

Unit 10

Lesson 6

Lesson Opener

Before the lesson, choose one of the following activities to write on the board or post on the *LANGUAGE! Live* Class Wall online.

- *Use the word* enforcing *in three sentences. Use it as a verb in one sentence, a noun in one sentence, and an adjective in another sentence.*
- *Use intransitive verbs to write five sentences about why uniforms can be a bad idea.*
- *Write one sentence about the way you dress on the weekends. Write one sentence about the way you dress for school. Combine the sentences using a conjunction to create a compound sentence.*

Reading

Objectives

- Determine and discuss the topic of a text.
- Determine and discuss the author's purpose.
- Use text features to preview text.

Passage Introduction

Direct students to page 268 in their Student Books. Discuss the content focus.

Content Focus

self-expression

We are about to learn more about how the way you dress is a form of self-expression.

Type of Text

Text can be divided into two categories: informational and literature. **Discuss the differences.** We just read a letter and uniform policy. Look at the first page of this text and the title. Predict what this text will be about. Once you have your prediction, it should be pretty easy to determine what type of text it is. Write your answer on the page.

Lesson 6 | Reading

Let's Focus: "Say Yes to Free Dress!"

Content Focus
self-expression

Type of Text
persuasive

Author's Name unknown

Author's Purpose to persuade

Big Ideas
Consider the following Big Ideas. Write your answer for each question.

Does clothing reflect who you are on the inside?

How does society affect the definition of *appropriate dress*?

Informational Preview Checklist: "Say Yes to Free Dress!" on pages 270–273.

- ☐ Title: What clue does it provide?
- ☐ Pictures: What additional information is added here?
- ☐ Headings: What information do they provide?
- ☐ Margin Information: What vocabulary is important to understand this story?
- ☐ Features: What other text features do you notice?

Enduring Understandings
After reading the text . . .

268 Unit 10

Author's Purpose

Have students glance at the text. Who is the author of the text? (unknown) Now that you have made your prediction about the type of text, you should know the author's purpose for writing—they are one in the same. Prior to reading, make an educated guess as to what the author's purpose for writing is. After we finish, you will return to this section and revise your answer if you need to. Have students write their responses on the page.

Background Information

Youth belong to groups. It is a fundamental need of adolescence. Socioeconomic class, gender, intelligence, conformity, morality, and ethnicity can be important in the formation of these groups. There are groups such as punks, emos, ravers, metalheads, goths, cowboys, jocks, and nerds. Groups express themselves through distinct styles and behaviors. What happens when one of these mediums of expression is taken away?

Big Ideas

Read the Big Idea questions aloud.

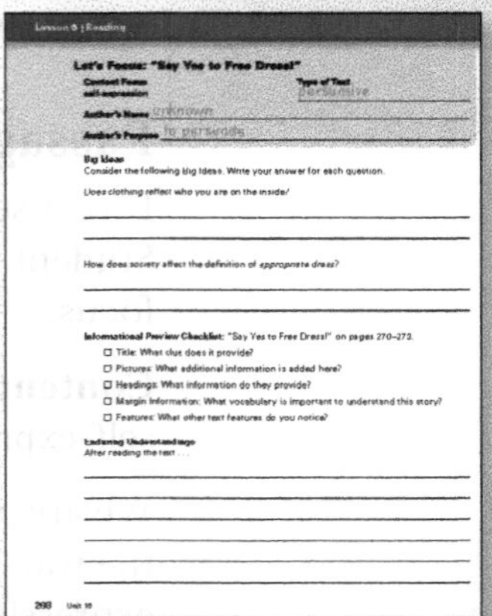

Big Ideas

Does clothing reflect who you are on the inside?

How does society affect the definition of *appropriate dress*?

As a class, consider the two Big Idea questions. After discussing each question, have students write an answer. We'll come back to these questions after we finish reading the text. You can add to your answers as you gain information and perspective.

Preview

Read the Preview Checklist on page 268. Follow the Preview Procedure outlined below.

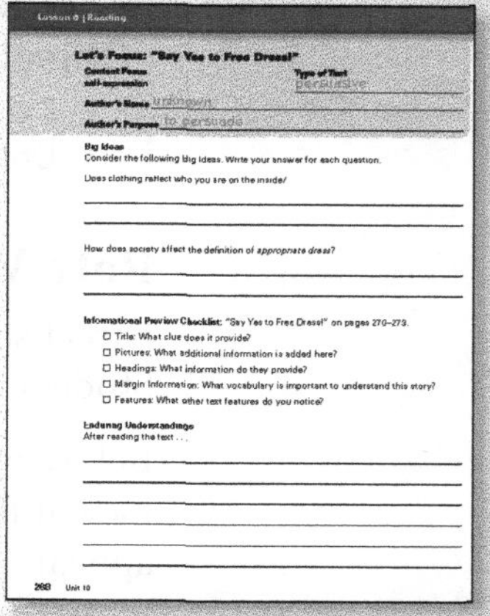

Lesson 6 | Reading

Let's Focus: "Say Yes to Free Dress!"

Content Focus self-expression

Type of Text persuasive

Author's Name unknown

Author's Purpose to persuade

Big Ideas

Consider the following Big Ideas. Write your answer for each question.

Does clothing reflect who you are on the inside?

How does society affect the definition of *appropriate dress*?

Informational Preview Checklist: "Say Yes to Free Dress!" on pages 270–273.

- ☐ Title: What clue does it provide?
- ☐ Pictures: What additional information is added here?
- ☐ Headings: What information do they provide?
- ☐ Margin Information: What vocabulary is important to understand this story?
- ☐ Features: What other text features do you notice?

Enduring Understandings

After reading the text . . .

268 Unit 10

Preview Procedure

- Group students with partners or in triads.
- Have students count off as 1s or 2s. The 1s will become the student leaders. If working with triads, the third students become 3s.
- The student leaders will preview the text in addition to managing the checklist and pacing.
- The 2s and 3s will preview the text with 1s.
- Direct 1s to open their Student Books to page 268 and 2s and 3s to open their Student Books to page 270. This allows students to look at a few different pages at one time without turning back and forth.

Direct students to page 270. Have students preview the text.

If necessary, guide students in a short preview using the following talking points.

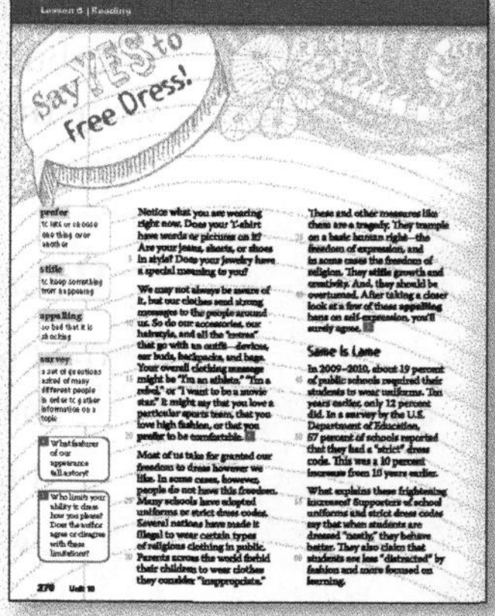

Lesson 6 | Reading

Say YES to Free Dress!

prefer to like or choose one thing over another

stifle to keep something from happening

appalling so bad that it is shocking

survey a set of questions asked of many different people in order to gather information on a topic

What features of our appearance tell a story?

Who limits your ability to dress how you please? Does the author agree or disagree with these limitations?

Notice what you are wearing right now. Does your T-shirt have words or pictures on it? Are your jeans, shorts, or shoes in style? Does your jewelry have a special meaning to you?

We may not always be aware of it, but our clothes send strong messages to the people around us. So do our accessories, our hairstyle, and all the "extras" that go with an outfit—devices, ear buds, backpacks, and bags. Your overall clothing message might be "I'm an athlete," "I'm a rebel," or "I want to be a movie star." It might say that you love a particular sports team, that you love high fashion, or that you prefer to be comfortable.

Most of us take for granted our freedom to dress however we like. In some cases, however, people do not have this freedom. Many schools have adopted uniforms or strict dress codes. Several nations have made it illegal to wear certain types of religious clothing in public. Parents across the world forbid their children to wear clothes they consider "inappropriate."

These and other measures like them are a tragedy. They trample on a basic human right—the freedom of expression, and in some cases the freedom of religion. They stifle growth and creativity. And, they should be overturned. After taking a closer look at a few of these appalling bans on self-expression, you'll surely agree.

Same Is Lame

In 2009–2010, about 19 percent of public schools required their students to wear uniforms. Ten years earlier, only 12 percent did. In a survey by the U.S. Department of Education, 57 percent of schools reported that they had a "strict" dress code. This was a 10 percent increase from 10 years earlier.

What explains these frightening increases? Supporters of school uniforms and strict dress codes say that when students are dressed "neatly," they behave better. They also claim that students are less "distracted" by fashion and more focused on learning.

270 Unit 10

What is the title of the text? ("Say Yes to Free Dress!") Did you notice anything creative that this author did to capture your attention while playing with words? (The title and headings all have rhyming words.) Which words rhyme in the title? (yes/dress) Let's read the rest of the headings looking for rhyming words. **Read headings with students.** (same/lame; belief/grief; hole/control) Pay special attention to the meanings of these headings because they provide insight into the author's position on free dress.

Vocabulary

Objectives

- Evaluate word knowledge.
- Determine the meaning of key passage vocabulary.

Rate Vocabulary Knowledge

Direct students to page 269 in their Student Books.

Before we read the text, let's take a look at the vocabulary words that appear in this text. Remind students that as you read each word in the first column aloud, they will write the word in the third column and then rate their knowledge of it. Display the Vocabulary Rating Scale poster or write the information on the board. Review the meaning of each rating.

Vocabulary Rating Scale

0—I have never heard the word before.

1—I have heard the word, but I'm not sure how to use it.

2—I am familiar with the word, but I'm not sure if I know the correct meaning.

3—I know the meaning of the word and can use it correctly in a sentence.

Lesson 6 | Vocabulary

Key Passage Vocabulary: "Say Yes to Free Dress!"

Read each word. Write the word in column 3. Then, circle a number to rate your knowledge of the word.

Read the Word	Part of Speech	Write the Word	Rate the Word
prefer	(v)	prefer	0 1 2 3
stifle	(v)	stifle	0 1 2 3
appalling	(adj)	appalling	0 1 2 3
survey	(n)	survey	0 1 2 3
increase	(n)	increase	0 1 2 3
contradict	(v)	contradict	0 1 2 3
individuality	(n)	individuality	0 1 2 3
ban	(v)	ban	0 1 2 3
valid	(adj)	valid	0 1 2 3
exaggeration	(n)	exaggeration	0 1 2 3

Unit 10 269

The points are not a grade; they are just there to help you know which words you need to focus on. By the end of this unit, you should be able to change all your ratings to a 3. That's the goal.

Read each word aloud. Have students repeat it, write it, and rate it. Then, have volunteers who rated a word *2* or *3* use the word in an oral sentence.

Preteach Vocabulary

Let's take a closer look at the words. Follow the Preteach Procedure below.

Preteach Procedure

This activity is intended to take only a short amount of time, so make it an oral exercise.

- Introduce each word as indicated on the word card.
- Read the definition and example sentences.
- Ask questions to clarify and deepen understanding.
- If time permits, allow students to share.

* If your students would benefit from copying the definitions, please have them do so in the vocabulary log in the back of the Student Books using the margin definitions in the passage selections. This should be done outside of instruction time.

prefer (v)

Let's read the first word together. *Prefer.*

Definition: If you *prefer* something, you like it or choose it over another thing. What means "to like or choose one thing over another"? (prefer)

Example 1: Some people like comedy movies, but I *prefer* dramas.

Example 2: Senior citizens who *prefer* warm weather sometimes retire to Florida.

Example 3: Just because a person *prefers* to be quiet does not mean he or she is shy.

Question 1: You always take the front seat on the bus. Do you *prefer* a seat further back? Yes or no? (no)

Question 2: Lydia's sister likes pop music, but Lydia likes country. Does Lydia *prefer* country? Yes or no? (yes)

Pair Share: Turn to your partner and tell what kind of pizza you *prefer.*

stifle (v)

Let's read the next word together. *Stifle.*

Definition: If you *stifle* something, you keep it from happening. What word means "to keep something from happening"? (stifle)

Example 1: It is difficult to *stifle* the giggles once you get them.

Example 2: If you try to not feel a certain way, you are trying to *stifle* your feelings.

Example 3: Teachers who like to lecture sometimes *stifle* debate or discussion in their classrooms.

Question 1: You *stifle* a yawn. Do you yawn? Yes or no? (no)

Question 2: You see a big crowd on the corner and are curious about what's happening, but you're late to a meeting, so you continue on your way. Do you *stifle* your curiosity? Yes or no? (yes)

Pair Share: Turn to your partner and tell what you wish people at ballgames would *stifle.*

appalling (adj)

Let's read the next word together. *Appalling.*

Definition: If something is *appalling*, it is so bad that it is shocking. What word means "so bad that it is shocking"? (appalling)

Example 1: On occasion, I spot some *appalling* outfits in the hallway.

Example 2: If the humor in a movie is so crude as to be *appalling*, I turn it off.

Example 3: I saw a woman fill her baby's bottle with soda at a restaurant. In my view, this is an example of *appalling* parenting.

Question 1: You give your friend a compliment, and it brightens her day. Was the compliment *appalling*? Yes or no? (no)

Question 2: The slave trade is alive and well in this "free" country. Is this information *appalling*? Yes or no? (yes)

Pair Share: Turn to your partner and discuss examples of public figures acting in *appalling* ways.

survey (n)

Let's read the next word together. *Survey.*

Definition: A *survey* is a set of questions you ask many different people in order to gather information on a topic. What word means "a set of questions asked of many different people in order to gather information on a topic"? (survey) This word can also be used as a verb. For example: *I surveyed my friends to see what everyone wanted for lunch.*

Example 1: Magazines conduct *surveys* to see what kinds of articles people like to read.

Example 2: After shopping at some stores, you can participate in an online *survey* about your experience and then get a percentage off your next purchase.

Example 3: *Surveys* show that many Americans get too little sleep.

Question 1: A friend is writing a newspaper story on superheroes and asks everyone in the school who their favorite superhero is. Is he taking a *survey*? Yes or no? (yes)

Question 2: Before you see a movie, you ask your best friend if she liked it. Have you taken a *survey*? Yes or no? (no)

Pair Share: Turn to your partner. Discuss ways you could use technology to conduct a *survey*.

increase (n)

Let's read the next word together. *Increase.*

Definition: An *increase* is a growth in size, number, or strength. What word means "a growth in size, number, or strength"? (increase)

Example 1: If you set aside 10 percent every time you earn or receive money, you will see an *increase* in your savings.

Example 2: There won't be an *increase* in the lake levels until we get a good rain.

Example 3: There has been an *increase* in football attendance this year; more fans than ever are going to games.

Question 1: More cars cut through the neighborhood on your street these days. Is there an *increase* in traffic on your street? Yes or no? (yes)

Question 2: Our precinct set a voter turnout record during the last election. Did the precinct see an *increase* in voting? Yes or no? (yes)

Pair Share: Turn to your partner and tell how you *increase* your energy when you're feeling sluggish.

contradict (v)

Let's read the next word together. *Contradict.*

Definition: To *contradict* something is to go against it or to say the opposite of it. What word means "to go against or to say the opposite of something"? (contradict)

Example 1: We all know that too much sugar and salt is bad for you. Nevertheless, junk-food companies often hire "experts" to *contradict* these facts.

Example 2: People who like to create a stir often *contradict* other people's ideas just to get a rise out of them.

Example 3: In a famous play by Shakespeare, a husband *contradicts* everything his wife says; he even says it's the moon when she points out the sun.

Question 1: You say the party is tonight, but your best friend insists it's next week. Is your friend *contradicting* you? Yes or no? (yes)

Question 2: You show up for a meeting at 7:00 a.m. Nobody's there. You see a flyer on the door that says the meeting is at 7:00 p.m. Does the flyer *contradict* what you thought you knew? Yes or no? (yes)

Pair Share: Turn to your partner. Take turns stating a fact and *contradicting* it.

individuality (n)

Let's read the next word together. *Individuality.*

Definition: *Individuality* is the state of being different from everyone else. What means "the state of being different from everyone else"? (individuality)

Example 1: In this country, we are allowed to express our *individuality* unless we do it in a way that hurts someone else.

Example 2: One reason teenagers argue with their parents is because they are trying to show their *individuality* and independence.

Example 3: You can express your *individuality* through your clothing, your words, and your actions.

Question 1: When they are on duty, soldiers must wear a uniform. Are they expressing their *individuality*? Yes or no? (no)

Question 2: You like art class because you can create artworks that reflect your feelings. Do you show your *individuality* through art? Yes or no? (yes)

Pair Share: Turn to your partner and name one way you express your *individuality.*

ban (v)

Let's read the next word together. *Ban.*

Definition: To *ban* something is to forbid it or to formally say that it must not be done, said, or used. What means "to forbid; to formally state that something must not be done, said, or used"? (ban)

Example 1: Most cities have *banned* smoking in public buildings.

Example 2: When someone is under house arrest, he or she is *banned* from leaving the property.

Example 3: In 2011, France *banned* ketchup in school cafeterias—except with French fries.

Question 1: Would most people support a *ban* on phones in public? Yes or no? (no)

Question 2: A city passed an ordinance that says "no bicycles on sidewalks." Were bikes *banned* on sidewalks? Yes or no? (yes)

Pair Share: What annoying behavior do you wish was *banned* in public? Tell your partner.

valid (adj)

Let's read the next word together. *Valid.*

Definition: If something is *valid*, it is logical or based on good, clear thinking. What word means "logical; based on good, clear thinking"? (valid)

Example 1: If you have a *valid* reason for being late, you will be excused.

Example 2: Vegetarians have many *valid* reasons for not eating meat, including respect for animals.

Example 3: If I said I deserved to be president of the United States because I am kind to animals, my thinking would not be *valid.*

Question 1: You ask for an A instead of a D because you did some of your homework. Is your reasoning *valid*? Yes or no? (no)

Question 2: The student council reduces the price of prom tickets in order to boost sales. Is the council's reasoning *valid*? Yes or no? (yes)

Pair Share: Turn to your partner and take turns stating reasons a player might miss basketball practice and telling whether each reason is *valid.*

exaggeration (n)

Let's read the last word together. *Exaggeration.*

Definition: An *exaggeration* is a stretching of the truth, or the act of making something seem bigger or more important than it really is. What means "a stretching of the truth; the act of making something seem bigger or more important than it really is"? (exaggeration)

Example 1: When someone says "I'm dying of hunger," it's usually an *exaggeration.*

Example 2: One of my friends is prone to *exaggeration*, so I think of her stories more as entertainment than as truth.

Example 3: In most cases, the phrase "You're a rock star" is a complete *exaggeration.*

Question 1: There's thunder, lightning, and rain. You call it a storm. Is this an *exaggeration*? Yes or no? (no)

Question 2: You're very warm. You say, "I'm burning up." Is this an *exaggeration*? Yes or no? (yes)

Pair Share: Turn to your partner and describe how your day is going. Use at least two *exaggerations.*

10

Reading

Objectives

- Read persuasive text.
- Monitor comprehension during text reading.

"Say Yes to Free Dress!"

Direct students to page 270 in their Student Books.

Now that we have previewed vocabulary, it's time to read. Good readers can read text of different lengths and difficulty levels. Good reading requires active participation: eyes on text, mind on message.

Guiding Students Toward Independent Reading

It is important that your students read as much and as often as they can. Assign readings that meet the needs of your students, based on your observations and data. This is a good opportunity to stretch your students. If students become frustrated, scaffold the reading with paired reading, choral reading, or a read-aloud.

Options for reading text:

- Teacher read-aloud
- Teacher-led or student-led choral read
- Paired read or independent read

Choose an option for reading text. Students read according to the option that you chose.

Review the purpose of the numbered squares in the text and prompt students to stop periodically and check comprehension.

If you choose to read the text aloud or chorally, use the following text boxes and stop to ask questions and have students answer them.

SE p. 270, paragraphs 1–2

Notice what you are wearing right now. Does your T-shirt have words or pictures on it? Are your jeans, shorts, or shoes in style? Does your jewelry have a special meaning to you?

We may not always be aware of it, but our clothes send strong messages to the people around us. So do our accessories, our hairstyle, and all the "extras" that go with an outfit—devices, ear buds, backpacks, and bags. Your overall clothing message might be "I'm an athlete," "I'm a rebel," or "I want to be a movie star." It might say that you love a particular sports team, that you love high fashion, or that you **prefer** to be comfortable.

1. What features of our appearance tell a story?

SE p. 270, paragraphs 3–4

Most of us take for granted our freedom to dress however we like. In some cases, however, people do not have this freedom. Many schools have adopted uniforms or strict dress codes. Several nations have made it illegal to wear certain types of religious clothing in public. Parents across the world forbid their children to wear clothes they consider "inappropriate."

These and other measures like them are a tragedy. They trample on a basic human right—the freedom of expression, and in some cases the freedom of religion. They **stifle** growth and creativity. And they should be overturned. After taking a closer look at a few of these **appalling** bans on self-expression, you'll surely agree.

2. Who limits your ability to dress how you please? Does the author agree or disagree with these limitations?

Same Is Lame

SE p. 270, paragraphs 5–6

In 2009–2010, about 19 percent of public schools required their students to wear uniforms. Ten years earlier, only 12 percent did. In a **survey** by the U.S. Department of Education, 57 percent of schools reported that they had a "strict" dress code. This was a 10 percent **increase** from 10 years earlier.

What explains these frightening increases? Supporters of school uniforms and strict dress codes say that when students are dressed "neatly," they behave better. They also claim that students are less "distracted" by fashion and more focused on learning.

SE p. 271, paragraph 1

These arguments may sound good. In reality, though, they aren't credible. In fact, they **contradict** the very idea of education itself! School is supposed to be a place of learning, growth, and development. But strict dress codes send mixed messages to kids. On one hand, kids are being told to "learn and grow!" On the other, they are being told to "stay the same!" This sort of contradiction can only lead to confusion in the minds of dress-code kids—who are also the adults of tomorrow.

3. What should happen at school?

SE p. 271, paragraphs 2–3

The sobering truth is this: if young people are taught to conform, or be like everyone else, they will continue to conform in adulthood. How will more sameness solve the world's many problems? We are in desperate need of creative, original thinking. We need new energy and new ideas. We need young people who are taught to be bold and different.

"By instituting a uniform policy," says a leading child psychologist, "schools are taking away kids' **individuality**." In a democracy such as ours—one that values individuality so highly—this type of action should be considered a crime! I take my hat off to those who have tried to cure the problems in education with uniforms, but, it will never work.

4. Would the child psychologist agree with the heading, Same Is Lame?

SE p. 271, paragraph 4

In truth, there is little proof to substantiate the benefits of school uniforms. According to the American Civil Liberties Union—an organization developed to defend and preserve the rights and liberties of individuals—there is no link between school uniforms and safety or good grades. Uniforms are simply an infringement on our rights as human beings. Add to that the fact that wearing a prescribed set of clothing every day alleviates free will, and you have a disastrous outcome. Administrators and teachers focus their attention on developing students' decision-making skills and ability to take responsibility for their actions. But both of these skills require real-world practice, something students would receive less of without the freedom to stand in front of their closet and choose what to present to their peers every day.

Belief Grief

SE p. 272, paragraph 1

In 2004, France **banned** certain religious clothing in schools and government buildings. Several other nations have passed similar laws. These laws center mainly on religious head coverings worn by Muslim women. Supporters of the laws say that wearing the veils or scarves encourages racism, especially after the events of September 11, 2001. (On that day, Muslim extremists attacked buildings in New York City and Washington, D.C., killing thousands.) Others say that religious clothing in public places challenges the idea that church and state should be separate.

5. How is the United States connected to the laws in France?

SE p. 272, paragraphs 2–4

Some of these concerns are **valid**. Religious clothing can bring up negative feelings in those who disagree with a religion's basic ideas. These negative feelings can sometimes lead to violence. And some people believe that religion should have a greater role in government.

But these concerns do not justify laws that ban religious clothing. The laws are quick fixes rather than real solutions. Instead of trying to prevent racism by getting rid of religious clothing, we should try to prevent racism through education. People should take the time to learn about other religions and to share their own beliefs in calm and non-threatening ways. Only this will reduce racism and violence for good. And only this will convince people that every religion has a few extremists but is mainly made up of regular folks who want to lead peaceful lives.

The bottom line is this: clothing doesn't create conflict, fear does. And we can't legislate fear away. We have to do the hard work of accepting each other, getting to know each other, and learning from each other. We need to learn how to make our differences a plus rather than a minus. Accepting all kinds of clothing is the necessary first step in this very long journey.

6. What needs to be part of the very long journey of acceptance?

SE p. 272, paragraphs 5–7

Black Hole of Control

Most parents mean well. They want their kids to grow up, be happy, do good work, and have healthy relationships. They want them to find their way in life and develop their gifts and talents. But they also want their kids to be "normal." They want their kids to reflect positively on their own parenting. Parents think of their children as walking billboards for their own success.

This may be a slight **exaggeration**. But it's true that most parents care what their kids look like on a day-to-day basis. It's also true that many parents have very different standards for dress and overall appearance than their children do.

page break

For example, a 2010 survey showed that nearly 40 percent of young people between the | ages of 18 and 29 have tattoos. By contrast, only 15 percent of people their parents' age have tattoos. These statistics reflect a trend that goes beyond tattoos. What was once considered taboo is quickly becoming the norm. This trend makes it hard for parents to let go of their "kids"—even those aged 18 to 29!

7. What do tattoos have to do with the way people dress?

SE p. 273, paragraphs 1–2

Naturally enough, this need for control expresses itself in parental rules about how a child may or may not dress. Most six-year-olds don't care how they dress. But by the time a child reaches middle school, the mood has shifted. Daily battles about clothes, makeup, and hairstyles become the norm. The louder the parent says NO, the louder the child says YES.

In fact, it's a natural reflex for a teen to say yes when a parent says no. In early adolescence, kids begin to separate from their parents. They go on a mission to find out who they are as individuals. The will to do this becomes even stronger as a teen matures. One very obvious and important way of asserting one's identity is by wearing unique—and sometimes startling—clothes and accessories.

8. How do you assert your identity?

SE p. 273, paragraph 3

Because it is a natural part of growing up, a teenager who wants to wear blue hair, ripped jeans, or a nose ring should be permitted to do so. True, there are some limits to this idea. No child—or adult—should wear clothes that are insulting or indecent. (We all know these types of clothing when we see them.) But if the fashion choice is harmless, it should be allowed. If a child wants to wear purple-striped jeans with an orange-and-black plaid top, his or her parents should say nothing but "Have a nice day!" Then, they should congratulate themselves on raising such a creative, adventuresome kid. Creative self-expression must be in their jeans.

9. Who determines whether dress is insulting or indecent?

SE p. 273, paragraph 4

> And remember, parents: the best way a child can learn is through making a mistake. If an outfit is a terrible choice, your kids' friends will definitely let them know!

10. What advice does the author give parents?

SE p. 273, paragraphs 5–6

> **The Skinny**
>
> If you've noticed a theme in this argument, it might be "Your clothes reflect who you are." People have been expressing themselves through clothing since the earliest humans realized they had a choice between buffalo skins and bear skins. Today, the choice might be between skinny jeans and wide-legged pants. But the stakes are the same. Any attempt to limit our basic freedom to dress—in a school, in a nation, or in a home—is an attempt to limit our very humanity.
>
> So, go ahead and make a statement. Explore who you are. Experiment with your style. Say "yes" to your own sense of dress. Self-expression is always in fashion.

11. What is "The Skinny" on the author's point of view? Do you agree or disagree?

For confirmation of engagement, have partners discuss the various ways people express themselves with clothing. Have volunteers share ideas with the class.

Unit 10

Lesson 7

Lesson Opener

Before the lesson, choose one of the following activities to write on the board or post on the *LANGUAGE! Live* Class Wall online.

- *Write a summary of the author's point of view in "Say Yes to Free Dress!"*
- *Make a list of adjectives describing the clothes you are wearing today.*
- *Write five sentences explaining what you would do to express yourself if you were unable to do so through clothing, accessories, makeup, or hair.*

Vocabulary

Objective

- Review key passage vocabulary.

Review Passage Vocabulary

Direct students to page 269 in their Student Books. Use the following questions to review the vocabulary words from "Say Yes to Free Dress!" Have students answer each question using the vocabulary word or indicating its meaning in a complete sentence.

Key Passage Vocabulary: "Say Yes to Free Dress!"

Read each word. Write the word in column 3. Then, circle a number to rate your knowledge of the word.

[illegible]	[illegible]	[illegible]	[illegible]
prefer	(v)	prefer	0 1 2 3
stifle	(v)	stifle	0 1 2 3
appalling	(adj)	appalling	0 1 2 3
survey	(n)	survey	0 1 2 3
increase	(n)	increase	0 1 2 3
contradict	(v)	contradict	0 1 2 3
individuality	(n)	individuality	0 1 2 3
ban	(v)	ban	0 1 2 3
valid	(adj)	valid	0 1 2 3
exaggeration	(n)	exaggeration	0 1 2 3

Unit 10 269

- The author of the text says clothes can show whether you *prefer* to be comfortable. What might you wear if you *prefer* to be comfortable? (If you prefer to be comfortable, you probably wear comfortable clothes like jeans, T-shirts, or sweats.) Does the author of the article *prefer* school uniforms to a lenient or free dress code? (No, the author does not prefer school uniforms; he or she prefers free dress.)
- The author says strict dress codes *stifle* what? (The author says strict dress codes stifle growth and creativity.) What would you say the author of this article is trying to *stifle*? (Possible responses: The author is trying to stifle strict dress codes. The author is trying to stifle opinions that are different from his or hers.)
- The author writes that strict dress codes are *appalling*. Based on this description, how do they affect him or her? (If he or she finds them appalling, they shock him or her.) Would you say this description is an *exaggeration*? Why or why not? (Yes; the author might find the dress codes annoying, but he or she probably isn't really appalled by them.)
- A *survey* shows that more schools use uniforms now than before. How was the survey most likely conducted? (To conduct the survey, someone probably asked many different schools if they used uniforms.) If you *surveyed* the students in our school, do you think they would agree with the author's main idea? Why or why not? (Possible response: Yes, surveying students would show that most students agree that free dress encourages self-expression.)

- According to the article, are dress codes *increasing*? Cite a fact to support your answer. (Yes, they are increasing; in 1999–2000, only 47 percent of schools had a strict dress code, but in 2009–2010, 57 percent of them did.) Schools that adopt uniforms believe that uniforms will *increase* what? (They believe uniforms will increase students' ability to focus.)
- What basic goal of education does the author say uniforms *contradict*? (The author says uniforms contradict the idea that students should be learning to express themselves.) How could you *contradict* the idea that uniforms tell students to "stay the same"? (Possible response: To contradict this idea, you could say that uniforms encourage students to express themselves in other ways besides clothing.)
- The author states that a democracy such as ours values *individuality*. What is the author saying we value? (If we value individuality, we value being ourselves.) Do you agree that we value *individuality*, or can you think of an example that *contradicts* this idea? (Responses will vary. Some students will say that we do value individuality because our laws tolerate some differences; others will say we really value being like everyone else—having the same clothes, phones, and cars as people who are "in.")
- In 2004, France *banned* some religious clothing. Could people wear this clothing in public places? (No; if the clothing was banned, they could not wear it.) What do governments hope to *stifle* by *banning* religious clothing? (By banning religious clothing, they hope to stifle expressions of racism.)
- According to the author, what makes some of these concerns about racism *valid*? (The author admits that events like 9/11 make concerns about racism valid.) What does the author say is a better way to address racism than *banning* certain types of clothes? (The author says taking the time to learn about other races and cultures is a better way to address racism than banning religious clothing.) Do you find the author's thinking *valid*? Why or why not? (Possible response: Yes, the author's thinking is valid because the more we learn about others, the more we understand and respect them.)

Assign online practice from the Text Training link on the left menu of your teacher dashboard.

- The author writes that kids are "walking billboards" for their parents' success as parents; he or she also writes that parents care what their kids look like. Which of these statements is an *exaggeration*? Why? (The first one is an exaggeration because it makes the situation sound far more extreme than it really is.) When the author writes that "any attempt to limit our basic freedom to dress . . . is an attempt to limit our very humanity," do you find it an *exaggeration*? Why or why not? (Possible response: Yes, it seems like an exaggeration because even when a student is wearing a uniform, he or she is still a human being.)

Reading

Objectives

- Determine how to respond to prompts.
- Use critical thinking skills to write responses to prompts about text.
- Support written answers with evidence from text.
- Use personal knowledge as evidence in support of an author's claim.
- Develop counterclaims against an author based on personal experience.

Critical Understandings: Direction Words *clarify, develop an argument, prove, support*

Let's review some prompts. Prompts are statements that require a constructed response, which can range from a list to a complete sentence to a paragraph or an essay. Good readers can take prompts and turn them into questions to help them understand what is being asked.

Write the words *clarify, develop an argument, prove,* and *support* on the board. Have students read the words aloud with you.

Direct students to pages 14 and 15 in their Student Books. It is critical to understand what the question is asking and how to answer it. Today, we will look at four direction words used in prompts.

Have students read about the four direction words in the chart with their partner.

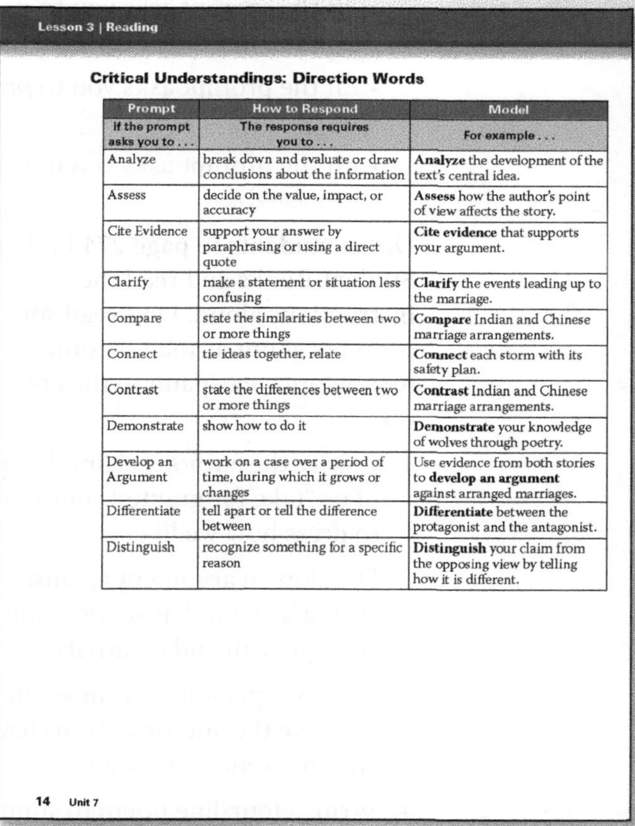

Lesson 3 | Reading

Critical Understandings: Direction Words

Prompt	How to Respond	Model
If the prompt asks you to . . .	The response requires you to . . .	For example . . .
Analyze	break down and evaluate or draw conclusions about the information	**Analyze** the development of the text's central idea.
Assess	decide on the value, impact, or accuracy	**Assess** how the author's point of view affects the story.
Cite Evidence	support your answer by paraphrasing or using a direct quote	**Cite evidence** that supports your argument.
Clarify	make a statement or situation less confusing	**Clarify** the events leading up to the marriage.
Compare	state the similarities between two or more things	**Compare** Indian and Chinese marriage arrangements.
Connect	tie ideas together, relate	**Connect** each storm with its safety plan.
Contrast	state the differences between two or more things	**Contrast** Indian and Chinese marriage arrangements.
Demonstrate	show how to do it	**Demonstrate** your knowledge of wolves through poetry.
Develop an Argument	work on a case over a period of time, during which it grows or changes	Use evidence from both stories to **develop an argument** against arranged marriages.
Differentiate	tell apart or tell the difference between	**Differentiate** between the protagonist and the antagonist.
Distinguish	recognize something for a specific reason	**Distinguish** your claim from the opposing view by telling how it is different.

14 Unit 7

Chart Reading Procedure

- Group students with partners or in triads.
- Have students count off as 1s or 2s. The 1s will become the student leaders. If working with triads, the third students become 3s.
- The student leaders will read the left column (Prompt) in addition to managing the time and turn-taking if working with a triad.
- The 2s will explain the middle column of the chart (How to Respond). If working in triads, 3s take turns explaining the middle column.
- The 1s read the model in the right column (Model), and 2s and 3s restate the model as a question.
- All students should follow along with their pencil eraser while others are explaining the chart.
- Students must work from left to right, top to bottom in order to benefit from this activity.

Check for understanding by requesting an oral response to the following questions.

- If the prompt asks you to *clarify*, the response requires you to . . . (make a statement or situation less confusing).
- If the prompt asks you to *develop an argument*, the response requires you to . . . (work on a case over a period of time, during which it grows or changes).
- If the prompt asks you to *prove*, the response requires you to . . . (give evidence to show that it is true).
- If the prompt asks you to *support*, the response requires you to . . . (help it succeed).

Direct students to page 274 in their Student Books and read the instructions aloud. Let's read some prompts about a small section of the text before we expand to the entire text.

1. Clarify the author's claim that most of us "take for granted" our freedom to dress how we like.
2. Develop an argument against the author's claim that school uniforms stifle growth and creativity.
3. Use your personal clothing choices to prove the author's claim that our clothing sends a message.
4. Write a four-line poem to support the author's claim that dress codes are bad.

We are going to focus on the first section of this text. We will practice answering prompts with these new direction words. Having a good understanding of the text from the

Lesson 7 | Reading

Critical Understandings

Reread the first section of "Say Yes to Free Dress!" Respond to each prompt using complete sentences. Refer to the chart on pages 14 and 15 to determine how to respond to each prompt.

1. Clarify the author's claim that most of us "take for granted" our freedom to dress how we like.
   The author is saying that because many of us have always had the freedom to dress how we like, we do not appreciate it. People who are forced to dress in a certain way would likely have a greater appreciation for the freedom to dress to express.
2. Develop an argument against the author's claim that school uniforms stifle growth and creativity.
   School uniforms do not stifle growth and creativity. In fact, they do the opposite. When students are no longer allowed to express themselves through clothing (a very easy form of expression), they are forced to develop new methods of expression—increasing creativity and, thus, personal growth.
3. Use your personal clothing choices to prove the author's claim that our clothing sends a message.
   Answers will vary but should be about the way in which clothing choices express who students are and what they like and/or don't like.
4. Write a four-line poem to support the author's claim that dress codes are bad.
   Answers will vary. Possible answer:
   Who am I and what do I stand for?
   Instead of telling you, I would rather show you.
   In this polo and khaki pants I am silenced.
   How I long to express. How I long to express.

274 Unit 10

beginning will help build a foundation for understanding the rest of the text and make it feel less difficult.

Guided Practice

Let's practice answering questions that are written as prompts. Remember to use the chart as reference.

1. Clarify the author's claim that most of us "take for granted" our freedom to dress how we like.

How should we respond according to the chart? (If the prompt asks you to *clarify*, the response requires that you make a statement or situation less confusing.) Now, turn the prompt into a question to confirm your understanding. Tell your partner the question. (What does the author mean when he or she says most of us "take for granted" our freedom to dress how we like?)

While providing partner time, write the sentence starter on the board.

The author is saying ______________________.

Have partners answer the question.

2. Develop an argument against the author's claim that school uniforms stifle growth and creativity.

How should we respond according to the chart? (If the prompt asks you to *develop an argument*, the response requires that you work on a case over a period of time, during which it grows or changes.) Now, turn the prompt into a question to confirm your understanding. Tell your partner the question. (What is the proof that school uniforms do not stifle growth and creativity?) Because you are being asked to work on a case over a period of time, you will need to pull in information from things you have learned in the past.

While providing partner time, write the sentence starter on the board.

School uniforms do not stifle growth and creativity. In fact, ______________
____.

Have partners answer the question.

3. Use your personal clothing choices to prove the author's claim that our clothing sends a message.

How should we respond according to the chart? (If the prompt asks you to *prove*, the response requires that you give evidence to show that it is true.) Now, turn the prompt into a question to confirm your understanding. Tell your partner the question. (What experiences from your personal clothing choices prove that our clothing sends a message?) Remember, you are using personal clothing experiences as proof. So think about this.

While providing partner time, write the sentence starter on the board.

The fact that______________________________ is proof that clothing sends a message.

Have partners answer the question.

4. Write a four-line poem to support the author's claim that dress codes are bad.

How should we respond according to the chart? (If the prompt asks you to *support*, the response requires that you help it succeed.) Now, turn the prompt into a question to confirm your understanding. Tell your partner the question. (What can be said to further indicate that dress codes are bad?)

Have partners write a poem.

Writing

Objective

- Demonstrate understanding of the story elements for writing.

Prepare to Write: Short Story

In Lesson 10, you will be tasked with writing a short story. Planning is an important step for writing, especially with longer writing assignments.

Direct students to page 275 in their Student Books and read the writing prompt. Walk through the planning template, modeling possible responses. Have partners discuss their ideas and complete the planning template.

Lesson 7 | Writing

Prepare to Write: Short Story

Imagine living in Kalba, a land where everything is gray and brown. Lives are governed by strict laws, and every day is predictably the same as the previous day. It's the only world you know until an unexpected event provides the opportunity for something different. Use the template to plan your short story.

Setting: Answers will vary.

When: 2413 Where: Kalba

Characters and attributes:

1. Samantha—16 years old, questions and challenges every rule
2. Warren—16 years old, follows the rules but quietly resents them
3. Miko—16 years old, from a different world full of color and individuality

Problem: life in Kalba is dreary; individualism is stifled; most people are very unhappy, but they are unwilling to try to speak out against the laws that restrict them

Solution: living in a world where individuality and creativity are allowed to flourish

Kick-off event (starts the story): a strange flying machine crashes in the woods behind Samantha's house, carrying someone from a very different land

Unit 10 275

Unit 10

Lesson 8

Lesson Opener

Before the lesson, choose one of the following activities to write on the board or post on the *LANGUAGE! Live* Class Wall online.

- *Use the word* exciting *in three sentences. Use it as a verb in one sentence, a noun in one sentence, and an adjective in another sentence.*
- *Write the dialogue of a conversation you think the author of "Say Yes to Free Dress!" might have with Principal Dogan. Remember to punctuate correctly.*
- *Expand one or more of these simple sentences, using the steps in Masterpiece Sentences.*

  I dress.

  I like clothes.

  I express myself.

  My clothes speak.

Reading

Objectives

- Establish a purpose for rereading text.
- Read a persuasive text.
- Monitor comprehension during text reading.
- Use critical thinking skills to write responses to prompts about text.
- Support written answers with evidence from text.
- Use personal knowledge as evidence in support of an author's claim.
- Develop counterclaims against an author based on personal experience.
- Use multiple texts to develop counterclaims against an argument.

Reading for a Purpose: "Say Yes to Free Dress!"

Good readers read text more than once to gain understanding. Nothing is wrong with you if you don't understand the text after the first read. Difficult text requires you to reread the text or parts of the text, especially when the vocabulary words are difficult or unfamiliar.

Let's preview the prompts to provide a purpose for rereading the text. You should recognize the direction words that we practiced in the last lesson.

Direct students to pages 276 and 277 in their Student Books. Have students read the prompts aloud with you.

1. Use the First Amendment to prove the author's claim that the freedom of expression is a basic human right.
2. Use personal experience to support the author's claim that in early adolescence kids begin to separate from their parents.
3. Write a new title for the passage in support of the author's claim that your clothes reflect who you are and send a message. Take notice of the headings and current title and what is similar before creating your title.

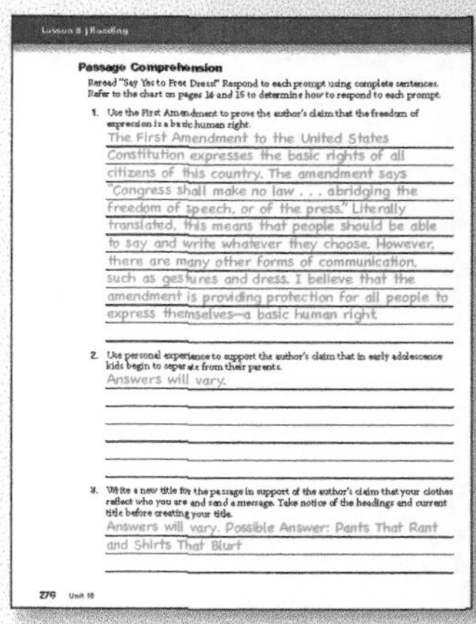

Lesson 8 | Reading

Passage Comprehension

Reread "Say Yes to Free Dress!" Respond to each prompt using complete sentences. Refer to the chart on pages 14 and 15 to determine how to respond to each prompt.

1. Use the First Amendment to prove the author's claim that the freedom of expression is a basic human right.

   The First Amendment to the United States Constitution expresses the basic rights of all citizens of this country. The amendment says "Congress shall make no law . . . abridging the freedom of speech, or of the press." Literally translated, this means that people should be able to say and write whatever they choose. However, there are many other forms of communication, such as gestures and dress. I believe that the amendment is providing protection for all people to express themselves—a basic human right.

2. Use personal experience to support the author's claim that in early adolescence kids begin to separate from their parents.

   Answers will vary.

3. Write a new title for the passage in support of the author's claim that your clothes reflect who you are and send a message. Take notice of the headings and current title before creating your title.

   Answers will vary. Possible Answer: Pants That Rant and Shirts That Blurt

276 Unit 10

4. Use text evidence from the NHS letter to develop an argument against the author's claim that laws and dress codes trample on a person's religious freedom.
5. Clarify the author's quote "Clothing doesn't create conflict, fear does."
6. Prove the author's point that parents have a hard time "letting go of their kids."

It's time to revisit the text. Good readers reread text for different purposes like answering critical thinking questions. Rereading text also builds fluency including accurate word recognition and speed.

Choose an option for reading text. Have students read the text according to the option that you chose.

Options for reading text:

- Teacher read-aloud
- Teacher-led or student-led choral read
- Paired read or independent read with bold vocabulary words read aloud

Direct students to page 270 in their Student Books or have them tear out the extra copy of the text from the back of their book.

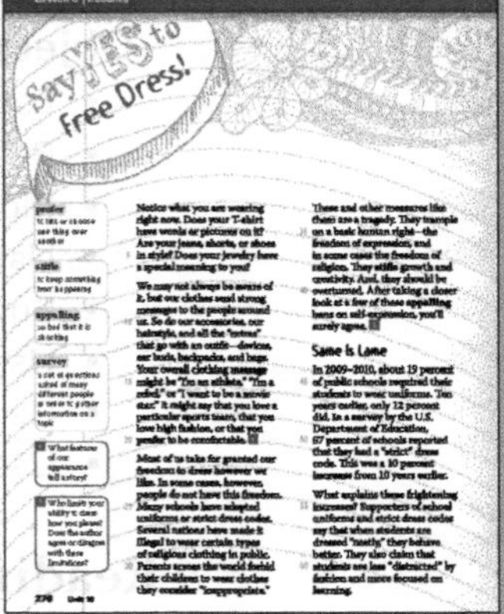

Note: To minimize flipping back and forth between the pages, a copy of each text has been included in the back of the Student Books. Encourage students to tear this out and use it when working on activities that require the use of the text.

Have students read the text.

Passage Comprehension

Write the words *clarify, develop an argument, prove,* and *support* on the board. Have students read the words aloud with you.

Direct students to pages 14 and 15 in their Student Books. It is critical to understand what the question is asking and how to answer it. Today, we will review four direction words used in prompts.

Lesson 3 | Reading

Critical Understandings: Direction Words

Prompt If the prompt asks you to . . .	How to Respond The response requires you to . . .	Model For example . . .
Analyze	break down and evaluate or draw conclusions about the information	**Analyze** the development of the text's central idea.
Assess	decide on the value, impact, or accuracy	**Assess** how the author's point of view affects the story.
Cite Evidence	support your answer by paraphrasing or using a direct quote	**Cite evidence** that supports your argument.
Clarify	make a statement or situation less confusing	**Clarify** the events leading up to the marriage.
Compare	state the similarities between two or more things	**Compare** Indian and Chinese marriage arrangements.
Connect	tie ideas together, relate	**Connect** each storm with its safety plan.
Contrast	state the differences between two or more things	**Contrast** Indian and Chinese marriage arrangements.
Demonstrate	show how to do it	**Demonstrate** your knowledge of wolves through poetry.
Develop an Argument	work on a case over a period of time, during which it grows or changes	Use evidence from both stories to **develop an argument** against arranged marriages.
Differentiate	tell apart or tell the difference between	**Differentiate** between the protagonist and the antagonist.
Distinguish	recognize something for a specific reason	**Distinguish** your claim from the opposing view by telling how it is different.

14 Unit 7

Have students read the chart on pages 14 and 15 with their partner. Check for understanding by requesting an oral response to the following questions.

- If the prompt asks you to *clarify,* the response requires you to . . . (make a statement or situation less confusing).
- If the prompt asks you to *develop an argument*, the response requires you to . . . (work on a case over a period of time, during which it grows or changes).
- If the prompt asks you to *prove,* the response requires you to . . . (give evidence to show that it is true).
- If the prompt asks you to *support,* the response requires you to . . . (help it succeed).

Let's practice answering questions that are written as prompts. Remember to use the chart as a reference. Don't forget, if the direction word is confusing, try to restate the prompt by using a question word.

Direct students to pages 276 and 277 in their Student Books.

Passage Comprehension

Reread "Say Yes to Free Dress!" Respond to each prompt using complete sentences. Refer to the chart on pages 14 and 15 to determine how to respond to each prompt.

1. Use the First Amendment to prove the author's claim that the freedom of expression is a basic human right.
   The First Amendment to the United States Constitution expresses the basic rights of all citizens of this country. The amendment says "Congress shall make no law . . . abridging the freedom of speech, or of the press." Literally translated, this means that people should be able to say and write whatever they choose. However, there are many other forms of communication, such as gestures and dress. I believe that the amendment is providing protection for all people to express themselves—a basic human right.

2. Use personal experience to support the author's claim that in early adolescence kids begin to separate from their parents.
   Answers will vary.

3. Write a new title for the passage in support of the author's claim that your clothes reflect who you are and send a message. Take notice of the headings and current title before creating your title.
   Answers will vary. Possible Answer: Pants That Rant and Shirts That Blurt

Passage Comprehension (*cont.*)

4. Use text evidence from the NHS letter and policy to develop an argument against the author's claim that laws and dress codes trample on a person's religious freedom.
   Bans on religious clothing have been established because such clothing encourages hatred and violence toward people simply because of religion. Banning the outward symbols of religion is intended to protect those who practice specific religions by keeping people from taking drastic measures. The dress code policy clearly states that exceptions to the rules can be made based on "sincerely held religious beliefs." This means that the dress code, and others like it, will not trample on religious freedoms.

5. Clarify the author's quote "Clothing doesn't create conflict, fear does."
   The author feels that religious clothing gets banned because some fear that it may lead to violence. We cannot create laws that make the fear go away. To eliminate fear, we need to accept each other, get to know each other, and learn from each other.

6. Prove the author's point that parents have a hard time "letting go of their kids."
   The author used a 2010 survey that showed that 40 percent of youth have tattoos, but a mere fraction of their parents have been "inked." The author felt that the survey regarding tattoos reflects a trend other than tattoos, which proves that parents are afraid to let their kids grow up and make their own decisions because they disagree with the popular trends.

Guided Practice

1. Use the First Amendment to prove the author's claim that the freedom of expression is a basic human right.

How should we respond according to the chart? (If the prompt asks you to *prove*, the response requires that you give evidence to show that it is true.) Now, turn the prompt into a question to confirm your understanding. Tell your partner the question. (What does the First Amendment say that proves the freedom of expression is a basic human right?)

Have students find the First Amendment on page 271. Generate a class discussion about the connection between the words in the amendment and freedom of expression. Explain that the first 10 amendments to the Constitution are considered to be the Bill of Rights, which outlines human rights for citizens of the United States that the government cannot take away from them.

Write the following sentence starters on the board.

The First Amendment to the United States Constitution expresses the basic rights of all citizens of this country. The amendment says ______________________.

Literally translated, this means ______________________.

However, ______________________.

Have students write the answer on the page.

Independent Practice

Have partners respond to the remaining prompts. For students who need more assistance, provide the following alternative questions.

Alternative questions:

2. What has happened in your life that proves the claim that in early adolescence kids begin to separate from their parents?
3. What can you call the passage to help say that clothes reflect who you are and send a message?
4. What is said in the NHS letter that disproves that laws and dress codes trample on a person's religious freedom?
5. What does "Clothing doesn't create conflict, fear does" mean?
6. What evidence from the text is proof that parents have a hard time "letting go of their kids"?

Unit 10

Lesson 9

Lesson Opener

Before the lesson, choose one of the following activities to write on the board or post on the *LANGUAGE! Live* Class Wall online.

- *Summarize your point of view of school uniforms.*
- *Using conjunctions, write two sentences about the changes when a uniform policy is adopted.*
- *Change the following sentences to active voice.*

  A letter was written by the students.

  A pair of designer shoes was stolen by gang members.

  The policy was violated by twenty students on the first day of school.

  My clothing is an expression of who I am.

Reading

Objectives

- Read with purpose and understanding.
- Answer questions to demonstrate comprehension of text.
- Identify and explain explicit details from text.
- Monitor comprehension during text reading.
- Objectively summarize text.
- Analyze a summary for accuracy and content.
- Analyze how an author distinguishes position from that of others.
- Analyze an author's response to conflicting viewpoints.
- Analyze the presentation of differing viewpoints on the same issue.
- Identify where texts disagree.
- Identify rhetorical fallacies in text.
- Determine the validity of an author's claims and counterclaims.
- Identify claims supported by evidence and those that aren't.
- Determine the double meaning of puns used by an author.

Close Reading of "Say Yes to Free Dress!"

Highlighters or colored pencils

Let's reread "Say Yes to Free Dress!" I will provide specific instructions on how to mark the text to help with comprehension.

Have students get out a highlighter or colored pencil.

Direct students to pages 278–282 in their Student Books.

Draw a rectangle around the title.

Circle the headings. What do you notice about the title and the headings? (rhyming)

Now, let's read the vocabulary words aloud.

- What's the first bold vocabulary word? (prefer) *Prefer* means "to like or choose one thing over another." I *prefer* jeans over slacks. Have partners use the word in a sentence.
- What's the next vocabulary word? (stifle) *Stifle* means "to keep something from happening." Lack of sleep can *stifle* my ability to get my work done. Have partners use the word in a sentence.

- Next word? (appalling) *Appalling* means "so bad that it is shocking." The youth's inability to communicate face-to-face is *appalling.* **Have partners use the word in a sentence.**
- Next word. (survey) *Survey* means "a set of questions asked of many different people in order to gather information on a topic." A lady at the mall asked me to participate in a *survey* about shopping. **Have partners use the word in a sentence.**
- Let's continue. (increase) *Increase* means "a growth in size, number, or strength." There will be an *increase* in lunch prices next year because food will become more expensive to buy. **Have partners use the word in a sentence.**
- Next word? (contradict) *Contradict* means "to go against or to say the opposite of something." Your actions should not *contradict* your message. **Have partners use the word in a sentence.**
- Let's continue. (individuality) *Individuality* means "the state of being different from everyone else." Your *individuality* is what makes you special. **Have partners use the word in a sentence.**
- Next word? (banned) *Banned* means "forbade; formally stated that something must not be done, said, or used." In some inner-city schools, officials *banned* cell phone use in schools; students and teachers can't even bring them inside the building. **Have partners use the word in a sentence.**
- Let's continue. (valid) *Valid* means "logical; based on good, clear thinking." The argument "just because" is not *valid* in any situation. **Have partners use the word in a sentence.**
- Last word. (exaggeration) *Exaggeration* means "a stretching of the truth; the act of making something seem bigger or more important than it really is." His *exaggeration* seems a lot like lying. **Have partners use the word in a sentence.**

Talk with a partner about any vocabulary word that is still confusing for you to read or understand.

As you reread the passage, you will monitor your understanding by circling the check marks or the question marks. Please be sure to draw a question mark over any confusing words, phrases, or sentences.

Options for rereading text.

- **Teacher read-aloud**
- **Teacher-led or student-led choral read**
- **Paired read or independent read with bold vocabulary words read aloud**

Choose an option for reading text. Have students read lines 1–20 according to the option that you chose. Pay attention to the arguments. Draw a star in the margin if you agree with what the author is saying.

When most of the students are finished, continue with the entire class. Let's see how well you understood what you read.

Close Reading

Read the text.

"Say Yes to Free Dress!"

Notice what you are wearing right now. Does your T-shirt have words or pictures on it? Are your jeans, shorts, or shoes in style? Does your jewelry have a special meaning to you?

We may not always be aware of it, but our clothes send strong messages to the people around us. So do our accessories, our hairstyle, and all the "extras" that go with an outfit—devices, ear buds, backpacks, and bags. Your overall clothing message might be "I'm an athlete," "I'm a rebel," or "I want to be a movie star." It might say that you love a particular sports team, that you love high fashion, or that you **prefer** to be comfortable.

Most of us take for granted our freedom to dress however we like. In some cases, however, people do not have this freedom. Many schools have adopted uniforms or strict dress codes. Several nations have made it illegal to wear certain types of religious clothing in public. Parents across the world forbid their children to wear clothes they consider "inappropriate."

These and other measures like them are a tragedy. They trample on a basic human right—the freedom of expression, and in some cases the freedom of religion. They **stifle** growth and creativity. And, they should be overturned. After taking a closer look at a few of these **appalling** bans on self-expression, you'll surely agree.

✓ ?

- Circle the check mark or the question mark for this text. Draw a question mark over any confusing words.
- Go to the title. Mark the synonym of *unregulated*. (free)
- Mark the gender-neutral word that means "clothing." (dress)
- On line 4, mark the words used to indicate that our clothes communicate or speak. (send strong messages)
- Go to line 6. Number the "extras." (1. devices; 2. ear buds; 3. backpacks; 4. bags)
- Number the six possible messages of clothing. (1. "I'm an athlete"; 2. "I'm a rebel"; 3. "I want to be a movie star"; 4. you love a particular sports team; 5. you love high fashion; 6. you prefer to be comfortable) In the margin, write the message spoken by your outfit today.
- Go to line 10. Mark the phrase that means "not appreciating the value of something." (take for granted)
- On the same line, mark the word that means "in whatever way." (however)
- Go to line 11. Mark the word that introduces a contradiction and means "on the other hand." (however)
- Go to line 14. Mark the word that means "do not allow." (forbid)
- On the same line, mark the synonym of *judge*. (consider)
- Go to line 15. Mark the word that means "not proper." (inappropriate) Circle the prefix that means "not." (in-)
- On line 16, mark the pronoun that refers to schools adopting uniforms, nations outlawing religious clothing, and parents forbidding inappropriate dress. (these) Mark the words indicating there are other examples. (and other measures like them)
- On the same line, mark the word that means "bad" but has a stronger connotation, more like a disaster. (tragedy)
- In the next sentence, mark the consecutive adjectives. (basic; human) Draw an arrow from each adjective to the word it describes. (human: right; basic: human right)
- Go to line 19. Mark the word that means "awful" but has a stronger connotation than *horrible*. (appalling)
- Go to line 20. Mark the rhetorical or leading language used to persuade the reader. (you'll surely agree)

Have students read the section Same Is Lame according to the option that you chose. While reading, pay attention to the arguments. Draw a star in the margin if you agree with what the author is saying.

When most of the students are finished, continue with the entire class. Let's see how well you understood the next section.

- Circle the check mark or the question mark for this text. Draw a question mark over any confusing words.
- Go to line 24. Mark the word that means "rigid" but has a stronger connotation than *firm*. (strict)
- In the same paragraph, mark the credible source used by the author to ensure he or she is taken seriously. (U.S. Department of Education)

Lesson 9 | Reading

Close Reading (*cont.*)

Same Is Lame

In 2009–2010, about 19 percent of public schools required their students to wear uniforms. Ten years earlier, only 12 percent did. In a **survey** by the U.S. Department of Education, 57 percent of schools reported that they had a "strict" dress code. This was a 10 percent **increase** from 10 years earlier.

What explains these frightening increases? Supporters of school uniforms and strict dress codes say that when students are dressed "neatly," they behave better. They also claim that students are less "distracted" by fashion and more focused on learning.

These arguments may sound good. In reality, though, they aren't credible. In fact, they **contradict** the very idea of education itself! School is supposed to be a place of learning, growth, and development. But strict dress codes send mixed messages to kids. On one hand, kids are being told to "learn and grow!" On the other, they are being told to "stay the same!" This sort of contradiction can only lead to confusion in the minds of dress-code kids—who are also the adults of tomorrow.

The sobering truth is this: if young people are taught to conform, or be like everyone else, they will continue to conform in adulthood. How will more sameness solve the world's many problems? We are in desperate need of creative, original thinking. We need new energy and new ideas. We need young people who are taught to be bold and different.

"By instituting a uniform policy," says a leading child psychologist, "schools are taking away kids' **individuality.**" In a democracy such as ours—one that values individuality so highly—this type of action should be considered a crime! I take my hat off to those who have tried to cure the problems in education with uniforms, but, it will never work.

In truth, there is little proof to substantiate the benefits of school uniforms. According to the American Civil Liberties Union—an organization developed to defend and preserve the rights and liberties of individuals—there is no link between school uniforms and safety or good grades. Uniforms are simply an infringement on our rights as human beings. Add to that the fact that wearing a prescribed set of clothing every day alleviates free will, and you have a disastrous outcome. Administrators and teachers focus their attention on developing students' decision-making skills and ability to take responsibility for their actions. But both of these skills require real-world practice, something students would receive less of without the freedom to stand in front of their closets and choose what to present to their peers every day.

✔ ?

Unit 10 279

- Circle the punctuation used to indicate that the exact word from the document is being used. (quotation marks)
- Mark the first claims of the opposition used by the author to establish reasons for the argument. (Supporters of school uniforms and strict dress codes say that when students are dressed "neatly," they behave better. They also claim that students are less "distracted" by fashion and more focused on learning.)
- Go to line 27. Circle the word that means "state to be true." (claim)
- Go to line 28. Circle the positive impact of being less distracted. (more focused on learning)
- Go to line 29. Mark the word with Latin origin that means "worthy to be believed." (credible)
- Go to lines 32 and 33. Mark the transition words that indicate a contradiction. (on one hand, on the other)
- Underline both sides of the contradiction. (Kids are being told to learn and grow; they are told to stay the same.) In the margin, write what is telling kids to "stay the same." (uniforms)
- Go to line 35. Mark the words that describe "kids." (the adults of tomorrow)
- Are the claims in this paragraph supported by evidence? (no) Are they valid? Write your answer in the margin. (Answers will vary.)
- Go to line 36. Mark the synonym of *serious*. (sobering)
- On the same line, use context to define *conform*. (be like everyone else) Circle the word that signals that a definition will follow. (or)

- Go to line 38. Mark the singular possessive noun. (world's) Draw an arrow to show what it owns. (problems)
- At the end of the same paragraph, number the things the world needs. (1. creative, original thinking; 2. new energy; 3. new ideas; 4. young people taught to be bold and different)
- Circle the adjective that cannot be used to describe the clothing in a school with uniforms. (different)
- Go to line 41. Mark the vague reference to an important person. (a leading child psychologist) In the margin, write what the author should have included for credibility purposes. (a name)
- Go to line 42. Mark the plural possessive noun. (kids') Draw an arrow to show what they own. (individuality)
- Go to line 43. Mark the phrase that explains our democracy. (one that values individuality)
- On the same line, mark the pronoun *this*. Draw a line to what *this* is referencing. (instituting a uniform policy)
- Mark the pun, or play on words, that uses an idiom that is related to clothing. (I take my hat off)
- Go to line 46. Mark the word that means "prove." (substantiate)
- Go to line 49. Mark the claim made by the author. (no link between school uniforms and safety or good grades) Mark the source she uses for this claim. (American Civil Liberties Union)
- Go to line 53. Mark the goal of administrators and teachers. (developing students' decision-making skills and the ability to take responsibility for their actions) In the margin, write why this is ironic in schools with uniforms. (Students don't even get to choose what they wear.)

Have students read the section Belief Grief according to the option that you chose. While reading, pay attention to the arguments. Draw a star in the margin if you agree with what the author is saying.

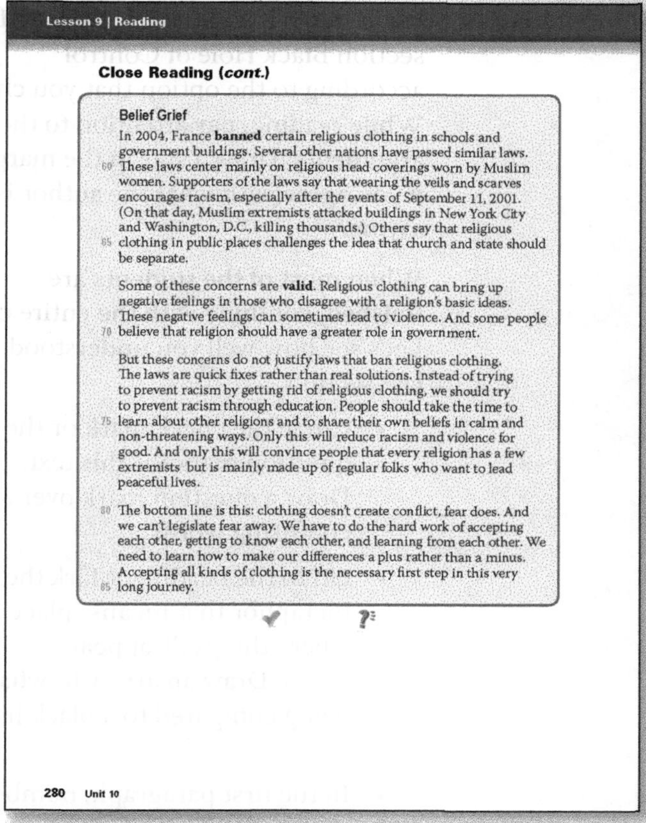

Lesson 9 | Reading

Close Reading (*cont.*)

Belief Grief

In 2004, France **banned** certain religious clothing in schools and government buildings. Several other nations have passed similar laws. These laws center mainly on religious head coverings worn by Muslim women. Supporters of the laws say that wearing the veils and scarves encourages racism, especially after the events of September 11, 2001. (On that day, Muslim extremists attacked buildings in New York City and Washington, D.C., killing thousands.) Others say that religious clothing in public places challenges the idea that church and state should be separate.

Some of these concerns are **valid**. Religious clothing can bring up negative feelings in those who disagree with a religion's basic ideas. These negative feelings can sometimes lead to violence. And some people believe that religion should have a greater role in government.

But these concerns do not justify laws that ban religious clothing. The laws are quick fixes rather than real solutions. Instead of trying to prevent racism by getting rid of religious clothing, we should try to prevent racism through education. People should take the time to learn about other religions and to share their own beliefs in calm and non-threatening ways. Only this will reduce racism and violence for good. And only this will convince people that every religion has a few extremists but is mainly made up of regular folks who want to lead peaceful lives.

The bottom line is this: clothing doesn't create conflict, fear does. And we can't legislate fear away. We have to do the hard work of accepting each other, getting to know each other, and learning from each other. We need to learn how to make our differences a plus rather than a minus. Accepting all kinds of clothing is the necessary first step in this very long journey.

✔ ?

280 Unit 10

When most of the students are finished, continue with the entire class. Let's see how well you understood what you read.

- Circle the check mark or the question mark for this text. Draw a question mark over any confusing words.
- Go to line 58. Mark the synonym of *outlawed*. (banned)
- Go to line 60. Circle the pronoun *these*. Draw an arrow to what *these* refers to. (similar laws) Draw another arrow to what they are similar to. (banned certain religious clothing)
- Go to line 62. Mark the verb that means "contributes to." (encourages)
- Go to line 63. Mark the synonym of *terrorists*. (extremists)
- On line 65, mark what should be separate. (church and state) In the margin, write what you think that means. (Government should not declare a religion.)
- On line 68, mark what can lead to violence. (negative feelings)
- On line 71, mark the word that means "make it right." (justify)
- In the third paragraph, number the author's solutions to racism. (1. prevent racism through education; 2. people should take time to learn about other religions; 3. people should share their own beliefs in calm and non-threatening ways.)
- On line 80, mark what creates conflict. (fear) In the margin, write whether you agree or disagree with this statement.
- Go to line 81. Mark the word that means "make laws." (legislate)
- Number the examples of hard work. (1. accepting each other; 2. getting to know each other; 3. learning from each other)
- On line 84, mark the pronoun *this*. Mark what *this* is referencing. (make our differences a plus) Circle the first step. (accepting all kinds of clothing)

Have students read lines 86–106 of the section Black Hole of Control according to the option that you chose. While reading, pay attention to the arguments. Draw a star in the margin if you agree with what the author is saying.

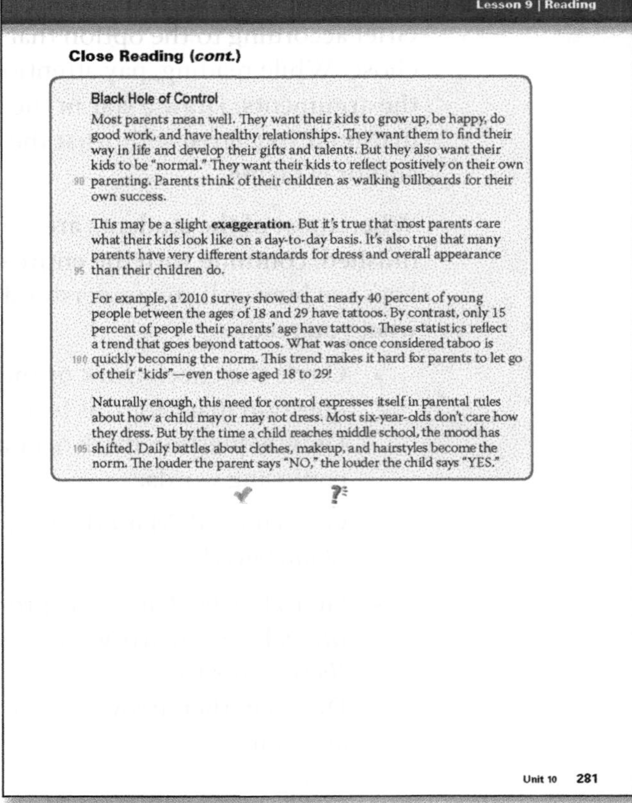

Lesson 9 | Reading

Close Reading (*cont.*)

Black Hole of Control

Most parents mean well. They want their kids to grow up, be happy, do good work, and have healthy relationships. They want them to find their way in life and develop their gifts and talents. But they also want their kids to be "normal." They want their kids to reflect positively on their own parenting. Parents think of their children as walking billboards for their own success.

This may be a slight **exaggeration**. But it's true that most parents care what their kids look like on a day-to-day basis. It's also true that many parents have very different standards for dress and overall appearance than their children do.

For example, a 2010 survey showed that nearly 40 percent of young people between the ages of 18 and 29 have tattoos. By contrast, only 15 percent of people their parents' age have tattoos. These statistics reflect a trend that goes beyond tattoos. What was once considered taboo is quickly becoming the norm. This trend makes it hard for parents to let go of their "kids"—even those aged 18 to 29!

Naturally enough, this need for control expresses itself in parental rules about how a child may or may not dress. Most six-year-olds don't care how they dress. But by the time a child reaches middle school, the mood has shifted. Daily battles about clothes, makeup, and hairstyles become the norm. The louder the parent says "NO," the louder the child says "YES."

Unit 10 281

When most of the students are finished, continue with the entire class. Let's see how well you understood the last section.

- Circle the check mark or the question mark for this text. Draw a question mark over any confusing words.
- Go to the heading. Mark the metaphor that means "place where things disappear." (Black Hole) Draw an arrow to what is being compared to a black hole. (parents)
- In the first paragraph, number the examples of what parents want for their kids. (1. want their kids to grow up; 2. be happy; 3. do good work; 4. have healthy relationships; 5. find their way in life; 6. develop their gifts and talents; 7. be "normal")
- Go to line 90. Mark the figurative language that means "an advertisement." (walking billboard)
- Go to line 92. Circle the pronoun *This*. Underline the idea that *this* refers to. (Parents think of their children as walking billboards of their own success.)
- Go to line 94. Mark the synonym of *guidelines*. (standards)
- Go to line 96. Mark the word that means "almost." (nearly)
- Go to line 99. Mark the word that means "a popular thing to do at any given time." (trend)
- Go to line 100. Mark the idiom that means "to stop controlling someone." (let go)
- On the same line, mark the punctuation used to show that something is by name only. (quotation marks)
- Go to line 105. Mark the synonym of *changed*. (shifted)

Have students read lines 107–125 of the section Black Hole of Control according to the option that you chose. While reading, pay attention to the arguments. Draw a star in the margin if you agree with what the author is saying.

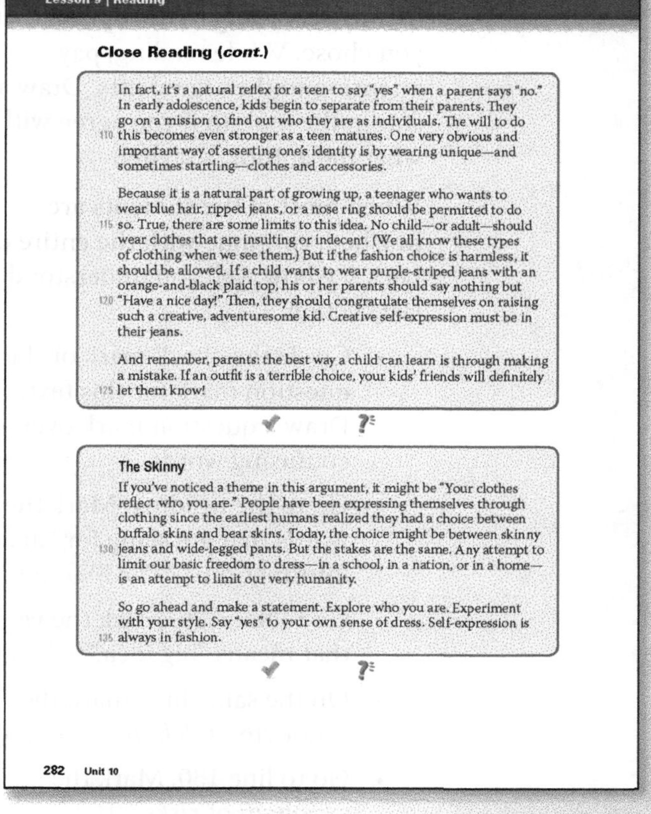

Lesson 9 | Reading

Close Reading (*cont.*)

In fact, it's a natural reflex for a teen to say "yes" when a parent says "no." In early adolescence, kids begin to separate from their parents. They go on a mission to find out who they are as individuals. The will to do this becomes even stronger as a teen matures. One very obvious and important way of asserting one's identity is by wearing unique—and sometimes startling—clothes and accessories.

Because it is a natural part of growing up, a teenager who wants to wear blue hair, ripped jeans, or a nose ring should be permitted to do so. True, there are some limits to this idea. No child—or adult—should wear clothes that are insulting or indecent. (We all know these types of clothing when we see them.) But if the fashion choice is harmless, it should be allowed. If a child wants to wear purple-striped jeans with an orange-and-black plaid top, his or her parents should say nothing but "Have a nice day!" Then, they should congratulate themselves on raising such a creative, adventuresome kid. Creative self-expression must be in their jeans.

And remember, parents: the best way a child can learn is through making a mistake. If an outfit is a terrible choice, your kids' friends will definitely let them know!

The Skinny

If you've noticed a theme in this argument, it might be "Your clothes reflect who you are." People have been expressing themselves through clothing since the earliest humans realized they had a choice between buffalo skins and bear skins. Today, the choice might be between skinny jeans and wide-legged pants. But the stakes are the same. Any attempt to limit our basic freedom to dress—in a school, in a nation, or in a home—is an attempt to limit our very humanity.

So go ahead and make a statement. Explore who you are. Experiment with your style. Say "yes" to your own sense of dress. Self-expression is always in fashion.

282 Unit 10

When most of the students are finished, continue with the entire class. Let's see how well you understood the last section.

- Circle the check mark or the question mark for this text. Draw a question mark over any confusing words.
- Go to line 107. Mark the synonym of *reaction.* (reflex)
- Go to line 109. Mark the word that means "an important assignment." (mission)
- Go to line 112. Mark the word that means "expressing." (asserting)
- Go to line 114. Mark the synonym of *allowed.* (permitted)
- On line 116, number the types of clothing no one should wear. (1. insulting; 2. indecent)
- Go to line 117. Mark the word that means "without harm." (harmless) Circle the suffix that means "without." (-less)
- Mark the pun that uses homophones, or words that sound the same but are spelled differently, instead of multiple meanings of the same word. (self-expression must be in their jeans) In the margin, write the correct spelling of the homophone. (genes)
- In the last paragraph, mark the best way to learn. (making a mistake)

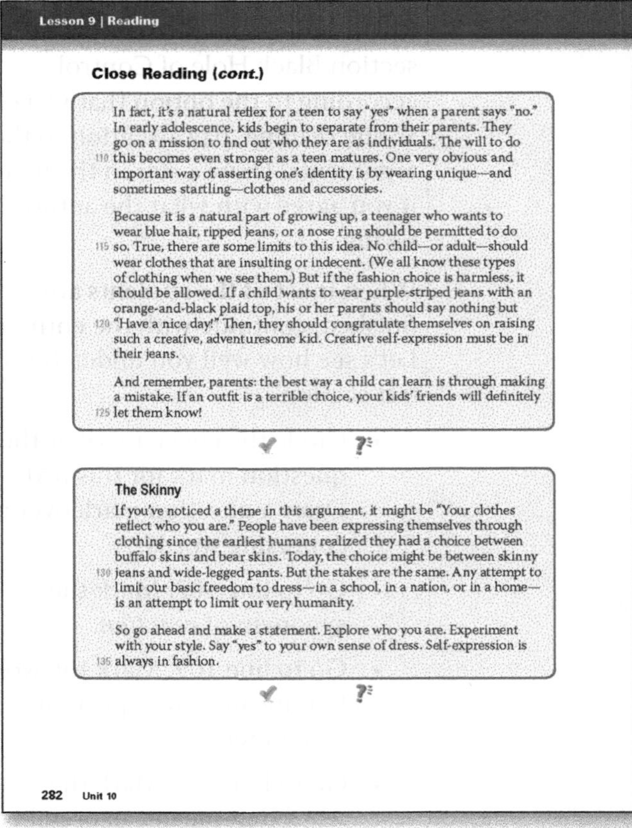
Lesson 9 | Reading

Close Reading (*cont.*)

In fact, it's a natural reflex for a teen to say "yes" when a parent says "no." In early adolescence, kids begin to separate from their parents. They go on a mission to find out who they are as individuals. The will to do this becomes even stronger as a teen matures. One very obvious and important way of asserting one's identity is by wearing unique—and sometimes startling—clothes and accessories.

Because it is a natural part of growing up, a teenager who wants to wear blue hair, ripped jeans, or a nose ring should be permitted to do so. True, there are some limits to this idea. No child—or adult—should wear clothes that are insulting or indecent. (We all know these types of clothing when we see them.) But if the fashion choice is harmless, it should be allowed. If a child wants to wear purple-striped jeans with an orange-and-black plaid top, his or her parents should say nothing but "Have a nice day!" Then, they should congratulate themselves on raising such a creative, adventuresome kid. Creative self-expression must be in their jeans.

And remember, parents: the best way a child can learn is through making a mistake. If an outfit is a terrible choice, your kids' friends will definitely let them know!

✓ ?

The Skinny

If you've noticed a theme in this argument, it might be "Your clothes reflect who you are." People have been expressing themselves through clothing since the earliest humans realized they had a choice between buffalo skins and bear skins. Today, the choice might be between skinny jeans and wide-legged pants. But the stakes are the same. Any attempt to limit our basic freedom to dress—in a school, in a nation, or in a home—is an attempt to limit our very humanity.

So go ahead and make a statement. Explore who you are. Experiment with your style. Say "yes" to your own sense of dress. Self-expression is always in fashion.

✓ ?

282 Unit 10

Have students read the section The Skinny according to the option that you chose. While reading, pay attention to the arguments. Draw a star in the margin if you agree with what the author is saying.

When most of the students are finished, continue with the entire class. Let's see how well you understood the last section.

- Circle the check mark or the question mark for this text. Draw a question mark over any confusing words.
- Go to the heading. Mark the words that are slang for "inside information." (The Skinny)
- Go to line 126. Mark the word that means "big idea." (theme)
- On the same line, mark the synonym of *debate.* (argument)
- Go to line 130. Mark the synonym of *risks.* (stakes)
- Go to line 132. Mark the word that means "quality of being human." (humanity)
- Mark the final pun, or play on words, used by the author. It is funny because a key word has multiple meanings. (Self-expression is always in fashion.)

Have partners compare text markings and correct any errors.

Summarize and Scrutinize

Direct students to page 283 in their Student Books. Read the instructions aloud, and have pairs summarize the texts. Then, have partners switch summaries and determine if the partner's summary is accurate and complete.

Regroup students who have chosen the same text and have groups complete the chart for their passage.

Bring partners back together and have them discuss the claims, evidence, and validity of the author's arguments. Generate a class discussion on which writer did a better job at persuasion. Use the following questions to foster conversation.

1. What are the conflicting viewpoints in the two texts?
2. Where do the authors disagree with each other?
3. Which author acknowledges the opposing viewpoint and which one doesn't?

Unit 10 Lesson 10

Lesson Opener

Before the lesson, choose one of the following activities to write on the board or post on the *LANGUAGE! Live* Class Wall online.

- *Write four sentences with at least two vocabulary words in each. Show you know the meanings. (prefer, stifle, appalling, survey, increase, contradict, individuality, ban, valid, exaggeration)*
- *Dress your avatar as though you were new to a school and wanted people to know about you without having to say a word. Explain your choices.*
- *Knowing the benefits of school uniforms, would you prefer to attend a school with or without a uniform policy? Explain.*

Vocabulary

Objective

- Review key passage vocabulary.

Recontextualize Passage Vocabulary

Direct students to page 269 in their Student Books. Use the following questions to review the vocabulary words from "Say Yes to Free Dress!"

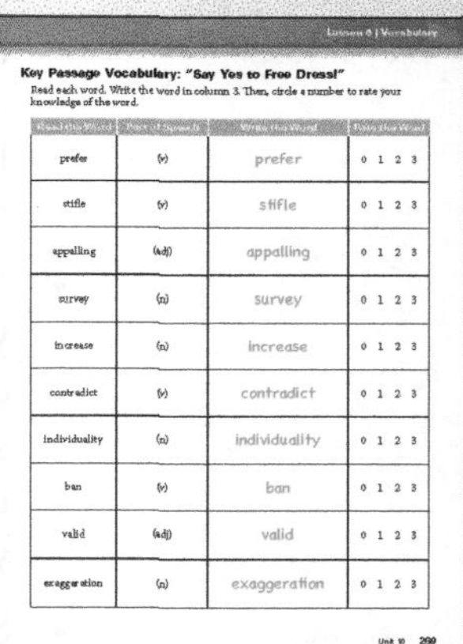

Lesson 6 | Vocabulary

Key Passage Vocabulary: "Say Yes to Free Dress!"

Read each word. Write the word in column 3. Then, circle a number to rate your knowledge of the word.

Read the Word	Part of Speech	Write the Word	Rate the Word
prefer	(v)	prefer	0 1 2 3
stifle	(v)	stifle	0 1 2 3
appalling	(adj)	appalling	0 1 2 3
survey	(n)	survey	0 1 2 3
increase	(n)	increase	0 1 2 3
contradict	(v)	contradict	0 1 2 3
individuality	(n)	individuality	0 1 2 3
ban	(v)	ban	0 1 2 3
valid	(adj)	valid	0 1 2 3
exaggeration	(n)	exaggeration	0 1 2 3

Unit 10 269

- You go to a new restaurant, open the menu, and see that a grilled cheese sandwich is $19. Do you find this *appalling*? (yes) Your mail carrier always whistles, and today is no different; he's whistling a cheerful tune. Do you find this *appalling*? (no) You smell something foul next door and peek over the fence. You see dozens of overflowing trash bags and realize your neighbor hasn't put his trash out in months. You find this what? (appalling)
- Your grandmother says you are growing like a weed. Is this an *exaggeration*? (yes) Your hair has grown half an inch in a month. Is this an *exaggeration*? (no) Your uncle owns a comedy club, and your friend is an aspiring comedian. You tell your uncle that your friend is the funniest person in the world. What is your claim? (an exaggeration)
- Your friend wears dark colors, but you like to wear bright ones. Do you *prefer* brighter colors? (yes) You like chicken salad but not tuna salad. Do you *prefer* tuna salad? (no) You can either walk or take the bus. It's a pretty day, and you need some fresh air, but you choose the bus. You what? (prefer the bus)
- You get a raise at work. Have you gotten an *increase* in pay? (yes) You turn the sound down on the radio. Is there an *increase* in volume? (no) Last year, there were 78 people in marching band; this year, there are 128. The band has seen a what? (increase)

- Your brother wakes up from a nap and his hair is standing straight up. You decide not to say anything because he looks grumpy. Do you *stifle* your comment? (yes) Your favorite player gets a slam-dunk to win the game, and you let out a holler. Do you *stifle* your joy? (no) You're playing hide and seek. The person who is "it" comes very, very close to where you are. You have to sneeze. What do you do? (stifle the sneeze)
- A movie star wears a certain brand of boots, and soon you see the boots on people everywhere. Are the people wearing that brand of boots expressing their *individuality*? (no) At our family reunions, everyone wears matching T-shirts. Are we trying to show our *individuality*? (no) You like to put together unique outfits from clothes you buy at resale shops. You do this to show your what? (individuality)
- You think a problem through on your own and then take action. Have you decided to take action based on a *survey*? (no) You ask 50 of your closest friends if they'll be available on a certain date for a birthday bash. Have you *surveyed* your friends? (yes) To find out how many students would eat breakfast at school if the cafeteria served it, the school should conduct a what? (survey)
- Your friend says he can't go running with you because it's raining, but it's clear and sunny outside. Is your friend's reason *valid*? (no) Your body aches and your throat is sore. You think you might be getting sick. Is this a *valid* assumption? (yes) A guy calls into a radio talk show and insists an asteroid is headed toward Earth and will destroy the planet in 12 hours. The caller's fears are probably not what? (valid)
- You say you can do more sit-ups than your cousin. He says he can do more than you. Has he *contradicted* you? (yes) You say koala bears are the cutest animals ever, and your best friend agrees. Has she *contradicted* you? (no) Your social studies teacher says India has the largest population of any country in the world, but you just read an article that said China's population was larger. You raise your hand and politely do what? (contradict the fact)
- Student groups may hold sales in the cafeteria during lunch hours. Have sales been *banned* in the cafeteria during lunch hours? (no) At your favorite swimming hole, the city put up a sign that says "No swimming." Has swimming been *banned* there? (yes) Wearing ear buds in class is not allowed. Ear buds in class are what? (banned)

Writing

Objectives

- Use multiple texts to write coherently.
- Use a process to write.
- Write a short story that contains the requisite story elements.
- Use a rubric to guide and evaluate writing.

Six Traits of Effective Writing

Direct students back to page 35 in their Student Books. Reread the Six Traits of Effective Writing.

We will continue to focus on writing with all six traits.

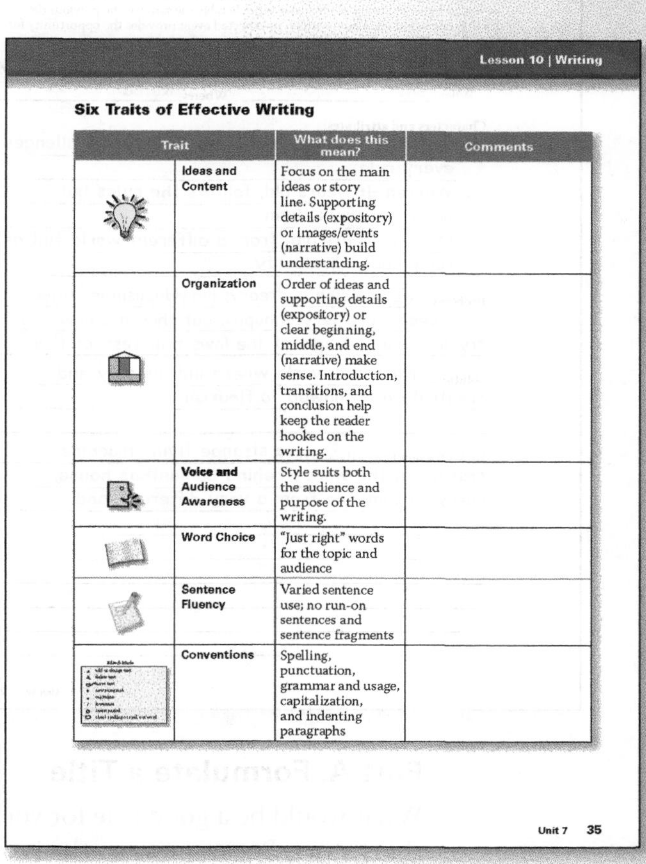

Lesson 10 | Writing

Six Traits of Effective Writing

Trait		What does this mean?	Comments
	Ideas and Content	Focus on the main ideas or story line. Supporting details (expository) or images/events (narrative) build understanding.	
	Organization	Order of ideas and supporting details (expository) or clear beginning, middle, and end (narrative) make sense. Introduction, transitions, and conclusion help keep the reader hooked on the writing.	
	Voice and Audience Awareness	Style suits both the audience and purpose of the writing.	
	Word Choice	"Just right" words for the topic and audience	
	Sentence Fluency	Varied sentence use; no run-on sentences and sentence fragments	
	Conventions	Spelling, punctuation, grammar and usage, capitalization, and indenting paragraphs	

Unit 7 35

Notebook paper

Writing a Short Story

Direct students back to their planning template, Prepare to Write, on page 275 in their Student Books. Briefly discuss their story ideas.

Direct students to page 284 in their Student Books.

Lesson 7 | Writing

Prepare to Write: Short Story

Imagine living in Kalba, a land where everything is gray and brown. Lives are governed by strict laws, and every day is predictably the same as the previous day. It's the only world you know until an unexpected event provides the opportunity for something different. Use the template to plan your short story.

Answers will vary.

Setting:

When: 2413 Where: Kalba

Characters and attributes:

1. Samantha—16 years old, questions and challenges every rule
2. Warren—16 years old, follows the rules but quietly resents them
3. Miko—16 years old, from a different world full of color and individuality

Problem: life in Kalba is dreary; individualism is stifled; most people are very unhappy, but they are unwilling to try to speak out against the laws that restrict them

Solution: living in a world where individuality and creativity are allowed to flourish

Kick-off event (starts the story): a strange flying machine crashes in the woods behind Samantha's house, carrying someone from a very different land

Unit 10 275

Lesson 10 | Writing

Developing a Short Story Answers will vary.

Refer to your notes on the Prepare to Write template on page 275.

Part A. Formulate a Title

Samantha and the Mysterious Flying Machine; An Unexpected Change: An Open Door

Part B. Begin the Story

Choose one of the following strategies for beginning your story. Circle your choice and write your opening line(s).

- Provide a where or when
- Provide an action
- Introduce a character
- Make a simple but interesting comment
- Start a dialogue

Opening line(s): "What on earth is that?" exclaimed Samantha's mother as she stood at her kitchen window.

"What did you see, Mother?" asked Samantha as she raced to the kitchen from her bedroom.

"I honestly don't know what I saw. It looked like a big cloth balloon, but it had colors and patterns unlike anything I have ever seen!"

284 Unit 10

Part A. Formulate a Title

What would be a good title for your story? You know the basic story line for my short story. Because Samantha is one of my main characters, I could put her name in the title: Samantha and the Mysterious Flying Machine. Because the flying machine is so unexpected, I could make my title a hint about how the story will unfold: An Unexpected Change: An Open Door. Talk with your partner about some ideas for a title and then write your working title in the space provided. Remember, this is a working title, and you may come up with a very different idea by the time you've finished your story. Give students time to discuss and decide on a working title for their story. Have volunteers share their titles.

Part B. Begin the Story

Direct students to the chart and review the different strategies for beginning a story. What would be an effective way to begin your story? I think I want to open my story with dialogue. I'll use dialogue to introduce the balloon that crashed in the woods behind Samantha's house. Look back at your "kick off" event and decide which strategy could be an effective way to introduce it. Write the draft of your opening lines and then read them aloud to your partner for feedback. Give students time to develop their opening and share it with their partners. **Monitor student progress and offer support and guidance to any students who struggle to write their opening lines.**

Part C. Introduce the Characters

Now that you've decided how your story will begin, you need to introduce your characters to your readers. Your Prepare to Write template contains your ideas about your three main characters. You should have decided on names for each character and determined some basic attributes. Did you introduce or reference a character in your opening lines? If so, consider moving directly into some background information on that character. Because I introduced Samantha in my opening lines, my next step will be to tell my readers more about her character. Then, I will introduce Miko, the stranger from another land. Finally, I will introduce Warren. He is Samantha's best friend, and she feels compelled to tell Warren and see what he thinks of her discovery in the woods. Develop a sequence of events that will allow you to logically introduce your three main characters. Jot down some notes and then discuss it with your partner. After talking through the sequence of events, write the scene. **Monitor student progress as they discuss their characters and begin to expand their opening scene. Provide support and guidance for any student who seems to be struggling to get his or her ideas written down.**

Lesson 10 | Writing

Developing a Short Story (*cont.*) Answers will vary.

Part C. Introduce the Characters

Sketch out how you will introduce the main characters to your readers.

Samantha: describe her rebellious nature and excitement about the unexpected event
Miko: Samantha will find Miko in the balloon's wreckage and describe her unique characteristics
Warren: have Samantha call him with her exciting news and introduce him as a quiet rebel
Samantha: intrigued by the mysterious object; hated the dull, colorless life; longed for something, anything out of the ordinary; going to find what just landed in the woods behind her house; spied the fallen object and was mesmerized by the brilliant colors and patterns. Saw a girl about her same age, but she definitely wasn't from Kalba.
Miko: pink hair; odd-shaped glasses; didn't know where she was
Samantha: thought it was a trick to get her in trouble; intrigued; wanted to share with Warren
Warren: discontented with life in Kalba; never got in trouble; quietly talked about a different life—something else

Unit 10 285

Part D. Describe the Problem

Now, develop the problem more fully. Create an urgent need for a solution by providing more details. In my story, I need to describe life in Kalba as intolerable. Life is dreary and drab, and everyone should want it to be different. Talk with your partner about the nature of the problem in your story. Then, take a few notes regarding the details and elaborations you want to add. **Monitor student progress as they discuss the problem and begin to elaborate with details and examples. Provide support and guidance for any student who seems to be struggling to describe his or her characters' situation.**

Lesson 10 | Writing

Developing a Short Story (*cont.*) Answers will vary.

Part D. Describe the Problem

Provide examples and elaborations to develop the problem.

Everything was the same in Kalba—houses, clothing, buildings, and streets.

Color was seen as frivolous and distracting—had a negative impact on productivity.

Citizens were forbidden to leave Kalba, and strangers were unheard of.

Part E. Develop the Solution

List the events that contribute to the solution and make it possible.

Samantha befriends Miko and hides her from the authorities.

Miko tells Samantha and Warren about her home and all of the freedoms enjoyed by her people.

They repair Miko's hot air balloon so she can return home.

They convince everyone in Kalba to demand changes starting with the brown and gray uniforms. They are successful in overturning the rules that stifled individuality and self-expression.

Part F. End the Story

Choose a strategy for ending your story. Circle your choice and write the closing lines of your short story.

- Make an emotional connection
- Focus on an important character
- Reiterate the story's message
- Reflect on the story's message

Closing sentences: Samantha stood on her front porch, waiting for Warren. They were going to the movies, a previously unheard of activity in Kalba. She ran her hand through her blue hair and smiled as she looked down at her purple and yellow shoes.

286 Unit 10

Part E. Develop the Solution

With the characters' situation fully developed, turn your attention to the solution. Develop a sequence of events that will lead to resolving the problem. **Share your notes on developing a solution.** Think quietly about your story's development and write down the events that will solve the issue. Then, talk through the sequence of events with your partner. Adjust your ideas based on their feedback. **Monitor student progress as they begin developing their sequence of events. As they discuss their solutions with their partners, circulate to ensure feedback is meaningful. Provide support and guidance for any student who seems to be struggling to develop a solution.**

Part F. End the Story

Discuss the strategies for writing an effective ending. After talking about each strategy, share your example of focusing on an important character. Give students a few minutes to think about how they want to end their story. After they have made their choice of strategy, have them write their closing lines in the space provided. Monitor student progress and provide guidance and support where needed. When students have finished writing their ending, have volunteers share their endings.

Notebook paper

Write

Have students consult the Six Traits of Writing: Fiction Rubric on page 551 as they write their story. If they struggle or need additional support in developing their story, use the following story as a model.

Six Traits of Writing: Fiction

	Ideas and Development	Organization	Voice and Audience Awareness	Word Choice	Sentence Fluency	Language Conventions
4	Clear plot events, as well as a readily identifiable conflict/problem and setting. The climax and resolution are clear. Rich details and sensory description make characters come to life. No irrelevant material.	Beginning grabs reader's attention. Logically sequenced plot. Story transitions link events. Conclusion caps off story and does not leave the reader hanging.	Strong sense of person and purpose behind the words. Brings story to life.	Words are specific, accurate, and vivid. Word choice enhances meaning and reader's enjoyment.	Writes complete sentences with varied sentence patterns and beginnings.	There are no major grammar errors. There are few errors in spelling, capitalization, or punctuation.
3	Identifiable plot events. Conflict/problem may not be entirely clear. The climax or resolution may not be clear. Some details/sensory description. Characters present but may not be fully developed. Setting may be missing. Limited irrelevant material.	Beginning interests reader. Plot somewhat logically sequenced but may lack one story element such as climax or satisfying conclusion. Story transitions link some events.	Some sense of person and purpose behind the words.	Words are correctly used but may be somewhat general and unspecific.	Writes complete sentences with some expansion. Limited variety.	There are a few grammar errors. There are a few errors in spelling, capitalization, or punctuation.
2	Limited plot and/or the conflict/problem is not clear. The setting, climax, and/or resolution may not be apparent. There are insufficient details and description. Characterization is weak. Too repetitious or too much irrelevant material.	Beginning does not capture reader's interest. Plot underdeveloped and two or more story elements (setting, initiating event, climax, resolution) missing. Story transitions missing.	Little sense of person and purpose behind the words.	Word choice limited. Words may be used inaccurately or repetitively.	Writes mostly simple and/or awkwardly constructed sentences. May include some run-ons and fragments.	There are many grammar or spelling errors. There are quite a few errors in capitalization and punctuation.
1	Does not address the prompt or the plot, conflict/problem are not discernible. Description, details, and characterization are missing.	Text has no evident structure. Lack of organization seriously interferes with meaning.	No sense of person or purpose behind the words.	Extremely limited range of words. Restricted vocabulary impedes message.	Numerous run-ons and/or sentence fragments interfere with meaning.	There are many spelling and grammar errors. There are many errors in capitalization and punctuation.

Writing Rubric: Fiction 551

Writing Rubric: Fiction

Sample Short Story

An Unexpected Change

"What on earth is that?" exclaimed Samantha's mother as she stood at her kitchen window.

"What did you see, Mother?" asked Samantha as she raced to the kitchen from her bedroom.

"I honestly don't know what I saw. It looked like a big cloth balloon, but it had colors and patterns unlike anything I have ever seen!"

Intrigued by the mysterious object, Samantha darted out the back door. She hated the dull, colorless life she led in Kalba. Everyone dressed in the same gray and brown outfits, and their regimented lives made Samantha want to scream. She longed for something, anything out of the ordinary, and now it had just landed in the woods behind her house! Her mother's words echoed through her head as she sprinted into the woods. "It had colors and patterns unlike anything I have ever seen!"

Finally, she spied the fallen object, and she was mesmerized by the brilliant colors and patterns. "Oh!" she exclaimed when she saw the object begin to move. Soon, a head appeared, and Samantha couldn't believe her eyes. She was pretty sure it was a girl, about her same age, but she definitely wasn't from Kalba. Her pink hair and odd-shaped glasses were a dead giveaway.

The stranger smiled and said, "Hi, I'm Miko. A storm blew me off course. Where am I?" She struggled to free herself from the balloon's canvas and soon came to stand next to Samantha.

Samantha had not said a word, and she eyed the stranger suspiciously. She wondered if this was just a trick to get her into trouble. Citizens of Kalba were not supposed to welcome strangers. In fact, they were supposed to turn them over to the authorities immediately. As a known troublemaker, Samantha thought this would be just like the police to see how she would handle this situation. Miko's appearance was so unusual that Samantha had to wonder if the authorities had that much creativity. Standing mute and motionless, all she could think of was calling Warren. She desperately needed to tell Warren. He was as discontented with life in Kalba as she was, yet he managed to never get in trouble. While he remained outwardly compliant, he often talked with Samantha about life beyond the reach of Kalba.

Before the two girls headed back to Samantha's house, they found a place to sit and talk. Samantha wanted to know all about Miko's world and knew she needed to warn Miko about life in Kalba. They sat for what seemed like hours. Miko described a world full of color, beauty, and variety. Everyone dressed differently, and the buildings were a blend of varying architectural styles. People decorated their shops and houses as a reflection of themselves. Samantha's life in Kalba stood in stark contrast to Miko's life. For the sake of efficiency and equality, every building and house looked exactly the same. The colors were dull and never varied. Everyone wore brown pants and dull gray shirts. While hair color might vary, no one dared to dye their hair or wear it in a different style. Because of the technological advances in Kalba, most jobs were basically the same. Workers oversaw the automation of a variety of tasks. Anything out of the ordinary was viewed as a distraction or a waste. Distractions affected productivity, and the focus of life in Kalba was efficiency and productivity. The leaders needed to make sure the citizens of Kalba never had the opportunity to experience life anywhere else. They monitored their borders carefully to ensure no strangers ever wandered into Kalba, especially strangers with tantalizing tales of life in other lands. Samantha knew the dangers facing Miko. She decided to help her fix her hot air balloon and escape. Hiding her would be a challenge because she would need her parents to feel the same way she did.

Each day, Samantha and Warren took varying paths into the woods behind her house. They worked with Miko to sew the torn canvas and repair the burner in the base of the balloon. Progress was slow but steady. As they worked, Miko would tell stories about her world, and the friends began to think about leaving Kalba. Leaving Kalba was an exciting yet sad thought. All of their friends and family lived in Kalba, and leaving would mean leaving forever. Even when they were away from Miko, Warren and Samantha would talk about the idea. One day, Samantha turned to Warren and said, "Wouldn't it be wonderful if we could bring Miko's world to Kalba?"

At first, Warren didn't understand what Samantha was suggesting. "Are you insane? No, don't bother answering that question. I already know the answer!" he exclaimed. Samantha, however, had planted a seed in his mind that he could not cast away. The next day, Warren told Samantha, "We need to find out how other people really feel about the laws and life in Kalba. We need to know if they feel like we feel, but they just don't show it." She loved the idea, especially because it contained risk. It was a violation of so many laws and that provided additional motivation for Samantha. She would love to live in a Kalba that mirrored Miko's world. Carefully, so carefully, they began to talk with their friends about discontentment and a desire for change. They were pleasantly surprised by their friends' deep desires for a different kind of life. The idea spread like wildfire, and soon people were talking about more than just desire. They were formulating a plan that would bring about change. If everyone would refuse to follow the laws, they had a chance of winning. A small handful could be easily stopped, but a united front would not be so easily suppressed.

Miko's balloon was finally ready for flight. She had hoped they would come with her, but they had other ideas. Their ideas were big, exciting, and scary. They waved good-bye to Miko as she quietly floated above the tree line and away to a distant horizon. A rally in the town square was set for that evening, and the crowd was truly amazing. As they looked around, they realized everyone was there. They had found natural dyes to use on their clothes and hair. For the first time in Samantha's life, she saw a kaleidoscope of colors in a sea of defiance. With the entire population in an uproar, the leaders of Kalba quickly realized they would have to capitulate. Elections followed, and soon Kalba had a very different team of leaders and a very different set of laws. Samantha found herself wondering if word of their changes would ever reach Miko. She knew Miko would be smiling if she ever learned about all of the changes. While residents of Kalba still embraced technology and efficiency, they also celebrated their individuality and creativity. Evidence of this could be seen on every street and on every face.

Samantha stood on her front porch, waiting for Warren. They were going to the movies, a previously unheard of activity in Kalba. She ran her hand through her blue hair and smiled as she looked down at her purple and yellow shoes.

Evaluate Writing

Direct students to page 287 in their Student Books and read the information in the checklist.

Notice that this checklist is the same as the one you used in Unit 9. This checklist is specifically for narrative writing. It is a tool you can use to evaluate your writing and make sure you are using good technique. Have individuals quickly assess their writing, then have partners evaluate each other's writing based on the checklist.

Note: Use Six Traits of Writing Scoring Rubric: Fiction on page 546 of this book to assess students' writing. A printable version is located online in the Teacher Resources.

Six Traits of Writing: Fiction

Lesson 10 | Writing

The Narrative Writer's Checklist

Trait	Yes	No	Did the writer . . . ?
Ideas and Content			include characters, setting, plot
			create an opening that grabs the reader's attention
			include enough description so that the reader can picture the characters and setting
			include dialogue between characters
			create a title for the story
Organization			create an initiating event, conflict (or rising action), and climax
			include a resolution, as well as a conclusion that ties everything up
			create a clear sequence of events
Voice and Audience Awareness			think about the audience and purpose for writing
			write in a clear and engaging way that makes the audience want to read the work; select a point of view (1st or 3rd person) and maintain it consistently
Word Choice			find a unique way to say things
			use words that are lively and specific to the content
Sentence Fluency			write complete sentences
			expand some sentences using the steps of Masterpiece Sentences
			use compound sentence elements and compound sentences
Conventions			capitalize words correctly:
			capitalize the first word of each sentence
			capitalize proper nouns, including people's names
			punctuate correctly:
			end sentences with a period, question mark, or exclamation mark
			use an apostrophe for possessive nouns and contractions
			use commas and/or semicolons correctly
			use grammar correctly:
			use the correct verb tense
			make sure the verb agrees with the subject in number
			use correct spelling

Unit 10 287

Reading

Objectives

- Self-correct as comprehension of text deepens.
- Answer questions to demonstrate comprehension of text.
- Engage in class discussion.
- Identify the enduring understandings from a piece of text.

Revisit Passage Comprehension

Direct students back to pages 276 and 277 in their Student Books. Have students review their answers and make any necessary changes. Then, have partners share their answers and collaborate to perfect them.

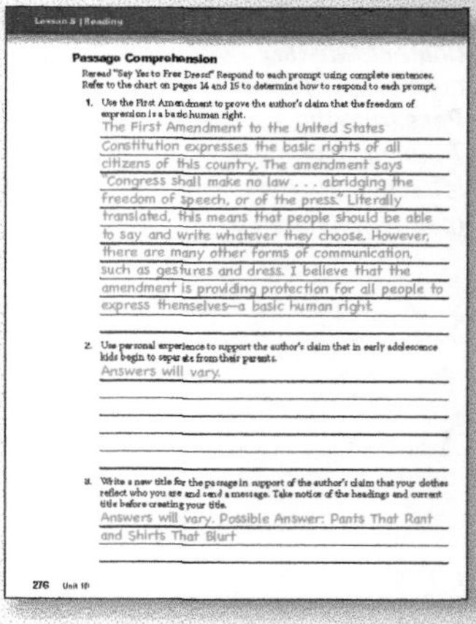

Author's Purpose

Direct students back to page 268 in their Student Books.

Let's review. What type of text is "Say Yes to Free Dress?" Fiction or nonfiction? (nonfiction) Every author has a purpose for writing. Why did the author write this text? What was his or her purpose? (inform; persuade) Record your answers. What was the author's point of view of school uniforms and dress codes? (They limit creativity and expression and therefore are not good.)

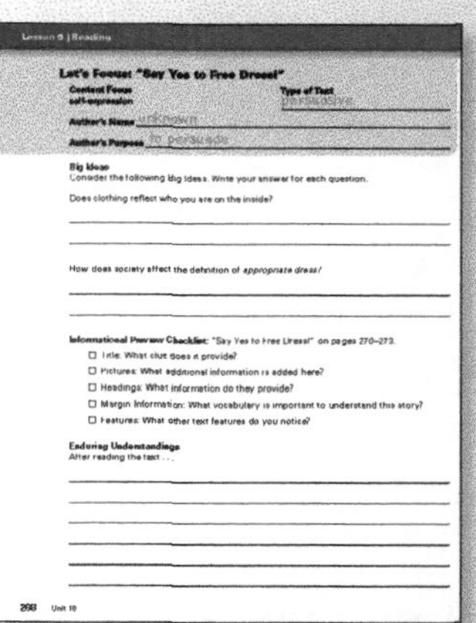

Enduring Understandings

Reread the Big Idea questions.

Does clothing reflect who you are on the inside?

How does society affect the definition of *appropriate dress*?

Generate a class discussion about the questions and the answers students came up with in Lesson 6. Have them consider whether their answers have changed any after reading the text.

Use the following talking points to foster conversation. Then, have students write their enduring understandings from the unit.

- There is an old proverb: "You can't judge a book by its cover." What do you think about that? We tend to judge people based on outward appearance—including clothing. Is it a fair assessment? Do we always have the opportunity to make our clothing reflect what we want it to?
- Does the definition of *appropriate dress* change over time? Does it change based on the circumstances? Think about what people wore 100 years ago. Think about what people wear to a restaurant on the beach as opposed to a restaurant downtown. With changing definitions, is it hard to know the answers?

What we read should make us think. Use our discussion and your thoughts about the text to determine what you will "walk away with." Has it made you think about a personal experience or someone you know? Has your perspective or opinion on a specific topic changed? Do you have any lingering thoughts or questions? Write these ideas as your enduring understandings. What will you take with you from this text?

Assign online Unit 10 ***Content Mastery*** *quizzes and* ***Power Pass*** *from the Text Training link on the left menu of your teacher dashboard.*

Discuss the enduring understandings with the class. If time permits, have students post a personal response from their enduring understandings to the online class wall.

Unit 11 Unit Plan

Primary Texts:
Excerpt from *The Good Earth*
by Pearl S. Buck

Text type: literature—novel

Excerpt from *Nectar in a Sieve*
by Kamala Markandaya

Text type: literature—novel

***LANGUAGE! Live* Online**

Grammar Practice

- Use participial phrases correctly.
- Use appositives correctly.
- Use commas correctly with appositives.
- Identify and correct errors in subject-verb agreement.
- Use *to be* verbs correctly.
- Identify and understand the function of conjunctive adverbs.

Vocabulary Practice

- Determine the meaning of derivations of words.
- Determine the meaning of puns, hyperboles, and aphorisms.

Content Mastery

- Demonstrate an understanding of . . .
  - word meaning by answering questions and using words in sentences.
  - participial phrases.
  - appositives.
  - subject-verb agreement.

Word Study

- Discuss the concept of Latin roots.
- Blend, read, and spell multisyllabic words with Latin roots port, form, rupt, and script/scribe; Latin prefixes de- and ex-; suffixes -ation, -ize, and -ary; and Latin prefixes com-, con-, cor-, col-, and in-, im-, il-, ir-.
- Read connected text to build fluency.

Lesson 1

Reading

- Determine and discuss the topic of a text.
- Determine and discuss the author's purpose.
- Use text features to preview text.

Vocabulary

- Evaluate word knowledge.
- Determine the meaning of key passage vocabulary.

Reading

- Read an excerpt from a novel.
- Monitor comprehension during text reading.

Lesson 2

Vocabulary

- Review key passage vocabulary.

Grammar

- Identify participial phrases and use them correctly.
- Differentiate between participial phrases and prepositional phrases.
- Identify appositives and the corresponding nouns they modify.

Writing

- Combine sentences using appositives.
- Use proper subject-verb agreement.

Lesson 6

Reading

- Determine and discuss the topic of a text.
- Determine and discuss the author's purpose.
- Use text features to preview text.

Vocabulary

- Evaluate word knowledge.
- Determine the meaning of key passage vocabulary.

Reading

- Read an excerpt from a novel.
- Monitor comprehension during text reading.

Lesson 7

Vocabulary

- Review key passage vocabulary.

Reading

- Determine how to respond to prompts.
- Use critical thinking skills to write responses to prompts about text.
- Support written answers with evidence from text.
- Compare characters across multiple texts.
- Cite text evidence in support of an opinion.

Writing

- Demonstrate an understanding of the components and structure of a compare-contrast essay.

Writing Project, Units 10–12: Narrative Writing

Lesson 3

Reading

- Reread text for comprehension.
- Establish a purpose for reading text.
- Use critical thinking skills to write responses to prompts about text.
- Support written answers with evidence from text.
- Determine the meaning of proverbs and adages.
- Analyze the way the setting shapes characters.
- Determine character point of view.
- Connect personal experience to text.

Lesson 4

Vocabulary

- Review key passage vocabulary.

Reading

- Read with purpose and understanding.
- Answer questions to demonstrate comprehension of text.
- Identify and explain explicit details from text.
- Monitor comprehension of text during reading.
- Identify flashbacks in literature.
- Analyze the contrasting points of view of characters within a story.
- Analyze the development of character traits over time.
- Track pronouns to their antecedents.
- Determine the meaning of figurative language in literature.
- Use synonyms and antonyms to deepen word knowledge.
- Determine the meaning of consecutive adjectives.

** See pg. 394 for additional lesson objectives.*

Lesson 5

Vocabulary

- Review key passage vocabulary.

Writing

- Use text to write coherent paragraphs in response to reading.
- Write a persuasive essay.

Reading

- Self-correct as comprehension of text deepens.
- Answer questions to demonstrate comprehension of text.
- Engage in class discussion.
- Identify the enduring understandings from a piece of text.

Lesson 8

Reading

- Establish a purpose for rereading text.
- Read an excerpt from a novel.
- Monitor comprehension during text reading.
- Use critical thinking skills to write responses to prompts about text.
- Support written answers with evidence from text.
- Compare and contrast characters across multiple texts.
- Compare and contrast points of view in multiple texts.

Lesson 9

Vocabulary

- Review key passage vocabulary.

Reading

- Read with purpose and understanding.
- Answer questions to demonstrate comprehension of text.
- Identify and explain explicit details from text.
- Monitor comprehension of text during reading.
- Analyze the contrasting points of view of characters within a story.
- Analyze the development of character traits over time.
- Track pronouns to their antecedents.
- Determine the meaning of figurative language in literature.
- Use synonyms and antonyms to deepen word knowledge.
- Objectively summarize text.

** See pg. 433 for additional lesson objectives.*

Lesson 10

Vocabulary

- Review key passage vocabulary.

Writing

- Use multiple texts to write coherently.
- Use a process to write.
- Write a compare-contrast essay.
- Compare and contrast a topic across two texts from different cultures.
- Use a rubric to guide and assess writing.

Reading

- Self-correct as comprehension of text deepens.
- Answer questions to demonstrate comprehension of text.
- Engage in class discussion.
- Identify the enduring understandings from a piece of text.

Unit 11 Lesson 1

Lesson Opener

Before the lesson, choose one of the following activities to write on the board or post on the *LANGUAGE! Live* Class Wall online.

- *Describe your dream spouse. What does he or she look like? What personality traits does he or she have?*
- *Write two sentences about a person you would like to date. Use the relative pronouns* who *or* whom *in each sentence.*
- *Use the word* distracting *in three sentences. Use it as a verb in one sentence, a noun in one sentence, and an adjective in another sentence.*

Reading

Objectives

- Determine and discuss the topic of a text.
- Determine and discuss the author's purpose.
- Use text features to preview text.

Passage Introduction

Direct students to page 289 in their Student Books. Discuss the content focus.

Content Focus
arranged marriage
Chinese culture

What do you think you will read about in this text? (Answers will vary.)

Type of Text

Text can be divided into two categories: informational and literature. Discuss the differences. Look at the first page of the text and determine what type of text it is. Write your answer on the page.

Unit 11

Lesson 1 | Reading

Let's Focus: Excerpt from *The Good Earth*

Content Focus
arranged marriage
Chinese culture

Type of Text
fiction—literature

Author's Name Pearl S. Buck

Author's Purpose to entertain; to increase awareness of women's roles in traditional Chinese culture

Big Ideas
Consider the following Big Idea questions. Write your answer for each question.

What factors are involved when choosing a lifelong mate?

What is the purpose of marriage?

Narrative Preview Checklist: the excerpt from *The Good Earth* on pages 291–298.

- ☐ Title: What clue does it provide about the passage?
- ☐ Pictures: What additional information is added here?
- ☐ Margin Information: What vocabulary is important to understand this story?

Enduring Understandings
After reading the text . . .

Unit 11 289

Author's Purpose

Have students glance at the text. Who is the author of the text? (Pearl S. Buck) Prior to reading, make an educated guess as to what the author's purpose for writing is. After we finish, you will return to this section and revise your answer if you need to. Have students write the answers on the page.

Play the Unit 11 Text Training video found in the Teacher Resources online.

Before we read the excerpt from *The Good Earth*, we will watch a short video to help build our background knowledge. **Play the Unit 11 Text Training video. Have partners discuss what they learned from the video.**

Note: If you are unable to play the video, Background Information about former marriage practices in China compared with the Western ideal of marriage can be found in the Teacher Resources online.

Read the Big Idea questions aloud.

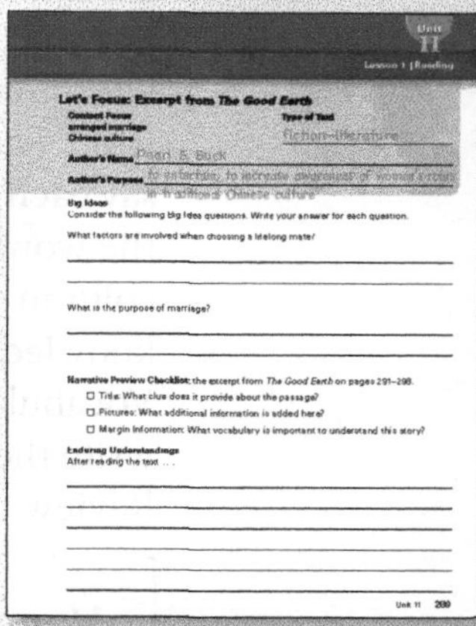

Big Ideas

What factors are involved when choosing a lifelong mate?

What is the purpose of marriage?

As a class, consider the two Big Idea questions. After discussing each question, have students write an answer. We'll come back to these questions after we finish reading the text. You can add to your answers as you gain information and perspective.

Preview

Read the Preview Checklist on page 289. Follow the Preview Procedure outlined below.

Preview Procedure

- Group students with partners or in triads.
- Have students count off as 1s or 2s. The 1s will become the student leaders. If working with triads, the third students become 3s.
- The student leaders will preview the text in addition to managing the checklist and pacing.
- The 2s and 3s will preview the text with 1s.
- Direct 1s to open their Student Books to page 289 and 2s and 3s to open their Student Books to page 291. This allows students to look at a few different pages at one time without turning back and forth.

Direct students to page 291. Have them preview the text.

If necessary, guide students in a short preview using the following talking points.

What is the title? (*The Good Earth*) What clue does the title provide about the text? (Answers will vary.) Pay close attention to the pictures for this text. What do you notice? What information do the pictures provide to help your comprehension? (Pictures help you create images in your mind's eye that allow you to imagine the story.)

Vocabulary

Objectives

- Evaluate word knowledge.
- Determine the meaning of key passage vocabulary.

Rate Vocabulary Knowledge

Direct students to page 290 in their Student Books. Let's take a look at the vocabulary words from the excerpt from *The Good Earth*. I am going to say each word aloud. You will repeat the word and write it in the third column. Then, you will rate your knowledge of the word. Display the Vocabulary Rating Scale poster or write the information on the board. Review the meaning of each rating.

Lesson 1 | Vocabulary

Key Passage Vocabulary: Excerpt from *The Good Earth*

Read each word. Write the word in column 3. Then, circle a number to rate your knowledge of the word.

Read the Word	Part of Speech	Write the Word	Rate the Word
fruition	(n)	fruition	0 1 2 3
fashion	(v)	fashion	0 1 2 3
delicately	(adv)	delicately	0 1 2 3
cease	(v)	cease	0 1 2 3
precious	(adj)	precious	0 1 2 3
recklessly	(adv)	recklessly	0 1 2 3
warped	(adj)	warped	0 1 2 3
divert	(v)	divert	0 1 2 3
mutinous	(adj)	mutinous	0 1 2 3
acknowledgment	(n)	acknowledgment	0 1 2 3

290 Unit 11

Vocabulary Rating Scale

0—I have never heard the word before.

1—I have heard the word, but I'm not sure how to use it.

2—I am familiar with the word, but I'm not sure if I know the correct meaning.

3—I know the meaning of the word and can use it correctly in a sentence.

Remember, the points are there to help you know which words you need to focus on. By the end of this unit, you should be able to change all your ratings to a 3. That's the goal.

Read each word aloud and have students repeat it, write it, and rate it. Then, have volunteers who rated a word *2* or *3* use the word in an oral sentence.

Preteach Vocabulary

Explain that you will now take a closer look at the words. Follow the Preteach Procedure outlined below.

Preteach Procedure

This activity is intended to take only a short amount of time, so make it an oral exercise.

- Introduce each word as indicated on the word card.
- Read the definition and example sentences.
- Ask questions to clarify and deepen understanding.
- If time permits, allow students to share.

* If your students would benefit from copying the definitions, please have them do so in the vocabulary log in the back of the Student Books using the margin definitions in the passage selections. This should be done outside of instruction time.

fruition (n)

Let's read the first word together. *Fruition.*

Definition: If something comes to *fruition*, it reaches completion and has a good outcome. What word means "completion; a good outcome"? (fruition)

Example 1: If your band works hard for months and finally lands a gig, your efforts have come to *fruition*.

Example 2: Hours of preparation in the kitchen can come to *fruition* in a scrumptious dinner.

Example 3: When a crop comes to *fruition*, it's harvest time.

Question 1: You plant some tomato seedlings in a pot on your balcony, but they don't get enough sun and die. Do the plants come to *fruition*? Yes or no? (no)

Question 2: You come up with a plan to drop some books near your locker so your cute locker neighbor will help you pick them up. The plan works! Does the plan come to *fruition*? Yes or no? (yes)

Pair Share: Turn to your partner and discuss what plan you have for today that you hope will come to *fruition*.

fashion (v)

Let's read the next word together. *Fashion.*

Definition: To *fashion* something is to make it or shape it. What means "to make; to shape"? (fashion)

Example 1: A skilled bow hunter can *fashion* her own bow from the branch of a tree.

Example 2: Wilderness campers sometimes *fashion* their own shelters from the materials available in nature.

Example 3: Pioneer girls didn't have store-bought toys, so they *fashioned* dolls from cornhusks and fabric scraps.

Question 1: Your mom buys a new doormat at the craft store. Did she *fashion* the mat? Yes or no? (no)

Question 2: Your aunt weaves natural fibers into doormats and sells them at crafts fairs. Does she *fashion* the mats? Yes or no? (yes)

Pair Share: You inherit a bag of colorful fabric strips from your grandmother. What wearable item could you *fashion* with them? Would it be fashionable? Tell your partner.

delicately (adv)

Let's read the next word together. *Delicately.*

Definition: If you do something *delicately*, you do it with a soft touch and great attention to detail. What means "with a soft touch and great attention to detail"? (delicately)

Example 1: In one of my favorite games, you stack blocks into a tower and then remove them from the tower one by one. If you don't remove a block *delicately*, the tower will collapse.

Example 2: My cousin's bridesmaids carried lovely bouquets that had been *delicately* arranged by a florist.

Example 3: To earn one scouting badge, a scout must *delicately* fashion a campfire and then light it with flint instead of matches.

Question 1: On small, ceramic eggs, you paint scenes that tell a story using tiny, detailed characters. Do you paint them *delicately*? Yes or no? (yes)

Question 2: A food truck owner is famous for tossing fried food and catching it in the carton he serves it in. Does he arrange the food *delicately*? Yes or no? (no)

Pair Share: Turn to your partner. Name something you do *delicately* each day.

3

cease (v)

Let's read the next word together. *Cease.*

Definition: If something *ceases*, it stops or comes to an end. What means "to stop; to come to an end"? (cease)

Example 1: Car alarms drive me crazy; thankfully, they *cease* after a few minutes of wailing.

Example 2: My neighbor's pet rooster seems to crow without *ceasing*.

Example 3: If you *cease* communicating with a close friend, the friendship may fade away.

Question 1: Wind speeds are increasing, and hail is starting to fall. Is the storm *ceasing*? Yes or no? (no)

Question 2: The guy next door has been revving his motorcycle in the driveway for 10 minutes. It's six in the morning. Do you wish the revving would *cease*? Yes or no? (yes)

Pair Share: Turn to your partner and share a strategy for getting the hiccups to *cease*.

precious (adj)

Let's read the next word together. *Precious.*

Definition: Something *precious* is very valuable, hard to get, and not to be wasted. What means "very valuable; hard to get and not to be wasted"? (precious)

Example 1: Tickets to a concert that sells out months in advance are *precious* and hard to come by.

Example 2: Parents of newborn triplets find just a few moments of quiet time *precious*.

Example 3: In a desert, water is *precious*.

Question 1: The resale store has rack after rack of used clothing. Is used clothing *precious*? Yes or no? (no)

Question 2: In your favorite book series, the hero uses a powerful weapon. It is the only weapon like it in the entire universe. Is the weapon *precious*? Yes or no? (yes)

Pair Share: Turn to your partner and describe a resource that you believe will be *precious* in 100 years, and what we can do today to help save it.

5

recklessly (adv)

Let's read the next word together. *Recklessly.*

Definition: If you do something *recklessly*, you do it carelessly or without concern for the harm that might be done. What means "carelessly; without concern for the harm that might be done"? (recklessly)

Example 1: If you drive *recklessly*, you will eventually cause an accident.

Example 2: *Recklessly* made business deals can cost companies large amounts of money.

Example 3: People who *recklessly* ignore the feelings of others usually have few friends.

Question 1: The battalion commander shared his carefully crafted battle plans with the officers. Were the plans made *recklessly*? Yes or no? (no)

Question 2: Campers ignore the fire ban and build a campfire near very dry grass. Is this done *recklessly*? Yes or no? (yes)

Pair Share: Turn to your partner and describe how a person might *recklessly* break up with someone.

warped (adj)

Let's read the next word together. *Warped.*

Definition: If something is *warped,* it is bent out of shape. What word means "bent out of shape"? (warped)

Example 1: Flooding can cause floorboards and wall paneling to become *warped.*

Example 2: I sometimes try to flatten the *warped* cover of a paperback book by putting another, heavier book on top of it.

Example 3: My favorite cookie sheet is old and *warped,* but it still bakes cookies to perfection.

Question 1: You find your old skateboard behind the shed. After years of weathering, its surface is cracked, bumpy, and uneven. Is it *warped*? Yes or no? (yes)

Question 2: You admire your uncle's new car by running a hand over the smooth surface of its hood. Is the hood *warped*? Yes or no? (no)

Pair Share: Turn to your partner and tell how a bike frame could get *warped.*

divert (v)

Let's read the next word together. *Divert.*

Definition: To *divert* something is to cause it to get off track or lose focus. What means "to cause someone or something to get off track or lose focus"? (divert)

Example 1: A farmer might build a dam to *divert* a stream to a different area of land.

Example 2: Deep ruts in a dirt road can *divert* a car's tires.

Example 3: It's hard for me to read in an airport because my attention is *diverted,* and I end up people-watching instead.

Question 1: You are taking a difficult test when the fire alarm goes off for a fire drill. Is your attention *diverted*? Yes or no? (yes)

Question 2: You are engrossed in a good movie. Someone knocks at the door, but you don't even hear it. Is your concentration *diverted* by the knocking? Yes or no? (no)

Pair Share: Turn to your partner and describe a sport, game, or musical instrument that you play well. Then, tell what happens if your focus is *diverted* while you do it.

8

mutinous (adj)

Let's read the next word together. *Mutinous.*

Definition: Someone who is *mutinous* strongly wants to rebel, or disobey someone in authority. What word means "strongly wanting to rebel, or disobey someone in authority"? (mutinous)

Example 1: Team members can feel *mutinous* when their leaders' rules are too strict.

Example 2: History shows that people who are oppressed eventually become *mutinous* and rise up against their oppressors.

Example 3: In the military, *mutinous* attitudes are not tolerated; total obedience is required.

Question 1: Your cousin scowls at his mom behind her back when she asks him to do something. Is he *mutinous*? Yes or no? (yes)

Question 2: You sometimes disagree with your mom's rules, but you understand why she sets them and don't really mind following them. Are you *mutinous*? Yes or no? (no)

Pair Share: Turn to your partner and tell about a movie, book, or TV character who acts in a *mutinous* way.

9

acknowledgment (n)

Let's read the last word together. *Acknowledgment.*

Definition: An *acknowledgment* is a sign or action that shows you know something is true. What word means "a sign or action that shows you know something is true"? (acknowledgment)

Example 1: A thank-you note is one form of *acknowledgment* that you appreciate a gift.

Example 2: Most employees appreciate *acknowledgment* of a job well done.

Example 3: When you order something online, you should receive *acknowledgment* of your order by e-mail.

Question 1: You mailed a package to your friend but never heard back. Did you receive *acknowledgment* that she got it? Yes or no? (no)

Question 2: You help a friend put together a slideshow presentation, and he lists your name in the credits. Did you receive *acknowledgment* for your help? Yes or no? (yes)

Pair Share: You are the producer of a new game show on TV. What clever or unusual method will the host use to show *acknowledgment* of a correct answer by one of the contestants? Tell your partner.

10

Reading

Objectives

- Read an excerpt from a novel.
- Monitor comprehension during text reading.

Excerpt from *The Good Earth*

Direct students to page 291 in their Student Books. Now that we have previewed vocabulary, it's time to read.

Guiding Students Toward Independent Reading

It is important that your students read as much and as often as they can. Assign readings that meet the needs of your students, based on your observations and data. This is a good opportunity to stretch your students. If students become frustrated, scaffold the reading with paired reading, choral reading, or a read-aloud.

Options for reading text:

- Teacher read-aloud
- Teacher-led or student-led choral read
- Paired read or independent read

Choose an option for reading the text. Have students read according to the option that you chose.

Remind students to pause at the numbers and consider the questions.

If you choose to read the text aloud or chorally, use the text in the following boxes and stop to ask questions and have students answer them.

SE p. 291, paragraph 1

It was Wang Lung's marriage day. At first, opening his eyes in the blackness of the curtains about his bed, he could not think why the dawn seemed different from any other. The house was still except for the faint, gasping cough of his old father, whose room was opposite to his own across the middle room. Every morning the old man's cough was the first sound to be heard. Wang Lung usually lay listening to it and moved only when he heard it approaching nearer and when he heard the door of his father's room squeak upon its wooden hinges.

1. Who does Wang Lung live with?

SE p. 291, paragraphs 2–4

But this morning he did not wait. He sprang up and pushed aside the curtains of his bed. It was a dark, ruddy dawn, and through a small square hole of a window, where the tattered paper fluttered, a glimpse of bronze sky gleamed. He went to the hole and tore the paper away.

"It is spring and I do not need this," he muttered.

He was ashamed to say aloud that he wished the house to look neat on this day. The hole was barely large enough to admit his hand and he thrust it out to feel of the air. A small soft wind blew gently from the east, a wind mild and murmurous and full of rain. It was a good omen. The fields needed rain for **fruition**. There would be no rain this day, but within a few days, if this wind continued, there would be water. It was good. Yesterday he had said to his father that if this brazen, glittering sunshine continued, the wheat could not fill in the ear. Now it was as if Heaven had chosen this day to wish him well. Earth would bear fruit.

2. What is the weather like on Wang Lung's wedding day? Why is that a problem?

SE p. 291, paragraph 5

page break

He hurried out into the middle room, drawing on his blue outer trousers as he went, and knotting about the fullness at his waist his girdle of blue cotton cloth. He left his upper body bare until he had heated water to bathe himself. He went into | the shed which was the kitchen, leaning against the house, and out of its dusk an ox twisted its head from behind the corner next the door and lowed at him deeply. The kitchen was made of earthen bricks as the house was, great squares of earth dug from their own fields, and thatched with straw from their own wheat. Out of their own earth had his grandfather in his youth **fashioned** also the oven, baked and black with many years of meal preparing. On top of this earthen structure stood a deep, round, iron cauldron.

3. How has the earth been good to Wang Lung and his father?

SE p. 292, paragraph 1

This cauldron he filled partly full of water, dipping it with a half gourd from an earthen jar that stood near, but he dipped cautiously, for water was precious. Then, after a hesitation, he suddenly lifted the jar and emptied all the water into the cauldron. This day he would bathe his whole body. Not since he was a child upon his mother's knee had anyone looked upon his body. Today one would, and he would have it clean.

4. What did Wang Lung treat himself to on his wedding day?

SE p. 292, paragraphs 2–3

He went around the oven to the rear, and selecting a handful of the dry grass and stalks standing in the corner of the kitchen, he arranged it **delicately** in the mouth of the oven, making the most of every leaf. Then from an old flint and iron he caught a flame and thrust it into the straw and there was a blaze.

This was the last morning he would have to light the fire. He had lit it every morning since his mother died six years before. He had lit the fire, boiled water, and poured the water into a bowl and taken it into the room where his father sat upon his bed, coughing and fumbling for his shoes upon the floor. Every morning for these six years the old man had waited for his son to bring in hot water to ease him of his morning coughing. Now father and son could rest. There was a woman coming to the house. Never again would Wang Lung have to rise summer and winter at dawn to light the fire. He could lie in his bed and wait, and he also would have a bowl of water brought to him, and if the earth were fruitful there would be tea leaves in the water. Once in some years it was so.

5. What is Wang Lung expecting of his new wife?

SE p. 293, paragraphs 1–2

And if the woman wearied, there would be her children to light the fire, the many children she would bear to Wang Lung. Wang Lung stopped, struck by the thought of children running in and out of their three rooms. Three rooms had always seemed much to them, a house half empty since his mother died.

Now the grandsons were coming, grandsons upon grandsons! They would have to put beds along the walls and in the middle room. The house would be full of beds. The blaze in the oven died down while Wang Lung thought of all the beds there would be in the half empty house, and the water began to chill in the cauldron. The shadowy figure of the old man appeared in the doorway, holding his unbuttoned garments about him. He was coughing and spitting and he gasped, "How is it that there is not water yet to heat my lungs?"

6. What else is Wang Lung expecting of his new wife?

SE p. 293, paragraphs 3–6

Wang Lung stared and recalled himself and was ashamed.

"This fuel is damp," he muttered from behind the stove. "The damp wind—"

The old man continued to cough perseveringly and would not **cease** until the water boiled. Wang Lung dipped some into a bowl, and then, after a moment, he opened a glazed jar that stood upon a ledge of the stove and took from it a dozen or so of the curled dried leaves and sprinkled them upon the surface of the water. The old man's eyes opened greedily and immediately he began to complain.

"Why are you wasteful? Tea is like eating silver."

7. How is tea like eating silver?

SE p. 293, paragraphs 7–8

"It is the day," replied Wang Lung with a short laugh. "Eat and be comforted."

The old man grasped the bowl in his shriveled, knotty fingers, muttering, uttering little grunts. He watched the leaves uncurl and spread upon the surface of the water, unable to bear drinking the **precious** stuff.

SE p. 294, paragraphs 1–6

"It will be cold," said Wang Lung.

"True—true—" said the old man in alarm, and he began to take great gulps of the hot tea. He passed into an animal satisfaction, like a child fixed upon its feeding. But he was not too forgetful to see Wang Lung dipping the water **recklessly** from the cauldron into a deep wooden tub. He lifted his head and stared at his son.

"Now there is water enough to bring a crop to fruit," he said suddenly.

Wang Lung continued to dip the water to the last drop. He did not answer.

"Now then!" cried his father loudly.

"I have not washed my body all at once since the New Year," said Wang Lung in a low voice.

8. How long has it been since Wang Lung washed his entire body?

SE p. 294, paragraphs 7–9

He was ashamed to say to his father that he wished his body to be clean for a woman to see. He hurried out, carrying the tub to his own room. The door was hung loosely upon a **warped** wooden frame and it did not shut closely, and the old man tottered into the middle room and put his mouth to the opening and bawled, "It will be ill if we start the woman like this—tea in the morning water and all this washing!"

"It is only one day," shouted Wang Lung. And then he added, "I will throw the water on the earth when I am finished and it is not all waste."

The old man was silent at this, and Wang Lung unfastened his girdle and stepped out of his clothing. In the light that streamed in a square block from the hole he wrung a small towel from the steaming water and he scrubbed his dark slender body vigorously. Warm though he had thought the air, when his flesh was wet he was cold, and he moved quickly, passing the towel in and out of the water until from his whole body there went up a delicate cloud of steam. Then he went to a box that had been his mother's and drew from it a fresh suit of blue cotton cloth. He might be a little | cold this day without the wadding of the winter garments, but he suddenly could not bear to put them on against his clean flesh. The covering of them was torn and filthy and the wadding stuck out of the holes, grey and sodden. He did not want this woman to see him for the first time with the wadding sticking out of his clothes. Later she would have to wash and mend, but not the first day. He drew over the blue cotton coat and trousers a long robe made of the same material—his one long robe, which he wore on feast days only, ten days or so in the year, all told. Then with swift fingers he unplaited the long braid of hair that hung down his back, and taking a wooden comb from the drawer of the small, unsteady table, he began to comb out his hair.

page break

9. What does Wang Lung wear on his wedding day?

SE p. 295, paragraphs 1–4

His father drew near again and put his mouth to the crack of the door.

"Am I to have nothing to eat this day?" he complained. "At my age the bones are water in the morning until food is given them."

"I am coming," said Wang Lung, braiding his hair quickly and smoothly and weaving into the strands a tasseled black silk cord.

Then after a moment he removed his long gown and wound his braid about his head and went out, carrying the tub of water. He had quite forgotten the breakfast. He would stir a little water into cornmeal and give it to his father. For himself he could not eat. He staggered with the tub to the threshold and poured the water upon the earth nearest the door, and as he did so he remembered he had used all the water in the cauldron for his bathing and he would have to start the fire again. A wave of anger passed over him at his father.

10. What did Wang Lung forget to do on his wedding day?

SE p. 295, paragraph 5

"That old head thinks of nothing except his eating and his drinking," he muttered into the mouth of the oven; but aloud he said nothing. It was the last morning he would have to prepare food for the old man. He put a very little water into the cauldron, | drawing it in a bucket from the well near the door, and it boiled quickly and he stirred meal together and took it to the old man.

page break

11. What else does Wang Lung expect of his new wife?

SE p. 296, paragraphs 1–2

Wang Lung went into his own room then, and drew about him again the long blue robe and let down the braid of his hair. He passed his hand over his shaven brow and over his cheeks. Perhaps he had better be newly shaven? It was scarcely sunrise yet. He could pass through the Street of the Barbers and be shaved before he went to the house where the woman waited for him. If he had the money he would do it.

He took from his girdle a small greasy pouch of grey cloth and counted the money in it. There were six silver dollars and a double handful of copper coins. He had not yet told his father he had asked friends to sup that night. He had asked his male cousin, the young son of his uncle, and his uncle for his father's sake, and three neighboring farmers who lived in the village with him. He had planned to bring back from the town that morning pork, a small pond fish, and a handful of chestnuts. He might even buy a few of the bamboo sprouts from the south and a little beef to stew with the cabbage he had raised in his own garden. But this only if there were any money left after the bean oil and the soybean sauce had been bought. If he shaved his head he could not, perhaps, buy the beef. Well, he would shave his head, he decided suddenly.

12. How did Wang Lung treat himself on his wedding day?

SE p. 296, paragraph 3

He left the old man without speech and went out into the early morning. In spite of the dark red dawn the sun was mounting the horizon clouds and sparkled upon the dew on the rising wheat and barley. The farmer in Wang Lung was **diverted** for an instant and he stooped to examine the budding heads. They were empty as yet and waiting for the rain. He smelled the air and looked anxiously at the sky. Rain was there, dark in the clouds, heavy upon the wind. He would buy a stick of incense and place it in the little temple to the Earth God. On a day like this he would do it.

SE p. 297, paragraph 1

He wound his way in among the fields upon the narrow path. In the near distance the grey city wall arose. Within that gate in the wall through which he would pass stood the great house where the woman had been a slave girl since her childhood, the House of Hwang. There were those who said, "It is better to live alone than to marry a woman who has been slave in a great house." But when he had said to his father, "Am I never to have a woman?" his father replied, "With weddings costing as they do in these evil days and every woman wanting gold rings and silk clothes before she will take a man, there remain only slaves to be had for the poor."

13. What is the background of Wang Lung's bride?

SE p. 297, paragraphs 2–4

His father had stirred himself, then, and gone to the House of Hwang and asked if there were a slave to spare.

"Not a slave too young, and above all, not a pretty one," he had said.

Wang Lung had suffered that she must not be pretty. It would be something to have a pretty wife that other men would congratulate him upon having. His father, seeing his **mutinous** face, had cried out at him, "And what will we do with a pretty woman? We must have a woman who will tend the house and bear children as she works in the fields, and will a pretty woman do these things? She will be forever thinking about clothes to go with her face! No, not a pretty woman in our house. We are farmers. Moreover, who has heard of a pretty slave who was virgin in a wealthy house? All the young lords have had their fill of her. It is better to be first with an ugly woman than the hundredth with a beauty. Do you imagine a pretty woman will think your farmer's hands as pleasing as the soft hands of a rich man's son, and your sun-black face as beautiful as the golden skin of the others who have had her for their pleasure?"

14. What criteria did Wang Lung's father require for his chosen wife?

SE p. 297, paragraph 5

Wang Lung knew his father spoke well. Nevertheless, he had to struggle with his flesh before he could answer. And then he said violently, "At least, I will not have a woman who is pock-marked, or who has a split upper lip."

SE p. 298, paragraphs 1–2

"We will have to see what is to be had," his father replied.

Well, the woman was not pock-marked nor had she a split upper lip. This much he knew, but nothing more. He and his father had bought two silver rings, washed with gold, and silver earrings, and these his father had taken to the woman's owner in **acknowledgment** of betrothal. Beyond this, he knew nothing of the woman who was to be his, except that on this day he could go and get her.

15. How much did Wang Lung's father pay for his wife?

For confirmation of engagement, have partners share two things they learned about arranged marriages in China.

Unit 11 Lesson 2

Lesson Opener

Before the lesson, choose one of the following activities to write on the board or post on the *LANGUAGE! Live* Class Wall online.

- *Write the dialogue between you and a spouse you have never met at your wedding. Don't forget the appropriate punctuation and to vary your verbs.*
- *Use transitive verbs to write five sentences about why arranged marriages are a good idea.*
- *Use the word* wedding *in three sentences. Use it as a verb in one sentence, a noun in one sentence, and an adjective in another sentence.*

Vocabulary

Objective

- Review key passage vocabulary.

Review Passage Vocabulary

Direct students to page 290 in their Student Books. Use the following questions to review the vocabulary words in the excerpt from *The Good Earth*. Have students answer each question using the vocabulary word or indicating its meaning in a complete sentence.

Lesson 1 | Vocabulary

Key Passage Vocabulary: Excerpt from *The Good Earth*

Read each word. Write the word in column 3. Then, circle a number to rate your knowledge of the word.

[illegible]	[illegible]	[illegible]	[illegible]
fruition	(n)	fruition	0 1 2 3
fashion	(v)	fashion	0 1 2 3
delicately	(adv)	delicately	0 1 2 3
cease	(v)	cease	0 1 2 3
precious	(adj)	precious	0 1 2 3
recklessly	(adv)	recklessly	0 1 2 3
warped	(adj)	warped	0 1 2 3
divert	(v)	divert	0 1 2 3
mutinous	(adj)	mutinous	0 1 2 3
acknowledgment	(n)	acknowledgment	0 1 2 3

290 Unit 11

- Wang Lung's fields need rain for *fruition*. What will *fruition* bring? (Fruition will bring crops.) In what way does Wang Lung hope his marriage will come to *fruition*? (Possible response: He hopes his marriage will come to fruition by producing many children—"grandsons upon grandsons.")
- Wang Lung's grandfather *fashioned* the family's oven out of the earth. What did he do to the oven? (If he fashioned it, he shaped it or made it.) What other objects had been *fashioned* from natural materials? (The house had been fashioned from the earth, and the roof had been fashioned from wheat.)
- What does Wang Lung arrange *delicately* in the oven? Why? (He arranges dry grass and stalks in the oven delicately, or with a soft touch and great attention to detail, in order not to waste a single leaf.) Would you say that Wang Lung's father looks for his shoes *delicately*? Why or why not? (No, he doesn't look for his shoes with a soft touch; instead, he fumbles for them. He is old and unwell, and basic movements are a challenge for him.)
- Wang Lung wishes his father's coughing would *cease*. What does he wish it would do? (He wishes it would stop.) When does it *cease*? (It ceases when the water finally boils.)

- Wang Lung puts tea leaves in his father's hot water. His father can't bring himself to drink the *precious* tea. Why? (He can't bring himself to drink the tea because tea leaves are hard to come by and shouldn't be wasted.) Why do you suppose so many items—kindling, tea leaves, water—are *precious* in Wang Lung's house? (Possible response: He and his father are poor. They rely solely on their crops for money and needed goods. It is spring now, so they haven't had any crops since last summer—and those might not have been very fruitful. Wang Lung seems very glad that rain is on its way.)
- Wang Lung pours water *recklessly* from the cauldron into a deep tub. What is he thinking about? What isn't he thinking about? (He is thinking of taking a bath. He isn't thinking about the consequences of wasting water.) Does his father approve of this *reckless* use of water? Why or why not? (No, he doesn't approve of his recklessness. He is afraid the water will be needed to water the crops.) When his father makes a comment about wasting water, does Wang Lung cease dipping the water? (No, he doesn't cease; he continues to fill the tub.)
- The door to Wang Lung's room hangs loosely on a *warped* wooden frame. Use your hand to show the line of the frame. (Students should make a wavy line in the air with their hand.) What does the *warped* frame allow Wang Lung's father to do? (The warped frame creates an opening through which his father can yell at him about his wasteful ways.)
- On his way out to get shaved, Wang Lung is *diverted*. What *diverts* him? (The budding heads on the wheat and barley divert him.) Had his father been successful in *diverting* Wang Lung from bathing? (No, his father did not divert Wang Lung from his bath; he finished taking it.)
- When his father had arranged for the marriage, he had requested a slave woman who was not pretty. Why did this make Wang Lung feel *mutinous*? (It made him feel like rebelling against his father because he wanted an attractive wife.) Can you imagine the woman herself feeling *mutinous* when her owner gives her to Wang Lung? Why or why not? (Possible responses: Yes, she might want to rebel against the marriage because Wang Lung is poor and she will have to work very hard; No, she is a slave and expects a hard life.)
- Wang Lung's father had taken a pair of earrings to the woman's owner in *acknowledgment* of the engagement. By doing this, he had been saying what? (By acknowledging the engagement, he had been saying that the engagement was real and the marriage would happen.) Does the excerpt end in *acknowledgment* of the couple's future happiness? (No; it does not let us know that a happy marriage will occur. It says the opposite—that Wang Lung knows nothing about his wife or his future.)

Grammar

Objectives

- Identify participial phrases and use them correctly.
- Differentiate between participial phrases and prepositional phrases.
- Identify appositives and the corresponding nouns they modify.

Participial Phrases

Words have multiple functions. You learned that some verbs can be used to describe nouns and answer the adjective questions *what kind* or *which one*. We called these verb forms *participles*. What are these verb forms called? (participles)

Write the following words on the board: *declining, warped.*

Consider these two words. They can both be participles. *Declining* is a present participle, and *warped* is a past participle. Think of how we could use these words to modify or describe a noun. What are some things that could decline? (Possible responses: grades, temperature) The *declining* temperature caused me to grab my coat as I headed to school. What kind of temperature? (declining) Turn to your partner and use *declining* in a sentence where it answers the *what kind* or *which one* question. Have volunteers share their sentences with the class.

Now, think about using *warped* in the same way. The *warped* wood made it difficult to close the door securely. What kind of wood? (warped) Turn to your partner and use *warped* in a sentence where it answers the *what kind* or *which one* question. Have volunteers share their sentences with the class.

A participial phrase is simply a group of words that describe a noun. The phrase begins with a participle and includes other words that create the phrase.

Direct students to page 299 in their Student Books. Read the information about participial phrases aloud.

Read the instructions for the activity.

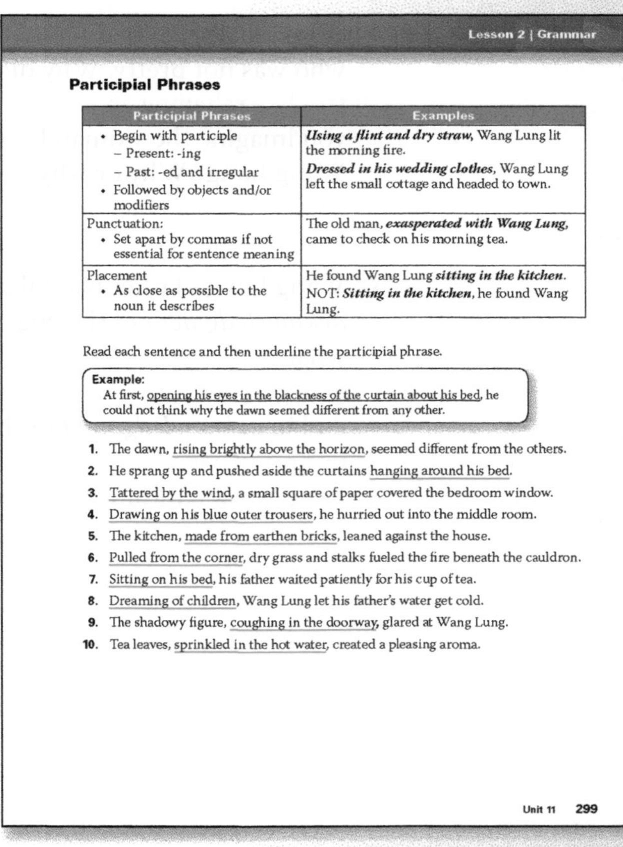

Lesson 2 | Grammar

Participial Phrases

Participial Phrases	Examples
• Begin with participle – Present: -ing – Past: -ed and irregular • Followed by objects and/or modifiers	***Using a flint and dry straw,*** Wang Lung lit the morning fire. ***Dressed in his wedding clothes,*** Wang Lung left the small cottage and headed to town.
Punctuation: • Set apart by commas if not essential for sentence meaning	The old man, ***exasperated with Wang Lung,*** came to check on his morning tea.
Placement • As close as possible to the noun it describes	He found Wang Lung ***sitting in the kitchen.*** NOT: ***Sitting in the kitchen,*** he found Wang Lung.

Read each sentence and then underline the participial phrase.

Example:
At first, opening his eyes in the blackness of the curtain about his bed, he could not think why the dawn seemed different from any other.

1. The dawn, rising brightly above the horizon, seemed different from the others.
2. He sprang up and pushed aside the curtains hanging around his bed.
3. Tattered by the wind, a small square of paper covered the bedroom window.
4. Drawing on his blue outer trousers, he hurried out into the middle room.
5. The kitchen, made from earthen bricks, leaned against the house.
6. Pulled from the corner, dry grass and stalks fueled the fire beneath the cauldron.
7. Sitting on his bed, his father waited patiently for his cup of tea.
8. Dreaming of children, Wang Lung let his father's water get cold.
9. The shadowy figure, coughing in the doorway, glared at Wang Lung.
10. Tea leaves, sprinkled in the hot water, created a pleasing aroma.

Unit 11 299

Model

Listen as I read the example: *At first, opening his eyes in the blackness of the curtain about his bed, he could not think why the dawn seemed different from any other.*

I have to find and underline the participial phrase within the sentence. I'm going to look for the subject noun or pronoun first and then see if I can find a group of words that modify the subject. Who or what? *He*. What did he do? *Could not think.*

Note: Negative terms like *not* are not a part of the verb; rather, they are adverbs. *Not* has been included here to simplify ruling out the main verb as a possible participle. You will teach negation in the next unit but can add clarification here if you think it will be helpful.

I have to remember the definition of a participial phrase: begins with a participle and is followed by objects and or modifiers. Immediately preceding the pronoun, I see a very long phrase that begins with *opening.* I know *opening* is not the verb, so it is a present participle. I'll keep reading to see if this group of words fits the definition. The entire phrase *opening his eyes in the blackness of the curtain about his bed* gives me information about the subject, *he.* I have underlined the entire phrase.

Listen as I read #1: *The dawn, rising brightly above the horizon, seemed different from the others.*

It helps to locate the kernel sentence, the subject noun and predicate verb. Who or what is this sentence about? *Dawn.* What did it do? *The dawn seemed.* Although *seemed* does not convey an action, it is serving as a link to the rest of the sentence. Finding the kernel sentence allows me to look for a phrase that describes a noun without confusing the participle with the main verb. I have to remember that sentences can contain more than one noun and one verb. Are there any describing words that tell me more about the dawn? Yes, and I see another present participle followed by a group of words—*rising brightly above the horizon.* What kind of dawn? One that is *rising brightly above the horizon.* I need to underline that phrase. As a way to check my thinking, I also see commas setting the phrase apart. Does the sentence make sense without the participial phrase? *The dawn seemed different from the others.* It makes perfect sense.

Guided Practice

Listen as I read #2: *He sprang up and pushed aside the curtains hanging around his bed.* Let's find the kernel sentence first. Who or what? (He) What did he do? (sprang and pushed) What did he push? (curtains) Which curtains? (hanging around his bed) What is the first word in that phrase? (hanging) What kind of a word is *hanging*? (present participle) It's a present participle, and it is followed by words that modify hanging. Underline the phrase *hanging around his bed.* In this sentence, the participial phrase modifies a noun that is not the subject noun. *Curtains* is the direct object because it answers the *pushed what* question.

Independent Practice

Have students complete the activity. Review the answers as a class.

Participial Phrase or Prepositional Phrase

You have worked a great deal with prepositions and prepositional phrases. Remember, a prepositional phrase begins with a preposition and includes an object. Listen to these examples: *in the water, on the table, with the class, for my mother, by the street, across the fields.*

Direct students to page 300 in their Student Books. Read the instructions for the activity and model the examples.

Lesson 2 | Grammar

Participial Phrase or Prepositional Phrase

Read each sentence and determine whether the underlined words form a participial phrase or a prepositional phrase. Sort the phrases into the chart below.

Examples:
Wang Lung dipped some water into the bowl.
Pushing aside the bed curtains, Wang Lung quickly rose to greet the morning.

1. On this morning, he wanted the house to look neat and tidy.
2. A small soft wind blew gently from the east.
3. The wind, blowing from the east, was murmurous and full of rain.
4. The thatched straw roof was made from their own wheat.
5. Filled with water, the cauldron hung above the earthen oven.
6. Walking behind the oven, he selected a handful of dry grass.
7. Striking an old flint and iron, he caught a flame and thrust it into the straw.
8. After this morning, he would not have to light the morning fire.
9. Coughing in the damp morning air, the old man waited for his morning cup of hot water.
10. Rising at dawn's first light, Wang Lung had lit the oven and heated the water.

Participial Phrases	Prepositional Phrases
Pushing aside the bed curtains	into the bowl
blowing from the east	On this morning
Filled with water	from the east
Walking behind the oven	from their own wheat
Striking an old flint and iron	above the earthen oven
Coughing in the damp morning air	of dry grass
Rising at dawn's first light	into the straw
	After this morning
	of hot water

300 Unit 11

Model

Listen as I read the first example: *Wang Lung dipped some water into the bowl.*

Into the bowl is underlined. It begins with a direction/position word that must be a preposition, so it must be a prepositional phrase. My next step is to write the phrase in the chart below under Prepositional Phrases.

Listen as I read the second example: *Pushing aside the bed curtains, Wang Lung quickly rose to greet the morning.*

Pushing aside the bed curtains is underlined. I have to decide if it's a participial phrase or a prepositional phrase. *Pushing* ends in -ing and it is an action, so I think this must be a participial phrase. It is describing Wang Lung. Next, I need to write the phrase in the chart underneath Participial Phrases.

Guided Practice

Listen as I read #1: *On this morning, he wanted the house to look neat and tidy.*

What words are underlined? (on this morning) Look carefully at how the phrase begins. Is the first word a participle or a preposition? (preposition) It is a preposition. What is our next step? (write the phrase in the chart underneath Prepositional Phrases)

Independent Practice

Have students complete the activity. Review the answers as a class.

Appositives

You have learned that nouns have a variety of jobs in a sentence. What are some of the jobs that nouns can have in a sentence? (subject, direct object, or object of the preposition) Sometimes, we can use nouns to further identify or explain other nouns. Unlike adjectives that offer descriptive details, sometimes another noun helps the reader understand the *who* or *what* better. Nouns used in this way are called appositives. What do you call nouns that serve to further identify other nouns? (appositives) Appositives offer us another way to vary the sentence structure while providing more specific details about a noun in a sentence.

Direct students to page 301 in their Student Books. Read the information about appositives and the first set of examples aloud.

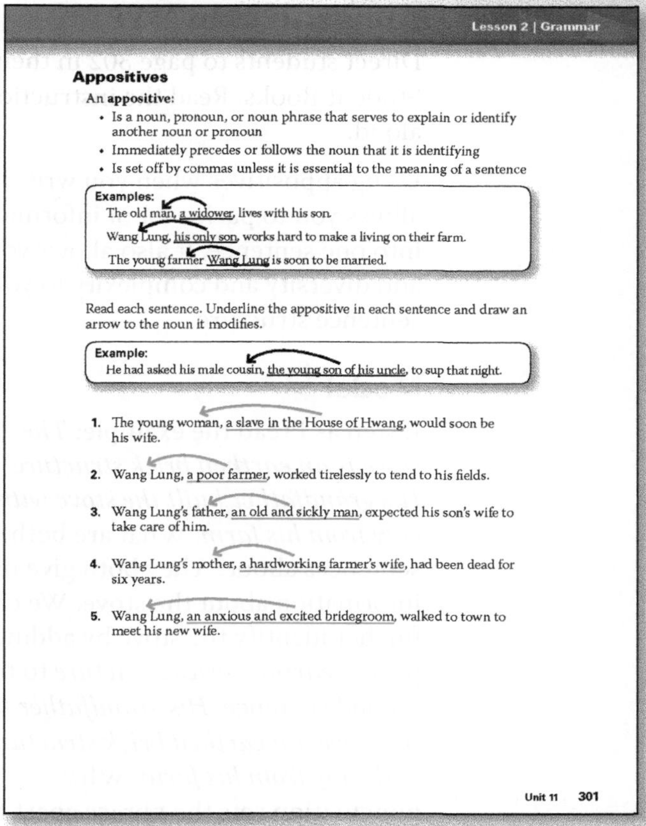
Lesson 2 | Grammar

Appositives

An **appositive**:

- Is a noun, pronoun, or noun phrase that serves to explain or identify another noun or pronoun
- Immediately precedes or follows the noun that it is identifying
- Is set off by commas unless it is essential to the meaning of a sentence

Examples:

The old man, a widower, lives with his son.

Wang Lung, his only son, works hard to make a living on their farm.

The young farmer Wang Lung is soon to be married.

Read each sentence. Underline the appositive in each sentence and draw an arrow to the noun it modifies.

Example:

He had asked his male cousin, the young son of his uncle, to sup that night.

1. The young woman, a slave in the House of Hwang, would soon be his wife.
2. Wang Lung, a poor farmer, worked tirelessly to tend to his fields.
3. Wang Lung's father, an old and sickly man, expected his son's wife to take care of him.
4. Wang Lung's mother, a hardworking farmer's wife, had been dead for six years.
5. Wang Lung, an anxious and excited bridegroom, walked to town to meet his new wife.

Unit 11 301

Model

Read the instructions for the activity.

Listen as I read the example: *He had asked his male cousin, the young son of his uncle, to sup that night.*

The first thing I need to do is identify the appositive, or the noun phrase that renames or further identifies another noun in the sentence. Who or what is the sentence about? *He* is the subject. What did he do? He *had asked*. Who did he ask? *His male cousin*. Does the sentence give me any more information about who *he* is? No. Does it give me any more information about the direct object *cousin*? Yes, it tells me he is the young son of his uncle. The phrase *the young son of his uncle* renames or further identifies the direct object *cousin*. Because it is a noun phrase that further identifies another noun, it is an appositive. I need to underline the phrase and then draw an arrow back to the noun that it renames. So, I draw an arrow back to *cousin*.

Guided Practice

Listen as I read #1: *The young woman, a slave in the House of Hwang, would soon be his wife.*

Who or what is the sentence about? (woman) Does the sentence give us details that identify her further? (yes) How does the sentence further explain her identity? (a slave in the House of Hwang) That's a noun phrase that adds information about the subject noun—an appositive. What is your next step? (underline the appositive) After underlining the appositive, what's your last step? (draw an arrow from the phrase to *woman*)

Independent Practice

Have students complete the activity. Review the answers as a class.

Writing

Objectives

- Combine sentences using appositives.
- Use proper subject-verb agreement.

Appositives in Writing

Direct students to page 302 in their Student Books. Read the instructions aloud.

Using appositives when you write allows you to pack a lot of information into one sentence. It also allows you to add diversity and complexity to your sentence structure.

Lesson 2 | Writing

Appositives in Writing

Write one sentence that combines each pair of sentences by turning one sentence into an appositive. Remember to correctly punctuate each new sentence.

Example:
The stove is an earthen brick structure.
His grandfather built the stove with clay from his farm.
His grandfather built the stove, an earthen brick structure, with clay from his farm.

1. Wang Lung's father is a feeble old man.
Wang Lung's father lives with him.
Wang Lung's father, a feeble old man, lives with him.
2. Wang Lung's new wife is a slave in the House of Hwang.
Wang Lung's new wife lives in town.
Wang Lung's new wife, a slave in the House of Hwang, lives in town.
3. Wang Lung is a dutiful son.
Wang Lung takes good care of his father.
Wang Lung, a dutiful son, takes good care of his father.
4. Arranged marriages are a common practice in rural China.
Arranged marriages are frowned upon in the Western world.
Arranged marriages, a common practice in rural China, are frowned upon in the Western world.
5. Wang Lung's bride is a poor slave.
The slave married Wang Lung for a chance for a better life.
Wang Lung's bride, a poor slave, married Wang Lung for a chance at a better life.

302 Unit 11

Model

Listen as I read the example: *The stove is an earthen brick structure. His grandfather built the stove with clay from his farm.* What are both sentences about? They both give us information about the stove. We can further identify the stove by adding the phrase *earthen brick structure* to the second sentence. *His grandfather built the stove, an earthen brick structure, with clay from his farm.* What punctuation sets the phrase apart from the rest of the sentence? Commas before and after the phrase are needed to properly punctuate the sentence. The rewritten sentence is a good reminder to look for ways to expand any noun in a sentence, not just the subject noun. In this sentence, *stove* answers the *built what* question, making it the direct object.

Guided Practice

Listen as I read #1: *Wang Lung's father is a feeble old man. Wang Lung's father lives with him.* What are both sentences about? (Wang Lung's father) How can you combine the information about Wang Lung's father in the first sentence with the second sentence? Turn and tell your partner how you would combine the two sentences. Remember: our combined sentence needs to have a noun phrase that renames or further identifies one of the nouns in the sentence. What is the new sentence? (Wang Lung's father, a feeble old man, lives with him.) What punctuation do we need within the sentence? (commas before and after the phrase) Check your sentence to make sure you've written it correctly.

Independent Practice

Have students complete the activity. Review the answers as a class.

Subject-Verb Agreement

Complex sentences that have multiple nouns and verbs can make it difficult to find the kernel sentence: the simple subject and predicate. To confirm understanding as a reader, it's important to be able to pull out the kernel sentence. You have to know who or what's being modified. It's also critical when you write sentences because the subject noun and verb work together in a special way. They have to agree in number. If the subject noun is singular, then the verb has to be singular as well. If the subject noun is plural, then the verb has to match. Sounds simple, but it isn't always simple.

Direct students to page 303 in their Student Books. Read the information on subject-verb agreement aloud, then read the instructions for the activity.

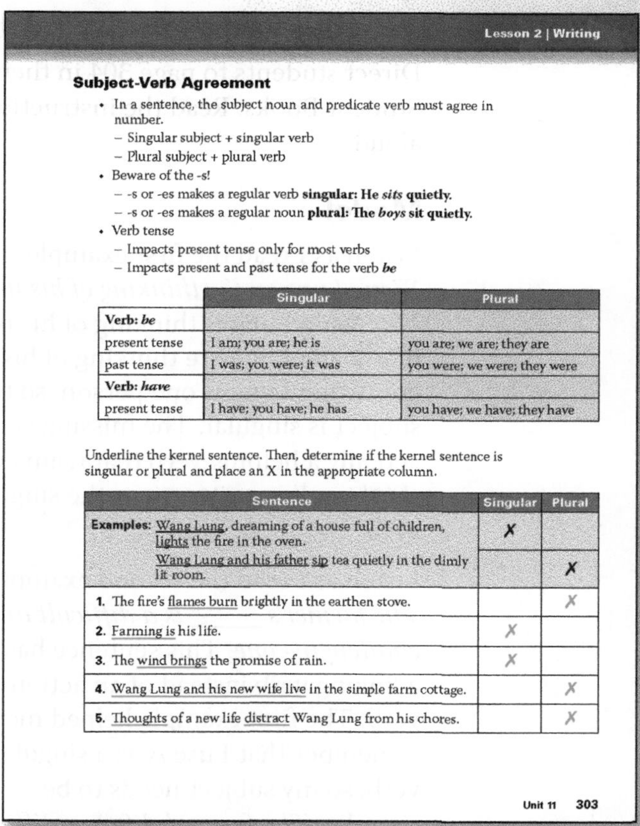

Lesson 2 | Writing

Subject-Verb Agreement

- In a sentence, the subject noun and predicate verb must agree in number.
  - Singular subject + singular verb
  - Plural subject + plural verb
- Beware of the -s!
  - -s or -es makes a regular verb **singular: He *sits* quietly.**
  - -s or -es makes a regular noun **plural: The *boys* sit quietly.**
- Verb tense
  - Impacts present tense only for most verbs
  - Impacts present and past tense for the verb *be*

	Singular	Plural
Verb: *be*		
present tense	I am; you are; he is	you are; we are; they are
past tense	I was; you were; it was	you were; we were; they were
Verb: *have*		
present tense	I have; you have; he has	you have; we have; they have

Underline the kernel sentence. Then, determine if the kernel sentence is singular or plural and place an X in the appropriate column.

Sentence	Singular	Plural
Examples: Wang Lung, dreaming of a house full of children, lights the fire in the oven.	✗	
Wang Lung and his father sip tea quietly in the dimly lit room.		✗
1. The fire's flames burn brightly in the earthen stove.		✗
2. Farming is his life.	✗	
3. The wind brings the promise of rain.	✗	
4. Wang Lung and his new wife live in the simple farm cottage.		✗
5. Thoughts of a new life distract Wang Lung from his chores.		✗

Unit 11 303

Model

Listen as I read the first example: *Wang Lung, dreaming of a house full of children, lights the fire in the oven.*

Who or what is this sentence about? The sentence contains multiple nouns, but *Wang Lung* is the subject noun. I need to see if the sentence tells me what he did. *Dreaming* can be a verb, but it doesn't make sense to say *Wang Lung dreaming.* It does make sense to say *Wang Lung lights.* The instructions tell me to underline the kernel sentence. Next, I have to figure out if it's singular or plural. Wang Lung is one person, so my verb needs to be singular as well. I need an -s on the verb to make it singular. I know that sounds complicated. I just need to remember if I can substitute *he, she,* or *it* as the subject, usually I need to add an -s to a present tense verb.

Listen to the next example: *Wang Lung and his father sip tea quietly in the dimly lit room.*

Who or what is this sentence about? Wang Lung and his father. What do they do? They sip. I need to underline *Wang Lung and his father sip.* My subject is more than one person, so it's plural. Because my subject is plural, I don't need to add anything to the verb. I placed an X in the Plural column.

Guided Practice

Listen as I read #1: *The fire's flames burn brightly in the earthen stove.*

Who or what is the sentence about? (flames) *Flames* is the subject noun. *Fire's* shows ownership or possession. It is describing flames. What do the flames do? (burn) They burn. What needs to be underlined? (flames burn) Our second question is whether it's singular or plural. Using *they* instead of *it* should provide a hint. What is it? (plural) Put your X in the Plural column.

Independent Practice

Have students complete the activity. Review the answers as a class.

Writing with Subject-Verb Agreement

Direct students to page 304 in their Student Books. Read the instructions aloud.

Lesson 2 | Writing

Writing with Subject-Verb Agreement

Complete each sentence with the correct form of the subject or verb to maintain subject-verb agreement.

Examples:
Wang Lung __is__ thinking of his new life. (to be)
The farmer's __life__ is a difficult and challenging one. (life)

1. Wang Lung and his father __talk__ about his new wife. (talk)
2. Children's __beds__ line the halls in Wang Lung's dreams. (bed)
3. In town, a young slave girl __waits__ for Wang Lung. (wait)
4. The residents of the House of Hwang __have__ gifts for Wang Lung and his new wife. (have)
5. The wedding __guests__ are eager for the ceremony to begin. (guest)
6. The band __plays__ music as the couple enters. (play)
7. The family of the slave girl __hopes__ she will be better off with Wang Lung. (hope)
8. Wang Lung's bath __takes__ longer than usual. (take)
9. Wang Lung and his bride __begin__ a new life together. (begin)
10. The festivities __last__ for several hours. (last)

304 Unit 11

Model

Listen as I read the first example: *Wang Lung _____ thinking of his new life.* Wang Lung is thinking of his new life. Wang Lung are thinking of his new life. Wang Lung is one person, so the subject is singular. The missing verb is actually a helping verb that teams with *thinking.* I've written *is* as the singular verb.

Listen as I read the second example: *The farmer's _____ is a difficult and challenging one.* This sentence has a linking verb instead of an action verb. The first example helped me remember that I use *is* as a singular verb, so my subject needs to be singular. *The farmer's life is a difficult and challenging one.* I wrote *life* as the correct subject. A good strategy is to read the sentence twice, using each derivation. Then, think about if the missing word needs to be singular or plural.

Guided Practice

Listen as I read #1: *Wang Lung and his father ______ about his new wife.* I'll read the sentence twice using each form of *talk*: *Wang Lung and his father talks about his new wife. Wang Lung and his father talk about his new wife.* Is the subject singular or plural? (plural) What does *plural* mean? (more than one) To make the verb agree, do you need to add an -s? (no) I can check it by substituting the plural pronoun *they*. I wouldn't say *They talks*. I would say *They talk*. Write the correct word and reread the sentence silently to yourself. You have to train your ears to detect the correct response. Ideally, it should *sound* right or *sound* wrong.

Independent Practice

Have students complete the activity. Review the answers as a class.

Unit 11 Lesson 3

Lesson Opener

Before the lesson, choose one of the following activities to write on the board or post on the *LANGUAGE! Live* Class Wall online.

- *Write five sentences about Wang Lung's life using participial phrases.*
- *Write five sentences about your best friend using appositives.*
- *Write a paragraph describing Wang Lung's wedding day. Use the word* wedded *as a verb and a participle.*

Reading

Objectives

- Reread text for comprehension.
- Establish a purpose for reading text.
- Use critical thinking skills to write responses to prompts about text.
- Support written answers with evidence from text.
- Determine the meaning of proverbs and adages.
- Analyze the way the setting shapes characters.
- Determine character point of view.
- Connect personal experience to text.

Reading for a Purpose: Excerpt from *The Good Earth*

It is time to answer some specific questions about the text. Because critical understanding requires active participation, we are going to read the text again. We will be reading for a specific purpose, which will help us pay attention to details that we may have missed the first time around.

Let's read some questions about the text to provide a purpose for rereading.

Direct students to pages 305 and 306 in their Student Books. Have students read the prompts aloud with you.

1. Support Wang Lung's father's theory about pretty girls focusing more on clothes than work with a real-life example.
2. Develop an argument against the arranged marriage from the bride's point of view. Support your answer with text evidence.
3. Prove that though *The Good Earth* is written in third person, it is told from Wang Lung's point of view. Support your answer with text evidence.
4. Prove that the setting shaped the main character, Wang Lung.
5. Clarify how lines 250–280 fit into the overall plot.
6. Clarify the adage "You get what you pay for" as it relates to Wang Lung in *The Good Earth*.

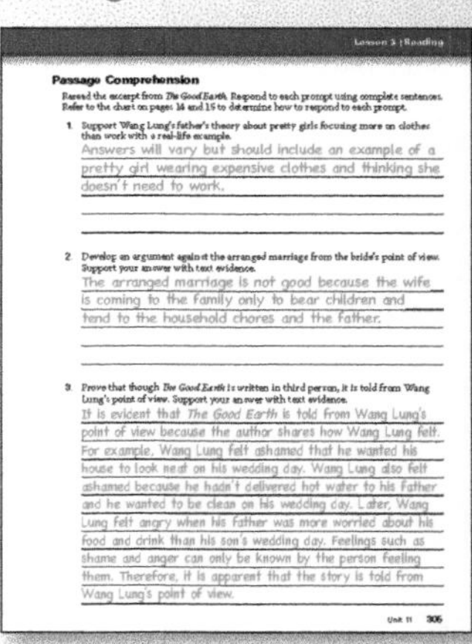

Lesson 3 | Reading

Passage Comprehension

Reread the excerpt from *The Good Earth*. Respond to each prompt using complete sentences. Refer to the chart on pages 14 and 15 to determine how to respond to each prompt.

1. Support Wang Lung's father's theory about pretty girls focusing more on clothes than work with a real-life example.
   Answers will vary but should include an example of a pretty girl wearing expensive clothes and thinking she doesn't need to work.
2. Develop an argument against the arranged marriage from the bride's point of view. Support your answer with text evidence.
   The arranged marriage is not good because the wife is coming to the family only to bear children and tend to the household chores and the father.
3. Prove that though *The Good Earth* is written in third person, it is told from Wang Lung's point of view. Support your answer with text evidence.
   It is evicent that *The Good Earth* is told from Wang Lung's point of view because the author shares how Wang Lung felt. For example, Wang Lung felt ashamed that he wanted his house to look neat on his wedding day. Wang Lung also felt ashamed because he hadn't delivered hot water to his father and he wanted to be clean on his wedding day. Later, Wang Lung felt angry when his father was more worried about his food and drink than his son's wedding day. Feelings such as shame and anger can only be known by the person feeling them. Therefore, it is apparent that the story is told from Wang Lung's point of view.

Unit 11 305

Direct students to pages 291–298 in their Student Books or have them tear out the extra copy of the excerpt from the back of their book.

> **Note:** To minimize flipping back and forth between the pages, a copy of each text has been included in the back of the Student Books. Encourage students to tear this out and use it when working on activities that require the use of the text.

Choose an option for reading text. Have students read the text according to the option that you chose.

Options for reading text:

- Teacher read-aloud
- Teacher-led or student-led choral read
- Paired read or independent read with bold vocabulary words read aloud

Passage Comprehension

Write the words *clarify, develop an argument, prove,* and *support* on the board. Have students read the words aloud with you.

It is critical to understand what the question is asking and how to answer it. Today, we will review four direction words used in prompts.

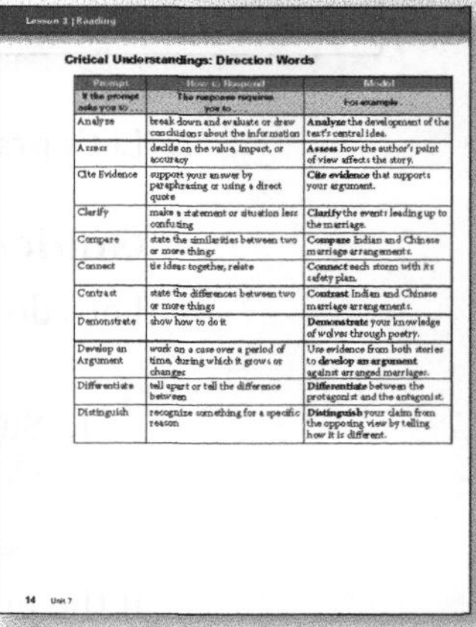

Have students review the words on the board in the chart on pages 14 and 15. Check for understanding by requesting an oral response to the following questions.

- If the prompt asks you to *clarify,* the response requires you to . . . (make a statement or situation less confusing).
- If the prompt asks you to *develop an argument,* the response requires you to . . . (work on a case over a period of time, during which it grows or changes).
- If the prompt asks you to *prove,* the response requires you to . . . (give evidence to show that it is true).
- If the prompt asks you to *support,* the response requires you to . . . (help it succeed).

Direct students to pages 305 and 306 in their Student Books.

Passage Comprehension

Reread the excerpt from *The Good Earth*. Respond to each prompt using complete sentences. Refer to the chart on pages 14 and 15 to determine how to respond to each prompt.

1. Support Wang Lung's father's theory about pretty girls focusing more on clothes than work with a real-life example.
Answers will vary but should include an example of a pretty girl wearing expensive clothes and thinking she doesn't need to work.

2. Develop an argument against the arranged marriage from the bride's point of view. Support your answer with text evidence.
The arranged marriage is not good because the wife is coming to the family only to bear children and tend to the household chores and the father.

3. Prove that though *The Good Earth* is written in third person, it is told from Wang Lung's point of view. Support your answer with text evidence.
It is evident that *The Good Earth* is told from Wang Lung's point of view because the author shares how Wang Lung felt. For example, Wang Lung felt ashamed that he wanted his house to look neat on his wedding day. Wang Lung also felt ashamed because he hadn't delivered hot water to his father and he wanted to be clean on his wedding day. Later, Wang Lung felt angry when his father was more worried about his food and drink than his son's wedding day. Feelings such as shame and anger can only be known by the person feeling them. Therefore, it is apparent that the story is told from Wang Lung's point of view.

Passage Comprehension (*cont.*)

4. Prove that the setting shaped the main character, Wang Lung.
The main character is Wang Lung, a Chinese farmer who lived with his father in the early 1900s. During that time period, farmers didn't have much—not even running water. Wang Lung didn't take anything for granted and wasted nothing. Wang Lung developed a caring nature from caring for his father and the land.

5. Clarify how lines 250–280 fit into the overall plot.
Lines 250–280 describe background information about the marriage arranged by Wang Lung's father. This information is a shift in time from the wedding day to a time before the wedding. This information helps the reader understand the plot because it provides information about Wang Lung's father's requirements versus Wang Lung's expectations of a wife.

6. Clarify the adage "You get what you pay for" as it relates to Wang Lung in *The Good Earth*.
"You get what you pay for" means that higher quality goods cost more for a reason. If you get something for a cheap price, it will not be of good quality. Wang Lung was poor and had very little money to offer a family for a bride. Therefore, Wang Lung was to wed a poor slave girl who was not pretty. She was also of a lower class than him.

Let's practice answering questions written as prompts that require critical thinking.

Guided Practice

Let's do the first two together.

1. Support Wang Lung's father's theory about pretty girls focusing more on clothes than work with a real-life example.

If the prompt asks you to *support*, what should you do? (help it succeed) Let's turn the prompt into a question to confirm our understanding. If we change the prompt into a question, what would it be? (What real-life example supports Wang Lung's father's theory about pretty girls?)

As students are thinking of an example, write the following sentence starters on the board.

Wang Lung's father believed that a pretty girl ________________.
________________ *is pretty and she* ________________
________________.

Have students answer the question.

2. Develop an argument against the arranged marriage from the bride's point of view. Support your answer with text evidence.

If the prompt asks you to *develop an argument,* what should you do? (Work on a case over time during which it grows or changes.) Let's turn the prompt into a question to confirm our understanding. If we change this to a question, what would it be? (Why might the bride be against an arranged marriage?)

As students refer to the text for evidence, write the following sentence starter on the board.

The arranged marriage is not good because ______________.

Your answers should relate information provided in the text. What kinds of information could be used to support your answer? **Discuss possible answers.**

- The bride may want to meet her husband first.
- The bride may not want to take care of Wang Lung's father.
- The bride may not want to go from a slave house to Wang Lung's house where she continues slave-like duties.
- The bride may prefer a wealthy husband.

Have partners answer the question.

Independent Practice

Have students respond to the remaining questions. For students who need more assistance, provide the following alternative questions.

Alternative questions:

3. What evidence proves that the excerpt is written from Wang Lung's point of view?
4. How did the time and place of the story influence Wang Lung's character?
5. How do lines 250–280 fit into the overall plot?
6. What does "You get what you pay for" mean in respect to Wang Lung?

Unit 11

Lesson 4

Lesson Opener

Before the lesson, choose one of the following activities to write on the board or post on the *LANGUAGE! Live* Class Wall online.

- *Dress your avatar as though you were getting married outside and didn't have much money. Explain your choices.*
- *Use present and past participles to explain why choosing your own mate is better than letting your parents choose your mate.*
- *Make a list of adjectives describing Wang Lung. Make another list of adjectives describing Wang Lung's father. Write two compound sentences using the adjectives.*

Reading

Objectives

- Read with purpose and understanding.
- Answer questions to demonstrate comprehension of text.
- Identify and explain explicit details from text.
- Monitor comprehension of text during reading.
- Identify flashbacks in literature.
- Analyze the contrasting points of view of characters within a story.
- Analyze the development of character traits over time.
- Track pronouns to their antecedents.
- Determine the meaning of figurative language in literature.
- Use synonyms and antonyms to deepen word knowledge.
- Determine the meaning of consecutive adjectives.
- Identify the conditional mood in literature.
- Determine the meaning of hyperboles.
- Determine the meaning of figurative language.
- Use noncount nouns correctly.
- Identify the past perfect tense and present perfect tense and understand the meanings.

Close Reading of the Excerpt from *The Good Earth*

Let's reread *The Good Earth*. I will provide specific instructions on how to mark the text that will help with comprehension.

Highlighters or colored pencils

Have students get out a highlighter or colored pencil.

Direct students to pages 307–314 in their Student Books.

Draw a rectangle around the title.

Now, let's read the vocabulary words aloud.

- What's the first bold vocabulary word? (fruition) *Fruition* means "completion; a good outcome." My plan for developing proficient readers will come to *fruition* if you work hard. Have partners use the word in a sentence.
- Next word? (fashioned) *Fashioned* means "made; shaped." My niece *fashioned* an entire outfit out of duct tape. Have partners use the word in a sentence.

- What's the next vocabulary word? (delicately) *Delicately* means "with a soft touch and great attention to detail." Be sure to handle the glasses *delicately*, or they will break. **Have partners use the word in a sentence.**
- Let's continue. (cease) *Cease* means "to stop; to come to an end." Without wind, windmills will *cease* their movement. **Have partners use the word in a sentence.**
- Next word? (precious) *Precious* means "very valuable; hard to get and not to be wasted." Water is *precious*, and it pains me to see people waste it. **Have partners use the word in a sentence.**
- Let's continue. (recklessly) *Recklessly* means "carelessly; without concern for the harm that might be done." If you behave *recklessly*, there are consequences. **Have partners use the word in a sentence.**
- Next word? (warped) *Warped* means "bent out of shape." Moisture caused the wood to become *warped*. **Have partners use the word in a sentence.**
- Let's continue. (diverted) *Diverted* means "caused someone or something to get off track or lose focus." The attention of the students was *diverted* by the flashing lights outside the window. **Have partners use the word in a sentence.**
- Next word? (mutinous) *Mutinous* means "strongly wanting to rebel, or disobey someone in authority." Many people become *mutinous* when rules seem to be strict and pointless. **Have partners use the word in a sentence.**
- Last word. (acknowledgment) *Acknowledgment* means "a sign or action that shows you know something is true." *Acknowledgment* for a job well done is motivational for many people. **Have partners use the word in a sentence.**

Talk with a partner about any vocabulary word that is still confusing for you to read consistently or understand its meaning.

You will reread the excerpt from *The Good Earth* one section at a time. After each section, you will monitor your understanding by circling the check mark if you understand the text or the question mark if you don't understand the text. I also want you to draw a question mark over any confusing words, phrases, or sentences.

Options for reading text:

- Teacher read-aloud
- Teacher-led or student-led choral read
- Paired read or independent read with bold vocabulary words read aloud

Choose an option for reading text. Have students read lines 1–22 according to the option that you chose.

When most of the students are finished, continue with the entire class. Let's see how well you understood what you read.

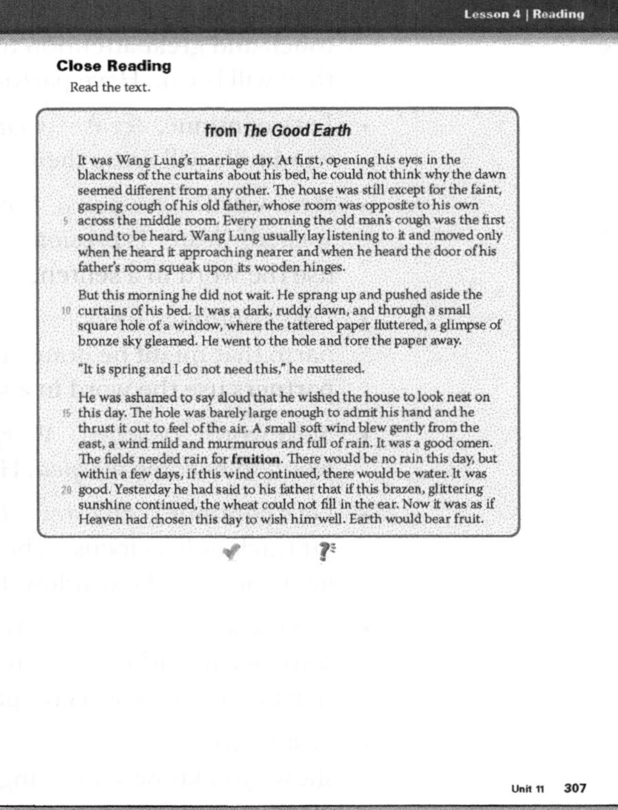

Lesson 4 | Reading

Close Reading

Read the text.

from *The Good Earth*

It was Wang Lung's marriage day. At first, opening his eyes in the blackness of the curtains about his bed, he could not think why the dawn seemed different from any other. The house was still except for the faint, gasping cough of his old father, whose room was opposite to his own across the middle room. Every morning the old man's cough was the first sound to be heard. Wang Lung usually lay listening to it and moved only when he heard it approaching nearer and when he heard the door of his father's room squeak upon its wooden hinges.

But this morning he did not wait. He sprang up and pushed aside the curtains of his bed. It was a dark, ruddy dawn, and through a small square hole of a window, where the tattered paper fluttered, a glimpse of bronze sky gleamed. He went to the hole and tore the paper away.

"It is spring and I do not need this," he muttered.

He was ashamed to say aloud that he wished the house to look neat on this day. The hole was barely large enough to admit his hand and he thrust it out to feel of the air. A small soft wind blew gently from the east, a wind mild and murmurous and full of rain. It was a good omen. The fields needed rain for **fruition**. There would be no rain this day, but within a few days, if this wind continued, there would be water. It was good. Yesterday he had said to his father that if this brazen, glittering sunshine continued, the wheat could not fill in the ear. Now it was as if Heaven had chosen this day to wish him well. Earth would bear fruit.

Unit 11 307

- Circle the check mark or the question mark for this section. Draw a question mark over any confusing words.
- Go to line 2. Mark the word that means "first light of day." (dawn) *Dawn* is an example of a noncount noun. With noncount nouns, we don't use a plural form of the word in common speech or writing.
- Go to line 3. Mark the synonym of *quiet.* (still)
- In the same sentence, mark the coordinate adjectives. (faint; gasping) Are the adjectives equal in weight or unequal? (equal) The comma indicates they are coordinate adjectives.
- Go to line 4. Mark the word *whose.* Draw an arrow to the noun the following words are clarifying. (father)
- Go to line 6. Circle the pronoun *it.* Draw an arrow to the noun that *it* refers to. (cough)
- Go to line 10. Mark the word that means "reddish color." (ruddy)
- Go to line 14. Underline the reason that Wang Lung was ashamed. (wished the house to look neat)
- Go to line 17. Mark the synonym of *whispering.* (murmurous)
- Go to line 20. Mark the word that means "extremely bold, extremely strong." (brazen)
- Reread the last paragraph. There are six noncount nouns. Circle them. (air, wind, rain, water, sunshine, wheat)

Have students read lines 23–51 according to the option that you chose.

When most of the students are finished, continue with the entire class. Let's see how well you understood what you read.

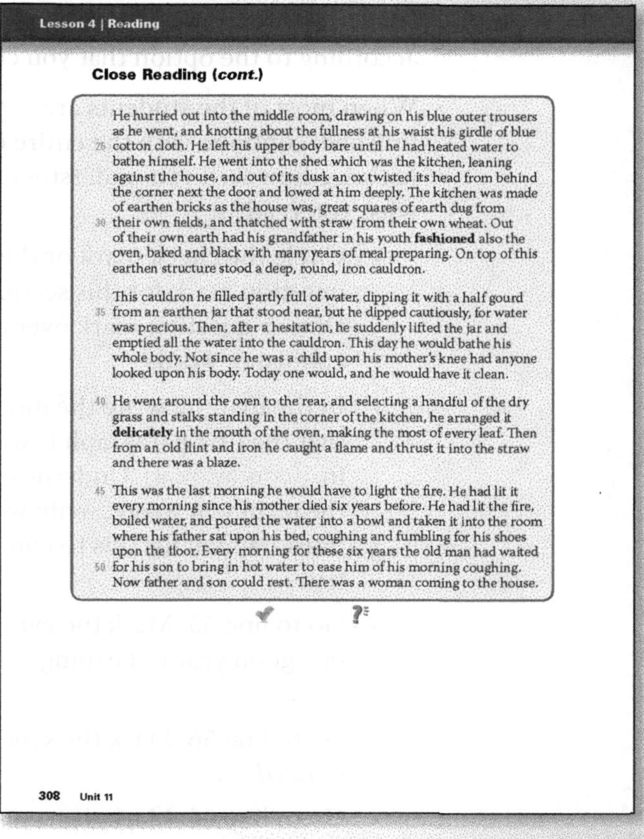

Lesson 4 | Reading

Close Reading (*cont.*)

He hurried out into the middle room, drawing on his blue outer trousers as he went, and knotting about the fullness at his waist his girdle of blue cotton cloth. He left his upper body bare until he had heated water to bathe himself. He went into the shed which was the kitchen, leaning against the house, and out of its dusk an ox twisted its head from behind the corner next the door and lowed at him deeply. The kitchen was made of earthen bricks as the house was, great squares of earth dug from their own fields, and thatched with straw from their own wheat. Out of their own earth had his grandfather in his youth **fashioned** also the oven, baked and black with many years of meal preparing. On top of this earthen structure stood a deep, round, iron cauldron.

This cauldron he filled partly full of water, dipping it with a half gourd from an earthen jar that stood near, but he dipped cautiously, for water was precious. Then, after a hesitation, he suddenly lifted the jar and emptied all the water into the cauldron. This day he would bathe his whole body. Not since he was a child upon his mother's knee had anyone looked upon his body. Today one would, and he would have it clean.

He went around the oven to the rear, and selecting a handful of the dry grass and stalks standing in the corner of the kitchen, he arranged it **delicately** in the mouth of the oven, making the most of every leaf. Then from an old flint and iron he caught a flame and thrust it into the straw and there was a blaze.

This was the last morning he would have to light the fire. He had lit it every morning since his mother died six years before. He had lit the fire, boiled water, and poured the water into a bowl and taken it into the room where his father sat upon his bed, coughing and fumbling for his shoes upon the floor. Every morning for these six years the old man had waited for his son to bring in hot water to ease him of his morning coughing. Now father and son could rest. There was a woman coming to the house.

308 Unit 11

- Circle the check mark or the question mark for this section. Draw a question mark over any confusing words.
- Go to line 23. Mark the synonym of *pants*. (trousers)
- Go to line 24. Mark the word that means "belt" or "band." (girdle)
- Go to line 26. Mark the location of the kitchen. (shed)
- Go to line 33. Mark the consecutive adjectives. (deep, round, iron) In the margin, write what kind of adjectives they are. (coordinate)
- In the same line, mark the word that means "large pot used over an open fire." (cauldron)
- Look at the first paragraph again. Circle the noncount nouns. (cloth, water, dusk, earth, straw, wheat)
- Go to line 35. Mark Wang Lung's limited resource. (water)
- Go to line 36. Mark the word that means "pause caused by uncertainty or doubt." (hesitation)
- Go to line 43. Mark the primitive tool for striking a fire. (flint)
- Go to line 46. Circle the amount of time that Wang Lung has been lighting the morning fire. (six years)
- Much of the last paragraph is written in the past perfect tense. This means that something occurred before another action. Mark the verb phrases in lines 45, 46, and 49 that are used in the past perfect tense. (had lit, had lit, had waited) Mark what was happening that changed the things that occurred in the past. (There was a woman coming to the house.)
- In the last paragraph, number the chores that Wang Lung would require of his new wife. (1. lit the fire; 2. boiled water; 3. poured the water into a bowl; 4. taken it into the room where his father sat upon his bed)

Have students read lines 52–78 according to the option that you chose.

When most of the students are finished, continue with the entire class. Let's see how well you understood what you read.

- Circle the check mark or the question mark for this section. Draw a question mark over any confusing words.
- In the margin, write the mood that the first paragraph is written in. (conditional) Underneath the term you wrote, write what must happen for this to come true. (marriage)
- Go to line 55. Mark the evidence of a good year of farming. (tea leaves in the water)
- Go to line 56. Mark the synonym of *tired*. (wearied)
- Go to line 66. Mark the synonym of *clothes*. (garments)
- Go to line 68. Mark the reason that Wang Lung was ashamed. (not water yet to heat my lungs)
- In this paragraph, we have been introduced to a second character in the story. Reread the first words that he spoke. Are he and Wang Lung approaching the day with the same attitude? (no) In the margin, contrast their attitudes. (Wang Lung: happy, excited; Father: ornery; confrontational)
- Go to line 72. Mark the synonym of *persistently*. (perseveringly)
- Go to line 77. Mark the verb specifically chosen by the author as a way to explain a character trait of the old man. (complain)
- Go to line 78. Mark the simile that indicates they are poor. (Tea is like eating silver.) Circle the two noncount nouns in the simile. (Tea; silver)

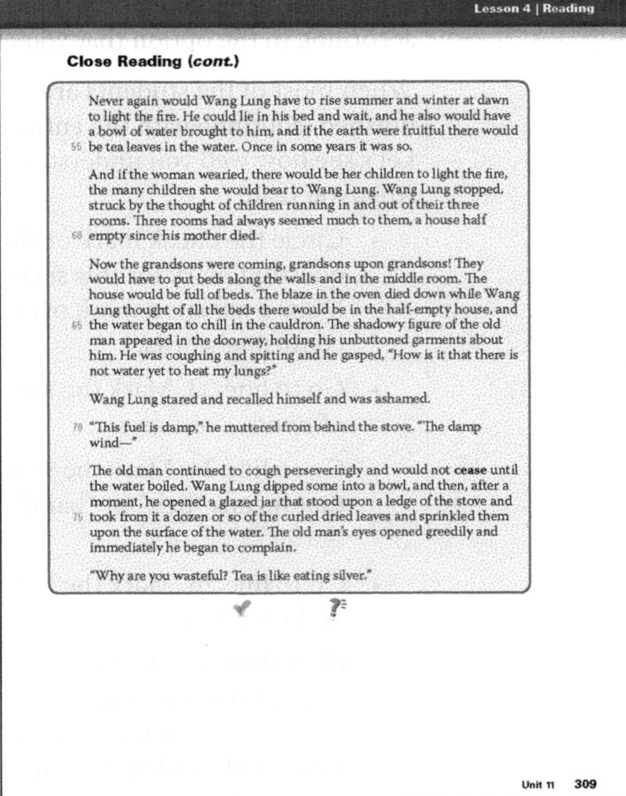

Lesson 4 | Reading

Close Reading (*cont.*)

Never again would Wang Lung have to rise summer and winter at dawn to light the fire. He could lie in his bed and wait, and he also would have a bowl of water brought to him, and if the earth were fruitful there would be tea leaves in the water. Once in some years it was so.

And if the woman wearied, there would be her children to light the fire, the many children she would bear to Wang Lung. Wang Lung stopped, struck by the thought of children running in and out of their three rooms. Three rooms had always seemed much to them, a house half empty since his mother died.

Now the grandsons were coming, grandsons upon grandsons! They would have to put beds along the walls and in the middle room. The house would be full of beds. The blaze in the oven died down while Wang Lung thought of all the beds there would be in the half-empty house, and the water began to chill in the cauldron. The shadowy figure of the old man appeared in the doorway, holding his unbuttoned garments about him. He was coughing and spitting and he gasped, "How is it that there is not water yet to heat my lungs?"

Wang Lung stared and recalled himself and was ashamed.

"This fuel is damp," he muttered from behind the stove. "The damp wind—"

The old man continued to cough perseveringly and would not **cease** until the water boiled. Wang Lung dipped some into a bowl, and then, after a moment, he opened a glazed jar that stood upon a ledge of the stove and took from it a dozen or so of the curled dried leaves and sprinkled them upon the surface of the water. The old man's eyes opened greedily and immediately he began to complain.

"Why are you wasteful? Tea is like eating silver."

Unit 11 309

Have students read lines 79–103 according to the option that you chose.

When most of the students are finished, continue with the entire class. Let's see how well you understood what you read.

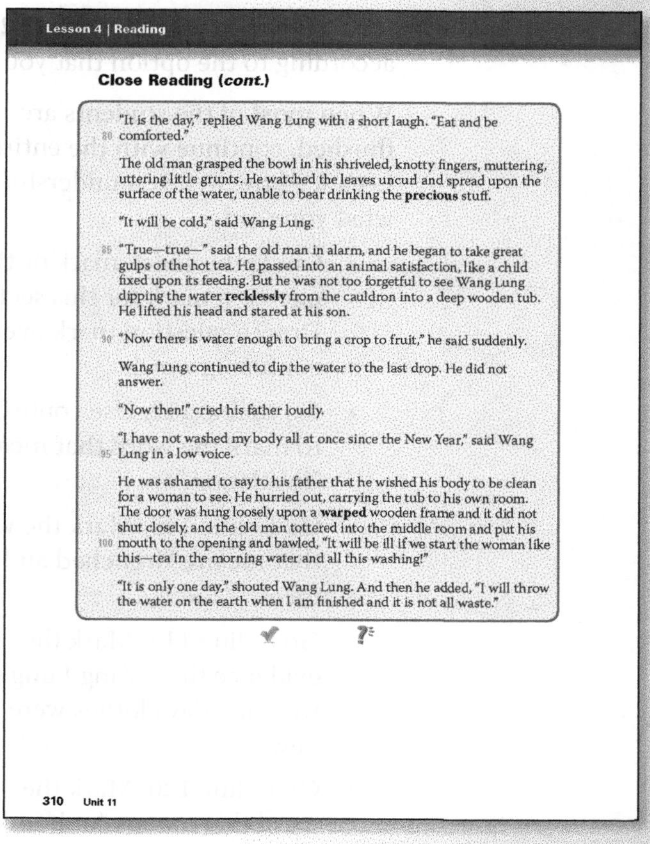

Lesson 4 | Reading

Close Reading (*cont.*)

"It is the day," replied Wang Lung with a short laugh. "Eat and be comforted."

The old man grasped the bowl in his shriveled, knotty fingers, muttering, uttering little grunts. He watched the leaves uncurl and spread upon the surface of the water, unable to bear drinking the **precious** stuff.

"It will be cold," said Wang Lung.

"True—true—" said the old man in alarm, and he began to take great gulps of the hot tea. He passed into an animal satisfaction, like a child fixed upon its feeding. But he was not too forgetful to see Wang Lung dipping the water **recklessly** from the cauldron into a deep wooden tub. He lifted his head and stared at his son.

"Now there is water enough to bring a crop to fruit," he said suddenly.

Wang Lung continued to dip the water to the last drop. He did not answer.

"Now then!" cried his father loudly.

"I have not washed my body all at once since the New Year," said Wang Lung in a low voice.

He was ashamed to say to his father that he wished his body to be clean for a woman to see. He hurried out, carrying the tub to his own room. The door was hung loosely upon a **warped** wooden frame and it did not shut closely, and the old man tottered into the middle room and put his mouth to the opening and bawled, "It will be ill if we start the woman like this—tea in the morning water and all this washing!"

"It is only one day," shouted Wang Lung. And then he added, "I will throw the water on the earth when I am finished and it is not all waste."

310 Unit 11

- Circle the check mark or the question mark for this section. Draw a question mark over any confusing words.
- Go to line 83. Mark the synonym of *accept* or *handle*. (bear)
- On the same line, mark the word that refers to *tea*. (stuff) What kind of noun is *stuff*? (noncount)
- Go to line 84. Mark what prompted Wang Lung's father to take great gulps of tea. (It will be cold.)
- Go to lines 86 and 87. Mark the simile used to describe the intense focus of the father's eating. (like a child fixed upon its feeding)
- Go to the middle of the page. Mark the hyperbole, or gross exaggeration, that is proof that Wang Lung's father thinks he is using too much water. (Now there is water enough to bring a crop to fruit.)
- Go to line 93. Mark the words that show that Father is upset about the water usage. (Now then!)
- Mark Wang Lung's rebuttal to his father. (I have not washed my body all at once since the New Year.) The verb phrase used in this sentence indicates an action happened at an unspecified time before now. The exact time is not important. This verb tense is called the present perfect tense. Circle the verb phrase. (have not washed)
- Go to line 96. Mark the descriptive word that has been purposefully used before by the author to explain a character trait of Wang Lung. (ashamed)
- Go to lines 96 and 97. Mark the reason that Wang Lung was ashamed. (that he wished his body to be clean for a woman to see)
- Go to line 100. Use context to mark the word that means "a bad habit." (ill)

Have students read lines 104–127 according to the option that you chose.

When most of the students are finished, continue with the entire class. Let's see how well you understood what you read.

- Circle the check mark or the question mark for this section. Draw a question mark over any confusing words.
- Go to line 112. Use context to mark the word that means "insulation." (wadding)
- Go to line 115. Mark the word that means "drenched and a mess." (sodden)
- Go to line 119. Mark the evidence that Wang Lung's wedding day clothes were not new. (ten days or so in the year)
- Go to line 120. Mark the word that means "unbraided." (unplaited)
- Go to line 123. Mark the words that mean "came closer." (drew near)
- Go to line 124. Mark the quote that means "I'm hungry." ("Am I to have nothing to eat this day?") Mark the verb used again by the author to explain a character trait of the father. (complained)
- Go to line 125. Mark the metaphor. (the bones are water) Circle the two things being compared. (bones; water)

Close Reading (*cont.*)

The old man was silent at this, and Wang Lung unfastened his girdle and stepped out of his clothing. In the light that streamed in a square block from the hole he wrung a small towel from the steaming water and he scrubbed his dark slender body vigorously. Warm though he had thought the air, when his flesh was wet he was cold, and he moved quickly, passing the towel in and out of the water until from his whole body there went up a delicate cloud of steam. Then he went to a box that had been his mother's and drew from it a fresh suit of blue cotton cloth. He might be a little cold this day without the wadding of the winter garments, but he suddenly could not bear to put them on against his clean flesh. The covering of them was torn and filthy and the wadding stuck out of the holes, grey and sodden. He did not want this woman to see him for the first time with the wadding sticking out of his clothes. Later she would have to wash and mend, but not the first day. He drew over the blue cotton coat and trousers a long robe made of the same material—his one long robe, which he wore on feast days only, ten days or so in the year, all told. Then with swift fingers he unplaited the long braid of hair that hung down his back, and taking a wooden comb from the drawer of the small, unsteady table, he began to comb out his hair.

His father drew near again and put his mouth to the crack of the door.

"Am I to have nothing to eat this day?" he complained. "At my age the bones are water in the morning until food is given them."

"I am coming," said Wang Lung, braiding his hair quickly and smoothly and weaving into the strands a tasseled black silk cord.

Have students read lines 128–147 according to the option that you chose.

When most of the students are finished, continue with the entire class. Let's see how well you understood what you read.

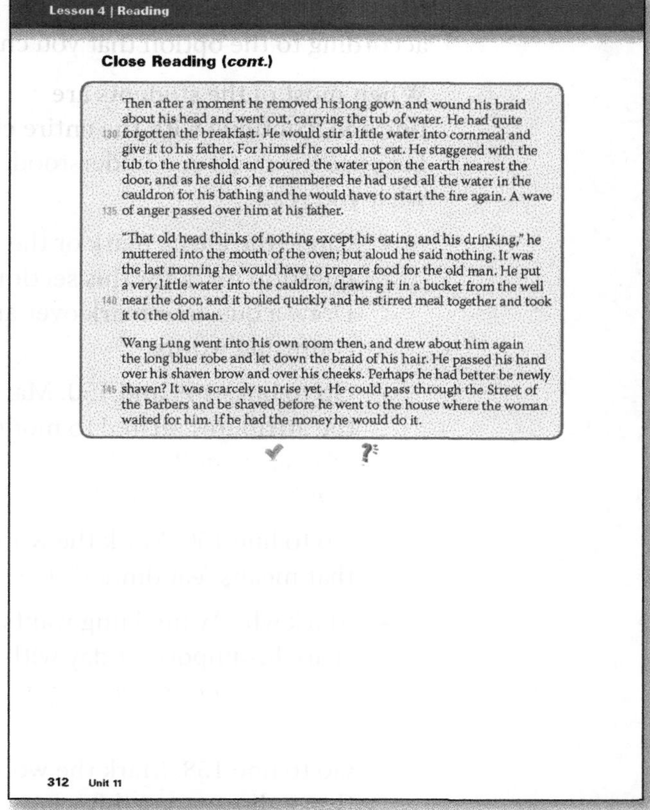

Lesson 4 | Reading

Close Reading (*cont.*)

Then after a moment he removed his long gown and wound his braid about his head and went out, carrying the tub of water. He had quite forgotten the breakfast. He would stir a little water into cornmeal and give it to his father. For himself he could not eat. He staggered with the tub to the threshold and poured the water upon the earth nearest the door, and as he did so he remembered he had used all the water in the cauldron for his bathing and he would have to start the fire again. A wave of anger passed over him at his father.

"That old head thinks of nothing except his eating and his drinking," he muttered into the mouth of the oven; but aloud he said nothing. It was the last morning he would have to prepare food for the old man. He put a very little water into the cauldron, drawing it in a bucket from the well near the door, and it boiled quickly and he stirred meal together and took it to the old man.

Wang Lung went into his own room then, and drew about him again the long blue robe and let down the braid of his hair. He passed his hand over his shaven brow and over his cheeks. Perhaps he had better be newly shaven? It was scarcely sunrise yet. He could pass through the Street of the Barbers and be shaved before he went to the house where the woman waited for him. If he had the money he would do it.

✓ ?

312 Unit 11

- Circle the check mark or the question mark for this section. Draw a question mark over any confusing words.
- Go to line 130. Mark the ritual that Wang Lung forgot on his wedding day. (breakfast)
- Go to line 133. Mark the reason that Wang Lung had to start another fire. (he had used all the water)
- In the second paragraph, mark the sentence that is used to show that Wang Lung was becoming frustrated with his father's attitude. (That old head thinks of nothing except his eating and his drinking.)
- Go to line 139. Mark the synonym of *retrieving.* (drawing)
- In the second paragraph, circle the two references to Wang Lung's father. (that old head; the old man)
- Go to line 145. Mark the synonym of *barely.* (scarcely)
- Go to line 147. Mark the noncount noun that affects whether Wang Lung will be cleanly shaven on his wedding day. (money)

Have students read lines 148–180 according to the option that you chose.

When most of the students are finished, continue with the entire class. Let's see how well you understood what you read.

- Circle the check mark or the question mark for this section. Draw a question mark over any confusing words.
- Go to lines 149 and 150. Mark the attributes related to money. (six, silver, dollars, double handful, copper, coins)
- Go to line 150. Mark the word that means "eat dinner." (sup)
- Mark who Wang Lung wants to share his important day with. (cousin, uncle, three neighboring farmers)
- Go to line 158. Mark the word that indicates one thing is conditional on another thing. (If)
- Go to line 159. Mark evidence that Wang Lung splurged on his wedding day. (he would shave his head, he decided suddenly)
- Go to line 160. Mark the phrase that means "quietly." (without speech)
- Go to line 164. Mark the words that mean "new crop." (budding heads)
- Go to lines 166 and 167. Mark the references to a tradition based on belief. (incense, little temple to the Earth God)
- Go to line 172. Mark the words that describe Wang Lung's future wife. (slave girl since her childhood)
- On the same line, mark the name of the wealthy slave house. (House of Hwang)
- Underline the text that is a flashback—events that happened prior to the wedding day. (from "There were those . . ." to ". . . he had said.")

Lesson 4 | Reading

Close Reading (*cont.*)

He took from his girdle a small greasy pouch of grey cloth and counted the money in it. There were six silver dollars and a double handful of copper coins. He had not yet told his father he had asked friends to sup that night. He had asked his male cousin, the young son of his uncle, and his uncle for his father's sake, and three neighboring farmers who lived in the village with him. He had planned to bring back from the town that morning pork, a small pond fish, and a handful of chestnuts. He might even buy a few of the bamboo sprouts from the south and a little beef to stew with the cabbage he had raised in his own garden. But this only if there were any money left after the bean oil and the soybean sauce had been bought. If he shaved his head he could not, perhaps, buy the beef. Well, he would shave his head, he decided suddenly.

He left the old man without speech and went out into the early morning. In spite of the dark red dawn the sun was mounting the horizon clouds and sparkled upon the dew on the rising wheat and barley. The farmer in Wang Lung was **diverted** for an instant and he stooped to examine the budding heads. They were empty as yet and waiting for the rain. He smelled the air and looked anxiously at the sky. Rain was there, dark in the clouds, heavy upon the wind. He would buy a stick of incense and place it in the little temple to the Earth God. On a day like this he would do it.

He wound his way in among the fields upon the narrow path. In the near distance the grey city wall arose. Within that gate in the wall through which he would pass stood the great house where the woman had been a slave girl since her childhood, the House of Hwang. There were those who said, "It is better to live alone than to marry a woman who has been slave in a great house." But when he had said to his father, "Am I never to have a woman?" his father replied, "With weddings costing as they do in these evil days and every woman wanting gold rings and silk clothes before she will take a man, there remain only slaves to be had for the poor."

His father had stirred himself, then, and gone to the House of Hwang and asked if there were a slave to spare.

"Not a slave too young, and above all, not a pretty one," he had said.

Unit 11 313

Have students read from line 181 to the end according to the option that you chose.

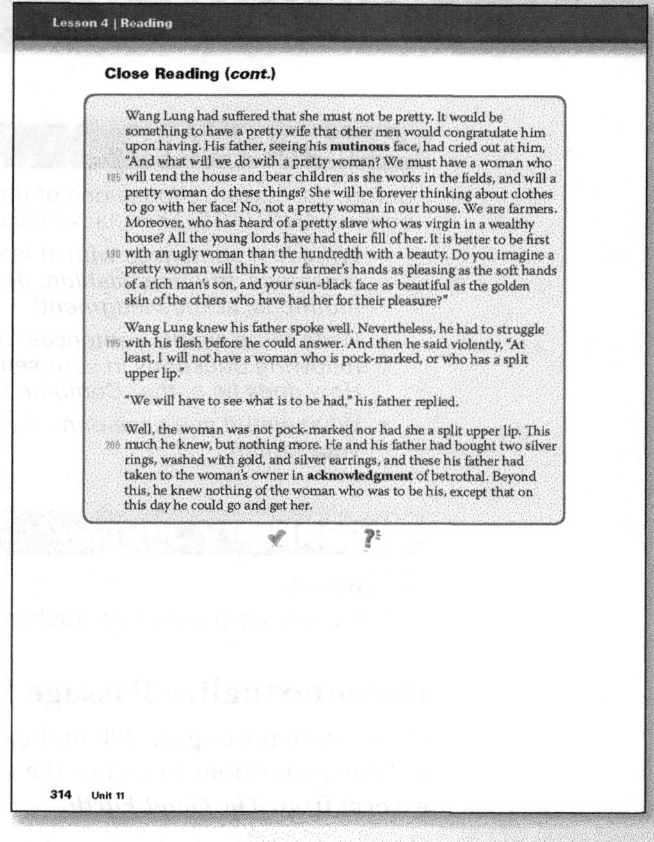

Lesson 4 | Reading

Close Reading (*cont.*)

Wang Lung had suffered that she must not be pretty. It would be something to have a pretty wife that other men would congratulate him upon having. His father, seeing his **mutinous** face, had cried out at him, "And what will we do with a pretty woman? We must have a woman who will tend the house and bear children as she works in the fields, and will a pretty woman do these things? She will be forever thinking about clothes to go with her face! No, not a pretty woman in our house. We are farmers. Moreover, who has heard of a pretty slave who was virgin in a wealthy house? All the young lords have had their fill of her. It is better to be first with an ugly woman than the hundredth with a beauty. Do you imagine a pretty woman will think your farmer's hands as pleasing as the soft hands of a rich man's son, and your sun-black face as beautiful as the golden skin of the others who have had her for their pleasure?"

Wang Lung knew his father spoke well. Nevertheless, he had to struggle with his flesh before he could answer. And then he said violently, "At least, I will not have a woman who is pock-marked, or who has a split upper lip."

"We will have to see what is to be had," his father replied.

Well, the woman was not pock-marked nor had she a split upper lip. This much he knew, but nothing more. He and his father had bought two silver rings, washed with gold, and silver earrings, and these his father had taken to the woman's owner in **acknowledgment** of betrothal. Beyond this, he knew nothing of the woman who was to be his, except that on this day he could go and get her.

✔ ?

314 Unit 11

When most of the students are finished, continue with the entire class. Let's see how well you understood what you read.

- Circle the check mark or the question mark for this section. Draw a question mark over any confusing words.
- In the first three lines, mark the evidence that Wang Lung accepted what his father said, but he disagreed with his father. (suffered that she must not be pretty, his mutinous face)
- At the end of the first paragraph, mark the attributes of a rich man's son. (soft hands, golden skin)
- Go to line 194. Mark the evidence that Wang Lung thought his father was correct. (knew his father spoke well)
- Go to line 195. Mark the evidence that Wang Lung was angry. (said violently)
- Go to lines 196 and 197. Mark Wang Lung's criteria for his wife. (I will not have a woman who is pock-marked, or who has a split upper lip.)
- Go to line 202. Mark the word that means "engagement or promise." (betrothal)
- Star the paragraph that is a return to the present time, i.e., the flashback is over. (Well, the woman . . .)
- The author has made it clear that the father's point of view regarding marriage and Wang Lung's point of view are different. Use the text on this page to write the differences at the bottom of the page. (father: wife should not be pretty, but a useful virgin; Wang Lung: wife should be pretty and something to be envied)

Have partners compare text markings and correct any errors.

Unit 11

Lesson 5

Lesson Opener

Before the lesson, choose one of the following activities to write on the board or post on the *LANGUAGE! Live* Class Wall online.

- *Write four sentences with at least two vocabulary words in each. Show you know the meanings. (fruition, fashion, delicately, cease, precious, recklessly, warped, divert, mutinous, acknowledgment)*
- *Write three simple sentences that describe Wang Lung's hygiene habits. Answer the following questions in your sentences: When does he bathe? Where does he bathe? How does he bathe? Combine the three sentences into one Masterpiece Sentence.*
- *What would you have done if you were Wang Lung and were tired of taking care of your father?*

Vocabulary

Objective

- Review key passage vocabulary.

Recontextualize Passage Vocabulary

Direct students to page 290 in their Student Books. Use the following questions to review the vocabulary words in the excerpt from *The Good Earth*.

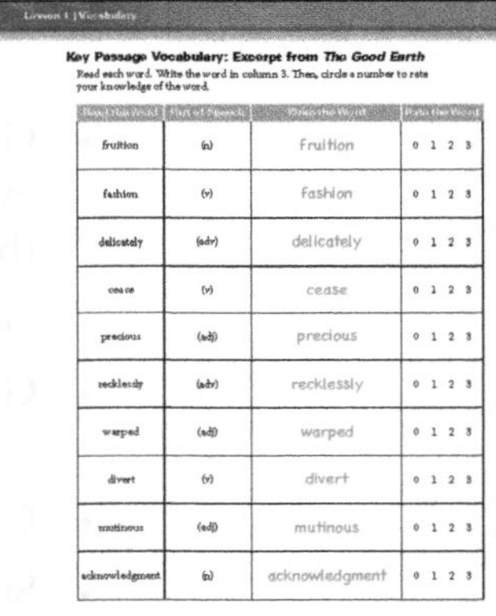

- You release the lever too late and the pinball drops into the hole. Did you *divert* the pinball? (no) Your friend sits way across the classroom. He's concentrating on an assignment. You signal to him but can't get his attention. Did you *divert* his attention? (no) Your family has the TV turned up. You need to study. You stuff cotton balls in your ears so your concentration won't be what? (diverted)
- If the wind picks up speed, will the tree branches *cease* waving? (no) The alarm goes off, and you push snooze. Does the buzzing *cease*? (yes) The people behind you in the movie are laughing and carrying on. You wish they would what? (cease)
- You pin tiny flowers carefully into your friend's hair for prom. Are you pinning them *delicately*? (yes) You toss a stack of old magazines into the recycling bin. Have you put them in the bin *delicately*? (no) You can't just shove the end of a thread through the eye of a needle. You have to do it how? (delicately)
- You plan a cookout in the park for your dad's birthday. It rains. Do your plans come to *fruition*? (no) You buy one of those clay "pets" whose "fur coat" grows from seeds inside the body. You water your "pet," and within days, it has a nice green covering. Did your pet's fur come to *fruition*? (yes) You've been e-mailing your favorite celebrity for three years, and he finally responded. Your efforts have come to what? (fruition)

- Your family has a grainy old video of your mother as a little girl. It's on tape and hasn't been digitized. Is the video *precious*? (yes) Your favorite flavor of chewing gum has been discontinued. You have one pack of it left. Is this pack of gum *precious* to you? (yes) It's a thousand years in the future. You own the last book known to humankind. What is the book? (precious)
- Your twin cousins are hard to control. They chase each other around the house, hurdling over your aunt's glass coffee tables at high speed. Do they behave *recklessly*? (yes) It takes your sister forever to get anywhere on a bike. She rides slowly and cautiously and stops for a full minute at every stop sign just to make sure there aren't any oncoming cars. Does she ride her bike *recklessly*? (no) You are so happy to be done with an assignment that you shut the file without saving it first. You have shut the file how? (recklessly)
- You can't get the CD to go into the player because you left it in the hot sun and it isn't flat anymore. Is it *warped*? (yes) The local dive restaurant is proud of its décor. The carpet is stained, the photos on the wall are crooked, and the tabletops are bumpy. Are the tabletops *warped*? (yes) The roof of the new museum is wavy. It's supposed to resemble water, but to you it just looks what? (warped)
- You write your state senator a letter expressing an opinion, and her office writes you back, thanking you for your input. Have you received *acknowledgment*? (yes) Your aunt is pouting because she didn't receive a thank-you note for the birthday gift she gave you. Does she want *acknowledgment*? (yes) Before rehearsal begins, the band director singles you out and praises your performance in a recent competition. What have you received? (acknowledgment)
- Your mom wakes you up at 4:00 a.m. and says she needs your help with the dog, who's sick and vomiting. Do you feel *mutinous*? (yes) The coach gives the team a break and cancels a grueling weight-training session. Do you feel *mutinous*? (no) A new law is passed that requires eight years of high school. How do you feel? (mutinous)
- You make a papier-mâché model of your best friend's head. Have you *fashioned* a model of your friend? (yes) You purchase a premade costume online. Have you *fashioned* your own costume? (no) You need a bench for a prop in the school play. You set a wooden plank across two cinder blocks. What have you done? (fashioned a bench)

Writing

Objectives

- Use text to write coherent paragraphs in response to reading.
- Write a persuasive essay.

Quick Write in Response to Reading

Direct students to pages 315 and 316 in their Student Books.

Lesson 5 | Writing

Quick Write in Response to Reading Answers will vary.

Is an arranged marriage a good thing or a bad thing? Write an essay in which you attempt to persuade the reader to accept your position. Your opening paragraph should state your position, and you should elaborate each claim in a body paragraph. Remember, each body paragraph needs a topic sentence. Use the concluding paragraph to restate your position without sounding repetitive.

In a culture that prides itself on individual rights and freedoms, arranged marriages strike a sour note. When considering the number of marriages that end in divorce, however, freedom of choice does not seem to be working very well. Love tends to ignore issues like family compatibility, religion, and upbringing. Placing the responsibility of "matchmaking" on someone else offers some unique benefits.

First, the process of arranging a marriage begins with an objective evaluation of personal strengths and weaknesses. Decisions that are meant to last a lifetime should be made rationally as opposed to emotionally. Romantic desires are fleeting and often create relationships that are more destructive than productive.

In marriages based on love, family incompatibility is rarely considered. However, when parents of both parties are involved in the marriage process, this is not an issue. They will advocate for relationships between families that have similar values and beliefs. As much as couples want to deny it, conflicts with in-laws can eventually destroy the relationship between husband and wife.

Finally, arranged marriages convey a deeper sense of obligation. Multiple people are involved in the final decision and consequently have a stake in the marriage's longevity. From its outset, newlyweds work more diligently

Unit 11 315

Lesson 5 | Writing

Quick Write in Response to Reading (*cont.*)

to establish a lasting and fulfilling relationship.

While it does not sound very romantic, a return to arranged marriages may be the best antidote to rising divorce rates. What we think we want is not always what we need, and allowing others to be involved in the decision-making process helps us avoid rash choices. Our current model seems to be broken and desperately in need of repair. Perhaps this is just the repair it needs.

316 Unit 11

Read the prompt and clarify instructions, spending a few minutes discussing the idea of arranged marriages. Challenge students to genuinely consider the pros as well as the cons of arranged marriages. Encourage students to use previously learned strategies from Unit 6 in their efforts to persuade.

Reading

Objectives

- Self-correct as comprehension of text deepens.
- Answer questions to demonstrate comprehension of text.
- Engage in class discussion.
- Identify the enduring understandings from a piece of text.

Revisit Passage Comprehension

Direct students back to pages 305 and 306 in their Student Books. Have students review their answers and make any necessary changes. Then, have partners share their answers and collaborate to perfect them.

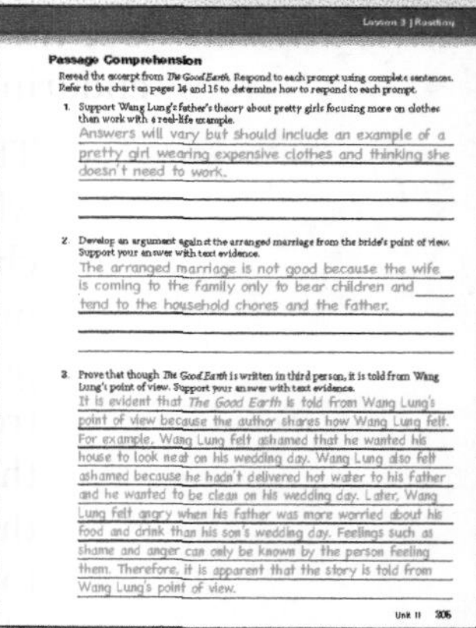

Passage Comprehension

Reread the excerpt from *The Good Earth*. Respond to each prompt using complete sentences. Refer to the chart on pages 14 and 15 to determine how to respond to each prompt.

1. Support Wang Lung's father's theory about pretty girls focusing more on clothes than work with a real-life example.
   Answers will vary but should include an example of a pretty girl wearing expensive clothes and thinking she doesn't need to work.

2. Develop an argument against the arranged marriage from the bride's point of view. Support your answer with text evidence.
   The arranged marriage is not good because the wife is coming to the family only to bear children and tend to the household chores and the father.

3. Prove that though *The Good Earth* is written in third person, it is told from Wang Lung's point of view. Support your answer with text evidence.
   It is evident that *The Good Earth* is told from Wang Lung's point of view because the author shares how Wang Lung felt. For example, Wang Lung felt ashamed that he wanted his house to look neat on his wedding day. Wang Lung also felt ashamed because he hadn't delivered hot water to his father and he wanted to be clean on his wedding day. Later, Wang Lung felt angry when his father was more worried about his food and drink than his son's wedding day. Feelings such as shame and anger can only be known by the person feeling them. Therefore, it is apparent that the story is told from Wang Lung's point of view.

Unit 11 306

Author's Purpose

Direct students back to page 289 in their Student Books. We just finished studying a fiction selection about an arranged marriage. Before discussing our enduring understandings, let's talk about the author's purpose. Why did this author write the text? **Provide sharing time. If necessary, elaborate or clarify their responses.** (The author's purpose is the reason that he or she wrote the text. Authors write for different purposes. They write to entertain, to persuade, or to inform or to teach. Knowing an author's purpose can help a reader understand a text better. This novel was written to entertain and to increase awareness about women's roles in Chinese culture.) **Have students correct their answer on their page as necessary.**

Unit 11

Lesson 1 | Reading

Let's Focus: Excerpt from *The Good Earth*

Content Focus
arranged marriage
Chinese culture

Type of Text
fiction—literature

Author's Name Pearl S. Buck

Author's Purpose to entertain; to increase awareness of women's roles in traditional Chinese culture

Big Ideas
Consider the following Big Idea questions. Write your answer for each question.

What factors are involved when choosing a lifelong mate?

What is the purpose of marriage?

Narrative Preview Checklist: the excerpt from *The Good Earth* on pages 291–298.

- ☐ Title: What clue does it provide about the passage?
- ☐ Pictures: What additional information is added here?
- ☐ Margin Information: What vocabulary is important to understand this story?

Enduring Understandings
After reading the text . . .

Unit 11 289

Enduring Understandings

Reread the Big Idea questions.

What factors are involved when choosing a lifelong mate?

What is the purpose of marriage?

Generate a class discussion about the questions and the answers students came up with in Lesson 1. Have them consider whether their answers have changed any after reading the text.

Use the following talking points to foster conversation. Then, have students write their enduring understandings from the unit.

- The tone of *The Good Earth* is opposite from the tone of "Say Yes to Free Dress!" where the author suggests that people stand up for their rights and freedom of choice. Through the story, we learned how marriages were arranged in China in the early 1900s. We also learned how economic standings determined who people could be paired with. Finally, we learned how women were viewed and treated based on their economic standing and physical appearance. How is the society we live in different from the society in *The Good Earth*? How is it the same? Do you think social class dictates future relationships in our society today? Are women still treated differently based on their social class and physical appearance?

What we read should make us think. Use our discussion and your thoughts about the text to determine what you will "walk away with." Has it made you think about a personal experience or someone you know? Has your perspective or opinion on a specific topic changed? Do you have any lingering thoughts or questions? Write these ideas as your enduring understandings. What will you take with you from this text?

Discuss the enduring understandings with the class. If time permits, have students post a personal response about their enduring understandings to the online class wall.

Lesson 6

Lesson Opener

Before the lesson, choose one of the following activities to write on the board or post on the *LANGUAGE! Live* Class Wall online.

- *Use the word* loving *in three sentences. Use it as a verb in one sentence, a noun in one sentence, and an adjective in another sentence.*
- *Use intransitive verbs to write five sentences about why arranged marriages are beneficial.*
- *Write one sentence about marrying for love. Write one sentence about marrying for money. Combine the sentences using a conjunction to create a compound sentence.*

Reading

Objectives

- Determine and discuss the topic of a text.
- Determine and discuss the author's purpose.
- Use text features to preview text.

Passage Introduction

Direct students to page 317 in their Student Books. Discuss the content focus.

Content Focus
arranged marriage
Indian culture

We just read a literary text about a particular topic in Chinese culture. Now, we will read a literary text about a similar topic in Indian culture.

Type of Text

Text can be divided into two categories: informational and literature. **Discuss the differences.**

Look at the first page of the text and determine what type of text it is. Write your answer on the page.

Lesson 6 | Reading

Let's Focus: Excerpt from *Nectar in a Sieve*

Content Focus
arranged marriage
Indian culture

Type of Text
fiction ~~literature~~

Author's Name Kamala Markandaya

Author's Purpose to entertain; to increase awareness of the traditional Indian culture

Big Ideas
Consider the following Big Idea questions. Write your answer for each question.

What role does economic status play in marriages today?

How have women's roles changed over time? Have those changes impacted men's roles in family and society?

Literary Preview Checklist: the excerpt from *Nectar in a Sieve* on pages 319–323.

- ☐ Title: What clue does it provide?
- ☐ Pictures: What additional information is added here?
- ☐ Margin Information: What vocabulary is important to understand this story?

Enduring Understandings
After reading the text . . .

Unit 11 317

Author's Purpose

Have students glance at the text. Who is the author of the text? (Kamala Markandaya) Prior to reading, make an educated guess as to what the author's purpose for writing is. After we finish, you will return to this section and revise your answers if you need to. **Have students write their responses on the page.**

Note: Determine if students need Background Information pertaining to life in India in the mid- to late 1900s. This can be found in the Teacher Resources online.

Big Ideas

Read the Big Idea questions aloud.

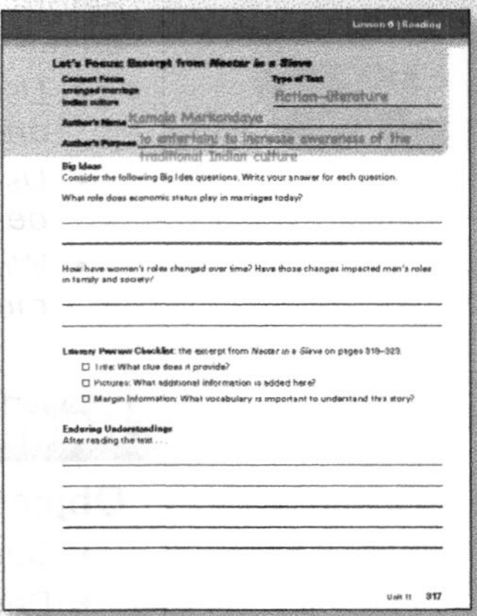
Lesson 6 | Reading

Let's Focus: Excerpt from *Nectar in a Sieve*

Content Focus
arranged marriage
Indian culture

Type of Text
fiction—literature

Author's Name Kamala Markandaya

Author's Purpose to entertain; to increase awareness of the traditional Indian culture

Big Ideas
Consider the following Big Idea questions. Write your answer for each question.

What role does economic status play in marriages today?

How have women's roles changed over time? Have those changes impacted men's roles in family and society?

Literary Preview Checklist: the excerpt from *Nectar in a Sieve* on pages 319–323.

- ☐ Title: What clue does it provide?
- ☐ Pictures: What additional information is added here?
- ☐ Margin Information: What vocabulary is important to understand this story?

Enduring Understandings
After reading the text . . .

Unit 11 317

Big Ideas

What role does economic status play in marriages today?

How have women's roles changed over time? Have those changes impacted men's roles in family and society?

As a class, consider the two Big Idea questions. After discussing each question, have students write an answer. We'll come back to these questions after we finish reading the text. You can add to your answers as you gain information and perspective.

Preview

Read the Preview Checklist on page 317. Follow the Preview Procedure outlined below.

Preview Procedure

- Group students with partners or in triads.
- Have students count off as 1s or 2s. The 1s will become the student leaders. If working with triads, the third students become 3s.
- The student leaders will preview the text in addition to managing the checklist and pacing.
- The 2s and 3s will preview the text with 1s.
- Direct 1s to open their Student Books to page 317 and 2s and 3s to open their Student Books to page 319. This allows students to look at a few different pages at one time without turning back and forth.

Direct students to page 319. Have students preview the text.

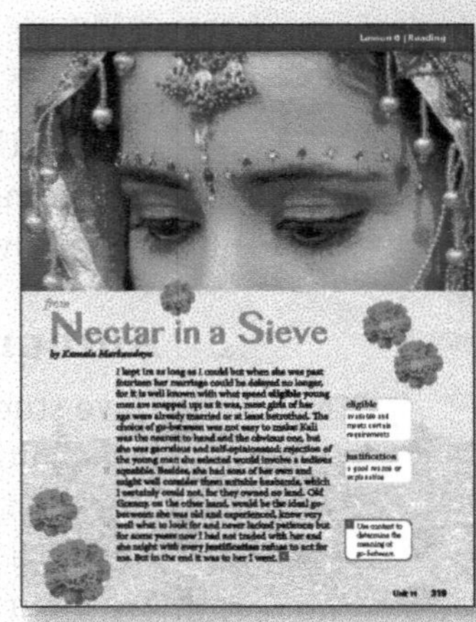
Lesson 6 | Reading

from *Nectar in a Sieve*
by Kamala Markandaya

Unit 11 319

If necessary, guide students in a short preview using the images in the text.

Vocabulary

Objectives

- Evaluate word knowledge.
- Determine the meaning of key passage vocabulary.

Rate Vocabulary Knowledge

Direct students to page 318 in their Student Books.

Before we read the text, let's take a look at the vocabulary words that appear in this excerpt. Remind students that as you read each word in the first column aloud, they will write the word in the third column and then rate their knowledge of it. Display the Vocabulary Rating Scale poster or write the information on the board. Review the meaning of each rating.

Lesson 6 | Vocabulary

Key Passage Vocabulary: Excerpt from *Nectar in a Sieve*

Read each word. Write it in column 3. Then, circle a number to rate your knowledge of the word.

Read the Word	Part of Speech	Write the Word	Rate the Word
eligible	(adj)	eligible	0 1 2 3
justification	(n)	justification	0 1 2 3
grudge	(n)	grudge	0 1 2 3
assess	(v)	assess	0 1 2 3
regretfully	(adv)	regretfully	0 1 2 3
preliminaries	(n)	preliminaries	0 1 2 3
retort	(n)	retort	0 1 2 3
hoist	(v)	hoist	0 1 2 3
procession	(n)	procession	0 1 2 3
decorous	(adj)	decorous	0 1 2 3

318 Unit 11

Vocabulary Rating Scale

0—I have never heard the word before.

1—I have heard the word, but I'm not sure how to use it.

2—I am familiar with the word, but I'm not sure if I know the correct meaning.

3—I know the meaning of the word and can use it correctly in a sentence.

The points are not a grade; they are just there to help you know which words you need to focus on. By the end of this unit, you should be able to change all your ratings to a 3. That's the goal.

Read each word aloud. Have students repeat it, write it, and rate it. Then, have volunteers who rated a word *2* or *3* use the word in an oral sentence.

Preteach Vocabulary

Let's take a closer look at the words. Follow the Preteach Procedure below.

Preteach Procedure

This activity is intended to take only a short amount of time, so make it an oral exercise.

- Introduce each word as indicated on the word card.
- Read the definition and example sentences.
- Ask questions to clarify and deepen understanding.
- If time permits, allow students to share.

* If your students would benefit from copying the definitions, please have them do so in the vocabulary log in the back of the Student Books using the margin definitions in the passage selections. This should be done outside of instruction time.

eligible (adj)

Let's read the first word together. *Eligible.*

Definition: If something is *eligible*, it is available and meets certain requirements. What means "available and meets certain requirements"? (eligible)

Example 1: If you are 16 and have passed drivers' ed, you are *eligible* for a driver's license.

Example 2: On a popular TV show, a group of women compete for the affection of the same *eligible* man.

Example 3: If a school athlete fails a class, he or she is no longer *eligible* to play.

Question 1: Only people with dark brown hair are eligible for the role of Snow White in the upcoming play. Are you *eligible*? Yes or no? (Answers will vary.)

Question 2: A friend asks you to the dance, but you've already got a date. Are you *eligible*? Yes or no? (no)

Pair Share: Turn to your partner and name three things that make someone *eligible* to be your friend.

1

justification (n)

Let's read the next word together. *Justification.*

Definition: A *justification* is a good reason or explanation for something. What word means "a good reason or explanation"? (justification)

Example 1: "The dog ate my homework" is a poor *justification* for turning an assignment in late.

Example 2: People who procrastinate, or put things off, come up with the most entertaining *justifications* for doing so.

Example 3: If you are late to class, I have total *justification* for marking you tardy.

Question 1: Your dog has chewed a hole in every sweater you own. Do you have *justification* for keeping him out of your room from now on? Yes or no? (yes)

Question 2: Your friend always tells you the truth. You ask her how your hair looks, and she says, "Awesome!" Do you have any *justification* for not believing her? Yes or no? (no)

Pair Share: The coach says, "OK, everybody, run five miles!" What's your reason for refusing his request? Tell your partner, then discuss whether the *justification* is valid.

2

grudge (n)

Let's read the next word together. *Grudge.*

Definition: If you have a *grudge,* you have bad feelings toward someone because of something he or she did in the past. What word means "bad feelings toward someone because of something he or she did in the past"? (grudge)

Example 1: Over time, holding a *grudge* can hurt you more than it hurts the person you're mad at.

Example 2: I sometimes hold a short *grudge* against people with full carts who get in the express lane at the grocery store.

Example 3: People who hold multiple *grudges* at once might want to ask themselves how their own actions or attitudes are creating conflicts with others.

Question 1: You're hungry, and a friend shares half his cereal bar with you. Does this cause you to hold a *grudge*? Yes or no? (no)

Question 2: A friend misinterprets the tone of a text you sent her, and she gets mad. Even after you explain, she stays mad. Is she holding a *grudge*? Yes or no? (yes)

Pair Share: Turn to your partner and tell two reasons it's not good to hold a *grudge.*

assess (v)

Let's read the next word together. *Assess.*

Definition: If you *assess* something, you think it through in order to make a decision or judgment about it. What word means "to think something through in order to make a decision or judgment about it"? (assess)

Example 1: You should *assess* the actual value of an item before you try to sell it online.

Example 2: Some people *assess* their chances of winning before they buy a lotto ticket; others don't.

Example 3: Before you make a commitment to any group or project, it's best to *assess* the amount of time you'll have to give.

Question 1: At the last minute, you decide to catch a cross-town bus to see a movie that starts in 15 minutes. Have you *assessed* your chances of arriving on time? Yes or no? (no)

Question 2: People hate playing cards with you because you take forever to make a play. Do you *assess* your hand before making a play? Yes or no? (yes)

Pair Share: Turn to your partner and tell why it's a good idea to *assess* a band's music before hiring it to play at prom.

regretfully (adv)

Let's read the next word together. *Regretfully.*

Definition: To do something *regretfully* is to do it in a way that shows you wish something wasn't true or wasn't happening. What word means "in a way that shows you wish something wasn't true or wasn't happening"? (regretfully)

Example 1: I've had a pretty good year; there aren't too many days I think back on *regretfully.*

Example 2: *Regretfully,* not everyone in this class will make an A+.

Example 3: If the lady at the deli says they're out of your favorite potato salad, you might frown *regretfully* and then order the fruit salad instead.

Question 1: It's your job as vice president of a company to write e-mails to people who applied for a job but did not get accepted. Might you sign those e-mails *Regretfully* yours? Yes or no? (yes)

Question 2: It's your birthday. You open a present and it's just what you were hoping for. Do you smile *regretfully*? Yes or no? (no)

Pair Share: You just stepped on and broke your partner's new phone. Turn to your partner and pretend you are handing the phone to him or her *regretfully.* 5

preliminaries (n)

Let's read the next word together. *Preliminaries.*

Definition: *Preliminaries* are activities that take place before an event. What word means "activities that take place before an event"? (preliminaries)

Example 1: Nurses go through certain *preliminaries* before giving a patient a shot, such as preparing the injection and swabbing the area with alcohol.

Example 2: Before taking a standardized test, you may be led through *preliminaries* of sharpening your pencil, clearing your desk, and opening your test booklet to the first page.

Example 3: If an athlete makes it to the Olympics, he or she has competed in many *preliminaries.*

Question 1: Before each round, the golf pro puts on his lucky hat, stretches, and texts his daughter. Are these activities *preliminaries*? Yes or no? (yes)

Question 2: Before she serves, Mia doesn't even bounce the tennis ball; she just serves it without thinking. Does she go through any *preliminaries*? Yes or no? (no)

Pair Share: Turn to your partner. Tell him or her your dream vacation destination. Identify three *preliminaries* you must attend to before going.

retort (n)

Let's read the next word together. *Retort.*

Definition: A *retort* is an angry or smart-aleck reply. What word means "an angry or smart-aleck reply"? (retort)

Example 1: If someone says you look nice, it would be rude to answer it with a *retort* like "You don't."

Example 2: An effective way to respond to a *retort* is to chuckle as if the person is joking.

Example 3: A sharp *retort* can sting, especially if it's not deserved.

Question 1: The team parent hands out frozen fruit bars after a hot practice. You say "Thanks!" Is this a *retort*? Yes or no? (no)

Question 2: A boy on the bus is staring at you. When you ask what he is looking at, he answers, "Not a whole lot." Is this a *retort*? Yes or no? (yes)

Pair Share: Role-play two little kids with your partner. One kid asks the other to come over to play. Take turns turning down the invitation, the first time regretfully and the second time with a *retort.*

hoist (v)

Let's read the next word together. *Hoist.*

Definition: To *hoist* something heavy is to lift or heave it. What means "to lift or heave, usually something heavy"? (hoist)

Example 1: After we pack all of our holiday decorations, we *hoist* the boxes onto the top shelf in the garage.

Example 2: Frequent fliers get used to *hoisting* their luggage into the overhead compartment.

Example 3: After a big victory, football players sometimes *hoist* the quarterback onto their shoulders in celebration.

Question 1: A princess sets a teacup lightly on a saucer. Has she *hoisted* it? Yes or no? (no)

Question 2: A crane lifts a marble statue and sets it on its base. Has the statue been *hoisted*? Yes or no? (yes)

Pair Share: Turn to your partner and tell about a holiday character, a superhero, or a movie hero who has been known to *hoist* things. Give an example.

procession (n)

Let's read the next word together. *Procession.*

Definition: A *procession* is a group of people moving forward as part of a public event. What word means "a group of people moving forward as part of a public event"? (procession)

Example 1: Graduates usually rehearse their *procession* into the auditorium before the big day arrives.

Example 2: The creepy play ended with all of the actors walking in a slow *procession* up the aisles.

Example 3: Our neighborhood Fourth of July parade begins with a *procession* of people dressed like early American colonists.

Question 1: You and some friends race each other to the end of the street. Is this a *procession*? Yes or no? (no)

Question 2: The homecoming court walks onto the football field two by two. Is this a *procession*? Yes or no? (yes)

Pair Share: Turn to your partner and describe a *procession* you've seen at a wedding or other ceremony.

9

decorous (adj)

Let's read the last word together. *Decorous.*

Definition: If something is *decorous*, it is polite, proper, and respectful. What means "polite, proper, and respectful"? (decorous)

Example 1: Before people have an arranged meeting with the Queen of England, they are given tips for how to be *decorous* in her presence.

Example 2: In the 1700s, men and women would give each other a *decorous* bow before and after dancing together.

Example 3: We should all treat senior citizens *decorously*; they've earned our respect.

Question 1: You're slurping your soup at a fancy dinner. Is your eating style *decorous*? Yes or no? (no)

Question 2: You grow impatient with your little brother and yell at him to hurry up or get left behind. Are you being *decorous*? Yes or no? (no)

Pair Share: Turn to your partner and name one event where *decorous* behavior is expected and one event where it might not be.

Reading

Objectives

- Read an excerpt from a novel.
- Monitor comprehension during text reading.

Excerpt from *Nectar in a Sieve*

Direct students to page 319–324 in their Student Books.

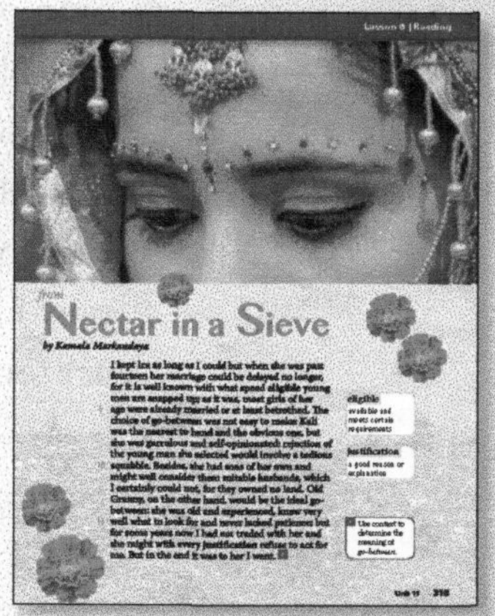

Now that we have previewed vocabulary, it's time to read.

> **Guiding Students Toward Independent Reading**
>
> It is important that your students read as much and as often as they can. Assign readings that meet the needs of your students, based on your observations and data. This is a good opportunity to stretch your students. If students become frustrated, scaffold the reading with paired reading, choral reading, or a read-aloud.
>
> Options for reading text:
>
> - Teacher read-aloud
> - Teacher-led or student-led choral read
> - Paired read or independent read

Choose an option for reading text. Students read according to the option that you chose.

Review the purpose of the numbered squares in the text and prompt students to stop periodically and check comprehension.

If you choose to read the text aloud or chorally, use the following text boxes and stop to ask questions and have students answer them.

SE p. 319, paragraph 1

I kept Ira as long as I could but when she was past fourteen her marriage could be delayed no longer, for it is well known with what speed **eligible** young men are snapped up; as it was, most girls of her age were already married or at least betrothed. The choice of go-between was not easy to make: Kali was the nearest to hand and the obvious one, but she was garrulous and self-opinionated: rejection of the young man she selected would involve a tedious squabble. Besides, she had sons of her own and might well consider them suitable husbands, which I certainly could not, for they owned no land. Old Granny, on the other hand, would be the ideal go-between: she was old and experienced, knew very well what to look for and never lacked patience; but for some years now I had not traded with her and she might with every **justification** refuse to act for me. But in the end it was to her I went.

1. Use context to determine the meaning of *go-between.*

SE p. 320, paragraphs 1–3

"A dowry of one hundred rupees," I said. "A maiden like a flower. Do your best for me and I shall be ever in your debt. This I ask you," I said, looking straight at her, "although Biswas takes my produce and for you there has been nothing."

"I bear you no **grudge**, Rukmani," she replied. "Times are hard and we must do what we can for ourselves and our children. I will do my best."

Thereafter never a week went by but she brought news of this boy or that, and she and I and Nathan spent long hours trying to **assess** their relative merits. At last we found one who seemed to fulfill our requirements: he was young and well favoured, the only son of his father from whom he would one day inherit a good portion of land.

2. What merit is Ira's mom looking for in her future son-in-law?

SE p. 320, paragraphs 4–6

"They will expect a large dowry," I said **regretfully**. "One hundred rupees will not win such a husband, we have no more."

"She is endowed with beauty," Old Granny said. "It will make up for a small dowry—in this case."

She was right. Within a month the **preliminaries** were completed, the day was fixed. Ira accepted our choice with her usual docility; if she fretted at the thought of leaving us and her brothers she showed no sign. Only once she asked a little wistfully how frequently I would be able to visit her, and, although I knew such trips would have to be very rare since her future home lay some ten villages away, I assured her not a year would pass without my going to see her two or three times.

3. How did Ira react to the news of her future husband?

SE p. 320, paragraphs 7–8

"Besides, you will not want me so often," I said. "This home, your brothers, are all you have known so far, but when you have your own home and your own children you will not miss these . . . . "

She nodded slightly, making no comment, yet I knew how bruised she must be by the imminent parting. My spirit ached with pity for her, I longed to be able to comfort her, to convince her that in | a few months' time her new home would be the most significant part of her life, the rest only a preparation . . . but before this joy must come the stress of parting, the loneliness of beginning a new life among strangers, the strain of the early days of marriage; and because I knew this the words would not come . . . .

page break

4. How is Ira's mom feeling about Ira's impending wedding day?

SE p. 321, paragraphs 1–2

Wedding day. Women from the village came to assist. Janaki, Kali, many I hardly knew. We went with Ira to the river and, when she was freshly bathed, put on her the red sari I had worn at my own wedding. Its rich heavy folds made her look more slender than she was, made her look a child . . . . I darkened her eyes with kohl and the years fell away more; she was so pitifully young I could hardly believe she was to be married, today.

The bridegroom arrived; his parents, his relatives, our friends, the priests. The drummer arrived and squatted outside awaiting permission to begin; the fiddler joined him. There should have been other musicians—a flautist, a harmonium player, but we could not afford these. Nathan would have nothing we could not pay for. No debts, he insisted, no debts. But I grudged Ira nothing: had I not saved from the day of her birth so that she should marry well? Now I brought out the stores I had put by month after month—rice and dhal and ghee, jars of oil, betel leaf, areca nuts, chewing tobacco and copra.

5. How is Ira's wedding different from a wedding in your culture?

SE p. 321, paragraphs 3–5

"I didn't know you had so much," said Nathan in amazement.

"And if you had there would be little enough," I said with a wink at the women, "for men are like children and must grab what they see."

I did not wait for his **retort**, hearing only the laughter that greeted his sally, but went out to speak to the drummer. Arjun, my eldest son, was sitting next to the man, cautiously tapping the drum with three fingers as he had been shown.

SE p. 322, paragraphs 1–3

"There is plenty of food inside," I said to him. "Go and eat while there is still some left."

"I can eat no more," he replied. "I have been feasting all day."

Nevertheless he had made provision for the morrow: I saw in his lap a bundle bulging with food; sugar syrup and butter had soaked through the cloth patchily.

6. Why is Arjun's bundle bulging with food?

SE p. 322, paragraphs 4–6

"Join your brothers," I said, **hoisting** him up. "The drummer is going to be busy."

He ran off, clinging tightly to his bundle. The wedding music began. Bride and groom were sitting uneasily side by side, Ira stiff in the heavy embroidered sari, white flowers in her hair, very pale. They did not look at each other. About them were packed some fourteen or fifteen people—the hut could hold no more. The remainder sat outside on palm leaves the boys had collected.

"What a good match," everybody said. "Such a fine boy, such a beautiful girl, too good to be true." It was indeed. Old Granny went about beaming: it was she who had brought the two parties together; her reputation as a matchmaker would be higher than ever. We none of us could look into the future.

7. What phrase foreshadows bad news for this couple?

SE p. 322, paragraph 7

So they were married. As the light faded two youths appeared bearing a palanquin for the newly married couple, lowered it at the entrance to the hut for them to step into. Now that it was time to go, Ira looked scared, she hesitated a little before entering: but already a dozen willing hands had lifted her in. The crowd, full of good feeling, replete with food and drunk with the music, vicariously excited, pressed round, eagerly thrusting over their heads garland after garland of flowers; the earth was spattered with petals. In the midst of the crush Nathan and I, Nathan holding out his hands to Ira in blessing, she with dark head bent low to receive it. Then the palanquin was lifted up, the torchbearers closed in, the musicians took their places. We | followed on foot behind, relatives, friends, well-wishers and hangers-on. Several children had added themselves to the company; they came after, jigging about in high glee, noisy and excited: a long, ragged tail-end to the **procession**. *(page break)*

8. What was the mood of the wedding? How was Ira feeling?

SE p. 323, paragraphs 1–2

> Past the fields, through the winding streets of the village we went, the bobbing palanquin ahead of us. Until we came at last to where, at a **decorous** distance, the bullock cart waited to take them away.
>
> Then it was all over, the bustle, the laughter, the noise. The wedding guests departed. The throng melted. After a while we walked back together to our hut. Our sons, tired out, were humped together asleep, the youngest clutching a sugary confection in one sticky fist. Bits of food lay everywhere. I swept the floor clean and strewed it with leaves. The walls showed cracks, and clods of mud had fallen where people had bumped against them, but these I left for patching in the morning. The used plantain leaves I stacked in one heap—they would do for the bullocks. The stars were pale in the greying night before I lay down beside my husband. Not to sleep but to think. For the first time since her birth, Ira no longer slept under our roof.

9. How was Ira's mom feeling?

For confirmation of engagement, have partners compare the point of view between *Nectar in a Sieve* and *The Good Earth*. Have volunteers share comparisons with the class.

Unit 11

Lesson 7

Lesson Opener

Before the lesson, choose one of the following activities to write on the board or post on the *LANGUAGE! Live* Class Wall online.

- *Write a summary of the author's point of view of arranged marriages.*
- *Write five sentences about Ira using appositives.*
- *Write five sentences explaining how it would feel to be sent from your home at age 14.*

Vocabulary

Objective

- Review key passage vocabulary.

Review Passage Vocabulary

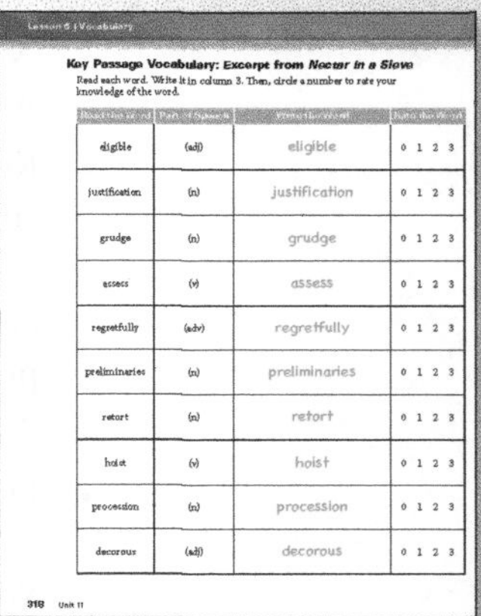

Key Passage Vocabulary: Excerpt from *Nectar in a Sieve*

Read each word. Write it in column 3. Then, circle a number to rate your knowledge of the word.

[illegible]	[illegible]	[illegible]	[illegible]
eligible	(adj)	eligible	0 1 2 3
justification	(n)	justification	0 1 2 3
grudge	(n)	grudge	0 1 2 3
assess	(v)	assess	0 1 2 3
regretfully	(adv)	regretfully	0 1 2 3
preliminaries	(n)	preliminaries	0 1 2 3
retort	(n)	retort	0 1 2 3
hoist	(v)	hoist	0 1 2 3
procession	(n)	procession	0 1 2 3
decorous	(adj)	decorous	0 1 2 3

318 Unit 11

Direct students to page 318 in their Student Books. Use the following questions to review the vocabulary words in the excerpt from *Nectar in a Sieve*. Have students answer each question using the vocabulary word or indicating its meaning in a complete sentence.

- This story is told by a mother who is looking for an *eligible* man for her daughter. What kind of man is she looking for? (She is looking for a man who is available for marriage and meets the family's criteria.) Why is a poor man not *eligible* for marriage to Ira? (A poor man is not eligible because he likely doesn't own land.)
- Rukmani hopes Old Granny will be their go-between but feels that Old Granny has every *justification* for saying no. Old Granny has every what for saying no? Use another word. (Old Granny has every reason to say no.) If Old Granny had wanted to say no, what would her main *justification* have been? (Her main justification, or reason, would have been that the mother had not traded with her for years.)
- Does Old Granny hold a *grudge* against the mother for not trading with her? Why or why not? (No, she doesn't have bad feelings toward the mother; she knows everyone must do what's best for their family.) Would it be a good idea to hire a go-between who held a *grudge* against your family? Why or why not? (If you hired a go-between who held a grudge against your family, she might arrange a very bad marriage for your daughter just to get even.)
- Old Granny, Rukmani, and her husband, Nathan, spend many long hours *assessing* different boys. What are they doing when they *assess* the boys? (When they assess the boys, they are thinking about them and deciding whether they are the right match for Ira.) If Ira were allowed to *assess* the candidates, do you think she would reach the same decisions? Why or why not? (Possible response: No, she would assess them differently. She would probably look for someone she felt attracted to rather than someone who was a good financial or social match.)

- Rukmani admits *regretfully* that the family of the boy they finally choose will expect a larger dowry than they can offer. How does she feel about this situation? (She wishes it wasn't true; she wishes it were different.) Does Old Granny feel *regretful* about young Ira's beauty? Why or why not? (No; she is glad that young Ira is beautiful because, in this case, it will make up for the smaller dowry her family can offer.)
- Wedding *preliminaries* are completed within a month. What are completed within a month? (Activities that must take place before the wedding are completed within a month.) What do you imagine some of these *preliminaries* are? (Possible response: The preliminaries might include finalizing the deal, making payment, planning the ceremony itself, and packing.)
- On the day of the wedding, Ira's father marvels at the abundant food. The mother responds that she had to hide it so the men wouldn't grab it. Do you consider her response a *retort*? Why or why not? (Yes, it is a retort; it is a smart-aleck answer.) How do we know that the husband's own *retort* was a clever one rather than an angry one? (We know that it was clever because people respond to it with laughter.) If your parent told you your marriage had been arranged, would you accept it or make a *retort*? (Responses will vary.)
- Rukmani comes across her eldest son, who has gathered a large amount of food supplies in his lap. Why must she *hoist* him to his feet? (She must hoist him because the food supplies make him even heavier than he already is.) After the ceremony, the bride and groom enter a palanquin, or a covered box carried on poles. After they enter it, must the palanquin be *hoisted*? Why or why not? (Yes, it must be hoisted, or lifted, in order to be carried.)
- Describe the *procession* following the palanquin. (The procession is made up of musicians, family members, relatives, friends, well-wishers, and hangers-on.) Where does the *procession* go? (The procession follows the palanquin through the village to the cart that is waiting to take them away.)
- Was the procession itself *decorous*? (No; it was noisy and bustling.) The people in the procession stop at a *decorous* distance from the cart. What do they want to give the bride and groom? (They want to give the couple respect and privacy.) Do you hope to have a *decorous* wedding or a more casual one? Why? (Responses will vary.)

Assign online practice from the Text Training link on the left menu of your teacher dashboard.

Reading

Objectives

- Determine how to respond to prompts.
- Use critical thinking skills to write responses to prompts about text.
- Support written answers with evidence from text.
- Compare characters across multiple texts.
- Cite text evidence in support of an opinion.

Critical Understandings: Direction Words *cite evidence, compare, contrast, demonstrate*

Let's review some prompts. Prompts are statements that require a constructed response, which can range from a list to a complete sentence to a paragraph or an essay.

Write the words *cite evidence, compare, contrast,* and *demonstrate* on the board. Have students read the words aloud with you.

Direct students to pages 14 and 15 in their Student Books. It is critical to understand what the question is asking and how to answer it. Today, we will look at four direction words used in prompts.

Have students read about the four direction words in the chart with their partner.

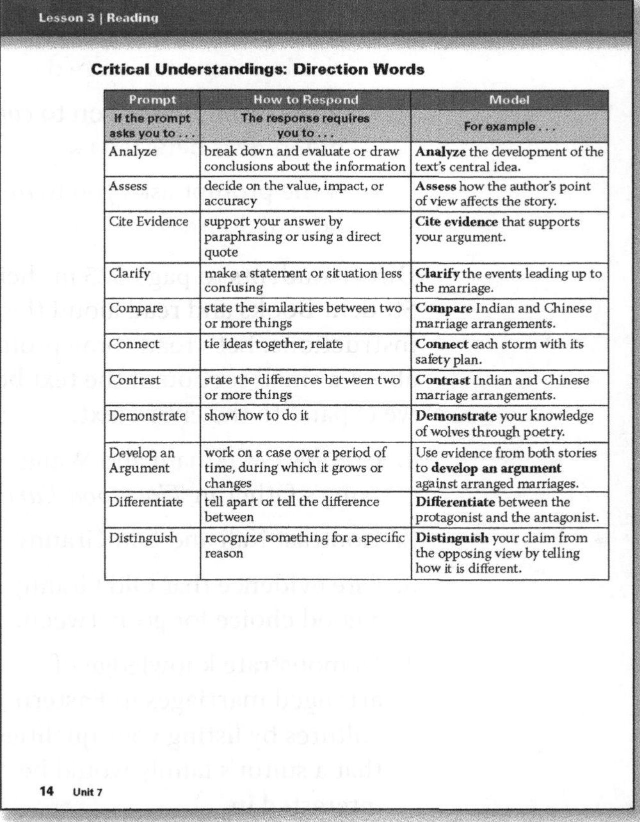

Lesson 3 | Reading

Critical Understandings: Direction Words

Prompt If the prompt asks you to . . .	How to Respond The response requires you to . . .	Model For example . . .
Analyze	break down and evaluate or draw conclusions about the information	**Analyze** the development of the text's central idea.
Assess	decide on the value, impact, or accuracy	**Assess** how the author's point of view affects the story.
Cite Evidence	support your answer by paraphrasing or using a direct quote	**Cite evidence** that supports your argument.
Clarify	make a statement or situation less confusing	**Clarify** the events leading up to the marriage.
Compare	state the similarities between two or more things	**Compare** Indian and Chinese marriage arrangements.
Connect	tie ideas together, relate	**Connect** each storm with its safety plan.
Contrast	state the differences between two or more things	**Contrast** Indian and Chinese marriage arrangements.
Demonstrate	show how to do it	**Demonstrate** your knowledge of wolves through poetry.
Develop an Argument	work on a case over a period of time, during which it grows or changes	Use evidence from both stories to **develop an argument** against arranged marriages.
Differentiate	tell apart or tell the difference between	**Differentiate** between the protagonist and the antagonist.
Distinguish	recognize something for a specific reason	**Distinguish** your claim from the opposing view by telling how it is different.

14 Unit 7

Chart Reading Procedure

- Group students with partners or in triads.
- Have students count off as 1s or 2s. The 1s will become the student leaders. If working with triads, the third students become 3s.
- The student leaders will read the left column (Prompt) in addition to managing the time and turn-taking if working with a triad.
- The 2s will explain the middle column of the chart (How to Respond). If working in triads, 3s take turns explaining the middle column.
- The 1s read the model in the right column (Model), and 2s and 3s restate the model as a question.
- All students should follow along with their pencil eraser while others are explaining the chart.
- Students must work from left to right, top to bottom in order to benefit from this activity.

Check for understanding by requesting an oral response to the following questions.

- If the prompt asks you to *cite evidence*, the response requires you to . . . (support your answer by paraphrasing or using a direct quote).
- If the prompt asks you to *compare*, the response requires you to . . . (state the similarities between two or more things).
- If the prompt asks you to *contrast*, the response requires you to . . . (state the differences between two or more things).
- If the prompt asks you to *demonstrate*, the response requires you to . . . (show how to do it).

Direct students to page 325 in their Student Books and read aloud the instructions. Let's read some prompts about a small section of the text before we expand to the entire text.

1. Compare Rukmani and Wang Lung's father in *The Good Earth.*
2. Contrast Kali and Old Granny.
3. Cite evidence that Old Granny was a good choice for go-between.
4. Demonstrate knowledge of arranged marriages in Eastern cultures by listing your qualities that a suitor's family would be interested in.

We are going to focus on lines 1–38 of the excerpt from *Nectar in a Sieve.*

Lesson 7 | Reading

Critical Understandings

Reread lines 1–38 of the excerpt from *Nectar in a Sieve*. Respond to each prompt using complete sentences. Refer to the chart on pages 14 and 15 to determine how to respond to each prompt.

1. Compare Rukmani and Wang Lung's father in *The Good Earth.*
   Rukmani and Wang Lung's father are similar because they are both farmers responsible for finding a suitable mate for their child. In both cases, poverty limits their choices because payment is agreed upon before marriage. In both cases, the parents arrange the marriage without much input from the children.
2. Contrast Kali and Old Granny.
   Kali is a matchmaker who lives nearby, but she could be difficult to work with and may want her sons who don't own land to be considered for Rukmani's daughter. On the other hand, Old Granny is a matchmaker who has experience and would be easier to work with but may be holding a grudge because Rukmani hasn't traded with her in a while.
3. Cite evidence that Old Granny was a good choice for go-between.
   Old Granny was a good choice because she worked hard and was in constant consultation with Rukmani and Nathan. Old Granny shares Rukmani's family values and worked long hours for weeks to find a husband who would inherit land in the future.
4. Demonstrate knowledge of arranged marriages in Eastern cultures by listing your qualities that a suitor's family would be interested in.
   Answers will vary but should include wealth, land, family values, work ethic, and/or fertility.

Unit 11 325

Guided Practice

Let's practice answering questions that are written as prompts. Remember to use the chart as reference.

1. Compare Rukmani and Wang Lung's father in *The Good Earth*.

How should we respond according to the chart? (If the prompt asks you to *compare*, the response requires that you state the similarities between two or more things.) Now, turn the prompt into a question to confirm your understanding. Tell your partner the question. (How are Ira's mom and Wang Lung's father alike?)

Have partners refer to the text to answer the question. As they are working, write the following sentence starter on the board.

Rukmani and Wang Lung's father are similar because ____________________ ____.

Complete the response as a class.

Let's move on to the next prompt.

2. Contrast Kali and Old Granny.

How should we respond according to the chart? (If the prompt asks you to *contrast*, the response requires that you state the difference between two or more things.) Now, turn the prompt into a question to confirm your understanding. Tell your partner the question. (How are Kali and Old Granny different?)

Have partners refer to the text to answer the question. As they are working, write the following sentence starters on the board.

Kali is a matchmaker who ______________________________
but ____.

On the other hand, Old Granny is a matchmaker who ______________

but ____.

Complete the response as a class.

Let's move on to the next prompt.

3. **Cite evidence that Old Granny was a good choice for go-between.**

How should we respond according to the chart? (If the prompt asks you to *cite evidence*, the response requires that you support your answer by paraphrasing or using a direct quote.) Now, turn the prompt into a question to confirm your understanding. Tell your partner the question. (What is the proof that Old Granny was a good choice?)

Have partners refer to the text to answer the question. As they are working, write the following sentence starter on the board.

Old Granny was a good choice because ________________________
____.

Have partners complete the response.

4. **Demonstrate knowledge of arranged marriages in Eastern cultures by listing your qualities that a suitor's family would be interested in.**

How should we respond according to the chart? (If the prompt asks you to *demonstrate*, the response requires that you show how to do it.) Now, turn the prompt into a question to confirm your understanding. Tell your partner the question. (What qualities do you possess that would make you a good candidate for a suitor in an arranged marriage?)

Generate a class list of what was important to Wang Lung, Wang Lung's father, Rukmani, and Old Granny. Then, have students answer the question with their personal qualities.

Writing

Objective

- Demonstrate an understanding of the components and structure of a compare-contrast essay.

Green and yellow highlighters or colored pencils

Compare-Contrast Essay Structure

In Lesson 10, you will be tasked with writing a compare-contrast essay. Planning is an important step for writing, especially with longer writing assignments.

Direct students to page 326 in their Student Books and read the instructions. Read the essay, and guide students to identify the key components of the essay. Have students use highlighters or colored pencils to identify the elements within the essay:

- thesis statement
- topic sentence of each paragraph
- body paragraphs
- concluding paragraph
- introductory paragraph

Lesson 7 | Writing

Compare-Contrast Essay Structure

Read the following essay. Follow the steps below.

- Highlight the thesis statement green.
- Highlight the topic sentence of each paragraph yellow.
- Label the body paragraphs.
- Label the concluding paragraph.
- Label the introductory paragraph.

Introductory Paragraph — Claire and Chad have been volunteers at the local community center for years. Both of them are reliable, energetic, and dedicated workers. Because of their unique strengths and weaknesses, they have very different roles at the center.

Body Paragraph — Claire possesses fabulous organizational skills. Implementing her ideas has saved the community center thousands of dollars and streamlined its operations. She created procedures for most of the activities that take place at the center, thus eliminating many of the problems that once plagued the facility. Because her abrupt attitude can rub people the wrong way, she enjoys working in the solitude of her office.

Body Paragraph — Chad, on the other hand, is very much a people person. While his organizational skills may be somewhat weak, he is very effective in dealing with the public. With his passion for the well-being of the community and his winning smile, he has worked tirelessly to get local businesses involved in the center. Through the submission of grant applications and securing business sponsorships, he has dramatically increased the center's budget. With these funds, the community center has been able to offer many different types of activities that appeal to a wide variety of citizens.

Concluding Paragraph — Facilities like the community center need volunteers with an array of skills and interests. Claire and Chad have been willing to donate their unique skill sets to the community center, and the community is definitely the better for it.

326 Unit 11

Discuss the topics of the two body paragraphs and the words used to indicate similarities and differences. Be sure to point out the positioning of similarities in the introductory paragraph only.

Unit 11 Lesson 8

Lesson Opener

Before the lesson, choose one of the following activities to write on the board or post on the *LANGUAGE! Live* Class Wall online.

- *Write five sentences describing Ira's wedding day using participial phrases.*
- *Write five sentences about Rukmani using appositives.*
- *Expand one or more of these simple sentences, using the steps in Masterpiece Sentences.*

  Ira bathes.

  Old Granny searches.

  Rukmani wept.

  Ira was scared.

Reading

Objectives

- Establish a purpose for rereading text.
- Read an excerpt from a novel.
- Monitor comprehension during text reading.
- Use critical thinking skills to write responses to prompts about text.
- Support written answers with evidence from text.
- Compare and contrast characters across multiple texts.
- Compare and contrast points of view in multiple texts.
- Cite text evidence when answering questions about text.

Reading for a Purpose: Excerpt from *Nectar in a Sieve*

Let's preview the prompts to provide a purpose for rereading the text. You should recognize the question words that we practiced in the last lesson.

Direct students to pages 327–329 in their Student Books. Have students read the prompts aloud with you.

1. Compare Ira's family values with Wang Lung's family values.
2. Contrast the goals of Rukmani with the goals of Wang Lung's father.
3. Use inferencing to compare and contrast the bride's point of view in both texts on arranged marriages.
4. Cite evidence to prove that Wang Lung's father and Ira's father had different roles in the family.
5. Demonstrate understanding of the life of Indian farmers by explaining the happenings of the wedding day.
6. Cite evidence to prove that Indian weddings are ceremonial.

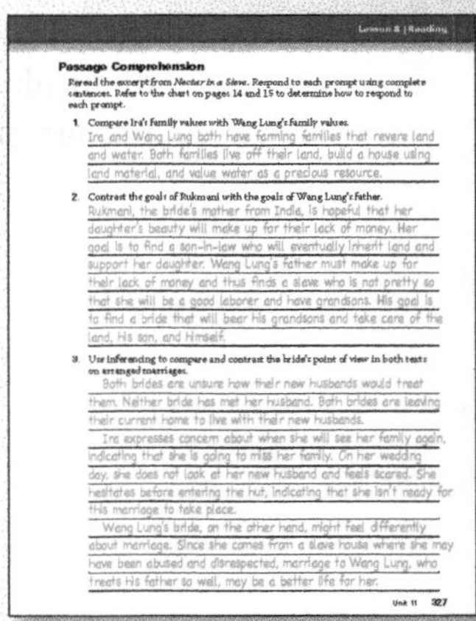

Lesson 8 | Reading

Passage Comprehension

Reread the excerpt from *Nectar in a Sieve*. Respond to each prompt using complete sentences. Refer to the chart on pages 14 and 15 to determine how to respond to each prompt.

1. Compare Ira's family values with Wang Lung's family values.

   Ira and Wang Lung both have farming families that revere land and water. Both families live off their land, build a house using land material, and value water as a precious resource.

2. Contrast the goals of Rukmani with the goals of Wang Lung's father.

   Rukmani, the bride's mother from India, is hopeful that her daughter's beauty will make up for their lack of money. Her goal is to find a son-in-law who will eventually inherit land and support her daughter. Wang Lung's father must make up for their lack of money and thus finds a slave who is not pretty so that she will be a good laborer and have grandsons. His goal is to find a bride that will bear his grandsons and take care of the land, his son, and himself.

3. Use inferencing to compare and contrast the bride's point of view in both texts on arranged marriages.

   Both brides are unsure how their new husbands would treat them. Neither bride has met her husband. Both brides are leaving their current home to live with their new husbands.

   Ira expresses concern about when she will see her family again, indicating that she is going to miss her family. On her wedding day, she does not look at her new husband and feels scared. She hesitates before entering the hut, indicating that she isn't ready for this marriage to take place.

   Wang Lung's bride, on the other hand, might feel differently about marriage. Since she comes from a slave house where she may have been abused and disrespected, marriage to Wang Lung, who treats his father so well, may be a better life for her.

Unit 11 327

It's time to reread the text.

Choose an option for reading text. Have students read the text according to the option that you chose.

Options for reading text:

- Teacher read-aloud
- Teacher-led or student-led choral read
- Paired read or independent read with bold vocabulary words read aloud

Direct students to pages 319–324 in their Student Books or have them tear out the extra copy of the excerpt from the back of their book.

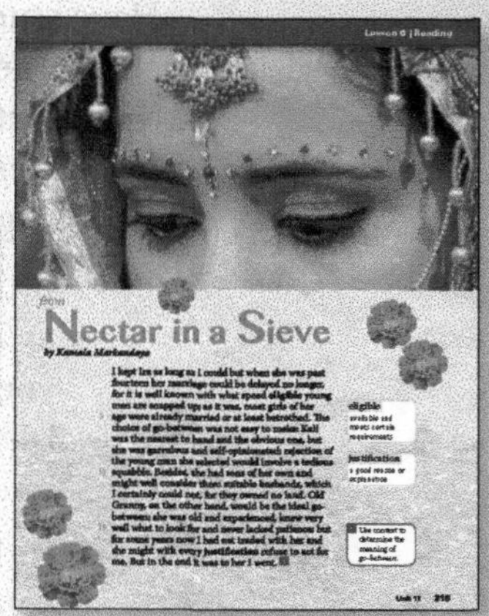

Note: To minimize flipping back and forth between the pages, a copy of each text has been included in the back of the Student Books. Encourage students to tear this out and use it when working on activities that require the use of the text.

Have students read the text.

Passage Comprehension

Write *cite evidence, compare, contrast,* and *demonstrate* on the board. Have students read the words aloud with you.

Direct students to pages 14 and 15 in their Student Books. It is critical to understand what the question is asking and how to answer it. Today, we will review four direction words used in prompts.

Lesson 3 | Reading

Critical Understandings: Direction Words

Prompt	How to Respond	Model
If the prompt asks you to . . .	The response requires you to . . .	For example . . .
Analyze	break down and evaluate or draw conclusions about the information	**Analyze** the development of the text's central idea.
Assess	decide on the value, impact, or accuracy	**Assess** how the author's point of view affects the story.
Cite Evidence	support your answer by paraphrasing or using a direct quote	**Cite evidence** that supports your argument.
Clarify	make a statement or situation less confusing	**Clarify** the events leading up to the marriage.
Compare	state the similarities between two or more things	**Compare** Indian and Chinese marriage arrangements.
Connect	tie ideas together, relate	**Connect** each storm with its safety plan.
Contrast	state the differences between two or more things	**Contrast** Indian and Chinese marriage arrangements.
Demonstrate	show how to do it	**Demonstrate** your knowledge of wolves through poetry.
Develop an Argument	work on a case over a period of time, during which it grows or changes	Use evidence from both stories to **develop an argument** against arranged marriages.
Differentiate	tell apart or tell the difference between	**Differentiate** between the protagonist and the antagonist.
Distinguish	recognize something for a specific reason	**Distinguish** your claim from the opposing view by telling how it is different.

14 Unit 7

Have students read the information about the four direction words with their partner. Check for understanding by requesting an oral response to the following questions.

- If the prompt asks you to *cite evidence,* the response requires you to . . . (support your answer by paraphrasing or using a direct quote).
- If the prompt asks you to *compare,* the response requires you to . . . (state the similarities between two things).
- If the prompt asks you to *contrast,* the response requires you to . . . (state the differences between two or more things).
- If the prompt asks you to *demonstrate,* the response requires you to . . . (show how to do it).

Let's practice answering questions that are written as prompts. Remember to use the chart as reference. Don't forget, if the direction word is confusing, try to restate the prompt by using a question word.

Direct students to pages 327–329 in their Student Books.

Lesson 8 | Reading

Passage Comprehension

Reread the excerpt from *Nectar in a Sieve*. Respond to each prompt using complete sentences. Refer to the chart on pages 14 and 15 to determine how to respond to each prompt.

1. Compare Ira's family values with Wang Lung's family values.
   Ira and Wang Lung both have farming families that revere land and water. Both families live off their land, build a house using land material, and value water as a precious resource.
2. Contrast the goals of Rukmani with the goals of Wang Lung's father.
   Rukmani, the bride's mother from India, is hopeful that her daughter's beauty will make up for their lack of money. Her goal is to find a son-in-law who will eventually inherit land and support her daughter. Wang Lung's father must make up for their lack of money and thus finds a slave who is not pretty so that she will be a good laborer and have grandsons. His goal is to find a bride that will bear his grandsons and take care of the land, his son, and himself.
3. Use inferencing to compare and contrast the bride's point of view in both texts on arranged marriages.
   Both brides are unsure how their new husbands would treat them. Neither bride has met her husband. Both brides are leaving their current home to live with their new husbands.
   Ira expresses concern about when she will see her family again, indicating that she is going to miss her family. On her wedding day, she does not look at her new husband and feels scared. She hesitates before entering the hut, indicating that she isn't ready for this marriage to take place.
   Wang Lung's bride, on the other hand, might feel differently about marriage. Since she comes from a slave house where she may have been abused and disrespected, marriage to Wang Lung, who treats his father so well, may be a better life for her.

Unit 11 327

328 Unit 11

Lesson 8 | Reading

Passage Comprehension (*cont.*)

4. Cite evidence to prove that Wang Lung's father and Ira's father had different roles in the family.
   Wang Lung's father had the responsibility to choose Wang Lung's wife and had a say in the goings on of the house. Wang Lung's father seemed to be the authority in the family. Wang Lung very much wanted to please his father.
   Ira's father seemed to support the wishes of Ira's mother. Ira's mother seemed to be the authority in the family and played a key role in arranging Ira's marriage. Although Ira's father insisted that they didn't go in debt for her wedding, her mom had saved for her wedding day since her birth without her father knowing. Ira was very connected to her mother, but not her father.
5. Demonstrate understanding of the life of Indian farmers by explaining the happenings of the wedding day.
   Farmers were poor and had little to eat as evidenced by the fact that Rukmani had been putting food away for the wedding for quite a while. They typically didn't have excess food, so it was surprising to Nathan that she was able to provide it. The lack of food is also proven by Arjun's attempt to pack food away for the next day. Farmers in India did not have running water, and thus Ira had to bathe in the river. The houses were small and shabby as evidenced by the fact that there was little room, leaves on the floor, and the walls were filled with holes from people bumping into them.

Guided Practice

Let's practice answering questions that are written as prompts. Let's read the first prompt.

> 1. Compare Ira's family values with Wang Lung's family values.

How should we respond according to the chart? (If the prompt asks you to *compare*, the response requires you to state the similarities between two or more things.) Now, turn the prompt into a question to confirm your understanding. Tell your partner the question. (How are Ira's family values similar to Wang Lung's family values?)

Lesson 8 | Reading

Passage Comprehension (*cont.*)

6. Cite evidence to prove that Indian weddings are ceremonial.
   Indian weddings are ceremonial, which is evidenced by Ira's wedding day rituals. Village women came to help Ira bathe in the river. Ira wore the same red sari that her mom wore at her wedding. Her mom put kohl, a kind of makeup, on her eyes and flowers in her hair. The groom's family, friends, and priests arrived. Musicians played drums and a fiddle. After the ceremony, the bride and groom were taken away on a palanquin, which is a bed-like platform attached to poles. They were carried through the village until they reached their cart powered by a bull that pulled them home.

Unit 11 329

We must realize that this prompt requires us to recall or revisit *The Good Earth* text in order to compare the values of both families.

Have partners refer to both texts to answer the question. As they are working, write the following sentence starters on the board.

> *Ira and Wang Lung both have farming families that* ____________. *Both families* ____.

Have partners complete the response.

Independent Practice

Have partners respond to the remaining prompts. For students who need more assistance, provide the following alternative questions.

Alternative questions:

2. How are Rukmani's goals different from the goals of Wang Lung's father?
3. What is the bride's perspective in both texts on arranged marriages? How are they the same? How are they different?
4. What proves that Wang Lung's father and Ira's father played different familial roles?
5. What was the life of Indian farmers like? What elements of the wedding ritual prove this?
6. What ceremonial events occurred during Ira's wedding day?

Unit 11

Lesson 9

Lesson Opener

Before the lesson, choose one of the following activities to write on the board or post on the *LANGUAGE! Live* Class Wall online.

- *In the story, Ira had to leave her home and start a family at age 14. Imagine you had to do the same. Contrast how you would be before leaving home and after leaving home. How you would be different after being forced to wed so young?*
- *Change the following sentences to active voice.*
  - *A marriage was arranged by Rukmani.*
  - *A groom was secured by Old Granny.*
  - *Music was played while the couple danced.*
  - *A red sari was worn by Ira.*
- *Write the dialogue of a conversation you think Rukmani had with Ira on the day she turned 14. Remember to punctuate correctly.*

Reading

Objectives

- Read with purpose and understanding.
- Answer questions to demonstrate comprehension of text.
- Identify and explain explicit details from text.
- Monitor comprehension of text during reading.
- Analyze the contrasting points of view of characters within a story.
- Analyze the development of character traits over time.
- Track pronouns to their antecedents.
- Determine the meaning of figurative language in literature.
- Use synonyms and antonyms to deepen word knowledge.
- Objectively summarize text.
- Analyze a summary for accuracy and content.
- Analyze how the setting influences the theme or message.
- Explain how the historical and cultural setting affects character development.
- Compare and contrast two cultural texts on the same topic.
- Determine the meaning of extended similes.

Close Reading of the Excerpt from *Nectar in a Sieve*

Highlighters or colored pencils

Let's reread the excerpt from *Nectar in a Sieve.* I will provide specific instructions on how to mark the text to help with comprehension.

Have students get out a highlighter or colored pencil.

Direct students to pages 330–333 in their Student Books.

Draw a rectangle around the title.

Now, let's read the vocabulary words aloud.

- What's the first bold vocabulary word? (eligible) *Eligible* means "available and meets certain requirements." If you pass your classes, you are *eligible* to participate in extracurricular activities. Have partners use the word in a sentence.

- What's the next vocabulary word? (justification) *Justification* means "a good reason or explanation." Rukmani had *justification* for keeping the food a secret from her husband. **Have partners use the word in a sentence.**
- Next word? (grudge) *Grudge* means "bad feelings toward someone because of something he or she did in the past." Holding a *grudge* against someone for a long time is unhealthy. **Have partners use the word in a sentence.**
- Let's continue. (assess) *Assess* means "to think something through in order to make a decision or judgment about it." Old Granny will *assess* the merits of the possible grooms. **Have partners use the word in a sentence.**
- Next word? (regretfully) *Regretfully* means "in a way that shows you wish something wasn't true or wasn't happening." I *regretfully* forgot to eat breakfast this morning; I am really hungry. **Have partners use the word in a sentence.**
- Let's continue. (preliminaries) *Preliminaries* means "activities that take place before an event." *Preliminaries* come before finals in track and field. **Have partners use the word in a sentence.**
- Next word? (retort) *Retort* means "an angry or smart-aleck reply." His *retort* made his friend feel bad. **Have partners use the word in a sentence.**
- Let's continue. (hoisting) *Hoisting* means "lifting or heaving, usually something heavy." *Hoisting* your car will allow the mechanics to work under your car. **Have partners use the word in a sentence.**
- Next word? (procession) *Procession* means "a group of people moving forward as part of a public event." Police blocked traffic to make way for the funeral *procession*. **Have partners use the word in a sentence.**
- Last word. (decorous) *Decorous* means "polite, proper, and respectful." Some teens need to practice the *decorous* habit of making eye contact when speaking to someone. **Have partners use the word in a sentence.**

Talk with a partner about any vocabulary word that is still confusing for you to read or understand.

As you reread the passage, you will monitor your understanding by circling the check marks or the question marks. Please be sure to draw a question mark over any confusing words, phrases, or sentences.

Options for rereading text.

- Teacher read-aloud
- Teacher-led or student-led choral read
- Paired read or independent read with bold vocabulary words read aloud

Choose an option for reading text. Have students read lines 1–24 according to the option that you chose.

When most of the students are finished, continue with the entire class. Let's see how well you understood what you read.

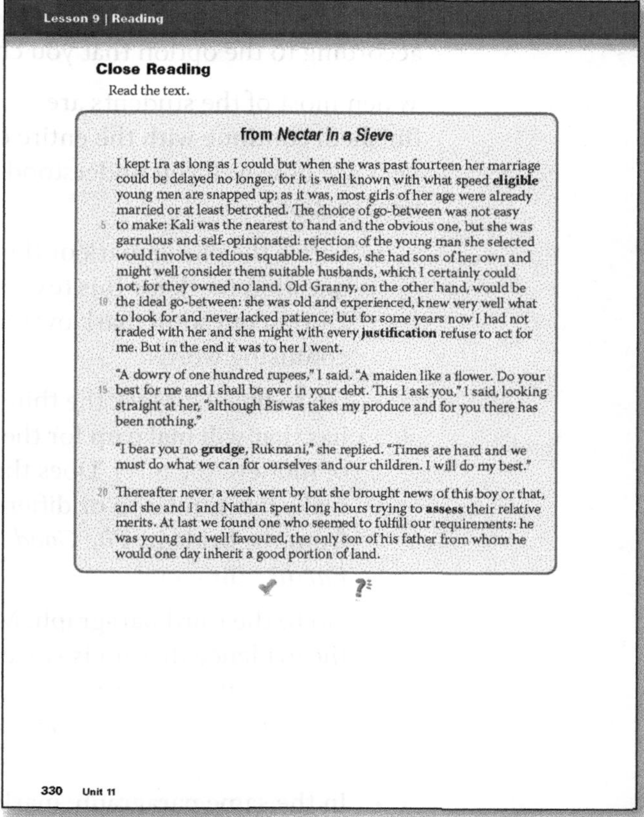

Lesson 9 | Reading

Close Reading

Read the text.

from *Nectar in a Sieve*

I kept Ira as long as I could but when she was past fourteen her marriage could be delayed no longer, for it is well known with what speed **eligible** young men are snapped up; as it was, most girls of her age were already married or at least betrothed. The choice of go-between was not easy to make: Kali was the nearest to hand and the obvious one, but she was garrulous and self-opinionated: rejection of the young man she selected would involve a tedious squabble. Besides, she had sons of her own and might well consider them suitable husbands, which I certainly could not, for they owned no land. Old Granny, on the other hand, would be the ideal go-between: she was old and experienced, knew very well what to look for and never lacked patience; but for some years now I had not traded with her and she might with every **justification** refuse to act for me. But in the end it was to her I went.

"A dowry of one hundred rupees," I said. "A maiden like a flower. Do your best for me and I shall be ever in your debt. This I ask you," I said, looking straight at her, "although Biswas takes my produce and for you there has been nothing."

"I bear you no **grudge**, Rukmani," she replied. "Times are hard and we must do what we can for ourselves and our children. I will do my best."

Thereafter never a week went by but she brought news of this boy or that, and she and I and Nathan spent long hours trying to **assess** their relative merits. At last we found one who seemed to fulfill our requirements: he was young and well favoured, the only son of his father from whom he would one day inherit a good portion of land.

330 Unit 11

- Circle the check mark or the question mark for this text. Draw a question mark over any confusing words.
- Go to line 4. Mark the word that means "engaged" or "promised." (betrothed)
- Go to line 6. Mark the synonym of *talkative.* (garrulous)
- Go to line 8. Mark the word that means "believe to be." (consider)
- Number three reasons why Rukmani didn't want to choose Kali as matchmaker. (1. garrulous; 2. self-opinionated; 3. sons of her own . . . owned no land)
- Number the reasons that Rukmani chose Old Granny as matchmaker. (1. old; 2. experienced; 3. knew very well what to look for; 4. never lacked patience)
- Go to lines 11 and 12. Mark the past perfect verb phrase. (had not traded)
- Go to line 14. Mark the synonym of *payment.* (dowry)
- Mark the amount of money in the dowry. (one hundred rupees)
- Underline the simile that compares Ira to a flower. (A maiden like a flower) Circle the word indicating it is a simile. (like)
- Go to lines 16 and 17. Mark Rukmani's reason for thinking Old Granny may hold a grudge. (Although Biswas takes my produce and for you there has been nothing.)
- Go to line 18. Mark the name of Ira's mother. (Rukmani)
- Go to line 21. Mark the name of Ira's father. (Nathan)
- Go to line 22. Mark the word that means "deserving qualities." (merits)
- Go to line 24. Mark the requirement for a groom that is an indication that Ira's family was not wealthy and needed to rely on the groom's family to take care of Ira. (inherit a good portion of land)

Have students read lines 25–45 according to the option that you chose.

When most of the students are finished, continue with the entire class. Let's see how well you understood the next section.

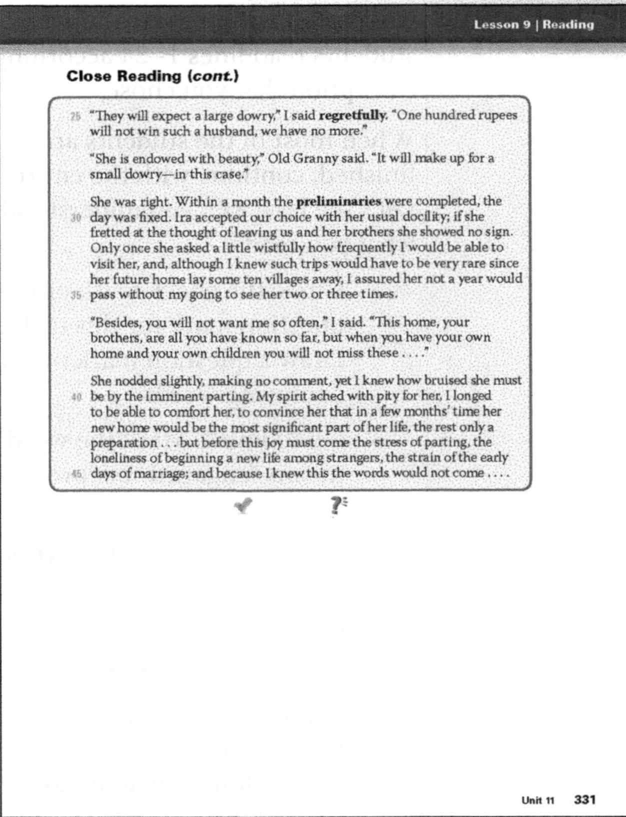
Lesson 9 | Reading

Close Reading (*cont.*)

"They will expect a large dowry," I said **regretfully**. "One hundred rupees will not win such a husband, we have no more."

"She is endowed with beauty," Old Granny said. "It will make up for a small dowry—in this case."

She was right. Within a month the **preliminaries** were completed, the day was fixed. Ira accepted our choice with her usual docility; if she fretted at the thought of leaving us and her brothers she showed no sign. Only once she asked a little wistfully how frequently I would be able to visit her, and, although I knew such trips would have to be very rare since her future home lay some ten villages away, I assured her not a year would pass without my going to see her two or three times.

"Besides, you will not want me so often," I said. "This home, your brothers, are all you have known so far, but when you have your own home and your own children you will not miss these . . . ."

She nodded slightly, making no comment, yet I knew how bruised she must be by the imminent parting. My spirit ached with pity for her, I longed to be able to comfort her, to convince her that in a few months' time her new home would be the most significant part of her life, the rest only a preparation . . . but before this joy must come the stress of parting, the loneliness of beginning a new life among strangers, the strain of the early days of marriage; and because I knew this the words would not come . . . .

Unit 11 331

- Circle the check mark or the question mark for this text. Draw a question mark over any confusing words.
- Go to line 27. Mark the thing Ira has that will make up for the lack of money. (beauty) Does this make her similar to or different from the bride in *The Good Earth*? (different)
- Go to the third paragraph. Mark the evidence that Ira is scared. (asked a little wistfully how frequently I would be able to visit her)
- In the same paragraph, mark the evidence that Ira is acting like it doesn't bother her. (usual docility; she showed no sign)
- Go to line 34. Mark the synonym of *guaranteed*. (assured)
- Go to line 39. Mark the word that means "hurt." (bruised)
- Go to line 40. Mark the word that means "happening soon." (imminent)
- Number the feelings that Rukmani is predicting before Ira can feel joy. (1. stress; 2. loneliness; 3. strain)
- Go to line 45. Mark the line that indicates Rukmani had been married at a young age and gone through a similar ordeal. (and because I knew this the words would not come)
- Think about Rukmani's point of view of Ira's marriage. Compare that with Ira's point of view. In the margin, write whether their points of view are the same or different. (same)

Have students read lines 46–73 according to the option that you chose.

When most of the students are finished, continue with the entire class. Let's see how well you understood what you read.

- Circle the check mark or the question mark for this text. Draw a question mark over any confusing words.
- Look at the first sentence. Is it a complete sentence? (no) What is missing? (a verb) Why would the author do this? (possible responses: for impact; to get to the point; to keep from using the passive voice)
- Go to line 47. Mark the location of Ira's bath. (river)
- Go to line 49. Mark the synonym of *thin*. (slender)
- Mark two things that Ira wore on her wedding day. (1. red sari; 2. kohl)
- Go to line 50. Mark the words indicating that the kohl made her look even younger. (the years fell away more)
- Go to line 54. Mark the punctuation used in place of a colon to indicate that examples are coming. (em dash)
- Go to line 55. Cross out the musicians that Ira's family could not afford. (a flautist, a harmonium player)
- Go to line 57. Mark the past perfect verb phrase used to indicate that something had been done in the past but was stopped because of another event. (had I not saved) What event caused the past action to stop? (wedding)
- Go to line 59. Mark the words that represent food and favors in the Indian culture. (dhal, ghee, betel leaf, areca nuts, copra) Circle the noncount nouns. (rice, dhal, ghee, betel leaf, copra) How do you know? (the pluralization of nuts)
- Go to line 62. Mark the evidence that Rukmani was proud of her wedding feast. (wink)
- Mark the simile that is extended by a clarification. (for men are like children and must grab what they see)
- Go to line 65. Mark the word that means "witty remark." (sally)
- Go to line 68. Mark the word *him*. Draw an arrow to the person *him* is referring to. (Arjun)
- Go to line 71. Mark the transition word that means "however." (nevertheless)
- Mark the past perfect verb phrase. (had made)
- Mark the word that means "a store or supply of something." (provision)

Lesson 9 | Reading

Close Reading (*cont.*)

Wedding day. Women from the village came to assist. Janaki, Kali, many I hardly knew. We went with Ira to the river and, when she was freshly bathed, put on her the red sari I had worn at my own wedding. Its rich heavy folds made her look more slender than she was, made her look a child . . . . I darkened her eyes with kohl and the years fell away more; she was so pitifully young I could hardly believe she was to be married, today.

The bridegroom arrived; his parents, his relatives, our friends, the priests. The drummer arrived and squatted outside awaiting permission to begin; the fiddler joined him. There should have been other musicians—a flautist, a harmonium player, but we could not afford these. Nathan would have nothing we could not pay for. No debts, he insisted, no debts. But I grudged Ira nothing: had I not saved from the day of her birth so that she should marry well? Now I brought out the stores I had put by month after month—rice and dhal and ghee, jars of oil, betel leaf, areca nuts, chewing tobacco and copra.

"I didn't know you had so much," said Nathan in amazement.

"And if you had there would be little enough," I said with a wink at the women, "for men are like children and must grab what they see."

I did not wait for his **retort**, hearing only the laughter that greeted his sally, but went out to speak to the drummer. Arjun, my eldest son, was sitting next to the man, cautiously tapping the drum with three fingers as he had been shown.

"There is plenty of food inside," I said to him. "Go and eat while there is still some left."

"I can eat no more," he replied. "I have been feasting all day."

Nevertheless he had made provision for the morrow: I saw in his lap a bundle bulging with food; sugar syrup and butter had soaked through the cloth patchily.

✔ ?

332 Unit 11

- Mark the word that means “the next day.” (morrow)
- On the same line, mark the punctuation used in place of a semicolon because the second sentence is an illustration or explanation of the first sentence. (colon)

Have students read lines 74 to the end according to the option that you chose.

When most of the students are finished, continue with the entire class. Let’s see how well you understood this section.

- Circle the check mark or the question mark for this text. Draw a question mark over any confusing words.
- Go to line 76. Mark the word that refers to Arjun’s food hoarding. (bundle)
- Go to line 77. Mark the word that means “nervously.” (uneasily)
- Go to line 81. Mark the past perfect verb phrase. (had collected)
- Go to line 83. Mark the idiom that means “almost unbelievable.” (too good to be true)
- Go to lines 85 and 86. Mark the foreshadowing evidence that Granny’s reputation could get tarnished. (none of us could look into the future)
- Go to line 88. Mark the word that means “bed-like platform strapped to poles for ease of carrying the bride and groom overhead.” (palanquin)
- Go to line 92. Mark the word that indicates people were feeling what the couple was feeling. (vicariously)
- Go to line 101. Mark the path of the procession. (Past the fields, through the winding streets, the bullock cart)
- Go to line 105. Mark the words that mean that the crowd thinned. (throng melted)
- Go to line 109. Mark the evidence that their house is made from the earth. (mud)
- Go to line 110. Mark the word that means “banana-like tree.” (plantain)
- Go to line 111. Mark the word that means “male cows.” (bullocks)
- Go to line 114. Mark evidence that Rukmani was missing Ira. (Ira no longer slept under our roof.)

Have partners compare text markings and correct any errors.

Lesson 9 | Reading

Close Reading (*cont.*)

“Join your brothers,” I said, **hoisting** him up. “The drummer is going to be busy.”

He ran off, clinging tightly to his bundle. The wedding music began. Bride and groom were sitting uneasily side by side, Ira stiff in the heavy embroidered sari, white flowers in her hair, very pale. They did not look at each other. About them were packed some fourteen or fifteen people—the hut could hold no more. The remainder sat outside on palm leaves the boys had collected.

“What a good match,” everybody said. “Such a fine boy, such a beautiful girl, too good to be true.” It was indeed. Old Granny went about beaming: it was she who had brought the two parties together; her reputation as a matchmaker would be higher than ever. We none of us could look into the future.

So they were married. As the light faded two youths appeared bearing a palanquin for the newly married couple, lowered it at the entrance to the hut for them to step into. Now that it was time to go, Ira looked scared, she hesitated a little before entering: but already a dozen willing hands had lifted her in. The crowd, full of good feeling, replete with food and drunk with the music, vicariously excited, pressed round, eagerly thrusting over their heads garland after garland of flowers; the earth was spattered with petals. In the midst of the crush Nathan and I, Nathan holding out his hands to Ira in blessing, she with dark head bent low to receive it. Then the palanquin was lifted up, the torchbearers closed in, the musicians took their places. We followed on foot behind, relatives, friends, well-wishers and hangers-on. Several children had added themselves to the company; they came after, jigging about in high glee, noisy and excited: a long, ragged tail-end to the **procession**.

Past the fields, through the winding streets of the village we went, the bobbing palanquin ahead of us. Until we came at last to where, at a **decorous** distance, the bullock cart waited to take them away.

Then it was all over, the bustle, the laughter, the noise. The wedding guests departed. The throng melted. After a while we walked back together to our hut. Our sons, tired out, were humped together asleep, the youngest clutching a sugary confection in one sticky fist. Bits of food lay everywhere. I swept the floor clean and strewed it with leaves. The walls showed cracks, and clods of mud had fallen where people had bumped against them, but these I left for patching in the morning. The used plantain leaves I stacked in one heap—they would do for the bullocks. The stars were pale in the greying night before I lay down beside my husband. Not to sleep but to think. For the first time since her birth, Ira no longer slept under our roof.

✔ ?

Unit 11 333

Summarize and Scrutinize

Unit 11 Background Information can be found in the Teacher Resources online.

Direct students to page 334 in their Student Books. Read the instructions for Part A aloud, and have pairs summarize the texts. Then, have partners switch summaries and determine if the partner's summary is accurate and complete.

Read the instructions for Part B aloud. Regroup students who have chosen the same text, and have groups answer the questions about the setting and characters.

> **Note:** Students will need to have seen the Unit 11 video or been given access to the Background Information to complete the assignment.

Bring partners back together, and have them discuss the differences in the settings and messages of the respective stories.

Lesson 9 | Reading

Summarize and Scrutinize Answers will vary.

Part A

Write an objective summary of one text from this unit. Your partner should choose the other text.

Passage: ____________________

Part B

Use information from the story and the unit video to respond to the following prompts.

Describe the historical and cultural setting, i.e., what was life like in the culture at the time the book was set? ____________________

Describe the life of the main family in the story. Be sure to include their financial situation.

In what way did the setting of the story affect the thoughts and feelings of the characters and the message of the story? ____________________

334 Unit 11

Unit 11 Lesson 10

Lesson Opener

Before the lesson, choose one of the following activities to write on the board or post on the *LANGUAGE! Live* Class Wall online.

- *Write four sentences with at least two vocabulary words in each. Show you know the meanings. (eligible, justification, grudge, assess, regretfully, preliminaries, retort, hoist, procession, decorous)*
- *Dress your avatar as though you were meeting a person who was paid by your parents to marry you. Explain your choices.*
- *Summarize your point of view of arranged marriages.*

Vocabulary

Objective

- Review key passage vocabulary.

Recontextualize Passage Vocabulary

Direct students to page 318 in their Student Books. Use the following questions to review the vocabulary words from the excerpt from *Nectar in a Sieve.*

Key Passage Vocabulary: Excerpt from *Nectar in a Sieve*

Read each word. Write it in column 3. Then, circle a number to rate your knowledge of the word.

Read the Word	Part of Speech	Write the Word	Rate the Word
eligible	(adj)	eligible	0 1 2 3
justification	(n)	justification	0 1 2 3
grudge	(n)	grudge	0 1 2 3
assess	(v)	assess	0 1 2 3
regretfully	(adv)	regretfully	0 1 2 3
preliminaries	(n)	preliminaries	0 1 2 3
retort	(n)	retort	0 1 2 3
hoist	(v)	hoist	0 1 2 3
procession	(n)	procession	0 1 2 3
decorous	(adj)	decorous	0 1 2 3

318 Unit 11

- Your dog is finicky. Before you give him a bath, you have to turn on his favorite Beatles song, give him two treats, and do your special handshake. If you don't do these things, he hides under the bed. Are these activities *preliminaries*? (yes) Mr. Matson is famous for jumping right into a lesson without conducting any "class business" first. Does he conduct *preliminaries*? (no) Before you can join the dance team, you have to show that you are skilled in ballet, tap, jazz, and hip-hop. These demonstrations are what? (preliminaries)
- You sit a perfect red autumn leaf on the ground and watch it glow. Are you *hoisting* the leaf? (no) You lug the last bag of canned goods into the soup kitchen pantry and shove it onto the shelf. Have you *hoisted* it? (yes) You are helping build a house for a family in need. You're in charge of the pallets of shingles for the roof. How do you get the pallets up to the guys on the roof? (hoist them)
- You can only buy one jacket, but you like two. You hold them side by side, think about the pros and cons of each one, and compare their prices. Are you *assessing* the jackets? (yes) Without thinking, you jump right into the swimming pool. Have you *assessed* the temperature? (no) You take a quiz in a magazine that will tell you what kind of personality you have. The quiz will what? (assess your personality type)

- Only juniors and seniors can try out for drum major. Are you *eligible* for this position? (Responses will vary.) People with perfect attendance can enter their names for a $100 raffle. Are you *eligible*? (Responses will vary.) The drama club is looking for a Chihuahua to play the role of a rich woman's dog in the upcoming play. Your Labrador-German Shepherd mix is not what? (eligible for the part)
- Your uncle belches after every meal and insists that it's natural. Is this a *decorous* habit? (no) Retired teacher Mrs. Estrada is being given an award during assembly. The senior class president gives her a little bow, offers his arm, and escorts her to the stage. Are his actions *decorous*? (yes) If you aren't sure how to behave in a given situation, it's probably best to err on the side of good manners and use what kind of words and actions? (decorous)
- You politely decline an invitation to a meeting of the earthworm society, and then you do a little dance to celebrate. Did you say "no" to the invitation *regretfully*? (no) You need a seven to win the game, but you roll a three. Do you make your final move *regretfully*? (yes) Your friends are having a movie-watching marathon, but you're stuck at home with the flu. You text them to have fun without you. How do you send the text? (regretfully)
- "Come here," you say to your niece. She responds, "Nanny, nanny, boo, boo." Is this a *retort*? (yes) You ask if you can have half of your friend's sandwich. She shrugs and hands you a half. Is this a *retort*? (no) The bus driver is in a bad mood. Sometimes she lets you off close to your house if you ask, but today you stay quiet. You don't want to hear her what? (retort)
- Your aunt offers you her awful banana pudding. You say you can't eat it because you have a toothache. Is this a true *justification* for saying no to the pudding? (no) Your dad is driving 20 miles over the speed limit. Does the police officer have *justification* for pulling him over? (yes) Your friend's feelings are hurt because her boyfriend stopped texting. Then, she finds out his phone got crushed by the wheel of a bus. This is a pretty good what for not calling? (justification)
- A complete stranger complimented you yesterday, and you still feel happy about it. Are you holding a *grudge*? (no) Your kitten scratched you yesterday, and today, you won't let her snuggle with you. Are you holding a *grudge*? (yes) Your ex is now dating a friend of yours, but you don't mind; they make a good couple. You don't have a what? (grudge)
- When the ice cream vendor comes onto your street, a mob of kids runs out to meet him. Is this a *procession*? (no) The teams file into the arena for opening ceremonies, wearing their uniforms and carrying team flags. Is this a *procession*? (yes) Your little sister is a flower girl in your aunt's wedding. She's the first one down the aisle. She leads the what? (procession)

Writing

Objectives

- Use multiple texts to write coherently.
- Use a process to write.
- Write a compare-contrast essay.
- Compare and contrast a topic across two texts from different cultures.
- Use a rubric to guide and assess writing.

Six Traits of Effective Writing

Direct students back to page 35 in their Student Books. Reread the Six Traits of Effective Writing.

We will continue to focus on writing with all six traits.

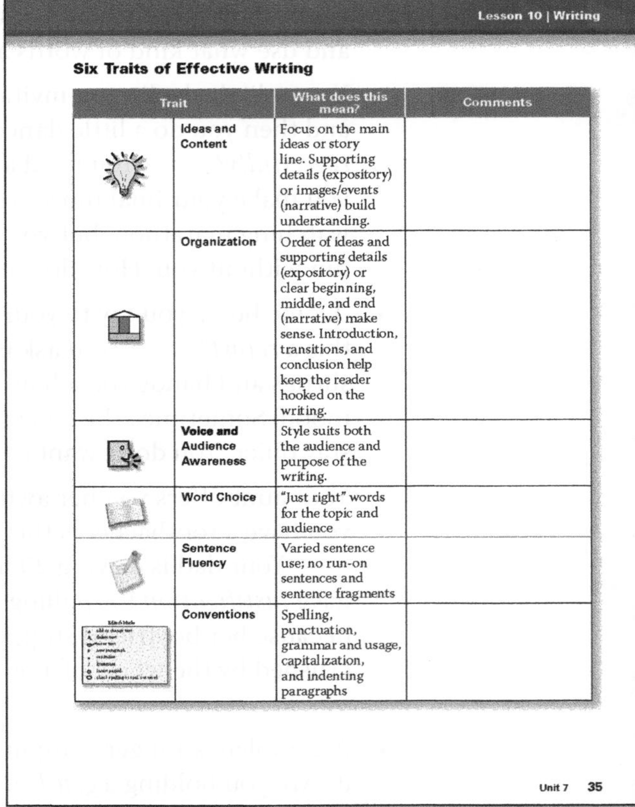

Lesson 10 | Writing

Six Traits of Effective Writing

Trait		What does this mean?	Comments
	Ideas and Content	Focus on the main ideas or story line. Supporting details (expository) or images/events (narrative) build understanding.	
	Organization	Order of ideas and supporting details (expository) or clear beginning, middle, and end (narrative) make sense. Introduction, transitions, and conclusion help keep the reader hooked on the writing.	
	Voice and Audience Awareness	Style suits both the audience and purpose of the writing.	
	Word Choice	"Just right" words for the topic and audience	
	Sentence Fluency	Varied sentence use; no run-on sentences and sentence fragments	
	Conventions	Spelling, punctuation, grammar and usage, capitalization, and indenting paragraphs	

Unit 7 35

Prepare to Write: Compare-Contrast Essay

Direct students to page 335 in their Student Books. Read the instructions for Part A and the prompt.

Part A. Study the Prompt

Guide students through identifying the topic, summarizing the directions, and understanding the purpose for writing.

Part B. Organize Information

Before you can write about the similarities and elaborate on the differences, you need to reexamine what you learned about each culture's approach to arranging a marriage. Work with students to generate the differences and similarities. Help them remember what they learned about the process in each culture and guide their note-taking in the Venn diagram in their Student Books.

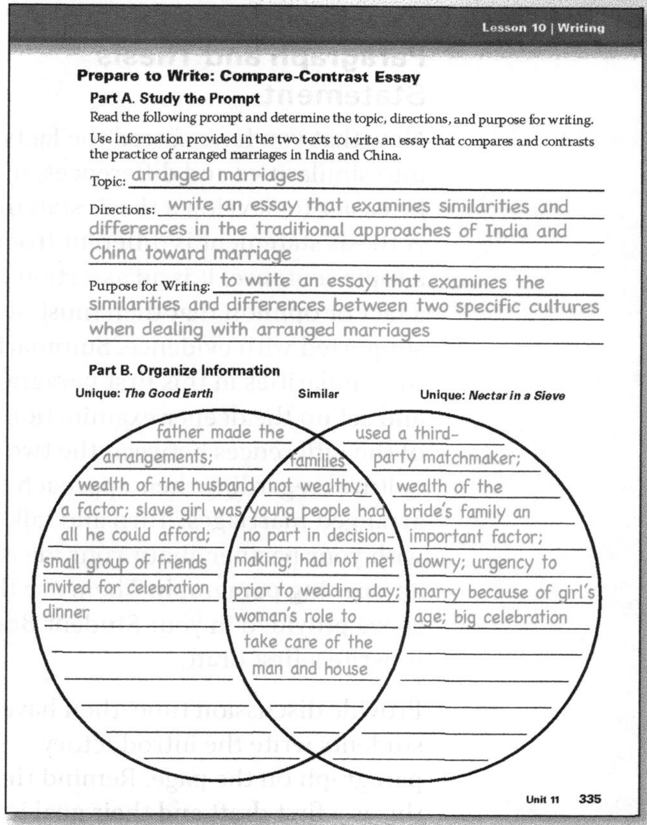

Lesson 10 | Writing

Prepare to Write: Compare-Contrast Essay

Part A. Study the Prompt

Read the following prompt and determine the topic, directions, and purpose for writing.

Use information provided in the two texts to write an essay that compares and contrasts the practice of arranged marriages in India and China.

Topic: arranged marriages

Directions: write an essay that examines similarities and differences in the traditional approaches of India and China toward marriage

Purpose for Writing: to write an essay that examines the similarities and differences between two specific cultures when dealing with arranged marriages

Part B. Organize Information

Unique: *The Good Earth*

father made the arrangements; wealth of the husband a factor; slave girl was all he could afford; small group of friends invited for celebration dinner

Similar

families not wealthy; young people had no part in decision-making; had not met prior to wedding day; woman's role to take care of the man and house

Unique: *Nectar in a Sieve*

used a third-party matchmaker; wealth of the bride's family an important factor; dowry; urgency to marry because of girl's age; big celebration

Unit 11 335

Part C. Write Introductory Paragraph and Thesis Statement

Now that you have sorted the facts into similarities and differences, it will be easier to develop a thesis statement. A thesis statement is different from a topic sentence. It is an assertion of a fact or opinion that then must be supported with evidence. Summarize the similarities in this first paragraph and set up the deeper examination of the differences between the two cultures regarding their approach to arranged marriages. Turn and talk with your partner about your ideas for an opening paragraph. Then, use the space provided in your Student Books to write a first draft.

Provide discussion time, then have students write the introductory paragraph on the page. Remind them this is a first draft and their goal is to get started. If students seem to struggle, provide them with the opening paragraph from the sample essay.

Prepare to Write: Compare-Contrast Essay (*cont.*)

Part C. Write Introductory Paragraph and Thesis Statement

The opening paragraph needs to contain an introduction to the topic. It should state the similarities between the two cultures and set the framework for examining the differences.

Answers will vary.

Marriage can be more of a commitment of assistance and money than a commitment of love. Marriages arranged by parents, without the consent of the betrothed, happen in many cultures. These arranged marriages, while common in many Asian cultures, can have quite different rituals and customs.

Part D. Write Body Paragraph Topic Sentences

Write the topic sentences for the two paragraphs that will focus on the differences within each culture.

Examining practices in the Indian culture: The path to marriage was quite structured and formal for a young girl living in India.

Examining practices in the Chinese culture: Wang Lung's road to marriage was much less formal and celebratory.

Part E. Write Concluding Paragraph

Restate your thesis by using a different topic sentence pattern. Summarize differences and commonalities. Close with a personal perspective to avoid sounding repetitive.

In some cultures, marriage is seen as an obligation or partnership. Romance does not enter the picture. Even though the steps may differ, young Chinese and Indian men and women can find themselves in a marriage arranged for them by others. While arranged marriages may not reflect the current realities of the cultures, these stories provide a vivid portrait of past realities. The idea of arranged marriages is a tough pill to swallow for youth who believe love is the answer and parents should not choose their life partner.

Part D. Write Body Paragraph Topic Sentences

With your thesis stated, now you need to move to developing the differences between the cultures. Discuss the unique elements found in *Nectar in a Sieve* in the first paragraph and those shared in *The Good Earth* in the second paragraph. Getting the topic sentence written for each paragraph will allow you to use the notes from the Venn diagram to develop each paragraph. Talk for a few minutes with your partner and then write your topic sentences. Consider the differences between the two when writing your sentences.

Monitor student progress as they discuss their ideas for topic sentences for the body paragraphs. If students seem to struggle, provide them with sample topic sentences to use as patterns for their essay.

Part E. Write Concluding Paragraph

You can write your concluding paragraph knowing the contrasting elements that will be shared in your body paragraphs. Look at your thesis statement and consider how you can reword it. Try to summarize your main points without simply repeating what you wrote in previous paragraphs. Because we're using two fictional texts to compare these two cultures, how much do you think we know about this practice in these two countries? Do we know if these practices are still in place today? Consider these questions as you write your concluding paragraph and add a perspective outside of the text.

Give students time to work independently to write their concluding paragraph. Call on several volunteers to share their original thesis statement and their topic sentence from their concluding paragraph. If students struggle, use elements from the sample essay to provide a model.

Write

You have worked through all of the steps for writing your essay. Now, use your notes to write the essay.

Have students consult the Six Traits of Writing: Literary Analysis Rubric on page 553 as they write their essay. If they struggle or need additional support in developing their essay, use the following essay as a model.

Six Traits of Writing: Literary Analysis

	Ideas and Development	Organization	Voice and Audience Awareness	Word Choice	Sentence Fluency	Language Conventions
4	States thesis clearly. Develops main ideas fully with elaborations. Direct quotations from text support ideas. All information pertinent to thesis.	Introduction contains thesis statement and cites title, author of work. Ideas logically sequenced. Transition sentences link ideas. Conclusion offers some evaluation of the work.	Strong sense of person and purpose behind the words. Brings topic to life.	Words are specific, accurate, and vivid. Word choice enhances meaning and reader's enjoyment.	Writes complete sentences with varied sentence patterns and beginnings.	There are no major grammar errors. There are few errors in spelling, capitalization, or punctuation.
3	States thesis clearly. Develops main ideas with some elaboration. May lack direct quotations from text to support ideas. Limited amount of irrelevant information.	Introduction contains thesis statement and cites title, author of work. Ideas mostly logically sequenced. Some linkage of main ideas. Formulaic conclusion may not offer evaluation of the work.	Some sense of person and purpose behind the words. Sense of commitment to the topic. Text may be too casual for purpose.	Words are correctly used but may be somewhat general and unspecific.	Writes complete sentences with some expansion. Limited variety.	There are a few grammar errors. There are a few errors in spelling, capitalization, or punctuation.
2	Does not state thesis clearly and/or minimal development of main ideas. No direct quotations to support ideas. Too repetitious or too much irrelevant information.	Introduction may not have clear thesis. Ideas not logically sequenced. Transitions may be missing. May lack conclusion, or conclusion is formulaic with no evaluation of the work.	Little sense of person and purpose behind the words. Very little engagement with the reader. Text may be too casual for purpose.	Word choice limited. Words may be used inaccurately or repetitively.	Writes mostly simple and/or awkwardly constructed sentences. May include some run-ons and fragments.	There are many grammar or spelling errors. There are quite a few errors in capitalization and punctuation.
1	Does not address the prompt or does not develop a thesis. Elaboration lacking or unrelated to a thesis.	No evident structure. Lack of organization seriously interferes with meaning.	No sense of person or purpose behind the words. No sense of audience.	Extremely limited range of words. Restricted vocabulary impedes message.	Numerous run-ons and/or sentence fragments interfere with meaning.	There are many spelling and grammar errors. There are many errors in capitalization and punctuation.

Writing Rubric: Persuasion 553

Writing Rubric: Persuasion

Sample essay:

Marriage can be more of a commitment of assistance and money than a commitment of love. Marriages arranged by parents, without the consent of the betrothed, happen in many cultures. These arranged marriages, while common in many Asian cultures, can have quite different rituals and customs.

The path to marriage was quite structured and formal for Ira, a young girl living in India. Time was seen as the enemy as a sense of urgency surrounded the process. A matchmaker negotiated the arrangements. She leveraged the young girl's beauty against a substantial dowry to win the approval of a handsome, land-owning groom. The bride's family organized a celebration dinner, and all of the guests joined in a formal send-off for the new couple.

Wang Lung's road to marriage was much less formal and celebratory. His father, as opposed to a matchmaker, arranged his wedding. Rather than the bride's dowry, his personal wealth restricted his possible choices. In this culture, the groom's family pursued the arrangement instead of the bride's family, and the prospective couple did not meet one another prior to their wedding day. Only a few close friends and relatives celebrated the wedding at a dinner hosted by the groom.

In some cultures, marriage is seen as an obligation or partnership. Romance does not enter the picture. Even though the steps may differ, young Chinese and Indian men and women can find themselves in a marriage arranged for them by others. While arranged marriages may not reflect the current realities of the cultures, these stories provide a vivid portrait of past realities. The idea of arranged marriages is a tough pill to swallow for youth who believe love is the answer and parents should not choose their life partner.

Evaluate Writing

Direct students to page 337 in their Student Books and read the information in the checklist. Notice that this checklist is a little different. It is specific to writing about literature you have read and using evidence from that literature in your writing. Use the tool to evaluate your writing and make sure you are using good writing technique. **Have individuals quickly assess their writing, then have partners evaluate each other's writing based on the checklist.**

Note: Use Six Traits of Writing Scoring Rubric: Literary Analysis on page 548 of this book to assess students' writing. A printable version is located online in the Teacher Resources.

Lesson 10 | Writing

The Literary Analysis Writer's Checklist

Trait	Yes	No	Did the writer . . . ?
Ideas and Content			clearly state the thesis of the essay
			analyze and evaluate the elements found in the literature
			focus each paragraph on the topic
			include effective support for the thesis by giving details, examples, explanations, and quotations from the texts
Organization			write an introductory paragraph that captures the reader's interest and cites the titles of the works and the names of the authors
			include in the introductory paragraph a clear viewpoint on the topic and a "map" for the essay that follows
			sequence body paragraphs logically and use transition sentences that make clear the relationship between the ideas
			write a conclusion that ties the analysis together and offers an evaluation of the particulars
Voice and Audience Awareness			think about the audience and purpose for writing
			write in a clear and engaging way that makes the audience want to read the work
Word Choice			find a unique way to say things; avoid sounding repetitive
			use words that are lively and specific to the content
Sentence Fluency			write complete sentences
			expand some sentences using the steps of Masterpiece Sentences
			use compound sentence elements and compound sentences
Conventions			capitalize words correctly:
			capitalize the first word of each sentence
			capitalize proper nouns, including people's names
			punctuate correctly:
			end sentences with a period, question mark, or exclamation mark
			use an apostrophe for possessive nouns and contractions
			use commas and/or semicolons correctly
			use grammar correctly:
			use the correct verb tense
			make sure the verb agrees with the subject in number
			use correct spelling

Unit 11 337

Six Traits of Writing: Literary Analysis

Reading

Objectives

- Self-correct as comprehension of text deepens.
- Answer questions to demonstrate comprehension of text.
- Engage in class discussion.
- Identify the enduring understandings from a piece of text.

Revisit Passage Comprehension

Direct students back to pages 327–329 in their Student Books. Have students review their answers and make any necessary changes. Then, have partners share their answers and collaborate to perfect them.

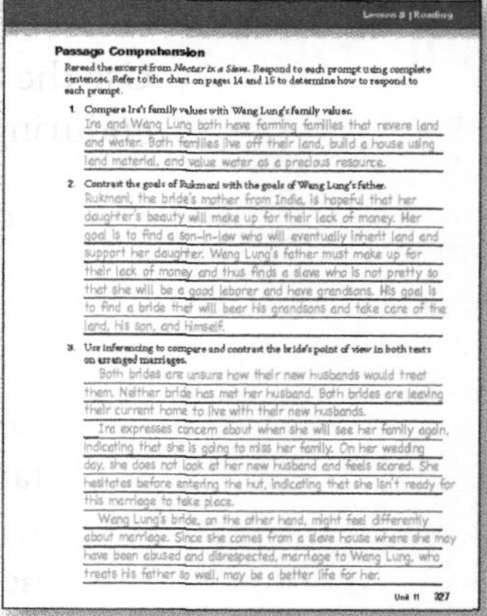

Lesson 8 | Reading

Passage Comprehension

Reread the excerpt from *Nectar in a Sieve*. Respond to each prompt using complete sentences. Refer to the chart on pages 14 and 15 to determine how to respond to each prompt.

1. Compare Ira's family values with Wang Lung's family values.
   Ira and Wang Lung both have farming families that revere land and water. Both families live off their land, build a house using land material, and value water as a precious resource.
2. Contrast the goals of Rukmani with the goals of Wang Lung's father.
   Rukmani, the bride's mother from India, is hopeful that her daughter's beauty will make up for their lack of money. Her goal is to find a son-in-law who will eventually inherit land and support her daughter. Wang Lung's father must make up for their lack of money and thus finds a slave who is not pretty so that she will be a good laborer and have grandsons. His goal is to find a bride that will bear his grandsons and take care of the land, his son, and himself.
3. Use inferencing to compare and contrast the bride's point of view in both texts on arranged marriages.
   Both brides are unsure how their new husbands would treat them. Neither bride has met her husband. Both brides are leaving their current home to live with their new husbands.
   Ira expresses concern about when she will see her family again, indicating that she is going to miss her family. On her wedding day, she does not look at her new husband and feels scared. She hesitates before entering the hut, indicating that she isn't ready for this marriage to take place.
   Wang Lung's bride, on the other hand, might feel differently about marriage. Since she comes from a slave house where she may have been abused and disrespected, marriage to Wang Lung, who treats his father so well, may be a better life for her.

Unit 11 327

Author's Purpose

Direct students back to page 317 in their Student Books. We just finished studying a fiction selection about an arranged marriage. Before discussing our enduring understandings, let's talk about the author's purpose. Why did this author write the text? **Provide sharing time. If necessary, elaborate or clarify their response.** (The author's purpose is the reason that he or she wrote the text. Authors write for different purposes. Authors write to entertain, to persuade, or to inform or to teach. Knowing an author's purpose can help a reader understand a text better. This novel was written to entertain and to increase awareness about arranged marriages in Indian culture.) **Have students correct their answer on their page as necessary.**

Lesson 8 | Reading

Let's Focus: Excerpt from *Nectar in a Sieve*

Content Focus
arranged marriage
Indian culture

Type of Text
fiction—literature

Author's Name Kamala Markandaya

Author's Purpose to entertain; to increase awareness of the traditional Indian culture

Big Ideas
Consider the following big idea questions. Write your answer for each question.

What role does economic status play in marriages today?

How have women's roles changed over time? Have those changes impacted men's roles in family and society?

Literary Preview Checklist: the excerpt from *Nectar in a Sieve* on pages 319–323.

- ☐ Title: What clue does it provide?
- ☐ Pictures: What additional information is added here?
- ☐ Margin Information: What vocabulary is important to understand this story?

Enduring Understandings
After reading the text . . .

Unit 11 317

Enduring Understandings

Reread the Big Idea questions.

What role does economic status play in marriages today?

How have women's roles changed over time? Have those changes impacted men's roles in family and society?

Generate a class discussion about the questions and the answers students came up with in Lesson 6. Have them consider whether their answers have changed any after reading the text.

Use the following talking points to foster conversation. Then, have students write their enduring understandings from the unit.

- Consider this quote from the epigraph, or preface, of the novel *Nectar in a Sieve.*

  "Work without hope draws nectar in a sieve,
  And hope without an object cannot live."

  Both novels on arranged marriages tell a story of hardworking agricultural families trying to make ends meet while struggling with life's adversities. "Work without hope draws nectar in a sieve" means that work without hope is like nectar—the best juice you can imagine—draining from a sieve or a sifter because it is hard to hold on to. Do you think the characters in these two novels are working without hope? Have you ever faced a situation where you felt that you were working without hope, unsure if you would taste the nectar of life before it slipped through the sieve?

What we read should make us think. Use our discussion and your thoughts about the text to determine what you will "walk away with." Has it made you think about a personal experience or someone you know? Has your perspective or opinion on a specific topic changed? Do you have any lingering thoughts or questions? Write these ideas as your enduring understandings. What will you take with you from this text?

Assign online Unit 11 ***Content Mastery*** *quizzes and* ***Power Pass*** *from the Text Training link on the left menu of your teacher dashboard.*

Discuss the enduring understandings with the class. If time permits, have students post a personal response from their enduring understandings to the online class wall.

Unit 12 Unit Plan

Primary Texts:

Part 1 of the Excerpt from *My Sister's Keeper*
by Jodi Picoult

Text type: literature—novel

Part 2 of the Excerpt from *My Sister's Keeper*
by Jodi Picoult

Text type: literature—novel

LANGUAGE! Live Online 

Grammar Practice
- Use phrasal verbs *be*, *do*, and *have* correctly.
- Identify and correct double negatives.
- Determine the meaning of punctuation.
- Identify and correct sentence fragments in writing.

Vocabulary Practice
- Determine the correct usage of multiple meaning words.
- Determine the meaning of foreign words used commonly in English.
- Increase depth of word knowledge through the use of analogies.

Content Mastery
- Demonstrate an understanding of . . .
  - word meaning by answering questions and using words in sentences.
  - phrasal verbs.
  - *be*, *do*, and *have* verbs.
  - the use of negative statements.

Word Study
- Blend, read, and spell multisyllabic words with Latin roots tract, cept, ject, and spect/spec; Latin prefixes contra-/counter-, ob-, and sub-; suffixes -ate and -ity; and Latin prefixes ad-, af-, ac-, at-, as-, ag-, and al-.
- Read connected text to build fluency.

Lesson 1

Reading
- Determine and discuss the topic of a text.
- Determine and discuss the author's purpose.
- Use text features to preview text.

Vocabulary
- Evaluate word knowledge.
- Determine the meaning of key passage vocabulary.

Reading
- Read an excerpt from a novel.
- Monitor comprehension during text reading.

Lesson 2

Vocabulary
- Review key passage vocabulary.

Grammar
- Determine the meaning of phrasal verbs.
- Differentiate between phrasal verbs and prepositional phrases.
- Recognize different functions of the verbs *do*, *have*, and *be*.

Writing
- Correctly use negation in writing.
- Recognize and correct double negatives in writing.

Lesson 6

Reading
- Determine and discuss the topic of a text.
- Determine and discuss the author's purpose.
- Use text features to preview text.
- Identify allusions to historical works (the Bible) in text.

Vocabulary
- Evaluate word knowledge.
- Determine the meaning of key passage vocabulary.

Reading
- Read an excerpt from a novel.
- Monitor comprehension during text reading.

Lesson 7

Vocabulary
- Review key passage vocabulary.

Reading
- Determine how to respond to prompts.
- Use critical thinking skills to write responses to prompts about text.
- Support written answers with evidence from text.
- Make connections between two texts.

Writing Project, Units 10–12: Narrative Writing 

Lesson 3	Lesson 4	Lesson 5
Reading • Establish a purpose for rereading literary text. • Use critical thinking skills to write responses to prompts about text. • Support written answers with evidence from text. • Compare and contrast characters within a story. • Compare the treatment of similar topics across multiple texts.	**Vocabulary** • Review key passage vocabulary. **Reading** • Read literature with purpose and understanding. • Answer questions to demonstrate comprehension of text. • Identify and explain explicit details from text. • Monitor comprehension of text during reading. • Determine the meaning of figurative language. • Identify allusions to other texts. • Identify the purpose of intensive pronouns. • Determine the meaning and purpose for proverbs in literature. • Identify personification. • Determine the meaning of novel words. • Determine the meaning and purpose of punctuation. ** See pg. 481 for additional lesson objectives.*	**Vocabulary** • Review key passage vocabulary. **Writing** • Use text to write coherent paragraphs in response to reading. • Write a descriptive essay. • Analyze character development and the relationship among characters within a story. **Reading** • Self-correct as comprehension of text deepens. • Answer questions to demonstrate comprehension of text. • Engage in class discussion. • Identify the enduring understandings from a piece of text.

Lesson 8	Lesson 9	Lesson 10
Reading • Establish a purpose for rereading literary text. • Monitor comprehension during text reading. • Use critical thinking skills to write responses to prompts about text. • Support written answers with evidence from text. • Analyze how a character in a story affects the plot. • Analyze how character point of view creates suspense. • Identify the points of view of multiple characters.	**Vocabulary** • Review key passage vocabulary. **Reading** • Read literature with purpose and understanding. • Answer questions to demonstrate comprehension of text. • Identify and explain explicit details from text. • Monitor comprehension of text during reading. • Identify puns in writing. • Identify sarcasm in writing. • Determine the meaning of figurative language. • Identify allusions to historical works (the Bible) in text. • Identify indefinite pronouns and determine their purpose. • Determine the meaning and purpose of conjunctive adverbs.	**Vocabulary** • Review key passage vocabulary. **Writing** • Use multiple texts to write coherently. • Use a process to write. • Write a character analysis with text evidence. • Analyze the character development in a story. • Use a rubric to guide and evaluate writing. **Reading** • Self-correct as comprehension of text deepens. • Answer questions to demonstrate comprehension of text. • Engage in class discussion. • Identify the enduring understandings from a piece of text.

Unit 12 Lesson 1

Lesson Opener

Before the lesson, choose one of the following activities to write on the board or post on the *LANGUAGE! Live* Class Wall online.

- *How much pain would you endure to help someone else? Explain your answer.*
- *Write five sentences describing your weekend using participial phrases.*
- *Change the following sentences to active voice:*
  A child was genetically created by her parents.
  The siblings were loved by the parents.
  Decisions were made by parents, not Anna.
  Intense pain was felt by Kate, but little pain was felt by Anna.

Reading

Objectives

- Determine and discuss the topic of a text.
- Determine and discuss the author's purpose.
- Use text features to preview text.

Passage Introduction

Direct students to page 339 in their Student Books. Discuss the content focus.

Unit 12

Lesson 1 | Reading

Let's Focus: Part 1 of the Excerpt from *My Sister's Keeper*

Content Focus
savior sibling
family dynamics

Type of Text
fiction—literature

Author's Name Jodi Picoult

Author's Purpose to entertain; to increase awareness of savior siblings

Big Ideas
Consider the following Big Idea questions. Write your answer for each question.

Should parents be able to make decisions for their minor children? Why or why not?

Is there a true "normal"? Or does the definition of *normal* change with circumstances? Explain.

Preview Checklist: Part 1 of the excerpt from *My Sister's Keeper* on pages 341–349.

- ☐ Title: What clue does it provide about the passage?
- ☐ Pictures: What additional information is added here?
- ☐ Margin Information: What vocabulary is important to understand this story?

Enduring Understandings
After reading the text . . .

Unit 12 339

Content Focus

savior sibling
family dynamics

What do you think you will read about in this text? (Answers will vary.)

Type of Text

Text can be divided into two categories: informational and literary. Discuss the differences. Look at the first page of the text and determine what type of text it is. Write your answer on the page.

Author's Purpose

Have students glance at the text. Who is the author of the text? (Jodi Picoult) Prior to reading, make an educated guess as to what the author's purpose for writing is. After we finish, you will return to this section and revise your answer if you need to. Have students write their responses on the page.

Play the Unit 12 Text Training video found in the Teacher Resources online.

Before we read the excerpt from *My Sister's Keeper,* we will watch a short video to help build our background knowledge. **Play the Unit 12 Text Training video. Have partners discuss what they learned from the video.**

Note: If you are unable to play the video, Background Information about leukemia can be found in the Teacher Resources online.

Read the Big Idea questions aloud.

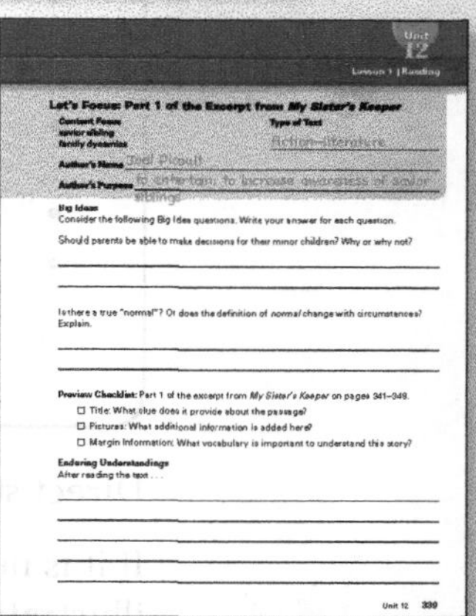
Unit 12

Lesson 1 | Reading

Let's Focus: Part 1 of the Excerpt from *My Sister's Keeper*

Content Focus savior sibling, family dynamics

Type of Text fiction—literature

Author's Name Jodi Picoult

Author's Purpose to entertain; to increase awareness of savior siblings

Big Ideas
Consider the following Big Idea questions. Write your answer for each question.

Should parents be able to make decisions for their minor children? Why or why not?

Is there a true "normal"? Or does the definition of *normal* change with circumstances? Explain.

Preview Checklist: Part 1 of the excerpt from *My Sister's Keeper* on pages 341–349.

- ☐ Title: What clue does it provide about the passage?
- ☐ Pictures: What additional information is added here?
- ☐ Margin Information: What vocabulary is important to understand this story?

Enduring Understandings
After reading the text . . .

Unit 12 339

Big Ideas

Should parents be able to make decisions for their minor children? Why or why not?

Is there a true "normal"? Or does the definition of *normal* change with circumstances? Explain.

As a class, consider the two Big Idea questions. After discussing each question, have students write an answer. We'll come back to these questions after we finish reading the text. You can add to your answers as you gain information and perspective.

Preview

Read the Preview Checklist on page 339. Follow the Preview Procedure outlined below.

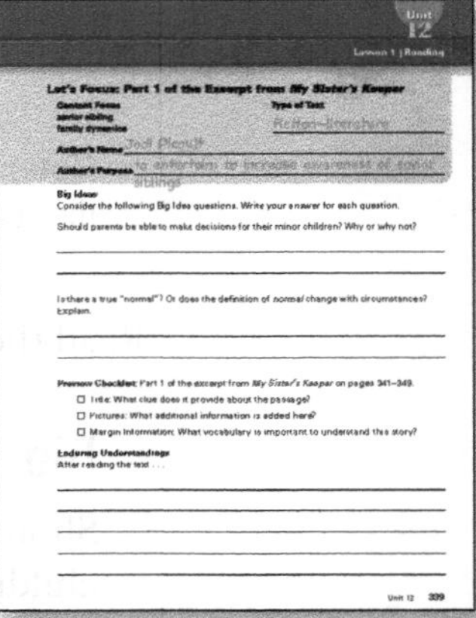

Preview Procedure

- Group students with partners or in triads.
- Have students count off as 1s or 2s. The 1s will become the student leaders. If working with triads, the third students become 3s.
- The student leaders will preview the text in addition to managing the checklist and pacing.
- The 2s and 3s will preview the text with 1s.
- Direct 1s to open their Student Books to page 339 and 2s and 3s to open their Student Books to page 341. This allows students to look at a few different pages at one time without turning back and forth.

Direct students to page 341. Have students preview the text.

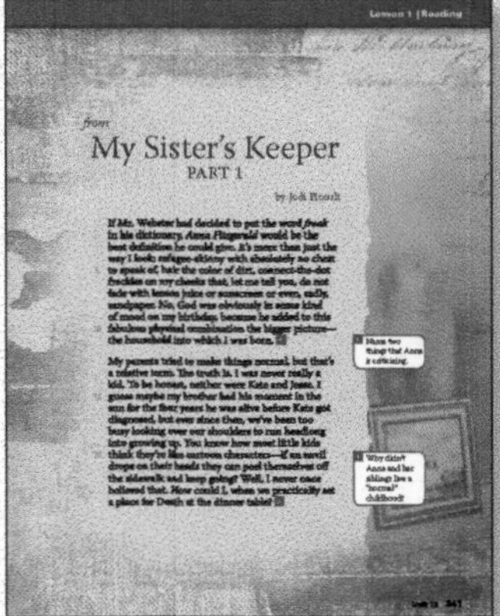

If it is necessary, guide students in a short preview using the illustrations. Explain that in many texts we read, illustrations don't offer much help. This is one of those texts.

Vocabulary

Objectives

- Evaluate word knowledge.
- Determine the meaning of key passage vocabulary.

Rate Vocabulary Knowledge

Direct students to page 340 in their Student Books. Let's take a look at the vocabulary words from Part 1 of the excerpt from *My Sister's Keeper.* I am going to say each word aloud. You will repeat the word and write it in the third column. Then, you will rate your knowledge of the word. Display the Vocabulary Rating Scale poster or write the information on the board. Review the meaning of each rating.

Vocabulary Rating Scale

0—I have never heard the word before.

1—I have heard the word, but I'm not sure how to use it.

2—I am familiar with the word, but I'm not sure if I know the correct meaning.

3—I know the meaning of the word and can use it correctly in a sentence.

Lesson 1 | Vocabulary

Key Passage Vocabulary: from *My Sister's Keeper,* Part 1

Read each word. Write the word in column 3. Then, circle a number to rate your knowledge of the word.

Read the Word	Part of Speech	Write the Word	Rate the Word
acute	(adj)	acute	0 1 2 3
donor	(n)	donor	0 1 2 3
drastically	(adv)	drastically	0 1 2 3
collapse	(v)	collapse	0 1 2 3
assume	(v)	assume	0 1 2 3
circumstance	(n)	circumstance	0 1 2 3
wince	(v)	wince	0 1 2 3
obstacle	(n)	obstacle	0 1 2 3
inferno	(n)	inferno	0 1 2 3
friction	(n)	friction	0 1 2 3

340 Unit 12

Remember, the points are there to help you know which words you need to focus on. By the end of this unit, you should be able to change all your ratings to a 3. That's the goal.

Read each word aloud and have students repeat it, write it, and rate it. Then, have volunteers who rated a word *2* or *3* use the word in an oral sentence.

Preteach Vocabulary

Explain that you will now take a closer look at the words. Follow the Preteach Procedure outlined below.

Preteach Procedure

This activity is intended to take only a short amount of time, so make it an oral exercise.

- Introduce each word as indicated on the word card.
- Read the definition and example sentences.
- Ask questions to clarify and deepen understanding.
- If time permits, allow students to share.

* If your students would benefit from copying the definitions, please have them do so in the vocabulary log in the back of the Student Books using the margin definitions in the passage selections. This should be done outside of instruction time.

acute (adj)

Let's read the first word together. *Acute.*

Definition: If something is *acute*, it is serious and severe; *acute* can also mean "sharp" or "very sensitive." What word means "serious; severe; sharp"? (acute)

Example 1: If you have *acute* pain low on your right side, you may have appendicitis.

Example 2: An *acute* infection needs the immediate attention of a doctor.

Example 3: Dogs have an *acute* sense of smell.

Question 1: A plane crash survivor is lost in the wilderness and hasn't eaten for three days. Is his hunger *acute*? Yes or no? (yes)

Question 2: An ambulance has rushed your neighbor to the hospital with chest pains. Is your neighbor's situation *acute*? Yes or no? (yes)

Pair Share: Turn to your partner and tell about someone you've seen on TV or in a movie who suffered from an *acute* illness or condition.

1

donor (n)

Let's read the next word together. *Donor.*

Definition: A *donor* is a person who gives something in order to help a person or group. What means "a person who gives something in order to help a person or group"? (donor)

Example 1: If you agree to be an organ *donor*, your healthy organs may be given to people who need them after you die.

Example 2: Blood *donors* voluntarily give a pint or more of blood at a time to be stored for later use.

Example 3: *Donors* have given money to the school to help pay for needed supplies and updates.

Question 1: You have your long hair cut off and you give it to an organization that makes wigs for cancer patients. Are you a hair *donor*? Yes or no? (yes)

Question 2: The idea of giving your organs to someone else makes you very uncomfortable. Will you probably become an organ *donor*? Yes or no? (no)

Pair Share: Turn to your partner and share your feelings about becoming an organ *donor*.

drastically (adv)

Let's read the next word together. *Drastically.*

Definition: If something happens *drastically*, it happens quickly and to a great degree. What means "quickly and to a great degree"? (drastically)

Example 1: As the cold front barreled through town, temperatures dropped *drastically.*

Example 2: Every sailor knows that conditions at sea can change *drastically.*

Example 3: Breaking a single bad habit can improve your life *drastically* in other areas too.

Question 1: A train goes around a long, slow bend. Does it change directions *drastically*? Yes or no? (no)

Question 2: Your math grade goes from an 83 to an 84. Has it improved *drastically*? Yes or no? (no)

Pair Share: Turn to your partner. Describe a situation in which your mood is likely to change *drastically.*

3

collapse (v)

Let's read the next word together. *Collapse.*

Definition: If something *collapses*, it falls down or falls apart suddenly. What means "to fall down or fall apart suddenly"? (collapse)

Example 1: If you don't fully extend a folding chair before you sit on it, it might *collapse.*

Example 2: When people get really bad news, they might feel as if the world has *collapsed* around them.

Example 3: It is the job of architects and engineers to make sure buildings don't *collapse.*

Question 1: One of the cheerleaders on the bottom level of a human pyramid gets a leg cramp. Might the pyramid *collapse*? Yes or no? (yes)

Question 2: On a campout, you take your time and put your tent up correctly. Is it likely to *collapse*? Yes or no? (no)

Pair Share: Turn to your partner and tell a funny story about a time something you were working on *collapsed.*

4

assume (v)

Let's read the next word together. *Assume.*

Definition: If you *assume* something, you believe it is true but haven't made sure it is. What means "to believe something is true without first making sure"? (assume)

Example 1: I always *assume* my students will do their best—and am surprised when they don't.

Example 2: People who *assume* the worst about others are often unhappy with themselves.

Example 3: If you *assume* others share your beliefs, you might say something offensive without realizing it.

Question 1: The corner store is open every morning at 8:00 a.m. Can you safely *assume* it's also open at 2:00 in the morning? Yes or no? (no)

Question 2: You see a guy in a green shirt. Should you *assume* green is his favorite color? Yes or no? (no)

Pair Share: Turn to your partner and tell about something you *assumed* was true when you were little.

5

circumstance (n)

Let's read the next word together. *Circumstance.*

Definition: A *circumstance* is an event or situation; the state of things. What means "an event or situation; the state of things"? (circumstance)

Example 1: Having a day off is one *circumstance* that helps people catch up on their sleep.

Example 2: Living in a house with someone who smokes cigarettes is a *circumstance* that can harm a person's own health.

Example 3: Bad rush hour traffic is a *circumstance* of city life.

Question 1: After the orthodontist tightens your braces, she gives you a note saying you should chew gum in school that day to keep your mouth from getting sore. Is this a special *circumstance*? Yes or no? (yes)

Question 2: You hardly ever go out to dinner, but your mom got a raise and wants to celebrate. Is this a special *circumstance*? Yes or no? (yes)

Pair Share: Tell your partner two *circumstances* that helped you reach a goal.

wince (v)

Let's read the next word together. *Wince.*

Definition: If you *wince*, you make a face in response to something painful or unpleasant. What word means "to make a face in response to something painful or unpleasant"? (wince)

Example 1: If you drag your fingernails across a chalkboard, people in the room may *wince*.

Example 2: Sucking on a sour lemon wedge makes me *wince*.

Example 3: When someone is trying to dig a splinter out of your finger, you might *wince*.

Question 1: You give yourself a paper cut. Do you *wince*? Yes or no? (yes)

Question 2: You see hot, fresh cookies on the kitchen counter. Do you *wince*? Yes or no? (no)

Pair Share: Turn to your partner and demonstrate *wincing*.

7

obstacle (n)

Let's read the next word together. *Obstacle.*

Definition: An *obstacle* is an object in someone's way. What means "an object that is in someone's way"? (obstacle)

Example 1: In an *obstacle* course, you have to figure out how to get around or over the objects in your path.

Example 2: A car wreck in the middle of an intersection creates an *obstacle* for other drivers.

Example 3: The defensive line was no *obstacle* for the quarterback; he simply passed the ball over their heads to his wide receiver.

Question 1: You are in the home stretch of a race, and there's nothing between you and the finish line. Is there an *obstacle* in your way? Yes or no? (no)

Question 2: A tree fell across the road in a windstorm, and you have to walk your bike around it. Is the tree an *obstacle*? Yes or no? (yes)

Pair Share: Turn to your partner and name an *obstacle* in the way of you making the honor roll.

inferno (n)

Let's read the next word together. *Inferno.*

Definition: An *inferno* is a fire blazing out of control. What word means "a fire blazing out of control"? (inferno)

Example 1: Bonfires can easily turn into *infernos*.

Example 2: The Great Chicago Fire of 1871 was a true *inferno*.

Example 3: Some forest fires grow into *infernos* that are impossible to contain.

Question 1: It's 103 degrees. The sun is pounding down. You're in the middle of the parking lot for marching band practice. Does it feel like an *inferno*? Yes or no? (yes)

Question 2: You try to light a candle, but the wick is damp. It gives one little spark and then sputters out. Is it an *inferno*? Yes or no? (no)

Pair Share: Turn to your partner and tell about an *inferno* you've seen in a movie or in the news.

friction (n)

Let's read the last word together. *Friction.*

Definition: *Friction* is disagreement or argument between people. What word means "disagreement or argument between people"? (friction)

Example 1: Friends in the middle of a misunderstanding are probably feeling *friction*.

Example 2: When there is *friction* in a household, pets may hide under a bed or in a closet.

Example 3: The best way to avoid *friction* with a loved one is to tell the truth kindly and directly; pouting never works.

Question 1: You're upset with your sister and refuse to pass her the salt at the dinner table. Is there *friction* between you? Yes or no? (yes)

Question 2: All the girls on the volleyball team work well together and support one another. Is there *friction* among the teammates? Yes or no? (no)

Pair Share: Turn to your partner and name two characters on a TV show between whom there is always *friction*.

10

Reading

Objectives

- Read an excerpt from a novel.
- Monitor comprehension during text reading.

Part 1 of the Excerpt from *My Sister's Keeper*

Direct students to page 341 in their Student Books. Now that we have previewed vocabulary, it's time to read.

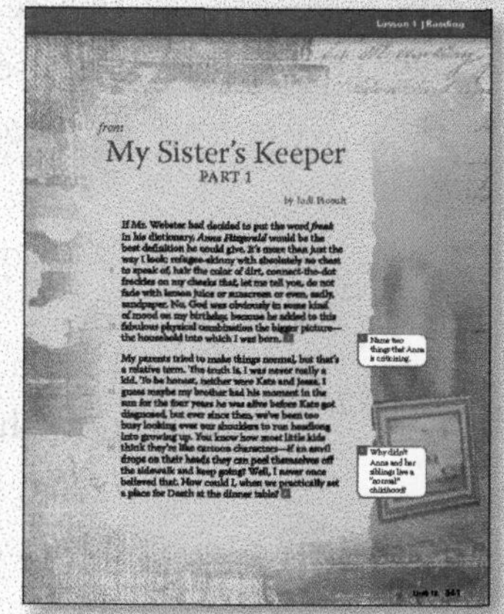

Guiding Students Toward Independent Reading

It is important that your students read as much and as often as they can. Assign readings that meet the needs of your students, based on your observations and data. This is a good opportunity to stretch your students. If students become frustrated, scaffold the reading with paired reading, choral reading, or a read-aloud.

Options for reading text:

- Teacher read-aloud
- Teacher-led or student-led choral read
- Paired read or independent read

Choose an option for reading the text. Have students read according to the option that you chose.

Remind students to pause at the numbers and consider the questions.

If you choose to read the text aloud or chorally, use the text in the following text boxes and stop to ask questions and have students answer them.

SE p. 341, paragraph 1

If Mr. Webster had decided to put the word *freak* in his dictionary, *Anna Fitzgerald* would be the best definition he could give. It's more than just the way I look: refugee-skinny with absolutely no chest to speak of, hair the color of dirt, connect-the-dot freckles on my cheeks that, let me tell you, do not fade with lemon juice or sunscreen or even, sadly, sandpaper. No, God was obviously in some kind of mood on my birthday, because he added to this fabulous physical combination the bigger picture—the household into which I was born.

1. Name two things that Anna is criticizing.

SE p. 341, paragraph 2

My parents tried to make things normal, but that's a relative term. The truth is, I was never really a kid. To be honest, neither were Kate and Jesse. I guess maybe my brother had his moment in the sun for the four years he was alive before Kate got diagnosed, but ever since then, we've been too busy looking over our shoulders to run headlong into growing up. You know how most little kids think they're like cartoon characters—if an anvil drops on their heads they can peel themselves off the sidewalk and keep going? Well, I never once believed that. How could I, when we practically set a place for Death at the dinner table?

2. Why didn't Anna and her siblings live a "normal" childhood?

SE p. 342, paragraph 1

Kate has **acute** promyelocytic leukemia. Actually, that's not quite true—right now she doesn't have it, but it's hibernating under her skin like a bear, until it decides to roar again. She was diagnosed when she was two; she's sixteen now. *Molecular relapse* and *granulocyte* and *portacath*—these words are part of my vocabulary, even though I'll never find them on any SAT. I'm an allogeneic **donor**—a perfect sibling match. When Kate needs leukocytes or stem cells or bone marrow to fool her body into thinking it's healthy, I'm the one who provides them. Nearly every time Kate's hospitalized, I wind up there, too.

3. Why does Anna end up in the hospital with Kate?

SE p. 342, paragraphs 2–4

None of which means anything, except that you shouldn't believe what you hear about me, least of all that which I tell you myself.

As I am coming up the stairs, my mother comes out of her room wearing another ball gown. "Ah," she says, turning her back to me. "Just the girl I wanted to see."

I zip it up and watch her twirl. My mother could be beautiful, if she were parachuted into someone else's life. She has long dark hair and the fine collarbones of a princess, but the corners of her mouth turn down, like she's swallowed bitter news. She doesn't have much free time, since a calendar is something that can change **drastically** if my sister develops a bruise or a nosebleed, but what she does have she spends at Bluefly.com, ordering ridiculously fancy evening dresses for places she is never going to go. "What do you think?" she asks.

4. Why do you think Anna's mom spends her free time like this?

SE p. 342, paragraph 5

The gown is all the colors of a sunset, and made out of material that swishes when she moves. It's strapless, what a star might wear sashaying down a red carpet—totally not the dress code for a suburban house in Upper Darby, RI. My mother twists her hair into a knot and holds it in place. On her bed are three other dresses—one slinky and black, one bugle-beaded, one that seems impossibly small. "You look . . . "

SE p. 343, paragraphs 1–6

Tired. The word bubbles right under my lips.

My mother goes perfectly still, and I wonder if I've said it without meaning to. She holds up a hand, shushing me, her ear cocked to the open doorway. "Did you hear that?"

"Hear what?"

"Kate."

"I didn't hear anything."

But she doesn't take my word for it, because when it comes to Kate she doesn't take anybody's word for it. She marches upstairs and opens up our bedroom door to find my sister hysterical on her bed, and just like that the world **collapses** again. My father, a closet astronomer, has tried to explain black holes to me, how they are so heavy they absorb everything, even light, right into their center. Moments like this are the same kind of vacuum; no matter what you cling to, you wind up being sucked in.

5. Why is Anna's mom worried?

SE p. 343, paragraphs 7–9

"Kate!" My mother sinks down to the floor, that stupid skirt a cloud around her. "Kate, honey, what hurts?"

Kate hugs a pillow to her stomach, and tears keep streaming down her face. Her pale hair is stuck to her face in damp streaks; her breathing's too tight. I stand frozen in the doorway of my own room, waiting for instructions: *Call Daddy. Call 911. Call Dr. Chance.* My mother goes so far as to shake a better explanation out of Kate. "It's Preston," she sobs. "He's leaving Serena for good."

page break

That's when we notice the TV. On the screen, a blond hottie gives a longing look to a woman crying almost as hard as my sister, and then he slams the | door. "But what hurts?" my mother asks, certain there has to be more to it than this.

SE p. 344, paragraph 1

"Oh my *God,*" Kate says, sniffling. "Do you have any idea how much Serena and Preston have been through? Do you?"

6. What is wrong with Kate?

SE p. 344, paragraphs 2–6

That fist inside me relaxes, now that I know it's all right. Normal, in our house, is like a blanket too short for a bed—sometimes it covers you just fine, and other times it leaves you cold and shaking; and worst of all, you never know which of the two it's going to be. I sit down on the end of Kate's bed. Although I'm only thirteen, I'm taller than her and every now and then people mistakenly **assume** I'm the older sister. At different times this summer she has been crazy for Callahan, Wyatt, and Liam, the male leads on this soap. Now, I guess, it's all about Preston. "There was the kidnapping scare," I volunteer. I actually followed that story line; Kate made me tape the show during her dialysis sessions.

"And the time she almost married his twin by mistake," Kate adds.

"Don't forget when he died in the boat accident. For two months, anyway." My mother joins the conversation, and I remember that she used to watch this soap, too, sitting with Kate in the hospital.

For the first time, Kate seems to notice my mother's outfit. "What are you *wearing*?"

"Oh. Something I'm sending back." She stands up in front of me so that I can undo her zipper. This mail-order compulsion, for any other mother, would be a wake-up call for therapy; for my mom, it would probably be considered a healthy break. I wonder if it's putting on someone else's skin for a while that she likes so much, or if it's the option of being able to send back a **circumstance** that just doesn't suit you. She looks at Kate, hard. "You're sure nothing hurts?"

7. What circumstance is Anna referring to?

SE p. 345, paragraphs 1–3

After my mother leaves, Kate sinks a little. That's the only way to describe it—how fast color drains from her face, how she disappears against the pillows. As she gets sicker, she fades a little more, until I am afraid one day I will wake up and not be able to see her at all. "Move," Kate orders. "You're blocking the picture."

So I go to sit on my own bed. "It's only the coming attractions."

"Well, if I die tonight I want to know what I'm missing."

8. Why does Kate want to see the previews?

SE p. 345, paragraphs 4–10

I fluff my pillows up under my head. Kate, as usual, has swapped so that she has all the funchy ones that don't feel like rocks under your neck. She's supposed to deserve this, because she's three years older than me or because she's sick or because the moon is in Aquarius—there's *always* a reason. I squint at the television, wishing I could flip through the stations, knowing I don't have a prayer. "Preston looks like he's made out of plastic."

"Then why did I hear you whispering his name last night into your pillow?"

"Shut up," I say.

"*You* shut up." Then Kate smiles at me. "He probably *is* gay, though. Quite a waste, considering the Fitzgerald sisters are—" **Wincing**, she breaks off mid-sentence, and I roll toward her.

"Kate?"

She rubs her lower back. "It's nothing."

It's her kidneys. "Want me to get Mom?"

SE p. 346, paragraph 1

"Not yet." She reaches between our beds, which are just far apart enough for us to touch each other if we both try. I hold out my hand, too. When we were little we'd make this bridge and try to see how many Barbies we could get to balance on it.

9. How does Anna comfort Kate?

SE p. 346, paragraphs 2–5

Lately, I have been having nightmares, where I'm cut into so many pieces that there isn't enough of me to be put back together.

My father says that a fire will burn itself out, unless you open a window and give it fuel. I suppose that's what I'm doing, when you get right down to it; but then again, my dad also says that when flames are licking at your heels you've got to break a wall or two if you want to escape. So when Kate falls asleep from her meds I take the leather binder I keep between my mattress and box spring and go into the bathroom for privacy. I know Kate's been snooping—I rigged up a red thread between the zipper's teeth to let me know who was prying into my stuff without my permission, but even though the thread's been torn there's nothing missing inside. I turn on the water in the bathtub so it sounds like I'm in there for a reason, and sit down on the floor to count.

If you add in the twenty dollars from the pawnshop, I have $136.87. It's not going to be enough, but there's got to be a way around that. Jesse didn't have $2,900 when he bought his beat-up Jeep, and the bank gave him some kind of loan. Of course, my parents had to sign the papers, too, and I doubt they're going to be willing to do that for me, given the circumstances. I count the money a second time, just in case the bills have miraculously reproduced, but math is math and the total stays the same. And then I read the newspaper clippings.

page break

Campbell Alexander. It's a stupid name, in my opinion. It sounds like a bar drink that costs too | much, or a brokerage firm. But you can't deny the man's track record.

10. What do you think Anna is saving up for?

SE p. 347, paragraphs 1–5

To reach my brother's room, you actually have to leave the house, which is exactly the way he likes it. When Jesse turned sixteen he moved into the attic over the garage—a perfect arrangement, since he didn't want my parents to see what he was doing and my parents didn't really want to see. Blocking the stairs to his place are four snow tires, a small wall of cartons, and an oak desk tipped onto its side. Sometimes I think Jesse sets up these **obstacles** himself, just to make getting to him more of a challenge.

I crawl over the mess and up the stairs, which vibrate with the bass from Jesse's stereo. It takes nearly five whole minutes before he hears me knocking. "What?" he snaps, opening the door a crack.

"Can I come in?"

He thinks twice, then steps back to let me enter. The room is a sea of dirty clothes and magazines and leftover Chinese take-out cartons; it smells like the sweaty tongue of a hockey skate. The only neat spot is the shelf where Jesse keeps his special collection—a Jaguar's silver mascot, a Mercedes symbol, a Mustang's horse—hood ornaments that he told me he just found lying around, although I'm not dumb enough to believe him.

Don't get me wrong—it isn't that my parents don't care about Jesse or whatever trouble he's gotten himself mixed up in. It's just that they don't really have time to care about it, because it's a problem somewhere lower on the totem pole.

11. Why don't Anna's parents have time to care about what Jesse is doing?

SE p. 348, paragraphs 1–4

Jesse ignores me, going back to whatever he was doing on the far side of the mess. My attention is caught by a Crock-Pot—one that disappeared out of the kitchen a few months ago—which now sits on top of Jesse's TV with a copper tube threaded out of its lid and down through a plastic milk jug filled with ice, emptying into a glass Mason jar. Jesse may be a borderline delinquent, but he's brilliant. Just as I'm about to touch the contraption, Jesse turns around. "Hey!" He fairly flies over the couch to knock my hand away. "You'll screw up the condensing coil."

"Is this what I think it is?"

A nasty grin itches over his face. "Depends on what you think it is." He jimmies out the Mason jar, so that liquid drips onto the carpet. "Have a taste."

For a still made out of spit and glue, it produces pretty potent moonshine whiskey. An **inferno** races so fast through my belly and legs I fall back onto the couch. "Disgusting," I gasp.

12. What is Jesse like?

SE p. 348, paragraphs 5–8

Jesse laughs and takes a swig, too, although for him it goes down easier. "So what do you want from me?"

"How do you know I want something?"

"Because no one comes up here on a social call," he says, sitting on the arm of the couch. "And if it was something about Kate, you would've already told me."

"It *is* about Kate. Sort of." I press the newspaper clippings into my brother's hand; they'll do a better job explaining than I ever could. He scans them, then looks me right in the eye. His are the palest shade of silver, so surprising that sometimes when he stares at you, you can completely forget what you were planning to say.

SE p. 349, paragraphs 1–2

"Don't mess with the system, Anna," he says bitterly. "We've all got our scripts down pat. Kate plays the Martyr. I'm the Lost Cause. And you, you're the Peacekeeper."

He thinks he knows me, but that goes both ways—and when it comes to **friction**, Jesse is an addict. I look right at him. "Says who?"

13. Predict what Anna wants from Jesse.

For confirmation of engagement, have partners share two things about Anna's life.

Unit 12 Lesson 2

Lesson Opener

Before the lesson, choose one of the following activities to write on the board or post on the *LANGUAGE! Live* Class Wall online.

- *Write five sentences about Anna using appositives.*
- *Use the word* caring *in three sentences. Use it as a verb in one sentence, a noun in one sentence, and an adjective in another sentence.*
- *Use intransitive verbs to write five sentences about why savior siblings could be a good thing.*

Vocabulary

Objective

- Review key passage vocabulary.

Review Passage Vocabulary

Direct students to page 340 in their Student Books. Use the following questions to review the vocabulary words in the first excerpt from *My Sister's Keeper*. Have students answer each question using the vocabulary word or indicating its meaning in a complete sentence.

Lesson 1 | Vocabulary

Key Passage Vocabulary: from *My Sister's Keeper*, Part 1

Read each word. Write the word in column 3. Then, circle a number to rate your knowledge of the word.

[illegible]	[illegible]	[illegible]	[illegible]
acute	(adj)	acute	0 1 2 3
donor	(n)	donor	0 1 2 3
drastically	(adv)	drastically	0 1 2 3
collapse	(v)	collapse	0 1 2 3
assume	(v)	assume	0 1 2 3
circumstance	(n)	circumstance	0 1 2 3
wince	(v)	wince	0 1 2 3
obstacle	(n)	obstacle	0 1 2 3
inferno	(n)	inferno	0 1 2 3
friction	(n)	friction	0 1 2 3

340 Unit 12

- Anna's sister Kate has an *acute* form of leukemia. What makes it *acute*? (It is acute because it is severe and life-threatening.) From what *acute* awareness does the whole family suffer, according to Anna? (Possible response: They suffer from an acute awareness that death is near.)
- What is Anna's role as Kate's *donor*? (Her role as a donor is to give Kate white blood cells, stem cells, and bone marrow from her own body when Kate needs them.) How does Anna feel about being a *donor*? Why? (Possible response: She seems to know giving Kate what she needs is the right thing to do, but she also resents that she has no say in how her body is being used.)
- If Kate's condition worsens, their mother's calendar changes *drastically*. How does it change? (If it changes drastically, it changes quickly and greatly.) How might a person feel after years and years of expecting everything to change *drastically* and for the worse at any moment? (When a person constantly expects drastic change over a long period of time, he or she might feel despair, fear, exhaustion, and maybe even anger.)
- When Anna and her mother hear Kate in hysterics, what bubble *collapses*? (The bubble that collapses is the one her mother was in, wearing a fancy dress and imagining some other life.) Why does Anna say the "world *collapses*" whenever Kate is in distress? (She means that the world of pretend normalcy shatters—that the harsh reality of Kate's situation comes crashing back into their minds.)

- People mistakenly *assume* Anna is the older sister. Why? (They believe she is older because she is taller than Kate.) Why might this assumption bother Anna? (Possible response: Being thought of as the older sister might bother Anna by reminding her of her great and unwanted responsibilities.) What do her parents seem to *assume* about Anna? (Her parents assume that Anna wants or doesn't mind the responsibilities she's been given.)
- What welcome *circumstance* do Anna and her mother find in the girls' bedroom? (They find that Kate is crying because of a soap opera.) What *circumstance* does Anna wish she and the whole family could return, like a dress that doesn't fit? (She wishes she could return the circumstance of Kate's illness.)
- While the sisters are talking, Kate *winces*. What does she do? Why? (She makes a face because of the pain she suddenly feels.) How is the *wince* different from her earlier hysterics? (She winces in silence.) Why do you think Kate *winces* instead of cries out? (Possible response: She may wince and stay silent because she doesn't want to draw attention to her condition.)
- What *obstacles* does Anna mention on her way up to Jesse's room? (She mentions all the objects blocking the stairway—four snow tires, some cartons, and a desk on its side.) What message do these *obstacles* send visitors? (The obstacles send the message that Jesse doesn't want anyone to reach his room—that he wants to be alone.)
- When Anna swallows the drink Jesse gives her, she feels an *inferno* in her throat. Describe what she feels. (She feels a strong burning sensation.) Why might Jesse want to experience such an *inferno* on a regular basis? (Possible response: The burning sensation might distract him from the emotional pain he's feeling.)
- Anna calls Jesse a *friction* addict. What does she mean? (She means that he's addicted to conflict.) Jesse thinks of Anna as the peacekeeper. How does she show him that she feels *friction* too? (When he calls her the peacekeeper, she challenges his response, disagreeing with his opinion of her.)

Grammar

Objectives

- Determine the meaning of phrasal verbs.
- Differentiate between phrasal verbs and prepositional phrases.
- Recognize different functions of the verbs *do, have,* and *be.*

Phrasal Verbs

In many of the previous units, you have worked with different kinds of phrases. Remember, a phrase is simply a group of related words within a sentence. What are some different types of phrases? (Possible responses: prepositional phrases, adjective phrases, adverbial phrases, appositives, participial phrases) In this lesson, we will work with verb phrases. We know that verb phrases can be made up of a helping verb and a main verb. Phrasal verbs are also a type of verb phrase.

Direct students to pages 350 and 351 in their Student Books.

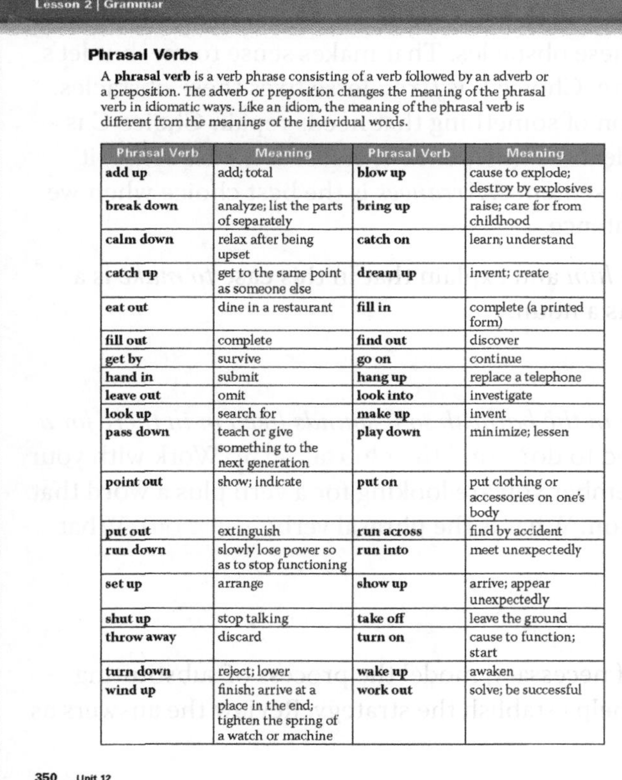

Lesson 2 | Grammar

Phrasal Verbs

A **phrasal verb** is a verb phrase consisting of a verb followed by an adverb or a preposition. The adverb or preposition changes the meaning of the phrasal verb in idiomatic ways. Like an idiom, the meaning of the phrasal verb is different from the meanings of the individual words.

Phrasal Verb	Meaning	Phrasal Verb	Meaning
add up	add; total	**blow up**	cause to explode; destroy by explosives
break down	analyze; list the parts of separately	**bring up**	raise; care for from childhood
calm down	relax after being upset	**catch on**	learn; understand
catch up	get to the same point as someone else	**dream up**	invent; create
eat out	dine in a restaurant	**fill in**	complete (a printed form)
fill out	complete	**find out**	discover
get by	survive	**go on**	continue
hand in	submit	**hang up**	replace a telephone
leave out	omit	**look into**	investigate
look up	search for	**make up**	invent
pass down	teach or give something to the next generation	**play down**	minimize; lessen
point out	show; indicate	**put on**	put clothing or accessories on one's body
put out	extinguish	**run across**	find by accident
run down	slowly lose power so as to stop functioning	**run into**	meet unexpectedly
set up	arrange	**show up**	arrive; appear unexpectedly
shut up	stop talking	**take off**	leave the ground
throw away	discard	**turn on**	cause to function; start
turn down	reject; lower	**wake up**	awaken
wind up	finish; arrive at a place in the end; tighten the spring of a watch or machine	**work out**	solve; be successful

350 Unit 12

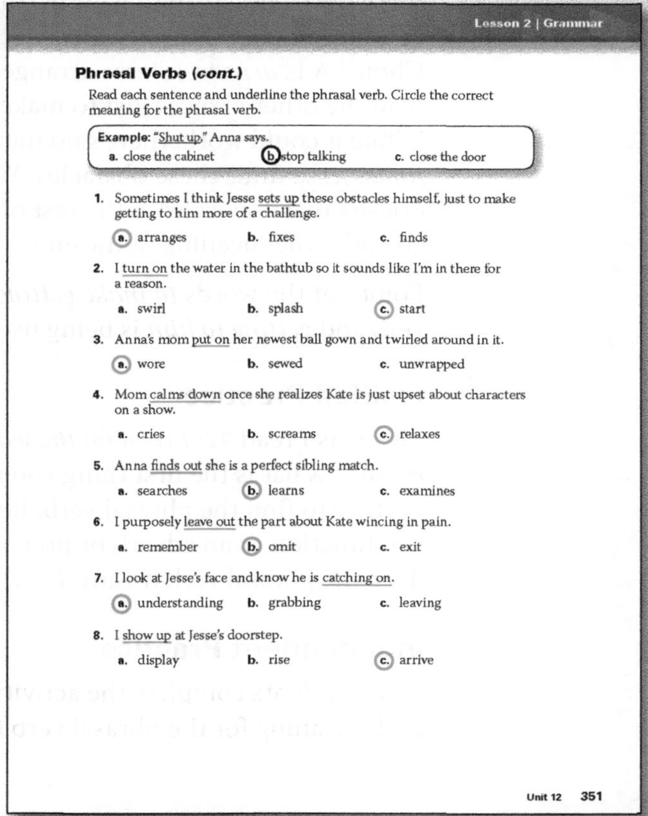

Lesson 2 | Grammar

Phrasal Verbs (*cont.*)

Read each sentence and underline the phrasal verb. Circle the correct meaning for the phrasal verb.

Example: "Shut up," Anna says.
a. close the cabinet (b.) stop talking c. close the door

1. Sometimes I think Jesse sets up these obstacles himself, just to make getting to him more of a challenge.
   (a.) arranges b. fixes c. finds
2. I turn on the water in the bathtub so it sounds like I'm in there for a reason.
   a. swirl b. splash (c.) start
3. Anna's mom put on her newest ball gown and twirled around in it.
   (a.) wore b. sewed c. unwrapped
4. Mom calms down once she realizes Kate is just upset about characters on a show.
   a. cries b. screams (c.) relaxes
5. Anna finds out she is a perfect sibling match.
   a. searches (b.) learns c. examines
6. I purposely leave out the part about Kate wincing in pain.
   a. remember (b.) omit c. exit
7. I look at Jesse's face and know he is catching on.
   (a.) understanding b. grabbing c. leaving
8. I show up at Jesse's doorstep.
   a. display b. rise (c.) arrive

Unit 12 351

Read the information in the chart. As you go through the chart, point out the idiomatic nature of phrasal verbs. Stress to your students that this chart reflects only a handful of the many phrasal verbs that are found in the English language.

Write the following sentences on the board and point out the difference between the phrasal verb and the verb + prepositional phrase.

> *He ran into an old friend.* (phrasal verb)
>
> *He ran into the garage to grab some tools.* (verb + prepositional phrase)

Read the instructions for the activity aloud.

Model

Listen as I read the example: *"Shut up," Anna says. Shut up* is the verb and it is a phrasal verb, so I need to underline it. Now, I have to figure out what it means. When I tell someone to "shut up," I want that person to be quiet or hush. I need to read each choice and see which one means the same thing. Choice A is *close the cabinet* and that's not right. Choice B is *stop talking* and that sounds right, but I want to read C just to make sure. Choice C is *close the door* and that's certainly not right. B, *stop talking,* is the correct answer, so I need to circle it.

Listen as I read #1: *Sometimes I think Jesse sets up these obstacles himself, just to make getting to him more of a challenge.* I need to look for a verb phrase where the verb is followed by a word that could function as a preposition or adverb. I can eliminate the verb *think* because it's all alone. The next verb I see is *sets* and it's followed by the word *up. Up these obstacles* makes no sense, so *up* must go with *sets.* Jesse sets up these obstacles. Turn to your partner and say what you think *sets up* means. Have a volunteer share his or her idea. Let's look at the choices and see what makes sense. Choice A is *arranges.* Jesse arranges these obstacles. That makes sense to me, but let's read the other choices just to make sure. Choice B is *fixes.* Jesse fixes these obstacles. While it could work, there's no mention of something that needs repair. Choice C is *finds.* Jesse finds these obstacles. While as an independent clause it makes sense, it doesn't make sense with the rest of the sentence. *Arranges* is the best choice when we consider the meaning of the entire sentence.

Point out the words *to make getting to him* and explain that in this case *to make* is a verb and *getting to him* is being used as a noun.

Guided Practice

Listen as I read #2: *I turn on the water in the bathtub so it sounds like I'm in there for a reason.* What is the first thing you need to do? (find the phrasal verb) Work with your partner to find the phrasal verb. Remember you are looking for a verb plus a word that can function as an adverb or preposition. What is the phrasal verb? (turn on) What does the phrasal verb mean? (start)

Independent Practice

Have students complete the activity. If necessary, model the process of substituting each meaning for the phrasal verb to help establish the strategy. Review the answers as a class.

Phrasal Verb or Prepositional Phrase

Direct students to page 352 in their Student Books. Read the instructions aloud.

Lesson 2 | Grammar

Phrasal Verb or Prepositional Phrase

Read each sentence and underline the phrasal verb or prepositional phrase. Write the underlined phrases in the correct column in the chart below.

Examples:
Anna ran across several interesting articles in the newspaper.
Kate ran across the street to visit a friend.

1. Nearly every time Kate's hospitalized, I wind up there, too.
2. An abandoned path winds up the mountain and across a small creek.
3. Decorative lights were hung in the trees and around the patio.
4. Kate plays down her discomfort so as not to alarm her mom.
5. Anna hung up after making an appointment to meet Campbell Alexander.
6. When he finds out what Anna is planning, Jesse is stunned.
7. Anna doesn't want to give up the fight for her sister's life, but she is tired of being in the hospital.
8. Jesse runs down the stairs and leaves his garage apartment.
9. Anna shows up at Mr. Alexander's office and expects him to help her.
10. Mom looks into Kate's eyes to make sure she's telling the truth.

Phrasal Verbs	Prepositional Phrases
ran across	across the street
wind up	up the mountain
plays down	across a small creek
hung up	in the trees
finds out	around the patio
give up	down the stairs
shows up	into Kate's eyes

352 Unit 12

Model

Listen as I read the first example: *Anna ran across several interesting articles in the newspaper. Ran* is the verb in this sentence because it answers the *what did Anna do* question. Now, I have to figure out if *ran across* is a phrasal verb, or if *across several interesting articles* is a prepositional phrase. It doesn't really make sense for *ran* to mean an action like jogging over articles in a newspaper. It makes more sense to consider *ran across* as a verb phrase that means "to find or locate." My last step is to write *ran across* in the chart under Phrasal Verbs.

Listen as I read the second example: *Anna ran across the street to visit a friend.* Again, *ran* is the main verb in this sentence because it answers the *what did Anna do* question. *Across the street* answers the *where* question and makes sense in the context of the sentence. I need to write *across the street* in the chart under Prepositional Phrases.

Guided Practice

Listen as I read #1: *Nearly every time Kate's hospitalized, I wind up there, too.* The first verb I see in this sentence is *is hospitalized,* but it's not followed by a word that could function as a preposition or adverb. What is the other verb in the sentence? (wind) *Wind* is the other verb. What word follows *wind*? (up) Is *up* a word that can function as a preposition or an adverb? (yes) It could answer the *where* question. In this sentence, does it make sense to be functioning as part of a phrasal verb or as an adverb or the beginning of a prepositional phrase? (part of a phrasal verb) *Wind up* is a phrasal verb. In this sentence, it means she has to be in the hospital along with her sister. What's your final step? (write *wind up* in the chart under Phrasal Verbs)

Independent Practice

Have students complete the activity. Review the answers as a class.

Verbs: *Be, Do, Have*

The verbs *be, do,* and *have* are verbs you use frequently. They are good examples of verbs that can function in a variety of ways. Often you read them, hear them, or use them as part of a verb phrase.

Direct students to page 353 in their Student Books. Read the information in the charts. To make the review more interactive, read the pronoun and have students provide the correct verb form. Use the sentences below each chart to help solidify the difference between functioning as the main verb and functioning within a verb phrase as a helping verb.

Lesson 2 | Grammar

Verbs: *Be, Do, Have*

Be	Past		Present		Future	
Person	**Singular**	**Plural**	**Singular**	**Plural**	**Singular**	**Plural**
First	I ***was***	we ***were***	I ***am***	we ***are***	I ***will be***	we ***will be***
Second	you ***were***	you ***were***	you ***are***	you ***are***	you ***will be***	you ***will be***
Third	he ***was***	they ***were***	she ***is***	they ***are***	it ***will be***	they ***will be***

Main Verb: She ***is*** an excellent tennis player.
Helping Verb: She ***is practicing*** her serve.

Do	Past		Present		Future	
Person	**Singular**	**Plural**	**Singular**	**Plural**	**Singular**	**Plural**
First	I ***did***	we ***did***	I ***do***	we ***do***	I ***will do***	we ***will do***
Second	you ***did***	you ***did***	you ***do***	you ***do***	you ***will do***	you ***will do***
Third	he ***did***	they ***did***	she ***does***	they ***do***	it ***will do***	they ***will do***

Main Verb: He ***does*** his chores before school each morning.
Helping Verb: He ***does get up*** earlier than his sister.

Have	Past		Present		Future	
Person	**Singular**	**Plural**	**Singular**	**Plural**	**Singular**	**Plural**
First	I ***had***	we ***had***	I ***have***	we ***have***	I ***will have***	we ***will have***
Second	you ***had***	you ***had***	you ***have***	you ***have***	you ***will have***	you ***will have***
Third	he ***had***	they ***had***	she ***has***	they ***have***	it ***will have***	they ***will have***

Main Verb: I ***have*** his letter in my hand.
Helping Verb: I ***have read*** his letter several times.

Unit 12 353

Direct students to page 354 in their Student Books.

Model

Listen as I read the first example: *Jesse is living in the attic above the garage.* My first step is to find a form of *be, have,* or *do* within the sentence and then decide if it's the main verb or a helping verb. The verb will either be an action verb or a linking verb, so I can start by asking *what does Jesse do*? Jesse is living. The third-person singular form of the verb *be* is *is. Is living* is a verb phrase where *is* functions as a helping verb. I underline the phrase and place a check mark in the Helping Verb column.

Listen as I read the second example: *Jesse's room is a mess. Room* is my subject and when I ask myself the verb question *what does it do*? I don't have an answer. In this sentence, the verb *is* is functioning as a connector or linking verb. There is no verb phrase, only the linking verb *is*. I underline the verb and place a check mark in the Main Verb column.

Guided Practice

Listen as I read #1: *Kate has acute promyelocytic leukemia.* What is the first step? (find a form of the verb *be, do,* or *have*) What is the verb in this sentence? (has) Is it part of a verb phrase or is it the main verb? (main verb) Underline the verb. What is the last step? (place a check mark in the Main Verb column)

Independent Practice

Have students complete the activity. Clarify the use of contractions in #7 and #9. Review the answers as a class.

Lesson 2 | Grammar

Verbs: *Be, Do, Have* (cont.)

Read each sentence and underline the form of ***be, do,*** or ***have*** that is used in the sentence. Determine if it is used as a main verb or helping verb and place a check mark in the appropriate column.

Sentences with *be, do,* or *have*	Main Verb	Helping Verb
Examples: Jesse is living in the attic above the garage.		✓
Jesse's room is a mess.	✓	
1. Kate has acute promyelocytic leukemia.	✓	
2. She was diagnosed as a toddler.		✓
3. My mother has long dark hair and the fine collarbones of a princess.	✓	
4. The gown is all the colors of a sunset, and made out of material that swishes when she moves.	✓	
5. My father, a closet astronomer, has tried to explain black holes to me.		✓
6. Her pale hair is stuck to her face in damp streaks.		✓
7. "Preston's leaving Serena for good," she sobs.		✓
8. Normal, in our house, is like a blanket too short for a bed.	✓	
9. "Move," Kate orders. "You're blocking the picture."		✓
10. "So what do you want from me?" Jesse asks.		✓

354 Unit 12

Writing

Objectives

- Correctly use negation in writing.
- Recognize and correct double negatives in writing.

Negative Statements

Let's continue our focus on the verb by examining the correct way to say or write a negative statement. One common way to express a negative involves verb phrases. What do I mean by a negative statement? A negative statement tells what someone did not do or say.

Direct students to pages 355 and 356 in their Student Books.

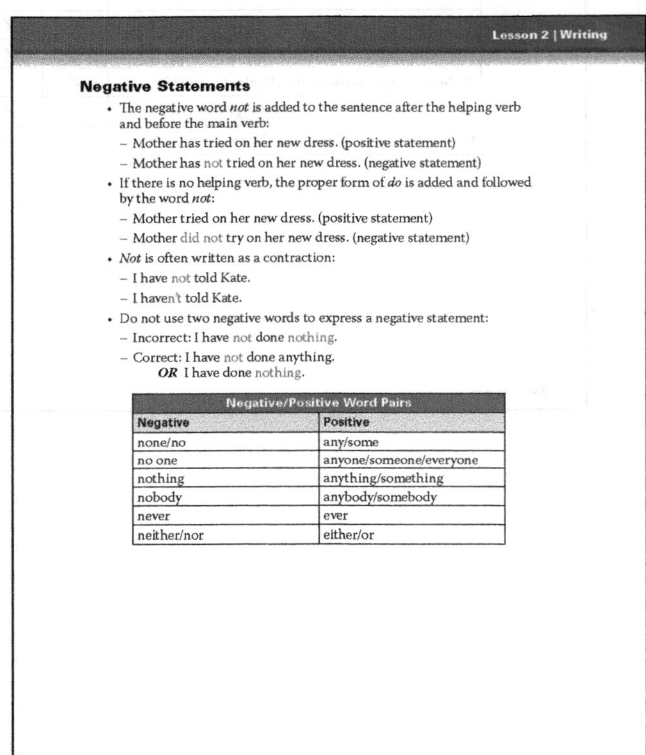

Lesson 2 | Writing

Negative Statements

- The negative word *not* is added to the sentence after the helping verb and before the main verb:
  – Mother has tried on her new dress. (positive statement)
  – Mother has not tried on her new dress. (negative statement)
- If there is no helping verb, the proper form of *do* is added and followed by the word *not*:
  – Mother tried on her new dress. (positive statement)
  – Mother did not try on her new dress. (negative statement)
- *Not* is often written as a contraction:
  – I have not told Kate.
  – I haven't told Kate.
- Do not use two negative words to express a negative statement:
  – Incorrect: I have not done nothing.
  – Correct: I have not done anything.
  OR I have done nothing.

Negative/Positive Word Pairs	
Negative	**Positive**
none/no	any/some
no one	anyone/someone/everyone
nothing	anything/something
nobody	anybody/somebody
never	ever
neither/nor	either/or

Unit 12 355

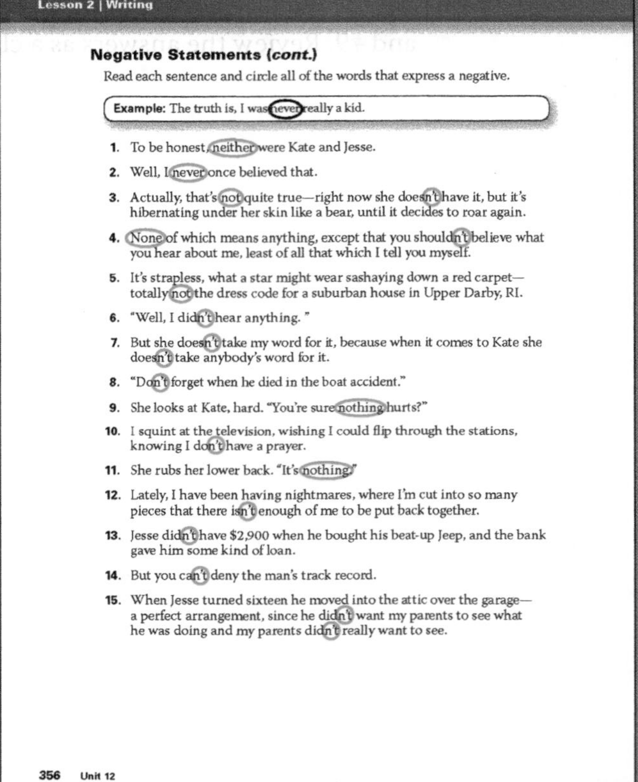

Lesson 2 | Writing

Negative Statements (*cont.*)

Read each sentence and circle all of the words that express a negative.

Example: The truth is, I was never really a kid.

1. To be honest, neither were Kate and Jesse.
2. Well, I never once believed that.
3. Actually, that's not quite true—right now she doesn't have it, but it's hibernating under her skin like a bear, until it decides to roar again.
4. None of which means anything, except that you shouldn't believe what you hear about me, least of all that which I tell you myself.
5. It's strapless, what a star might wear sashaying down a red carpet—totally not the dress code for a suburban house in Upper Darby, RI.
6. "Well, I didn't hear anything."
7. But she doesn't take my word for it, because when it comes to Kate she doesn't take anybody's word for it.
8. "Don't forget when he died in the boat accident."
9. She looks at Kate, hard. "You're sure nothing hurts?"
10. I squint at the television, wishing I could flip through the stations, knowing I don't have a prayer.
11. She rubs her lower back. "It's nothing."
12. Lately, I have been having nightmares, where I'm cut into so many pieces that there isn't enough of me to be put back together.
13. Jesse didn't have $2,900 when he bought his beat-up Jeep, and the bank gave him some kind of loan.
14. But you can't deny the man's track record.
15. When Jesse turned sixteen he moved into the attic over the garage—a perfect arrangement, since he didn't want my parents to see what he was doing and my parents didn't really want to see.

356 Unit 12

Read the information about negatives. Work through the bullets, giving students an opportunity to work with their partners to create negative statements that follow each pattern. Possible sentences to use with students:

- Kate and Anna were talking in their bedroom. (Kate and Anna were not talking in their bedroom.)
- Kate helped Anna when she was sick. (Kate did not help Anna when she was sick.)
- Jesse cleaned up his room. (Jesse hasn't cleaned up his room.)

Work through the chart of negative and positive word pairs, helping students understand how to avoid using a double negative.

Read the instructions for the activity aloud.

Model

Listen as I read the example: *The truth is, I was never really a kid.* Our task is to find words that express a negative, so my first thought is to look for the word *not.* I don't see it in this sentence. What I do see is the word *never.* It is listed in the chart of negative/positive word pairs, so I have circled it. Recognizing words that express a negative help me avoid saying or writing a double negative.

Guided Practice

Listen as I read #1: *To be honest, neither were Kate and Jesse.* What negative word do you see in this sentence? (neither) *Neither* is listed in the chart as a word that can express a negative. What's your next step? (circle *neither*)

Independent Practice

Have students complete the activity. Clarify the use of contractions in #3, #4, #6–8, #10, and #12–15. Review the answers as a class.

Double Negatives

Direct students to page 357 in their Student Books. Read the instructions aloud. Explain that in writing, two negatives make a positive, and this must be avoided.

Model

Listen as I read the example: *Mother hasn't gotten no new dresses today.* That sentence just sounds wrong. I don't need both negative terms in this sentence to properly express the thought. It's important that I can identify the negative terms in this sentence in order to be able to correct it. I can leave the contracted form of *not* and replace *no* with any: *Mother hasn't gotten any new dresses today.* Or, I can take out the contracted form of *not* and leave *no*: *Mother has gotten no new dresses today.* Both of these are correct forms of a negative statement.

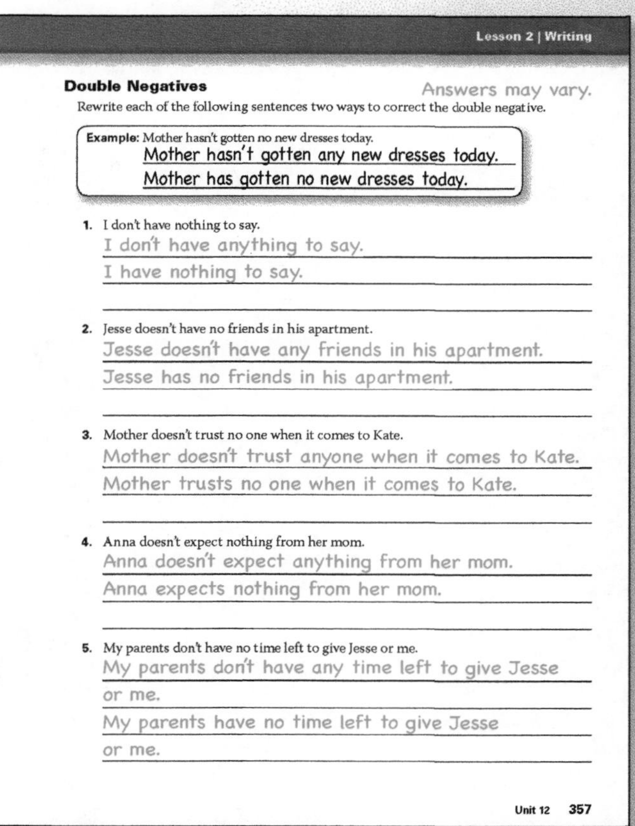
Lesson 2 | Writing

Double Negatives Answers may vary.

Rewrite each of the following sentences two ways to correct the double negative.

Example: Mother hasn't gotten no new dresses today.
Mother hasn't gotten any new dresses today.
Mother has gotten no new dresses today.

1. I don't have nothing to say.
I don't have anything to say.
I have nothing to say.

2. Jesse doesn't have no friends in his apartment.
Jesse doesn't have any friends in his apartment.
Jesse has no friends in his apartment.

3. Mother doesn't trust no one when it comes to Kate.
Mother doesn't trust anyone when it comes to Kate.
Mother trusts no one when it comes to Kate.

4. Anna doesn't expect nothing from her mom.
Anna doesn't expect anything from her mom.
Anna expects nothing from her mom.

5. My parents don't have no time left to give Jesse or me.
My parents don't have any time left to give Jesse or me.
My parents have no time left to give Jesse or me.

Unit 12 357

Guided Practice

Listen as I read #1: *I don't have nothing to say. Don't* and *nothing* create the double negative. How can you correct the double negative and still use *not*? (I don't have anything to say.) Write that as your first corrected sentence. **Pause briefly to give students time to write the sentence.** How can you correct the double negative without using *not* or the contraction *don't*?
(I have nothing to say.) Write that down as your second correction. **Pause briefly to give students time to write the second sentence.**

Independent Practice

Have students complete the activity. Review the answers as a class.

Unit 12 Lesson 3

Lesson Opener

Before the lesson, choose one of the following activities to write on the board or post on the *LANGUAGE! Live* Class Wall online.

- *Write one sentence about Anna's health. Write one sentence about Kate's health. Combine the sentences using a conjunction to create a compound sentence.*
- *Describe a time when you needed someone. Who did you need and what did you need him or her for?*
- *Use present and past participles to explain why you think it is right for Anna's parents to expect her to help her sister in any way she can.*

Reading

Objectives

- Establish a purpose for rereading literary text.
- Use critical thinking skills to write responses to prompts about text.
- Support written answers with evidence from text.
- Compare and contrast characters within a story.
- Compare the treatment of similar topics across multiple texts.

Reading for a Purpose: Part 1 of the Excerpt from *My Sister's Keeper*

It is time to answer some more specific questions. Because critical understanding requires active participation, we are going to read the text again. This time, we will be reading for a specific purpose, which will help us pay attention to details that we may have missed the first time around. Let's read some questions about the text to provide a purpose for rereading.

Direct students to pages 358 and 359 in their Student Books. Have students read the prompts aloud with you.

1. Compare and contrast Anna and Kate.
2. Contrast Anna with Jesse.
3. Cite evidence to prove that Kate's illness is life-threatening.
4. Demonstrate understanding of the relationship between Anna and Kate through an illustration.
5. Cite evidence to prove that Anna is in conflict regarding her sister's illness.
6. Compare the section Black Hole of Control in Unit 10's "Say Yes to Free Dress!" to the Fitzgeralds' black hole.

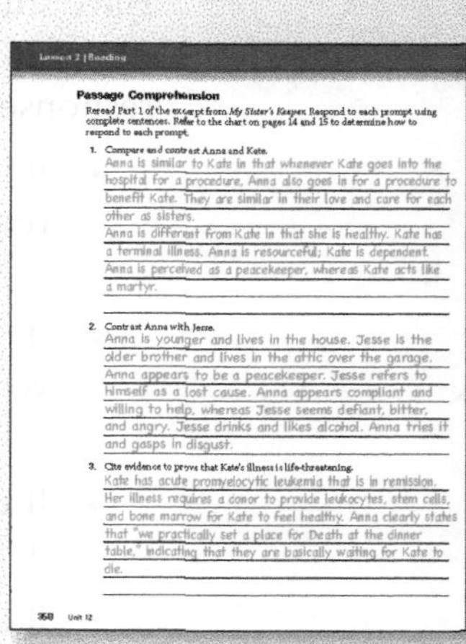

Lesson 3 | Reading

Passage Comprehension

Reread Part 1 of the excerpt from *My Sister's Keeper*. Respond to each prompt using complete sentences. Refer to the chart on pages 14 and 15 to determine how to respond to each prompt.

1. Compare and contrast Anna and Kate.
   Anna is similar to Kate in that whenever Kate goes into the hospital for a procedure, Anna also goes in for a procedure to benefit Kate. They are similar in their love and care for each other as sisters.
   Anna is different from Kate in that she is healthy. Kate has a terminal illness. Anna is resourceful; Kate is dependent. Anna is perceived as a peacekeeper, whereas Kate acts like a martyr.
2. Contrast Anna with Jesse.
   Anna is younger and lives in the house. Jesse is the older brother and lives in the attic over the garage. Anna appears to be a peacekeeper. Jesse refers to himself as a lost cause. Anna appears compliant and willing to help, whereas Jesse seems defiant, bitter, and angry. Jesse drinks and likes alcohol. Anna tries it and gasps in disgust.
3. Cite evidence to prove that Kate's illness is life-threatening.
   Kate has acute promyelocytic leukemia that is in remission. Her illness requires a donor to provide leukocytes, stem cells, and bone marrow for Kate to feel healthy. Anna clearly states that "we practically set a place for Death at the dinner table," indicating that they are basically waiting for Kate to die.

358 Unit 12

Direct students to page 341 in their Student Books or have them tear out the extra copy of the excerpt from the back of their book.

Lesson 1 | Reading

from

My Sister's Keeper

PART 1

by Jodi Picoult

If Mr. Webster had decided to put the word *freak* in his dictionary, *Anna Fitzgerald* would be the best definition he could give. It's more than just the way I look: refugee-skinny with absolutely no chest to speak of, hair the color of dirt, connect-the-dot freckles on my cheeks that, let me tell you, do not fade with lemon juice or sunscreen or even, sadly, sandpaper. No, God was obviously in some kind of mood on my birthday, because he added to this fabulous physical combination the bigger picture—the household into which I was born.

My parents tried to make things normal, but that's a relative term. The truth is, I was never really a kid. To be honest, neither were Kate and Jesse. I guess maybe my brother had his moment in the sun *for* the four years he was alive before Kate got diagnosed, but ever since then, we've been too busy looking over our shoulders to run headlong into growing up. You know how most little kids think they're like cartoon characters—if an anvil drops on their heads they can peel themselves off the sidewalk and keep going? Well, I never once believed that. *How* could I, when we practically set a place for Death at the dinner table?

Name two things that Anna is criticizing.

Why didn't Anna and her siblings live a "normal" childhood?

Unit 12 341

> **Note:** To minimize flipping back and forth between the pages, a copy of each text has been included in the back of the Student Books. Encourage students to tear this out and use it when working on activities that require the use of the text.

Choose an option for reading text. Have students read the text according to the option that you chose.

Options for reading text:

- Teacher read-aloud
- Teacher-led or student-led choral read
- Paired read or independent read with bold vocabulary words read aloud

Passage Comprehension

Write the words *cite evidence, compare, contrast,* and *demonstrate* on the board. Have students read the words aloud with you.

Direct students to pages 14 and 15 in their Student Books. It is critical to understand what the question is asking and how to answer it. Today, we will review four direction words used in prompts.

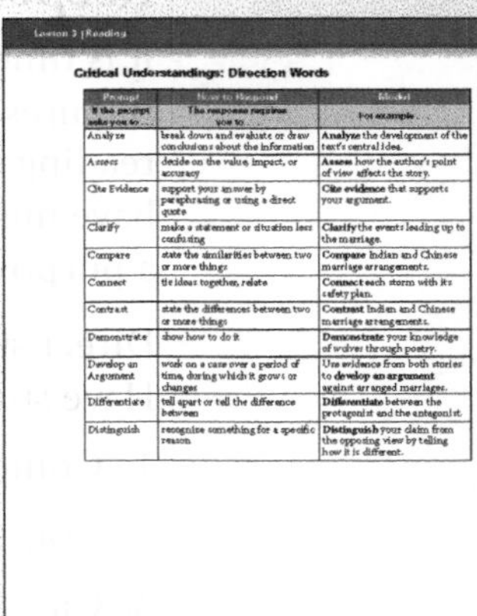

Lesson 3 | Reading

Critical Understandings: Direction Words

Prompt If the prompt asks you to . . .	How to Respond The response requires you to . . .	Model For example . . .
Analyze	break down and evaluate or draw conclusions about the information	**Analyze** the development of the text's central idea.
Assess	decide on the value, impact, or accuracy	**Assess** how the author's point of view affects the story.
Cite Evidence	support your answer by paraphrasing or using a direct quote	**Cite evidence** that supports your argument.
Clarify	make a statement or situation less confusing	**Clarify** the events leading up to the marriage.
Compare	state the similarities between two or more things	**Compare** Indian and Chinese marriage arrangements.
Connect	tie ideas together, relate	**Connect** each storm with its safety plan.
Contrast	state the differences between two or more things	**Contrast** Indian and Chinese marriage arrangements.
Demonstrate	show how to do it	**Demonstrate** your knowledge of wolves through poetry.
Develop an Argument	work on a case over a period of time, during which it grows or changes	Use evidence from both stories to **develop an argument** against arranged marriages.
Differentiate	tell apart or tell the difference between	**Differentiate** between the protagonist and the antagonist.
Distinguish	recognize something for a specific reason	**Distinguish** your claim from the opposing view by telling how it is different.

14 Unit 7

Have students review the words on the board in the chart on pages 14 and 15. Check for understanding by requesting an oral response to the following questions.

- If the prompt asks you to *cite evidence,* the response requires you to . . . (support your answer by paraphrasing or using a direct quote).
- If the prompt asks you to *compare,* the response requires you to . . . (state the similarities between two or more things).
- If the prompt asks you to *contrast,* the response requires you to . . . (state the differences between two or more things).
- If the prompt asks you to *demonstrate,* the response requires you to . . . (show how to do it).

Direct students to pages 358 and 359 in their Student Books.

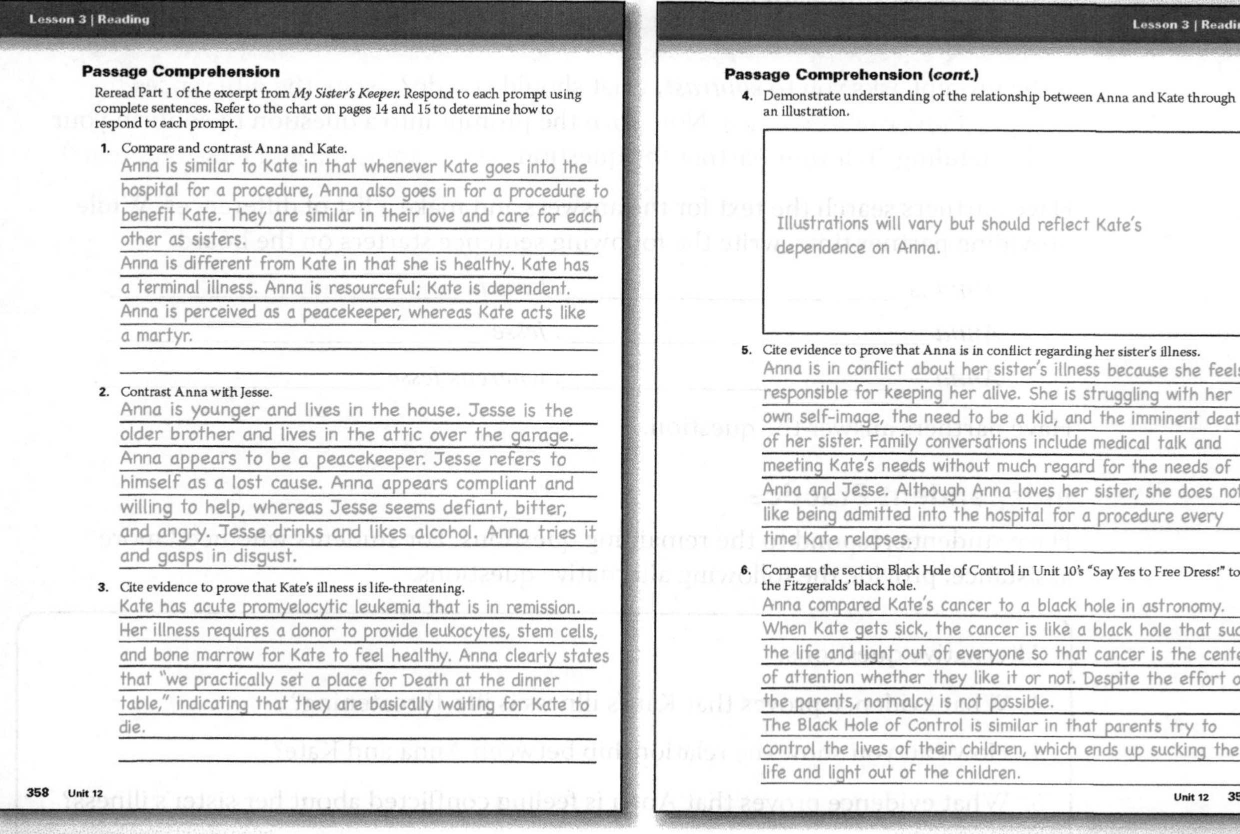

Lesson 3 | Reading

Passage Comprehension

Reread Part 1 of the excerpt from *My Sister's Keeper.* Respond to each prompt using complete sentences. Refer to the chart on pages 14 and 15 to determine how to respond to each prompt.

1. Compare and contrast Anna and Kate.
   Anna is similar to Kate in that whenever Kate goes into the hospital for a procedure, Anna also goes in for a procedure to benefit Kate. They are similar in their love and care for each other as sisters.
   Anna is different from Kate in that she is healthy. Kate has a terminal illness. Anna is resourceful; Kate is dependent. Anna is perceived as a peacekeeper, whereas Kate acts like a martyr.
2. Contrast Anna with Jesse.
   Anna is younger and lives in the house. Jesse is the older brother and lives in the attic over the garage. Anna appears to be a peacekeeper. Jesse refers to himself as a lost cause. Anna appears compliant and willing to help, whereas Jesse seems defiant, bitter, and angry. Jesse drinks and likes alcohol. Anna tries it and gasps in disgust.
3. Cite evidence to prove that Kate's illness is life-threatening.
   Kate has acute promyelocytic leukemia that is in remission. Her illness requires a donor to provide leukocytes, stem cells, and bone marrow for Kate to feel healthy. Anna clearly states that "we practically set a place for Death at the dinner table," indicating that they are basically waiting for Kate to die.

358 Unit 12

Lesson 3 | Reading

Passage Comprehension (*cont.*)

4. Demonstrate understanding of the relationship between Anna and Kate through an illustration.
   Illustrations will vary but should reflect Kate's dependence on Anna.
5. Cite evidence to prove that Anna is in conflict regarding her sister's illness.
   Anna is in conflict about her sister's illness because she feels responsible for keeping her alive. She is struggling with her own self-image, the need to be a kid, and the imminent death of her sister. Family conversations include medical talk and meeting Kate's needs without much regard for the needs of Anna and Jesse. Although Anna loves her sister, she does not like being admitted into the hospital for a procedure every time Kate relapses.
6. Compare the section Black Hole of Control in Unit 10's "Say Yes to Free Dress!" to the Fitzgeralds' black hole.
   Anna compared Kate's cancer to a black hole in astronomy. When Kate gets sick, the cancer is like a black hole that sucks the life and light out of everyone so that cancer is the center of attention whether they like it or not. Despite the effort of the parents, normalcy is not possible.
   The Black Hole of Control is similar in that parents try to control the lives of their children, which ends up sucking the life and light out of the children.

Unit 12 359

Let's practice answering questions written as prompts that require critical thinking.

Guided Practice

1. Compare and contrast Anna and Kate.

There are two direction words in this prompt. If the prompt asks you to *compare*, what should you do? (state the similarities between two or more things) If the prompt asks you to *contrast*, what should you do? (state the differences between two or more things) Now, turn the prompt into two questions to confirm your understanding. Tell your partner the questions. (How are Anna and Kate similar? How are Anna and Kate different?)

Have partners search the text for the answers and make a list of the similarities and differences. While providing partner time, write the following sentence starters on the board.

Anna is similar to Kate in that ______________________.

Anna is different from Kate in that ______________________.

Have partners answer the questions.

2. Contrast Anna with Jesse.

If the prompt asks you to *contrast,* what should you do? (state the differences between two or more things) Now, turn the prompt into a question to confirm your understanding. Tell your partner the question. (How are Anna and Jesse different?)

Have partners search the text for the answers and make a list of differences. While providing partner time, write the following sentence starters on the board.

Anna is ________________. *Jesse is* ________________.

Anna ________________. *Jesse* ________________.

Anna ________________, *whereas Jesse* ________________.

Have partners answer the question.

Independent Practice

Have students respond to the remaining questions. For students who need more assistance, provide the following alternative questions.

Alternative questions:

3. What evidence proves that Kate's illness is life-threatening?
4. How can you show the relationship between Anna and Kate?
5. What evidence proves that Anna is feeling conflicted about her sister's illness?
6. How is the section Black Hole of Control from Unit 10 similar to the Fitzgeralds' black hole?

Unit 12

Lesson 4

Lesson Opener

Before the lesson, choose one of the following activities to write on the board or post on the *LANGUAGE! Live* Class Wall online.

- *Dress your avatar as though you were spending the day with someone who is dying. Explain your choices.*
- *Write five sentences about your weekend using common phrasal verbs.*
- *Write three past-tense sentences describing a day in the life of Anna. Use a form of* be *in one sentence, a form of* have *in one sentence, and a form of* do *in one sentence.*

Reading

Objectives

- Read literature with purpose and understanding.
- Answer questions to demonstrate comprehension of text.
- Identify and explain explicit details from text.
- Monitor comprehension of text during reading.
- Determine the meaning of figurative language.
- Identify allusions to other texts.
- Identify the purpose of intensive pronouns.
- Determine the meaning and purpose for proverbs in literature.
- Identify personification.
- Determine the meaning of novel words.
- Determine the meaning and purpose of punctuation.
- Identify indefinite pronouns and determine their purpose.
- Determine the meaning and purpose of conjunctive adverbs.
- Identify the meaning of verbs in the present perfect tense.

Close Reading of Part 1 of the Excerpt from *My Sister's Keeper*

Let's reread Part 1 of the excerpt from *My Sister's Keeper.* I will provide specific instructions on how to mark the text that will help with comprehension.

Highlighters or colored pencils

Have students get out a highlighter or colored pencil.

Direct students to pages 360–367 in their Student Books.

Draw a rectangle around the title.

Now, let's read the vocabulary words aloud.

- What's the first bold vocabulary word? (acute) *Acute* means "serious; severe; sharp." I was in *acute* pain after the car accident. **Have partners use the word in a sentence.**
- What's the next vocabulary word? (donor) *Donor* means "a person who gives something in order to help a person or group." Organ and tissue *donors* often save lives. **Have partners use the word in a sentence.**
- Next word? (drastically) *Drastically* means "quickly and to a great degree." Getting a zero on one assignment will *drastically* decrease your average. **Have partners use the word in a sentence.**

- Let's continue. (collapses) *Collapses* means "falls down or falls apart suddenly." One gust of wind and a house of cards *collapses.* Have partners use the word in a sentence.
- Next word? (assume) *Assume* means "to believe something is true without first making sure." I *assume* you come to school every day because you want to learn. Am I wrong? Have partners use the word in a sentence.
- Let's continue. (circumstance) *Circumstance* means "an event or situation; the state of things." The *circumstance* that led me to become a teacher was the poor state of literacy in this country. Have partners use the word in a sentence.
- Next word? (wincing) *Wincing* means "making a face in response to something painful or unpleasant." The patient was *wincing* at the sight of blood, but the doctor was used to it. Have partners use the word in a sentence.
- Let's continue. (obstacles) *Obstacles* means "objects that are in someone's way." Hurdlers jump over the *obstacles* on the track to get to the finish line. Have partners use the word in a sentence.
- Next word? (inferno) *Inferno* means "a fire blazing out of control." The *inferno* burned down the entire city block. Have partners use the word in a sentence.
- Last word. (friction) *Friction* means "disagreement or argument between people." *Friction* between friends is often temporary because they are willing to forgive and forget. Have partners use the word in a sentence.

Talk with a partner about any vocabulary word that is still confusing for you to read consistently or understand its meaning.

You will read Part 1 of the excerpt from *My Sister's Keeper* one section at a time. After each section, you will monitor your understanding by circling the check mark if you understand the text or the question mark if you don't understand the text. I also want you to draw a question mark over any confusing words, phrases, or sentences.

Options for reading text:

- Teacher read-aloud
- Teacher-led or student-led choral read
- Paired read or independent read with bold vocabulary words read aloud

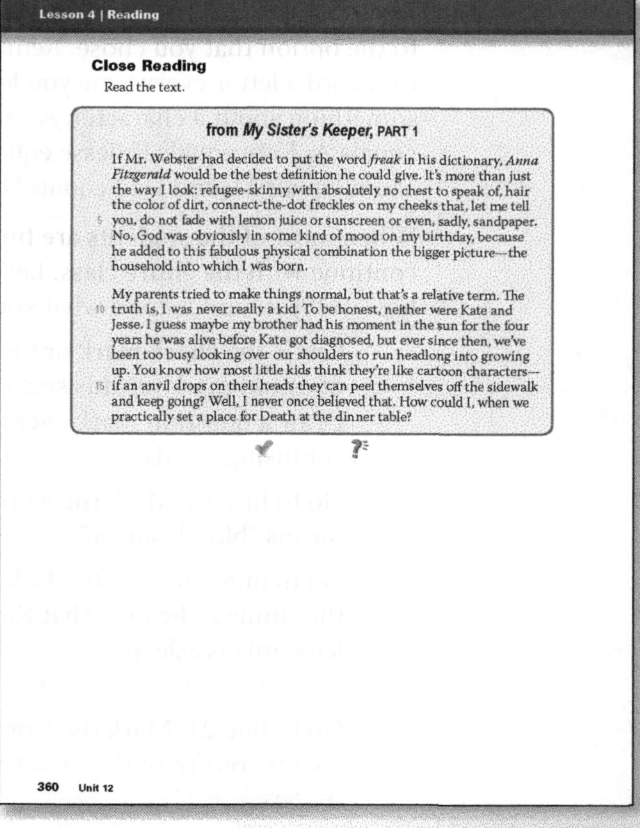
Lesson 4 | Reading

Close Reading

Read the text.

from *My Sister's Keeper*, PART 1

If Mr. Webster had decided to put the word *freak* in his dictionary, *Anna Fitzgerald* would be the best definition he could give. It's more than just the way I look: refugee-skinny with absolutely no chest to speak of, hair the color of dirt, connect-the-dot freckles on my cheeks that, let me tell you, do not fade with lemon juice or sunscreen or even, sadly, sandpaper. No, God was obviously in some kind of mood on my birthday, because he added to this fabulous physical combination the bigger picture—the household into which I was born.

My parents tried to make things normal, but that's a relative term. The truth is, I was never really a kid. To be honest, neither were Kate and Jesse. I guess maybe my brother had his moment in the sun for the four years he was alive before Kate got diagnosed, but ever since then, we've been too busy looking over our shoulders to run headlong into growing up. You know how most little kids think they're like cartoon characters—if an anvil drops on their heads they can peel themselves off the sidewalk and keep going? Well, I never once believed that. How could I, when we practically set a place for Death at the dinner table?

✔ ?

360 Unit 12

Choose an option for reading text. Have students read lines 1–17 according to the option that you chose. Pay attention to the traits for each character. Follow this process. When you learn something about Anna, record an A in the margin. When you learn something about Kate, record a K. Record a J for Jesse, an M for Mom, and a D for Dad. You will revisit these characters' traits for a later writing assignment.

When most of the students are finished, continue with the entire class. Let's see how well you understood what you read.

- Circle the check mark or the question mark for this section. Draw a question mark over any confusing words.
- Go to line 1. Mark the author of the first American dictionary. (Mr. Webster)
- Go to line 3. Mark the word that means "a person who has left his or her home to escape war or persecution." (refugee) Circle the punctuation mark used to indicate that though *refugee* is a noun, it is working with the word *skinny* as an adjective.
- Go to lines 7 and 8. Mark what Anna believes is the biggest reason she is a freak. (the household into which I was born)
- Go to line 9. Mark the word used to indicate that the definition of something is only known in relationship to something else. (relative)
- Go to line 11. Mark the idiom that means "brief time of attention from others." (moment in the sun)
- Go to line 12. Mark the word that means "identified a disease." (diagnosed)
- Go to line 13. Mark the idiom that means "watching for danger." (looking over our shoulders)
- Go to line 15. Mark the word that means "heavy block of iron or steel." (anvil)
- Go to line 17. Mark the presence in their household that kept Anna from being a kid. (Death)

Have students read lines 18–39 according to the option that you chose. Remember to record a letter every time you learn something about a character. Anna equals A; Kate equals K; Jesse equals J; Mom equals M; and Dad equals D.

When most of the students are finished, continue with the entire class. Let's see how well you understood what you read.

- Circle the check mark or the question mark for this section. Draw a question mark over any confusing words.
- Go to line 18. Mark the word that means "blood cancer." (leukemia)
- Go to lines 19 and 20. Mark the simile indicating that Kate's leukemia is asleep. (hibernating under her skin like a bear)
- Go to line 21. Mark the word that means "return of the disease." (relapse)
- Go to line 23. Use context clues to define *allogeneic donor*. (a perfect sibling match) Circle the punctuation mark that signals an explanation. (em dash)
- Go to line 24. Mark the word that means "disease-fighting cells." (leukocytes)
- In the same sentence, mark the words that mean "cells that maintain the ability to replicate themselves and form other cells of the body." (stem cells)
- In the same sentence, mark the words that mean "tissue deep inside the bones." (bone marrow)
- Go to line 25. Mark the reason that Anna ends up in the hospital with Kate. (I'm the one who provides them.)
- Go to line 27. Mark the indefinite pronoun indicating nothing specific. (anything)
- Go to line 28. Mark the evidence that Anna is not truthful all the time. (least of all that which I tell you myself) Circle the intensive pronoun that is unnecessary and being used for emphasis. (myself)
- Go to lines 32 and 33. Mark what would make Anna's mom beautiful. (if she were parachuted into someone else's life)
- Go to line 35. Mark the transition word that indicates a reason is coming. (since)
- Go to line 36. Mark what changes based on Kate's health. (calendar)
- Go to lines 38 and 39. Mark the evidence that Anna's mom escapes reality by shopping. (ordering ridiculously fancy evening dresses for places she is never going to go) In the margin, write a word to describe Anna's mom. (Answers will vary.)

Close Reading (*cont.*)

Kate has **acute** promyelocytic leukemia. Actually, that's not quite true—right now she doesn't have it, but it's hibernating under her skin like a bear, until it decides to roar again. She was diagnosed when she was two; she's sixteen now. *Molecular relapse* and *granulocyte* and *portacath*—these words are part of my vocabulary, even though I'll never find them on any SAT. I'm an allogeneic **donor**—a perfect sibling match. When Kate needs leukocytes or stem cells or bone marrow to fool her body into thinking it's healthy, I'm the one who provides them. Nearly every time Kate's hospitalized, I wind up there, too.

None of which means anything, except that you shouldn't believe what you hear about me, least of all that which I tell you myself.

As I am coming up the stairs, my mother comes out of her room wearing another ball gown. "Ah," she says, turning her back to me. "Just the girl I wanted to see."

I zip it up and watch her twirl. My mother could be beautiful, if she were parachuted into someone else's life. She has long dark hair and the fine collarbones of a princess, but the corners of her mouth turn down, like she's swallowed bitter news. She doesn't have much free time, since a calendar is something that can change **drastically** if my sister develops a bruise or a nosebleed, but what she does have she spends at Bluefly.com, ordering ridiculously fancy evening dresses for places she is never going to go. "What do you think?" she asks.

✔ ?

Have students read lines 40–71 according to the option that you chose. Remember to record a letter every time you learn something about a character. Anna equals A; Kate equals K; Jesse equals J; Mom equals M; and Dad equals D.

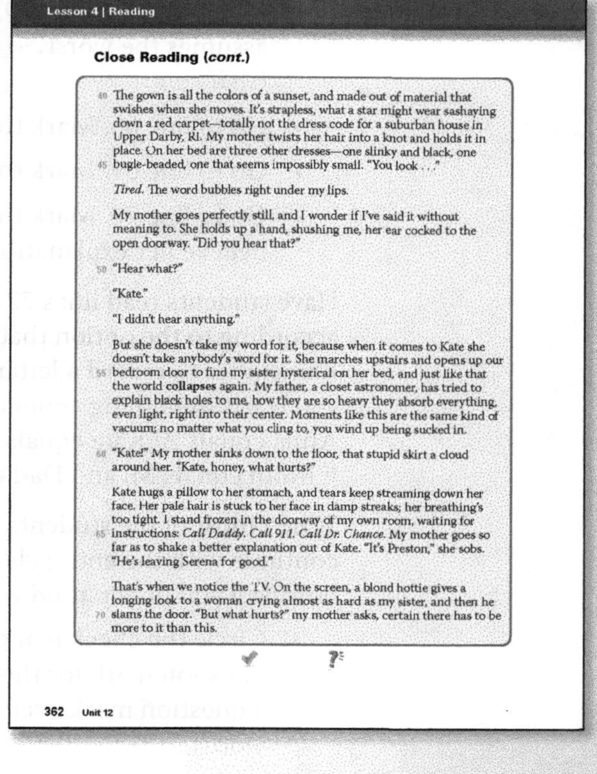

Lesson 4 | Reading

Close Reading (*cont.*)

The gown is all the colors of a sunset, and made out of material that swishes when she moves. It's strapless, what a star might wear sashaying down a red carpet—totally not the dress code for a suburban house in Upper Darby, RI. My mother twists her hair into a knot and holds it in place. On her bed are three other dresses—one slinky and black, one bugle-beaded, one that seems impossibly small. "You look . . ."

Tired. The word bubbles right under my lips.

My mother goes perfectly still, and I wonder if I've said it without meaning to. She holds up a hand, shushing me, her ear cocked to the open doorway. "Did you hear that?"

"Hear what?"

"Kate."

"I didn't hear anything."

But she doesn't take my word for it, because when it comes to Kate she doesn't take anybody's word for it. She marches upstairs and opens up our bedroom door to find my sister hysterical on her bed, and just like that the world **collapses** again. My father, a closet astronomer, has tried to explain black holes to me, how they are so heavy they absorb everything, even light, right into their center. Moments like this are the same kind of vacuum; no matter what you cling to, you wind up being sucked in.

"Kate!" My mother sinks down to the floor, that stupid skirt a cloud around her. "Kate, honey, what hurts?"

Kate hugs a pillow to her stomach, and tears keep streaming down her face. Her pale hair is stuck to her face in damp streaks; her breathing's too tight. I stand frozen in the doorway of my own room, waiting for instructions: *Call Daddy. Call 911. Call Dr. Chance.* My mother goes so far as to shake a better explanation out of Kate. "It's Preston," she sobs. "He's leaving Serena for good."

That's when we notice the TV. On the screen, a blond hottie gives a longing look to a woman crying almost as hard as my sister, and then he slams the door. "But what hurts?" my mother asks, certain there has to be more to it than this.

362 Unit 12

When most of the students are finished, continue with the entire class. Let's see how well you understood what you read.

- Circle the check mark or the question mark for this section. Draw a question mark over any confusing words.
- Go to the first paragraph. Mark the dress code violation. (the gown)
- Go to line 43. Mark the setting of the story. (Upper Darby, RI)
- Go to lines 44 and 45. Number the attributes of the dresses on the bed. (1. slinky and black; 2. bugle-beaded; 3. impossibly small) Circle the punctuation mark used to indicate that though *bugle* is a noun, it is working with the word *beaded* as an adjective.
- On line 45, mark the punctuation used to indicate an inability to finish the sentence. (ellipses)
- Go to line 46. Mark the evidence that Anna doesn't say the word *tired,* though she thinks it. (The word bubbles right under my lips.) In the margin, write the name of the text treatment that indicates something is thought, but not spoken. (italics)
- Go to line 47. Circle the pronoun *it.* Draw an arrow to the word that *it* refers to. (tired)
- Go to lines 49 and 50. Mark the two words that refer to the same thing—though it hasn't been named. (that, what) Mark the word in the next line that also refers to the same thing. (anything) Circle the indefinite pronoun used to indicate nothing specific. (anything)
- Go to line 53. Mark the idiom that means "believe me." (take my word for it)
- Mark the evidence that Anna's mom has trust issues. (when it comes to Kate she doesn't take anybody's word for it)
- In the margin, write the one thing that can transform Anna's mom from fun-loving and playful to serious. (problems with Kate)
- Go to line 55. Mark the word that means "uncontrollable extreme emotion." (hysterical)
- Go to line 59. Mark the proof that nobody in the family can escape Kate's problem. (no matter what you cling to, you wind up being sucked in)
- Go to lines 60 and 61. Mark the metaphor. (that stupid skirt a cloud around her) Circle the two things being compared. (skirt; cloud)

- In paragraphs 8 and 9, mark the evidence that when Kate is crying, her family assumes the worst. (Kate, honey, what hurts; Call Daddy. Call 911. Call Dr. Chance.)
- Go to line 66. Mark the tactic used by Kate's mom to get her to talk. (shake)
- Go to line 69. Mark the word that means "wishful." (longing)
- Go to line 70. Mark the evidence that Kate's mom has trust issues and doesn't believe her explanation. ("But what hurts?")

Have students read lines 72–96 according to the option that you chose. Remember to record a letter every time you learn something about a character. Anna equals A; Kate equals K; Jesse equals J; Mom equals M; and Dad equals D.

When most of the students are finished, continue with the entire class. Let's see how well you understood what you read.

- Circle the check mark or the question mark for this section. Draw a question mark over any confusing words.
- Go to lines 74 and 75. Mark the simile indicating that daily life is not quite adequate in their household. (Normal, in our house, is like a blanket too short for a bed.) Circle the word indicating it is a simile. (like)
- Go to line 79. Mark evidence that Anna is younger than Kate. (people mistakenly assume I'm the older sister)

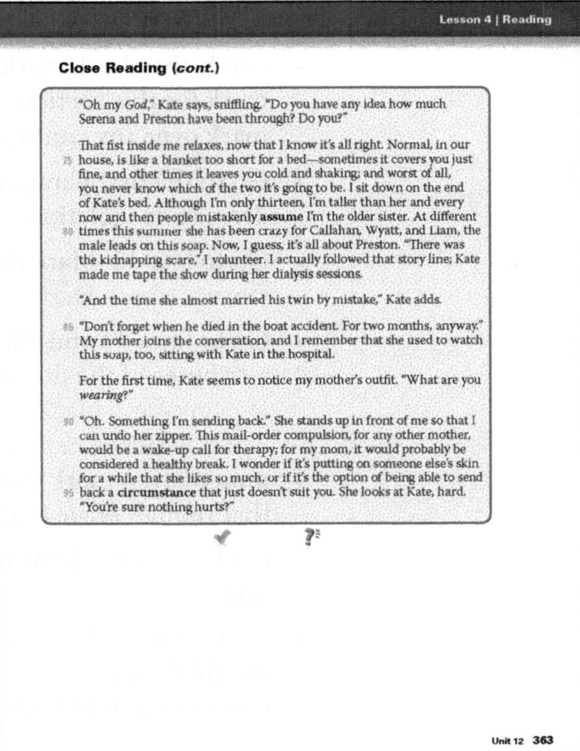

Lesson 4 | Reading

Close Reading (*cont.*)

"Oh my *God*," Kate says, sniffling. "Do you have any idea how much Serena and Preston have been through? Do you?"

That fist inside me relaxes, now that I know it's all right. Normal, in our house, is like a blanket too short for a bed—sometimes it covers you just fine, and other times it leaves you cold and shaking; and worst of all, you never know which of the two it's going to be. I sit down on the end of Kate's bed. Although I'm only thirteen, I'm taller than her and every now and then people mistakenly **assume** I'm the older sister. At different times this summer she has been crazy for Callahan, Wyatt, and Liam, the male leads on this soap. Now, I guess, it's all about Preston. "There was the kidnapping scare," I volunteer. I actually followed that story line; Kate made me tape the show during her dialysis sessions.

"And the time she almost married his twin by mistake," Kate adds.

"Don't forget when he died in the boat accident. For two months, anyway." My mother joins the conversation, and I remember that she used to watch this soap, too, sitting with Kate in the hospital.

For the first time, Kate seems to notice my mother's outfit. "What are you *wearing*?"

"Oh. Something I'm sending back." She stands up in front of me so that I can undo her zipper. This mail-order compulsion, for any other mother, would be a wake-up call for therapy; for my mom, it would probably be considered a healthy break. I wonder if it's putting on someone else's skin for a while that she likes so much, or if it's the option of being able to send back a **circumstance** that just doesn't suit you. She looks at Kate, hard. "You're sure nothing hurts?"

Unit 12 363

- Go to line 80. Mark the present perfect tense verb phrase used to indicate that the action happened at an unspecific time in the past. (has been)
- On the same line, mark the idiom that means "likes a lot." (crazy for)
- Go to line 83. Mark the word that is a type of medical treatment to filter the blood when the kidneys no longer work well. (dialysis)
- Go to line 87. Mark the word used to refer to a daytime dramatic television show about a group of people. (soap)
- In paragraph 5, mark the word that is said in a different tone or with exaggeration. (wearing) In the margin, write the name of the text treatment that indicates something is spoken this way. (italics)
- Go to line 91. Mark the words *this mail-order compulsion*. In the margin, write what the author is referring to. (ordering ball gowns and sending them back)
- Circle the word that means "strong desire." (compulsion)
- Go to line 95. In the margin, write what circumstance the author is alluding to. (Kate's cancer)

Have students read lines 97–123 according to the option that you chose. Remember to record a letter every time you learn something about a character. Anna equals A; Kate equals K; Jesse equals J; Mom equals M; and Dad equals D.

When most of the students are finished, continue with the entire class. Let's see how well you understood what you read.

- Circle the check mark or the question mark for this section. Draw a question mark over any confusing words.
- Go to lines 97 and 98. Mark the evidence that Kate puts on a show for her mom to keep her from worrying. (sinks a little; color drains from her face)
- Go to line 103. Mark the reason that Kate wants to see the previews. (if I die tonight I want to know what I'm missing)
- Go to line 105. Mark the novel word that has been made up by the author. (funchy) In the margin, write what you think that word means based on context. (Answers will vary.)
- Go to line 109. Mark the idiom that means "unlikely to succeed." (I don't have a prayer.)
- Go to line 111. Mark word that usually indicates time, but does not in this case. (then) In this sentence, *then* is a conjunctive adverb. It is an adverb being used like a conjunction—connecting one sentence or clause to another one.
- Go to line 114. Mark the word that is said in a different tone or with exaggeration. (You) In the margin, write the name of the text treatment that indicates something is spoken this way. (italics)
- Go to line 115. Mark the evidence that Kate is in pain. (wincing)
- Go to line 119. Mark the contraction. (it's) In the margin, write what *it* is referring to. (Kate's pain; what's bothering Kate)
- Underline Anna's hypothesis. (It's her kidneys.)
- On the same line, mark the evidence that Anna is afraid. (Want me to get Mom?)
- Go to line 121. Mark evidence that Anna loves her sister. (I hold out my hand, too.)

Lesson 4 | Reading

Close Reading (*cont.*)

After my mother leaves, Kate sinks a little. That's the only way to describe it—how fast color drains from her face, how she disappears against the pillows. As she gets sicker, she fades a little more, until I am afraid one day I will wake up and not be able to see her at all. "Move," Kate orders. "You're blocking the picture."

So I go to sit on my own bed. "It's only the coming attractions."

"Well, if I die tonight I want to know what I'm missing."

I fluff my pillows up under my head. Kate, as usual, has swapped so that she has all the funchy ones that don't feel like rocks under your neck. She's supposed to deserve this, because she's three years older than me or because she's sick or because the moon is in Aquarius—there's *always* a reason. I squint at the television, wishing I could flip through the stations, knowing I don't have a prayer. "Preston looks like he's made out of plastic."

"Then why did I hear you whispering his name last night into your pillow?"

"Shut up," I say.

"*You* shut up." Then Kate smiles at me. "He probably is gay, though. Quite a waste, considering the Fitzgerald sisters are—" **Wincing**, she breaks off mid-sentence, and I roll toward her.

"Kate?"

She rubs her lower back. "It's nothing."

It's her kidneys. "Want me to get Mom?"

"Not yet." She reaches between our beds, which are just far apart enough for us to touch each other if we both try. I hold out my hand, too. When we were little we'd make this bridge and try to see how many Barbies we could get to balance on it.

✔ ?

364 Unit 12

Have students read lines 124–147 according to the option that you chose. Remember to record a letter every time you learn something about a character. Anna equals A; Kate equals K; Jesse equals J; Mom equals M; and Dad equals D.

When most of the students are finished, continue with the entire class. Let's see how well you understood what you read.

- Circle the check mark or the question mark for this section. Draw a question mark over any confusing words.
- Go to line 124. Mark the evidence that Anna is overwhelmed with saving her sister's life. (nightmares)
- Go to lines 126 and 127. Mark the proverb Anna thinks of when she looks at her situation. (a fire will burn itself out, unless you open a window and give it fuel) Mark what Anna compares herself to. (fire) Mark the transition phrase used later to mean that Anna doesn't want her fire to be extinguished. (but then again)
- Go to line 128. Mark the example of personification in which nonliving objects take on human qualities. (flames are licking at your heels)
- Go to line 129. Mark the transition word used to connect the idea of breaking a wall to escape to what Anna is about to do. (so)
- Go to lines 130 and 131. Mark Anna's actions after Kate falls asleep. (take the leather binder . . . and go into the bathroom for privacy)
- In the third paragraph, number the two things Anna keeps in the binder. (1. \$136.87; 2. newspaper clippings)
- Go to line 143. Mark the synonym for *multiplied*. (reproduced)
- Go to line 146. Mark the word that means "declare untrue." (deny)
- Go to line 147. Mark the term used to mean the accomplishments of an individual. (track record)

Lesson 4 | Reading

Close Reading (*cont.*)

Lately, I have been having nightmares, where I'm cut into so many pieces that there isn't enough of me to be put back together.

My father says that a fire will burn itself out, unless you open a window and give it fuel. I suppose that's what I'm doing, when you get right down to it; but then again, my dad also says that when flames are licking at your heels you've got to break a wall or two if you want to escape. So when Kate falls asleep from her meds I take the leather binder I keep between my mattress and box spring and go into the bathroom for privacy. I know Kate's been snooping—I rigged up a red thread between the zipper's teeth to let me know who was prying into my stuff without my permission, but even though the thread's been torn there's nothing missing inside. I turn on the water in the bathtub so it sounds like I'm in there for a reason, and sit down on the floor to count.

If you add in the twenty dollars from the pawnshop, I have \$136.87. It's not going to be enough, but there's got to be a way around that. Jesse didn't have \$2,900 when he bought his beat-up Jeep, and the bank gave him some kind of loan. Of course, my parents had to sign the papers, too, and I doubt they're going to be willing to do that for me, given the circumstances. I count the money a second time, just in case the bills have miraculously reproduced, but math is math and the total stays the same. And then I read the newspaper clippings.

Campbell Alexander. It's a stupid name, in my opinion. It sounds like a bar drink that costs too much, or a brokerage firm. But you can't deny the man's track record.

✔ ?

Unit 12 365

Have students read lines 148–177 according to the option that you chose. Remember to record a letter every time you learn something about a character. Anna equals A; Kate equals K; Jesse equals J; Mom equals M; and Dad equals D.

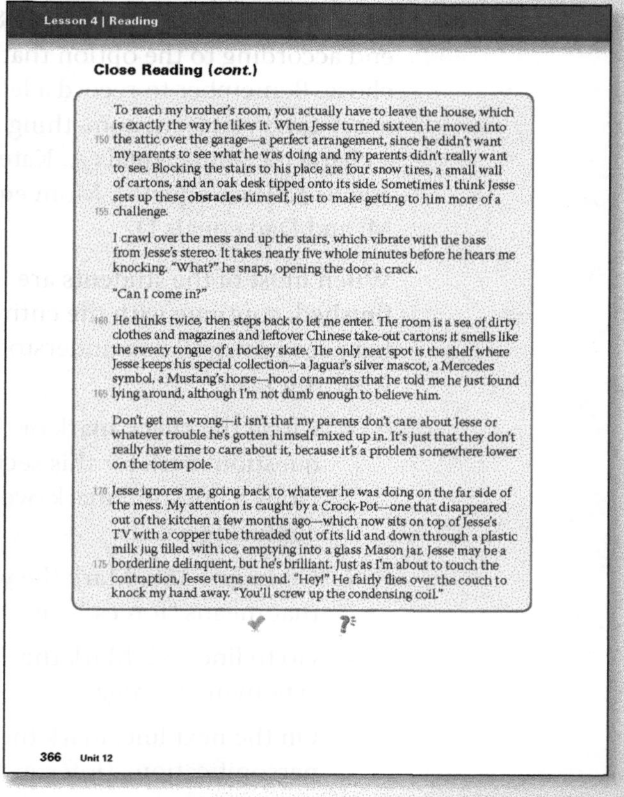

Lesson 4 | Reading

Close Reading (*cont.*)

To reach my brother's room, you actually have to leave the house, which is exactly the way he likes it. When Jesse turned sixteen he moved into the attic over the garage—a perfect arrangement, since he didn't want my parents to see what he was doing and my parents didn't really want to see. Blocking the stairs to his place are four snow tires, a small wall of cartons, and an oak desk tipped onto its side. Sometimes I think Jesse sets up these **obstacles** himself, just to make getting to him more of a challenge.

I crawl over the mess and up the stairs, which vibrate with the bass from Jesse's stereo. It takes nearly five whole minutes before he hears me knocking. "What?" he snaps, opening the door a crack.

"Can I come in?"

He thinks twice, then steps back to let me enter. The room is a sea of dirty clothes and magazines and leftover Chinese take-out cartons; it smells like the sweaty tongue of a hockey skate. The only neat spot is the shelf where Jesse keeps his special collection—a Jaguar's silver mascot, a Mercedes symbol, a Mustang's horse—hood ornaments that he told me he just found lying around, although I'm not dumb enough to believe him.

Don't get me wrong—it isn't that my parents don't care about Jesse or whatever trouble he's gotten himself mixed up in. It's just that they don't really have time to care about it, because it's a problem somewhere lower on the totem pole.

Jesse ignores me, going back to whatever he was doing on the far side of the mess. My attention is caught by a Crock-Pot—one that disappeared out of the kitchen a few months ago—which now sits on top of Jesse's TV with a copper tube threaded out of its lid and down through a plastic milk jug filled with ice, emptying into a glass Mason jar. Jesse may be a borderline delinquent, but he's brilliant. Just as I'm about to touch the contraption, Jesse turns around. "Hey!" He fairly flies over the couch to knock my hand away. "You'll screw up the condensing coil."

366 Unit 12

When most of the students are finished, continue with the entire class. Let's see how well you understood what you read.

- Circle the check mark or the question mark for this section. Draw a question mark over any confusing words.
- Go to line 150. Mark the location of Jesse's room. (attic over the garage)
- Go to lines 151 and 152. Mark the evidence that Jesse gets ignored a lot. (parents didn't really want to see)
- Mark the evidence that Jesse doesn't want visitors. (blocking the stairs; Jesse sets up these obstacles himself) Circle the intensive pronoun in line 154 used for emphasis. (himself)
- Number the obstacles set by Jesse. (1. four snow tires; 2. a wall of cartons; 3. oak desk tipped onto its side)
- Go to line 157. Mark the evidence that Anna really wants to see her brother and what she needs is important. (It takes nearly five whole minutes)
- Go to line 158. Mark the evidence that Jesse doesn't want to be bothered. ("What?" he snaps, opening the door a crack.)
- Go to line 160. Mark the idiom that means "weighs his options carefully." (thinks twice)
- In the next sentence, mark the metaphor used to describe Jesse's room. (a sea of dirty clothes and magazines and leftover Chinese take-out cartons)
- Mark the figurative language used to mean that his room stinks. (smells like the sweaty tongue of a hockey skate)
- Go to lines 168 and 169. Mark the words used to mean "not as important." (lower on the totem pole)
- Go to line 175. Mark the adjectives used to describe Jesse. (delinquent; brilliant) Mark the adjective that comes before *delinquent* that is used to explain that he is not quite a true delinquent. (borderline)
- Go to line 176. Mark the word that means "weird-looking machine." (contraption) Underline the description of the contraption. (a Crock-Pot with a copper tube threaded out of its lid and down through a plastic milk jug filled with ice, emptying into a glass Mason jar)

Have students read from line 178 to the end according to the option that you chose. Remember to record a letter every time you learn something about a character. Anna equals A; Kate equals K; Jesse equals J; Mom equals M; and Dad equals D.

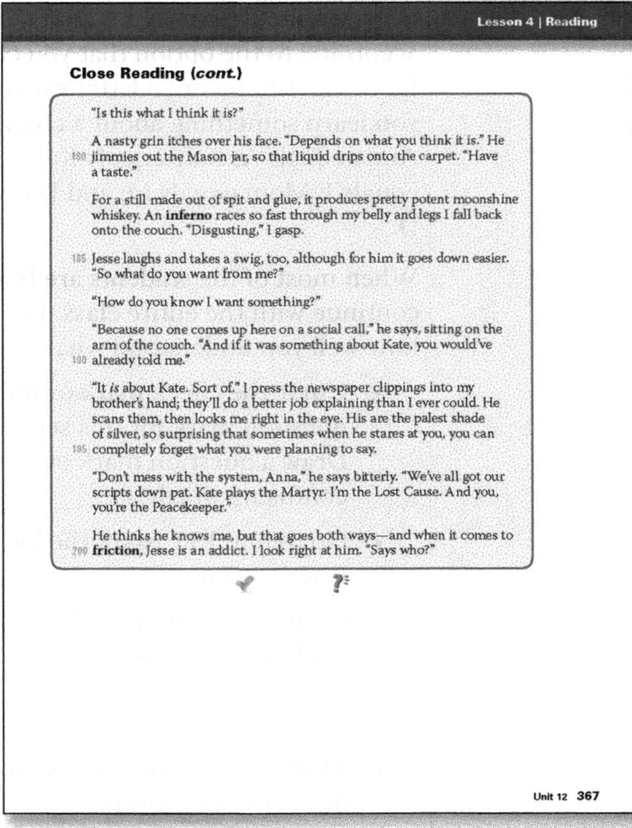

Lesson 4 | Reading

Close Reading (*cont.*)

"Is this what I think it is?"

A nasty grin itches over his face. "Depends on what you think it is." He jimmies out the Mason jar, so that liquid drips onto the carpet. "Have a taste."

For a still made out of spit and glue, it produces pretty potent moonshine whiskey. An **inferno** races so fast through my belly and legs I fall back onto the couch. "Disgusting," I gasp.

Jesse laughs and takes a swig, too, although for him it goes down easier. "So what do you want from me?"

"How do you know I want something?"

"Because no one comes up here on a social call," he says, sitting on the arm of the couch. "And if it was something about Kate, you would've already told me."

"It *is* about Kate. Sort of." I press the newspaper clippings into my brother's hand; they'll do a better job explaining than I ever could. He scans them, then looks me right in the eye. His are the palest shade of silver, so surprising that sometimes when he stares at you, you can completely forget what you were planning to say.

"Don't mess with the system, Anna," he says bitterly. "We've all got our scripts down pat. Kate plays the Martyr. I'm the Lost Cause. And you, you're the Peacekeeper."

He thinks he knows me, but that goes both ways—and when it comes to **friction**, Jesse is an addict. I look right at him. "Says who?"

Unit 12 367

When most of the students are finished, continue with the entire class. Let's see how well you understood what you read.

- Circle the check mark or the question mark for this section. Draw a question mark over any confusing words.
- Go to line 180. Mark the word that means "forces." (jimmies)
- Go to line 182. Mark the synonym of *strong*. (potent)
- On the next line, mark the personification. (inferno races)
- Go to line 192. Mark the contraction that means "they will." (they'll) Draw an arrow to what *they* is referring to. (newspaper clippings)
- Go to line 196. Mark the synonym of *angrily*. (bitterly)
- Go to line 197. Mark the word that means "someone who suffers rather than gives up what she believes in." (Martyr) This is an allusion to a happening in a famous book. What is the book, and who is the martyr? Write your answers in the margin. (Bible; Jesus)
- On the same line, mark Jesse's description of himself indicating that his parents have given up on him. (Lost Cause)
- Go to line 200. Mark the word that means "a person who has a constant need for a substance or activity." (addict)
- Mark the proof that Anna is no longer interested in keeping the peace. (Says who?) What is the author trying to create with this statement? (suspense)

Have partners compare text markings and correct any errors.

Unit 12

Lesson 5

Lesson Opener

Before the lesson, choose one of the following activities to write on the board or post on the *LANGUAGE! Live* Class Wall online.

- *Write four sentences with at least two vocabulary words in each. Show you know the meanings. (acute, donor, drastically, collapse, assume, circumstance, wince, obstacle, inferno, friction)*
- *Write three simple sentences that describe Anna's sister. Answer the following questions in your sentences: Which one? What kind? How does she feel? Combine the three sentences into one Masterpiece Sentence.*
- *What would you have done if you were Anna and didn't want to go to the hospital anymore?*

Vocabulary

Objective

- Review key passage vocabulary.

Recontextualize Passage Vocabulary

Direct students to page 340 in their Student Books. Use the following questions to review the vocabulary words in the first excerpt from *My Sister's Keeper*.

- Your prom date picks you up wearing a velvet tux with ruffles down the front. Might you *wince*? (yes) Someone tells you "good job" after you give a presentation. Does this make you *wince*? (no) The nurse isn't very gentle when she sticks the needle in your arm. It hurts. What do you do? (wince)
- You slam a window and smash your finger in it. Is your pain *acute*? (yes) You have the sniffles. Is your illness *acute*? (no) You have a sudden high fever, a searing pain in your stomach, and the chills. You should immediately see a doctor because your symptoms are what? (acute)
- Are there usually *obstacles* on an airport runway? (no) Your baby brother leaves his toys everywhere. You are constantly tripping over them. Are they *obstacles*? (yes) In a famous movie about a kid who gets left home alone, two burglars try to enter the house. What does the kid set up to stop them? (obstacles)
- Your visually impaired uncle can now see, thanks to a retina transplant. Did he get the retinas from a *donor*? (yes) In a famous Christmas story, a mean-spirited creature steals presents and decorations from local villagers. Are the villagers *donors*? (no) In a famous children's book, a tree gives everything it has to make a boy's life better—its fruit, its branches, and finally its trunk. The tree is a what? (donor)

- You set up a tripod securely and fasten your camera on it to take a family photo. Does the tripod *collapse*? (no) You're making a pillow fort with your little sister, and she jumps on the roof. Does it *collapse*? (yes) You pull the perfect apple from the bottom of the stack at the grocery store. What does the stack do? (collapse)
- You thought you and your sister were going to a movie on your own, but now you learn that her friend is going. You don't like the friend. Is this an awkward *circumstance*? (yes) Grass grows every spring. Would you call the growing of the grass a *circumstance*? (no) The holiday turkey gets burned. Your dad goes to the chicken place to get fried chicken instead. You love turkey and are bummed by this unexpected what? (circumstance)
- Whenever your friends argue, you try to get them to calm down and get along. Do you like *friction*? (no) One of your friends, in particular, is a drama queen. She loves to be at the center of big conflicts. Does she thrive on *friction*? (yes) Some reality TV shows are all about family members who don't get along. These shows are cashing in on what? (family friction)
- The front door opens and then shuts. Do you *assume* someone else who lives in your house has passed through the door? (yes) You wake up, and it's pitch dark. Do you *assume* it's morning? (no) Your friend said to meet her at the bowling alley at 2:00. You thought you knew which one, but now it's twenty after and she's still not there. You may have what? (assumed you knew which bowling alley she meant)
- It's a chilly day. You zip up your jacket and pull up your hood. Do you feel as if you're in an *inferno*? (no) You take a bite of the hottest salsa that has ever crossed your lips. Your mouth is on fire. Could you describe the sensation as an *inferno*? (yes) You're watching a forest fire blaze out of control on the news. What are you watching? (an inferno)
- At the last second, you put on a bracelet before leaving for school. Has your outfit changed *drastically*? (no) You are about to go to a carnival with friends, but then you get an emergency call from your cousin who is in trouble and needs your help. Have your plans changed *drastically*? (yes) Ten minutes ago, it was sunny and calm; now it's pouring rain. The weather has changed how? (drastically)

Writing

Objectives

- Use text to write coherent paragraphs in response to reading.
- Write a descriptive essay.
- Analyze character development and the relationship among characters within a story.

Quick Write in Response to Reading

Direct students to page 368 in their Student Books. Read the prompt and clarify directions. Have students talk with their partner about the relationship between Anna and Kate. Encourage them to use details from the text in describing the traits of each character.

Lesson 5 | Writing

Quick Write in Response to Reading Answers will vary.

Kate's illness has had a dramatic impact on her relationship with her siblings. Describe the relationship between Anna and Kate. Consider what you know about their personalities and character traits and how these traits impact their relationship.

Anna and Kate have a very complicated relationship. While they seem to share genuine affection for one another, Kate's illness has reversed the traditional roles of older and younger sister. Kate is frail emotionally as well as physically. Her outburst regarding characters on a television show reveals a level of immaturity. Anna takes on a more mature role in this scene by helping Kate think about past events on the show. She takes the lead in shifting the conversation to the outrageous things that have happened in the past to these characters on the soap opera. She even succeeds in shifting her mother's focus from worry to laughter. Kate confides in Anna instead of worrying their mother with every ache and pain. She turns to Anna for comfort, as evidenced by the long-standing habit of holding hands to create a bridge with their arms.

Anna clearly worries about her sister and quickly shifts into crisis mode whenever necessary. She sees Kate growing weaker and worries that Kate may eventually fade away. Anna is the only person who can provide what Kate needs most desperately, healthy cells to fight the cancer in her own blood cells. Even though she loves her sister deeply, Anna seems to resent having her childhood snatched away from her. Her role in Kate's medical treatment is leading to nightmares. Anna is planning something that will probably upset her current relationship with Kate and the entire family.

Even though she is the younger sister, Anna looks and acts older. She is clearly stronger emotionally and, in some ways, more mature than her older sister. She has been thrust into a role of tremendous responsibility, and that role is placing a strain on her relationship with her sister, Kate.

368 Unit 12

Reading

Objectives

- Self-correct as comprehension of text deepens.
- Answer questions to demonstrate comprehension of text.
- Engage in class discussion.
- Identify the enduring understandings from a piece of text.

Revisit Passage Comprehension

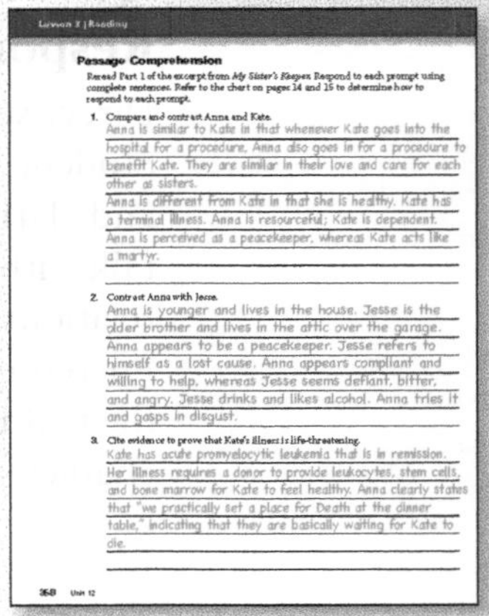

Direct students back to pages 358 and 359 in their Student Books. Have students review their answers and make any necessary changes. Then, have partners share their answers and collaborate to perfect them.

Author's Purpose

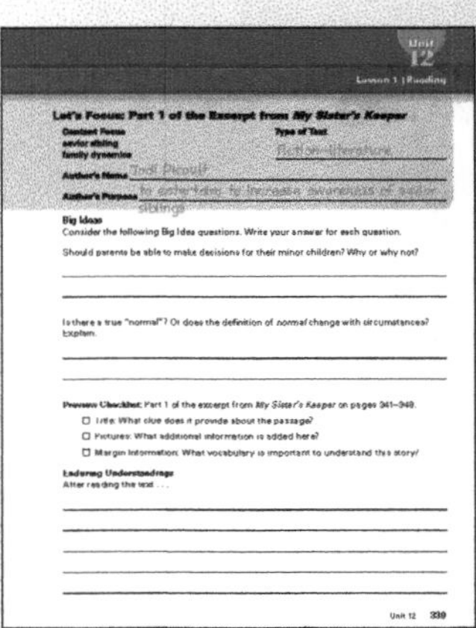

Direct students back to page 339 in their Student Books. We just finished studying a fiction selection about a child diagnosed with cancer and what the parents have done to save her life. Before discussing our enduring understandings, let's talk about the author's purpose. Why did this author write the text? Provide sharing time. If necessary, elaborate or clarify their responses. (The author's purpose is the reason that he or she wrote the text. Authors write for different purposes. Authors write to entertain, to persuade, or to inform or to teach. Knowing an author's purpose can help a reader understand a text better. This novel was written to entertain and to get people to look at an issue from multiple perspectives.) Have students correct their answers on their page as necessary.

Enduring Understandings

Reread the Big Idea questions.

Should parents be able to make decisions for their minor children? Why or why not?

Is there a true "normal"? Or does the definition of *normal* change with circumstances? Explain.

Generate a class discussion about the questions and the answers students came up with in Lesson 1. Have them consider whether their answers have changed any after reading the text. Use the following talking points to foster conversation. Then, have students write their enduring understandings from the unit.

- Children are minors in most states until they turn 18 years old. According to state laws, a minor is a ward of his or her parents or of the state—meaning that the parent or state is responsible for the child and thus can make decisions for the child. Are there decisions that a minor should make on his or her own? Are there decisions that are probably best that parents or caretakers be involved in?

- In the story, Anna claims that "normal" is relative. Is it difficult to see people and families drastically different from your own as being normal? Do we judge other people based on our definition of *normal*? Is that fair?

Has this text made you think about a personal experience or someone you know? Has your perspective or opinion on a specific topic changed? Do you have any lingering thoughts or questions? Write these ideas as your enduring understandings.

Discuss the enduring understandings with the class. If time permits, have students post a personal response about their enduring understandings to the online class wall.

Unit 12

Lesson 6

Lesson Opener

Before the lesson, choose one of the following activities to write on the board or post on the *LANGUAGE! Live* Class Wall online.

- *Imagine you are Anna and wanted your brother's support. How would you convince him?*
- *Write five sentences to describe your morning routine using common phrasal verbs.*
- *Write one sentence about sickness. Write one sentence about scientific discovery. Combine the sentences using a conjunction to create a compound sentence.*

Reading

Objectives

- Determine and discuss the topic of a text.
- Determine and discuss the author's purpose.
- Use text features to preview text.
- Identify allusions to historical works (the Bible) in text.

Passage Introduction

Direct students to page 369 in their Student Books. Discuss the content focus.

Content Focus
savior sibling
family dynamics

We are going to continue reading an excerpt from *My Sister's Keeper.*

Type of Text

You should already know the type of text we are about to read because it is a continuation of the excerpt from *My Sister's Keeper.* Write your answer on the page.

Lesson 6 | Reading

Let's Focus: Part 2 of the Excerpt from *My Sister's Keeper*

Content Focus
savior sibling
family dynamics

Type of Text
fiction—literature

Author's Name Jodi Picoult

Author's Purpose to entertain; to increase awareness of savior siblings

Big Ideas
Consider the following Big Idea questions. Write your answer for each question.

Is it ethical to hurt one person to help another? Explain.

How do you decide whether to accept a given circumstance or fight it with everything you can?

Preview: Part 2 of the excerpt from *My Sister's Keeper* on pages 371–375.
Predict what will happen in this excerpt based on your knowledge of Part 1.

Enduring Understandings
After reading the text . . .

Unit 12 369

Author's Purpose

Have students glance at the text. Who is the author of the text? (Jodi Picoult) Prior to reading, make an educated guess as to what the author's purpose for writing is. Maybe you have changed your mind after reading Part 1. After we finish, you will return to this section and revise your answer if you need to. Have students write their responses on the page.

Background Information

Review Part 1 of *My Sister's Keeper* as a class. Now that you have read the first excerpt from *My Sister's Keeper,* let's delve into the meaning of the title a bit. What do you think the title means? Discuss responses.

The phrase *my sister's keeper* comes from the Biblical reference *my brother's keeper,* which means "being responsible for the welfare of a sibling." Anna is clearly responsible for her sister's health; her parents expect her to save her sister's life—it is her life's purpose.

When you think of the title, what predictions do you have? Discuss responses.

Big Ideas

Read the Big Idea questions aloud.

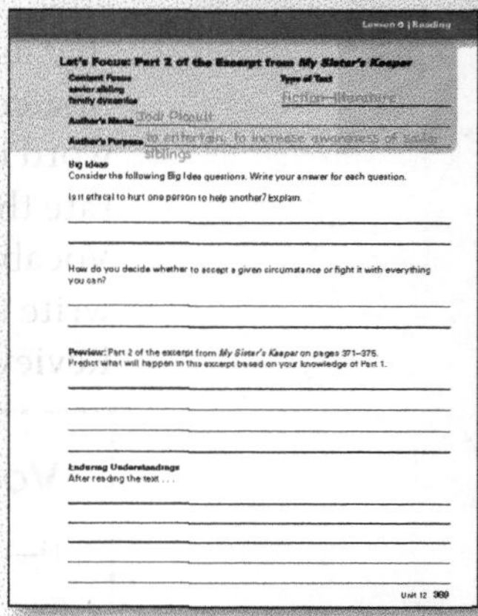

Lesson 6 | Reading

Let's Focus: Part 2 of the Excerpt from *My Sister's Keeper*

Content Focus
savior sibling
family dynamics

Type of Text
fiction—literature

Author's Name Jodi Picoult

Author's Purpose to entertain; to increase awareness of savior siblings

Big Ideas
Consider the following Big Idea questions. Write your answer for each question.

Is it ethical to hurt one person to help another? Explain.

How do you decide whether to accept a given circumstance or fight it with everything you can?

Preview: Part 2 of the excerpt from *My Sister's Keeper* on pages 371–375.
Predict what will happen in this excerpt based on your knowledge of Part 1.

Enduring Understandings
After reading the text . . .

Unit 12 369

> **Big Ideas**
>
> Is it ethical to hurt one person to help another? Explain.
>
> How do you decide whether to accept a given circumstance or fight it with everything you can?

As a class, consider the two Big Idea questions. After discussing each question, have students write an answer. We'll come back to these questions after we finish reading the text. You can add to your answers as you gain information and perspective.

Preview

Read the Preview section on page 369. Have students make a prediction.

Vocabulary

Objectives

- Evaluate word knowledge.
- Determine the meaning of key passage vocabulary.

Rate Vocabulary Knowledge

Direct students to page 370 in their Student Books.

Before we read the text, let's take a look at the vocabulary words that appear in this text. Remind students that as you read each word in the first column aloud, they will write the word in the third column and then rate their knowledge of it. Display the Vocabulary Rating Scale poster or write the information on the board. Review the meaning of each rating.

Vocabulary Rating Scale

0—I have never heard the word before.

1—I have heard the word, but I'm not sure how to use it.

2—I am familiar with the word, but I'm not sure if I know the correct meaning.

3—I know the meaning of the word and can use it correctly in a sentence.

Lesson 6 | Vocabulary

Key Passage Vocabulary: from *My Sister's Keeper*, Part 2

Read each word. Write the word in column 3. Then, circle a number to rate your knowledge of the word.

Read the Word	Part of Speech	Write the Word	Rate the Word
lacking	(adj)	lacking	0 1 2 3
interrupt	(v)	interrupt	0 1 2 3
verdict	(n)	verdict	0 1 2 3
consume	(v)	consume	0 1 2 3
primitive	(adj)	primitive	0 1 2 3
tenacity	(n)	tenacity	0 1 2 3
automatically	(adv)	automatically	0 1 2 3
exalted	(adj)	exalted	0 1 2 3
(on) behalf	(n)	(on) behalf	0 1 2 3
experimental	(adj)	experimental	0 1 2 3

370 Unit 12

The points are not a grade; they are just there to help you know which words you need to focus on. By the end of this unit, you should be able to change all your ratings to a 3. That's the goal.

Read each word aloud. Have students repeat it, write it, and rate it. Then, have volunteers who rated a word *2* or *3* use the word in an oral sentence.

Preteach Vocabulary

Let's take a closer look at the words. Follow the Preteach Procedure below.

Preteach Procedure

This activity is intended to take only a short amount of time, so make it an oral exercise.

- Introduce each word as indicated on the word card.
- Read the definition and example sentences.
- Ask questions to clarify and deepen understanding.
- If time permits, allow students to share.

* If your students would benefit from copying the definitions, please have them do so in the vocabulary log in the back of the Student Books using the margin definitions in the passage selections. This should be done outside of instruction time.

lacking (adj)

Let's read the first word together. *Lacking.*

Definition: If something is *lacking,* it is missing something or doesn't have enough of something. What means "missing something; not having enough of something"? (lacking)

Example 1: In a family of singers, the one child who can't carry a tune may feel *lacking.*

Example 2: Leaders who treat their followers as if they are *lacking* do not succeed in motivating them.

Example 3: Shy, quiet people sometimes feel *lacking* in a crowded, social situation.

Question 1: Only skilled dancers make the chorus line in the musical. You make the chorus line. Are your dance skills *lacking*? Yes or no? (no)

Question 2: You show up at a friend's quinceañera in tattered jeans. Might her mother look at you as if you are *lacking*? Yes or no? (yes)

Pair Share: Turn to your partner and state one thing a person could tell himself or herself in a situation where he or she is made to feel *lacking.*

interrupt (v)

Let's read the next word together. *Interrupt.*

Definition: If you *interrupt* someone, you say or do something that causes him or her to stop doing what he or she is doing. What word means "to say or do something that causes another person to stop doing something"? (interrupt)

Example 1: It is difficult to have an enjoyable conversation with a person who constantly *interrupts* what you say.

Example 2: If you must *interrupt* someone, it's best to begin by saying "I'm sorry, but . . ."

Example 3: A loud, sudden noise can *interrupt* a person's train of thought.

Question 1: You are talking to a friend on the phone when your friend's little brother starts crying and she has to go. Has the crying *interrupted* your conversation? Yes or no? (yes)

Question 2: Your grandmother can talk continuously without stopping. Do you sometimes find it necessary to *interrupt* her? Yes or no? (yes)

Pair Share: Talk about the weather with your partner. Take turns *interrupting* each other.

2

verdict (n)

Let's read the next word together. *Verdict.*

Definition: A *verdict* is a decision, a judgment, or a ruling. What word means "a decision, a judgment, or a ruling"? (verdict)

Example 1: If a jury's *verdict* is "guilty," a person on trial will be convicted of the crime.

Example 2: When a group of friends votes on what movie to see, they reach a *verdict* in a democratic way.

Example 3: Parents sometimes reach decisions in private and then announce the *verdict* to their kids.

Question 1: All the news shows and Web sites condemn a young movie star for his actions. Has the press reached a *verdict* on his behavior? Yes or no? (yes)

Question 2: You do a toothpaste taste test on your friends for a science project. They all agree Sparkle White brand tastes best. Have they reached a *verdict*? Yes or no? (yes)

Pair Share: With your partner, get together with another pair. Try to reach a *verdict* about the best pizza in town.

3

consume (v)

Let's read the next word together. *Consume.*

Definition: To *consume* is to take something in or to read and process information. What word means "to take in; to read or process information"? (consume)

Example 1: People who love reading murder mysteries can sometimes *consume* several in a single sitting.

Example 2: Politicians often have assistants who *consume* the news and then give them summaries or briefings on it.

Example 3: If you *consume* book after book after book, you might be called a bookworm.

Question 1: You read dozens of online reviews before you buy anything. Do you *consume* the reviews? Yes or no? (yes)

Question 2: You watch an entire TV series in one weekend. Have you *consumed* it? Yes or no? (yes)

Pair Share: Turn to your partner and tell how you *consume* information about your favorite celebrity, athlete, or public figure.

primitive (adj)

Let's read the next word together. *Primitive.*

Definition: If something is *primitive*, it is simple and old-fashioned, or it is an early model of something. What word means "simple and old-fashioned; an early model of something"? (primitive)

Example 1: Orville and Wilbur Wright's flying contraption was a *primitive* airplane.

Example 2: A sundial is a *primitive* type of clock.

Example 3: Using an abacus—a device with beads that move along rods—is a *primitive* way to do math.

Question 1: The computer crashes, so your mom suggests that you use her old typewriter to write your paper instead. Would that be a *primitive* way to write? Yes or no? (yes)

Question 2: Your Aunt Yolanda buys a new phone whenever a new model is released. Does she enjoy *primitive* technology? Yes or no? (no)

Pair Share: Turn to your partner. Describe a machine or gadget in your home that you consider *primitive*, but that someone still uses.

5

tenacity (n)

Let's read the next word together. *Tenacity.*

Definition: *Tenacity* is stubbornness, or the quality of not giving up easily. What word means "stubbornness; the quality of not giving up easily"? (tenacity)

Example 1: An athlete who won't rest until she breaks her personal record has *tenacity.*

Example 2: People who are passionate about a cause and devote their lives to it have *tenacity.*

Example 3: If a person has too much *tenacity*, he or she might be viewed by others as inflexible or narrow-minded.

Question 1: You ask your mother over and over if you can get your nose pierced, and she finally says yes. Do you have *tenacity*? Yes or no? (yes)

Question 2: Your friend volunteers for a political campaign, but when it starts to look like her candidate will lose, she quits. Does she have *tenacity*? Yes or no? (no)

Pair Share: Turn to your partner. Tell him or her about someone you know of who shows great *tenacity.*

automatically (adv)

Let's read the next word together. *Automatically.*

Definition: If you do something *automatically*, you do it without thinking. What word means "without thinking"? (automatically)

Example 1: If I stub my toe, I say "Ouch!" *automatically.*

Example 2: Food commercials are designed to make you feel hungry *automatically.*

Example 3: If you point and shout "Look!" most people will *automatically* do as you say.

Question 1: You think the shower water is warm but when you step in, it's ice cold. Do you *automatically* get out? Yes or no? (yes)

Question 2: Someone asks you what your favorite movie is. You think about it for a minute or two, and then give your answer. Have you answered *automatically*? Yes or no? (no)

Pair Share: Turn to your partner and describe something you do *automatically* when you wake up in the morning.

exalted (adj)

Let's read the next word together. *Exalted.*

Definition: If something is *exalted*, it is of high value or status. What word means "of high value or status"? (exalted)

Example 1: The deeds of *exalted* war heroes are described in history books.

Example 2: Some people consider meeting the king or queen of a country an *exalted* privilege.

Example 3: Humans of all ages have worshipped their *exalted* gods in formal services.

Question 1: Your friend has posters of her favorite movie star all over her walls and ceiling. Does this actor have *exalted* status in your friend's eyes? Yes or no? (yes)

Question 2: Nobody wants to sit with Thad at lunch. Is he an *exalted* lunch partner? Yes or no? (no)

Pair Share: Turn to your partner and tell whom it would be your most *exalted* honor to meet.

(on) behalf (n)

Let's read the next word together. *Behalf.*

Definition: If you do something on *behalf* of someone else, you do it in his or her place or to help that person. What word means "in someone's place or to help someone"? (behalf)

Example 1: If an important person cannot be at a ceremony to receive an award, a representative might accept it on his or her *behalf.*

Example 2: If you are speaking on someone else's *behalf*, be sure not to add your own opinions or ideas.

Example 3: A substitute teacher might give you an assignment on my *behalf.*

Question 1: A young boy has a rare disease, and his mother works hard to raise funds for new treatments. Is she working on his *behalf*? Yes or no? (yes)

Question 2: Your friend wants to ask someone out but is too shy. You ask the person out yourself but don't tell your friend. Do you ask the person out on your friend's *behalf*? Yes or no? (no)

Pair Share: Tell your partner what award you would most like to receive. Then, take turns giving a brief speech to accept the award on each other's *behalf.*

9

experimental (adj)

Let's read the last word together. *Experimental.*

Definition: If something is *experimental*, it uses new methods or ideas that may or may not work. What word means "using new methods or ideas that may or may not work"? (experimental)

Example 1: Some cancer patients are given *experimental* drugs to see if they work.

Example 2: If you come up with an *experimental* way to kill mosquitoes, you might try selling your idea to people on the Gulf Coast in summertime.

Example 3: Companies will sometimes pay volunteers to participate in an *experimental* weight-loss program.

Question 1: Your friend has a proven method of studying Spanish vocabulary; it works every time. Is the method *experimental*? Yes or no? (no)

Question 2: You describe your own fashion sense as *experimental*. Are you likely to try new combinations of clothing items and accessories? Yes or no? (yes)

Pair Share: Turn to your partner. Together, come up with an *experimental* method of making new friends. How would you test the method?

Reading

Objectives

- Read an excerpt from a novel.
- Monitor comprehension during text reading.

Part 2 of the Excerpt from *My Sister's Keeper*

Direct students to page 371 in their Student Books.

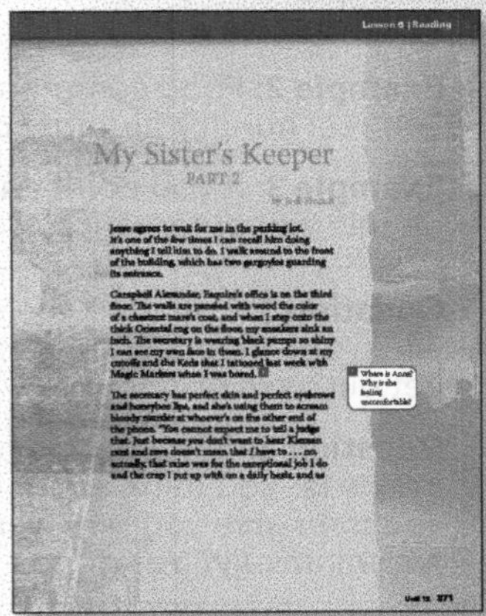

Now that we have previewed vocabulary, it's time to read.

Guiding Students Toward Independent Reading

It is important that your students read as much and as often as they can. Assign readings that meet the needs of your students, based on your observations and data. This is a good opportunity to stretch your students. If students become frustrated, scaffold the reading with paired reading, choral reading, or a read-aloud.

Options for reading text:

- Teacher read-aloud
- Teacher-led or student-led choral read
- Paired read or independent read

Choose an option for reading text. Students read according to the option that you chose.

Review the purpose of the numbered squares in the text and prompt students to stop periodically and check comprehension.

If you choose to read the text aloud or chorally, use the following text boxes and stop to ask questions and have students answer them.

SE p. 371, paragraphs 1–2

Jesse agrees to wait for me in the parking lot. It's one of the few times I can recall him doing anything I tell him to do. I walk around to the front of the building, which has two gargoyles guarding its entrance.

Campbell Alexander, Esquire's office is on the third floor. The walls are paneled with wood the color of a chestnut mare's coat, and when I step onto the thick Oriental rug on the floor, my sneakers sink an inch. The secretary is wearing black pumps so shiny I can see my own face in them. I glance down at my cutoffs and the Keds that I tattooed last week with Magic Markers when I was bored.

1. Where is Anna? Why is she feeling uncomfortable?

SE p. 371, paragraph 3

The secretary has perfect skin and perfect eyebrows and honeybee lips, and she's using them to scream bloody murder at whoever's on the other end of the phone. "You cannot expect me to tell a judge that. Just because *you* don't want to hear Kleman rant and rave doesn't mean that *I* have to . . . no, actually, that raise was for the exceptional job I do and the crap I put up with on a daily basis, and as | a matter of fact, while we're on—" She holds the phone away from her ear; I can make out the buzz of disconnection. "Bastard," she mutters, and then seems to realize I'm standing three feet away. "Can I help you?"

page break

SE p. 372, paragraph 1

She looks me over from head to toe, rating me on a general scale of first impressions, and finding me severely **lacking**. I lift my chin and pretend to be far more cool than I actually am. "I have an appointment with Mr. Alexander. At four o'clock."

2. What is the secretary basing her first impression on?

SE p. 372, paragraphs 2–6

"Your voice," she says. "On the phone, you didn't sound quite so . . . "

Young?

She smiles uncomfortably. "We don't try juvenile cases, as a rule. If you'd like I can offer you the names of some practicing attorneys who—"

I take a deep breath. "Actually," I **interrupt**, "you're wrong. Smith v. Whately, Edmunds v. Womens and Infants Hospital, and Jerome v. the Diocese of Providence all involved litigants under the age of eighteen. All three resulted in **verdicts** for Mr. Alexander's clients. And those were just in the past *year*."

The secretary blinks at me. Then a slow smile toasts her face, as if she's decided she just might like me after all. "Come to think of it, why don't you just wait in his office?" she suggests, and she stands up to show me the way.

3. How does Anna get the secretary to change her mind?

SE p. 372, paragraph 7

Even if I spend every minute of the rest of my life reading, I do not believe that I will ever manage to **consume** the sheer number of words routed high and low on the walls of Campbell Alexander, Esquire's office. I do the math—if there are 400 words or so on every page, and each of those legal | books are 400 pages, and there are twenty on a shelf and six shelves per bookcase—why, you're pushing nineteen million words, and that's only partway across the room.

page break

SE p. 373, paragraphs 1–3

I'm alone in the office long enough to note that his desk is so neat, you could play Chinese football on the blotter; that there is not a single photo of a wife or a kid or even himself; and that in spite of the fact that the room is spotless, there's a mug full of water sitting on the floor.

I find myself making up explanations: it's a swimming pool for an army of ants. It's some kind of **primitive** humidifier. It's a mirage.

I've nearly convinced myself about that last one, and am leaning over to touch it to see if it's real, when the door bursts open. I practically fall out of my chair and that puts me eye to eye with an incoming German shepherd, which spears me with a look and then marches over to the mug and starts to drink.

4. What personality traits of Anna are evident in the office?

SE p. 373, paragraphs 4–6

Campbell Alexander comes in, too. He's got black hair and he's at least as tall as my dad—six feet—with a right-angle jaw and eyes that look frozen over. He shrugs out of a suit jacket and hangs it neatly on the back of the door, then yanks a file out of a cabinet before moving to his desk. He never makes eye contact with me, but he starts talking all the same. "I don't want any Girl Scout cookies," Campbell Alexander says. "Although you do get Brownie points for **tenacity**. Ha." He smiles at his own joke.

"I'm not selling anything."

He glances at me curiously, then pushes a button on his phone. "Kerri," he says when the secretary answers. "What is this doing in my office?"

SE p. 374, paragraphs 1–2

"I'm here to retain you," I say.

The lawyer releases the intercom button. "I don't think so."

5. How does Alexander receive Anna's offer?

SE p. 374, paragraphs 3–9

"You don't even know if I have a case."

I take a step forward; so does the dog. For the first time I realize it's wearing one of those vests with a red cross on it, like a St. Bernard that might carry rum up a snowy mountain. I **automatically** reach out to pet him. "Don't," Alexander says. "Judge is a service dog."

My hand goes back to my side. "But you aren't blind."

"Thank you for pointing that out to me."

"So what's the matter with you?"

The minute I say it, I want to take it back. Haven't I watched Kate field this question from hundreds of rude people?

"I have an iron lung," Campbell Alexander says curtly, "and the dog keeps me from getting too close to magnets. Now, if you'd do me the **exalted** honor of leaving, my secretary can find you the name of someone who—"

6. What connects Campbell Alexander to Kate?

SE p. 374, paragraphs 10–11

But I can't go yet. "Did you really sue God?" I take out all the newspaper clippings, smooth them on the bare desk.

A muscle tics in his cheek, and then he picks up the article lying on top. "I sued the Diocese of Providence, on **behalf** of a kid in one of their orphanages who needed an **experimental** treatment involving fetal tissue, which they felt violated Vatican II. However, it makes a much better headline to say that a nine-year-old is suing God for being stuck with the short end of the straw in life." I just stare at him. "Dylan Jerome," the lawyer | admits, "wanted to sue God for not caring enough about him."

page break

SE p. 375, paragraph 1

A rainbow might as well have cracked down the middle of that big mahogany desk. "Mr. Alexander," I say, "my sister has leukemia."

7. What gives Anna hope?

SE p. 375, paragraphs 2–4

> "I'm sorry to hear that. But even if I were willing to litigate against God again, which I'm not, you can't bring a lawsuit on someone else's behalf."
>
> There is way too much to explain—my own blood seeping into my sister's veins; the nurses holding me down to stick me for white cells Kate might borrow; the doctor saying they didn't get enough the first time around. The bruises and the deep bone ache after I gave up my marrow; the shots that sparked more stem cells in me, so that there'd be extra for my sister. The fact that I'm not sick, but I might as well be. The fact that the only reason I was born was as a harvest crop for Kate. The fact that even now, a major decision about me is being made, and no one's bothered to ask the one person who most deserves it to speak her opinion.
>
> There's way too much to explain, and so I do the best I can. "It's not God. Just my parents," I say. "I want to sue them for the rights to my own body."

8. What is Anna's life like?

For confirmation of engagement, have partners share their opinions about Anna's purpose in life and her decision not to fulfill this. Have volunteers share opinions with the class.

Unit 12 Lesson 7

Lesson Opener

Before the lesson, choose one of the following activities to write on the board or post on the *LANGUAGE! Live* Class Wall online.

- *Write a summary sentence about Anna's request of the lawyer.*
- *Make a list of adjectives describing Anna. Use three of them in sentences.*
- *Write five sentences about Anna using negative statements.*

Vocabulary

Objective

- Review key passage vocabulary.

Review Passage Vocabulary

Direct students to page 370 in their Student Books. Use the following questions to review the vocabulary words from Part 2 of the excerpt from *My Sister's Keeper*. Have students answer each question using the vocabulary word or indicating its meaning in a complete sentence.

Lesson 6 | Vocabulary

Key Passage Vocabulary: from *My Sister's Keeper*, Part 2

Read each word. Write the word in column 3. Then, circle a number to rate your knowledge of the word.

Read the Word	Part of Speech	Write the Word	Rate the Word
lacking	(adj)	lacking	0 1 2 3
interrupt	(v)	interrupt	0 1 2 3
verdict	(n)	verdict	0 1 2 3
consume	(v)	consume	0 1 2 3
primitive	(adj)	primitive	0 1 2 3
tenacity	(n)	tenacity	0 1 2 3
automatically	(adv)	automatically	0 1 2 3
exalted	(adj)	exalted	0 1 2 3
(on) behalf	(n)	(on) behalf	0 1 2 3
experimental	(adj)	experimental	0 1 2 3

370 Unit 12

- Mr. Alexander's secretary finds Anna *lacking*. What is her opinion of Anna? (Her opinion is that Anna is not very important.) Earlier, we learned that Anna finds herself *lacking* too. How so? (She feels physically lacking: she describes herself as "refugee-skinny" and flat-chested with dirt-colored hair and freckles.)
- What is the secretary doing when Anna *interrupts* her? (She is about to tell Anna the names of some attorneys who try juvenile cases.) Why does Anna feel compelled to *interrupt* her? (She feels compelled to interrupt the secretary because Mr. Alexander has, in fact, tried juvenile cases in the past.)
- What were the *verdicts* in the juvenile cases Mr. Alexander tried? (The judge ruled in favor of his clients in all three cases.) What do you predict Mr. Alexander's *verdict* on taking Anna's case will be? (He will probably decide to take the case.)
- In the attorney's office, Anna sees more books than she will ever be able to *consume*. In other words, more books than she will ever be able to what? (It is more books than she will ever be able to read.) What has she clearly *consumed* in preparation for her meeting with Mr. Alexander? (She has clearly consumed information about his trial record.)

- While she waits for Mr. Alexander to come into the office, she sees a mug of water on the floor and imagines it is some kind of *primitive* humidifier. How else could you describe such a humidifier? (The humidifier is old-fashioned or outdated.) Imagine that it's 200 years in the future. What other objects or devices in the office will be considered *primitive* at that point in time? (Possible response: The books on the shelves, the paper files in the file cabinet, and the phone with the intercom will be considered old-fashioned in 200 years.)
- Mr. Alexander has noticed Anna's *tenacity.* What has he noticed about her? (He has noticed that she doesn't give up.) What final outcome do you think Anna's *tenacity* will lead to in this story? (Possible response: Her tenacity will lead to her winning the court case against her parents.)
- What does Anna do to the dog *automatically*? (She reaches out to pet the dog without thinking.) When Mr. Alexander says "Don't," what does Anna do *automatically*? (She puts her hand back to her side without thinking.) Do service dogs do certain things *automatically*? Why or why not? (Yes, they help their humans in certain ways automatically because they are trained to do so.)
- Mr. Alexander asks Anna to do him the "*exalted* honor" of leaving. Why is this such an insult? (It's an insult because he's saying that her leaving his presence would be of high value to him.) Instead of leaving, Anna produces newspaper clippings that tell about the attorney's *exalted* accomplishments. What is the most *exalted* one of all? (Mr. Alexander apparently sued God and won.)
- At first, Mr. Alexander misunderstands Anna and thinks she's visiting him on *behalf* of her sister. If she were, what would she be doing there? (If she were there on behalf of her sister, she would be asking the attorney to represent Kate.) Anna, however, wants Mr. Alexander to act on whose *behalf*? (She wants him to act on her behalf.)
- One of the clippings describes a case in which a sick boy was being denied *experimental* treatment. What kind of treatment would this be? (An experimental treatment is a new method that may or may not work.) If the lawyer takes Anna's case, how might it be *experimental*? (A young girl's attempt to sue her parents for the rights to her own body may or may not work.)

Assign online practice from the Text Training link on the left menu of your teacher dashboard.

Reading

Objectives

- Determine how to respond to prompts.
- Use critical thinking skills to write responses to prompts about text.
- Support written answers with evidence from text.
- Make connections between two texts.

Critical Understandings: Direction Words *assess, connect, illustrate, synthesize*

Let's review some prompts.

Write the words *assess, connect, illustrate,* and *synthesize* on the board. Have students read the words aloud with you.

Direct students to pages 14 and 15 in their Student Books. It is critical to understand what the question is asking and how to answer it. Today, we will look at four direction words used in prompts.

Have students read about the four direction words in the chart with their partner.

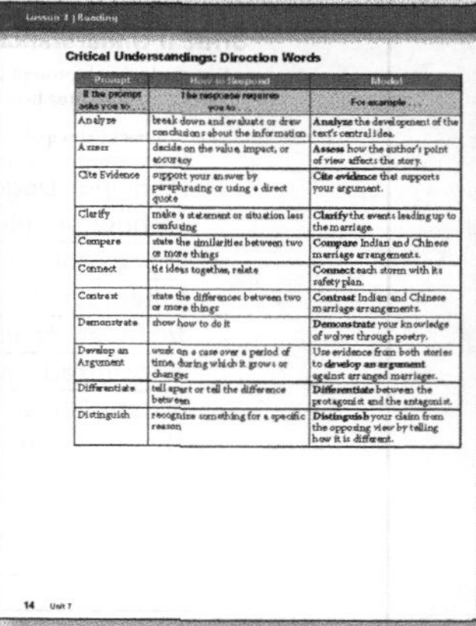

Lesson 3 | Reading

Critical Understandings: Direction Words

Prompt	How to Respond	Model
If the prompt asks you to . . .	The response requires you to . . .	For example . . .
Analyze	break down and evaluate or draw conclusions about the information	**Analyze** the development of the text's central idea.
Assess	decide on the value, impact, or accuracy	**Assess** how the author's point of view affects the story.
Cite Evidence	support your answer by paraphrasing or using a direct quote	**Cite evidence** that supports your argument.
Clarify	make a statement or situation less confusing	**Clarify** the events leading up to the marriage.
Compare	state the similarities between two or more things	**Compare** Indian and Chinese marriage arrangements.
Connect	tie ideas together, relate	**Connect** each storm with its safety plan.
Contrast	state the differences between two or more things	**Contrast** Indian and Chinese marriage arrangements.
Demonstrate	show how to do it	**Demonstrate** your knowledge of wolves through poetry.
Develop an Argument	work on a case over a period of time, during which it grows or changes	Use evidence from both stories to **develop an argument** against arranged marriages.
Differentiate	tell apart or tell the difference between	**Differentiate** between the protagonist and the antagonist.
Distinguish	recognize something for a specific reason	**Distinguish** your claim from the opposing view by telling how it is different.

14 Unit 7

Chart Reading Procedure

- Group students with partners or in triads.
- Have students count off as 1s or 2s. The 1s will become the student leaders. If working with triads, the third students become 3s.
- The student leaders will read the left column (Prompt) in addition to managing the time and turn-taking if working with a triad.
- The 2s will explain the middle column of the chart (How to Respond). If working in triads, 3s take turns explaining the middle column.
- The 1s read the model in the right column (Model), and 2s and 3s restate the model as a question.
- All students should follow along with their pencil eraser while others are explaining the chart.
- Students must work from left to right, top to bottom in order to benefit from this activity.

Check for understanding by requesting an oral response to the following questions.

- If the prompt asks you to *assess,* the response requires you to . . . (decide on the value, impact, or accuracy).
- If the prompt asks you to *connect,* the response requires you to . . . (tie ideas together, relate).
- If the prompt asks you to *illustrate,* the response requires you to . . . (use examples to demonstrate or prove).
- If the prompt asks you to *synthesize,* the response requires you to . . . (combine information in a logical way).

Direct students to pages 376 and 377 in their Student Books and read the instructions aloud.

Lesson 7 | Reading

Critical Understandings

Respond to each prompt using complete sentences. Refer to the chart on pages 14 and 15 to determine how to respond to each prompt.

1. Connect Principal Dogan's quote "How we dress does matter" with the secretary's first impression of Anna.

   Principal Dogan believes that dress is important to how people are perceived. The secretary's first impression of Anna is that she is too young to be taken seriously. Anna is dressed in cutoffs and tattooed tennis shoes. Her dress causes her to be discounted and dismissed, indicating that how she dressed has an impact on how she is perceived by the secretary.

2. Illustrate Anna's maturity during her visit to the lawyer's office.

   Anna is mature in the lawyer's office as evidenced by her persuasive, no-nonsense tone when speaking to the secretary and the lawyer. Her knowledge of the lawyer's past cases represents diligent research and conviction—both of which are mature traits. Anna is not intimidated or dissuaded by the lawyer as others her age likely would have been.

376 Unit 12

Lesson 7 | Reading

Critical Understandings (*cont.*)

3. Synthesize the information in the last three paragraphs of the first excerpt with the first paragraph of the second excerpt to determine what Jesse values.

   Jesse values friction and the life of his sister Anna over the freedoms he has become used to. They all have their roles, and it is a life he has settled into because he is pretty much left to himself to do as he pleases. However, when he realizes that Anna is serious and wants to "rock the boat," he cannot resist the temptation to see what happens and let her voice be heard.

4. Assess Anna's statement ". . . I'm not sick, but I might as well be."

   Anna's belief that she might as well be sick is valid because of the amount of time she spends in the hospital. Anna describes nurses holding her down to stick her, bruises and a deep bone ache, and shots to increase stem cells. These are not the typical medical experiences of a healthy child, which indicates that Anna spends as much time in the hospital as a sick person does. She experiences symptoms of a sick person even though she has no disease.

Unit 12 377

Let's read some prompts about the text.

1. Connect Principal Dogan's quote "How we dress does matter" with the secretary's first impression of Anna.
2. Illustrate Anna's maturity during her visit to the lawyer's office.
3. Synthesize the information in the last three paragraphs of the first excerpt with the first paragraph of the second excerpt to determine what Jesse values.
4. Assess Anna's statement ". . . I'm not sick, but I might as well be."

Guided Practice

Let's practice answering questions that are written as prompts. Remember to use the chart as reference. Let's respond to the first prompt together.

1. Connect Principal Dogan's quote "How we dress does matter" with the secretary's first impression of Anna.

First, tell your partner how to respond according to the chart. (If the prompt asks you to *connect*, the response requires you to tie ideas together.) Which text is Principal Dogan's quote from? (North High School letter) Let's turn the prompt into a question to confirm understanding. (How is the quote "How we dress does matter" related to the secretary's impression of Anna?)

We need to know what the secretary was thinking and how that changed things. With your partner, look for the answers to the following questions.

- What was the secretary's first impression of Anna? Did Anna's appearance have something to do with this?

Have partners search the text for the answers. While providing partner time, write the following sentence starters on the board.

Principal Dogan believes ________________________________.

The secretary's first impression of Anna ___________________.

Her dress causes ______________________________________.

Have partners answer the question.

Let's move on to the next prompt.

2. Illustrate Anna's maturity during her visit to the lawyer's office.

How should we respond according to the chart? (If the prompt asks you to *illustrate*, the response requires you to use examples to demonstrate or prove.) Now, turn the prompt into a question to confirm your understanding. Tell your partner the question. (What evidence proves that Anna was mature while visiting the lawyer's office?)

Have partners search the text for the answers. While providing partner time, write the following sentence starter on the board.

Anna is mature in the lawyer's office as evidenced by ____________________ ____________.

Have partners answer the question.

3. Synthesize the information in the last three paragraphs of the first excerpt with the first paragraph of the second excerpt to determine what Jesse values.

How should we respond according to the chart? (If the prompt asks you to *synthesize*, the response requires you to combine information in a logical way.) Now, turn the prompt into a question to confirm your understanding. Tell your partner the question. (What does Jesse value?)

Have partners search both excerpts for the answers. While providing partner time, write the following sentence starter on the board.

Jesse values ______________________________ *over*_________________.

Have partners answer the question.

4. Assess Anna's statement ". . . I'm not sick, but I might as well be."

Remind your partner how to respond to the direction word according to the chart. (If the prompt asks you to *assess*, the response requires you to decide on the value, impact, or accuracy.) Turn the prompt into a question to confirm understanding. (Is Anna's statement ". . . I'm not sick, but I might as well be" accurate?)

Have students search the excerpt for evidence to prove Anna might as well be sick. While providing partner time, write the following sentence starter on the board.

Anna's belief that she might as well be sick is/is not valid because ________ ______________________.

Have partners answer the question.

Unit 12

Lesson 8

Lesson Opener

Before the lesson, choose one of the following activities to write on the board or post on the *LANGUAGE! Live* Class Wall online.

- *Write five sentences describing Anna's trip to the lawyer's office using participial phrases.*
- *Write five sentences about Anna's mom using appositives.*
- *Expand one or more of these simple sentences, using the steps in Masterpiece Sentences.*

  Anna helped Kate.

  Kate's parents needed help.

  Jesse rebelled.

  Anna was born.

Reading

Objectives

- Establish a purpose for rereading literary text.
- Monitor comprehension during text reading.
- Use critical thinking skills to write responses to prompts about text.
- Support written answers with evidence from text.
- Analyze how a character in a story affects the plot.
- Analyze how character point of view creates suspense.
- Identify the points of view of multiple characters.

Reading for a Purpose: Part 2 of the Excerpt from *My Sister's Keeper*

Let's read the text again to gain understanding.

First, we'll preview the prompts to provide a purpose for rereading the text. You should recognize the question words that we practiced in the last lesson.

Direct students to pages 378–380 in their Student Books. Have them read the prompts aloud with you.

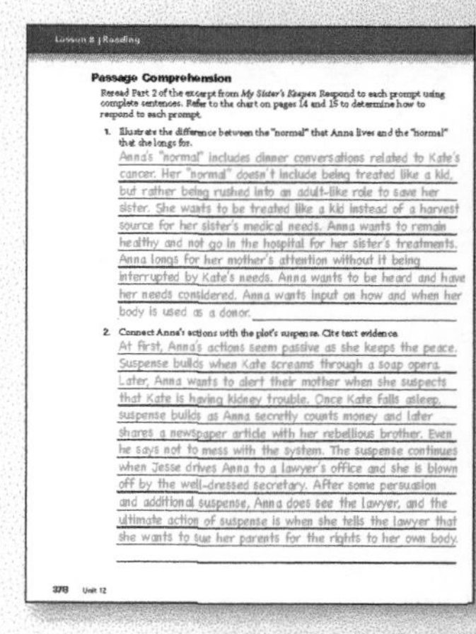

Lesson 8 | Reading

Passage Comprehension

Reread Part 2 of the excerpt from *My Sister's Keeper.* Respond to each prompt using complete sentences. Refer to the chart on pages 14 and 15 to determine how to respond to each prompt.

1. Illustrate the difference between the "normal" that Anna lives and the "normal" that she longs for.

   Anna's "normal" includes dinner conversations related to Kate's cancer. Her "normal" doesn't include being treated like a kid, but rather being rushed into an adult-like role to save her sister. She wants to be treated like a kid instead of a harvest source for her sister's medical needs. Anna wants to remain healthy and not go in the hospital for her sister's treatments. Anna longs for her mother's attention without it being interrupted by Kate's needs. Anna wants to be heard and have her needs considered. Anna wants input on how and when her body is used as a donor.

2. Connect Anna's actions with the plot's suspense. Cite text evidence.

   At first, Anna's actions seem passive as she keeps the peace. Suspense builds when Kate screams through a soap opera. Later, Anna wants to alert their mother when she suspects that Kate is having kidney trouble. Once Kate falls asleep, suspense builds as Anna secretly counts money and later shares a newspaper article with her rebellious brother. Even he says not to mess with the system. The suspense continues when Jesse drives Anna to a lawyer's office and she is blown off by the well-dressed secretary. After some persuasion and additional suspense, Anna does see the lawyer, and the ultimate action of suspense is when she tells the lawyer that she wants to sue her parents for the rights to her own body.

378 Unit 12

1. Illustrate the difference between the "normal" that Anna lives and the "normal" that she longs for.
2. Connect Anna's actions with the plot's suspense. Cite text evidence.
3. Illustrate Anna's reason for suing her parents for the rights to her own body.
4. Synthesize Kate's point of view and Anna's parents' points of view to convince Anna to keep things as is.
5. Connect Kate to Campbell Alexander.
6. Use both excerpts to assess Anna's case for the rights to her own body.

It's time to revisit the text.

Choose an option for reading text. Have students read the text according to the option that you chose.

Options for reading text:

- Teacher read-aloud
- Teacher-led or student-led choral read
- Paired read or independent read with bold vocabulary words read aloud

Direct students to page 371 in their Student Books or have them tear out the extra copy of the excerpt from the back of their book.

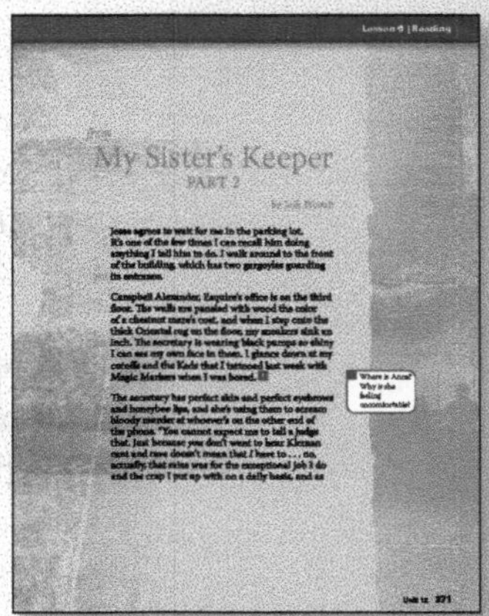

Note: To minimize flipping back and forth between the pages, a copy of each text has been included in the back of the Student Books. Encourage students to tear this out and use it when working on activities that require the use of the text.

Have students read the text.

Passage Comprehension

Write the words *assess, connect, illustrate,* and *synthesize* on the board. Have students read the words aloud with you.

Direct students to pages 14 and 15 in their Student Books. It is critical to understand what the question is asking and how to answer it. Today, we will review four direction words used in prompts.

Have students read about the four words in the chart on pages 14 and 15 with their partner. Check for understanding by requesting an oral response to the following questions.

- If the prompt asks you to *assess,* the response requires you to . . . (decide on the value, impact, or accuracy).
- If the prompt asks you to *connect,* the response requires you to . . . (tie ideas together, relate).
- If the prompt asks you to *illustrate,* the response requires you to . . . (use examples to demonstrate or prove).
- If the prompt asks you to *synthesize,* the response requires you to . . . (combine information in a logical way).

Lesson 3 | Reading

Critical Understandings: Direction Words

Prompt	How to Respond	Model
If the prompt asks you to . . .	**The response requires you to . . .**	**For example . . .**
Analyze	break down and evaluate or draw conclusions about the information	**Analyze** the development of the text's central idea.
Assess	decide on the value, impact, or accuracy	**Assess** how the author's point of view affects the story.
Cite Evidence	support your answer by paraphrasing or using a direct quote	**Cite evidence** that supports your argument.
Clarify	make a statement or situation less confusing	**Clarify** the events leading up to the marriage.
Compare	state the similarities between two or more things	**Compare** Indian and Chinese marriage arrangements.
Connect	tie ideas together, relate	**Connect** each storm with its safety plan.
Contrast	state the differences between two or more things	**Contrast** Indian and Chinese marriage arrangements.
Demonstrate	show how to do it	**Demonstrate** your knowledge of wolves through poetry.
Develop an Argument	work on a case over a period of time, during which it grows or changes	Use evidence from both stories to **develop an argument** against arranged marriages.
Differentiate	tell apart or tell the difference between	**Differentiate** between the protagonist and the antagonist.
Distinguish	recognize something for a specific reason	**Distinguish** your claim from the opposing view by telling how it is different.

14 Unit 7

Let's practice answering questions that are written as prompts. Remember to use the chart as reference. Don't forget, if the direction word is confusing, try to restate the prompt by using a question word.

Direct students to pages 378–380 in their Student Books.

Passage Comprehension

Reread Part 2 of the excerpt from *My Sister's Keeper.* Respond to each prompt using complete sentences. Refer to the chart on pages 14 and 15 to determine how to respond to each prompt.

1. Illustrate the difference between the "normal" that Anna lives and the "normal" that she longs for.
   Anna's "normal" includes dinner conversations related to Kate's cancer. Her "normal" doesn't include being treated like a kid, but rather being rushed into an adult-like role to save her sister. She wants to be treated like a kid instead of a harvest source for her sister's medical needs. Anna wants to remain healthy and not go in the hospital for her sister's treatments. Anna longs for her mother's attention without it being interrupted by Kate's needs. Anna wants to be heard and have her needs considered. Anna wants input on how and when her body is used as a donor.

2. Connect Anna's actions with the plot's suspense. Cite text evidence.
   At first, Anna's actions seem passive as she keeps the peace. Suspense builds when Kate screams through a soap opera. Later, Anna wants to alert their mother when she suspects that Kate is having kidney trouble. Once Kate falls asleep, suspense builds as Anna secretly counts money and later shares a newspaper article with her rebellious brother. Even he says not to mess with the system. The suspense continues when Jesse drives Anna to a lawyer's office and she is blown off by the well-dressed secretary. After some persuasion and additional suspense, Anna does see the lawyer, and the ultimate action of suspense is when she tells the lawyer that she wants to sue her parents for the rights to her own body.

Passage Comprehension (*cont.*)

3. Illustrate Anna's reason for suing her parents for the rights to her own body.
   Anna was genetically created to be a perfect tissue match to her sister Kate. The intention of doing so was to keep Kate alive by using Anna's stem cells and bone marrow whenever the need arises. The text says "my own blood seeping into my sister's veins; the nurses holding me down to stick me for white cells Kate might borrow; the doctor saying they didn't get enough the first time around. The bruises and the deep bone ache after I gave up my marrow; the shots that sparked more stem cells in me, so that there'd be extra for my sister. The fact that I'm not sick, but I might as well be. The fact that the only reason I was born was as a harvest crop for Kate. The fact that even now, a major decision about me is being made, and no one's bothered to ask the one person who most deserves it to speak her opinion."

4. Synthesize Kate's point of view and Anna's parents' points of view to convince Anna to keep things as is.
   Kate has been sick most of her life. She is constantly in pain and needing help to regain her strength. Anna provides this for her so she can live. Kate's parents do not want to watch a child die if there is anything at all they can do to prevent it. They created Anna for this purpose, and she should therefore fulfill her duty. If Anna sues for her rights, Kate will likely die and this will be hard on everyone . . . most of all Anna.

Guided Practice

Let's practice answering questions that are written as prompts. Let's read the first prompt together.

> 1. Illustrate the difference between the "normal" that Anna lives and the "normal" that she longs for.

How should we respond according to the chart? (If the prompt asks you to *illustrate,* the response requires you to use examples to demonstrate or prove.) Turn the prompt into a question to confirm understanding. Tell your partner the question. (What examples from the text prove that Anna's normal is different from the normal she longs for?)

Passage Comprehension (*cont.*)

5. Connect Kate to Campbell Alexander.
   Both Kate and Campbell Alexander have an illness and rely on another being to keep them alive. Kate has leukemia and relies on Anna for tissue and bone marrow. Campbell has an iron lung and relies on a service dog to keep him away from magnets that could affect his lung.

6. Use both excerpts to assess Anna's case for the rights to her own body.
   Anna's case has merit considering she has no say so in what happens to her own body. She was born as a harvest crop for her sister. She was created to be an identical tissue match so that she could give leukocytes, stem cells, and bone marrow to her sister as they are needed. She spends a great deal of time in the hospital saving her sister's life instead of living hers. Anna should be given the right to decide if she wants to help her sister or not, like other donors.

Have partners search the text for the answers. While providing partner time, write the following sentence starters on the board.

Anna's normal includes ___________. Her normal doesn't include ______.

Anna longs for _________________________________.

Anna wants ___________________________________.

Have partners answer the question.

Independent Practice

Have partners respond to the remaining prompts. For students who need more assistance, provide the following alternative questions.

Alternative questions:

2. How are Anna's actions related to the suspense in the story? *or* How did Anna's actions make you feel excited or worried about what would happen next?
3. What evidence proves that Anna should have rights to make medical decisions about her own body?
4. According to Kate and Anna's parents, why might they want Anna to keep things as is?
5. What is the relationship between Campbell Alexander and Kate?
6. What are the merits behind Anna's case for the rights to her own body?

Unit 12

Lesson 9

Lesson Opener

Before the lesson, choose one of the following activities to write on the board or post on the *LANGUAGE! Live* Class Wall online.

- *In the story, Anna was genetically created to be a tissue match to her sister in an attempt to save her sister's life. How would you change after finding out that was the reason you were born?*
- *Use the word* saving *in three sentences about Anna. Use it as a verb in one sentence, a noun in one sentence, and an adjective in another sentence.*
- *Write the dialogue of a conversation you think Anna had with her mom when she returned from the lawyer's office. Remember to punctuate correctly.*

Reading

Objectives

- Read literature with purpose and understanding.
- Answer questions to demonstrate comprehension of text.
- Identify and explain explicit details from text.
- Monitor comprehension during text reading.
- Identify puns in writing.
- Identify sarcasm in writing.
- Determine the meaning of figurative language.
- Identify allusions to historical works (the Bible) in text.
- Identify indefinite pronouns and determine their purpose.
- Determine the meaning and purpose of conjunctive adverbs.

Close Reading of Part 2 of the Excerpt from *My Sister's Keeper*

Highlighters or colored pencils

Let's reread Part 2 of the excerpt from *My Sister's Keeper.* I will provide specific instructions on how to mark the text to help with comprehension.

Have students get out a highlighter or colored pencil.

Direct students to pages 381–385 in their Student Books.

Draw a rectangle around the title.

Star the word used to indicate this is a part of a novel. (from)

Circle the words used to indicate this is a continuation. (PART 2)

Now, let's read the vocabulary words aloud.

- What's the first bold vocabulary word? (lacking) *Lacking* means "missing something; not having enough of something." If you don't eat vegetables, your diet is seriously *lacking.* Have partners use the word in a sentence.
- What's the next vocabulary word? (interrupt) *Interrupt* means "to say or do something that causes another person to stop doing something." Don't *interrupt* others during class discussions; it is rude. Have partners use the word in a sentence.
- Next word? (verdicts) *Verdicts* means "decisions, judgments, or rulings." The jury's *verdicts* on the multiple charges allowed the criminal to go free. Have partners use the word in a sentence.

- Let's continue. (consume) *Consume* means "to take in; to read or process information." When there is a tragedy, I *consume* as much information as I can so I am informed about the events. Have partners use the word in a sentence.
- Next word? (primitive) *Primitive* means "simple and old-fashioned; an early model of something." Some may consider handwritten letters a *primitive* form of communication. Have partners use the word in a sentence.
- Let's continue. (tenacity) *Tenacity* means "stubbornness; the quality of not giving up easily." *Tenacity* will help you achieve your goals. Have partners use the word in a sentence.
- Let's continue. (automatically) *Automatically* means "without thinking." The next song plays *automatically* once you begin playing the album. Have partners use the word in a sentence.
- Next word? (exalted) *Exalted* means "of high value or status." Upperclassmen feel that they have *exalted* status. Have partners use the word in a sentence.
- Next word? (behalf) *Behalf* means "in someone's place or to help someone." On *behalf* of all the teachers, I say it will give us great joy to watch you graduate. Have partners use the word in a sentence.
- Last word. (experimental) *Experimental* means "using new methods or ideas that may or may not work." Medical insurance does not pay for *experimental* procedures. Have partners use the word in a sentence.

Talk with a partner about any vocabulary word that is still confusing for you to read or understand.

As you reread the passage, you will monitor your understanding by circling the check marks or the question marks. Please be sure to draw a question mark over any confusing words, phrases, or sentences.

Options for rereading text:

- Teacher read-aloud
- Teacher-led or student-led choral read
- Paired read or independent read with bold vocabulary words read aloud

Choose an option for reading text. Have students read lines 1–18 according to the option that you chose. Pay attention to the traits for each character. Follow this process. When you learn something about Anna, record an A in the margin. When you learn something about Kate, record a K. Record a J for Jesse, an M for Mom, and a D for Dad. You will revisit these characters' traits for a later writing assignment.

Lesson 9 | Reading

Close Reading

Read the text.

from *My Sister's Keeper,* PART 2

Jesse agrees to wait for me in the parking lot. It's one of the few times I can recall him doing anything I tell him to do. I walk around to the front of the building, which has two gargoyles guarding its entrance.

Campbell Alexander, Esquire's office is on the third floor. The walls are paneled with wood the color of a chestnut mare's coat, and when I step onto the thick Oriental rug on the floor, my sneakers sink an inch. The secretary is wearing black pumps so shiny I can see my own face in them. I glance down at my cutoffs and the Keds that I tattooed last week with Magic Markers when I was bored.

The secretary has perfect skin and perfect eyebrows and honeybee lips, and she's using them to scream bloody murder at whoever's on the other end of the phone. "You cannot expect me to tell a judge that. Just because *you* don't want to hear Kleman rant and rave doesn't mean that *I* have to . . . no, actually, that raise was for the exceptional job I do and the crap I put up with on a daily basis, and as a matter of fact, while we're on—" She holds the phone away from her ear; I can make out the buzz of disconnection. "Bastard," she mutters, and then seems to realize I'm standing three feet away. "Can I help you?"

✔ ?

Unit 12 381

When most of the students are finished, continue with the entire class. Let's see how well you understood what you read.

- Circle the check mark or the question mark for this text. Draw a question mark over any confusing words.
- Go to line 1. Mark the evidence that Anna wants to do this on her own. (Jesse agrees to wait for me in the parking lot.)
- Go to line 5. Mark the description of the color of the walls. (chestnut mare's coat)
- Go to line 7. Mark how shiny the secretary's shoes are. (so shiny I can see my own face in them)
- Go to line 8. Mark the evidence that Anna felt underdressed. (I glance down at my cutoffs and the Keds that I tattooed) Circle the word that means "take a quick look." (glance)
- Go to line 13. Mark the idiom that means "shout angrily and wildly." (rant and rave)
- Mark the idiom that means "to complain very loudly." (scream bloody murder)
- Go to line 17. Mark the synonym of *mumbles*. (mutters)

Have students read lines 19–42 according to the option that you chose. Remember to record a letter every time you learn something about a character. Anna equals A; Kate equals K; Jesse equals J; Mom equals M; and Dad equals D.

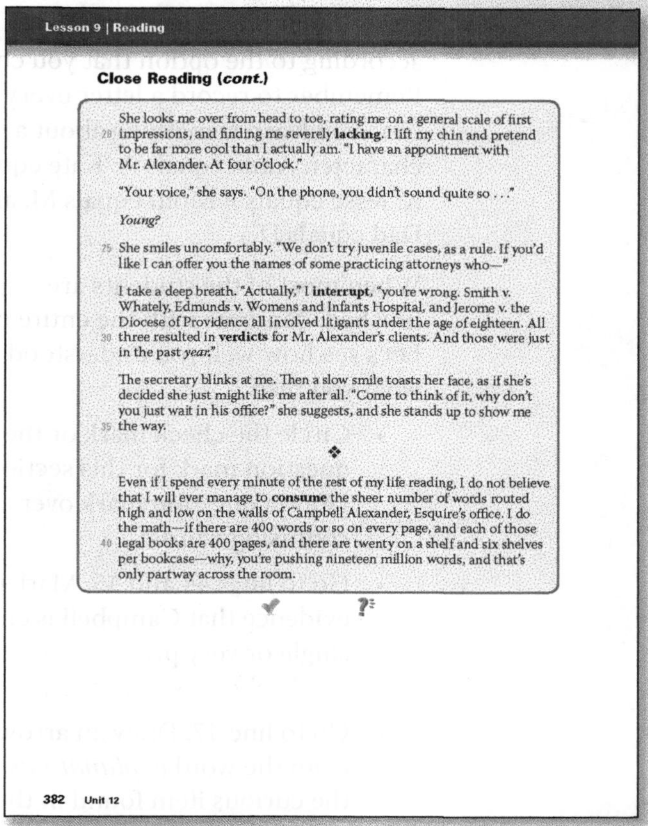

Lesson 9 | Reading

Close Reading (*cont.*)

She looks me over from head to toe, rating me on a general scale of first impressions, and finding me severely **lacking**. I lift my chin and pretend to be far more cool than I actually am. "I have an appointment with Mr. Alexander. At four o'clock."

"Your voice," she says. "On the phone, you didn't sound quite so . . ."

Young?

She smiles uncomfortably. "We don't try juvenile cases, as a rule. If you'd like I can offer you the names of some practicing attorneys who—"

I take a deep breath. "Actually," I **interrupt**, "you're wrong. Smith v. Whately, Edmunds v. Womens and Infants Hospital, and Jerome v. the Diocese of Providence all involved litigants under the age of eighteen. All three resulted in **verdicts** for Mr. Alexander's clients. And those were just in the past *year*."

The secretary blinks at me. Then a slow smile toasts her face, as if she's decided she just might like me after all. "Come to think of it, why don't you just wait in his office?" she suggests, and she stands up to show me the way.

❖

Even if I spend every minute of the rest of my life reading, I do not believe that I will ever manage to **consume** the sheer number of words routed high and low on the walls of Campbell Alexander, Esquire's office. I do the math—if there are 400 words or so on every page, and each of those legal books are 400 pages, and there are twenty on a shelf and six shelves per bookcase—why, you're pushing nineteen million words, and that's only partway across the room.

✔ ?

382 Unit 12

When most of the students are finished, continue with the entire class. Let's see how well you understood what you read.

- Circle the check mark or the question mark for this section. Draw a question mark over any confusing words.
- Go to line 20. Mark the body language that displays confidence. (lift my chin)
- Go to line 23. Mark the punctuation that indicates that the secretary didn't finish her sentence. (. . . [ellipses])
- Go to line 24. Mark what Anna is thinking. (Young?) How do you know she is just thinking it? (italics; no quotes)
- Go to line 25. Underline the secretary's untrue claim. (We don't try juvenile cases, as a rule.)
- Go to line 29. Mark the word that means "people involved in lawsuits." (litigants)
- Go to lines 29 and 30. Mark the reason Anna has chosen Mr. Alexander. (All three resulted in verdicts for Mr. Alexander's clients.)
- Go to line 31. Mark the word that Anna said in a different tone or with exaggeration. (year) How do you know? (italics)
- Go to line 32. Mark the body language that shows surprise. (blinks at me)
- Mark the body language that shows that the secretary is warming up to Anna and may change her mind. (slow smile toasts her face) **Use context to discuss the meaning of *toasts*.**
- Go to line 41. Mark the word that means "approaching." (pushing)
- Based on this last paragraph, write something you know about Anna in the margin. (smart; good at math)

Have students read lines 43–66 according to the option that you chose. Remember to record a letter every time you learn something about a character. Anna equals A; Kate equals K; Jesse equals J; Mom equals M; and Dad equals D.

When most of the students are finished, continue with the entire class. Let's see how well you understood what you read.

- Circle the check mark or the question mark for this section. Draw a question mark over any confusing words.
- Go to lines 44 and 45. Mark the evidence that Campbell is either single or very private. (not a single photo of a wife or a kid)
- Go to line 47. Draw an arrow from the word *explanations* to the curious item found in the office. (mug full of water)
- Mark evidence that Anna has a good imagination. (swimming pool for an army of ants)
- Go to line 48. Mark the word that means "an optical illusion, something that you believe you see but that isn't really there" (mirage)
- Based on Anna's explanations, write something you know about her in the margin. (curious; imaginative)
- Go to line 51. Circle the explanation for the mug full of water. (German shepherd)
- Go to lines 55 and 56. Mark the physical trait that indicates that Campbell Alexander isn't very caring. (eyes that look frozen over)
- Go to lines 58 and 59. Mark Campbell's sarcastic comment intended to make Anna feel young and insignificant. ("I don't want any Girl Scout cookies")
- Go to line 60. Mark the pun used because of the younger level of the Girl Scouts and the idiom that means "praise and approval." (Brownie points)
- Go to line 61. Mark the indefinite pronoun. (anything)
- Go to line 63. Circle the pronoun used to make Anna feel completely insignificant. (this) In the margin, write what *this* refers to. (Anna)
- Go to line 64. Mark the word that means "hire." (retain)

Lesson 9 | Reading

Close Reading (*cont.*)

I'm alone in the office long enough to note that his desk is so neat, you could play Chinese football on the blotter; that there is not a single photo of a wife or a kid or even himself; and that in spite of the fact that the room is spotless, there's a mug full of water sitting on the floor.

I find myself making up explanations: it's a swimming pool for an army of ants. It's some kind of **primitive** humidifier. It's a mirage.

I've nearly convinced myself about that last one, and am leaning over to touch it to see if it's real, when the door bursts open. I practically fall out of my chair and that puts me eye to eye with an incoming German shepherd, which spears me with a look and then marches over to the mug and starts to drink.

Campbell Alexander comes in, too. He's got black hair and he's at least as tall as my dad—six feet—with a right-angle jaw and eyes that look frozen over. He shrugs out of a suit jacket and hangs it neatly on the back of the door, then yanks a file out of a cabinet before moving to his desk. He never makes eye contact with me, but he starts talking all the same. "I don't want any Girl Scout cookies," Campbell Alexander says. "Although you do get Brownie points for **tenacity.** Ha." He smiles at his own joke.

"I'm not selling anything."

He glances at me curiously, then pushes a button on his phone. "Kerri," he says when the secretary answers. "What is this doing in my office?"

"I'm here to retain you," I say.

The lawyer releases the intercom button. "I don't think so."

"You don't even know if I have a case."

✓ ?

Unit 12 383

Have students read lines 67–91 according to the option that you chose. Remember to record a letter every time you learn something about a character. Anna equals A; Kate equals K; Jesse equals J; Mom equals M; and Dad equals D.

Lesson 9 | Reading

Close Reading (*cont.*)

I take a step forward; so does the dog. For the first time I realize it's wearing one of those vests with a red cross on it, like a St. Bernard that might carry rum up a snowy mountain. I **automatically** reach out to pet him. "Don't," Alexander says. "Judge is a service dog."

My hand goes back to my side. "But you aren't blind."

"Thank you for pointing that out to me."

"So what's the matter with you?"

The minute I say it, I want to take it back. Haven't I watched Kate field this question from hundreds of rude people?

"I have an iron lung," Campbell Alexander says curtly, "and the dog keeps me from getting too close to magnets. Now, if you'd do me the **exalted** honor of leaving, my secretary can find you the name of someone who—"

But I can't go yet. "Did you really sue God?" I take out all the newspaper clippings, smooth them on the bare desk.

A muscle tics in his cheek, and then he picks up the article lying on top. "I sued the Diocese of Providence, on **behalf** of a kid in one of their orphanages who needed an **experimental** treatment involving fetal tissue, which they felt violated Vatican II. However, it makes a much better headline to say that a nine-year-old is suing God for being stuck with the short end of the straw in life." I just stare at him. "Dylan Jerome," the lawyer admits, "wanted to sue God for not caring enough about him."

A rainbow might as well have cracked down the middle of that big mahogany desk. "Mr. Alexander," I say, "my sister has leukemia."

"I'm sorry to hear that. But even if I were willing to litigate against God again, which I'm not, you can't bring a lawsuit on someone else's behalf."

✓ ?

When most of the students are finished, continue with the entire class. Let's see how well you understood what you read.

- Circle the check mark or the question mark for this section. Draw a question mark over any confusing words.
- Go to line 70. Mark an X on the action that Alexander forbids Anna to do to the dog. (pet him)
- On the same line, mark the ironic name of the dog. (Judge)
- Underline the lawyer's sarcastic comment. ("Thank you for pointing that out to me.")
- Go to line 74. Mark the idiom that means "withdraw a comment that could hurt someone's feelings." (take it back)
- Go to line 76. Mark the word that means "a little rudely." (curtly)
- Underline Judge's purpose. (keeps me from getting too close to magnets)
- Go to line 78. Mark the punctuation used to indicate that the person was interrupted while talking. (— [em dash])
- Go to line 80. Mark the word that means "empty." (bare)
- Go to line 83. Mark the place the nine-year-old lived. (orphanages)
- On the same line, mark the word that means "related to an unborn human." (fetal)
- Go to line 84. Mark the conjunctive adverb used in place of the conjunction but. (However)
- Go to line 86. Mark the idiom that means "less desirable situation." (short end of the straw)
- Go to line 88. Mark evidence that Anna is feeling hopeful. (a rainbow) Draw an arrow to what has given her hope. (wanted to sue God for not caring enough about him) In the margin, write who Anna doesn't think cares enough about her. (her parents)
- Go to line 90. Mark the word that means "fight in court." (litigate)
- Go to line 91. Mark the relative clause that changes the meaning of the sentence. (which I'm not)
- In the margin, write who Campbell thinks Anna is visiting his office for. (Kate)

Have students read lines 92 to the end according to the option that you chose. Remember to record a letter every time you learn something about a character. Anna equals A; Kate equals K; Jesse equals J; Mom equals M; and Dad equals D.

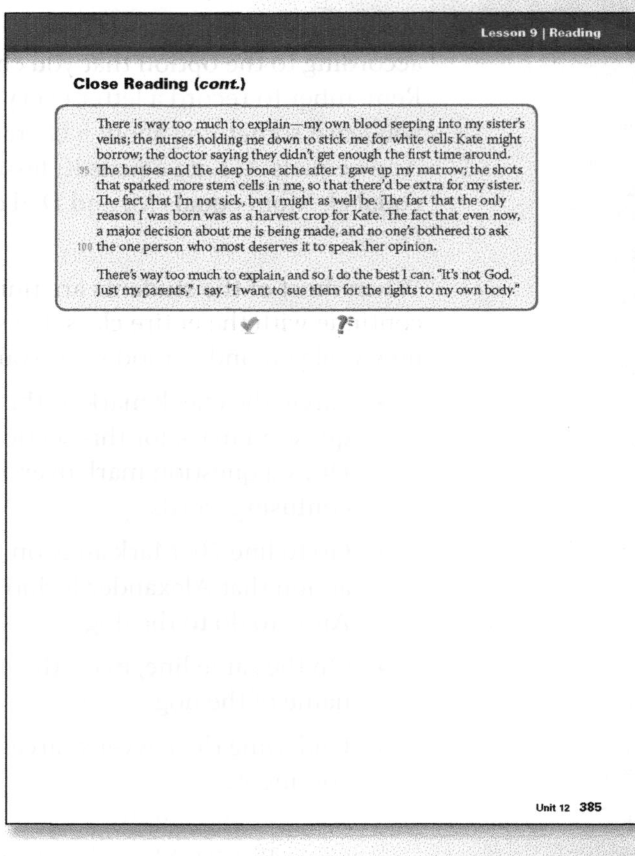

Lesson 9 | Reading

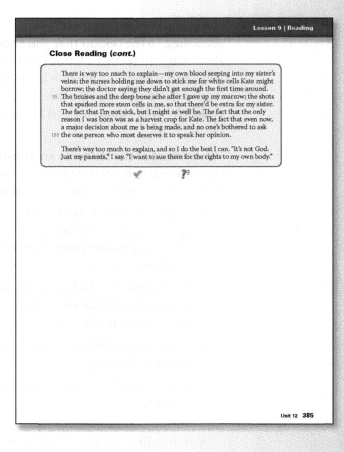

Close Reading (*cont.*)

There is way too much to explain—my own blood seeping into my sister's veins; the nurses holding me down to stick me for white cells Kate might borrow; the doctor saying they didn't get enough the first time around. The bruises and the deep bone ache after I gave up my marrow; the shots that sparked more stem cells in me, so that there'd be extra for my sister. The fact that I'm not sick, but I might as well be. The fact that the only reason I was born was as a harvest crop for Kate. The fact that even now, a major decision about me is being made, and no one's bothered to ask the one person who most deserves it to speak her opinion.

There's way too much to explain, and so I do the best I can. "It's not God. Just my parents," I say. "I want to sue them for the rights to my own body."

Unit 12 385

When most of the students are finished, continue with the entire class. Let's see how well you understood what you read.

- Circle the check mark or the question mark for this section. Draw a question mark over any confusing words.
- In the first paragraph, number the reasons that Anna wants to sue her parents for medical emancipation. (1. my own blood seeping into my sister's veins; 2. nurses holding me down; 3. doctors saying that they didn't get enough; 4. bruises and deep bone ache after I gave my bone marrow; 5. shots that sparked more stem cells in me; 6. I'm not sick, but I might as well be; 7. harvest crop for Kate; 8. no one's bothered to ask opinion)
- Go to line 98. Mark the phrase that means "organ donor." (harvest crop)
- Go to line 100. Mark the word that means "is worthy or qualifies for." (deserves)
- Go to line 102. Mark the word that means "make a legal claim against." (sue)
- At the bottom of the page, explain why the author chose to wait so long to explain why Anna was saving money? (to create suspense; to develop the characters)

Have partners compare text markings and correct any errors.

Unit 12 Lesson 10

Lesson Opener

Before the lesson, choose one of the following activities to write on the board or post on the *LANGUAGE! Live* Class Wall online.

- *Write four sentences with at least two vocabulary words in each. Show you know the meanings. (lacking, interrupt, verdict, consume, primitive, tenacity, automatically, exalted, experimental, (on) behalf)*
- *Dress your avatar as though you were meeting someone important and wanted to appear more mature than you really are. Explain your choices.*
- *Summarize your point of view of savior siblings.*

Vocabulary

Objective

- Review key passage vocabulary.

Recontextualize Passage Vocabulary

Direct students to page 370 in their Student Books. Use the following questions to review the vocabulary words from Part 2 of the excerpt from *My Sister's Keeper*.

Key Passage Vocabulary: from *My Sister's Keeper*, Part 2

Read each word. Write the word in column 3. Then, circle a number to rate your knowledge of the word.

Read the Word	Part of Speech	Write the Word	Rate the Word
lacking	(adj)	lacking	0 1 2 3
interrupt	(v)	interrupt	0 1 2 3
verdict	(n)	verdict	0 1 2 3
consume	(v)	consume	0 1 2 3
primitive	(adj)	primitive	0 1 2 3
tenacity	(n)	tenacity	0 1 2 3
automatically	(adv)	automatically	0 1 2 3
exalted	(adj)	exalted	0 1 2 3
(on) behalf	(n)	(on) behalf	0 1 2 3
experimental	(adj)	experimental	0 1 2 3

370 Unit 12

- You put the phone on speaker and let your friend talk while you get some homework done. Have you *interrupted* your friend? (no) The fire alarm goes off in the middle of Mr. Rodriguez's lecture. Does the alarm *interrupt* his talk? (yes) You're trapped in a boring conversation with someone at a party. You silently hope that someone will do what? (come up and interrupt the conversation)
- You use a trash can lid instead of a real sled to slide down a snowy hill. Is the trash can lid a *primitive* sled? (yes) Your grandmother insists on making popcorn by pouring kernels into a pan of hot oil and covering the pan. Compared to microwave popcorn, is her method *primitive*? (yes) Whenever you e-mail your great aunt, she responds with handwritten, snail-mailed letters. Her method of communication is more what than yours? (primitive)
- In a famous movie series about some kids at a boarding school, one of the professors always glares down his nose at the kids as if they were scum. Does he find them *lacking*? (yes) Your brother worships the quarterback on his favorite football team. Does he find the athlete *lacking*? (no) Nobody's home, and the fridge is almost empty. You fix yourself a plain ham sandwich for dinner—just bread and ham. You find this meal what? (lacking)
- If I assigned you 300 pages of reading tonight, would you be able to *consume* it all? (probably not) Your sister reads dozens of celebrity gossip magazines every week. Does she *consume* them? (yes) You're taking an online course. Before you take the final test, you have to read eight lessons' worth of material. You have to do what? (consume the material)

- Your friend panics when he gets called on in class, so you try to answer questions for him. Do you answer on his *behalf*? (yes) You've inherited a vast fortune from a long-lost relative. Until you're 18, though, you can't have access to it. A lawyer is handling the money for you. Is the lawyer handling the money on your *behalf*? (yes) Someone calls and asks for your sister, but she's not home. You take a message on her what? (behalf)
- When you get a cold, you take an old-fashioned approach. You drink hot tea with honey and get a good night's sleep. Are these treatments *experimental*? (no) You read online that you can improve your brain power by eating 10 bananas and doing 500 push-ups every day. Would you consider this strategy *experimental*? (yes) In the 1950s, the Russians sent several unmanned spacecraft to the moon but did not successfully land them. What were these attempts? (experimental)
- Every month, a group of students petitions the administration for permission to leave campus for lunch. They have been doing this for three years. Does the group have *tenacity*? (yes) Serena wanted to learn to knit but decided it was too hard after two rows. Does she have *tenacity*? (no) You start a letter-writing campaign asking to meet the president of the United States in person. What are you going to need for this effort? (tenacity)
- The first time you tied your shoes on your own, did you do it *automatically*? (no) But now, you don't have to think about how to do it. What is it? (automatic) Marvin has a habit of cracking his knuckles before he plays the trumpet. Does he crack his knuckles *automatically*? (yes) When you touch a hot stove, how do you pull your hand away? (automatically)
- Is the science fiction hero who saves the planet from alien forces an *exalted* figure? (yes) Is the Nobel Peace Prize an *exalted* honor? (yes) You're a rock star. You walk onstage and the crowd goes wild. How do you feel? (exalted)
- You wonder whether time travel is possible. Is this a *verdict*? (no) Martha asks three friends what color looks best on her. All three say blue. Is "blue" the *verdict*? (yes) The judge on a TV show decides that the defendant is guilty. "Guilty" is the judge's what? (verdict)

Writing

Objectives

- Use multiple texts to write coherently.
- Use a process to write.
- Write a character analysis with text evidence.
- Analyze the character development in a story.
- Use a rubric to guide and evaluate writing.

Six Traits of Effective Writing

Direct students back to page 35 in their Student Books. Reread the Six Traits of Effective Writing.

We will continue to focus on writing with all six traits.

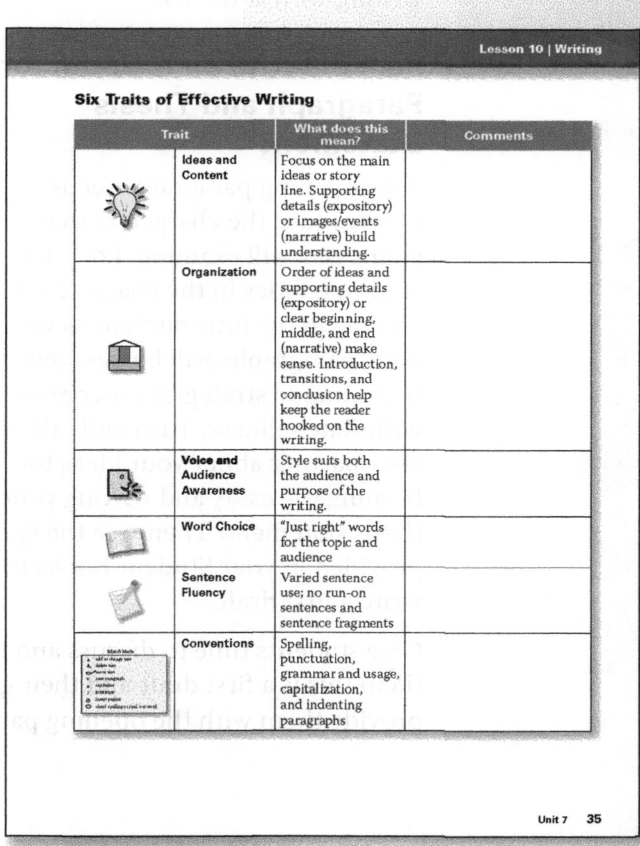
Lesson 10 | Writing

Six Traits of Effective Writing

Trait		What does this mean?	Comments
	Ideas and Content	Focus on the main ideas or story line. Supporting details (expository) or images/events (narrative) build understanding.	
	Organization	Order of ideas and supporting details (expository) or clear beginning, middle, and end (narrative) make sense. Introduction, transitions, and conclusion help keep the reader hooked on the writing.	
	Voice and Audience Awareness	Style suits both the audience and purpose of the writing.	
	Word Choice	"Just right" words for the topic and audience	
	Sentence Fluency	Varied sentence use; no run-on sentences and sentence fragments	
	Conventions	Spelling, punctuation, grammar and usage, capitalization, and indenting paragraphs	

Unit 7 35

Prepare to Write: Character Analysis Essay

Direct students to pages 386–389 in their Student Books. Read the instructions for Part A and the prompt.

Part A. Study the Prompt

Read the prompt and work through the topic, directions, and purpose for writing with students.

Part B. Write an Introductory Paragraph and Thesis Statement

Your opening paragraph needs to introduce the characters that your essay will examine. Look for commonalities in the characters to include in the introduction as your body paragraphs will be devoted to their unique strategies for coping with Kate's illness. Turn and talk with your partner about your ideas for framing the essay and writing your thesis statement. Then, use the space provided in your Student Books to write a first draft.

Lesson 10 | Writing

Prepare to Write: Character Analysis Essay

Part A. Study the Prompt Answers will vary.

Read the following prompt and determine the topic, directions, and purpose for writing.

Each character in the Fitzgerald family has developed unique ways to cope with Kate's illness. Write an essay that uses text evidence to describe Mom's, Jesse's, and Anna's coping mechanisms. If you were a member of the Fitzgerald family, which coping mechanism would you adopt?

Topic: characters' coping mechanisms

Directions: write a multiparagraph essay that describes the different coping mechanisms; choose the character most like myself

Purpose for Writing: use text evidence to gain a deeper understanding of characters and make a personal connection to one of the characters in the text

Part B. Write an Introductory Paragraph and Thesis Statement

The opening paragraph needs to contain an introduction to the topic. It should state the similarities between the characters and their coping mechanisms and set the framework for examining and documenting the differences.

Everyone in the Fitzgerald household is suffering from leukemia, even though Kate has the only official diagnosis. Kate's mom, brother, and sister have all developed strategies for dealing with the strain and darkness of Kate's disease. Their coping mechanisms, however, are not necessarily healthy for anyone in the long run.

386 Unit 12

Give students time to discuss and then write their initial thoughts on paper. Remind them this is a first draft and their goal is to get started. If students seem to struggle, provide them with the opening paragraph from the sample essay.

Part C. Organize Information

You probably have ideas about the characters and how they deal with Kate's sickness, but you need to find documentation within the text. Skim through the scenes and pull details from the text that support the coping mechanisms you have identified for each character.

Guide students through one example of text evidence dealing with Mom. Allow them to work independently or with a partner if they are able to complete the chart. If they need more guidance, work with the whole group or a small group and fill in the chart together.

Lesson 10 | Writing

Prepare to Write: Character Analysis Essay (*cont.*)

Part C. Organize Information

Character	Coping Mechanism	Text Evidence
Mom	focuses only on Kate; trusts only herself with Kate; escapes by ordering evening gowns	when it comes to Kate, she doesn't take anybody's word for it; don't really have time to care about Jesse or Anna; one word bubbles up: tired; ordering ridiculously fancy evening dresses for places she is never going to go
Jesse	attention-getting, self-destructive behaviors	he didn't want my parents to see what he was doing and my parents didn't really want to see; (stolen) hood ornaments; troubles he's gotten himself mixed up in; Jesse may be a borderline delinquent, but he's brilliant. For a still made out of spit and glue, it produces pretty potent moonshine whiskey; "I'm the Lost Cause"
Anna	inner strength; dependability; humor; a need to be in control of her own body	You're the Peacekeeper—"says who?"; every now and then people mistakenly assume I'm the older sister; I stand frozen in the doorway of my own room waiting for instructions; that fist inside me relaxes; There was the kidnapping scare (in the soap opera); sue them (parents) for the rights to my own body

Unit 12 387

Part D. Write Body Paragraph Topic Sentences

Now that you have taken some examples from the text, you should have a better idea of how you plan to describe each character's coping mechanisms. Discuss your ideas about each character and their unique set of behaviors. After talking for a few minutes with your partner, write a topic sentence for each body paragraph that launches your description of their behaviors.

Monitor student progress as they discuss their ideas for topic sentences for the body paragraphs. If students seem to struggle, provide them with sample topic sentences to use as patterns for their essay.

Lesson 10 | Writing

Prepare to Write: Character Analysis Essay (*cont.*)

Part D. Write Body Paragraph Topic Sentences

Write a topic sentence that introduces each character:

Mom: Mrs. Fitzgerald is completely consumed by Kate's illness.

Jesse: Jesse is constantly searching for behavior outrageous enough to garner his parents' attention away from Kate's illness.

Anna: Anna is the glue that holds the family together, yet even she is growing weary of her role as savior.

388 Unit 12

Part E. Write a Conclusion

Close your essay by summarizing the characters' behaviors. Look at your thesis statement and consider how you can reword it. Try to summarize your main points without simply repeating what you wrote in previous paragraphs. Incorporate your thoughts on which character you would most be like if you were a Fitzgerald.

Give students time to work independently to write their concluding paragraph. Have volunteers share their original thesis statement and their topic sentence from their concluding paragraph. If students struggle to get their thoughts on paper, use elements from the sample essay to provide a model.

Lesson 10 | Writing

Prepare to Write: Character Analysis Essay (*cont.*)

Part E. Write a Conclusion Answers will vary.

Restate your thesis by using a different topic sentence pattern. Summarize the characters' different strategies for coping. Close by adding your personal perspective on the character you would be like if you were a Fitzgerald.

The Fitzgeralds are managing their lives and Kate's illness to the best of their abilities. Kate's battle with leukemia places ever-increasing strain on their coping mechanisms. Mrs. Fitzgerald's singular focus on Kate pushes her other children further and further from her viewpoint. Jesse's rebellious behaviors have not helped him deal with the seriousness of his sister's illness. Anna is desperately searching for someone to fight for her. She struggles with her own value when measured against her sister's. Their strategies are dysfunctional and complex. I would like to think I would be strong and resilient like Anna, but I think I would be more like Mrs. Fitzgerald. Filled with the confidence that only I know what my child needs, I would spend each day focused on her and her alone. Allowing myself a fanciful flight in evening gowns and party dresses would be enough of an escape to recharge my batteries. When families battle life-threatening diseases like leukemia, everyone in the family is a casualty of the war.

Unit 12 389

Write

Notebook paper

You have worked through all of the steps for writing your essay. Now, use your notes and the paragraph elements from your Student Book to write the essay.

Have students consult the Six Traits of Writing: Literary Analysis Rubric on page 553 as they write their analysis. If they struggle or need additional support in developing their analysis, use the following essay as a model.

Six Traits of Writing: Literary Analysis

	Ideas and Development	Organization	Voice and Audience Awareness	Word Choice	Sentence Fluency	Language Conventions
4	States thesis clearly. Develops main ideas fully with elaborations. Direct quotations from text support ideas. All information pertinent to thesis.	Introduction contains thesis statement and cites title, author of work. Ideas logically sequenced. Transition sentences link ideas. Conclusion offers some evaluation of the work.	Strong sense of person and purpose behind the words. Brings topic to life.	Words are specific, accurate, and vivid. Word choice enhances meaning and reader's enjoyment.	Writes complete sentences with varied sentence patterns and beginnings.	There are no major grammar errors. There are few errors in spelling, capitalization, or punctuation.
3	States thesis clearly. Develops main ideas with some elaboration. May lack direct quotations from text to support ideas. Limited amount of irrelevant information.	Introduction contains thesis statement and cites title, author of work. Ideas mostly logically sequenced. Some linkage of main ideas. Formulaic conclusion may not offer evaluation of the work.	Some sense of person and purpose behind the words. Sense of commitment to the topic. Text may be too casual for purpose.	Words are correctly used but may be somewhat general and unspecific.	Writes complete sentences with some expansion. Limited variety.	There are a few grammar errors. There are a few errors in spelling, capitalization, or punctuation.
2	Does not state thesis clearly and/or minimal development of main ideas. No direct quotations to support ideas. Too repetitious or too much irrelevant information.	Introduction may not have clear thesis. Ideas not logically sequenced. Transitions may be missing. May lack conclusion, or conclusion is formulaic with no evaluation of the work.	Little sense of person and purpose behind the words. Very little engagement with the reader. Text may be too casual for purpose.	Word choice limited. Words may be used inaccurately or repetitively.	Writes mostly simple and/or awkwardly constructed sentences. May include some run-ons and fragments.	There are many grammar or spelling errors. There are quite a few errors in capitalization and punctuation.
1	Does not address the prompt or does not develop a thesis. Elaboration lacking or unrelated to a thesis.	No evident structure. Lack of organization seriously interferes with meaning.	No sense of person or purpose behind the words. No sense of audience.	Extremely limited range of words. Restricted vocabulary impedes message.	Numerous run-ons and/or sentence fragments interfere with meaning.	There are many spelling and grammar errors. There are many errors in capitalization and punctuation.

Writing Rubric: Persuasion 553

Writing Rubric: Persuasion

Sample Character Analysis

Everyone in the Fitzgerald household is suffering from leukemia, even though Kate has the only official diagnosis. Kate's mom, her brother, and her sister have all developed strategies for dealing with the strain and darkness of Kate's disease. Their coping mechanisms, however, are not necessarily healthy for anyone in the long run.

Mrs. Fitzgerald is completely consumed by Kate's illness. She trusts no one but herself to know what Kate needs and when she needs it. Anna tells us, "when it comes to Kate, she doesn't take anybody's word for it." She pays little attention to Anna and Jesse because she must focus so much attention on Kate. She sacrifices her health by devoting all of her attention to Kate. Even when modeling an extravagant gown, "tired" is the descriptive word that "bubbles up." Because her life is completely controlled by Kate's medical condition, she has no sense of a schedule. Her single escape, if just for moment, is "ordering ridiculously fancy evening dresses for places she is never going to go."

Jesse is constantly searching for behavior outrageous enough to garner his parents' attention. Every day for Jesse is filled with diversions that prevent him from dealing with the reality of Kate's illness. He has comfortably adopted the role of the "borderline delinquent" or "lost cause." He lives in the attic above the garage where his parents cannot "see what he was doing." They love Jesse, but they "didn't really want to see" what Jesse was doing. Stolen hood ornaments and a homemade still help decorate his room. His self-destructive behavior offers no support to the family and increases the chances for more heartache for his family and himself.

Anna is the glue that holds the family together, yet even she is growing weary of her role as provider. Her responsible demeanor and physical stature encourage people to mistakenly assume she's "the older sister." Whenever Kate has a medical emergency, Anna stands "frozen waiting for instructions." She is always up to the task, even when it includes donating her bone marrow or taking shots to encourage her body to produce more stem cells. She uses humor to diffuse emotionally charged scenes. When Kate is sobbing hysterically about soap opera characters, Anna highlights the absurdities of the show's plot. Her mother is able to push aside her panicky feelings by joining in the conversation as well. Anna is "the peacekeeper," but suing her parents for the rights to her own body will bring an end to that role.

The Fitzgeralds are managing their lives and Kate's illness to the best of their abilities. Kate's battle with leukemia places ever-increasing strain on their coping mechanisms. Mrs. Fitzgerald's singular focus on Kate pushes her other children further and further from her viewpoint. Jesse's rebellious behaviors have not helped him deal with the seriousness of his sister's illness. Anna is desperately searching for someone to fight for her. She struggles with her own value when measured against her sister's. Their strategies are dysfunctional and complex. I would like to think I would be strong and resilient like Anna, but I think I would be more like Mrs. Fitzgerald. Filled with the confidence that only I know what my child needs, I would spend each day focused on her and her alone. Allowing myself a fanciful flight in evening gowns and party dresses would be enough of an escape to recharge my batteries. When families battle life-threatening diseases like leukemia, everyone in the family is a casualty of the war.

Evaluate Writing

Direct students to page 390 in their Student Books and read the information in the checklist.

Notice that this checklist is the same one you used last unit. This checklist is specifically for analyzing literature. It is a tool you can use to evaluate your writing and make sure you are using good technique. **Have individuals quickly assess their writing, then have partners evaluate each other's writing based on the checklist.**

Note: Use Six Traits of Writing Scoring Rubric: Literary Analysis on page 548 of this book to assess students' writing. A printable version is located online in the Teacher Resources.

Six Traits of Writing: Literary Analysis

Lesson 10 | Writing

The Literary Analysis Writer's Checklist

Trait	Yes	No	Did the writer . . .?
Ideas and Content			clearly state the thesis of the essay
			analyze and evaluate the elements found in the literature
			focus each paragraph on the topic
			include effective support for the thesis by giving details, examples, explanations, and quotations from the texts
Organization			write an introductory paragraph that captures the reader's interest and cites the titles of the works and the names of the authors
			include in the introductory paragraph a clear viewpoint on the topic and a "map" for the essay that follows
			sequence body paragraphs logically and use transition sentences that make clear the relationship between the ideas
			write a conclusion that ties the analysis together and offers an evaluation of the particulars
Voice and Audience Awareness			think about the audience and purpose for writing
			write in a clear and engaging way that makes the audience want to read the work
Word Choice			find a unique way to say things; avoid sounding repetitive
			use words that are lively and specific to the content
Sentence Fluency			write complete sentences
			expand some sentences using the steps of Masterpiece Sentences
			use compound sentence elements and compound sentences
Conventions			capitalize words correctly:
			capitalize the first word of each sentence
			capitalize proper nouns, including people's names
			punctuate correctly:
			end sentences with a period, question mark, or exclamation mark
			use an apostrophe for possessive nouns and contractions
			use commas and/or semicolons correctly
			use grammar correctly:
			use the correct verb tense
			make sure the verb agrees with the subject in number
			use correct spelling

390 Unit 12

Reading

Objectives

- Self-correct as comprehension of text deepens.
- Answer questions to demonstrate comprehension of text.
- Engage in class discussion.
- Identify the enduring understandings from a piece of text.

Revisit Passage Comprehension

Direct students back to pages 378–380 in their Student Books. Have students review their answers and make any necessary changes. Then, have partners share their answers and collaborate to perfect them.

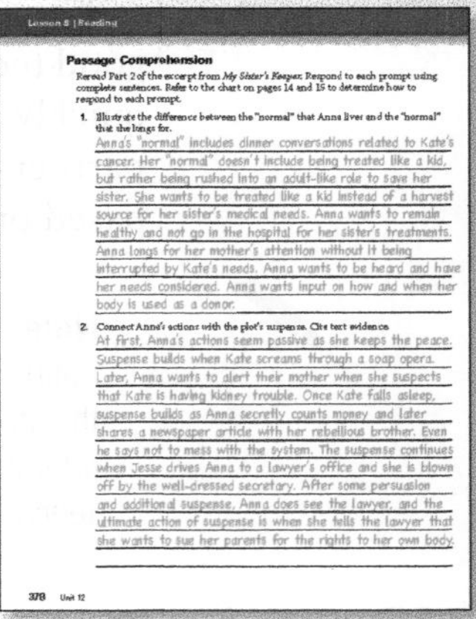

Enduring Understandings

Direct students back to page 369 in their Student Books. Reread the Big Idea questions.

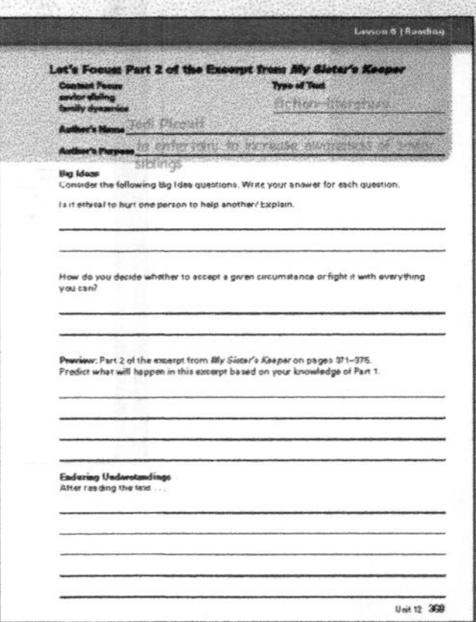

Is it ethical to hurt one person to help another? Explain.

How do you decide whether to accept a given circumstance or fight it with everything you can?

Generate a class discussion about the questions and the answers students came up with in Lesson 6. Have them consider whether their answers have changed any after reading the text.

Use the following talking points to foster conversation. Then, have students write their enduring understandings from the unit.

- If we define *abuse* as repetitively "inflicting pain on another human being," are savior siblings ethical?
- The advancement of science means that people who are ill or dying can live long past the time they would have lived otherwise. Some people believe this is going against the will of God or the universe. Other people believe that it is through these powers that scientists and doctors have been able to perform such "miracles." Is there a time when it is OK to give up on the life of another person? What would you sacrifice to save a loved one?

What we read should make us think. Use our discussion and your thoughts about the text to determine what you will "walk away with." Has it made you think about a personal experience or someone you know? Has your perspective or opinion on a specific topic changed? Do you have any lingering thoughts or questions? Write these ideas as your enduring understandings. What will you take with you from this text?

Assign online Unit 12 ***Content Mastery*** *quizzes and* ***Power Pass*** *from the Text Training link on the left menu of your teacher dashboard.*

Discuss the enduring understandings with the class. If time permits, have students post a personal response from their enduring understandings to the online class wall.

Additional Resources

Posters 538
Writing Rubrics 544
Sight Words 549
Vocabulary 550
Research and Evidence of Effectiveness 552
Index 556

Posters

Reading

Posters can also be printed from the Teacher Resources online.

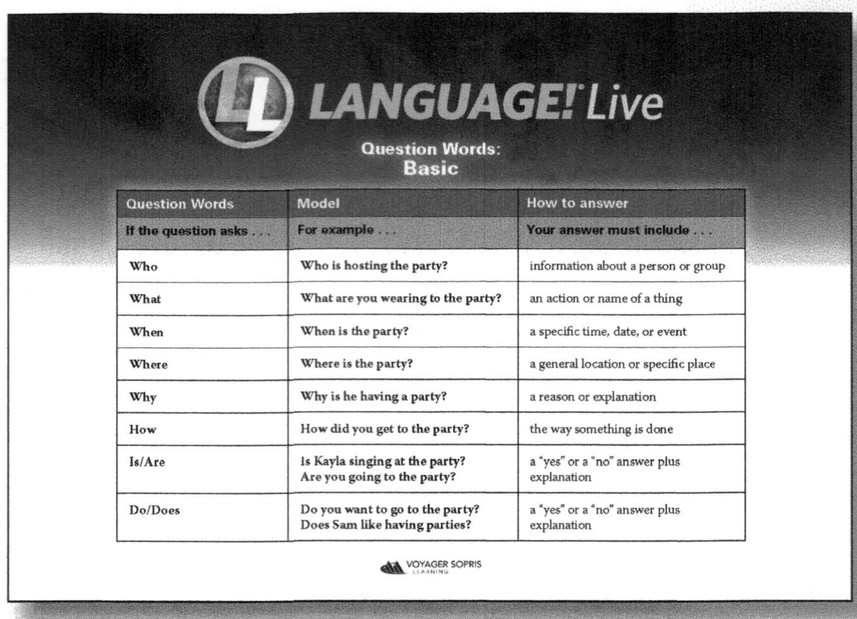

LANGUAGE! Live

Question Words: Basic

Question Words	Model	How to answer
If the question asks . . .	For example . . .	Your answer must include . . .
Who	Who is hosting the party?	information about a person or group
What	What are you wearing to the party?	an action or name of a thing
When	When is the party?	a specific time, date, or event
Where	Where is the party?	a general location or specific place
Why	Why is he having a party?	a reason or explanation
How	How did you get to the party?	the way something is done
Is/Are	Is Kayla singing at the party? Are you going to the party?	a "yes" or a "no" answer plus explanation
Do/Does	Do you want to go to the party? Does Sam like having parties?	a "yes" or a "no" answer plus explanation

VOYAGER SOPRIS LEARNING

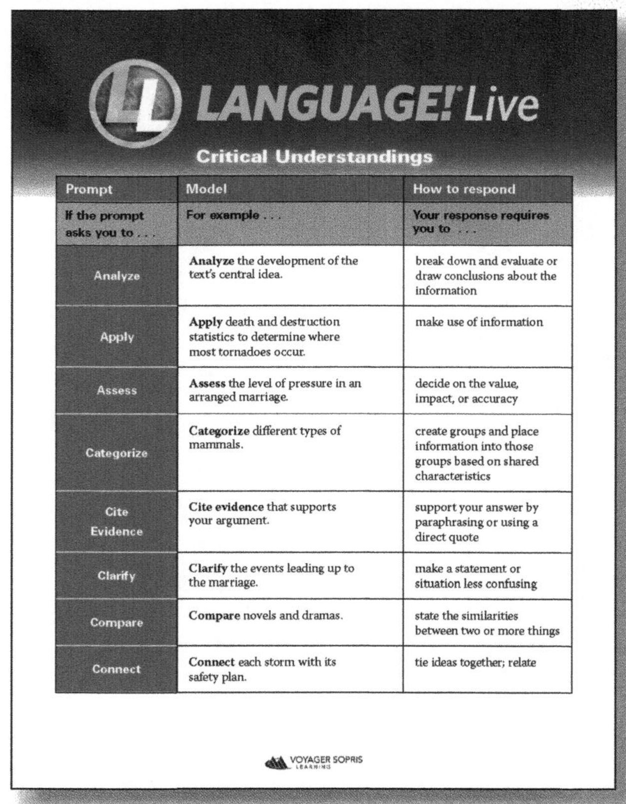

LANGUAGE! Live

Critical Understandings

Prompt	Model	How to respond
If the prompt asks you to . . .	For example . . .	Your response requires you to . . .
Analyze	**Analyze** the development of the text's central idea.	break down and evaluate or draw conclusions about the information
Apply	**Apply** death and destruction statistics to determine where most tornadoes occur.	make use of information
Assess	**Assess** the level of pressure in an arranged marriage.	decide on the value, impact, or accuracy
Categorize	**Categorize** different types of mammals.	create groups and place information into those groups based on shared characteristics
Cite Evidence	**Cite evidence** that supports your argument.	support your answer by paraphrasing or using a direct quote
Clarify	**Clarify** the events leading up to the marriage.	make a statement or situation less confusing
Compare	**Compare** novels and dramas.	state the similarities between two or more things
Connect	**Connect** each storm with its safety plan.	tie ideas together; relate

VOYAGER SOPRIS LEARNING

Reading

Posters can also be printed from the Teacher Resources online.

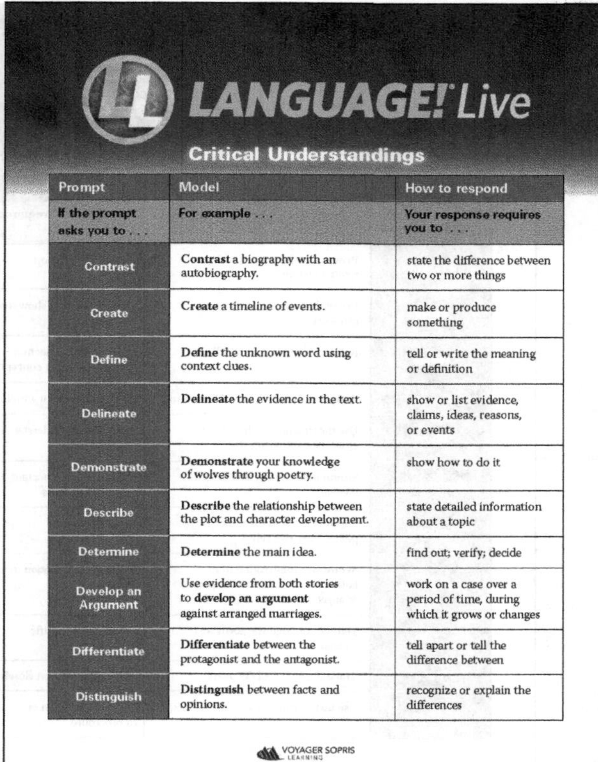

LANGUAGE! Live

Critical Understandings

Prompt	Model	How to respond
If the prompt asks you to . . .	For example . . .	Your response requires you to . . .
Contrast	**Contrast** a biography with an autobiography.	state the difference between two or more things
Create	**Create** a timeline of events.	make or produce something
Define	**Define** the unknown word using context clues.	tell or write the meaning or definition
Delineate	**Delineate** the evidence in the text.	show or list evidence, claims, ideas, reasons, or events
Demonstrate	**Demonstrate** your knowledge of wolves through poetry.	show how to do it
Describe	**Describe** the relationship between the plot and character development.	state detailed information about a topic
Determine	**Determine** the main idea.	find out; verify; decide
Develop an Argument	Use evidence from both stories to **develop an argument** against arranged marriages.	work on a case over a period of time, during which it grows or changes
Differentiate	**Differentiate** between the protagonist and the antagonist.	tell apart or tell the difference between
Distinguish	**Distinguish** between facts and opinions.	recognize or explain the differences

VOYAGER SOPRIS LEARNING

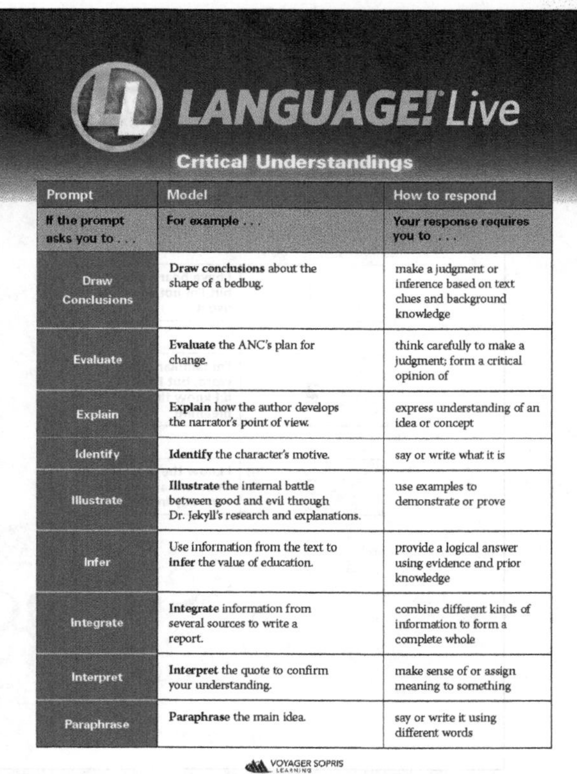

LANGUAGE! Live

Critical Understandings

Prompt	Model	How to respond
If the prompt asks you to . . .	For example . . .	Your response requires you to . . .
Draw Conclusions	**Draw conclusions** about the shape of a bedbug.	make a judgment or inference based on text clues and background knowledge
Evaluate	**Evaluate** the ANC's plan for change.	think carefully to make a judgment; form a critical opinion of
Explain	**Explain** how the author develops the narrator's point of view.	express understanding of an idea or concept
Identify	**Identify** the character's motive.	say or write what it is
Illustrate	**Illustrate** the internal battle between good and evil through Dr. Jekyll's research and explanations.	use examples to demonstrate or prove
Infer	Use information from the text to **infer** the value of education.	provide a logical answer using evidence and prior knowledge
Integrate	**Integrate** information from several sources to write a report.	combine different kinds of information to form a complete whole
Interpret	**Interpret** the quote to confirm your understanding.	make sense of or assign meaning to something
Paraphrase	**Paraphrase** the main idea.	say or write it using different words

VOYAGER SOPRIS LEARNING

Posters

Reading

Posters can also be printed from the Teacher Resources online.

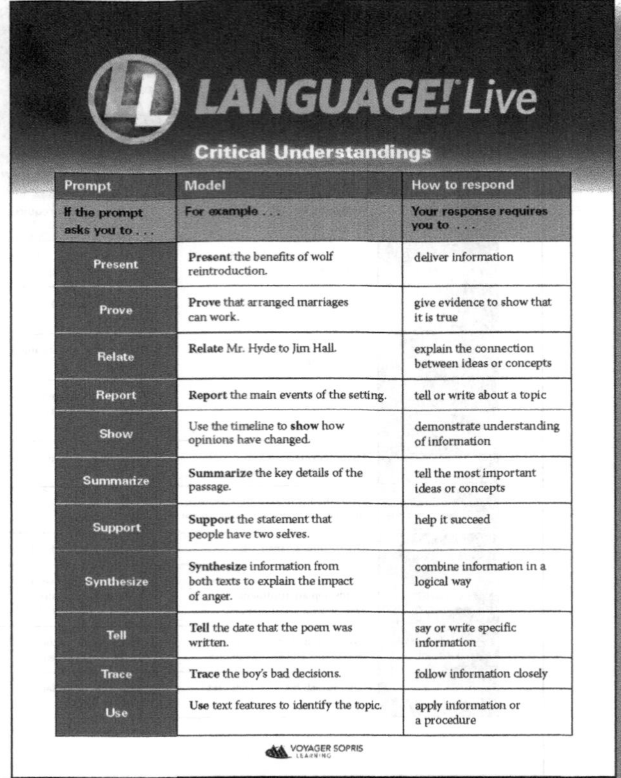

LANGUAGE! Live

Critical Understandings

Prompt	Model	How to respond
If the prompt asks you to . . .	For example . . .	Your response requires you to . . .
Present	**Present** the benefits of wolf reintroduction.	deliver information
Prove	**Prove** that arranged marriages can work.	give evidence to show that it is true
Relate	**Relate** Mr. Hyde to Jim Hall.	explain the connection between ideas or concepts
Report	**Report** the main events of the setting.	tell or write about a topic
Show	Use the timeline to **show** how opinions have changed.	demonstrate understanding of information
Summarize	**Summarize** the key details of the passage.	tell the most important ideas or concepts
Support	**Support** the statement that people have two selves.	help it succeed
Synthesize	**Synthesize** information from both texts to explain the impact of anger.	combine information in a logical way
Tell	**Tell** the date that the poem was written.	say or write specific information
Trace	**Trace** the boy's bad decisions.	follow information closely
Use	**Use** text features to identify the topic.	apply information or a procedure

VOYAGER SOPRIS LEARNING

Vocabulary

Posters can also be printed from the Teacher Resources online.

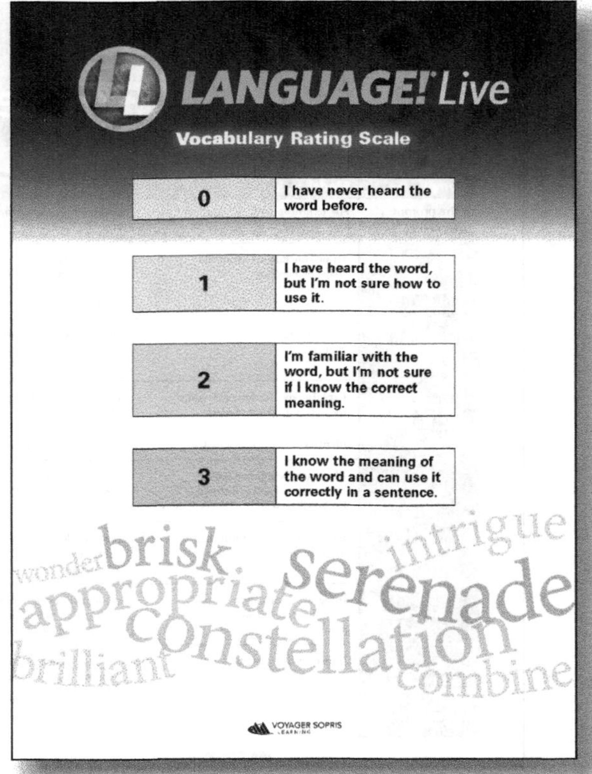

LANGUAGE! Live

Vocabulary Rating Scale

0	I have never heard the word before.
1	I have heard the word, but I'm not sure how to use it.
2	I'm familiar with the word, but I'm not sure if I know the correct meaning.
3	I know the meaning of the word and can use it correctly in a sentence.

Grammar

Posters can also be printed from the Teacher Resources online.

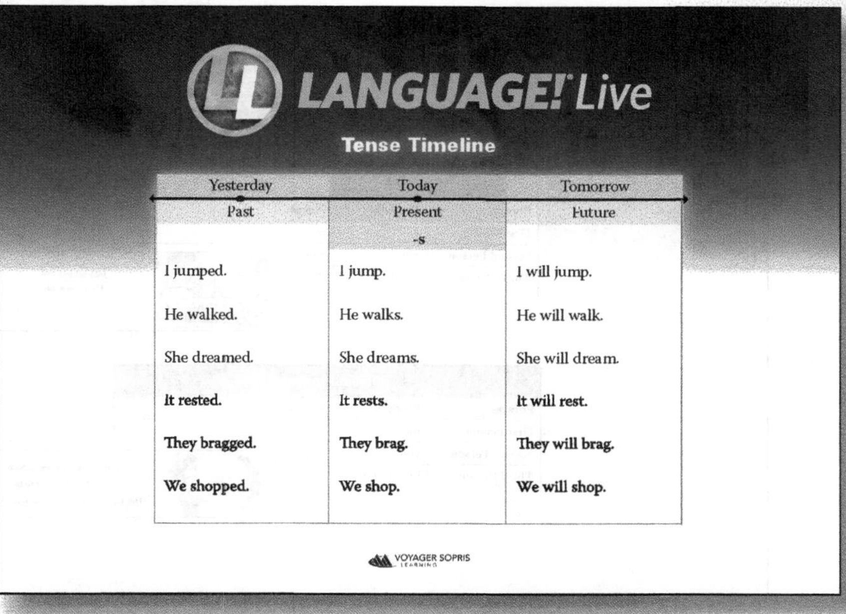

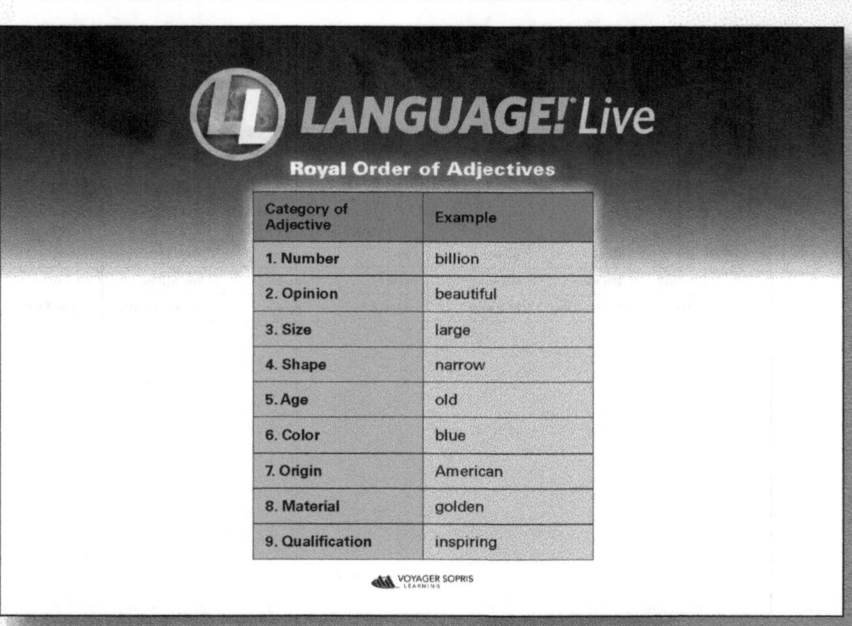

Posters

Grammar

Posters can also be printed from the Teacher Resources online.

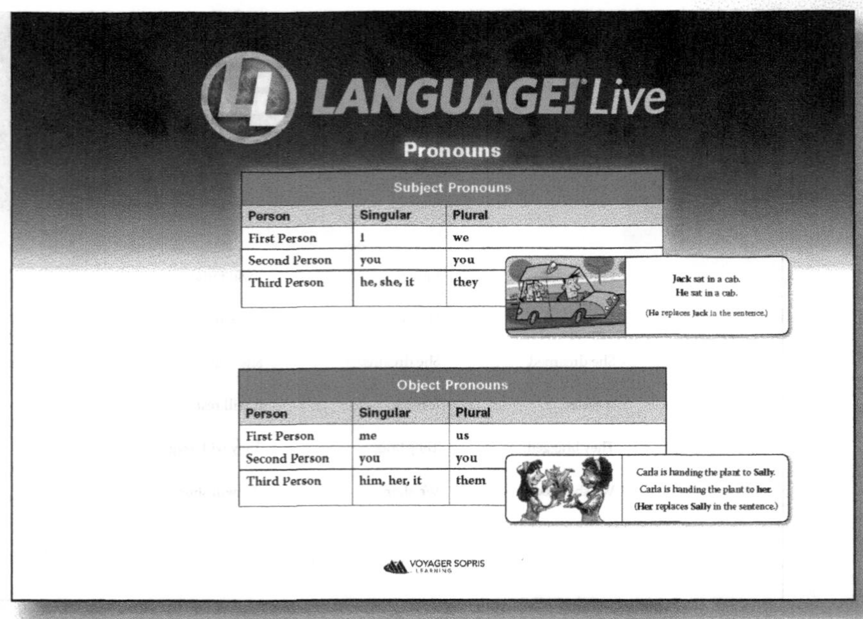

LANGUAGE! Live

Pronouns

Subject Pronouns		
Person	**Singular**	**Plural**
First Person	I	we
Second Person	you	you
Third Person	he, she, it	they

Jack sat in a cab.
He sat in a cab.
(He replaces Jack in the sentence.)

Object Pronouns		
Person	**Singular**	**Plural**
First Person	me	us
Second Person	you	you
Third Person	him, her, it	them

Carla is handing the plant to Sally.
Carla is handing the plant to her.
(Her replaces Sally in the sentence.)

VOYAGER SOPRIS LEARNING

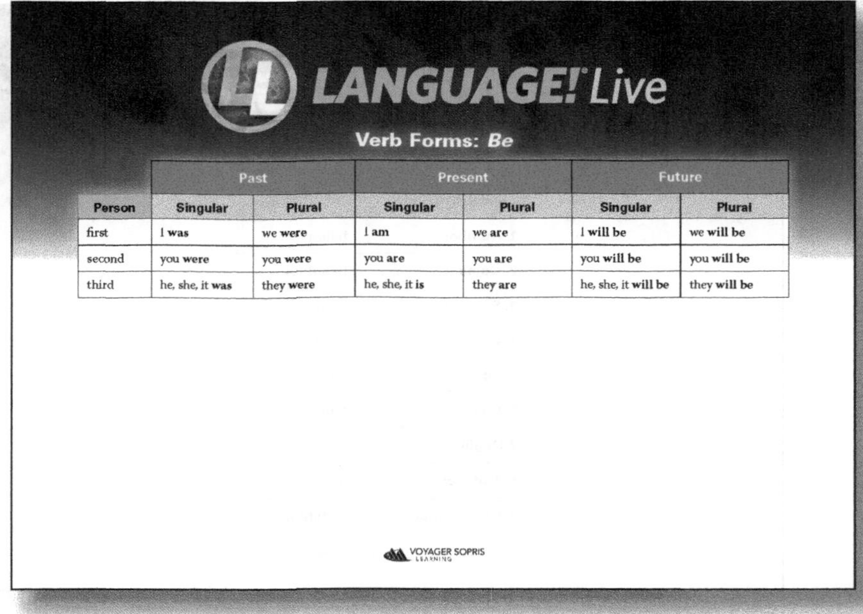

LANGUAGE! Live

Verb Forms: *Be*

	Past		Present		Future	
Person	**Singular**	**Plural**	**Singular**	**Plural**	**Singular**	**Plural**
first	I **was**	we **were**	I **am**	we **are**	I **will be**	we **will be**
second	you **were**	you **were**	you **are**	you **are**	you **will be**	you **will be**
third	he, she, it **was**	they **were**	he, she, it **is**	they **are**	he, she, it **will be**	they **will be**

VOYAGER SOPRIS LEARNING

Writing

Posters can also be printed from the Teacher Resources online.

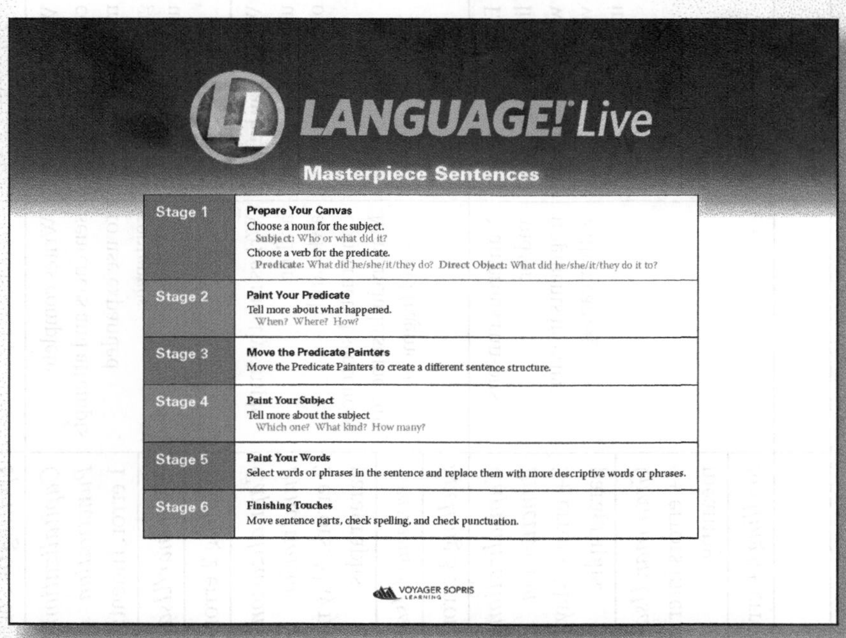

	Ideas and Development	Organization	Voice and Audience Awareness	Word Choice	Sentence Fluency	Language Conventions
4	Focuses on the topic. Main idea (topic sentence) is clear and well supported with details and elaboration (examples, evidence, and explanations).	Topic sentence clearly states main idea. Ideas are clear and logically organized. Contains concluding sentence.	The words have a strong sense of person and purpose. Brings topic to life.	Words are specific to the content, accurate, and vivid. Word choice enhances meaning and the reader's enjoyment.	Writes complete sentences and varies sentence structure.	*Capitalization & Punctuation* No errors. Indents paragraphs. *Grammar/Usage* 0–1 error *Spelling* 0–1 error
3	Mostly focuses on the topic. Sentences supporting the main idea (topic sentence) may be general rather than detailed and specific.	Topic sentence states main idea. Organization mostly clear and logical. May contain concluding sentence.	The words have some sense of person and purpose.	Words are correctly used but may be somewhat general and unspecific.	Writes complete sentences and attempts to use expanded sentences.	*Capitalization & Punctuation* 1 error. Indents paragraphs. *Grammar/Usage* 2 errors *Spelling* 2 errors
2	Main idea (topic sentence) is unclear and/or lacks sufficient support.	Structure may not be entirely clear or logical. Paragraph may seem more like a list and/or be hard to follow.	The words have little sense of person and purpose.	Words may be used inaccurately or repetitively.	Writes mostly simple and/or awkwardly constructed sentences. May include some run-ons and fragments.	*Capitalization & Punctuation* 2 errors. May not indent paragraphs. *Grammar/Usage* 3 errors *Spelling* 3 errors
1	Does not address prompt and/or lacks a topic sentence. Supporting details are absent or do not relate to topic.	No evident structure. Lack of organization seriously interferes with meaning.	The words have no sense of person or purpose. No sense of audience.	Extremely limited range of words. Restricted vocabulary impedes message.	Numerous run-ons and/or fragments interfere with meaning.	*Capitalization & Punctuation* 3+ errors. May not indent paragraphs. *Grammar/Usage* 4+ errors interfere with meaning *Spelling* 4+ errors
Value						

Comments ______________________________

Six Traits of Writing: Expository

	Ideas and Development	Organization	Voice and Audience Awareness	Word Choice	Sentence Fluency	Language Conventions
4	The paper is very clear and well focused. Supporting details make the paper very easy to understand and interesting.	Ideas are very clearly organized. All parts of the essay (introduction, body, and conclusion) work together to support the thesis.	The writer's voice is distinctive and shows an interest in the topic. The writer knows who his or her audience is.	Words are used correctly and are very well chosen. They create pictures in the reader's mind.	Sentences have an easy flow and rhythm. Transitions are very smooth.	*Capitalization & Punctuation* No errors. Indents paragraphs. *Grammar/Usage* 0–1 error *Spelling* 0–1 error
3	The paper is clear and well focused. Supporting details make the paper easy to understand.	Ideas are clearly organized. The paper includes all parts of an essay (introduction, body, and conclusion).	The writer's voice is natural and shows an interest in the topic. The writer knows who his or her audience is.	Words are used correctly. Some words may be a bit general.	Sentences are formed correctly and are varied in structure. Transitions are clear.	*Capitalization & Punctuation* 1 error. Indents paragraphs. *Grammar/Usage* 2 errors *Spelling* 2 errors
2	The paper has a clear thesis. The ideas are somewhat developed, but there are only a few details.	Ideas are fairly well organized. The paper includes all parts of an essay (introduction, body, and conclusion).	The writer's voice is natural, but the writer is not fully engaged in the topic. At times, the writer's viewpoint may be vague.	Most words are used correctly. A few words are too general. Some words are repeated.	Sentences are formed correctly, although they may be similar in structure. Most transitions are clear.	*Capitalization & Punctuation* 2 errors. May not indent paragraphs. *Grammar/Usage* 3 errors *Spelling* 3 errors
1	The thesis of the paper is unclear or missing. The paper is poorly developed and/or confusing.	Ideas are not clearly organized. The paper may be missing an introduction or a conclusion.	The writer seems uninterested in the topic and unaware of his or her audience.	Most words are used incorrectly, many are too general or frequently repeated.	The sentences do not flow well and lack structure. They are short and choppy or long and confusing.	*Capitalization & Punctuation* 3+ errors. May not indent paragraphs. *Grammar/Usage* 4+ errors interfere with meaning *Spelling* 4+ errors
Value						

Comments ____________________

	Ideas and Development	Organization	Voice and Audience Awareness	Word Choice	Sentence Fluency	Language Conventions
4	Clear plot events, as well as a readily identifiable conflict/problem and setting. The climax and resolution are clear. Rich details and sensory description make characters come to life. No irrelevant material.	Beginning grabs reader's attention. Logically sequenced plot. Story transitions link events. Conclusion caps off story and does not leave the reader hanging.	Strong sense of person and purpose behind the words. Brings story to life.	Words are specific, accurate, and vivid. Word choice enhances meaning and reader's enjoyment.	Writes complete sentences with varied sentence patterns and beginnings	*Capitalization & Punctuation* No errors. Indents paragraphs. *Grammar/Usage* 0–1 error *Spelling* 0–1 error
3	Identifiable plot events. Conflict/problem may not be entirely clear. The climax or resolution may not be clear. Some details/sensory description. Characters present but may not be fully developed. Setting may be missing. Limited irrelevant material.	Beginning interests reader. Plot somewhat logically sequenced but may lack one story element such as climax or satisfying conclusion. Story transitions link some events.	Some sense of person and purpose behind the words.	Words are correctly used but may be somewhat general and unspecific.	Writes complete sentences with some expansion. Limited variety.	*Capitalization & Punctuation* 1 error. Indents paragraphs. *Grammar/Usage* 2 errors *Spelling* 2 errors
2	Limited plot and/or the conflict/problem is not clear. The setting, climax, and/or resolution may not be apparent. There are insufficient details and description. Characterization is weak. Too repetitious or too much irrelevant material.	Beginning does not capture reader's interest. Plot under-developed and two or more story elements (setting, initiating event, climax, resolution) missing. Story transitions missing.	Little sense of person and purpose behind the words.	Word choice limited. Words may be used inaccurately or repetitively.	Writes mostly simple and/or awkwardly constructed sentences. May include some run-ons and fragments.	*Capitalization & Punctuation* 2 errors. May not indent paragraphs. *Grammar/Usage* 3 errors *Spelling* 3 errors
1	Does not address the prompt OR the plot, conflict/problem are not discernible. Description, details, and characterization are missing.	Text has evident structure. Lack of organization seriously interferes with meaning.	No sense of person or purpose behind the words.	Extremely limited range of words. Restricted vocabulary impedes message.	Numerous run-ons and/or sentence fragments interfere with meaning.	*Capitalization & Punctuation* 3+ errors. May not indent paragraphs. *Grammar/Usage* 4+ errors interfere with meaning *Spelling* 4+ errors
Value						

Comments ____________________

Six Traits of Writing: Persuasion

	Ideas and Development	Organization	Voice and Audience Awareness	Word Choice	Sentence Fluency	Language Conventions
4	Clearly states a position on the issue. Fully develops main ideas with evidence, examples, and explanations that are compelling. No irrelevant information.	Introduction clearly states position. Ideas logically sequenced. Transition sentences link ideas. Conclusion ties essay together and gives reader something to think about. Follows required format.	Strong sense of person and purpose behind the words. Brings issue to life.	Words are specific, accurate, and vivid. Word choice enhances meaning and reader's enjoyment.	Writes complete sentences with varied sentence patterns and beginnings	*Capitalization & Punctuation* No errors. Indents paragraphs. *Grammar/Usage* 0–1 error *Spelling* 0–1 error
3	States a position on the issue. Develops main ideas adequately with some evidence, examples, and explanations. Limited irrelevant information.	Introduction states position. Ideas mostly logically sequenced. Some linkage among ideas. Conclusion ties essay together. Follows required format.	Some sense of person and purpose behind the words. Sense of commitment to the issue. Text may be too casual for the purpose.	Words are correctly used but may be somewhat general and unspecific.	Writes complete sentences with some expansion. Limited variety.	*Capitalization & Punctuation* 1 error. Indents paragraphs. *Grammar/Usage* 2 errors *Spelling* 2 errors
2	Does not state a clear position on the issue and/or does not support main ideas with sufficient evidence, examples, and explanations. May be too repetitious or too much irrelevant information.	Introduction may not state a position. Ideas not logically sequenced. Transition sentences missing. Conclusion may be missing. Does not follow required format.	Little sense of person and purpose behind the words. Very little engagement with reader. Text may be too casual for the purpose.	Word choice limited. Words may be used inaccurately or repetitively.	Writes mostly simple and/or awkwardly constructed sentences. May include some run-ons and fragments.	*Capitalization & Punctuation* 2 errors. May not indent paragraphs. *Grammar/Usage* 3 errors *Spelling* 3 errors
1	Does not address the prompt OR does not develop a position. Elaboration lacking or unrelated to the issue.	Text has no evident structure. Lack of organization seriously interferes with meaning.	No sense of person or purpose behind the words. No sense of audience.	Extremely limited range of words. Restricted vocabulary impedes message.	Numerous run-ons and/or sentence fragments interfere with meaning.	*Capitalization & Punctuation* 3+ errors. May not indent paragraphs. *Grammar/Usage* 4+ errors interfere with meaning *Spelling* 4+ errors
Value						

Comments ______________________________

	Ideas and Development	Organization	Voice and Audience Awareness	Word Choice	Sentence Fluency	Language Conventions
4	States thesis clearly. Develops main ideas fully with elaborations. Direct quotations from text support ideas. All information pertinent to thesis.	Introduction contains thesis statement and cites title, author of work. Ideas logically sequenced. Transition sentences link ideas. Conclusion offers some evaluation of the work.	Strong sense of person and purpose behind the words. Brings topic to life.	Words are specific, accurate, and vivid. Word choice enhances meaning and reader's enjoyment.	Writes complete sentences with varied sentence patterns and beginnings	*Capitalization & Punctuation* No errors. Indents paragraphs. *Grammar/Usage* 0–1 error *Spelling* 0–1 error
3	States thesis clearly. Develops main ideas with some elaboration. May lack direct quotations from text to support ideas. Limited amount of irrelevant information.	Introduction contains thesis statement and cites title, author of work. Ideas mostly logically sequenced. Some linkage of main ideas. Formulaic conclusion may not offer evaluation of the work.	Some sense of person and purpose behind the words. Sense of commitment to the issue. Text may be too casual for purpose.	Words are correctly used but may be somewhat general and unspecific.	Writes complete sentences with some expansion. Limited variety.	*Capitalization & Punctuation* 1 error. Indents paragraphs. *Grammar/Usage* 2 errors *Spelling* 2 errors
2	Does not state thesis clearly and/or minimal development of main ideas. No direct quotations to support ideas. Too repetitious or too much irrelevant information.	Introduction may not have clear thesis. Ideas not logically sequenced. Transitions may be missing. May lack conclusion, or conclusion in formulaic with no evaluation of the work.	Little sense of person and purpose behind the words. Very little engagement with the reader. Text may be too casual for purpose.	Word choice limited. Words may be used inaccurately or repetitively.	Writes mostly simple and/or awkwardly constructed sentences. May include some run-ons and fragments.	*Capitalization & Punctuation* 2 errors. May not indent paragraphs. *Grammar/Usage* 3 errors *Spelling* 3 errors
1	Does not address the prompt OR does not develop a thesis. Elaboration lacking or unrelated to a thesis.	No evident structure. Lack of organization seriously interferes with meaning.	No sense of person or purpose behind the words. No sense of audience.	Extremely limited range of words. Restricted vocabulary impedes message.	Numerous run-ons and/or sentence fragments interfere with meaning.	*Capitalization & Punctuation* 3+ errors. May not indent paragraphs. *Grammar/Usage* 4+ errors interfere with meaning *Spelling* 4+ errors
Value						

Comments ______________________________

____

____

____

Sight Words

The following sight words are introduced by Unit and cumulatively reviewed online in Word Training and reinforced in Text Training.

Unit 1	Unit 2	Unit 3	Unit 4	Unit 5	Unit 6
hour	break	someone	ago	status	important
night	wear	news	behind	symbol	traffic
friend	hear	open	weight	energy	prove
though	buy	fiction	custom	plastic	afford
walk	loud	watch	building	bridge	guide
cover	listen	son	vision	carry	pause
special	student	river	color	young	mountains
family	talk	aunt	area	touch	toward
near	idea	able	piece	whole	table
wild	spread	refer	usual	early	money
four	truth	tower	heard	column	voice
perfect	vary	menu	during	several	cried
gone	engine	poor	honor	iron	guard
tomorrow	laugh	abroad	honest	course	guess
women	oil	against	half	certain	guest
Unit 7	**Unit 8**	**Unit 9**	**Unit 10**	**Unit 11**	**Unit 12**
spirit	steady	system	interesting	fragile	achieve
scene	period	ability	similar	opposite	practical
strength	distinct	information	article	science	structure
mighty	powerful	citizen	capture	official	optional
purpose	convince	mobile	creature	relief	dilemma
angle	popular	imagine	opinion	equation	surface
field	brilliant	focused	finally	government	material
notice	known	among	general	distance	instrument
figure	island	heavy	region	heart	paragraph
minutes	machine	circle	believe	probably	represent
ocean	brought	measure	exercise	length	clothes
nothing	thousand	ready	develop	present	either
busy	beautiful	captain	journal	colleague	character
business	beauty	curtain	journey	courage	education
villain	debt	language	guarantee	nuisance	extraordinary

Vocabulary

The following words are passage vocabulary explicitly taught in Text Training.

abruptly	U3	cherish	U8	diagnose	U5	govern	U6
access	U6	circumstance	U12	discrimination	U6	grudge	U11
acknowledgment	U11	clamor	U5	distinct	U9	habitat	U7
acquire	U4	collapse	U12	distracted	U10	hamper	U6
acute	U12	commit	U1	divert	U11	harmony	U6
adjust	U4	compel	U7	donor	U12	healthy	U2
advantage	U7	competition	U7	drastically	U12	hesitation	U3
ailment	U5	compromise	U7	drone	U4	hoist	U11
allergy	U2	concentrate	U3	economy	U7	identify	U1
allow	U2	conditions	U5	elaborate	U5	ignorant	U7
alter	U7	conflict	U9	eligible	U11	image	U9
alternative	U5	consist	U1	embarrass	U2	immobile	U8
anticipation	U5	consistency	U5	emphasis	U4	impact	U6
appalling	U10	conspicuous	U3	encounter	U7	implement	U9
apparent	U8	consultation	U10	enforce	U10	implicated	U8
apply	U5	consume	U12	enhance	U10	impose	U6
appropriate	U10	contradict	U10	enthusiastically	U4	incident	U9
ascent	U7	contribution	U6	envy	U4	increase	U10
aspect	U7	controversial	U9	euphoric	U5	indicate	U3
assess	U11	converse	U8	eventually	U4	individuality	U10
assume	U12	convict	U1	evidence	U1	inevitable	U4
attend	U9	correspondence	U4	exaggeration	U10	inferno	U12
automatically	U12	counsel	U8	exalted	U12	inhibition	U9
avoid	U1	course	U8	exchange	U4	innocence	U1
aware	U1	dazed	U1	experimental	U12	insecurity	U7
awkward	U3	debate	U4	exploitation	U6	inspiration	U5
balance	U2	declare	U1	falter	U3	instinctively	U4
ban	U10	decline	U7	fashion	U11	interrupt	U12
barren	U1	decorous	U11	fiber	U1	interval	U3
beckon	U8	defy	U6	formula	U9	introduce	U4
(on) behalf	U12	delicately	U11	frail	U2	invaluable	U5
cancel	U2	deny	U3	friction	U12	invent	U6
casual	U3	dependable	U3	fruition	U11	involved	U9
cease	U11	deserve	U3	functional	U4	irrelevant	U6
challenge	U9	design	U4	furnished	U2	isolation	U4
charge	U2	devise	U8	garment	U3	justification	U11

juvenile	U1	preserve	U1	stifle	U10
lacking	U12	previously	U9	stoop	U2
latch	U2	primitive	U12	straight	U2
lecture	U5	principle	U10	strategy	U5
legacy	U6	priority	U10	strict	U3
leisure	U3	procession	U11	suede	U2
lonely	U2	promotion	U7	survey	U10
lurk	U2	prone (to)	U9	suspect	U1
maintain	U8	prospect	U6	suspend	U6
massive	U6	punch	U2	tenacity	U12
media	U9	pursue	U7	trace	U1
motionless	U4	qualify	U5	transform	U6
motivated	U5	rashness	U8	transport	U9
murmur	U4	reaction	U9	truancy	U10
mutinous	U11	reassuring	U5	unique	U1
obstacle	U12	recklessly	U11	urge	U9
obtain	U9	reconsider	U8	vainly	U7
omission	U8	regretfully	U11	valid	U10
opportunity	U5	regulations	U3	vast	U1
ornery	U3	release	U2	vengeance	U7
outcome	U5	relocation	U7	verdict	U12
passive	U6	research	U9	warped	U11
peculiar	U3	resemblance	U3	wince	U12
penalty	U8	reside	U8	witness	U1
perish	U8	resist	U10		
permit	U2	resolve	U8		
persistence	U7	resources	U6		
policy	U6	restore	U8		
populated	U4	restrain	U7		
portion	U5	restrictive	U10		
possession	U3	retort	U11		
precious	U11	savor	U4		
prefer	U10	seldom	U8		
preliminaries	U11	sin	U2		
premises	U1	sought	U8		
presentable	U2	standard	U9		

Research and Evidence of Effectiveness

Alliance for Excellent Education (2010). *Issue brief – There's a crisis in America's high schools.* Alliance for Excellent Education: Washington, DC. Retrievable from: http://www.all4ed.org/about_the_crisis

Archer, A. L., Gleason, M. M., & Vachon, V. (2003). Decoding and fluency: Foundation skills for older struggling readers. *Learning Disability Quarterly, 26*(2), 89-101.

August, D., & Shanahan, T. (Eds.) (2006) Developing Literacy in Second-Language Learners: Report of the National Literacy Panel on Language-Minority Children and Youth. Mahwah, NJ: Lawrence Erlbaum.

Balfanz, R., & Herzog, L. (2006). *Keeping middle grades students on track to graduation. Part A: Early identification.* Paper presented at the Annual Meeting of the American Educational Research Association, San Francisco, CA.

Bhattacharya, A., & Ehri, L. (2004). Graphosyllabic analysis helps adolescent struggling readers read and spell words. *Journal of Learning Disabilities, 37*(4), 331-348.

Biancarosa, C., & Snow, C. E. (2006). Reading next—A vision for action and research in middle and high school literacy:A report to Carnegie Corporation of New York (2nd ed.). Washington, DC: Alliance for Excellent Education.

Boardman, A. G., Roberts, G., Vaughn, S., Wexler, J., Murray, C. S., & Kosanovich, M. (2008). *Effective instruction for adolescent struggling readers: A practice brief.* Portsmouth, NH: RMC Research Corporation, Center on Instruction. Available from: http://www.centeroninstruction.org/files/Adol%20Struggling%20Readers%20Practice%20Brief.pdf

Byrd, M. (2001). Technology helps increase reading scores. *Media & Methods, 37*(3), 12-15.

Calhoon, M. B. (2005). Effects of a peer-mediated phonological skill and reading comprehension program on reading skill acquisition of middle school students with reading disabilities. *Journal of Learning Disabilities*, 38(5), 424–433.

Calhoon, M.B., & Petscher Y. (2013). Individual and group sensitivity to remedial reading program design: Examining reading gains across three middle school reading projects. *Reading and Writing, 26*(4), 565-592.

Calhoon, M.B., Sandow, A., & Hunter, C.V. (2010) Reorganizing the instructional reading components: Could there be a better way to design remedial reading programs to maximize middle school students with reading disabilities' response to treatment? *Annals of Dyslexia, 60*, 57–85.

Carnegie Council on Advancing Adolescent Literacy. (2010). Time to act: An agenda for advancing adolescent literacy for college and career success. New York, NY: Carnegie Corporation of New York.

Cheung, A. C., & Slavin, R. E. (2011). *The effectiveness of education technology for enhancing reading achievement: A meta-analysis.* Best Evidence Encyclopedia, John Hopkins University School of Education's Center for Data-Driven Reform in Education and the Institute of Education Sciences, U.S. Department of Education. Retrievable from: www.bestevidence.org

Curtis, M. (2004). Adolescents who struggle with word identification: Research and practice. In T. Jetton & J. Dole (Eds.), *Adolescent literacy research and practice* (pp. 119-134). New York: Guilford.

Curtis, M., & Longo, A.M. (1999) *When adolescents can't read: Methods and materials that work.* Cambridge, MA: Brookline Books.

Denson, K. (2008). *Passport Reading Journeys effectiveness with ninth grade students identified for reading improvement instruction in an urban high school.* Dallas, TX: Voyager Expanded Learning, Inc.. Retrievable from: http://www.voyagerlearning.com

Deshler, D. D., Palincsar, A. S., Biancarosa, G., & Nair, M. (2007). *Informed choices for struggling adolescent readers: A researched-based guide to instructional programs and practices.* Newark, DE: International Reading Association.

Ehri, L. (2004). Teaching phonemic awareness and phonics: An explanation of the National Reading Panel meta-analysis. In P. McCardle. and L. Chhabra, (Eds.), *The Voice of Evidence in Reading Research* (pp. 153-186). Baltimore, MD: Brookes Publishing Company.

Fletcher, J. M., Lyon, G. R., Barnes, M., Stuebing, K. K., Francis, D. J., Olson, R. K., ... & Shaywitz, B. A. (2002). Classification of learning disabilities: An evidenced-based evaluation. In R. Bradley, L. Danielson, & D. P. Hallahan (Eds.). *Identification of learning disabilities: Research to practice* (pp. 185-250). Mahwah, NJ: Erlbaum.

Fletcher, J. M., Lyon, G. R., Fuchs, L. S., & Barnes, M. A. (2007). *Learning disabilities: From identification to intervention.* New York, NY: Guilford.

Foorman, B. R., Francis, D. J., Fletcher, J. M., Schatschneider, C., & Mehta, P. (1998). The role of instruction in learning to read: Preventing reading failure in at-risk children. *Journal of Educational Psychology, 90*(1), 37-55.

Foorman, B. R., & Torgesen, J. K. (2001). Critical elements of classroom and small group instruction promote reading success in all children. *Learning Disabilities Research & Practice 16(4),* 203-212.

Guskey, T. R. (1997). *Implementing mastery learning.* Belmont, CA: Wadsworth Publishing.

Hall, T. E., Hughes, C. A., & Filbert, M. (2000). Computer assisted instruction in reading for students with learning disabilities: A research synthesis. *Education and Treatment of Children, 23*(3), 173-193.

Hook, P. E., Macaruso, P., & Jones, S. (2001). Efficacy of fast forward training on facilitating acquisition of reading skills by children with reading difficulties—a longitudinal study. *Annals of Dyslexia, 51,* 75-96.

Kamil, M. L., Borman, G. D., Dole, J., Kral, C. C., Salinger, T., & Torgesen, J. (2008). *Improving adolescent literacy: Effective classroom and intervention practices: A Practice Guide* (NCEE #2008-4027). Washington, DC: National Center for Education Evaluation and Regional Assistance, Institute of Education Sciences, U.S. Department of Education.

Kluger, A., & Adler, S. (1993). Person-versus computer-mediated feedback. *Computers in Human Behavior, 9*(1), 1-16.

Kulik, J. A. (1994). Meta-analytic studies of findings on computer-based instruction. In E. L. Baker and H. F. O'Neil, Jr. (Eds.). *Technology assessment in education and training.* Hillsdale, NJ: Lawrence Erlbaum.

Lee, C.D., & Spratley, A. (2010). *Reading in the disciplines: The challenges of adolescent literacy.* New York, NY: Carnegie Corporation of New York. Available from: http://carnegie.org/fileadmin/Media/Publications/PDF/tta_Lee.pdf

Lovett, M.W., Lacerenza, L., De Palma, M., & Frijters, J.C. (2012) Evaluating the efficacy of remediation for struggling readers in high school. *Journal of Learning Disabilities, 45*(2), 151-169

Lyon, G. R. (1995). Toward a definition of dyslexia. *Annals of Dyslexia,* 45, 3-27.

MacArthur, C. A., Ferretti, R. P., Okolo, C. M., & Cavalier, A. R. (2001). Technology applications for students with literacy problems: A critical review. *The Elementary School Journal, 101,* 273-301.

Moats, L. C. (2010). *Speech to print: Language essentials for teachers.* Baltimore: Paul Brookes.

Morris, R. D., Lovett, M.W., Wolf, M., Sevcik, R.A., Steinbach, K.A., Frijters, J.C. & Shapiro, M.B. (2012) Multiple-component remediation for developmental reading disabilities: IQ, socioeconomic status, and race as factors in remedial outcome. *Journal of Learning Disabilities,* 45(2), 99-127.

Nagy, W.E., & Anderson, R.C. (1984). How many words are there in printed English? *Reading Research Quarterly, 19,* 304-330.

National Association of State Boards of Education (2005). *Reading at risk: How states can respond to the crisis in adolescent literacy.* Alexandria, VA: Author. Available from http://www.centeroninstruction.org/files/Reading_At_Risk_Full_Report.pdf

National Center for Education Statistics (2009). *The nation's report card: Reading 2009* (NCES 2010–458). Washington, DC: Institute of Education Sciences, U.S. Department of Education.

National Institute for Literacy (2007). *What content area teachers should know about adolescent literacy.* Jessup, MD: EdPubs. Retrievable from: http://lincs.ed.gov/publications/pdf/adolescent_literacy07.pdf

National Joint Committee on Learning Disabilities (2008). *Adolescent Literacy and Older Students with Learning Disabilities* [Technical Report]. Retrieved from: www.asha.org/policy

National Longitudinal Transition Study II. (2003). *National Center for Special Education Research at the Institute of Education Sciences.* Washington, DC: U.S. Department of Education.

National Reading Panel (2000). *Teaching children to read: An evidence-based assessment of the scientific research literature on reading and its implications for reading instruction.* National Institute of Child Health and Human Development, Washington, D.C.

Niemiec, C. P., & Ryan, R. M. (2009). Autonomy, competence, and relatedness in the classroom: Applying self-determination theory to educational practice. *Theory and Research in Education 7*(2), 133-144.

Reed, D. K., & Vaughn, S. (2010). Reading interventions for older students. In T. A. Glover & S. Vaughn (Eds.), *Response to intervention: Empowering all students to learn, a critical account of the science and practice* (pp. 143-186). New York, NY: Guilford Press.

Scammacca, N., Roberts, G., Vaughn, S., Edmonds, M., Wexler, J., Reutebuch, C. K., & Torgesen, J. (2007). *Reading interventions for adolescent struggling readers: A meta-analysis with implications for practice.* Portsmouth, NH: RMC Research Corporation, Center on Instruction.

Scarborough, HS and Brady, SA 2002. Toward a common terminology for talking about speech and reading: A glossary of the "phon" words and some related terms. *Journal of Literacy Research, 34*(3), 299–334

Schacter, J. (1999). *The impact of educational technology on student achievement: What the most current research has to say.* Milken Exchange on Educational Technology, Santa Monica, CA. Retrievable from: http://www.eric.ed.gov/PDFS/ED430537.pdf

Schatschneider, C., Buck, J., Torgesen, J., Wagner, R., Hassler, L., Hecht, S., & Powell-Smith, K. (2004). A Multivariate Study of Individual Differences in Performance on the Reading Portion of the Florida Comprehensive Assessment Test:A Preliminary Report. Technical report #5 , Florida Center for Reading Research

Shankweiler, D., Lundquist, E., Katz, L., Stuebing, K. K., Fletcher, J. M., Brady, S., ...Shaywitz, B. A. (1999). Comprehension and decoding: Patterns of association in children with reading difficulties. *Scientific Studies of Reading,* 3, 69-94.

Slavin, R. E., Cheung, A., Groff, C., & Lake, C. (2008). Effective reading programs for middle and high schools: A best-evidence synthesis. *Reading Research Quarterly, 43*(3), 290-322.

Snow, C. E., & Biancarosa, G. (2003). *Adolescent literacy and the achievement gap: What do we know and where do we go from here?* New York: Carnegie Corporation of New York.

Soe, K., Koki, S., & Chang, J. M. (2000). *Effect of computer-assisted instruction (CAI) on reading achievement: A meta-analysis.* Pacific Resources for Education and Learning: Honolulu, HI. Retrievable from: http://www.prel.org/products/products/effect-cai.htm

Tillman, P. S. (2010). *Computer-assisted instruction (CAI) and reading acquisition: A synthesis of the literature.* Retrievable from: http://teach.valdosta.edu/are/TillmanPLRFinal.pdf

Torgesen, J.K. (2004). Avoiding the devastating downward spiral: The evidence that early intervention prevents reading failure. *American Educator, 28,* 6-19.

Torgesen, A.W., Alexander, R. K., Wagner, C. A., Rashotte, K., Conway, T., & Rose, E. (2001). Intensive remedial instruction for children with severe reading disabilities: Immediate and long-term outcomes from two instructional approaches. *Journal of Learning Disabilities, 34,* 33-58.

Torgesen, J. K., Wagner, R. K., Rashotte, C. A., Herron, J., & Lindamood, P. (2010). Computer-assisted instruction to prevent early reading difficulties in students at risk for dyslexia: Outcomes from two instructional approaches. *Annals of Dyslexia, 60*(1), 40-56, doi:10.1007/s11881-009-0032-y

Tsesmeli, S. N., & Seymour, P. H. K. (2009). The effects of training of morphological structure on spelling derived words by dyslexic adolescents. *British Journal of Psychology, 100,* 565-592.

Vadasy, P. F., Sanders, E. A., & Tudor, S. (2007). Effectiveness of paraeducator supplemented individual instruction: Beyond basic decoding skill. *Journal of Learning Disabilities, 40*(6), 508-524.

Vaughn, S., Gersten, R., & Chard, D. J. (2000). The underlying message in LD intervention research: Findings from research syntheses. *Exceptional Children, 67*(1), 99-114.

Vellutino, F. R., Tunmer, W. E., Jaccard, J. J., & Chen, R. (2007). Components of reading ability: Multivariate evidence for a convergent skills model of reading development. *Scientific Studies of Reading, 11*(1), 3-32.

Index

abbreviations, using, 220, 222, 306, 307

action verbs, 472

active voice, 208–210

adages, 309

adjectives

- adjective clauses, 204–208, 311
- applying/using, 113, 115, 261, 309, 310, 346, 383, 489
- comparative, 70, 170
- consecutive, 344, 397
- coordinate, 119, 121, 396
- descriptive language with, 73, 266, 399
- function of, 385
- relative clauses as, 203–205
- superlative, 67, 70
- verbs as, 293–295

adverbial phrases, 469

adverbs

- adverb clauses, 206, 207–208
- applying/using, 112, 113, 114, 115, 117, 255
- conjunctive, 487, 523
- function of, 204, 383, 470, 471

agreement. *See* subject-verb agreement

allusion, 490

analyze (prompt), 26, 242, 243, 244, 249, 299, 301

antagonist, 30, 262–263

antonyms, using, 220, 221, 304

apostrophes, 98–99

appositives, 385–387

argument. *See* develop an argument (prompt)

argument essay, 74–76

assess (prompt), 26, 28, 242, 243, 246, 249, 299, 509, 510, 512, 515

audio versus print, 157

author's point of view. *See* point of view

author's purpose, 5, 43, 81, 128, 130, 189, 229, 232, 272, 277, 315, 318, 361, 366, 407, 409, 447, 452, 494, 496

background knowledge, 5, 11, 43, 81, 130, 189, 232, 277, 318, 367, 410, 439, 453, 497

backstory, 27–28. *See also* flashback

Big Ideas, 5, 41, 43, 77, 81, 125, 130, 184, 189, 229, 232, 273, 277, 315, 318, 361, 367, 408, 410, 448, 453, 494, 497, 534

body language, 521

body paragraphs, 427, 444, 528, 529

book title, analyzing, 6, 44, 82, 131, 188, 233, 317, 319, 344, 367, 497

brainstorming, 242

C

capitalization, 131, 153

captions, 190

cause and effect, 69

central idea, 126, 218

chant, 131, 153–154, 166, 175

character analysis essay, 528–532

characters

- analyzing, 268, 483, 484, 485, 486, 487, 488, 489, 493, 520, 521, 522, 523, 524
- antagonist/protagonist, 30, 262–263
- identifying, 127, 151, 355

chart reading procedure, 56, 152, 243, 334, 424, 509

choral reading

- applying/using, 12, 49, 87, 136, 195, 238, 283, 324, 372, 415, 459, 502
- as reading type, 12, 26, 33, 49, 61, 66, 87, 106, 111, 136, 162, 195, 212, 217, 238, 248, 254, 283, 299, 303, 324, 338, 343, 372, 391, 395, 415, 429, 434, 459, 478, 482, 502, 514, 519

chronological order, 26, 261, 272

cite evidence, 423, 424, 426, 428, 430, 478. *See also* evidence, using

claim, 62. *See also* overgeneralization

clarify (prompt), 56, 57, 58, 61, 62, 106, 107, 333, 334, 335, 339, 391

clauses, 19–20, 33. *See also* dependent clauses; independent clauses; relative clauses

close reading, 31–37, 65–70, 110–121, 161–176, 216–225, 252–263, 302–311, 342–350, 394–403, 433–438, 481–489, 518–524
colon, 437, 438
commas, 23, 24, 101, 102, 104, 119, 120, 121, 205, 241, 242, 386, 396
common nouns, 224
comparative adjectives, 70, 170. *See also* adjectives
compare (prompt), 423, 424, 425, 430, 431–432, 478, 479
compare-contrast essay, 427, 443–445
complex sentences, 24, 103–104, 387
compound object, 20
compound predicate, 20
compound sentences, 20
compound subject, 20
compound words, 70
comprehension. *See also* reading, reading for a purpose
  asking/answering questions (*See* questions)
  close reading, 31–37, 65–70, 110–121, 161–176, 216–225, 252–263, 302–311, 342–350, 394–403, 433–438, 481–489, 518–524
  demonstrating, 41, 77, 125, 184, 229, 272, 315, 361, 407, 447, 494, 534
  monitoring, 32, 49, 66, 111, 136, 162, 217, 238, 254, 303, 324, 343, 395, 415, 434, 482, 502, 519
concluding paragraph, 427, 444–445, 530
conclusion, 75, 181, 269
conditional mood (state), 176, 398
conflict, 30, 127, 236, 240, 253, 260, 347, 468, 492
conjunctions, 20, 67, 68, 487. *See also specific kinds of conjunctions*
conjunctive adverbs, 487, 523
connect (prompt), 509, 510, 511, 515
connotation, 67, 224, 344
content focus, 4, 42, 43, 80, 129, 188, 231, 276, 317, 366, 409, 452, 496
context clues, 57, 58, 220, 224, 259, 400, 484
contractions, using, 98–99, 205, 473, 475, 487, 490
contradictions, 344, 345
contrast (prompt), 214, 423, 424, 425, 430, 478, 479, 480
contrast essay, 180–183
coordinate adjectives, 119, 121, 396. *See also* adjectives
coordinating conjunctions, 20. *See also* conjunctions
craft, author's. *See* author's purpose
critical understandings, 56–59, 151–155, 242–246, 333–336, 423–426, 509–512. *See also* prompts

degrees of meaning. *See* vocabulary
demonstrate (prompt), 423, 424, 426, 430, 478
dependent clauses, 21–22, 23, 24, 100, 203–205. *See also* clauses
descriptive language, 73, 266, 399. *See also* adjectives
develop an argument (prompt), 333, 334, 335, 339, 391, 393
dialogue, 49, 158, 166, 238, 241–242, 259, 266, 268–269, 354
dialogue balloon versus thought balloon, 233, 238
diary, 227
differentiate (prompt), 242, 243, 245, 249, 299
direction words, 56–59, 61, 106, 151–152, 153, 157, 159, 212, 242–246, 249, 299, 333–334, 339, 391, 423, 430, 478, 479, 509, 512, 515. *See also* prompts; *specific direction words; specific question words*
direct objects, 103, 119, 206, 207, 208, 209, 220, 296, 383, 385, 386
distinguish (prompt), 26, 27
double negatives, 474, 475–476

editing. *See* revising
educated guess. *See* predictions, making
elaborations, 40, 73, 356. *See also* supporting details
ellipses, 176, 218, 485, 521

Index

em dash, 70, 114, 256, 307, 437, 484, 523

emphasis, 70, 114, 154, 167, 174, 306, 307, 484, 489, 521

enduring understandings, 41, 77, 125–126, 184–185, 229–230, 273, 315–316, 361–362, 408, 448, 494–495, 534–535

epic tales, 121

epigraph, 195, 216, 218, 448

essay. *See* multiparagraph essay

evaluate (prompt), 26, 152, 155, 157, 212

evidence, using, 25, 33, 36, 57, 58, 59, 61, 63, 67, 68, 70, 73, 74, 75, 98, 105, 106, 107, 108, 112, 113, 114, 116, 117, 118, 120, 121, 153, 154, 156, 159, 160, 164, 165, 166, 168, 169, 170, 171, 172, 174, 175, 211, 215, 248, 258, 259, 260, 261, 262, 305, 306, 334, 335, 337, 339, 340, 345, 390, 391, 393, 398, 400, 402, 403, 436, 437, 438, 444, 446, 484, 485, 486, 487, 488, 489, 513, 520, 522, 523, 529. *See also* cite evidence; prompts

exaggeration, 35, 36, 118, 306, 323, 332, 343, 399, 486, 487. *See also* hyperbole

fables, 126

factual mood. *See* indicative mood

fact versus opinion, 308, 444

fairy tales, 126

fallacies, 305

fiction, 4, 5, 80, 81, 129–130, 189, 231, 272, 276, 407, 444, 447, 494

figurative language, 34, 35, 348. *See also* metaphors; personification; similes; idioms

flashback, 26, 27–28, 244, 272, 402, 403

fluency, building, 73, 514

foreshadowing, 30, 36, 114, 115, 164, 169, 258, 419, 438

formatting, 266

future tense. *See* tense

genres, 189, 231. *See also* text type

gerunds, 292–293

gothic novel, 231

grammar
- adjectives (*See* adjectives)
- adverbs (*See* adverbs)
- appositives, 385–386
- conjunctions (*See* conjunctions)
- direct objects, 103, 119, 206, 207, 208, 209, 220, 296, 383, 385, 386
- gerunds, 292–293
- importance of, 73
- multiple functionality, 206, 292, 382
- nouns (*See* nouns)
- participles, 293–295, 382–384
- phrases versus clauses, 19–20, 100, 203
- plurals, 292, 387–389
- prepositions, 19 (*See also* prepositional phrases)
- pronouns (*See* pronouns)
- relative clauses, 101–102, 203–208, 523
- subject-verb agreement, 387–389
- tense (*See* tense)
- verbs (*See* verbs)

graphic novel, 231, 232, 238, 241–242, 252, 254, 272

graphic organizers
- story map, 127
- Venn diagram, 443, 444

guided highlighting. *See* close reading

guided practice
- grammar, 20, 22, 99, 101–102, 205, 206–207, 208, 293, 294, 383, 384, 385, 470, 471, 473
- reading, 28, 58–59, 63, 107–108, 154–155, 159, 214–215, 244–246, 250–251, 300–301, 335–336, 340–341, 392, 425–426, 431–432, 479–480, 511–512, 516–517
- vocabulary, 55
- writing, 23, 24, 104, 209, 297, 386, 388, 389, 475–476

headings, 190, 219, 319, 348

helping verbs, 19, 208, 209, 292–293, 294, 388, 469, 472

homophones, 117, 172, 173, 308, 349

how (question word), 204, 208

how many (question words), 204

hyperbole, 36, 399. *See also* exaggeration

hypothetical mood. *See* subjunctive mood

idioms, using, 36, 257, 308, 346, 348, 438, 469, 483, 485, 486, 487, 489, 520, 522, 523
illustrate (prompt), 509, 510, 511, 515, 516
illustrations. *See* pictures/illustrations
imperative mood, 120
imperative statement, 225
indefinite pronouns, 218, 484, 485, 522
independent clauses, 21–22, 24, 100, 103, 203, 470. *See also* clauses
independent practice
  grammar, 20, 22, 99, 102, 205, 207, 208, 293, 295, 383, 384, 386, 470, 471, 473
  reading, 29, 63, 108, 160, 215, 251, 301, 341, 393, 432, 480, 517
  vocabulary, 55
  writing, 23, 24, 104, 209, 297, 387, 388, 389, 475, 476
independent reading, 12, 26, 33, 49, 61, 66, 87, 106, 111, 136, 162, 195, 212, 217, 238, 248, 254, 283, 299, 303, 324, 338, 343, 372, 391, 395, 415, 429, 434, 459, 478, 482, 502, 514, 519
indicative mood, 121
informational text, 42–43, 126, 189, 229, 276, 317, 366, 409, 452
integrate (prompt), 152, 153, 157, 159, 212
intensive pronouns, 174, 484, 489
interrogative mood, 121
interrogative statement, 176
intransitive verbs, 295, 296
introduction (in writing), 73, 74, 75, 181, 427, 444, 528
introductory paragraphs, 180, 181, 268, 427, 444, 528
irony, 263, 346, 523
irrelevant facts, 58, 203, 214

journal. *See* diary

kernel sentence, 383, 387
key details. *See* summarizing

leading language. *See* rhetorical language
leading question, 116, 157
legend, 129–130
lesson openers, 4, 17, 25, 31, 38, 42, 52, 60, 65, 71, 80, 97, 105, 110, 122, 129, 149, 156, 161, 177, 188, 202, 211, 216, 226, 231, 239, 247, 252, 264, 276, 290, 298, 302, 312, 317, 331, 337, 342, 351, 366, 380, 390, 394, 404, 409, 421, 428, 433, 440, 452, 467, 477, 481, 491, 496, 507, 513, 518, 525
letter writing, 314, 405, 519, 525, 526
linking verbs, 19, 294, 388, 472
literary fiction. *See* fiction
literary meaning, 246
literary text/literature. *See* text type
logical errors. *See* fallacies

main idea, 64, 73, 331
mapping, 74, 75, 181, 268–269
Masterpiece Sentences, 208, 269
metaphors, 34, 36, 121, 125, 348, 400, 485, 489
misleading language. *See* fallacies
modeling
  grammar, 19, 21, 99, 101, 204, 206, 207, 292–293, 294, 382–383, 384, 385, 470, 471, 472
  reading, 27–28, 58, 62–63, 107, 153–154, 158, 213–214
  vocabulary, 55
  writing, 23, 24, 103, 209, 210, 268, 386, 387, 388, 475
modifiers. *See* adjectives
mood, 35, 113, 120, 121, 226, 329, 398, 419, 441, 459

Index

moral, 126, 151
multiparagraph essay, 73, 180. *See also* *specific kinds of essays*
multiple-meaning words, 245, 292, 304, 305, 349, 350
myths, 121

naming words. *See* nouns
narrative, 267–271
narrative box, 233, 238, 241, 252, 253, 258
negative statements, writing, 474–475
noncount nouns, 396, 397, 398, 399, 401, 437
nonexamples, 309
nonfiction, 42, 49, 80, 129, 189, 229, 231, 276, 315, 361. *See also* text type
nonrestrictive clause, 101. *See also* relative clauses
note taking, 74, 181, 355, 356, 443, 444
nouns
- adjectives as (*See* adjectives)
- appositives, 385
- common, 224
- function of, 98, 206, 385
- noncount, 396, 397, 398, 399, 401, 437
- noun clauses, 206–208
- noun phrase, 101–102, 104
- participial phrases, 382–384
- possessive, 98–99, 346
- relative clauses as, 206–207
- singular versus plural, 292, 387–389
- verbs as, 292–293

novel, 407, 447, 448, 494
novel meanings, words with, 487

objective summary, 64, 213–214
object of the preposition, 102, 103, 206, 305, 385
opinion. *See* perspective; point of view
overgeneralization, 305

P

paired reading, 12, 26, 33, 49, 61, 66, 87, 106, 111, 136, 162, 195, 212, 217, 238, 248, 254, 283, 299, 303, 324, 338, 343, 372, 391, 395, 415, 429, 434, 459, 478, 482, 502, 514, 519
panels, 233, 255–262
paragraphs
- body, 427, 444, 528, 529
- concluding, 427, 444–445, 530
- introductory, 180, 181, 268, 427, 444, 528
- multiparagraph essay (*See* multiparagraph essay)
- using, 427

parentheses, 309
participial phrases, 382–384
participles, 293–295, 382–384
passage comprehension. *See* comprehension; reading, asking/answering questions
passive voice, 208–209
past participle, 293, 382
past perfect tense. *See* tense
past tense. *See* tense
period, 98
personification, 34, 70, 113, 488, 490
perspective, 5, 16, 40, 41, 43, 44, 81, 126, 130, 185, 189, 239, 273, 277, 316, 318, 362, 367, 408, 410, 444, 448, 453, 495, 497, 534
persuasion, 75, 76, 361
phrasal verbs, 469–471. *See also* verbs
phrases, 19–20, 100, 203, 344, 469. *See also* participial phrases; phrasal verbs; prepositional phrases
pictures/illustrations, 231, 367
plot summary outline, 11, 30
plurals, 292, 387–389
point of view, 16, 30, 40, 62, 67, 96, 113, 124, 128, 130, 148, 158, 175, 180, 272, 403, 436
position statement, 74, 180
possessive nouns, 98–99, 346
predicate, 19, 103, 383. *See also* simple predicate
predicate noun, 206

predictions
making, 189, 232, 277, 278, 317, 318, 366, 409, 452, 496, 497
sharing, 15, 43, 190
prefixes, 42–43, 69, 70, 100, 119, 170, 220, 225, 296, 309, 344
prepositional phrases, 19, 207, 208, 253, 384, 469, 471
prepositions, 19, 470, 471
present (prompt), 56, 57, 59, 61, 106, 107
present participle, 293, 294, 382, 383
present perfect tense. *See* tense
present tense. *See* tense
preteaching vocabulary, 8–10, 46–48, 84–86, 133–135, 192–194, 235–237, 280–282, 321–323, 369–371, 412–414, 456–458, 499–501
Preview Checklist, 6, 44, 82, 131, 190, 233, 278, 319, 367, 410, 454
previewing text, 6, 44, 82, 131, 190, 233, 278, 319, 367, 410, 454, 497
prewriting. *See* writing, preparing to
prior knowledge. *See* background knowledge
problem, 127, 151, 356. *See also* conflict
prompts. *See also specific prompts*
figurative language (*See* figurative language)
function of, 56, 151
questions as, 26–29, 58–59, 107–109, 153–155, 213–215, 244–246, 300–301, 335–336, 392–393, 431–432, 479–480, 511–512
responding to, 25, 56, 57, 63, 153, 160, 215, 243, 251, 334, 341, 432, 510, 517 (*See also* critical understandings; direction words; purpose, reading for)
for writing (*See* quick writing)
pronouns
function of, 34, 35, 37, 40, 67, 68, 163, 218, 257, 305, 306, 344, 346, 347, 396
indefinite pronouns, 218, 484, 485, 522
intensive pronouns, 174, 484, 489
participial phrases, 382–383
point of view with, 16, 40, 175, 256, 258
reflexive pronouns, 119, 220, 305
relative, 100–101, 103, 204–205
verb forms and, 472
proof. *See* evidence, using
protagonist, 30, 262–263
prove (prompt), 56, 57, 59, 61, 106, 333, 334, 335, 339, 340, 391
proverb, 81, 125, 126, 255, 488
punctuation, 23, 73, 242, 266. *See also specific types of punctuation*
puns, 304, 305, 346, 349, 350, 522
purpose
author's purpose, 5, 43, 81, 128, 130, 189, 229, 232, 272, 277, 315, 318, 361, 366, 407, 409, 447, 452, 494, 496
reading for, 25–26, 60–61, 105–106, 156–157, 211–212, 247–248, 298–299, 337–338, 390–391, 428–429, 477–478, 513–514

Q

questions. *See also specific question words*
asking/answering, 12–15, 49–51, 58–59, 87–96, 137–148, 153–155, 157–160, 195–201, 283–289, 325–330, 340–341, 372–379, 416–420, 425–426, 459–466, 479–480, 503–506 (*See also* prompts, questions as)
question words, 57, 61, 157, 247, 249, 339, 428, 430, 510, 513, 515. *See also specific question words and prompts*
quick writing, 40, 124, 228, 314, 406, 493
quotation marks, 241, 242, 257, 260, 345, 348

R

read-alouds, 12, 26, 33, 49, 61, 66, 87, 106, 111, 136, 162, 195, 212, 217, 238, 248, 254, 283, 299, 303, 324, 338, 343, 372, 391, 395, 415, 429, 434, 459, 478, 482, 502, 514, 519
reading
asking/answering questions, 12–15, 26–28, 49–51, 58–59, 87–96, 107–108, 137–148, 153–155, 157–160, 195–201, 283–289, 300–301, 325–330, 335–336, 340–341, 372–379, 392–393, 416–420, 425–426, 431–432, 459–466, 479–480, 503–506
author's purpose, 5, 43, 81, 128, 130, 189, 229, 232, 272, 277, 315, 318, 361, 366, 407, 409, 447, 452, 494, 496, 513–514

Index

background knowledge, 5, 11, 43, 81, 130, 189, 232, 277, 318, 367, 410, 439, 453, 497
Big Ideas, 5, 41, 43, 77, 81, 125, 130, 184, 189, 229, 232, 273, 277, 315, 318, 361, 367, 408, 410, 448, 453, 494, 497, 534
close reading, 31–37, 65–70, 110–121, 161–176, 216–225, 252–263, 302–311, 342–350, 393–403, 433–438, 481–489, 518–524
content focus, 4, 42, 43, 80, 129, 188, 231, 276, 317, 366, 409, 452, 496
critical understandings, 56–59, 151–155, 242–246, 333–336, 423–426, 509–512
direction words (*See* direction words)
enduring understandings, 41, 77, 125–126, 184–185, 229–230, 273, 315–316, 351–362, 408, 448, 494–495, 534–535
main idea (*See* main idea)
monitoring comprehension (*See* comprehension)
point of view, 16, 30, 62, 67, 96, 113, 124, 128, 130, 148, 158, 175, 180, 272, 403, 436
previewing text, 6, 44, 82, 131, 190, 233, 278, 319, 367, 410, 454, 497
prompts, responding to (*See* prompts)
question words, 57, 61, 157, 247, 249, 339, 428, 430, 510, 513, 515
reading for a purpose, 25–26, 60–61, 105–106, 156–157, 211–212, 247–248, 298–299, 337–338, 390–391, 428–429, 477–478
response to reading, 40, 124, 228, 314, 406, 493
text type (*See* text type)

recontextualizing vocabulary, 38–39, 71–72, 122–123, 177–178, 226–227, 264–265, 312–313, 351–352, 404–405, 440–441, 491–492, 525–526

reflexive pronouns, 119, 220, 305

relate (prompt), 242, 243, 244, 249, 250–251, 299, 300–301

relative clauses, 101–104, 203–208, 523

relative pronouns, 100–101, 103, 204–205. *See also specific relative pronouns*

rereading, 25, 31, 58, 60–61, 65, 66, 105, 110, 111, 161, 162, 211, 216, 247, 252, 254, 298, 302, 337, 342, 343, 390, 394, 395, 428–429, 433, 434, 477, 481, 513, 514, 518, 519

resolution, 127, 262. *See also* solution

restrictive clause, 101. *See also* relative clauses

retelling, 11

reviewing vocabulary, 17–18, 31–32, 52–53, 65–66, 97–98, 110–111, 149–150, 161–162, 202–203, 216–217, 239–240, 253–254, 290–291, 302–303, 331–332, 342–343, 380–381, 394–395, 421–422, 433–434, 467–468, 481–482, 507–508, 518–519

revising, 103, 209

rhetorical fallacies. *See* fallacies

rhetorical language, 344

rhyme/rhyming, 319

rhythm, 131

sarcasm, 258, 522, 523

semicolon, 438

sentence frames, 22, 23, 54, 55, 154, 159, 188, 244

sentences
complex, 24, 103–104, 387
compound, 20
fluency with, 73
kernel sentence, 383, 387
Masterpiece Sentences, 208, 269
structure of, 73, 181, 209
topic sentences, 73, 427, 444, 529
writing, 22–23

sentence starters, 28, 29, 58, 59, 63, 107–108, 109, 155, 160, 215, 245, 246, 251, 300–301, 335, 340, 392, 393, 425, 426, 432, 479, 480, 511, 512, 517

sequencing, 355, 356

setting, 112, 127, 151, 255, 258, 259, 268

shadowing, 260. *See also* foreshadowing

short story, 80, 336, 354–359. *See also* fiction

similes, 113, 398, 399, 435, 437, 484, 486, 489. *See also* figurative language

simple predicate, 387

simple subject, 387

singular nouns, 387–389

six traits of writing. *See* writing, traits of

solution, 127, 151, 356. *See also* resolution

spelling, importance of, 73

story elements, 30, 127, 128

story map, 127
subject, 19, 103, 206, 208, 383, 385, 387. *See also* simple subject
subjective wording, 306, 308
subject-verb agreement, 387–389
subjunctive mood, 121
subjunctive wording, 307
subordinating conjunctions, 20–23, 24, 100, 114, 203–204
suffixes, 36, 67, 68, 70, 112, 113, 115, 117, 221, 255, 292, 293, 349, 384, 387
summarize (prompt), 152, 155, 157, 212, 213–214
summarizing, 64, 75, 127, 151, 181, 262, 350, 439, 444, 530
superlative adjectives, 67, 70. *See also* adjectives
supernatural fiction, 80, 81, 231. *See also* fiction
support (prompt), 333, 334, 336, 339, 391, 392
supporting details, 64, 73
suspense, creating, 37, 81, 113, 169, 255, 261, 272, 490, 524
symbol/symbolic terminology, 150, 168, 176, 309, 311
synonyms, using, 33, 34, 35, 68, 70, 113, 114, 116, 117, 118, 119, 120, 121, 163, 164, 165, 166, 175, 220, 221, 222, 224, 225, 245, 256, 304, 306, 307, 309, 310, 311, 344, 345, 347, 348, 349, 350, 396, 397, 398, 399, 401, 435, 436, 437, 488, 490, 520
synthesize (prompt), 56, 57, 58, 61, 63, 106, 107, 509, 510, 512, 515

tales, 128, 148
tense
- future, 176
- past, 37, 54, 165, 293
- past perfect, 397, 435, 437, 438
- present, 165, 387
- present perfect, 399, 486

text features, 49, 153, 190, 211, 214, 233
text structure, 246
text type
- fiction versus nonfiction, 4, 80, 129, 231
- informational, 42–43, 126, 189, 229, 276, 317, 366, 409, 452
- literature, 4, 42, 80, 96, 126, 129, 148, 183, 189, 231, 246, 276, 317, 366, 409, 446, 452, 533 (*See also specific kinds of literature*)

that (relative pronoun), 100, 204, 206
theme, 126–128, 151, 263
thesis statements, 180, 427, 444, 528
thought balloon versus dialogue balloon, 233, 238
topic sentences, 73, 427, 444, 529
trace (prompt), 152, 154, 157, 158, 212
transition words/phrases, 27, 67, 68, 69, 70, 73, 113, 115, 168, 170, 172, 215, 220, 223, 252, 258, 345, 437, 484, 488
transitive verbs, 296, 297

Unit Plans, 2–3, 78–79, 186–187, 274–275, 364–365, 450–451

Venn diagram, 443, 444
verbs
- action, 472
- function of, 116
- helping, 19, 208, 209, 292–293, 294, 388, 469, 472
- identifying, 347, 437
- linking, 19, 294, 388, 472
- painting, 208, 269
- properties of, 295–297
- tense (*See* tense)
- verb forms, 472–473
- verb phrases, 19–20
- verbs as adjectives, 293–295
- verbs as nouns, 292–293

video, 5, 81, 189, 277, 367, 453
vocabulary
- antonyms (*See* antonyms)
- compound words, 70
- degrees of meaning, 53–55

Index

figurative language (*See* figurative language)
key terms (*See* recontextualizing vocabulary; reviewing vocabulary)
multiple-meaning words, 245, 292, 304, 305, 349, 350
preteaching, 8–10, 46–48, 84–86, 133–135, 192–194, 235–237, 280–282, 321–323, 369–371, 412–414, 456–458, 499–501
rating knowledge of, 7, 45, 83, 132, 191, 234, 279, 320, 368, 411, 455, 498
recontextualizing, 38–39, 71–72, 122–123, 177–178, 226–227, 264–265, 312–313, 351–352, 404–405, 440–441, 491–492, 525–526
reviewing, 17–18, 31–32, 52–53, 65–66, 97–98, 110–111, 149–150, 161–162, 202–203, 216–217, 239–240, 253–254, 290–291, 302–303, 331–332, 342–343, 380–381, 394–395, 421–422, 433–434, 467–468, 481–482, 507–508, 518–519
synonyms (*See* synonyms)

what (question word), 107, 206, 208
what kind (question words), 204, 208, 293, 294, 382
when (question word), 204, 208, 252
where (question word), 204, 208, 253
where (relative pronoun), 204
which (relative pronoun), 100, 204, 206
which one (question words), 104, 204–205, 207, 208, 293, 294, 382
who (question word), 208
who (relative pronoun), 100, 101, 206
whom (relative pronoun), 100, 101, 206
whose (relative pronoun), 100
why (question word), 204
word choice, 33, 34, 35, 36, 37, 73, 266, 269
word picture. *See* figurative language
writing
active versus passive voice, 208–210
appositives in, 386–387
Big Ideas in, 181
capitalization, 131, 153
checklist, 76, 183, 271, 360, 446, 533
conclusions, 75, 181, 269
conventions in, 73, 266
direction words (*See* direction words)
essays (*See* multiparagraph essay)
evaluating, 76, 183, 271, 360, 446, 533
figurative language (*See* figurative language)
letters, 314, 405, 519, 525, 526
Masterpiece Sentences, 208, 269
negatives, 474–476
organization of, 73, 443, 529
paragraphs (*See* paragraphs)
preparing to, 74–75, 180–181, 267–269, 336, 355, 427, 528–530
punctuation (*See* punctuation)
quick write in response to reading, 40, 124, 228, 314, 406, 493
revising, 103, 209
sentence starters (*See* sentence starters)
spelling (*See* spelling)
subject-verb agreement in, 387–389
summarizing, 64
thesis statements, 180, 427, 444, 528
topic sentences (*See* topic sentences)
traits of, 73, 75, 179, 182, 266, 270, 353, 357, 442, 445, 527, 531